ECHOES
from the Past

World History to the 16th Century

Senior Author

Garfield Newman
Curriculum Consultant
York Region District School Board

Authors

Elizabeth Graham
Lecturer, Institute of Archaeology
University College, London (UK)

Rick Guisso
Chair, Department of East Asian Studies
University of Toronto

Elizabeth McLuhan
Curator, Royal Ontario Museum, Toronto

Osman Mohamed
Archaeologist
Formerly with Somali Academy
of Science and Arts

David Pendergast
Curator Emeritus
Royal Ontario Museum, Toronto

James Reilly
Associate Professor, Department of Near East
and Middle Eastern Civilizations
University of Toronto

Gerald Schaus
Chair and Professor, Department of
Archaeology and Classical Studies
Wilfrid Laurier University, Waterloo, Ontario

Christopher Simpson
Professor, Department of Archaeology
and Classical Studies
Wilfrid Laurier University, Waterloo, Ontario

John Topic
Department of Anthropology
Trent University, Peterborough, Ontario

Narendra Wagle
Director and Professor, Centre for
South Asian Studies
University of Toronto

McGraw-Hill Ryerson Limited

Toronto Montréal Burr Ridge, IL Dubuque, IA, Madison, WI New York San Francisco St. Louis
Bangkok Bogotá Caracas Kuala Lumpur Lisbon London Madrid Mexico City Milan New Delhi
Santiago Seoul Singapore Sydney Taipei

McGraw-Hill
Ryerson Limited

A Subsidiary of The **McGraw·Hill** *Companies*

COPIES OF THIS BOOK
MAY BE OBTAINED BY
CONTACTING:

McGraw-Hill Ryerson Ltd.

WEBSITE:
http://www.mcgrawhill.ca

E-MAIL:
orders@mcgrawhill.ca

TOLL FREE FAX:
1-800-463-5885

TOLL FREE CALLS:
1-800-565-5758

OR BY MAILING YOUR
ORDER TO:
McGraw-Hill Ryerson
Order Department
300 Water Street, Whitby
Ontario, L1N 9B6

Please quote the ISBN and
title when placing your
order

Echoes from the Past: World History to the 16th Century

ISBN 0-07-088739-X

www.mcgrawhill.ca

2 3 4 5 6 7 8 9 0 TRI 0 9 8 7 6 5 4 3 2

Printed and bound in Canada

Care has been taken to trace ownership of copyright material contained in this text. The publisher
will gladly take any information that will enable them to rectify any reference or credit in subsequent printings.

National Library of Canadian Cataloguing in Publication Data
Main entry under title:
Newman, Garfield
 Echoes from the past: world history to the 16th century

Includes index.
ISBN 0-07-088739-X

History, Ancient. 2. Middle Ages – History. 3. History, Modern – 16th century. I. Guisso, Rick. II. Title.

D21.N49 2001   909   C2001-930768-3

Publisher: Patty Pappas
Associate Editors: Ellen Munro, Dyanne Rivers
Supervising Editor: Crystal Shortt
Copy Editors: Gail Copeland, Alan Simpson
Feature Writers: Stephanie Smith Abram, Patty Pappas
Permissions Editor: Jacqueline Donovan
Production Co-ordinator: Paula Lowes
Editorial Assistants: Joanne Murray, Erin Parton
Interior/Cover Design: Dave Murphy/ArtPlus Ltd.
Electronic Page Make-Up: Barb Neri/ArtPlus Ltd.
Illustrations/Maps: ArtPlus Ltd., Deborah Crowle, Sue LeDoux, Ken Suzana
Cover Image: Courtesy of the Ontario Science Centre
Back Cover Image: Courtesy of Robert Harding Picture Library

Reviewers

Michael Butler
Head of History
Northern Secondary School
Toronto, Ontario

James Ellsworth
Program Co-ordinator –
Assessment and Accountability
Grand Erie District School Board
Brantford, Ontario

Helen Hatton
Professor of History, University of
Toronto, Erindale Campus
Mississauga, Ontario

Charles Leskun
Head of History
St. Aloysius Gonzaga
Secondary School
Georgetown, Ontario

Marilynn Mathews-Dickson
History Teacher
Canterbury High School
Ottawa, Ontario

Rob McGarrigle
History Teacher, St. Francis
Xavier Secondary School
Hammond, Ontario

Donna McIntyre
History Teacher, Southwood
Secondary School
Cambridge, Ontario

Connie McMaster
Head of History, Sir Wilfrid
Laurier Secondary School
London, Ontario

David Neelin
History Teacher, East York
Collegiate Institute
Toronto, Ontario

Peter Rogers
Teacher-Librarian,
Cardinal Newman
Secondary School
Hamilton, Ontario

George Sherwood
Head of History
North Albion Collegiate
Toronto, Ontario

Al Skeoch
Head of History (retired)
Parkdale Collegiate
Toronto, Ontario

Dominic Talarico
Head of History, Earl of March
Secondary School
Kanata, Ontario

Fil Walker
History Teacher, Huron Heights
Secondary School
Newmarket, Ontario

Peter Wren
Head of History, Madonna
Catholic Secondary School,
Toronto, Ontario

Advisory Board

Anneli Andre-Barrett
Teacher, The Woodlands School,
Mississauga, Ontario

Nick Brune
Teacher, Iroquois Ridge
High School,
Oakville, Ontario

Michael Butler
History Department Head
Northern Secondary School
Toronto, Ontario

Colleen Chandler
History Department Head,
Mother Theresa Catholic
Secondary School,
Scarborough, Ontario

Reg Hawes
Senior Tutor, Ontario Institute for
Studies in Education and the
University of Toronto Schools,
University of Toronto,
Toronto, Ontario

Dick Holland
Pre-Service Instructor, Secondary
Education, Ontario Institute for
Studies in Education of the
University of Toronto,
Toronto, Ontario

Mary Ann Kainola
Teacher, Oakwood Collegiate,
Toronto, Ontario

Nigel Lee
History Department Head
Cameron Heights Collegiate
Kitchener, Ontario

Lela Lilko
History Department Head
Central Peel Secondary School
Brampton, Ontario

Darcy Mintz
Teacher, Cameron
Heights Collegiate,
Kitchener, Ontario

John Montgomery
Former History Department
Head, Eastview Secondary
School, Barrie, Ontario

Paul Sydor
Teacher, West Elgin
Secondary School,
West Lorne, Ontario

Joe Tersigni
Teacher, Our Lady of Lourdes
High School,
Guelph, Ontario

About the Authors

Elizabeth Graham (Ch. 13, The Aztecs)

Elizabeth is Lecturer in Mesoamerican archaeology at the Institute of Archaeology, University College London (UK). Until 1999 she was Associate Professor of Anthropology at York University, where she had been on staff for more than a decade. She has specialized in the archaeology of the Maya and of Mesoamerica in general since 1972, when she began excavations in Belize, the principal area of her research. She is the author of over 60 publications, including a monograph on the archaeology of southern Belize as well as book chapters, scholarly papers, book reviews, and popular articles on the Aztec Civilization.

Rick Guisso (Chs. 10–11, China, Japan)

Rick was educated at the Universities of Toronto and Kyoto and obtained his doctorate from Oxford University in 1975. He is the author of several books on traditional China and has taught Chinese, Japanese and Korean history at both the University of Waterloo and University of Toronto. He has a special interest in the history of Women in East Asia and he is currently Chair of the department of East Asian Studies at the University of Toronto.

Elizabeth McLuhan (Chs. 15–17, The Middle Ages)

Elizabeth has taught Medieval History at the University of Toronto, including courses on Pagans and Christians, and the Conversion of Europe in the Early Middle Ages. She is currently completing her Ph.D. at the Centre for Medieval Studies of the University of Toronto where she was recipient of the Senior Doctoral Teaching Associateship for her research on medieval Christianity. She has presented papers internationally and has worked for over twenty years in the cultural and heritage field, curating art and history exhibitions for a wide range of institutions including the Art Gallery of Ontario. Currently, she is a curator at the Royal Ontario Museum.

Osman Mohamed (Ch. 8, African Kingdoms)

Osman is a former archaeologist with the Somali Academy of Science and Arts. He received his Ph.D. from the University of Georgia. Dr. Mohamed has done research in Somalia and taught African history, archaeology, and cultural heritage management. He has published a chapter on Somali cultural heritage entitled "Starting From Scratch: The Past, Present, and Future Management of Somalia's Cultural Heritage" with Steven Brandt, in *Plundering Africa's Past*, edited by Peter R. Schmidt and Roderick J. McIntosh.

David Pendergast (Ch. 12, The Maya)

David Pendergast was the Royal Ontario Museum's curator responsible for Maya archaeological research from 1964 until his retirement in 1999. During that time, he directed excavations at Altun Ha and Lamanai in Belize, as well as several smaller sites in the country. He has also done archaeological fieldwork in the United States, Mexico, Guatemala, and Cuba. He is the author of more than 230 publications, including books, monographs, book chapters, scholarly articles, and popular works, which have appeared in Canada, the Unites States and around the world A Fellow of the Royal Society of Canada, he is now Curator Emeritus at the ROM and Adjunct Curator, The Ancient Americas, at the George R. Gardiner Museum in Toronto. In addition Dr. Pendergast is Adjunct Professor of Anthropology at York University, Conjunct Professor in Anthropology at Trent University, and an associate of the Institute of Archaeology, University College, London.

James Reilly (Ch. 7, The Islamic Middle East)

James Reilly is an Associate Professor of Middle Eastern and Islamic History in the Department of Near and Middle Eastern Civilizations at the University of Toronto. He specializes in the social and economic history of the Middle East, and is the author of studies on Syria during the period of Ottoman rule.

Gerald Schaus (Chs. 3–4, Greece)

Gerry Schaus is Chair and Professor of the Department of Archaeology and Classical Studies at Wilfrid Laurier University. His expertise is in Greek archaeology with a specialty in the study of Greek pottery. Dr. Schaus is currently publishing the results of five seasons of work in the Sanctuary of Athena at Stymphalos in the Arkadian Mountains of southern Greece. He has excavated for more than 25 years in the Mediterranean region, including Greece, Italy, and Libya.

Christopher Simpson (Chs. 5–6, Rome)

Chris was elected Fellow of the Society of Antiquaries of London in 1989 and is currently a Professor in the Dept. of Archaeology and Classical Studies at Wilfrid Laurier University. Dr Simpson is a Roman historian and archaeologist specializing in early Roman Imperial history (Augustus, Tiberius, Caligula, Claudius); Italian archaeology (San Giovanni di Ruoti; and at Cosa). Chris has published one book and over 50 articles.

John Topic (Ch. 14, The Inca)

John is currently with the Department of Anthropology at Trent University, Peterborough. His area of expertise is Andean Archaeology and Ethnohistory. Dr Topic has worked in Peru since 1969. From 1981 to 1989 John worked in the northern highlands of Peru directing a large project that surveyed and excavated a number of sites near the modern town of Huamachuco. Since 1998 John has been involved in the study of the ancient oracle, Catequil. Through both documentary sources and archaeological survey, Dr. Topic has identified seven sites in Ecuador as associated with the Incaic diffusion of the cult. John's research has been supported by the Social Sciences and Humanities Research Council of Canada and the National Science Foundation (US).

Narendra Wagle (Ch. 9, India)

N.K. Wagle is Professor of History and Director of the Centre for South Asian Studies, University of Toronto. After obtaining his Ph.D. from the School of Oriental and African Studies, University of London (UK), Professor Wagle taught at the University of Virginia and Skidmore College, before joining the University of Toronto. He is the author and editor of eighteen books, written thirty-five book chapters and refereed articles in scholarly journals. His recently published books are: *Society at the Time of the Buddha, Writers Editors and Reformers: Political and Social Transformations of Maharashtra 1830-1930, Religion, Nationality and Region and Approaches to Jain Studies: Logic, Philosophy, Rituals and Symbols*

Acknowledgements

Echoes from the Past is dedicated to my children, Mathew, Geoffery, and Nikita, and the youth of Canada in the hope that the study of ancient civilizations will help them to develop an appreciation for the richness of world cultures and an awareness of history's travesties. May they learn from the past, strive to live harmoniously in the present, and work to shape the future.

One day I arrived home to be greeted by my four year old daughter Nikita, her blue eyes beaming with excitement as she showed me her new lengha given to her by her best friend Amrit. Nikita, dressed in a traditional North Indian formal garment, is a young girl with a Nona, a Teta, a Zio, and a grandma and grandpa, who enjoys Japanese food and is learning to speak French and Italian. Nikita is quintessentially Canadian. She represents the diversity of cultures of which Canada is comprised. As citizens living in one of the most ethnically diverse countries in the world, Canadians owe a collective debt of gratitude to the ancient cultures explored in the pages of *Echoes from the Past*.

Developing a textbook that deals with the history of the world must draw on the talents of many people. The entire editorial staff at McGraw-Hill Ryerson is an amazing group to work with. Melanie Myers, V.P. and Editorial Director, provided on-going support for the project. Patty Pappas has the unique ability to guide a project from its inception with humour, passion and professionalism. Ellen Munro, who demonstrated patience, insight and love of the arts, steered the project from the outset. Ellen was ably assisted by Dyanne Rivers who guided the final units from draft to polished text. Crystal Shortt, as usual, was instrumental in ensuring that the book made it from the minds of the authors to the designers, resulting in a stunning design. Jacqueline Donovan handled the Herculean task of chasing down permissions with incredible aplomb. Finally, Jennifer Burnell, although not directly involved in the text, has come to understand the intricacies of curriculum design like a seasoned and highly skilled teacher. Her work in guiding the creation of the Teacher's Resource is without equal.

Echoes from the Past represents the most current research into the history of ancient civilizations largely due to the efforts of the author team. I feel incredibly fortunate to have worked with a team of scholars, all of whom have earned international reputations for their work. In addition to the contributions of the author team I would like to thank the reviewers and the advisory board who provided encouragement, valid criticisms and useful directions which helped to ensure that the text would meet the needs of teachers and students.

I extend my deepest appreciation to my best friend, Laura Gini-Newman. Laura's passion for teaching and learning has helped to make me a better educator. More importantly, Laura's love and support, her tolerance of long hours, and her willingness to join me in excursions to museums, through the Maya jungles in search of pyramids, and to educational conferences is deeply appreciated.

To all those who have played a role in the creation of *Echoes from the Past: World History to the 16th Century*, thank you!

Garfield Newman
April 2001

Contents

A Tour of Your Textbook   xii
Prologue: An Introduction to Historical Inquiry   2
What is History   4
Methods of Historical Inquiry   4
Archaeology and the Study of History   6
Analyzing Historical Research   12
Social History   13
Cause and Effect: The Importance of Chronology   14
Lifelong Skills through the Study of History   16
Chapter Review   18

UNIT ONE THE NEAR EAST   20
Unit Overview   21

Chapter 1 *The March to Civilization*   22
Time Line: The March to Civilization   24
In Search of Our Ancestors   25
In the Field…:
  The Stones and Bones of Mary Leakey   27
Daily Life in the Upper Paleolithic Age   31
The Neolithic Revolution   35
Characteristics of a Civilization   36
Mesopotamia: The Cradle of Civilization   39
The History of the Imagination:
Myths and Legends:
  Gilgamesh and Enkidu: A Story of Epic
  Proportions   46
Evaluating Civilizations   49
Chapter Review   50

Chapter 2 *Egypt and Israel*   52
Time Line: Egypt and Israel   54
Continuity and Change in Egyptian History   55
The Rise of the Nation of Egypt   56
The Old Kingdom   57
The Middle Kingdom   58
Political, Legal, and Economic Structures   59

The New Kingdom   63
Egyptian Military Traditions   64
Intellectual Life   68
Pushing the Boundaries: Developments
in Science and Technology:
  From Here to Eternity: The Mummification
  Process   70
Continuity and Convention in Egyptian Art   75
Social Structure: Daily Life in Egypt   76
Stability Through Education   80
Ancient Israel   82
Biography:
  Nebuchadnezzar: A Force to be
  Reckoned With   84
The Evolution of the Jewish Faith   86
Rites of Passage:
  Sons and Daughters of the Commandment   88
Chapter Review   90
Unit Review   92

UNIT TWO THE MEDITERRANEAN   94
Unit Overview   95

Chapter 3 *Greece in the Heroic Age*   96
Time Line: Greece in the Heroic Age   98
The Earliest Civilization in Europe:
  The Minoans   99
External Forces   102
The Earliest Greeks: The Mycenaeans   104
In the Field…:
  Heinrich Schliemann: Hero or Fraud?   107
The Archaic Period   110
Government in Greece   113
Foundations of Democratic Rule   114
The Persian Wars: Greece Unites…   119
Early Greek Art: Cross-Cultural Influences   123
Chapter Review   126

Chapter 4 *Classical Greece*   128

Time Line: Classical Greece   130

Athens Builds an Empire   131

The Peloponnesian War   133

The Classical Moment   136

The Road to Persia: Alexander the Great   138

The Hellenistic Age   141

The History of the Imagination:

Myths and Legends:

    Legends of Alexander the Great   142

Greek Culture   145

Daily Life in Classical Athens   150

The Greatness of the Greeks   158

Chapter Review   160

Chapter 5 *The Rise of Rome*   162

Time Line: The Rise of Rome   164

Geography: The Italian Peninsula   165

The Etruscans: Forerunners of the Romans   166

The Roman Republic   168

External Forces: The Punic Wars,

    264-146 BCE   172

Republican Law and Legislation   177

The Decline of the Roman Republic   178

Daily Life in the Republic   180

Rites of Passage:

    Portraits for Posterity: Death, Art,

    and Ancestors   182

Pushing the Boundaries: Developments

in Science and Technology:

    Concrete: Bigger Better Buildings   186

Roman Republican Art and Architecture   188

The End of the Roman Republic   189

Chapter Review   190

Chapter 6 *The Roman Empire*   192

Time Line: The Roman Empire   194

From Republic to Empire   195

Buildings and Public Works   203

Beliefs   208

Biography:

    Tacitus: Roman Historian   210

The Empire at its Height   213

The Beginning of the End   216

Chapter Review   222

Unit Review   224

UNIT THREE THE ISLAMIC
MIDDLE EAST AND AFRICA   226

Unit Overview   **227**

Chapter 7 *The Islamic Middle East*   228

Time Line: The Islamic Middle East   230

Geography and Trade   231

Muhammad and Islam   232

The Growth of Empire   236

Social History   241

Biography:

    Khadija   246

The Arts   249

The History of the Imagination:

Myths and Legends:

    The Arabian Nights   250

Science and Technology   253

Pushing the Boundaries: Developments

in Science and Technology:

    Algebra: Another Islamic Innovation   254

Chapter Review   258

Chapter 8 *African Kingdoms*   260

Time Line: African Kingdoms   262

Ancient Civilizations in Northeast Africa:

    The Kingdom of Kush   263

The Kingdom of Axum   267

The East African City-states   270

Civilizations in Central Africa   274

The Royal Kingdoms of West Africa   276

The Rise of Ghana   277

In the Field…:

   Gertrude Caton-Thompson and

   Great Zimbabwe   278

The Rise of the Mali Kingdom   282

The Songhay Empire   284

Chapter Review   288

Unit Review   290

UNIT FOUR ASIA   292

Unit Overview   293

Chapter 9 *India*   294

Time Line: India   296

The Origin of the Indus Valley Civilization   297

The Political History of Ancient India   301

Muslim Rule in India   307

Political Union: The Mughal Empire   308

Religious Traditions in Ancient India   311

Buddhism   313

Rites of Passage:

   A Vedic Wedding   314

Cross-Cultural Interaction in India:

   Hindus and Muslims   317

Education in Ancient India: Promoting Stability   317

Trade   318

Indian Literature and Art   320

Social Structures: Daily Life in Ancient India   321

Chapter Review   324

Chapter 10 *China*   326

Time Line: China   328

Prehistory of China   329

Change and Continuity in China   330

The Classical Age   332

Confucius   333

The First Empire   337

In the Field:

   A Work in Progress: The Tomb of

   Qin Shihuang   338

The Golden Age of China   346

Daily Life in the Capital   350

The Last Empire   355

Pushing the Boundaries: Developments

in Science and Technology:

   Fire Medicine: The Accidental Invention

   of Gunpowder   356

Chapter Review   362

Chapter 11 *Japan*   364

Time Line: Japan   366

Geography of Japan   367

Japanese History: Change and Continuity   367

The Growth of the Empire   368

Chinese Influence and the Great Change   372

The Heian Period   374

The Kamakura Shogunate   377

Biography:

   Minamoto Yoritomo: The First Shogun   378

The Mongol Invasions:

   Challenge and Response   382

The Ashikaga Shogunate   383

Warrior Culture   386

Warrior Culture on the Brink of Change   388

The Coming of the Europeans   388

Chapter Review   390

Unit Review   392

UNIT FIVE THE AMERICAS   394

Unit Overview   395

Chapter 12 *The Maya*   396

Time Line: The Maya   398

Geography and History of the Maya World   399

The Growth of Empire   400

Beliefs   404

The History of the Imagination:

Myths and Legends:

   The Quiché Creation Myth   405

Social History of the Maya 408
Maya Literature and Art 412
Maya Science and Technology 415
Pushing the Boundaries: Developments
in Science and Technology:
   Maya Mathematics 418
The Maya Economy 420
Chapter Review 422

Chapter 13 *The Aztecs* 424
Time Line: The Aztecs 426
Geography of the Aztec World 427
The Origins of the Aztecs 429
Religion and Beliefs 432
Social History 436
Biography:
   Montezuma II 440
The Arts and Sciences 444
Aztec Economics 449
Chapter Review 454

Chapter 14 *The Inca* 456
Time Line: The Inca 458
Geography of the Inca World 459
Origins of the Inca 460
Inca History 461
Rites of Passage:
   Some Inca Rituals 464
Military History 468
Inca Religion 470
Social History 472
The Arts and Sciences 478
In the Field…:
   John Topic 480
Chapter Review 486
Unit Review 488

UNIT SIX THE MIDDLE AGES 490
Unit Overview 491

Chapter 15 *The Early Middle Ages* 492
Time Line: The Early Middle Ages 494
From Roman Empire to Early Middle Ages 495
The Byzantine Empire 495
Warriors and Warbands 500
The Church in the Early Middle Ages 503
The Merovingians 506
The Carolingians 508
The History of the Imagination:
Myths and Legends:
   Chanson de Roland: A Song of Deeds 512
Iberia 514
The British Isles 515
In the Field…:
   *Proof of Life: The Archaeological Search
   for Arthur* 518
The Vikings 520
Slaves and Serfs 521
The Role of Women 522
The Birth of Modern Languages 523
Chapter Review 524

Chapter 16 *The High Middle Ages* 526
Time Line: The High Middle Ages 528
From Early Middle Ages to High Middle Ages 529
Social Upheaval and Reorganization 530
Wars and Conflicts 531
The Crusades 536
New Economic Growth 538
New Learning 541
New Art and Architecture 542
New Religious Spirit 545
Life in the High Middle Ages 547
Rites of Passage:
   The Apprenticeship of a Knight 548
Women in Medieval Society 554
Population Growth and Expansion 556
Chapter Review 558

Chapter 17 *The Late Middle Ages* — 560

Time Line: The Late Middle Ages — 562

Plague and Hardship — 563

Commerce and Trade — 570

Changes in Warfare — 570

The Hundred Years' War — 572

The New Media of the Late Middle Ages — 575

Biography:

    The Hero of Orléans — 576

The Church in the Late Middle Ages — 579

Pushing the Boundaries: Developments in Science and Technology:

    The Printing Press: Invention of the Millennium — 580

Society and Government — 586

Chapter Review — 590

Unit Review — 592

UNIT SEVEN TOWARD THE MODERN AGE — 594

Unit Overview — 595

Chapter 18 *The Renaissance* — 596

Time Line: The Renaissance — 598

From Middle Ages to Renaissance — 599

The Emergence of the Renaissance — 600

Humanism — 606

Renaissance Ideas — 607

Renaissance Art and Architecture — 609

Biography:

    Leonardo da Vinci: "Tell me if anything at all was done" — 614

The Renaissance and the Individual — 617

Technology and the Modern Age — 621

The History of the Imagination:

Myths and Legends:

    Hunting Witches — 622

Renaissance Ideas in Northern Europe — 624

Chapter Review — 628

Chapter 19 *Epilogue* — 630

Time Line: Seeds of the Global Village — 632

The Modern Age Arrives — 633

From Isolation to Global Village — 633

Early Trading Networks — 634

European Knowledge of the World — 634

Foundations of European Exploration — 636

Globalization — 637

Early Contact — 638

The Role of Slavery — 640

The Grand Exchange — 642

The Process of Acculturation — 643

Chapter Review — 646

Unit Review — 648

MAPS

Unit One

Human Migration — 25

Levees on the Euphrates River in Mesopotamia — 40

Ancient Egypt and its Neighbouring States — 55

Ancient Israel: The Journeys of Abraham and Moses — 83

Unit Two

The Ancient Greek World — 100

The Greek Colonies — 112

The Persian Wars — 120

The Athenian Empire — 131

The Peloponnesian War, 431–404 BCE — 134

The Empire of Alexander the Great — 141

The Italian Peninsula — 165

Etruscan Italy ca. 1000 BCE — 166

Roman Territory 500-146 BCE — 174

The End of the Roman Empire — 217

Unit Three

The Spread of Islam to the Sixteenth Century — 231

Ancient Northeast Africa 263

The Nile Valley: Ancient Kush and Axum 264

Ancient Settlements on the East Coast
of Africa 271

Great Zimbabwe ca. 1400 275

Trans-Saharan Trade Routes of the
Fourteenth Century 281

Three Trading Empires of Ancient West Africa 284

Unit Four

Ancient India 297

The Gupta Empire and Delhi Sultanate 307

Ancient Trade Routes 319

China Under the Shang and Zhou Dynasties 329

China in the Han and Qin Dynasties 341

Ancient Japan 367

Mongol Invasions of Japan 382

Unit Five

The Maya World 399

The Aztec Empire of Meso-America 427

The Valley of Mexico 431

The Inca Empire 459

Expansion of the Inca Empire 467

Unit Six

Justinian's Conquests 497

Migration of the Huns and Germanic Tribes 501

Conquests of Clovis 506

Charlemagne's Empire in About 800 510

Division of the Carolingian Empire, 843 511

Christian Reconquest of Iberia 514

Kingdom of Alfred the Great, 886 516

England in 1066 533

Routes of the Crusades 538

Spread of the Black Death, 1347–1352 564

The Hundred Years' War, 1337-1453 574

The Great Schism, 1378-1417 583

Unit Seven

Italy, 1454 601

Spanish and Portuguese Exploration
and Conquest: 1400-1550 637

APPENDIX

Methods of Historical Inquiry

Archaeological Interpretation and the Historian 650

Writing Historical Biographies 652

Analyzing Art: A Window on the Past 654

Techniques for Historical Research 656

Working with Primary Documents 658

Writing a History Essay 660

History's Place in Your Future Career 662

Glossary **666**

Credits **674**

Index **680**

A Tour of Your Textbook

Welcome to *Echoes from the Past*. This textbook provides you with an interesting and in-depth coverage of societies and civilizations up to the 16th century. The Prologue is set up as a separate element that will give you the background to take full advantage of this course. To understand the book's structure, begin by taking a tour of the following pages.

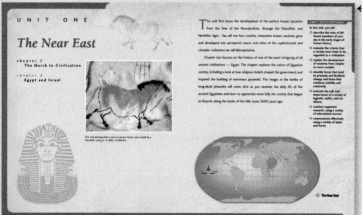

Unit Opener

- A striking photo with caption opens each unit and introduces students to the content.
- An opening paragraph captures student interest with a fascinating aspect to be developed.
- Unit Expectations lists curriculum expectations covered throughout the unit.
- A world map identifies the locale of the civilization covered in the unit.

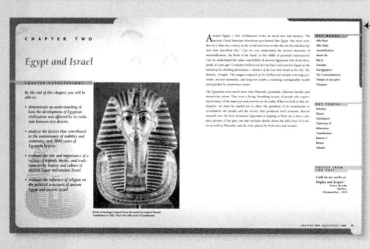

Chapter Opener

- Each chapter begins with an engaging photo or painting accompanied by a brief caption that sets a visual stage for the chapter.
- Students are provided with a list of curriculum expectations.
- The introductory paragraph invites you into the topic and clearly indicates what you will be studying in the chapter.
- Key Words and Key People are listed and always typed in bold when first introduced in the chapter.

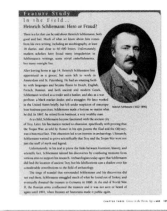

Time Line

- Each chapter lists the main events of the history of each civilization in chronological order.

Feature Study

- Key features that will enrich the content with glimpses of real people and how they lived and worked.
- Look for these headings: Biography, In the Field…, Rites of Passage, The History of the Imagination: Myths and Legends, and Pushing the Boundaries: Developments in Science and Technology.

Marginal Feature

- These shorter features appear periodically to present interesting bits of historical information that are relevant to the content.
- Look for these headings: Time Frames, Ancient Oddities, Medieval Miscellany, Scripts & Symbols, The Past at Play, and Current Research and Interpretations.

Review...Recall...Reflect

- These questions allow students to pause periodically to check their understanding of facts and ideas.

Web Connections

- Encourages students to explore topics further through the Internet. McGraw-Hill Ryerson monitors these sites and adds new ones regularly.

Maps

- Excellent detailed maps, following rules of geography.

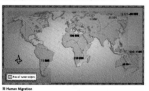

Chapter Review

- Activities are designed to reinforce the development of knowledge and skills outlined in the Achievement Chart.
- Chapter Summary — briefly reviews curriculum expectations covered by the chapter's content
- Reviewing the Significance of Key People, Concepts, and Events — activities provide students with opportunities to demonstrate a broad understanding of key content.
- Doing History: Thinking about the Past — suggests ways for students to demonstrate critical thinking, creative thinking, and inquiry skills.
- Applying Your Learning — provides opportunities to apply learning in creative activities.
- Communicating Your Learning — activities require students to demonstrate communication skills through speaking, writing, and the use of visuals.

Unit Review

- Activities allow students to demonstrate understanding of material listed in key curriculum expectations.
- Grading the Civilizations — facilitates the evaluation of characteristics, development, and interactions of several civilizations.
- The Role of Individuals in History — students can evaluate the contributions of individuals and groups to the development of political, military, religious, legal, and cultural endeavours.
- Understanding Chronology — students can better understand change in history when they learn the sequence of events.
- Cause and Effect in History — activities to help students identify the cause-and-effect relationships within the chronology of key historical events.

Methods of Historical Inquiry

- Located in the Appendix, students can access these strategies and ideas as needed.
- Methods covered:
  Archaeological Interpretation and the Historian
  Writing Historical Biographies
  Analyzing Art: A Window on the Past
  Techniques for Historical Research
  Working with Primary Documents
  Writing a History Essay
  History's Place in Your Future Career

An Introduction to Historical Inquiry

By the end of this chapter, you will be able to:

- *demonstrate an understanding of the use and importance of chronology and cause and effect relationships in the study of history*

- *demonstrate an understanding of the steps in the process of historical interpretation and analysis*

- *demonstrate an awareness of the role of continuity and change in history*

- *demonstrate an understanding of how key interpretations of world history have shaped the way history has been studied*

Archaeology takes teamwork and people with specialized skills. Here, a dig team is working on a recent excavation in Montréal.

Welcome to a journey to the distant past. Through the pages of *Echoes from the Past: World History to the 16th Century*, the voices of people great and small will rise again as you learn about their daily lives and how their legacy is reflected in our twenty-first century world. The Roman philosopher Cicero wrote, "Not to know what took place before you were born is to remain forever a child." Imagine knowing nothing about what went on before you were born, with no idea of the life your parents or grandparents lived. What if you had no understanding of how Canada and its culture developed. In effect, you would suffer from "cultural amnesia" — unaware of your heritage and your past. You would be totally confused by the world around you, because you would be unaware of the civilizations that have come and gone and how they shaped your life. Such a lack of knowledge of history can be the seedbed of prejudice and intolerance.

The study of **history** can also be a vital tool in the development of skills critical to success in many occupations. Students of history must learn how to ask probing questions, locate relevant information, analyze historical data, and think creatively. They must draw conclusions and present their findings in an appealing way. Equipped with the ability to carry out independent research and analysis, think critically and creatively, and communicate effectively, students of history gain not only a sound understanding of the world around them, but also skills that are highly valued in the workplace.

KEY WORDS

history

primary source

secondary source

historiography

archaeology

stratigraphy

radiocarbon dating

bias

chronology

cause and effect
   relationship

BCE

CE

VOICES FROM THE PAST

History is not what you thought. It is what you can remember!
   W.C. Sellar and R.J. Yeatman, *1066 and All That*

WHAT IS HISTORY?

The American historian Barbara Tuchman once asked the question "When does history happen?" In other words, is what happened last week history or is it merely the past? Does the past become history only once it has been interpreted by historians? Understanding the discipline of history is a very complex challenge involving issues such as how historians select data to study, conflicting interpretations, and what biases are brought to the subject at hand. Historians attempt to make sense of the past often with limited information, and always with the challenge of viewing distant cultures through the lenses of our modern world.

Change and Continuity in History

History is a discipline that focuses on the study of *change* over time, and is most concerned with the question *why?* Historians gather facts in order to understand why events occurred and the impact these events had on society. In some cases, continuity and stability — the lack of change — occupy the historian's attention. How is it, in a world of constant change, that some aspects of some societies and cultures remain surprisingly stable? Is continuity a good thing or does it lead to stagnation, causing a country or society to fall behind other parts of the world that have embraced change? Throughout *Echoes from the Past,* you will read about how significant turning points in world history led to important changes. Think about which aspects of the civilizations you study provided continuity and stability. How did these institutions sustain themselves for long periods of time, and why was the stability they offered vital to the survival of the society? Are there examples of when continuity was detrimental to a society?

METHODS OF HISTORICAL INQUIRY

Gathering the Evidence

The path to understanding the past is a bit like an obstacle course. The first hurdle facing historians is determining the focus of study. They review what has already been written, and then generate a list of probing questions. By taking the time to formulate questions, historians are able to focus their research and make a monumental task more manageable. Once they have a focus, historians begin hunting down data. Data are often sparse and hard to find, especially about people who had no rank or power. Historians rely on two types of resources when gathering information. **Secondary sources** — books, journals, film — are accounts of the past based on research and analysis. They help provide a context for research and are important starting points. Secondary sources help the historian see how others have interpreted the past and which biases may have shaped their views. The study of how history has been written is referred to as **historiography**; you could call it "the history of history."

Critically important to the study of history are **primary sources**, accounts recorded at the time of an event, which may include diaries, eyewitness accounts, government records, ships' logs, or newspaper articles. Primary sources can also be non-written data such as pottery pieces (also called potsherds) or other artifacts found by archaeologists, cave paintings, or the remains of an ancient religious site. Whether written or unwritten, primary sources are raw, unprocessed data that historians interpret as they try to reconstruct the past. So, is history independent of historians or created by them? Can a truly objective history ever be written, or are all accounts of the past subject to the biases of those who wrote them? Understanding that all historical accounts must be scrutinized carefully is an important lesson for students of history.

You will always find secondary sources in a library. What primary sources might you find there as well?

Reconstructing the Past

Just as change occurs over time, so does our understanding of the past change as the result of new interpretations and knowledge. Historians are not alone in the quest to reconstruct the past. Other disciplines such as **archaeology**, anthropology, ethnology, economics, geography, and the sciences play important roles.

Legends and History

At some point in our lives, we have all been fascinated by a legend. Whether through the stories of King Arthur or Robin Hood, King Solomon's Mines, the epic of Gilgamesh, or the search for Atlantis, we are drawn to the excitement and intrigue of legends. Unlike myths, which deal with the divine, and humanity's relationship with the divine, the central characters of legends are human, and the stories usually have a basis in fact. Often legends deal with the achievements of great leaders, the exploits of great warriors, or the wisdom of great sages and magicians. Although the characters take on superhuman qualities and the events are distorted, legends remain more than fanciful stories. Legends can act as signposts to historians and archaeologists by capturing the imagination and preserving the essence of the character, event, or society portrayed. From there, the great challenge is to separate fact from fiction. Some dedicate much of their lives to unearthing the history underlying a legend, as did Heinrich Schliemann with the legends of Troy and Mycenae. In some cases, the rewards have been astounding; in others, the quest continues.

Review...Recall...Reflect

1. What are the major challenges historians face in writing history?

2. How would you define the study of history?

3. What role can legends play in helping us to uncover the past?

ARCHAEOLOGY AND THE STUDY OF HISTORY

Archaeology provides scholars with the primary data necessary to answer certain questions. As archaeology is a means to an end, rather than an end in itself, it is most often problem oriented. Archaeologists do excavations to solve a problem or test a hypothesis. The artifacts that they gather become a primary source for anthropologists, ethnologists, paleontologists, biologists, and historians. In short, archaeology is the set of methods used to extract information regarding the past from the earth and sea.

Several factors come into play when archaeologists decide when and where to dig. Whether a particular site actually yields important information is often a matter of luck. The next step is to think about the questions to be answered.

Before the excavation can begin, a "dig team" must be assembled. The team will usually consist of a field director who is a trained and licensed archaeologist, a number of supervisors who have some training and experience, and the crew, interested

An archaeological dig requires people with a wide range of skills.

people with minimal experience. Depending on the site, other professionals such as photographers and surveyors may also be brought in. For the analysis of the artifacts, the talents of a wide variety of people are needed. Experts on zoology examine bones and animal remains. Botanists examine plant remains. Geographers do soil analysis. Even pathologists and other medical specialists may be called in if a human body is unearthed.

While the top layers of earth are removed, close attention is paid to the soil, in case a stain or an artifact appears. A variety of things leave tell-tale stains in the soil. Some stains are left by the decaying posts of a wooden structure. Other stains are made by hearths (fireplaces) and middens (garbage pits), both extremely valuable sources of information. Middens often yield bits of pottery, carbonized seeds, bones, and other remnants of daily life. As stains and artifacts are discovered, they are recorded in field notes and their locations marked on graph paper in a grid pattern. The artifacts are placed in labelled bags, and the stains are analyzed. When features such as middens or hearths are discovered, the soil is screened to ensure that no artifacts are accidentally discarded.

Archaeology is essentially destruction: once a site has been excavated, it can never be reworked. Accurate and meticulous notes are essential. Throughout the dig, each member of the team maintains a field journal to record the date, identify the square on the grid being excavated, and describe any finds, impressions, and observations. Graph paper is used to map each square which, when plotted on a master map, helps to create an accurate picture of the whole site. At the end of the season, the field director and assistants collate the information gathered each day by members of the team. The work in the field represents only about one quarter of the archaeologist's work: three quarters of the time is spent in the laboratory analyzing the mountain of primary data collected each season.

For the work of the archaeologist to be of value, the primary data and the completed analysis must be published. Ontario law requires all archaeologists granted licences to prepare a site report at the end of each season in order to get their licences renewed for the next year. Site reports, which include descriptions and photographs of the areas excavated, are made available to scholars and, eventually, the general public.

Underwater Archaeology: A Unique Challenge

Treasures of the past are found under water as well as underground. For as long as people have used water as a means of transportation, there have been shipwrecks. Many of these ships and their contents remain well preserved, lying at the bottom of a sea, an ocean, or a lake. While the rewards of underwater archaeology can be great, the challenges of the work can be daunting. Essentially the same archaeological principles are applied in underwater projects as on land sites, but with several additional challenges. First, conventional diving can be done only to a depth of about 35 m, and even then, divers can only stay down for a relatively short period of time. On average, underwater archaeologists spend about four hours a day under water. Another factor underwater archaeologists contend with is limited mobility. A fully equipped diver working under water lacks the dexterity of someone on land. This problem is compounded by the limited visibility that can result from sediment in the water or simply a lack of light. Finally, the recovered artifacts require immediate treatment to prevent them from decomposing

Compiling and analyzing data collected from the site of the recent discovery of the palace of Queen Cleopatra of Egypt will occupy archaeologists on land and in the water for many years to come.

once they are removed from the protective silt or sand. Despite the challenges faced in underwater archaeology, magnificent finds have convinced archaeologists that the effort is, indeed, worthwhile.

The Story of the Hamilton and Scourge

When the War of 1812 broke out between the Canadas and the United States, the Great Lakes quickly became a war zone. Control of the waterways was essential if troops and supplies were to be moved quickly and easily. To build up their fleets on the lakes, both sides enlisted merchant schooners, which were converted to armed vessels. Two of these schooners, the *Diana* and the *Lord Nelson* were refitted and renamed the *Hamilton* and the *Scourge*.

Early in the morning of 8 August 1813, an American squadron sat anchored off present-day St. Catharines, Ontario, waiting to attack the British at first light. Suddenly, and without warning, a violent squall came up, capsizing the *Hamilton* and *Scourge* and sending 53 members of a crew of 72 to a watery grave. The two schooners came to rest on the bottom

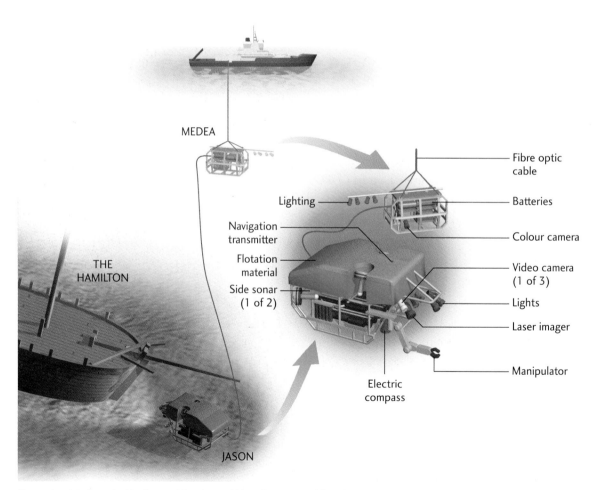

MEDEA

THE HAMILTON

Lighting

Navigation transmitter

Flotation material

Side sonar (1 of 2)

Electric compass

JASON

Fibre optic cable

Batteries

Colour camera

Video camera (1 of 3)

Lights

Laser imager

Manipulator

Recovering data from the *Hamilton* and *Scourge* would have been impossible without the remote-controlled vehicle Jason.

of the lake, 91 m below the surface. For the next 160 years, the two vessels lay lost and undisturbed in the dark, cold waters of Lake Ontario.

Until recently, a search for the *Hamilton* and *Scourge* was beyond the realm of possibility. At 91 m, the water is too deep, dark, and cold for divers to explore using standard underwater archaeological methods. The development of deep-water photography by remote control now allows access to depths formerly unattainable. In 1973, a brief exploration using an ROV (remotely operated vehicle) and sonar revealed that the vessels were still intact and in a remarkable state of preservation. The fresh water, constant near-freezing temperatures, and utter darkness were all key factors in the preservation of the ships and their contents. In 1982, a detailed survey of the *Hamilton* and *Scourge* was carried out by the *Hamilton-Scourge* Society in conjunction with the National Geographic Society. Using cameras mounted on a remote-controlled vehicle, archaeologists took 1900 still photographs and recorded 26 hours of videotape. The well-preserved ships and artifacts will ultimately provide researchers with an abundance of documentation on the construction of schooners in the early nineteenth century. The remarkable collection of artifacts lying with the vessels includes cannon still on the deck, cutlasses crossed above guns, shot (ammunition) resting in the shot racks, and boarding axes still in their racks, just as they were over 185 years ago when the vessels went down. The *Hamilton* and *Scourge* Project was one of the most important underwater archaeological projects in the world.

Analyzing Artifacts

To an archaeologist, the artifacts recovered during an excavation are primary data, much like a diary is a primary source to a historian. Artifacts are the key to a wealth of information about the society being studied, but unlocking that information requires careful analysis. Artifacts can be broken down into two main categories: organic remains, remnants of living things such as plants and animals, and inorganic remains such as stone tools or pottery.

The best preserved organic artifacts are found in dry, hot regions, such as deserts; in freezing conditions, such as Arctic regions; or in waterlogged places, such as peat bogs or the bottom of the sea. Decay caused by micro-organisms destroys underwater artifacts unless the objects lie in water that is near freezing or buried in silt. Many interesting finds

Organic matter, including human bodies, remains well-preserved in freezing conditions. This is the body of a young Inca girl who was sacrificed and frozen in the Andes Mountains about 500 years ago.

This 45-year-old woman from the Roman town of Herculaneum died during the volcanic eruption of Mt. Vesuvius in 79 CE. She was found buried under volcanic material, on the beach near her home. Due to the action of bacteria and the elements, all that remains are her bones and her jewels.

have been made in peat bogs, which are acidic. The acid causes bones to decay, while the moisture and the peat preserve the flesh. Bodies of animals and people found in bogs are remarkably well preserved, but have no bones.

One of the tasks in analyzing organic material is to determine its source. Was it from the local environment or was it a product of human activity and brought to the site? For example, people choose different types of wood for building and for making a fire. Wood used in buildings may have been brought from some distance, while firewood is more likely to have been found in the local environment.

Human remains present a special challenge to the archaeologist. Much can be learned about a people by studying their skeletal remains. The first goal in the analysis of human remains is to determine the age and sex of the person. The age of young children and teens can be determined within one year by examining their teeth. The age of young adults is determined by examining the fusion between the ends and shafts of long bones. Determining the age of adults is much less precise since it is done by studying tooth wear, which can be affected by several things. Sex can be determined by bone structure. Males tend to have heavier and larger bones. The pelvis of a female is structurally different from that of a male in order to allow childbearing.

A special area of study is paleopathology, the study of ancient diseases. Childhood diseases often leave evidence of slowed growth in the bones or other changes to the skeleton. For example, rickets causes bowed legs, a protruding chest, and brittle bones. Other diseases such as syphilis, arthritis, tuberculosis, and leprosy cause noticeable deformation and destruction of bone. Bones that show abnormal wear often reveal the occupation of a person. Other injuries can be associated with specific activities. Weapons also leave specific marks: swords leave narrow cuts, spears leave clearly defined holes, and clubs leave crushed and shattered bones.

A great deal of information can be learned from stone tools and pottery. A microscopic examination of the edges of a stone tool will often reveal evidence of its use. For example, tools used for cutting plant stems may have silica gloss on them from the silica in plants. Stones used to make tools were not randomly selected, but were quarried to obtain the proper type and quality. Flint, chert, and obsidian are all popular stones used in the ancient world. In some instances, stone quarried hundreds of kilometres from a site has been discovered even though similar types of stone were found locally. The most plausible explanation for this is that high-quality stone was prized and traded.

Pottery, the most common of all archaeological finds, has been used for over 10 000 years. Potsherds are abundant because baked clay preserves well, and because pots were cheap, everyday objects that were discarded when broken. Even a few pieces of ancient pottery can supply a great deal of information: the type of pot, how much the clay was worked, the techniques used in making and decorating, the firing conditions, artistic style, and sometimes even the name of the potter.

Methods of Dating Artifacts

When an archaeological find occurs, the first thing determined is the age of both the artifacts and the site. The archaeologist can choose from a variety of dating techniques, and while few of these allow for absolute dating, approximate and relative ages can be obtained. Recent improvements in dating techniques have made them an especially valuable tools for unmasking historical forgeries.

Review...Recall...Reflect

1. Briefly outline the stages archaeologists go through in preparing and executing a dig.

2. What additional factors must the underwater archaeologist contend with?

3. How have improved dating techniques assisted in exposing frauds?

Stratigraphy

A commonly used method of dating is **stratigraphy**, the study of the layers (strata) of archaeological remains at a site. It is based on the principle that the most recent materials are found at or just below the surface. Materials found are progressively older as the dig goes deeper. The consecutive periods of the occupation of a site can be distinguished and differentiated, with each layer revealing the lives of the inhabitants.

Many methods of dating are limited by the need to know the location and context of the artifact. Professor Willard F. Libby, the American chemist who discovered the principles of **radiocarbon dating**, raised these limitations in 1949. Radiocarbon dating determines the age of organic material by measuring the level of the radioisotope carbon 14 (C^{14}). Carbon 14 is formed by neutrons interacting with the earth's nitrogen. This process creates radiocarbon, which is equally distributed throughout the atmosphere. All living things absorb radiocarbon throughout their lives, and at the moment of death, the process is reversed and the radiocarbon begins to decay at a constant rate. The rate of decay can accu-

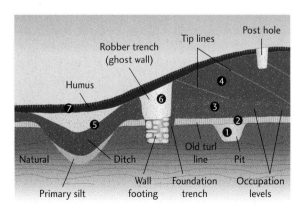

Stratigraphy can reveal the ages and other information about the layers (strata) of the occupation of an archaeological site. Where does the earliest occupation lie?

rately disclose the age of material up to 40 000 years old. When 5730 years have passed after the death of an organism, the radiocarbon level is at exactly one half of the original level, and after another 5730 years it is, again, exactly half. Decay of the radiocarbon will continue according to this formula. Measuring the radiocarbon can establish the stage of decay and thus indicate the amount of time elapsed since the death of the organism. Radiocarbon dating is the most popular archaeological technique for dating organic materials and probably the most effective.

ANALYZING HISTORICAL RESEARCH

The data archaeologists gather is only one of the sources a historian draws upon when attempting to reconstruct the past. Legends, as we have seen, can be a rich source of inspiration and a good starting point. Written records provide the historian with even more material. It is important to keep in mind that the fact that an eyewitness wrote an account at the time does not always mean that it can be accepted as true. For example, in 1554, on a voyage to Guinea, John Lock recorded that he saw elephants and dragons engaged in mortal combat, but neglected to explain that his crew had hidden in a tree when an anteater appeared. The reason why details like this were recorded or left out lies in the mental baggage carried by both explorers and the readers of their reports.

Mental baggage refers to the preconceived ideas that lead people to interpret events or draw conclusions in a way that meets their expectations. The merchants who funded the voyage would never have believed the story of the anteater since none had ever been reported before. However, people fully expected that there would be dragons in faraway exotic places. To ensure funding for future voyages, the report told

of events that the merchants could imagine, and avoided aspects of the truth that might have seemed like lies or exaggeration. From this example, we see that when analyzing primary documents, historians must take into account the mental baggage of both the intended audience and the writer.

Understanding Bias in History

It has been said that history is written by the winners. This expression points to another factor historians must be aware of — **bias**. For example, after Richard III of England lost his throne during the Wars of the Roses, he was portrayed as an evil and corrupt king. The first accounts of his reign must, however, be examined carefully since they were written by historians working for Richard's archrival Henry Tudor. They were biased in Henry's favour since he had won the war. Bias is the point of view that people tend to bring to a situation and consequently makes it difficult or impossible for them to judge fairly. Diary entries and newspaper accounts, while preserving the details of an event, may reflect the biases of the writer. When dealing with primary documents, the historian must carefully analyze both the facts and the source.

Aside from drawing on archaeological information and other primary sources, historians also rely on secondary sources. Secondary sources are accounts written after an event, and are generally based on information contained in primary sources or other secondary sources. Secondary sources can give the historian a framework, or context, within which to work. By drawing on the work of other historians, the task can become more manageable. Secondary sources can vary from ancient texts to recent publications. A work such as the *Histories* by Herodotus, a historical account of the Greek-Persian Wars, is considered a secondary source even though it was written over 2400 years ago.

King Richard III of England received a lot of "bad press" after his death. Over the years, historians have revealed a somewhat better, less-biased image of Richard.

History is like a jigsaw puzzle for which we have only some of the pieces to re-create the picture. In addition to missing pieces, historians are often faced with the task of choosing what to stress and what to ignore. The aim of most historians is to interpret events objectively in order to reconstruct the past as accurately as possible. Despite the best efforts to remain objective, historical writing is always affected by the historian's own biases. By choosing to emphasize one cause over another, or focus on one aspect of a situation while overlooking another, historians can sometimes reveal this bias. Bias will always remain a part of the writing of history, but it can make history more interesting. The challenge falls to the student of history to discover the bias of the author being consulted. It is because historians can never be absolutely certain about the past that

makes history alive with controversy. Students of history can join in the quest to know the past by exploring, challenging, and questioning other historians.

SOCIAL HISTORY

History is not just the story of political power struggles and military campaigns. This would ignore the majority of the people who make up the past. It focuses only on those with wealth and power. But in order to have a fuller picture of the past, historians can also study religious life, economic trends, technological change, artistic achievement, and the social fabric of the people. This means the realities of everyday life — the homes, clothing, food, health, festivals, and music of the people. This social history tries to reflect the lives of women, men and children from all classes. The poor also have a past. Because written records generally deal with the wealthy and

This is one artist's reconstruction of a marketplace in the city of Harappa, an important trading centre of the Indus Valley civilization, ca. 2200 BCE. Do you think reconstructions like this are helpful to our understanding of the distant past?

powerful, the historian often relies on the work of archaeologists to complete the picture of earlier times. For those societies that left little or no written record, the work of the archaeologist is vital to the historian who hopes to delve into the daily life of earlier civilizations.

Reconstructing the Past

The historian must act much like a detective, piecing together the events of the past based on limited bits of information. Consequently, interpretation and speculation are often involved. Whether a museum curator, historian, anthropologist, or a writer of historical fiction — no one can ever appreciate the past in all its fascinating detail. Instead, those who deal with the past attempt to present as complete a picture as possible based on available facts and interpretations. Whether reading a history book, touring a museum, or exploring a reconstructed historical site, we are benefiting from years of research, analysis, and interpretation by many talented and dedicated professionals.

CAUSE AND EFFECT: THE IMPORTANCE OF CHRONOLOGY

Chronology, the placing of events into the order in which they occurred, allows us to understand how events of history unfolded. For example, in studies of the history of ancient Egypt, two of the most famous images are the Great Pyramids at Giza and the gold head of Tutankhamun. Yet, by the time of Tutankhamun's reign, the Great Pyramid was already 1200 years old. Tutankhamun would himself have gazed upon the magnificent pyramid as a wondrous monument of the distant past. As students of history, we must keep people and events within the correct chronological order.

Beyond maintaining an accurate perspective on the past, understanding chronology helps us see causal relationships among events. Can Canadians understand the tensions between French and English Canada without knowing about earlier events such as the execution of Louis Riel or the Conscription Crisis? These events illustrate **cause and effect relationships**. Understanding history depends on understanding the relationships between events. For instance, how the victory of the Greeks over the Persians contributed to the cultural and political achievements of the Classical Age. How did the Crusaders shape the future of Europe, even though they failed to meet their goals. Understanding the connections between events is part of the study and enjoyment of history.

From BC to BCE and AD to CE

When Roman Catholicism became the dominant religion of Europe, the recording of time was aligned with the life of Jesus Christ. All time prior to the birth of Christ was expressed as *Before Christ* (BC) as in 450 BC. Time after the birth of Christ was expressed as *Anno Domini* (AD), which is Latin for "In the Year of Our Lord." Someone referring to the year 2000 AD is in fact saying the two-thousandth year "of our Lord Jesus Christ." To a non-Christian, this method of reckoning time makes little sense. On the Muslim calendar, 2001 ad is the year 1422 AH (*Anno Hejirae* — "In the year of the Hijra.") The Hijra was the Prophet Muhammad's departure from Mecca to Medina. According to the Jewish calendar, 2000 is 5761; and on the Chinese calendar, it is 4699.

We now recognize the cultural bias behind the BC/AD system and the need for more globally acceptable chronological terms. Since the most widely used calendar is, in fact, the one based on the Christian keeping of time, it has been adopted for international use. It is increasingly common now to refer to time as Before the Common Era (BCE) or in the Common Era (CE). For example, the date of the Greek-Persian War, formerly referred to as 480 BC, is now referred to as 480 BCE, while the beginning of the first crusade, formerly listed as AD 1092, is now referred to as 1092 CE.

Conflicting Interpretations: The History of History

The study of the history of history? Yes indeed. In universities, entire courses are now devoted to historiography, the study of how history has been written.

What is the truth about Louis XIV? Time, and the times, have a way of changing the truth. Even the best, most thorough historian can be the victim of her or his own bias.

Historiography recognizes that all history is the product of historians, their own interpretations of the past. Two historians, reading the same documents and examining the same artifacts, can arrive at very different views of the same events. When we read a history book, we must always take into account when the book was written and who wrote it. For example, Louis XIV, the absolute ruler of France in the seventeenth century, was heralded by the eighteenth-century writer Voltaire as the greatest monarch ever to have ruled France. During the 1930s, when dictatorships were threatening to overrun Europe, biographies of Louis were highly critical. Where does the truth about Louis XIV lie? To what degree were these conflicting views products of the times in which they were written rather than accounts of the reign of Louis XIV?

Liberal, Marxist, and Post-Modern Historians

Throughout the nineteenth and much of the twentieth century, liberal and Marxist interpretations dominated historical writing. A liberal view of history is characterized by a sense of inevitable progress. Liberal historians tend to see history as unfolding in a progressive manner, each generation building on the accomplishments of previous generations for the greater good. Even catastrophes such as World War II hold lessons from which we learn and move forward. The Marxist view sees history as the struggle between classes — rich and poor, the powerful and the powerless. Marxist historians tend to focus on the struggles of the common people against the tyranny and oppression of those with power. They see history as moving toward an ultimate conflict that will see the overthrow of the elite and the shifting of power to the people.

The 1990s saw post-modernism entering into the writing of history. Traditional divisions of history have either been replaced or become more refined through questions asked by post-modern scholars. Post-modernism refers to a view of history that emphasizes the role of the historian in creating history. Post-modern historians question the traditional search for historical truth, claiming that historical truth is relative and so no particular account can ever claim to be true.

Post-modernism celebrates diversity, and rejects monolithic world views like liberalism, Marxism, religions, and so on. In an age of post-modern thought, history is becoming increasingly fragmented as multiple views are now put forward, each with its relative view of truth. Some of the intriguing questions raised by post-modern historians include: Whose history are we telling? Is history from the point of view of women, labour, or the gay community different from "mainstream history"? Is each of the views equally valid? If history is relative and there are no historical truths, then is there any point to the study of history? Can men write about women's history? Can western historians write about Asian history? Is there a discipline that transcends (overrides) gender, race, and class, allowing trained historians to write authoritative history in any area? These and many other questions are being hotly debated in universities all over the world. *Echoes from the Past: World History to the 16th Century* has been written by leading scholars from several universities. As you read the chapters on various civilizations, see if you can determine which interpretation dominates each view of the past, or whether you can detect any bias.

Review...Recall...Reflect

1. Why is it important that we watch for biases when reading history?

2. Why are historians beginning to use the terms BCE and CE rather than BC and AD when referring to historical dates?

3. How is the writing of history shaped by the historian's own time and place?

LIFELONG SKILLS THROUGH THE STUDY OF HISTORY

Much of this chapter has focused on the gathering and analyzing of data and information, whether archaeological or historical. The historian's craft is one of research, analysis, and synthesis. Using the information they have managed to assemble, historians present their particular version of what happened in the past.

History is not simply a matter of knowing names, dates, and events. Historical studies involve gathering information from a variety of primary and secondary sources, analyzing the information, and synthesizing the material into a coherent account. Many skills are required to be successful in history. Students of history must develop good research skills in order to collect the necessary information. This entails knowing where to look for information, how to read efficiently, and how to make good notes. Organizational skills are also essential. Information must be well-organized if an intelligible and effective essay or seminar is to be presented.

For research to pay off, the student of history must be able to analyze effectively and evaluate information. Often, too much information is available and choices must be made about what is necessary and what is not. Analysis requires good thinking skills. Thinking creatively allows the historian to see patterns where none appear to exist, and to come up with innovative and new interpretations.

Finally, gathering and analyzing information is of limited value if it is not clearly presented. Presenting a lucid picture of the past requires a synthesis of the information — a bringing together of facts and ideas into a coherent interpretation. The ability to write and speak effectively is also helpful. *Echoes from the Past* will give you lots of opportunities to create, present, and evaluate your own interpretations of history.

Creativity and Collaboration

Developing your ability to think creatively and collaborate with others will be an asset in not only the study of history, but also in whatever career you choose. Because history involves much more than remembering historical dates and events, being able to interpret creatively is critical. Thinking creatively means reading and interpreting information in new and original ways, often drawing conclusions not obvious to others. The ability to think creatively is also an invaluable asset when planning and preparing a presentation, designing a display, or creating a skit or role-play based on history. The creativity you develop through this course could help you write a piece of historical fiction, script a historical movie, design a museum display, or write a groundbreaking interpretation of a particular period. The section entitled Careers in History, in the Methods of Historical Inquiry Appendix will show you how the study of history can enter into many challenging and exciting careers.

The aims of *Echoes from the Past: World History to the 16th Century* are to enrich your understanding of the past and introduce you to a variety of ancient and medieval cultures. Many civilizations are brought to life with hundreds of photographs, maps, diagrams, and Feature Studies. *Echoes from the Past: World History to the 16th Century* will broaden your knowledge of the past and the world around you, while helping you to develop skills that will be critical for your success in any future studies and careers.

Chapter Review

Chapter Summary

In this chapter, we have seen:

- that history is the study of change, continuity, and cause and effect relationships from the past
- that historians often develop conflicting interpretations of the past depending on the biases, point of view, or historiographical school of thought
- that the study of history is a complex task involving careful analysis of a variety of primary and secondary sources
- how acquiring and practising skills related to history will be valuable tools throughout our lives, both in various careers and in understanding our world

Reviewing the Significant Concepts (Knowledge/Understanding)

1. Understanding history requires knowledge of the following concepts and an understanding of their significance in the study of history. In your notes or in your *World History Handbook,* identify and explain the historical significance of three from each column.

   Concepts

history	change and continuity
primary sources	secondary sources
historiography	archaeology
stratigraphy	radiocarbon dating
bias	cause and effect relationships

2. What challenges did the discovery of the *Hamilton* and *Scourge* present to archaeologists? Why was it worth their efforts?

Doing History: Thinking About the Past (Thinking/Inquiry)

1. Why can it be said that archaeology is a means to an end but not an end in itself?

2. Why must historians be aware of bias? Is it possible to write history entirely free of bias?

Applying Your Learning (Application)

1. Prepare a chart with the following headings to summarize the information that can be obtained from various types of artifacts.

   Organic Remains   Human Remains   Tools and Pottery

2. If you had the opportunity to lead an archaeological expedition based on a legend, which legend would you choose? Write a one-paragraph rationale to explain your selection.

Communicating Your Learning (Communication)

1. How did this chapter change your view of history? What elements related to the study of history were new to you? Do you find history as described in this chapter more appealing than the study of names and dates? In a paragraph, respond to two of these questions.

2. In the *History's Place in Your Future Career* section of the Appendix, there is a chart illustrating history-related careers. Re-create some of this chart by finding an image to represent history, and images of six to eight careers you think you might be interested in pursuing. Working in a small group, combine your images around an image for history and create a "Visual History Career Web."

UNIT ONE

The Near East

chapter 1
The March to Civilization

chapter 2
Egypt and Israel

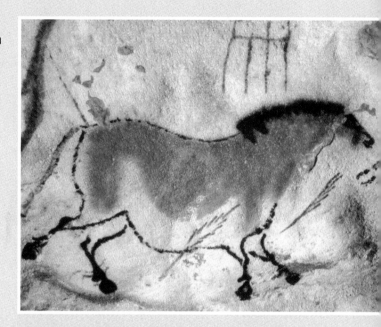

This rock painting from a cave at Lascaux, France, was created by a Paleolithic artist ca. 15 000–13 000 BCE.

This unit first traces the development of the earliest human societies from the time of the Neanderthals, through the Paleolithic and Neolithic Ages. You will see how creative, innovative human societies grew and developed into permanent towns and cities of the sophisticated and complex civilization we call Mesopotamia.

Chapter two focuses on the history of one of the most intriguing of all ancient civilizations — Egypt. The chapter explores the nature of Egyptian society, including a look at how religious beliefs shaped the government and inspired the building of enormous pyramids. The images in the tombs of long-dead pharaohs will come alive as you examine the daily life of the ancient Egyptians and learn to appreciate more fully the society that began to flourish along the banks of the Nile some 5000 years ago.

UNIT EXPECTATIONS

In this unit, you will:

O describe the roles of different members of society in the early stages of human history

O evaluate the criteria that a society must meet to be regarded as a civilization

O explain the development of societies from simpler to more complex

O identify forces that tend to promote and facilitate change and those that reinforce stability and continuity

O evaluate the role and importance of a variety of legends, myths, and traditions

O conduct organized research, using a variety of information sources

O communicate effectively using a variety of styles and forms

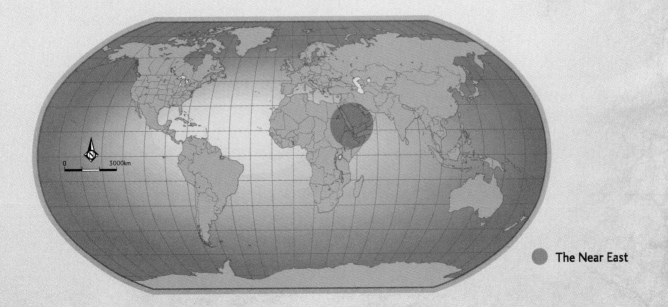

0   3000km

The Near East

The March to Civilization

By the end of this chapter, you will be able to:

- *explain the development of societies from simpler to more complex*

- *describe the roles of different members of society in the early stages of human history*

- *demonstrate an understanding of the bases of authority in Paleolithic, Neolithic, and early Mesopotamian society*

- *evaluate the criteria that a society must meet to be regarded as a civilization*

Caves in Valltorta Gorge in Spain display figures of Paleolithic hunters with their weapons. What kinds of weapons do they appear to be using?

When did human history begin? Did it begin when the first cities were built 5000 years ago or when the first hunter-gatherer societies appeared? The term **prehistory** is often used when we refer to early human societies that did not leave written records. This could be taken to mean that human societies that do not have writing have no history, or even that these societies experienced little significant change. It could lead to misconceptions such as that North American Aboriginal societies were unchanging until the arrival of Europeans, or that early humans, such as the **Cro-Magnons**, made no technological innovations that led to significant change. This could also encourage false ideas about cultures and societies that record their past in other ways.

Some would say that human history began with the arrival of the first fully human beings about 50 000 years ago. From that point on, human societies have evolved and become increasingly complex. During the period between 50 000 BCE and 10 000 BCE, virtually every corner of the earth was populated. Over the next several millennia, unique and diverse cultures reflected the physical environment in which they developed. This chapter examines life among our early ancestors, the **Neanderthals**. We then focus on the development of early human societies during the **Paleolithic Age**, and conclude with a look at the Neolithic Revolution and the essential elements of a civilization.

KEY WORDS

prehistory

Paleolithic Age

society

barter

Neolithic Revolution

civilization

Mesopotamia

Urban Revolution

cuneiform

ziggurat

KEY PEOPLE

Neanderthals

Cro-Magnons

Homo sapiens sapiens

Sumerians

King Hammurabi

Assyrians

VOICES FROM THE PAST

Ugh?

Anonymous

TIME LINE: THE MARCH TO CIVILIZATION

	4 million years ago	*Australopithecus*, the first upright hominid appears
Homo erectus appears	1.7 million years ago	
	400 000 years ago	*Homo sapiens* replaces Homo erectus
Neanderthals appear throughout Europe	100 000 years ago	
	50 000 years ago	Anatomically modern humans begin to move out of Africa into Europe, displacing Neanderthals
Great Leap Forward occurs with a burst of creative innovations in art and technology	35 000 years ago	
	20 000 years ago	Bow and arrow is developed, improving the success of Paleolithic hunters
Neolithic Revolution occurs, leading to the first permanent towns and the domestication of plants and animals	ca. 9000 BCE	
	ca. 4500 BCE	Earliest civilizations begin to emerge in river valleys of Mesopotamia, Egypt, India, and Asia
Cuneiform, the earliest known form of writing, is developed in Mesopotamia	ca. 3500 BCE	
	ca. 2900 BCE	Sumerian civilization dominates Mesopotamia

IN SEARCH OF OUR ANCESTORS

According to the most recent scientific and archaeological evidence, it appears that the earliest hominid biped (primate walking upright on two feet) to whom humans can trace their ancestry lived about 4 million years ago. By 1.7 million years ago, brain and body size, as well as other changes, were significant enough to suggest that the earlier primate named *Australopithecus* had been replaced by a new species, *Homo erectus*. By 1.2 million years ago, it appears that all hominids except *Homo erectus* had become extinct.

Over the next 500 000 years, *Homo erectus* continued to evolve in the direction of modern humans, acquiring a larger brain and rounder skull but still

This scene is one artist's conception of how early hominids appeared, walking upright on the plains of Tanzania 3.6 milllion years ago.

with thicker skulls and brow ridges than we have today. By 400 000 years ago, the changes were again significant enough for *Homo erectus* to be reclassified as *Homo sapiens* ("wise man").

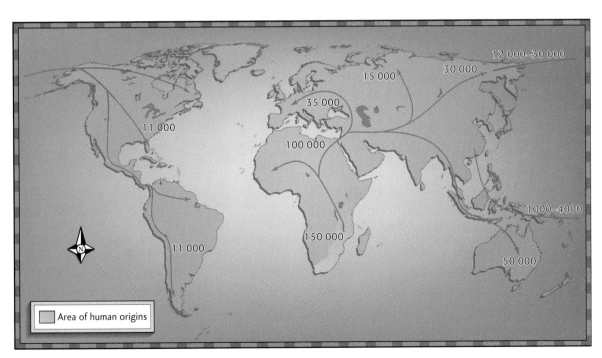

12 000–30 000

30 000

15 000

35 000

11 000

100 000

150 000

11 000

1000–4000

50 000

Area of human origins

■ Human Migration

This map indicates the routes of early human migration and the times when humans arrived at various areas of the world. The numbers are approximate, in thousands of years. When did humans arrive in North America?

By 100 000 years ago, humans had settled in three distinct populations, all of which were *Homo sapiens*. In Europe and the Near East, there were people we call *Homo sapiens neanderthalensis*, or **Neanderthals**. Africa was populated by anatomically modern humans (***Homo sapiens sapiens***) and in Asia, there was another group of people for whom we still have too few fossils to make a clear definition. Sometime around 50 000 years ago, the anatomically modern Africans began to invade Europe. Initially it was believed that the Neanderthals had evolved into *Homo sapiens sapiens*. But scientists are now quite certain that the invasion of *Homo sapiens sapiens* led to the assimilation, if not extinction, of the Neanderthals. Eventually, *Homo sapiens sapiens*, our direct ancestors, inhabited all parts of the world, reaching Australia 40 000 years ago, the Americas 12 000 years ago, the Arctic 10 000 years ago, and the Pacific Islands a scant 2000 years ago.

The Neanderthals

The people we call Neanderthals lived between 100 000 and 40 000 years ago at a time when Europe and Asia were in the grip of the last ice age. The Neanderthals, who were named after the Neander Valley in Germany, where the first skeleton was found in 1856, were a powerfully built people. If it were possible to meet some Neanderthals, their physical appearance would immediately tell us that they were not human beings of today. From a distance, you would notice that Neanderthals were heavy-set people with an average height of 160 cm and a weight of about 73 kg. Their arms and legs would seem stubby, since their forearms and lower legs were shorter than ours. These creatures were also heavily muscled, especially at the shoulders and neck. As you drew nearer, you might be struck by their facial features. Neanderthal eyebrows rested on prominently bulging, bony ridges, while their nose, jaws, and teeth protruded forward. The lower jaw sloped back so that the Neanderthals had no chin, and their eyes lay sunken in deep sockets. Finally, if you were to shake hands with a Neanderthal, you would feel the firm grip of a large and powerful hand.

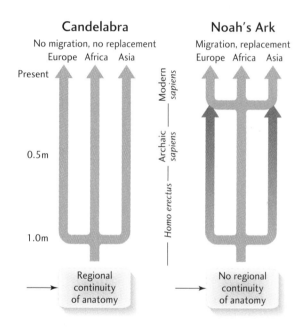

Views of Human Origins

Which view makes sense to you? The Candelabra model sees all populations of Homo erectus as originating in Africa one million years ago and migrating to Asia, Europe and so on.

The Noah's Ark model sees Homo erectus coming from Africa one million years ago, then being replaced in the Old World by migrations of anatomically modern humans.

In the Field...

The Stones and Bones of Mary Leakey

By the time of her death in 1996, at age 83, Mary Douglas Nicol Leakey had received numerous awards and honours, and was world renowned as an archaeologist, paleoanthropologist, author and artist. Others in her field said that she set the standard for the excavation and documentation of Paleolithic finds. Mary's meticulous records and her tireless unearthing of stones and bones inspired many others to start thinking about who the early humans were, not just where they were. Her son, Richard Leakey, a paleontologist himself, said that for much of her early career she laboured in the shadows while her husband, Louis, got most of the publicity. According to Richard, Mary was at the centre of the research. He would know, since he, his two brothers, their nannies and several Dalmatians usually accompanied Mary to her work.

Mary did not have a formal education, but she did have drive and curiosity to spare. She also had a family background that had exposed her to archaeology at an early age and predisposed her to thoughtful examination of her surroundings. Both Mary's parents were artists. Wherever the family lived, Mary's father pursued his avid, amateur interest in archaeology. One of his best friends was Howard Carter, the man who discovered Tutankhamun's tomb.

Mary's father died when she was 13 and her mother's attempts to settle her down in school were not successful. When she was 17, Mary wrote to a number of archaeologists offering to help at digs. An archaeologist named Dorothy Liddell, took her up on her offer and Mary dug and provided sketches for publication. Mary soon met a well-known archaeologist named Louis Leakey; the two were married in 1936 and made their home and workplace in Africa.

Until 1959, Mary and Louis worked at a variety of sites in Kenya and Tanzania. Louis was often distracted by other pursuits, but Mary persevered with a commitment to detail that resulted in several important finds. She also changed the scientific community's mind about human evolution. Before Mary Leakey documented her work, it was assumed that Asia would be found to be the site of human evolution. The Leakey discoveries made Africa our cradle.

What did Mary find? In 1948 she located the first fossil ape ever found. Dated between 16 and 20 million years old, people hoped that this would prove to be some sort of missing link between humans and apes. It wasn't, but it was thought to be an ancestor of both humans and apes. Only three others have been found since.

In 1959, after years of excavating in Olduvai Gorge, Mary discovered the skull of a 1.75 million-year-old hominid. At the time it was both the first of its species and the oldest hominid ever found.

These discoveries brought the Leakeys honours, financial support, the support of scientists, and a lot of attention. Mary shied away from the limelight and let Louis be the star. After Louis died in 1972, Mary continued to work, and established a site at Laetoli, just south of Olduvai. Then in 1978, Mary made an extremely exciting find: hominid foot prints that had been hardened in volcanic ash about 3.6-million-years ago! The absence of tools at the site led Mary to postulate that bipedalism (two-footedness) preceded the use of tools – the opposite of what had previously been thought.

Mary Leakey's most important discoveries were made here, in the Olduvai Gorge in Tanzania, Africa "the cradle of man."

Formidable to the end, Mary believed that archaeologists should spend more time looking for concrete evidence and less time making hypotheses.

Activities

1. Look up archaeologist, paleoanthropologist, and paleontologist in a dictionary. In your own words, write a definition for each. Which of these career options attracts you the most? Explain.

2. Defend or reject the last sentence of this feature. What are the roadblocks to uncovering the real story of human evolution?

Neanderthal Society?

Although we know that Neanderthal males worked together to track and kill large game, it is much less certain that they lived in any kind of formal social relationship. The world of the Neanderthals was harsh; life was lived on a day-to-day survival basis. It is likely that males lived largely separate from females and children, hunting and scavenging in small groups. However Neanderthals lived, it was not a society as we know it. The Neanderthal world was one of small groups thinly spread over the landscape. Mating between males and females was random, with no permanent relationship or family unit. In fact, outside the small group, there was seldom any interaction with others.

Within the small Neanderthal group, there was no formal leadership, no rules or laws people were expected to follow. If there was any primitive religion, it involved few rituals and no moral codes to guide life. Evidence gathered from Neanderthal sites suggests that their lives were lived on a very short-term basis with little organization. Although they wore clothes, they relied primarily on wraps to keep them warm, and there is no indication that they wore personal adornment to signify any type of social hierarchy. One definition of a **society** is a "system of human organizations that generates distinctive cultural patterns and usually provides protection, security, and continuity for its members." Using this definition, it would seem there is little reason to describe Neanderthals as living in a society.

The image of Neanderthals as excellent big-game hunters is only partially correct, for although they did track and kill game such as the woolly mammoth and the woolly rhinoceros, they also scavenged for food. Neanderthal males seem to have been scavengers as much as they were hunters, as suggested by the horse heads excavated at many Neanderthal sites. The head is the least desirable part of the horse, and would likely have been left by other predators after they had killed and eaten the prime meat. Neanderthal males scavenging for food would have taken the head back to the camp to be shared with others. Most probably, Neanderthals were opportunistic hunters and scavengers, tracking game when available, and at other times relying on the remains left by other predators.

Neanderthals probably lived by both hunting game and scavenging remains left by other predators. Females and children gathered plants that grew nearer the caves.

While males scavenged and hunted, females and children spent more time close to the cave fire, preparing plant foods they had gathered and animal scraps brought to them by males. Given the uncertainty of the hunt, the gathering done by women and children was critical to the survival of Neanderthals.

Did Neanderthals hold any religious beliefs? It has generally been assumed that they held no spiritual beliefs, but the discovery of Neanderthal burials has led some to speculate that they may, in fact, have had some kind of primitive beliefs. Given the absence of grave goods, it seems that if the Neanderthals did have any primitive beliefs, they certainly had no rituals associated with them.

WEB CONNECTION

http://www.mcgrawhill.ca/links/echoes

Go to the web site above to find out more about Neanderthals.

The skeletal remains of Neanderthals reveal the stresses of a difficult life. Most children died in childbirth or in the first few years of life, and 80 percent of adults died before the age of 40. Many suffered from a variety of ailments or permanent injuries inflicted during their struggle to survive. Neanderthals seem to have devised few ways to make their lives easier, relying instead on their physical strength to carry out the necessary tasks. Homes were simple, food never certain, and death a constant companion.

What happened to the Neanderthal people? It is quite likely that their demise came at the hands of invading, anatomically modern humans from Africa. *Homo sapiens sapiens* had better weapons and tools, products of their superior intelligence and ingenuity. After inhabiting Europe and the Near East for 60 000 years, the Neanderthals were wiped out within a couple of thousand years by the killing, disease, and displacement brought by *Homo sapiens sapiens*. Some have suggested that the Neanderthals were assimilated by the invading people from Africa. This would appear unlikely, as there is no fossil evidence of a *Homo sapiens sapiens*-Neanderthal hybrid. In fact, the fossil evidence shows that within 2000 years, the Neanderthals had been completely replaced by *Homo sapiens sapiens*. Even if interbreeding did take place, there is some evidence to suggest that the offspring would not have survived, since the pelvic structure of the female Neanderthal suggests a 12-month pregnancy, rather than the 9-month cycle normal for *Homo sapiens*. In the end, the invasion of modern humans (us) from Europe and Asia appears to have caused the extinction of the Neanderthals.

Paleolithic spearheads made of antler, from Willendorf, Austria and dated 30 000 years ago.

The Great Leap Forward: Complex Societies

Sometime around 35 000 years ago, a process of monumental significance began. Some scientists have called this process "The Great Leap Forward." Two fundamental changes occurred: the development of modern anatomy, and the beginning of innovative behaviour.

After millions of years during which the changes in hominids were imperceptibly slow, changes began to occur that would clearly set humans apart from all other animals. Humankind experienced a burst of innovation and creativity. The achievements of humanity in the past 35 000 years are astounding, especially when we consider that in the previous 60 000 years, Neanderthal culture had remained virtually unchanged.

The curiosity, ingenuity, and creativity of *Homo sapiens sapiens* produced a vast array of crafted materials. Tools were made of thin stone blades struck from larger stones, and some were mounted on wooden shafts to make spears. Most tools of *Homo sapiens* had a specific purpose: there were needles and awls for making clothing, mortars and pestles for preparing food, and axes for cutting wood. Eventually, more sophisticated weapons were developed, such as barbed harpoons, darts, spear throwers, and bows and arrows. The development of these more advanced weapons allowed hunting large and powerful animals such as wild pigs, reindeer, horses, and bison. Watercraft may also have appeared, since places such as Australia were settled for the first time. Perhaps even more significant than the advances in tools and weapons was the development of trade and aesthetic appreciation. The long-distance trade that developed was not only for raw materials, but also for ornaments. Aside from the crafted objects of personal adornment, sculpture and painting began to appear as well. For the first time in history, there is evidence of an appreciation of beauty. Modern humanity had arrived.

Review…Recall…Reflect

1. What evidence suggests that the Neanderthals and *Homo sapiens sapiens* were not the same people?

2. Describe how a Neanderthal would look compared with modern humans.

3. Why was innovative behaviour important to the development of early human societies?

DAILY LIFE IN THE UPPER PALEOLITHIC AGE

Perhaps the greatest change brought about by the Great Leap Forward was the development of human societies, over the course of what we call the Paleolithic Age. This term comes from the Greek words *paleo,* meaning *"old,"* and *lithos,* "stone," and, hence, an alternative title is the "Old Stone Age."

Roles in Paleolithic Society

Role	Function	Sphere of Influence
warrior	protection	society
hunter	provide food and clothing	family unit
spiritual leader	religion and ritual	society
healer	medicine and healing	society
artist	storytelling, adornment	society
gatherer	provide food	family unit
mentor	guidance, teaching	society

Human societies would grow in complexity and develop social hierarchies, alliances, marriage customs, religious rituals, and a refined sense of artistic beauty.

During the Upper Paleolithic period (50 000 to 10 000 years ago) people lived in small groups or bands of five to ten families. They were nomadic or semi-nomadic and lived by hunting and gathering. They were very aware of their surroundings and in tune with nature. Since success often depended on a communal effort, the social relationships within the band were also close.

Unlike the earlier Neanderthals, early modern humans such as the Cro-Magnons in Europe carefully cultivated relationships with other bands, sometimes scattered over hundreds of kilometres. Each year, likely in the summer or early fall, several bands would come together to arrange marriages, **barter** for raw materials, weapons, clothing or other goods, and carry out initiation rites. In order to keep the bloodline strong, it was important that the young people marry outside their own band, and at these gatherings of as many as several hundred people, marriages were arranged. Bands formed alliances with the exchange of exotic goods ranging from sharksí teeth and shells to Baltic amber. As winter neared, the bands would disperse to the protected valleys where they had stored food and could find some protection from the icy winter winds.

Another sign of the increasing complexity of Paleolithic groups was the stratification of society. There was leadership now, and the beginnings of social class. We find evidence of social hierarchy in the great variations in Paleolithic graves. For the first time in human history, personal adornment begins to appear, and it was by no means equally enjoyed. Hierarchy within Paleolithic societies had much to do with age and experience, and with gender, as men

began to exercise control over society. Wisdom and knowledge came to be prized traits, along with the essential qualities for effective leadership.

Role of Women and Men in Paleolithic Societies

Advances resulting from the Great Leap Forward made the men of the Upper Paleolithic period much more effective big-game hunters than their Neanderthal predecessors. Among the most significant developments were better hunting strategies resulting from closer cooperation, improved speech, and more lethal weapons. So successful were the strategies of early modern humans, people were able to survive comfortably on the food they hunted and gathered, without relying on scavenging. People such as the Cro-Magnons managed to plan ahead, storing food for the winter.

This very lifelike heard of bulls was painted by a Paleolithic artist who was skilled at portraying motion and direction. The artist has used the figure of one bull to frame an entrance within the cave.

Improvements in technology led to better weapons and better tools for skinning and preparing food, scraping skins, and — for the first time — sewing better-fitting clothes to provide much more protection from the harsh winter weather. Cro-Magnons were so successful at hunting big game that they were able to adapt to changes in their environment.

Hunters stalked whatever game was available. In Europe, men hunted mammoths, aurochs, bison, reindeer, wild cattle, horses, and red deer. In South America, it was llamas, giant sloths, and an ostrich-like bird called a rhea. In Australia, emus, wallabies, kangaroos, and large marsupials were the prized animals. Early hunters used a variety of techniques to capture large game, including driving the animals into natural enclosures or forcing them over cliffs, or into marshes or tar pits. The appearance of the bow and arrow about 20 000 BCE allowed hunters freedom to stalk animals with even greater success.

Ancient ODDITIES

In northeastern Asia, in Siberia, there is an archaeological site called Berelekh, famous for a so-called "mammoth cemetery" containing more than 140 well-preserved mammoths. The giant mammals died there during spring flooding.

Despite the males' increasing success at hunting big game, we must be careful not to overemphasize the importance of hunting and, consequently, men in society. Our view of Paleolithic society has been coloured by cave paintings of heroic hunters, and the fact that weapons preserve better than sewn leather bags or baskets made for gathering. The gathering of food was done mostly by women and children and accounted for approximately 60 to 70 percent of the Upper Paleolithic diet. Women were virtually assured of returning from their foraging with a full sack of food, while the men could never be certain whether the hunt would be a success. No wonder there was such rejoicing when a major kill was made. Women would spend a large portion of their time gathering food, which included various roots, potatoes, fruits, sweet berries, honey, and shellfish. Studies of the teeth of Paleolithic skeletons suggest that the bulk of the diet was vegetables.

The role of women extended far beyond the vital responsibility of food gatherer. Women in Paleolithic societies made clothing from the hides of animals and nurtured the young. Once past their childbearing years, older women would have advised younger women, passing on wisdom and stories handed down from generation to generation. Whether acting as mothers or grandmothers, women were essential to the health and survival of Paleolithic societies.

When discussing Paleolithic society, there is always the danger of oversimplifying gender roles. Women, who normally gathered in hunter-gatherer societies, also captured small game, reptiles, birds, and insects to supplement the diet of the family or band. On occasion, some women probably accompanied men on a hunt, helping to drive animals from the bushes, or paddling canoes while men fished. On the other hand, men tracking game would have gathered food along the way, even if primarily to feed themselves on the hunt. Other tasks, such as gathering firewood, cannot be assigned exclusively to one gender.

Art, Ideas, and Beliefs in the Paleolithic Age

The clearest expression of the creativity and ingenuity of Upper Paleolithic people lies in their art. During the Upper Paleolithic period, a cultural explosion occurred. Tools began to be carved with beauty as well as utility; pendants were made from horse teeth, and jewelry made of shell was worn by the living and the dead. Sculptures of plump, large-breasted women — perhaps symbolizing fertility — were common. The most remarkable artistic achievements of the Upper Paleolithic period were the vibrant cave paintings, some of which depict animals that are now extinct.

Small sculptures such as this, called the Venus of Willendorf, were common in the Paleolithic Age. The large breasts and wide hips of these female figures probably are meant to symbolize fertility.

Among the most famous of the cave paintings are those in the Lascaux Caves, in south-central France. The paintings, dating to 15 000 BCE, are the work of experienced artists. The painters often made use of irregularities in the cave walls to add a three-dimensional effect to their art. For example, a concavity was used to form the belly of a pregnant cow. In other instances, the figures of animals were intentionally distorted to give the viewer a more striking perspective. Scaffolding as high as five metres, was built to allow artists to paint the ceilings of the caves. After first outlining a silhouette of the figure in charcoal, the artist then created the picture using paint made from charcoal, clay, minerals, ochre, and other materials. The images, deep in the caves, were executed by the light of animal-fat lamps. No one is certain how the caves were used, although some believe they were part of rituals related to hunting magic. The significance of the paintings for us is that they capture and preserve the creativity of the Paleolithic people. Despite the primitive nature of the paintings, they manage to portray the beauty and strength of the animals, and convey movement and depth.

Religion

Paintings, such as those at Lascaux, clearly indicate a special reverence and awe for certain animals. This suggests that, for the first time in human history, people were expressing the beginnings of religious beliefs. Further evidence of religion comes from another cave in France called Trois-Frères. Here, in what is called the Chapel of the Lioness, a cave lion engraved on a stalagmite shows signs of being repeatedly struck, as if to kill it symbolically. It is thought that the Chapel of the Lioness might have been a ritual meeting place of Paleolithic hunters.

The technological innovations and artistic expression of the people of the Paleolithic period clearly set them apart from the earlier Neanderthals. After millions of years of evolution, humans acquired the knowledge and ability to change their environment according to their needs.

THE NEOLITHIC REVOLUTION

The **Neolithic Revolution** or New Stone Age (*neo is Greek for "new"*), refers to the period after 9000 BCE when ground and polished stone tools primarily were used. At this time, people started abandoning a semi-nomadic lifestyle to begin farming. The agricultural revolution was a further manifestation of the Great Leap Forward. Using the same innovative and creative spirit, people learned to harness nature by planting crops and domesticating animals. Several factors contributed to the shift from hunting and gathering to agriculture.

The first and most obvious factor is that, by the end of the last ice age, around 9000 BCE, people had learned a great deal about plants and animals. After observing animals at water holes or caring for injured animals, men may have decided to corral some of them. Meanwhile, women may have tried to grow some of the wild grains they gathered. Perhaps they noticed that where a basket of grain had spilled, new stalks began to grow, or noticed shoots sprouting from a midden (garbage pit). Whatever the process, men and women learned that, rather than simply rely on luck, they could control their food supply. Another factor contributing to the rise of agriculture was the end of the ice age, which resulted in a warmer, wetter climate. This led to a widespread abundance of wild grasses, including the ancestors of today's grains. A rise in population also accompanied the end of the ice age. The increase in population density led to increasing competition for land, which would eventually give the survival edge to agriculturists. On average, hunters and gatherers require 16 km^2 per person, whereas the same area can accommodate 100 agriculturists. The early farmers gained numerical superiority and eventually displaced the remaining hunter-gatherers.

The animals first domesticated were cattle, sheep, goats, and pigs. Of these, cattle were the most important as they supplied meat, leather, and milk — from which cheese and butter were made. When animals were slaughtered, nothing was wasted. Dishes were prepared using the udder, tripe (stomach), brains, bone, head, feet, tails, blood, and even gristle. Similarly, the weeds that grew in the grain fields were harvested along with the grain and often incorporated into the pottage (thick soup). Two of the drinks enjoyed by Neolithic farmers were beer made from barley, and mead, an alcoholic beverage made by allowing honey and water to ferment. Mead was often flavoured with wild fruit and herbs.

Improved tools allowed for better and more efficient agriculture. Using a sickle made of flint blades placed in a curved segment of an antler, a family could harvest enough wheat in ten days to last them six months. Land could also be cleared more quickly with the improved tools. Axes made of flint could cut down a pine tree with a diameter of 17 cm in five minutes. The invention of the hoe allowed tilling of the soil. During the late Neolithic period, the development of metallurgy also produced a wider range of tools. Copper could now be used to make sharper knives, elegant drinking vessels, spits, buckets, and cauldrons.

The Neolithic Revolution resulted in a profound shift in society. People abandoned their semi-nomadic lifestyle and, instead, built permanent towns and cities. Some left the fields altogether, choosing to specialize in various crafts. As people began to take up different occupations, society became more hierarchical; a class system developed. The domestication of animals and the planting of crops freed people from the endless pursuit of food, allowing further development of art, music, sports, and other leisure activities. It also enabled the development of more complex religions; society could now afford to maintain a priestly class that made no material contribution. The establishment of permanent cities and complex religions brought about the building of elaborate religious sites and tombs. In the process of shifting from hunting and gathering to farming, people laid the foundations for **civilization**.

Neolithic megaliths (Greek for "big stones") like Stonehenge on Salisbury Plain in England were created ca. 2800-1500 BCE. Similar structures are found in other parts of Europe as well. Their exact purpose is unknown. Were they used as astronomical observatories or religious rituals?

CHARACTERISTICS OF A CIVILIZATION

Between 4500 and 1000 BCE, civilizations developed independently in many parts of the world, ranging from **Mesopotamia** and Egypt in the Near East, to China in the Far East, and the Maya in Meso-America. The emergence of civilization in all cases was the result of subsequent revolutions; an **Urban Revolution** followed the Neolithic Revolution. The Urban Revolution was characterized by the development of large, densely populated settlements that were socially and economically diverse. In Neolithic societies, there was little to differentiate members of society. Everyone farmed and common ownership of land was important to the survival of the group at large. The development of urban societies saw much

greater differentiation of the population. People began to specialize, taking on roles such as ruler, trader, metal smith, scribe — as well as farmer, fisher, and herder. These diverse urban communities developed into what are generally accepted as the earliest civilizations.

The process and pace at which various civilizations developed differed in each case, but there are several characteristics commonly accepted as indications that a society is "civilized." These include: the emergence of a centralized government, agricultural intensification, specialization of occupations, a stratified class structure, merchants and trade, the development of science and a form of writing, and the development of a state religion.

Let us take a closer look at each of these characteristics.

Centralized Government

One of the cornerstones of any civilization is a central body that passes laws and regulates society. In pre-civilized societies, individuals took it upon themselves to correct a wrong that they or a member of their family or clan had suffered. Warfare was on a small scale, consisting of informal raids carried out by small groups. Over several thousand years, power became concentrated in a small, powerful group of people that was recognized as having the right to insist that others obey the laws and regulations it created. Initially, political authority rested with a citizen assembly guided by a group of elders. In these early governments, decisions were made on a consensual basis, since the idea of a majority vote was unknown. In times of crisis, societies tended to place themselves under the authority of a dictator, or single ruler. Over time, different types of leadership emerged, including monarchies (rule by divine right), kingship (rule appointed or inherited), and democracies (leaders chosen by vote). In a civilization, the government takes on the role of adjudicator of disputes and rectifier of wrongs. Warfare becomes an organized response of the state to external threat. Internal conflicts between citizens are settled by the government.

Agricultural Intensification

One of the most important areas of concern that early governments supervised was the planning and coordination of irrigation projects, building of dikes to reclaim land, and development of a calendar system to plan the planting and harvesting of crops. Through these efforts, there was a dramatic increase in agricultural productivity, a more secure year-round food supply, and the creation of leisure time.

Specialization in Occupations

With a dramatic increase in food production, societies were able to use their surplus food and time to support those engaged in other pursuits. As civilizations developed, so too did the need for specialization. The increasingly complex society would need specialists: tax collectors to gather the resources the government needed to function; record keepers to maintain inventories of food and other goods; judges to ensure that people obeyed the law. New, specialized trades could now develop: weavers, carpenters, coppersmiths, goldsmiths, tanners, bakers, brewers, and teachers. Increased food production also allowed time for people to create and enjoy works of art and architecture, to compose poetry and legends, and to explore music.

Class Structure

As centralized governments developed and specialized trades emerged, equality among the people of Neolithic and Paleolithic societies was lost. No longer did individuals have equal access to land. Over time, the concept of private ownership of land developed. This was accompanied by a desire to accumulate more land, hire others to work the land, and, eventually, the enslavement of some to carry out much of the manual labour. Once the concept of private land ownership became ingrained, an unequal distribution of wealth followed, leading to the formation of classes. In early civilizations, a very sharp division between nobles and commoners developed, usually with no real middle class. As distinct classes emerged, the wealthy nobility began to monopolize governments.

Characteristics of Civilization

Merchants and Trade

Trade itself was not new to early civilizations. What was new was the nature of trade. Prior to the development of early civilizations, trade was generally between bands and consisted of raw materials such as obsidian, amber, and shells. As new specialized trades developed, trade shifted to manufactured goods, including luxury items prized by the wealthy elite as important status symbols — rare dyes, ivory carvings, and precious stones. There was a change not only in what was traded, but also how trade took place. Along with the specialized trades, was the development of a merchant class that produced nothing, but earned wealth by helping to facilitate the exchange of goods. With the rise of a merchant class, shops and markets arose; bartering became more complex, which led to the development of currency. Long-distance trade developed, and with it, the movement of more people from place to place, civilization to civilization.

Development of Science and Writing

For practical reasons, and at times out of pure curiosity, people in early civilizations began to invest time in exploring the natural world. Important advancements were made in metallurgy and the invention of the wheel, baked bricks, mortar, simple machines, and specialized tools.

Most of the earliest examples of writing we have are concerned with the accounting for and ownership of goods. With surpluses of food and other commodities came the need to keep track of such things as: how much grain was available in the government storehouses; who owned the cattle on a given area of land and how many head did they have; how many cattle would be traded for how many chickens or sheep? The need to measure the amounts of food and other goods being stored and traded led to the development of systems of weights and measures. Writing was now important for the recording of laws and religious texts.

State Religion

What was the relationship between the emergence of civilizations and the development of religions? Today, we may argue that religion is not essential for a society to be civilized. When the first civilizations were developing, however, there was a very strong link between religion and the authority of the central government. In most cases, religion legitimized the authority of the government. The government, in turn, protected and promoted the religion. Without the gods to sanctify a social order that gave some members of society authority over others, it would have been very difficult to convince people to surrender their place in a more equal society. This is not to suggest that the religions of early civilizations were concocted purely to support the power of the elite. The religions of these civilizations were legimate expressions of their beliefs and spiritual needs.

Several elements that some may consider essential for a civilization could more appropriately be labelled by-products of civilization. They are the marks of a highly organized and specialized society. A complex and highly organized religion, for example, is not essential to a civilization, nor is a rigid class structure. Similarly, refined art and music, advanced architecture, and even systems of education are not essential for a society to be considered civilized. They are, however, characteristic of some great civilizations.

1. How did the roles of men and women differ in Paleolithic societies?

2. Why is the Neolithic Revolution considered one of the most significant turning points in human history?

3. Seven essential elements of any civilization are described here. List these seven elements in order of importance from the most important to the least important and defend your ranking.

Rivers and Civilizations

The earliest civilizations — Mesopotamia, Egypt, India, and China — had at least one common characteristic: they developed along river valleys. Mesopotamia grew up along the banks of the Tigris and Euphrates rivers, Egypt drew its life from the Nile, India's earliest civilization sprung from the Indus River Valley, and Chinese civilization originated along the mighty Yellow River. All of these relied on rivers for a steady source of water, fertile soil, and fish to supplement their diet. In most cases, the rivers also served as an easy means of communication, facilitating trade and the exchange of ideas.

The decision of early farmers to settle in the river valleys and attempt to control and utilize rivers had profound implications for the rise of early civilizations. The great river valleys of the world provided the key ingredients for the world's first civilizations to flourish.

MESOPOTAMIA: THE CRADLE OF CIVILIZATION

The earliest of all civilizations arose in a land the Greeks would later call Mesopotamia. Mesopotamia means "land between the rivers," and refers to the area between the Tigris and Euphrates rivers (in present-day Iraq). It was in this region that humans first abandoned their nomadic lifestyle and began to form permanent settlements. The changes that occurred in the river valleys of the Tigris and Euphrates were revolutionary. Codified laws, the concept of kingship, the building of places to worship the gods, writing, and even the wheel were all first developed by the Mesopotamians.

In ancient times, the southern part of Mesopotamia was known as Sumer and the northern area was called Akkad. Eventually, the two regions were unified under Babylonian leadership and became known as Babylonia.

The land of Mesopotamia is essentially a bleak alluvial plain that receives too little rainfall for crops to mature. The climate is hot and dry, and the soil is arid and sterile if not cared for properly. The land

> **TIME FRAMES**
> **THE ANCIENT NEAR EAST**
>
> Neolithic Era
>   ca. 9000–4000 BCE
> Mesopotamia
>   Uruk ca. 4500–3100 BCE
>   Sumer ca. 2800–1800 BCE
>   Akkad ca. 2340–2180 BCE
>   Babylon ca. 1830–539 BCE
>   Assyrian Empire 1100–612 BCE
>   Ancient Iran ca. 5000–331 BCE
>   Achaemenid Persia 559–331 BCE

contains no minerals and almost no stone or timber for building. The soil is baked by the long, hot summers, causing vegetation to wither and die. During the winter, stormy south winds brought unpredictable downpours that turned the river valleys into slippery mud. Spring was the most dangerous time for those living in Mesopotamia. Spring rains combined with the melting snows from the neighbouring Zagros Mountains and made the Tigris and Euphrates rivers swell, often causing catastrophic flooding.

So, what attracted settlers to this seemingly inhospitable region? The answer lies in the natural levees along the course of the Euphrates River. Natural levees are embankments produced by the build-up of sediment over thousands of years of flooding. The levee surface slopes gently downward away from the river. The highest and safest ground on a flood plain is along the portion of the levee adjacent to the river. Aside from the protection it provided, the silty sediment of the levees was fertile and easily drained, planted, irrigated, and cultivated. Adding to the richness of the area around the levees were the swamps that teemed with fish and waterfowl and produced an abundance of reeds. In the spring, the reeds provided excellent food for sheep and goats, and when mature, were an important building material. It was around these natural levees that the first settlers in Mesopotamia saw promise, and established permanent settlements.

While the natural levees did hold promise, this could only be realized with irrigation and better drainage. The land between the rivers and streams was desert and swampland, and this proved to be a great hindrance to the unity of Mesopotamia.

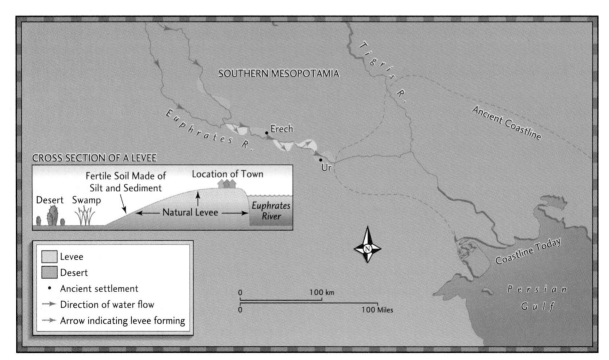

■ **Levees in the Euphrates River in Mesopotamia**

The fertile soil deposited on levees made it possible for people to grow enough food for themselves and create settlements. Why did the first cities form on rivers?

Communication was difficult and dangerous. Unlike the predictable Nile River in Egypt, the Tigris and Euphrates were givers of both life and death. Sudden floods often ravaged Mesopotamian villages without warning.

The People

Mesopotamian civilization was the product of a cross-fertilization of four distinct ethnocultural groups. The **Sumerians**, who arrived about 3000 BCE from central Asia, were the first to develop writing, and large social organizations. These would become the first cities of the world. Throughout the history of Mesopotamia, Semitic-speaking peoples arrived from the Syrian desert; the Akkadians arrived ca. 2600 BCE and the Amorites, ca. 2200 BCE. The third major cultural group to settle in Mesopotamia were the Indo-Europeans, represented by the Luvians and the Hittites. These migrations took place around 2000 BCE. Finally, the Hurrians, who were a people from the Caucasus, in Asia, began migrating to Mesopotamia around 1800 BCE. The study of ancient Mesopotamia is the study of several distinct peoples who settled the area.

The Growth of the Empire

For much of its history, Mesopotamia was a collection of independent states. Although Mesopotamia would eventually become unified, it occurred much later than in neighbouring Egypt. The early government of the towns and villages was democratic. An administrative bureaucracy was established to look after an increasingly complex society. The government built and maintained roads and canals, enforced laws, and settled disputes. As the towns grew and prospered, rivalries developed that led to intermittent wars. During times of war, many Mesopotamian villages found it necessary to appoint one of their strongest and ablest warriors to lead them to victory. The Sumerian title for king was *lugal,* meaning "big man." Although the appointment was initially temporary, the frequency of wars led to the decline of democratic government and the rise of a monarchical system in which kingship was hereditary and despotic.

Sumerian figures such as these surprised-looking worshippers (ca. 2700-2500 BCE) have been found in temples excavated in Iraq. Their wide eyes are probably meant to indicate that they are in the presence of a god.

Sumerian Society

The Sumerians were the dominant culture in Mesopotamia between 2900 and 2400 BCE. Their society was divided into four main classes. The top class was the nobility, comprised of the king and his family, the chief priests, and the high palace officials. The king's prominent role in society was further enhanced when it was given a religious dimension. Although the king was never deified, kingship itself was believed to be one of the basic institutions of human life created by the gods. The power of the king was not derived from brute strength. It was divinely ordained. The king and other members of the nobility owned the most and best land.

Those men and women who worked for the nobility in exchange for the use of the land were known as "free clients." These people were dependent on the nobility for their livelihood and were a major portion of Sumerian society. Commoners were free citizens who owned their own land and were not dependent on the nobility. Among this group were those who produced and traded a wide range of goods. Talented artisans created beautiful goldwork, ceramic bowls, and even board games. Others were involved in the day-to-day administration of the empire, making sure that the land was properly irrigated, laws were followed and enforced, and taxes were collected. The fourth group in Sumerian society was the slave population.

The Akkadians

The basic social, economic, and intellectual framework of Mesopotamia was established during the period of Sumerian domination. Despite repeated attempts to attain mastery over lower Mesopotamia, however, the Sumerians were never successful. Instead, the unification of lower Mesopotamia was accomplished by a Semitic chieftain named Sargon. After conquering the Sumerians in 2331 BCE, Sargon established his capital at Akkad, from which the Akkadians took their name. Sargon's greatest achievement was finally to unify Mesopotamia and spread Mesopotamian culture throughout the area known as the Fertile Crescent. The Fertile Crescent is a belt of rich farmland that stretches from Mesopotamia northeast to Syria and southwest to Egypt. The dynasty established by Sargon was short-lived; by 2200 BCE, the Akkadians fell to invading barbarians.

The Babylonians

Mesopotamia was eventually reunited by another Semitic people known as the Babylonians. The Babylonians used their central location to dominate trade and, eventually, establish control over all of Mesopotamia. Guiding Babylon's rise was the talented **King Hammurabi**, who came to the throne ca. 1750 BCE. He established Babylon as the leading power in Mesopotamia by conquering Akkad and Assyria, gaining control of both the north and the south. The most lasting and famous element of Hammurabi's reign was his law code. This code was inscribed on a stone pillar set up in public for all to see. On the pillar, Hammurabi is depicted receiving his authority from the god Shamash. The laws of ancient Babylon were not only considered divinely

King Hammurabi receiving the Law from Shamash, ca. 1750 BCE.

inspired, but also were clearly written out to form a consistent body of laws.

Hammurabi's laws tell us much about life in ancient Mesopotamia. The punishments were designed to fit the crimes. This code was the origin of the concept of an eye for an eye and a tooth for a tooth. For example, if a son struck his father, the son's hand was cut off; if someone were to break another's bone, they would have the same bone broken. The consequences of these laws, however, differed according to rank. Members of the nobility faced much more lenient penalties, often being required only to pay a fine.

Despite the talents and efforts of Hammurabi, Mesopotamia was not to remain united for long. By 1550 BCE, the Babylonian kingdom was in decline and the unity of Mesopotamia was again crumbling.

The Assyrians

For the next seven hundred years, Mesopotamia experienced turmoil and uncertainty. The invasion of the warlike Hurrians was but one of the events that contributed to centuries of chaos. Finally, in the tenth century BCE, Assyria began to emerge as the dominant force. Led by Assurnasirpal II and drawing on the best army in the Near East, Assyria was able to reunite Mesopotamia and establish the first true empire the world had ever seen. Using boasts such as, "I built a pillar over against his city gate, and I flayed all the chief men... and I covered the pillar with their skins; some I walled up within the pillar, some I impaled upon the pillar on stakes... and I cut off the limbs of the officers," the Assyrians soon became the most feared army in the Near East. By the seventh century BCE, the Assyrians had established an empire stretching from the Persian Gulf north and west to Syria, Palestine, and Egypt.

THE Past AT PLAY

The site of the great Sumerian city of Ur has provided an enormous amount of archaeological evidence of life in Mesopotamia during the third millennium BCE, including an example of the Royal Game of Ur. This was a racing game for two people that used a decorated gaming board and circular pieces that resembled a cross between checkers and dominoes.

The power of fear was insufficient to hold together the Assyrian Empire. The Assyrians overextended themselves and terrorized all that they had conquered. It was only a matter of time before the subject states rose up in revolt. The revolts began to occur in the late seventh century BCE, and by the end of the century, the collapse of the Assyrian Empire was complete. Although Babylon would later enjoy a short-lived resurgence, it too had passed its prime and was in decline. By 539 BCE, Mesopotamia had become a part of the vast Persian Empire, which stretched from the Indus River to the Mediterranean Sea.

The Persian leader Cyrus the Great replaced Assyrian rule by fear with tolerance and fairness. Differences in religion were accepted, taxes imposed on subject peoples were fair, and local officials were retained in the administration of the Persian Empire — reporting to Persian governors called *satraps*. This benevolent rule brought stability to the Persian Empire, which would survive some 800 years before the Greeks under Alexander the Great conquered it.

Many would say that the greatest contribution of Mesopotamia to western civilization was the invention of writing. Writing allowed the transmission of wisdom and knowledge, the codification of laws, and the keeping of records to facilitate trade. The earliest writing we have found dates to 3500 BCE and was discovered at the ancient Mesopotamian city of Uruk.

The written language of the Mesopotamians was developed by the Sumerians and is called **cuneiform**, which means "wedge-shaped." A scribe would record information by pressing a wedge-shaped stylus into a slab of soft clay. Other writing materials included stone and chisel, metal and chisel, and paint on glazed terracotta (red clay). Before the development of cuneiform script, written communication was in the form of pictograms. At this point, writing was used only for record keeping, and thus only concrete words (nouns) such as "ox," "grain," and "sheep" were needed. As society became more complex, the language evolved, enabling signs to be used to depict homonyms (words that sound the same and are spelled the same but mean different things e.g., "bow," "light") and, eventually, abstract thoughts. In time, the system of cuneiform writing spread to Persia and Egypt, and for centuries was the only international script. It was a great vehicle for the growth and spread of civilization and the exchange of ideas among cultures.

Science and Technology

Writing was only one of the many advances credited to the ancient Mesopotamians. By developing a variety of tools and techniques, the Mesopotamians were the first to make a prosperous living based on large-scale agriculture. The earliest and, perhaps, most significant development came in the fourth millennium BCE, when a Sumerian crafter built the first known wheeled vehicle. The design, using solid wooden wheels, allowed oxen to pull three times as much weight as before. Aside from the use of wheeled vehicles, Mesopotamian farmers developed seeder-plows and pickaxes to make their work easier and more efficient. The Mesopotamians became talented bakers, brewers, weavers, and tanners. Some of their buildings, constructed of mud-brick and tile, were so well built that they survive today.

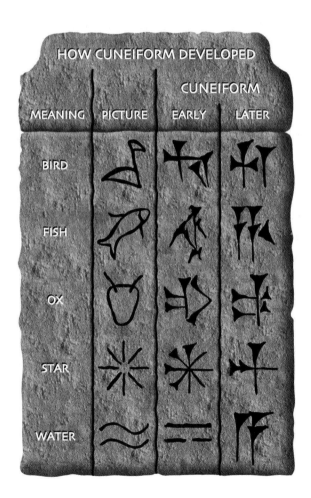

Could you make a sentence with these words? What's missing?

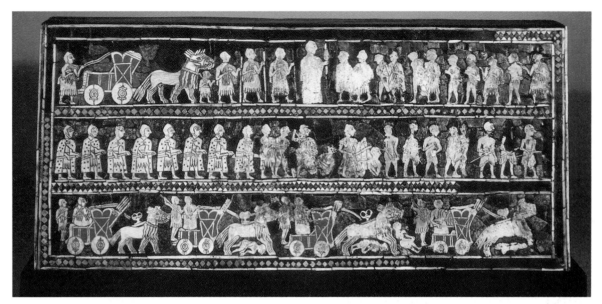

This panel from a tomb in the ancient Sumerian city of Ur show us soldiers, priests, and charioteers on the first known wheeled vehicles.

Beliefs

Mesopotamian religion is the oldest in the world for which written records exist. It was a polytheistic religion comprising some 3600 various gods and demigods. This vast number of deities reflects the diversity from region to region. Despite the differences in the representation of the gods and the varieties found in the local towns, all of Mesopotamia shared essentially the same religion. The five most prominent deities were Enlil, the supreme god and god of the air; Ishtar, the mother goddess of fertility and life; An, the god of heaven; Enki, the god of the underworld and the water; and Shamash, the sun god and the giver of law. The names used here are Sumerian. Throughout Mesopotamian history, the names would change but the basic functions remained the same.

The History of the Imagination: Myths and Legends

Gilgamesh and Enkidu: A Story of Epic Proportions

Like all legends, the incredible story of Gilgamesh and Enkidu is built around a larger than life real personality. As in great epics, the saga has both historic and mythic elements. This legend has given historians, anthropologists and sociologists plenty to think about.

Gilgamesh was a real king in Uruk in Babylonia and probably reigned about 2700 BCE. Many stories and myths surround him and endow him with beauty, strength, courage and an unsurpassed physical presence. Gilgamesh was said to be two-thirds divine and one-third human. He was revered for his accomplishments, yet his people complained and suffered under his overzealous leadership. Apparently, as king, Gilgamesh thought it was his right to control everything, even the right to sleep with any bride before the groom had a chance.

Gilgamesh

The gods heard the people's moaning and so created Enkidu. Physically, he looked like Gilgamesh, but shorter and broader. Valiant and innocent, Enkidu lived among the animals before the people of Uruk discovered him. He was seduced into human contact by a temple courtesan and taught human ways. With his strength and good heart, Enkidu was seen as a good match for Gilgamesh, someone who could be a worthy companion and subdue the king's baser tendencies. Enkidu was taken to the home of a bride, where it was known Gilgamesh was to visit. Enkidu blocked the way and the two men wrestled and fought each other like bulls. Eventually, the fighting stopped. The two men embraced and began an epic friendship that would see them through several exciting and terrifying adventures.

Unfortunately, in their exuberance, both Gilgamesh and Enkidu made the gods angry, and were punished by the killing of Enkidu. Humanized by his close relationship with Enkidu and grieving for his lost friend, Gilgamesh journeyed through the Underworld crying, "Death and life I wish to know".

The story is an amazing glimpse of life and thought several millennia ago. But, the themes are timeless and provide an interesting link between an ancient civilization and ourselves. Originally written on a series of twelve clay tablets, the stories were lost and unknown from the advent of Christianity until 1853, when fragments were excavated at Nineveh (modern northern Iraq). Other significant things about the epic of Gilgamesh and Enkidu include:

- it is the first known work of great literature

- it is the first known epic poem

- the tablets provide the name Sin-leqi-unninni — the earliest known author

- it mentions a great flood within a story similar to the one about Noah's Ark.

Activities

1. Why do people turn some of their leaders into legends.

2. List the timeless themes that seem evident from this short glimpse of the epic of Gilgamesh and Enkidu.

3. Look up a full retelling of the epic (try the Internet or a collection of myths) and present a visual representation of one of the episodes.

The oldest written records of a story of creation date back to ancient Mesopotamia. The creation of the universe was conceived in human terms, explaining life to the Mesopotamians as they knew it: a story created by people for people. The main creation roles were played by four gods: An, the god of heaven; Enlil, the air god; Enki, the water god; and the Earth goddess who had various names, such as Nammu. These supreme deities planned and created the main components of the universe and then delegated these components to their offspring to rule.

Ziggurats: Temples to the Gods

According to the beliefs of the ancient Mesopotamians, it was vitally important that the gods be honoured by religious ceremonies. These ceremonies were performed by the priests in sacred temples. Like most Mesopotamian architecture, temples were constructed of mud brick. Constant threat of flooding meant that the temples had to be placed on platforms. Over time, the temples evolved into the imposing structures known as **ziggurats**. This was a stack of platforms decreasing in size from bottom to top. The structure resembled the step pyramids of the Egyptians except that a small chapel sat on top of the ziggurat. Ziggurats ranged from one to seven platforms and were decorated with painted stucco and coloured, glazed bricks. To further enhance their appearance, the structures were often planted with flowers, shrubs, and trees.

One of the most famous ziggurats was the Tower of Babel. The original structure was destroyed and rebuilt several times. The final restoration was undertaken by Nebuchadnezzar, who hoped to raise the tower up to heaven. Once completed, the Tower of Babel was called one of the great wonders of the ancient world. This ziggurat's temple was perched almost 100 m above ground. The base measured 91 m on each side and covered half a square kilometre. Surrounding the massive structure were storehouses and apartments for the priests who served the temple.

The Ziggurat of Ur was built ca. 2000 BCE

Review...Recall...Reflect

1. Explain why the earliest civilizations developed in river valleys.

2. How did geography shape the nature of ancient Mesopotamian society?

3. For each of the seven elements of a civilization described above, provide an example from ancient Mesopotamia.

Mesopotamia's Lasting Legacy

There are many reasons why Mesopotamia has been called the cradle of civilization. It was in the river valleys of the Tigris and Euphrates that people first abandoned their nomadic way of life and began to build permanent homes and villages. This settlement led to an increasingly complex society that developed the concept of kingship and the city-state. Mesopotamia was also the birthplace of writing, astronomy (including the seasonal equinoxes), and a written legal code. Even the wheel, one of the most revolutionary technological advancements in history, was a product of the ingenuity of the ancient Mesopotamians. We are the inheritors of all this and much more. Later civilizations would borrow heavily from the Mesopotamians, taking their ideas and building upon them.

EVALUATING CIVILIZATIONS

Throughout the pages of *Echoes from the Past: World History to the 16th Century,* you will learn about the development of several civilizations. There are, of course, other civilizations not discussed. The process of selection involved value judgements, and your class will also have to make judgements when it decides which of these civilizations to study in the limited time available. How do we judge a civilization? Should a civilization be judged on the grandeur of the monuments it leaves behind? Should it be judged by the lasting contributions it makes in science, technology, and the arts? Or is a

civilization measured by the breadth of land it occupies and the number of people it represented? Perhaps, some consideration should be given to the quality of life enjoyed by the people of a civilization. Is a civilization that conquered huge areas and built impressive monuments and buildings with the sweat of slaves greater than one that left few monuments but gave all members of society basic human rights? There are no easy answers to these questions, but they are worth thinking about as you study ancient civilizations of the world.

History Continues to Unfold

The quest to understand the origins of modern humans continues in many fascinating ways. Some anthropologists are focusing their research on the evolution of the human mind and human consciousness. This is leading to questions such as: When in human evolution did consciousness as we experience it today develop? What evolutionary advantages would the mind provide for humans in their struggle to survive? Current scientific research into the brain is helping us to understand our ancestors as well as ourselves.

Current Research and Interpretations

Despite mountains of research both in the field of archaeology and in science laboratories, the origins of modern humans remain hotly debated. The very first human skeletons discovered were Neanderthal, so named because the skeletons were found in the Neander Valley in Germany. Ever since their discovery, the fate of Neanderthals has been a controversial issue, and still, a century and a half later, there is no definitive answer. Are they the distant ancestors of modern humans or are they an evolutionary dead end? Some believe that Neanderthals blended with anatomically modern humans moving out of Africa and were eventually absorbed through interbreeding. Others, citing a variety of physiological evidence, argue that Neanderthals could not have bred with modern humans and were in fact decimated by modern humans, ultimately pushed to extinction.

Chapter Review

Chapter Summary

In this chapter, we have seen:

- that development from the earliest upright hominid to modern humans took place over four million years
- that human societies evolved from the simple social organizations of the Neanderthals to the highly complex organizations of the ancient Mesopotamians
- how the basis of authority reflected the nature of the society, and that how this authority was granted changed over time
- how ancient Mesopotamia provides us with an excellent model of a civilization

Reviewing the Significance of Key People, Concepts, and Events (Knowledge/Understanding)

1. Understanding the Paleolithic Age, the Neolithic Revolution, and the importance of Mesopotamia as the worldís first civilization requires a knowledge of the following concepts and events and an understanding of their significance in the development of early civilizations. In your notes, identify and explain the historical significance of three from each column.

People	Concepts	Events
Neanderthals	prehistory	The Great Leap Forward
Cro-Magnons	barter	Paleolithic Society
Homo sapiens sapiens	civilization	Neolithic Revolution
Sumerians	cuneiform	Urban Revolution
King Hammurabi		
Assyrians		

2. Create a chart that compares the bases of authority in early human societies with societies at the time of the Neolithic and Urban Revolutions and ancient Mesopotamia.

3. Outline the different roles played by individuals in a Paleolithic society. You can organize this information using brief summaries, a mind map with small bits of information, or paragraphs.

Doing History: Thinking About the Past (Thinking/Inquiry)

1. Speculate as to why religion emerged in early human societies. Was this due to the development of greater intellectual capacity or a product of superstition and unexplained occurrences, or some other reason? Defend your answer in a paragraph.

2. How would you rank the civilization of Mesopotamia? To answer this, review how you ranked the seven essential elements of a civilization. Write two paragraphs arguing for or against considering Mesopotamia a great early civilization.

Applying Your Learning (Application)

1. Describe the typical diet of Paleolithic societies in one of the following ways:
   - prepare a grocery list
   - create an imaginary dialogue between a man and a woman in which they discuss gathering food and preparing a meal
   - create a menu for a hypothetical restaurant called Café Lascaux

2. Create a poster that highlights what you consider to be the most significant innovations from the Palaeolithic Age to the civilization of Mesopotamia. Your poster should include at least four innovations, arranged chronologically. In a short caption of not more than 50 words, explain the impact of each innovation on economic structures (how goods were produced, distributed, exchanged).

Communicating Your Learning (Communication)

1. Prepare a time line outlining major developments in human history from the emergence of *Homo sapiens* (400 000 years ago) to the Neolithic Revolution. Your time line must include five to seven dates and include visuals/symbols to make it attractive.

2. Explain how the Neolithic Revolution changed life in human societies. You can depict the change through a pair of mind maps, columns, contrasting sketches, or paragraphs that explain the change.

Egypt and Israel

By the end of this chapter, you will be able to:

- *demonstrate an understanding of how the development of Egyptian civilization was affected by its isolation between two deserts*

- *analyze the factors that contributed to the maintenance of stability and continuity over 3000 years of Egyptian history*

- *evaluate the role and importance of a variety of legends, myths, and traditions in the history and culture of ancient Egypt and ancient Israel*

- *evaluate the influence of religion on the political structures of ancient Egypt and ancient Israel*

British archaeologist Howard Carter discovered the tomb of Pharoah Tutankhamun in 1922. This is the coffin mask of Tutankhamun.

A ncient Egypt — few civilizations evoke as much awe and mystery. The ancient Greek historian Herodotus proclaimed that Egypt "has more wonders in it than any country in the world and more works that are beyond description than anywhere else." Can we ever understand the ancient mysteries of mummification, the Book of the Dead, or the riddle of pyramid construction? Can we understand the values and beliefs of ancient Egyptians who lived thousands of years ago? Countless Hollywood movies have used ancient Egypt as the backdrop for thrilling adventures — *Raiders of the Lost Ark, Death on the Nile, The Mummy, Stargate*. The images conjured up by Hollywood include towering pyramids, ancient mummies, and long-lost tombs containing unimaginable wealth and guarded by mysterious curses.

The Egyptians were much more than Pharaohs, pyramids, elaborate burials, and mysterious curses. They were a living, breathing society of people who experienced many of the same joys and sorrows we do today. When we look at this civilization, we must be careful not to allow the grandeur of its monuments to overshadow the people and the society that produced such treasures. Recent research into the lives of ancient Egyptians is helping to flesh out a more complete picture of the past, one that includes details about the daily lives of workers as well as Pharaohs, and the roles played by both men and women.

KEY WORDS

Nile River

Nile Delta

mummification

Amon-Re

Ma'at

mastaba

hieroglyphics

Ten Commandments

Temple of Jerusalem

Diaspora

KEY PEOPLE

Imhotep

Djoser

Hatshepsut

Tuthmosis III

Akhenaton

Tutankhamun

Ramses II

Moses

Yahweh

VOICES FROM THE PAST

Look on my works ye Mighty and despair!
Percy Bysshe Shelley,
Ozymandias, 1819

TIME LINE: ANCIENT EGYPT AND ISRAEL

	ca. 3100 BCE	King Menes unites the kingdoms of Upper and Lower Egypt
Beginning of the Old Kingdom and the Age of the Pyramids	ca. 2690 BCE	
	ca. 2600–2500 BCE	Pyramids at Giza built
First Intermediate Period begins when internal strife leads to civil war	2181 BCE	
	2050 BCE	Middle Kingdom begins, a period of expansion of the Egyptian empire
Second Intermediate Period when the Hyksos invade and occupy Egypt	1780 BCE	
	ca. 1550 BCE	New Kingdom, considered the Golden Age of Egypt
Reign of Hatshepsut, one of only four women Pharaohs to rule ancient Egypt	ca. 1470 BCE	
	ca. 1450 BCE	Reign of Tuthmosis III, who greatly expands the territories ruled by Egypt
Reign of Akhenaton	1350 BCE	
	1334 BCE	Reign of Tutankhamun, Akhenaton's religious revolution is reversed
Reign of Ramses II, period of the Exodus of Jews from Egypt	1297 BCE	
	1069 BCE	Third Intermediate Period
Persians conquer and rule Egypt	525 BCE	
	332 BCE	Alexander the Great defeats the Persians and is hailed a saviour by the Egyptians
Cleopatra VII is crowned Queen of Egypt	50 BCE	
	30 BCE	Egypt becomes part of the Roman empire after the suicide of Cleopatra VII and Mark Antony

CONTINUITY AND CHANGE IN EGYPTIAN HISTORY

Isolated and protected by deserts on each side, Egyptian society evolved slowly, sheltered from outside influences. Inspired by the constant rhythm of the Nile, rising and receding eternally, the Egyptians developed a culture in which stability, not change, was the primary goal. Living in an age of rapid, continuous change, we may, at times, struggle to understand a society that sought stability and frowned upon change. Certainly, changes did occur over time — in the mummification process, and in the burial practices of the Pharaohs. Trade grew and expanded, bringing new ideas and goods into Egyptian society. Change was slow and cautious, however, as the Egyptians were careful not to disrupt the rhythm of life along the banks of the Nile.

Geography: Life on the Nile

The Nile Valley

There were several important geographic influences on Egyptian culture and civilization. The most important of these was the **Nile River**. The wealth of Egypt depended entirely on the water of the Nile, often referred to as the "gift of the Nile." Rainfall in

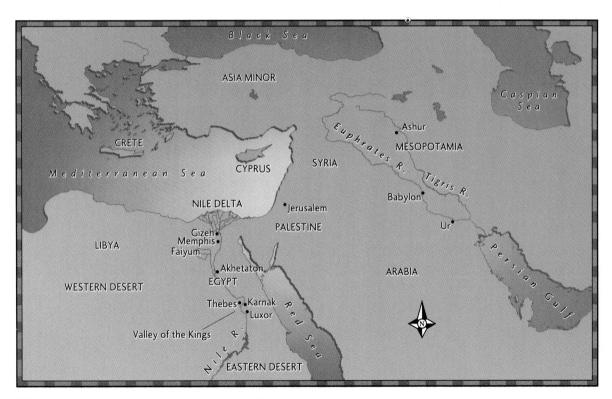

■ **Ancient Egypt and its Neighbouring States**

1. How did the geography of Ancient Egypt both isolate and protect it?

2. How did geography affect the stability of the Ancient Egyptian state?

the Nile Valley is negligible, and rainfall in the Nile Delta is only 100–200 mm per year. It was the flooding of the Nile upon which the fortunes of Egypt depended.

The waters of the Nile River come from the convergence of the White Nile and the Blue Nile. The Blue Nile, fed by the summer monsoons in Ethiopia, lead to the flooding of the Nile. This flooding occurs annually between July and October. The receding waters leave behind a rich alluvial soil, which makes the Nile River Valley a fertile and productive region.

Unlike other major rivers such as the Tigris and the Euphrates, which often underwent violent and unpredictable flooding, the Nile was usually a benevolent and predictable ally. The Egyptians were able to plan with some certainty the planting and harvesting of crops. If the water levels were higher than usual, however, serious damage could occur. Conversely, water levels that did *not* reach their usual heights could lead to drought and famine. The Nile was a force that the Egyptians both revered and feared.

The Nile Delta and the Faiyum

Aside from the Nile Valley, two other regions in Egypt were extensively cultivated and settled. The area in which the Nile empties into the Mediterranean Sea is known as the **Nile Delta**. The Nile Delta is the largest area of fertile land in Egypt and, consequently, encompassed many of the major centres of ancient Egypt. Lake Moeris, which lies at the end of a branch of the Nile, is at the centre of an oasis known as the **Faiyum**. Through extensive irrigation, the ancient Egyptians were able to make the Faiyum the third largest area of settlement and agriculture in Egypt.

Deserts and Egypt's Isolation

Perhaps the greatest irony of Egypt is that the very lush and fertile Nile Valley is sandwiched between two inhospitable deserts, the Western Desert and the Eastern Desert. The isolation these desolate areas created protected Egypt from invasion, while also insulating Egyptians from outside influences. It is hardly surprising that the civilization that developed was conservative and remarkably stable for most of its long history.

The significance of the deserts went beyond their acting as a buffer against outside influences. They were important sources of minerals and building supplies, including copper, gold, tin, alabaster, limestone, amethyst, and natron, the drying agent used in the **mummification** process.

The Mediterranean

Another geographic feature that significantly shaped Egyptian history was the Mediterranean Sea, Egypt's major outlet for trade. The extensive trade routes that were established allowed Egypt to obtain a wide diversity of goods. Trade was also a key factor in the exchange of cultures. One cannot help but notice the tremendous influence the Egyptians had on the architecture and art of the Greeks, especially the Minoans and Mycenaeans.

THE RISE OF THE NATION OF EGYPT

With the unification of Egypt under King Menes in about 3100 BCE, the history of one of the world's great civilizations began — one that would last over three thousand years. Egyptian history is generally divided into three eras, each characterized by its own accomplishments. The Old Kingdom, from

2686 BCE to 2150 BCE, was the age of the pyramids. The Middle Kingdom, from about 2050 BCE to 1700 BCE, was a time when Egypt greatly expanded its political and economic boundaries. The New Kingdom, spanning the years from around 1550 BCE to 1070 BCE, was the Golden Age of Egypt.

THE OLD KINGDOM

Prior to 3100 BCE, Egypt was probably a collection of unorganized societies. Lower Egypt, or the Delta Kingdom, was ruled by a monarchy symbolized by the red crown; the white crown represented the power of Upper Egypt. The legendary **King Menes** is believed to have been the first to unite Egypt and wear the double crown symbolizing the unity of the two kingdoms. Between 3100 BCE and 2700 BCE, Menes and his heirs were able to consolidate their power and achieve absolute rule in Egypt. By the time of the Old Kingdom, the king was ruler of all of Egypt and considered a god. He was the supreme ruler of all affairs, secular and religious.

| Red Crown | Double Crown | White Crown |

The Crowns of the Pharaohs of Egypt

The Old Kingdom reached its peak during the Fourth Dynasty (a dynasty is a series of rulers belonging to the same family). By engaging in trade throughout much of the Mediterranean, and by mining

copper in the Sinai Peninsula, the Egyptians acquired tremendous wealth in both material goods and new ideas. Timber from Syria, wine and oil from Crete, and the potter's wheel from Mesopotamia were all introduced to Egypt during the Old Kingdom.

> **TIME FRAMES**
> **EGYPTIAN HISTORY**
>
> Predynastic Period 3300–2960 BCE
> Early Dynastic Period 2960–2649 BCE
> Old Kingdom 2649–2150 BCE
> Middle Kingdom 1991–1700 BCE
> New Kingdom 1550–1070 BCE
> Late Dynastic Period 688–343 BCE
> Ptolemaic Period 332–30 BCE

The greatest symbols of the wealth of the Old Kingdom, however, were the three massive pyramids at Giza. Built between 2600 and 2500 bce, these pyramids were the chief undertaking of the kings of the Fourth Dynasty — Khufu (also known as Cheops), Khafre, and Menkure. To this day, these monumental structures stand as testimonials to the greatness of Egypt during the Old Kingdom.

Imhotep: An Egyptian Genius

Seldom were the lives and accomplishments of individuals other than Pharaohs recorded by the Egyptians. One worthy exception was **Imhotep**, a man whom historians have called a genius. Imhotep's contributions to Egyptian society were so profound that he was essentially deified, and rose to serve at the right hand of the Pharaoh **Djoser**. Living during the reign of Djoser, in the Third Dynasty (ca. 2686–2613 BCE), the brilliant Imhotep was the first individual (non-ruler) whose life has been recorded and passed on through history. On a statue of Imhotep in the royal funeral complex, we see the extent of his titles and the roles he played. The inscription reads: "The Chancellor of the King of Lower Egypt, the first after the King of Upper Egypt, administrator of the great palace, hereditary lord, the High Priest of Heliopolis, Imhotep the builder, the sculptor, and the maker of stone vases."

Evidently, Imhotep was all this and more. He was the founder of the Egyptian system of medicine — highly regarded for hundreds of years as the best of the ancient world. He was also the architect who designed and supervised the construction of the world's first stone building, and the first pyramid (also made entirely of stone blocks). In fact, the Step Pyramid created by Imhotep for the Pharaoh Djoser was the embodiment of Egyptian religious beliefs — it captured for eternity the majesty of Pharaonic Egypt. Imhotep's genius did not end with the creation of a huge and eternal tomb for the Pharaoh. Inside the tomb, Imhotep immortalized in stone every aspect of life within the royal palace at about

The Step Pyramid of Djoser, the first monumental architecture in Egypt, built ca. 2650 BCE.

2650 BCE. From the furnishings of the palace and everyday goods such as straw baskets and metal pots, to the exploits of the Pharaoh, his family, and Imhotep himself, all were captured and frozen in time in carefully sculpted stone images. In the end, the Step Pyramid emerged as the first piece of monumental architecture created by an artist. Imhotep's vision was to create a tomb that used space and design to capture the essence of the life of a Pharaoh, not merely a place to hold his final remains.

THE MIDDLE KINGDOM

The strong central government that had allowed Egypt to flourish, broke down at the end of the Old Kingdom period, as local and provincial officials became increasingly powerful. The resulting civil wars thrust Egypt into 150 years of anarchy, now referred to as the First Intermediate Period. By 2050 BCE, Egypt was reunited under Theban kings who would rule for the next 250 years. These monarchs initially ruled at Thebes and eventually moved their capital to Memphis. Theban supremacy was also reflected in the rise to national prominence of the god Amon. Amon had been a local Theban deity, but during the Middle Kingdom, he was merged with the Sun god Re to become **Amon-Re**, an Egyptian national god.

Throughout the Middle Kingdom, the economic and political boundaries of Egypt were expanded. By encouraging social mobility through the promotion of members of the middle class, the rulers of the Middle Kingdom were able to curtail the ambitions of the local princes. As a result, Egypt experienced two centuries of peace and stability during which the nation prospered.

External Relations: The Hyksos Invasion

Egypt's success was to be punctured by the invasion of the Hyksos, a warlike people, most likely from the area of what is now Syria and Palestine. While the Egyptians were culturally equal or superior to any of the civilizations of the Mediterranean, they lagged behind some in technological development. The Egyptian army, using copper weapons, was no match for the improved bows, horse-drawn chariots, and bronze weapons of the Hyksos. Although the method of conquest is uncertain, the superior technology of the Hyksos was surely a factor in their ability to take over the administration of Egypt. For 150 years, the Hyksos ruled Egypt using the existing infrastructure. In the end, the Egyptians came to master the new weapons, and drove the Hyksos out of Egypt. Egypt emerged from the Second Intermediate Period strengthened and revitalized.

The Role of Trade in Promoting Change

By the time of the New Kingdom, Egypt was engaged in a vast trading network that centred on the Mediterranean Sea but reached as far as northern Europe, subtropical Africa, and the Near East. A recently discovered and excavated trading vessel dated to the fourteenth century BCE, has contributed greatly to our understanding of the cosmopolitan world of the late Bronze Age. The ship was discovered at Ulu Burun, off the coast of modern-day Turkey, by a Turkish sponge diver in 1982. The vessel was found to carry a variety of items, including copper ingots from Cyprus, Mycenaean pottery from Greece, tin ingots from Asia Minor, amber beads from the Baltic, and glass and ivory from Syria. It is believed that ships such as this followed a circular pattern as they plied the waters of the Mediterranean. Setting out from Egypt, such a vessel would have travelled first to Syria and Palestine and then on to Cyprus, the Aegean Sea, and, occasionally, as far west as Sardinia, before heading back toward North Africa and Egypt.

The interchange of such a variety of cultures had a far greater significance than the simple exchange of material goods. It was through trade that ideas, forms of artistic expression, technology, and building methods were spread. It is not surprising to find that the Egyptians owed much to the Mesopotamians for their concepts of mathematics and writing. Early Greek art and medicine owed a great deal to the Egyptians. The calendar we use today was derived from the Roman (Julian) calendar, which was also borrowed from the Egyptians. Although Egypt was a conservative society in which change was slow, trade and the exchange of ideas ensured that Egyptian civilization did not remain completely static, but was always evolving.

POLITICAL, LEGAL, AND ECONOMIC STRUCTURES

Political Structures and Traditions

Central to the development of Egypt's political institutions was the concept of the god-king. From relatively early in the history of ancient Egypt, the Pharaoh was believed to be the earthly embodiment of the god Horus, son of Amon-Re. To deny this would be to undercut the entire structure and basis of authority of Egyptian kings. The accepted partial divinity of the king allowed him to mediate between gods and people, perform the religious rituals central to Egyptian beliefs, and perhaps most importantly, to remain separate from his subjects and rule with divine right. Deriving power from the gods ensured considerable stability since there were few challengers to the king's authority, and the word of the king was seen to be divinely inspired. Despite the appearance of absolute power, the king was expected to rule over Egypt subject to **Ma'at**. Although pictured as a woman with an ostrich feather, Ma'at was the goddess and symbol of the equilibrium of the universe. The king was expected to govern according to the principles of Ma'at, and to the precedents set by earlier kings. Kings attempting to alter society radically would be seen as destroying the equilibrium that was so important to the tradition-bound Egyptians; this could lead to a civil war or some other challenge to authority.

The Past AT PLAY

Egyptians were sociable people who enjoyed playing games. Board games were especially popular, including one called *Senet*, a racing game in which players tried to reach the realm of the gods. Another game called *Snake* used a snake-shaped board. Other games, more familiar to us, such as chess and backgammon, were also popular.

Succession

To ensure the purest line of succession, a Pharaoh passed on the throne to the eldest son born of the Principal Queen, or Great Royal Wife. This was usually the eldest daughter of the previous king and, therefore, the sister of the ruling king. If the king and the Great Royal Wife had no son to inherit the throne, succession would pass to a son of a secondary wife, who would then legitimize his claim to the throne by marrying the Great Royal Daughter. This would be the daughter of the king and the Principal Queen, or, if they had no daughter, the Principal Queen herself — the stepmother of the new king.

The Pharaoh owned all the land of Egypt, the people, and their possessions. Any personal wealth enjoyed by the Egyptian people was considered a result of the generosity of the king. Beneath the king was a hierarchy of government officials that advised him, enforced the laws, pleased the gods, oversaw the construction of the pyramids and tombs, sought trade opportunities, and collected taxes. These civil servants were often rewarded well for their efforts, receiving grants of land and other valuable goods. Many top-ranking officials were quite wealthy and able to prepare fairly elaborate burial tombs for themselves.

Among the most important of these government officials were the scribes who recorded the deeds of the Pharaohs, real or imagined, and kept stock of supplies. The value of the scribes is reflected in the fact that, most often, a scribe filled the role of vizier, or prime minister to the king. The vizier served several important roles. First, and above all else, the viziers were the advisors to the king from whom they received their orders, and to whom they were directly responsible. Viziers were also responsible for overseeing the entire administration of government, and served as the head of the judiciary. Next to the king, the vizier was the most important government official in Egypt. Beneath the vizier, were a number of minor officials who collected taxes, supervised agriculture and the granaries, coordinated trading expeditions, oversaw the construction of public works (including the pyramids and later tombs of the Pharaohs), managed the justice system, and supervised matters of public health. By the time of the Old Kingdom, Egypt was already a complex, bureaucratic state in which a centralized government was vital to stability and prosperity.

Legal Traditions

Egyptian law, like virtually all other areas of life, was governed by religious principles. The Egyptians believed that law was infused into the world by the gods at the time of creation. The goddess Ma'at personified the essential foundations of Egyptian law, which represented truth, righteousness, and justice. According to Ma'at, the goal of all people was to find and maintain the correct balance and order of the universe. This ideal seems to have been a central part of the lives of most Egyptians — they were generally a very law-abiding people, who sought harmony and stability in their lives. As the head of the court of justice, the vizier was a priest of Ma'at, as were the officials who administered the judicial system.

Generally, Egyptian laws were fair and humane compared with those of other ancient civilizations. They were also applied equally to all people, regardless of class or gender. The law emphasized protecting the family — providing protection to children and wives, who could divorce their husbands or be guaranteed compensation should their husbands divorce them. The Egyptians had no codified body of laws. Instead, their legal system was based on precedents (previous cases). Each Pharaoh strove to govern in accordance with Ma'at, and the courts ensured that the laws applied were consistent with past practices.

While the laws of Egypt were fair and equitably applied, punishments could often be quite severe. Two principles seem to have guided Egyptians in determining the appropriate punishment for a crime: that a severe punishment would act as a deterrent and that, in some cases, disgrace was more effective than death. Minor crimes were often punished with 100 lashes and forced labour in the mines and quarries. Escape attempts could lead to ears and noses being amputated. Men who raped a freeborn woman were castrated. Corrupt officials had their hands amputated, and those who released military secrets had their tongues cut out. For those who committed crimes punishable by death, there were several options for their execution. Some were devoured by crocodiles; those of high status were allowed to commit suicide; and children who killed their parents had pieces of their flesh cut away, were placed on a bed of thorns, and burned alive. Parents who killed their children were forced to hold the dead child for three days and nights. Deserters from the army were publicly disgraced but could erase the humiliation by performing a courageous deed.

WEB CONNECTION

http://www.mcgrawhill.ca/links/echoes

Go to the web site above to find out more about the history of ancient Egypt.

Economic Structure

Ancient Egypt's economic system could best be described as a mixed system blending elements of a traditional economy, a market economy, and a command economy. Despite being a relatively simple economy based primarily on the annual production of staple foods, a complex system of trade developed. The Pharaoh retained absolute control over the means of production and the distribution of wealth. Egyptian prosperity and stability were dependent on abundant harvests and the ability to manage food supplies in order to survive years in which harvests declined. The abundance of food supplies — not the size of the royal treasury — was the measure of Egypt's wealth. Full granaries, plenty of wildlife and fish, and thriving herds were the signs of prosperous times. These were the images used in the tombs of the Pharaohs to illustrate the wealth of their reigns.

Agricultural production was organized to provide a stable food supply for both the living and the dead. Any surplus was used in trade with neighbouring peoples. An enormous amount of labour was needed to construct huge public works such as temples, royal tombs, and pyramids. Everyone could be asked to contribute to the Pharaoh's building projects, but officials, scribes, or artisans seldom were required to fulfill this role. Instead, the majority of labour came from Egypt's poor; this led to the creation of a class of serfs, who although not slaves, had little control over their own lives.

The Granger Collection, New York.

Farming in the Afterlife

Throughout nearly all of ancient Egypt, trade, both within the country and with neighbouring countries, was carried out through the barter system.

Widespread use of coinage would not come until the time of the Romans. The Egyptians sold goods, paid salaries, collected taxes, and even paid interest on loans entirely through the exchange of goods. As trade became increasingly complex, they developed a refined system of barter, which used an arbitrary standard (initially wheat), against which all goods were measured and adjustments made when necessary. For example, a peasant wanting to purchase new pottery might offer some dried fish in exchange. If the potter demanded slightly more for the pottery than the fish, the difference could be made up with a small amount of wheat. After around 1580 BCE, the Egyptians used gold, silver, and copper as arbitrary standards, and introduced a system of weights and measures. Despite these developments, the use of coinage as a generally accepted medium of exchange would still be a thousand years away.

One of the features of ancient Egypt that contributed to the remarkable stability and continuity of the society was the passing of skilled trades from father to son. Few Egyptians grew up exploring a variety of career options. Instead, children would learn the trades of their parents, becoming skilled artisans who would then pass on the secrets of their trade to their children. Little is known about individual artisans, despite the numerous examples of fine sculpture, countless tomb paintings, and many impressive public works. The anonymity of Egyptian artists is, in part, due to the system of production used in most trades. Artisans did not work independently; they were part of a team in a specialized workshop. Each item was produced in the workshop by several artisans who either worked together on the piece or passed it along the line. Complex works, such as furniture, were first designed by a master artisan, and then each part was crafted and polished by other artisans before completion. Similar organization was

Why do you think scribes, like this man, were given high status in Egyptian society?

used in the building of monumental structures; master planners designed and supervised the building, while skilled artisans each contributed to the project by shaping building blocks, carving sculptures, or painting walls.

Review...Recall...Reflect

1. List and describe three ways that the environment shaped Egyptian culture and society.

2. Explain the meaning and significance of the double crown of Egypt. Why do you think Egypt became a united kingdom earlier than Mesopotamia?

3. Briefly explain how the political, economic, and legal structures of ancient Egypt were shaped by religious beliefs.

THE NEW KINGDOM

Egyptian civilization reached its apex during the New Kingdom. It was during these five centuries that Egypt experienced its Golden Age, building an empire and producing fine works of art. The New Kingdom was also a period dominated by several larger-than-life characters.

Hatshepsut

From the reign of Menes to the arrival of Alexander the Great over 2700 years later, only four women ever ruled Egypt. Three of these women ruled only for a brief period while a dynastic crisis was being solved. The reign of **Hatshepsut**, who ruled in her own right for a significant period of time, is unique in the history of ancient Egypt. Given the very masculine nature of Egyptian kings, the small number of women rulers is not surprising. The king was believed to be the son of the god Re, and was associated with male symbols such as the bull. The queen was seen as the daughter of Re and was associated with the vulture-goddess. Consequently, the offices of the king and queen were complementary yet fundamentally different. They were not interchangeable, so the reign of any woman in Pharaonic Egypt was a significant departure from tradition.

Historians have called Hatshepsut the first powerful female leader. When her husband Tuthmosis II died, Hatshepsut became regent for her young stepson, **Tuthmosis III**. Rather than govern in his name until he was old enough to assume the throne, Hatshepsut declared herself the female king of Egypt. Statues and paintings often show Hatshepsut wearing a beard to symbolize her power. The reign of Egypt's most famous woman has been described as a period of peace, stability, and prosperity. During her reign,

Hatshepsut expanded trade, sending a trading mission to the country of Punt on the Red Sea (likely today's Somalia) from which Egypt received ebony, ivory, and incense. Hatshepsut also embarked on an ambitious building program that included her own massive tomb at Deir al-Bahari, and two huge obelisks at the Great Temple of Karnak, near Luxor. After ruling for nearly fifteen years, Hatshepsut was succeeded by the stepson whom she had earlier deposed. It is unclear whether Tuthmosis III waited until his stepmother's death to reclaim the throne, or deposed her. What is clear is that some time near the end of his reign, Tuthmosis III ordered the removal of all references to and images of Hatshepsut from many monuments, and the smashing of statues that depicted her as king. Interestingly, her earlier images as queen in female dress and adornments went untouched. Was this an act of revenge, or was it simply an attempt to erase the uncomfortable fact of a woman assuming the role of a male king?

Queen Hatshepsut's Funerary Temple. This enormous temple complex was built during her reign ca. 1470 BCE.

Tuthmosis III

As a young boy, Tuthmosis III inherited the throne of Egypt from his father, but the real power lay in the hands of his stepmother, Hatshepsut. By the time he assumed control of the throne, Tuthmosis III was in his mid to late twenties. It would appear that he made wise use of his early years, training in the military — he has even been referred to as the "Napoleon of Egypt," because of his many military campaigns. Much of the wealth of the New Kingdom came from tribute paid by the people subjugated during Tuthmosis III's conquests. Evidence of the tremendous wealth generated by Tuthmosis's successful conquests can be seen in the burst of building activity, both public and private, that occurred during this period.

EGYPTIAN MILITARY TRADITIONS

By the time of Tuthmosis III, Egypt had earned a well-deserved reputation for having one of the best-trained armies in the Near East. Ironically, the Egyptians were actually among the least warlike people of ancient times. The bounty of the Nile Valley provided for their needs, and the deserts on either side served as natural barriers to their enemies. The wealth of ancient Egypt did, however, attract the attention of greedy neighbours who sought to seize control of the rich and fertile country. The success of the Hyksos invasion alerted the Egyptians to the need for a strong army to defend against future attacks. Fighting abroad was always viewed with anxiety, since nothing was more distressing to an Egyptian than the thought of dying away from home and being buried in a foreign land. Later in the New Kingdom, the powerful army did begin to expand Egypt's boundaries through conquests, but as in the past, mercenaries made up a significant part of the Egyptian army.

The Egyptian army was a highly trained and disciplined fighting machine. With each military campaign, the Egyptians invoked the power of the gods to ensure their victory. Wars were fought with great pomp and ceremony, with trumpeters leading the army into battle. At the head of the attack was the Pharaoh's chariot, carrying a flag decorated with a ram's head and the sun, symbolic of the god Amon-Re.

These clay figures of soldiers were found in a royal tomb. The Pharoah's army was needed to guard him in the afterlife.

Akhenaton's Challenge to Authority

In the midst of unparalleled wealth and power, the Egyptians faced an attempted religious revolution. Amonhotep IV, who changed his name to **Akhenaton**, concentrated his energies on reforming Egyptian religion. Akhenaton opposed the worship of Amon-Re, traditionally the supreme god of the Egyptians. In place of Amon-Re, Akhenaton sponsored the worship of Aton. To promote the new cult, he took the name Akhenaton, meaning "he who serves Aton," and built a new capital city called Akhetaton ("Place of the Glory of Aton") far from the major urban centres of Egypt. Akhenaton also had the temples of other gods closed and their possessions confiscated. These actions have since caused some to refer to Akhenaton as the first monotheist (believer in one god). This term is somewhat inaccurate since the Egyptian people were still expected to worship the Pharaoh while the royal family worshipped Aton. Akhenaton defined his new religion through hymns, some of which are preserved on the walls of tombs in the city he founded. Here is a sample of Akhenaton's writing:

> Splendid you rise in heaven's lightland,
>
> O living Aton, creator of life!
>
> When you have dawned in eastern lightland,
>
> You fill every land with your beauty.

Akhenaton's break with Egyptian traditions can also be seen in the art of his reign. Unlike other Pharaohs, who insisted on idealized representations of themselves, Akhenaton is portrayed with all of his human flaws: a slight pot-belly, and an oddly shaped head. There are also depictions of tender moments between Akhenaton and his wife and children — scenes rare in Egyptian art.

This relief sculpture shows Akhenaton, his wife and three of their children. Do you think the Pharoah and his family actually looked like this? How are the children portrayed?

Akhenaton's preoccupation with reforming Egyptian religion left him little time to govern the empire built by his predecessors. In fact, once his new city was built, Akhenaton vowed never to leave it. In essence, he had refused to fill the traditional role of the Pharaoh — leading the army into battle or attending to matters of the state that required him to travel outside his new city. By the time of his death, the Egyptian empire was crumbling from neglect, and while still a dominant power, Egyptian civilization had begun its long decline.

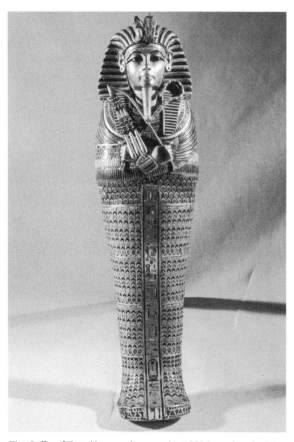

The Coffin of Tutankhamun, discovered in 1922 by archaeologist Howard Carter.

Tutankhamun

Tutankhamun came to power as a young child under the name Tutankhaton. It is likely that he was the son of Akhenaton and a minor wife. When Akhenaton died, the only surviving members of the royal family were two children, Tutankhaton and his half-sister Ankhesenpaton. A marriage of the two youngsters was hastily arranged, and the ten-year-old Tutankhaton ascended to the throne.

It is unclear how big a role Tutankhaton played in the destruction of his father's new religion and the restoration of traditional beliefs. He may have been well aware of the strife that had befallen Egypt and, guided by his advisors, sought to restore stability by halting the religious revolution. He may also have simply accepted the dictates of his advisors who, either for the good of Egypt or for their own personal ambitions, sought to reverse Akhenaton's changes.

Within a few years of coming to the throne, Tutankhaton had changed his name to Tutankhamun, signalling a rejection of the cult of Aton and a return to traditional Egyptian religion. He also restored the priests and moved the capital of Egypt back from exile in Akhetaton to Thebes. Tutankhamun's short rule ended suddenly when he died from an apparent blow to the head at the age of eighteen. The sudden and unexpected death of the young Pharaoh created a problem, since the preparation of a Pharaoh's tomb took many years to complete. Having no completed tomb in which to lay the mummy of Tutankhamun, a nearly completed tomb of a member of the nobility was used instead. This may explain why the tomb of King Tut, as he has come to be known, lay undisturbed until its dramatic discovery in 1922; perhaps grave robbers thought it was not worth the effort.

Tutankhamun should be remembered as the Pharaoh who restored traditional Egyptian religion. As successor to Akhenaton, it was Tutankhamun and his advisors who destroyed the cult of Aton. He is, however, better known for the unsurpassed wealth found in his tomb. The treasures Howard Carter found in 1922 included gold inlaid furniture, lavish jewelry, and a solid-gold coffin.

Ramses II

By the time of **Ramses II**, 60 years after Tutankhamun, Egypt was in its twilight years. During his 67-year reign, Ramses II constructed more buildings and colossal statues than any other Egyptian king. Among his greatest monuments are the two huge temples at Abu Simbel. In the 1960s, these were the focus of a massive undertaking to save them from being submerged beneath the artificial lake that was created with the construction of the Aswan High Dam. The salvage operation involved dismantling the temple facades by cutting them into huge blocks and moving them 210 m away from the river. The operation took four years and cost $40 million.

The statues of Ramses II in the Valley of the Kings

Not long after the reign of Ramses II, Egypt was invaded and eventually fell under the rule of foreigners. During the next thousand years, Nubians, Assyrians, Persians, Greeks, and Romans would govern the state of Egypt. Despite being subjected to the rule of foreigners, the grandeur of Egypt has never been lost.

Continuity in Egyptian Religious Traditions

In attempting to understand Egyptian culture and society, no factor is more significant than religion. The Egyptians were a deeply religious people for whom the sacred and the secular were inseparable. Religion was an integral part of all aspects of Egyptian life.

A society whose existence is closely linked to nature often shows a special reverence for it. The religion of early Egypt had its roots in the worship of nature deities, and the first gods to arise were frequently represented in animal form. In time, gods in human form became fused with earlier ideas, resulting in an interesting mix of human bodies and animal attributes.

Myths and Legends in Ancient Egypt

Like the Mesopotamians before them, the Egyptians considered those responsible for creation the most important gods. This is the case with most creation stories. According to Egyptian mythology, the earth was created when a primeval hill, the first solid matter, emerged from the waters of chaos. This was a natural assumption for ancient Egyptians, as they often saw islands of mud appearing in the Nile, or existing areas becoming islands during the annual inundation (floods). Atum, the creator-god, simply emerged standing on the first hill that rose from the water. He was "the perfect one" and self-begotten. He then ejected from his being Shu, the air, and Tefenet, the moisture. Next, he separated the sky from the earth and Geb, the earth, and Nut, the sky, came into being. Geb and Nut then joined and had children: the gods Osiris, Isis, Seth, and Nephthys. This group of deities formed the first unit in the divine hierarchy of gods.

National gods began to emerge during the Middle Kingdom. The most significant of these was Amon, the local god of Thebes and favoured god of the Theban kings. The other deities common to the Egyptians were the gods of the dead, including Osiris, Anubis, Horus, and Thoth.

[INTELLECTUAL LIFE

The Egyptians had a very complex explanation for their existence. Aside from the physical body, each individual had a *ka*, *ba*, and *akh*. According to Egyptian beliefs, infants were placed in the mother's womb after being created on a potter's wheel by the god Khnum. For each human crafted, Khnum also made a spiritual duplicate. This was called the ka. The ka was stored in the heart, and at death, was separated from the body. It would inhabit the tomb of the individual to be near the body in which it had spent its life. Like the living body from which it had come, the ka would need items such as food, clothing, perfume, and furniture.

| Horus | Osiris | Isis |

These are some of the more important gods of the Egyptians. On the left is Horus, son of Isis and Osiris, wearing the double crown of Egypt. On the right is Isis, wife/sister of Osiris and protector of children. In the centre is Osiris, god of the earth, whose rebirth symbolized the eternal, yearly cycle of the Nile River.

The ba was a non-physical element unique to each person. It entered the body at the time of birth and left the body at death. The ba is best described as a person's character or personality, and was depicted as a human-headed bird. When someone died, his or her mummy needed to be transformed into a form that could exist in the afterworld. This form was called the akh. The transformation took place through the use of magical spells said over the mummy.

A concept central to Egyptian religion was that of Ma'at. This was essentially order, truth, and justice — qualities the Egyptians believed were put in the world at the time of creation. Only by living in accordance with Ma'at could the Egyptians achieve harmony with the gods and be assured entry into the hereafter.

The Afterlife

The Egyptian concept of the afterlife is a reflection of their zeal for life and their optimistic outlook. The Egyptians saw the afterlife as a duplication of the best moments on Earth. They expected that, in their afterlife, they would be engaged in the activities they enjoyed most, such as fishing, hunting, feasting, and sailing. Death to the Egyptians was not an end, but a beginning.

The concept of an afterlife was common to all Egyptians, regardless of their social status. The preparation for the afterlife varied considerably depending on whether the individual was royal, noble, or a peasant. For all, however, there were two basic requirements. First, the body must be preserved in a lifelike form; second, the deceased must be provided with the items necessary for a life in the hereafter. The goods provided ranged from the few simple possessions of a peasant to the elaborate storehouse of treasures that accompanied the kings and queens. Royal tombs commonly held large food supplies, furniture, tools, weapons, chests full of clothes, jewelry, and games. All Egyptians, whether rich or poor, believed that the essence of the deceased continued to be tied to this world even after death. This essence, or the ka, returned via the preserved body and received its sustenance from the food, drink, and material possessions left in the tomb.

Hunting Game in the Afterlife

Egyptian Burial Practices

Central to Egyptian religious beliefs was the need to preserve the body. It is likely that mummification was a stage in the development of Egyptian burial practices. The earliest people to settle in the Nile Valley buried their dead in pit-graves dug in the hot desert sands bordering Egypt. The rainless climate and dryness of the sand around the body caused a natural process of desiccation whereby the body fluids were absorbed by the sand, preventing the body from decaying.

Pushing the Boundaries: Developments in Science and Technology

From Here to Eternity: The Mummification Process

A desire to preserve the body after death was central to Egyptian religion and beliefs about the afterlife. Egyptians expected that the afterlife would be spent enjoying the best that this life had to offer: fishing, hunting, feasting, sailing, and so on. There were two basic requirements for the afterlife: a body preserved in its lifelike form, and a supply of goods to last through eternity. Egyptians also believed that in death, their spiritual double, the ka, would reside near their body, and have the same needs — food, clothing, perfume, furniture — as their living body had.

Mummification in Egypt probably began about 2400 BCE, and continued into the Greco-Roman period. Some of our best information came from the Greek historian Herodotus, who documented the process in 450 BCE. Preserving bodies became a fully developed craft with its own guild of practitioners. It was also a religious rite presided over by a priest who uttered chants and prayers while wearing a jackal mask to represent Anubis, the god of embalming.

How to Make a Mummy

1. The brain, considered useless, was removed through the nostrils with an iron hook and discarded. What could not be reached was dissolved by chemicals.

2. The presiding priest turned the body onto its right side, made an incision on the left, and removed all the major organs except the heart. Because the heart was considered the seat of intelligence and the ka's bodily home, it was left in place.

3. The liver, lungs, stomach and intestines were cleaned, then dried with a substance called natron. The organs were then placed in four separate canopic jars, usually made

Canopic Jars: The baboon, Hapi, guarded the lungs; Duamutefla, the jackal protected the stomach; the falcon, Qebehsenuef looked after the intestines; Imseti, a man, cared for the liver.

of limestone, calcite, or clay. The lid of each jar was shaped to look like one of Horus' four sons. (Natron, obtained from dried-up riverbeds, is a compound of four salts: sodium carbonate, sodium bicarbonate, sodium chloride, and sodium sulfate. It draws water out and creates a hostile environment for bacteria.)

4. The body was washed with wine and the cavity stuffed with different materials: linen, Nile mud, sawdust, or lichen, plus aromatic substances such as myrrh. It was covered with more natron and dried for up to 70 days.

5. Once dried, the body was washed in oils and spices; the mouth and nose were cleaned and stuffed with linen, and the eyelids were stuffed with small onions or linen pads. The body incision was closed and covered with a plate, sometimes gold.

6. Finally, the body was wrapped in several layers of linen that had been coated with resins and oils. Amulets and jewelry were hidden amongst the layers. Towards the time of the Middle Kingdom, it was customary to place a mask over the face. Usually the masks were made of cartonnage (papyrus or linen coated with plaster), or sometimes wood. Silver and gold were for royalty.

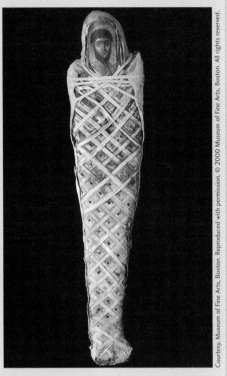

By the time the Romans ruled Egypt (first century CE), mummy masks (like King Tutankhamun's) could be realistic painted portraits. This young man was from a place called the Faiyum, in northern Egypt.

Activities

1. Explain how mummification suited the Egyptian notions of the afterlife. Would mummification suit your beliefs? Why or why not?

2. The mummy has provided much inspiration for books, movies, stories, and exhibits. Pick one medium and imagine you have to pitch the concept to a publisher, producer, or gallery. Explain why you think this would interest the public.

As Egyptian burials became more elaborate, the body of the deceased came to be placed in a lined tomb. Since the bodies were no longer covered by sand, desiccation did not occur naturally and the bodies decomposed. As a consequence, the Egyptians developed an artificial means to duplicate what had previously happened naturally — mummification. Initially, the Egyptians simply wrapped the body of the deceased in resin-soaked linens to preserve a lifelike form. Eventually, a more elaborate process was devised that enabled them to prevent the body from decaying. This process was lengthy and expensive and, therefore, the special reserve of royalty and the nobility. Peasants continued to rely on the natural desiccation that occurred when the deceased were buried in pit-graves in the sand.

An Egyptian Funeral

The funerals of Egypt's elite were lengthy and elaborate affairs. When someone died, a period of loud mourning took place. The female relatives of the deceased, as well as paid mourners, would bare their breasts and walk through the streets crying out in grief. They would be followed by male relatives who were also bare to the waist and pounding their chests in sorrow. Later, there would be a more composed procession in which the body was transferred from the home to the embalmers where the mummification took place. This process took about 70 days to complete. Once the process of mummification was completed, the mummy was returned to the family and the final procession to the tomb would begin. In this procession, the mummy was placed on a sledge drawn by oxen. A second sledge followed, carrying the canopic jars containing the deceased's preserved internal organs. At the rear of the procession, were the servants who carried objects the deceased would need in the afterlife. Upon arrival at the tomb, a priest would touch the mummy's eyes, and the grave goods were lowered into place through the roof since there was no entrance. Once everything was in place, the entire structure was roofed over. Some tombs were massive and elaborate structures designed to imitate palace facades. Later tombs for royalty were surrounded by smaller tombs containing the bodies of followers, and, possibly, mortuary chapels, where offerings were brought.

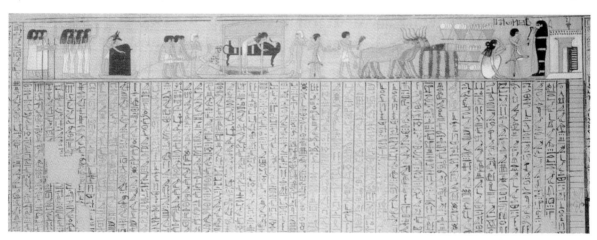

The Opening of the Mouth Ceremony and the explanation of it in hieroglyphics. In this ceremony, the mouth of the dead is opened to allow the deceased to breath again (seen on the right).

By the beginning of the Old Kingdom, Egyptian kings were assumed to be the living embodiment of Horus, the son of the god Osiris. Obviously, a person of such stature had to be laid to rest in a tomb that reflected this status. Thus, the pyramid evolved. The choice of the pyramid shape may have been an attempt to re-create the primeval mound the Egyptians believed had emerged from the waters of chaos at the time of creation. Over 40 pyramids have been discovered in Egypt, mostly from the Old Kingdom, although some from the end of the Middle Kingdom and the New Kingdom have also been found.

Scripts & Symbols λ μ ν ο π θ υ ρ σ τ υ ϖ ω ξ ψ ζ α β χ ε δ φ γ

The ancient Egyptians had more than one form of writing. Besides the well-known hieroglyphics (from the Greek words hieros, "sacred," and glyphe, "carving"), there was a simplified script called demotic (from the Greek demotikos, "people"). Hieroglyphics were used for religious or state purposes and demotic was for everyday use.

The earliest pyramids were, in fact, a series of **mastabas** (oblong tombs) stacked one on top of the other. The famous Step Pyramid at Saqqara, built for King Djoser, began as a single mastaba on which five additional mastabas, descending in size, were placed. Customarily, the burial chamber of the king remained underground.

Pyramid construction reached its climax with the building of King Khufu's tomb at Giza. Known as the Great Pyramid, this structure rose 146 m and had sides 238 m long. In total, the base of the Great Pyramid covers six hectares. It is constructed of 2.5 million stone blocks, each weighing on average 2.5 t. This remains the largest stone structure in the world. Construction was completed during the 23 years of Khufu's reign, without the aid of the wheel, lifting devices, or draft animals.

By the time of the New Kingdom, the Pharaohs had come to realize that building massive pyramids was a mistake. Nothing better advertised to grave robbers where a deceased Pharaoh and his riches could be found than these monuments rising majestically from the desert. In hopes of eternal security, the Pharaohs of the New Kingdom chose two quiet, hidden valleys they believed would be safe from robbers. These valleys near Luxor we now call the Valley of the Kings and the Valley of the Queens.

1. Original mastaba
2. Burial chamber

A schematic view of the Step Pyramid of Djoser, ca. 2650 BCE.

Here, the Pharaohs had elaborate tombs cut deep into the valley walls. The tombs had high corridors brightly painted with inscriptions from various religious texts such as the *Book of What Is in the Underworld*. These corridors led to burial chambers and side chambers that contained the royal grave goods. The burial chamber was covered with scenes from the life of the deceased, designed to convince the gods that he or she had led a good life in accordance with Ma'at. The ceiling of the burial chamber was often covered with a map of the heavens.

1. Silhouette with original facing stone
2. Relieving blocks
3. Airshafts
4. King's chamber
5. So-called queen's chamber
6. False tomb chamber
7. Grand gallery
8. Thieves' tunnel?
9. Entrance

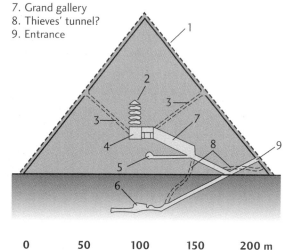

| 0 | 50 | 100 | 150 | 200 m |
| 0 | 200 | 400 | 600 m | |

A cross-section view of the Great Pyramid of Khufu, ca. 2600 BCE.

Temples

Not all of the Egyptians' time and effort went into building tombs for the Pharaohs. A great deal of time was devoted to the construction of temples dedicated to the gods. These massive structures, usually made of sandstone, were designed to be experienced from the inside during a ceremony — not as a means to decorate the landscape. All Egyptian temples had the same basic features: a monumental gateway, a roofless colonnaded court, a great hall with a ceiling resting on massive sandstone columns, and a private sanctuary of the god. The massive temple was, in turn, part of an even larger complex that included living quarters, workshops, a school, a sacred pool, granaries, and other storehouses. These religious complexes contained all the necessary facilities to support a community dedicated to serving the god. The largest and most famous of these temples is the Temple of Amon at Karnak. In this temple, 134 pillars — all displaying scenes of the king worshipping Amon — stand like a forest.

Review...Recall...Reflect

1. With the concept of a god-king, the importance of having a strong Pharaoh was crucial to Egypt's stability. Respond to this statement using the Pharaohs of the New Kingdom to support your answer.

2. Outline the funeral process for a wealthy ancient Egyptian from the time of death, through the mummification process, to the final laying to rest in the tomb.

3. How did the concept of Ma'at help to shape the way Pharaohs governed and the way in which people lived their lives?

CONTINUITY AND CONVENTIONS IN EGYPTIAN ART

The art of the ancient Egyptians reveals a very conservative people. Conservatism was one of three key factors that shaped Egyptian art. The other two were that virtually all art was produced for religious purposes, and that the Pharaoh was the chief patron and subject of the arts. Egyptian art was not innovative, but sought to remain unchanged by following traditions established during the Old Kingdom. The resistance to change inherent in Egyptian art reflects a quest for permanence achieved through conventions and idealizations. The fact that Egyptian art followed these conventions, remaining nearly unchanged for over three thousand years, is in itself impressive. Art, for the Egyptians, served to capture for eternity the ideal form of the individual represented.

Ancient ODDITIES

The Egyptians made mummies out of more that just people. Several different animals — including dogs, cats (which were sacred), and even bulls — were also preserved, placed in coffins, buried in tombs, and given funerals. When a favourite cat died, members of its human family would shave off their eyebrows as a sign of respect.

Sculpture

The most majestic works of art produced by the Egyptians were their statues. Egyptian sculpture ranged in size from small models to colossal statues such as the Sphinx (20 m high and 73 m long) and the statues of Ramses II (20 m high). Egyptian

statues generally looked straight ahead and were not engaged in any activity; they are rigid and without emotion. While Egyptian sculpture may not have had the lifelike qualities of later Greek statues, it did capture the grandeur of the Pharaohs for all time.

What characteristics of this statue make it less than lifelike?

Carved Relief and Painting

Two artistic forms commonly found in the tombs of the Pharaohs and the nobility are reliefs and wall paintings. Both served a similar purpose: to convey to the gods the character of the deceased, or to illustrate the activities to be enjoyed in the afterlife. Carved reliefs are pictures that are cut into stone.

Paintings were generally considered second best, and were usually done in tombs where poor rock surfaces made relief work difficult. In some cases, paintings were selected over reliefs because they were less costly and time consuming.

Egyptian artists were not particularly concerned with perspective. Instead, they produced mathematically precise paintings and reliefs that conveyed the necessary information. Realism was the least of the artist's concerns. Aside from the contrived stance and the disproportionate size of the figures, Egyptian paintings show many other examples of how information took precedence over realism. For example, Egyptian artists often used what is called false transparency. In a picture showing a side view of someone dipping a ladle into a pot, the viewer would not be able to see what is in the pot or the ladle. The Egyptian artist made both the contents and the ladle visible — as if the pot were made of glass —to provide necessary information.

It is important to view Egyptian art from the Egyptians' perspective, not ours. The task set before the ancient Egyptian artist was to capture for eternity the essence and character of the deceased. In this conservative society, artists were not supposed to be innovators.

SOCIAL STRUCTURE: DAILY LIFE IN EGYPT

History is often a record of the lives and exploits of the powerful and the wealthy. They won the battles; they built the tombs; they were the focus of society and reaped its benefits. Understanding the life of the masses has, in recent years, become of greater concern to historians. Ethnohistory is a new and challenging field that combines various disciplines such as archaeology, anthropology, and historical studies to unearth a part of our past that has often been neglected. To do a civilization justice, we must look at all levels of society and all the elements that made up the daily lives and routines of all the people.

The bountiful harvest that was collected annually in the Nile Valley and the security afforded by Egypt's relative isolation gave all Egyptians, regardless of their station in life, a comfortable existence. Recent studies of Egyptian daily life offer a fascinating perspective on a lifestyle of well over 3000 years ago. This perspective was supplied by the wealth of funerary offerings found in the tombs: agricultural implements, domestic items, colourful and lively paintings, and small figurines engaged in all sorts of everyday activities.

An artisan, merchant, trader, or a common labourer in ancient Egypt would have lived in a one-storey mud-brick home that looked no different from the rest of the dusty yellow houses on the crowded street. These houses had four, square rooms with only window slits to ensure privacy and cool shelter from the hot midday sun. Furnishings would have been simple — reed mats and cushions, sometimes a wooden chest or a table. This was home to an average ancient Egyptian.

Agriculture

The Nile dictated everyone's life. At the beginning of the year, when the Nile flooded, dams and canals had to be maintained and repaired. As much of this valuable water as possible had to be retained for the time after the Nile had receded. The river also left behind fertile soil, and as soon as surveyors had marked out the land with ropes, labourers sowed the seeds. Grains such as barley and wheat, and vegetables such as onions, leeks, lettuce, radishes, gourds, melons, peas, and lentils grew well in these fertile areas. Planting did not take much time because the soil was usually soft and wet. Children and labourers drove herds of animals over the saturated earth to churn up the ground and stamp in the seeds. During the rest of the growing season, the crops were cultivated and the livestock herded to the fields to graze. Then the tax collectors and scribes descended on the fields to calculate the yield and assess taxes. The harvest would end up in the landowner's kitchen, the town market, or given to the labourers as payment.

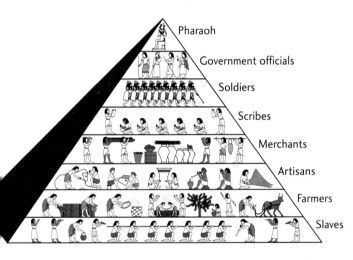

The structure of ancient Egyptian society.

The Family

The home was the refuge and gathering place for the family — a place to wash the dust away and eat and sleep. Children were fed and dressed simply and allowed few extravagances. Mothers or elder sisters cared for the children until they were four to six years old, when they were sent off to be educated. Children would be taught either in a teaching room by a priest or by their father, who would pass on all he knew about his trade or occupation.

The Role of Women

Our knowledge of ancient Egyptian life comes mainly from tomb decorations, and this includes what we know about the role of women in Egyptian society. Women were generally well treated and enjoyed considerable legal rights compared with women in other ancient civilizations. At least in theory, women shared the same legal rights as men, including the right to own and dispose of land and property, the right to seek a divorce, and the right to initiate a court case or serve as a witness. These legal rights allowed women to be economically independent. It appears that women's primary social role was in domestic life. The fact that female skin is coloured yellow in wall paintings, rather than the much darker skin tones of men, may indicate that women led a sheltered life, out of the sun. In early tomb decorations, women are often missing from culturally important work. At times, their role seems purely decorative, since they are usually depicted in ideal, slender and young form. Later, women were depicted much more often and in more elaborate clothing. Women did not hold important titles, had little political power, were usually illiterate, and were barred from intellectual and government life.

While a woman's role in society at large was limited, the home was the wife's domain. In fact, the common title for a married woman in ancient Egypt was *nebet per*, meaning "the lady of the house." In the ancient book *Instructions in Wisdom*, Egyptian men are cautioned:

Do not control your wife in her house,
When you know she is efficient;
Don't say to her: "Where is it? Get it!"
When she has put it in the right place.
Let your eye observe in silence,
Then you will recognize her skill.

Women took great pride in managing the household and raising their children. Although there were few career opportunities outside the home, Egyptian women faced few restrictions in public. When going out, perhaps to visit the market, women were not required to wear any kind of covering over their faces as in some ancient cultures. At home, the baking of bread and brewing of beer, both for family consumption and as offerings to the dead, occupied much of a woman's time.

Aside from the daily routine of running the household, a woman's main function in society was to bear and raise children. Children were so important to the ancient Egyptians that early marriages were encouraged so women could have children while they were young. Infertility was dreaded. A woman who was unable to conceive would make pleas to the gods and goddesses of fertility and childbirth: Bes, Taweret, and, especially, Hathor. Women would resort to spells, amulets, and herbal remedies in order to conceive. For couples who were, despite their best efforts, unable to bear children, adopting a child was considered the proper course of action. Despite their general love of children, there were occasions when pregnancy was not wanted, and ancient Egyptian recipes for contraception appear to have had some effectiveness.

The Role of Men

The husband was the head of the family and passed on the inheritance to his children. Marriage property was agreed upon by a marriage settlement, and did not necessarily follow a rigid pattern. Men were not restricted in the number of wives they could have, but economics usually dictated that one man took only one wife. The priests also exerted a powerful moral influence, and although harems and concubines existed, sexual excesses were not evident in everyday social life. The man of the household was the labourer, the craftsperson, or the official. Since the father was the holder of the office or the occupation, he passed this on to his sons. It took many generations to acquire the skills and secrets of a

The Granger Collection, New York.

This figure of a brewer making beer was found in a tomb.

trade, and sons were expected to continue the tradition. Change was not encouraged, because this involved risk.

Clothing of the Commoner

A day in the fields would begin early, making use of the cooler hours. The labourer wore as little as possible — a pleated or knotted loincloth made of very light material or, perhaps, nothing at all. Workers may have worn wigs to protect their heads from the sun. Children and servant girls often wore only an amulet around their neck or a string of beads around their waist. The women wore long, close-fitting robes made of a light, almost transparent linen that was easy to clean and good protection against the heat. Among the commoners, going barefoot was preferable.

Foods and Festivals

The fall season was a time for festivals since food had been assured until the next year. The people were relieved of their agricultural duties, and were now involved in community jobs such as building temples and tombs. Festivals were joyous occasions for young and old, rich and poor. Reasons for celebrating included religious festivals, political events, the butchering of an ox, or the end of a successful hunt in the marshes.

A banquet or a festival required preparation. The room was decorated with flowers and perfumed, the food was prepared, and the entertainment arranged. The kitchen would be full of servants busily preparing the festival fare: a freshly slaughtered ox; an assortment of roasted or boiled game, such as wild goat, gazelle, quail, duck, and fish; and vegetables that were in season, such as leeks, melons, onion, beans, chickpeas, lettuce, and radishes.

Seasonings for the meat and vegetables would include garlic, onions, beer, milk, and wine. There would also be a wide selection of wild and cultivated fruits, among these grapes, figs, dates, and pomegranates. Pastries and cakes were shaped and decorated with preserves and sweetened with honey. The guests could help themselves directly from the heaping plates placed on tables or offered to them by servants. Food was eaten using many different types of bread to clean up the plate.

Clothing and Jewelry of the Upper Classes

A love of functional ornament was obvious in the clothing of the wealthier Egyptians — it was practical yet elegant. Their jewelry was a means of personal expression. The sophistication in dress and jewelry increased with the importance of rank or family.

Men wore a loincloth, just as did the lower classes, but covered it with a full linen tunic with sleeves, secured by an elegant belt. Although sandals were not very comfortable, they were also indicative of aristocratic stature. To insult their enemies, Pharaohs often wore pictures of them on the soles of their shoes.

The women wore clothing similar to that of the women of the lower classes, but the cloth was finer and decorated with lively patterns and bright colours. The finest, softest cloth was, of course, kept for the queen. Jewelry could actually reflect a break from traditional Egyptian art because jewellers were less bound by convention and rules than other artists. Their work demonstrates a skill that has never been surpassed. Using gold, silver, agate, jasper, garnet, amethyst, and turquoise in fanciful engraved or twisted forms, the Egyptians fashioned exquisite accent pieces. This jewelry was stored in finely crafted boxes of ivory or wood covered in gold.

Cosmetics

Beside the jewelry box was another box of materials and utensils needed to apply cremes and make-up. Fashionable eyes were almond shaped, with eyebrows and eyelids made up in blue, green, or dark grey. Men and women applied this heavy make-up for two reasons: beauty and protection from dust, infection, and the glare of the sun and sand. Women smoothed a red, fat-based paint over their lips, and after bathing — which was done frequently — they applied perfume. The barber would come during this time to shave men's heads, because short hair was much easier to keep clean and more comfortable in the confines of their own homes. Wigs worn in public would be made from real hair or dyed black wool. The women wore shoulder-length hair that was braided and usually ornamented with a band or jewelry.

A plaster sculpture of Queen Nefertiti. Her eye make-up was both for beauty and protection.

STABILITY THROUGH EDUCATION

Education played a crucial role in the stability and continuity of ancient Egypt. All children, regardless of social class, received at least some education. One of the texts central to the education of Egypt's youth was *Instructions in Wisdom,* a moral and ethical guide. One of the primary goals of the ancient Egyptian educational system was to ensure that the youth grew up to exhibit self-control and good manners, and be contributing members of society. By the age of fourteen, children were streamed into the careers of their parents, with boys either joining their fathers in the fields or workshops, and girls learning from their mothers the proper way to run a household.

The sons of priests, Pharaohs, and administrative families were educated in a more formal manner, but these classes also passed on the father's position. Literacy was of great importance in running the highly bureaucratic Egyptian society. Teaching children to read and write was a priority. Children learned two types of writing: the rewriting of existing poetry and prose, and business writing. Business writing was required for the varied tasks that gave the scribe his rank and importance in society. Mathematics also received considerable attention in the curriculum. Overall, the Egyptian system of education was highly respected in the ancient world for its efforts at creating a well-rounded individual who could become a valuable member of society.

Science and Technology

The conservatism and practicality of the Egyptians are also evident in their scientific and technical achievements. They created what was needed and refined it until it was practical and could be used efficiently. Examples of this very practical nature include the development of Egyptian writing, medicine, their techniques for preserving the dead for thousands of years, and a calendar that allowed the Egyptians to predict accurately the yearly flooding of the Nile.

WEB CONNECTION

http://www.mcgrawhill.ca/links/echoes

Go to the web site above to learn more about Egyptian hieroglyphics.

Writing

The ancient Egyptians' form of writing, known as **hieroglyphics**, dates back to the earliest periods of their history. It is thought that the Egyptians likely borrowed from the Mesopotamians, who had developed cuneiform script — a script that had evolved from a series of pictographs. The Mesopotamians developed a more comprehensive system of writing to replace pictographs, but Egyptian hieroglyphics retained their pictographic nature. By about 3100 BCE, the Egyptians had a fully developed written language that used a combination of ideograms (symbols that express a whole word or idea) and phonograms (symbols that suggest a particular sound).

At the time of the New Kingdom, there were about 700 hieroglyphs in common usage, of which about 100 remained strictly visual, while the rest were phonograms. The system of hieroglyphic writing, while aesthetically pleasing and well-suited to the adornment of temples and tombs, proved impractical for day-to-day use. From the earliest period, scribes adapted hieroglyphic symbols in order to create handwriting known as hieratic writing. This simplified form of hieroglyphics was more suited to rapid writing using a brush on wood or a reed pen on papyrus. A further refinement of hieratic script occurred around 700 BCE when the demotic, or popular script, came into use for secular matters such as letters, accounts, and record keeping.

The Rosetta Stone carried the same text in full Egyptian hieroglyphics, Egyptian demotic script, and Greek. How would having these three forms of writing make deciphering hierogyphics possible?

As ancient Egyptian civilization waned, hieroglyphics faded from use. The last recorded use of hieroglyphics is found on the Temple of Isis at Philae dating to 394 CE. By this time, hieroglyphics were a mysterious text used only by a few priests who kept their meaning secret. It was not until the nineteenth century, when Jean François Champollion cracked the hieroglyphic code, that we were able to unlock the secrets of ancient Egyptian writing.

Medicine

Names marked on Egyptian tombs clearly indicate that there were doctors in Egyptian society. Medicine was a literate profession, and medical knowledge was recorded from a very early date, the oldest text dating back to 2000 BCE. These accumulated texts were a mixture of observation, medical and surgical descriptions, diagnosis, and prescriptions. They contain medical knowledge, plus observations mingled with nonsense, magic, and religion. Some of the inaccuracies stem from an inadequate knowledge of anatomy and the belief that disease was imposed as a punishment by the gods.

Some common medical problems that appear in the texts — and can easily be verified by examination of mummies — are worm infestations, arthritis, smallpox, tuberculosis, and gallstones. The medicines concocted were made of beer, milk, oil, plants, herbs, and animal substances. Bandages, splints, and disinfectants were used and doctors usually treated and stitched open wounds.

The texts comprised a sacred and unchangeable wisdom that was greater than the abilities of the doctors. This resulted in a stagnation of the development of medicine since no further research or modification was seen to be necessary. Resourcefulness and practicality were part of the Egyptians' mentality, as was the confining conservatism. They created the tools necessary to live a comfortable life in the Nile Valley.

Egypt's Legacy

One of the great achievements of Egyptian culture was its longevity. For over two thousand years, Egypt remained a dominant political and cultural force in the Near East. In fact, its influence spread throughout the Mediterranean, helping to shape, first, Minoan culture and, later, the culture of mainland Greece. As one of the world's first civilizations and one of the earliest powers to dominate the eastern Mediterranean, Egypt played a critical role in the development of the Near East. Although conservative, the ancient Egyptians made significant advances in many fields, including art, architecture, and technology. In the end, although we may marvel at the pyramids and be intrigued by the tombs and treasures of the Pharaohs, we must not lose sight of the ancient Egyptians as a people. They had a rich and vibrant society whose customs and traditions reflected their dependence on nature and their optimistic view of the afterlife.

[ANCIENT ISRAEL

Most of our information regarding the early history of Israel comes from the Old Testament, the first part of the Bible. According to this text, nomadic tribes wandered into Palestine from the east about 1900 BCE. Each tribe was led by a patriarch, of which Abraham is the most famous. God is said to have appeared before Abraham at a place called Harran, a city east of the Euphrates River, and to have given him the following instructions: "Leave your own country, your kinsmen, and your father's house, and go to a country that I will show you. I will make you into a great nation." According to the Old Testament, when Abraham arrived at the city of Shechem in Canaan, God again appeared to him and said: "I give this land to your descendants."

Later, Abraham's grandson Jacob, who took the name Israel, meaning "God ruled," organized the people into 12 tribes. Some of these tribes remained in Canaan while others, perhaps fleeing drought and famine, settled in Egypt and became subjects of the Pharaohs. To these numbers were added many slaves taken captive by the Egyptians during their conquest of Canaan in the fifteenth through thirteenth centuries BCE.

Perhaps the most important and famous part of the history of Israel concerns **Moses**, who led the Israelites out of bondage in Egypt. The oppression suffered by the Israelites was considerable. Under Ramses II, Egypt was undergoing its most ambitious period of construction since the days of the pyramids. Much of the labour required was supplied by conscripted foreigners, like the Israelites. They were forced to serve in the army, till the fields, pave the roads, build temples, and construct a new palace and two new cities. In the face of harsh treatment, many wanted to escape their oppression by Egypt. Some time around the end of the thirteenth century BCE, there was a mass migration of Israelites from Egypt (called the Exodus) under the leadership of a man with the Egyptian name Moses. Moses organized the tribes of Israel into a confederation bound by a covenant (a solemn agreement) to a god named **Yahweh**. According to the Old Testament, Moses received instructions directly from Yahweh, including what are called the **Ten Commandments**, a body of laws based on right conduct and stating, above all, "Thou shalt have no other gods before me." For the first time, the Israelites were united under one god (monotheism)

and the foundations were laid for the religion that would profoundly shape Western civilization.

The Israelites established themselves in Palestine, and in 1230 BCE, guided by Joshua, the successor to Moses, invaded Canaan and took the city of Jericho by siege. Despite being delivered from Egypt and led to victory by Joshua, the Israelites still had no central government, and over the years, the tribes drifted apart. Eventually, about 1020 BCE, a man named Saul became the first king of the Israelites and led them against their greatest enemy, the Philistines. Under David, Saul's successor, the Israelites captured the city of Jerusalem and extended the kingdom's boundaries to its greatest extent.

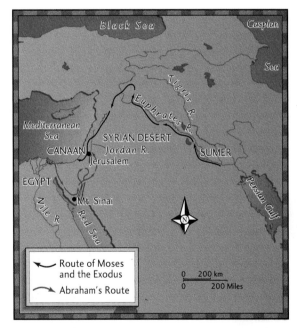

■ **Ancient Israel: The Journeys of Abraham and Moses**

1. Which rivers did Abraham have to cross?

2. What famous mountain did the Israelites and Moses journey past?

Biography

Nebuchadrezzar II: A Force to be Reckoned With

Nebuchadrezzar II (also known as Nebuchadnezzar), King of Babylon from 605 to 562 BCE, was a formidable leader. His reign was chronicled by ancient writers in several Books of the Old Testament, in the historical works of the Roman-Jewish writer Josephus, and in the text known as the Apocrypha, as well as by modern scholars.

Some ancient texts portray Nebuchadrezzar as mad, and this characterization has been used in several later works of art and literature about him. It is possible that the taint of madness came from Nebuchadrezzar's immense capacity for both wanton destruction and brilliant rebuilding. Following in his father's footsteps, Nebuchadrezzar pursued a military policy of expansion. His aim was to have no opposition from "horizon to sky," and so his army was always on the move, taking over an ever-widening circle of states through Syria, Palestine, Arabia, Judah, and even Egypt. The attacks were not always successful, and he faced rebellion within his own army. He was always a force to be reckoned with.

Nebuchadrezzar captured Jerusalem twice. The first time was 597 BCE. Typically, when Nebuchadrezzar invaded an area, the siege was quite complete: physical destruction was extensive, anything of value (property, wealth, and people) was deported out of the area to Babylon. Someone loyal to Babylon was then left in charge of the decimated region. Unfortunately for Jerusalem, the man left in charge, Zedebiah, did not remain loyal to Nebuchadrezzar, so the second invasion, in 587–586 BCE, was even more horrible than the first.

In II Kings 25: 8-12 of the Old Testament, it is reported that virtually nothing was left standing in Jerusalem. Even the sacred and beloved Temple of Solomon was burned to the ground. All the people fled or were deported. This ended the days of the First Temple and began the Jewish Diaspora, the dispersion of the Jewish people from their homeland, which would go on for centuries.

While he was a ruthless military strategist, Nebuchadrezzar was also known for his skilful diplomacy (despite the destruction in Jerusalem, he is not portrayed as totally bad in Jewish tradition) and his numerous building projects. Many temples were constructed during his reign, along with canals and fortifications. Nebuchadrezzar will always be remembered for directing the largest ziggurat project of them all — the Hanging Gardens of Babylon, one of the wonders of the ancient world.

All that remains of Nebuchadrezzar's Hanging Gardens of Babylon are these foundation blocks. It was certainly one of the largest ziggurats ever built.

Activities

1. What would have been the consequences of the tactics that Nebuchadrezzar used to defeat his enemies? Explain the effects of these tactics on the people and any future government.

2. Look up one of the following:
   - the opera *Nabucco* by G. Verdi
   - II Kings (Old Testament)
   - Diaspora
   - Hanging Gardens of Babylon

   Write a brief summary of your topic and its significance. Create a poster that captures this significance.

David's son Solomon is best remembered for his wisdom and skilful administration. He has also been credited with writing some of the books of the Bible, including Proverbs, Ecclesiastes, and the Song of Solomon, although it is quite certain that these were written much later. Solomon ruled at a time when many Near Eastern powers were weak, and he was able to maintain peace through a series of alliances and by increasing the size of the standing army he equipped with chariots.

The greatest monument to Solomon's rule was the **Temple of Jerusalem**, which he had built to house the Arc of the Covenant, a sacred box used to hold the holy text called the Torah. The temple has been described as "a marvel of cedar beams, cast-bronze pillars, ivory- panelled doors, golden vessels, and carved stone ornaments..." This magnificent temple was destroyed during a Babylonian invasion, rebuilt in the sixth century BCE, and destroyed again in 70 CE by the Romans. All that remains today is a part of the western wall of the outer court (now called the Wailing Wall). Solomon's other great building was his

Thousands come from around the world to pray at the Wailing Wall in Jerusalem.

new palace, said to be sufficiently large to house his 700 wives and to have stables for 12 000 horses!

Following the death of Solomon, the Kingdom of Israel split in two. While the northern part retained the name of Israel, the southern half, with Jerusalem as its capital, became known as Judah. Weakened by internal divisions, Israel was conquered by the powerful Assyrians in 722 BCE, and its leaders dispersed throughout the Assyrian Empire. The scattered people became known as the ten lost tribes of Israel. Judah was all that remained of the former kingdom of Israel, and it too would fall. In 586 BCE, Judah fell to Chaldea, or New Babylon, and the captives were deported to Babylon. Slowly, the Israelites trickled back into Palestine, but the Kingdom of Israel had passed.

Review...Recall...Reflect

1. Explain the primary purpose/function of art in ancient Egypt and how this purpose influenced the nature of the art produced.

2. How did the conservative nature of ancient Egypt affect the development of the sciences?

3. Create a timeline that captures the important dates in the development of Hebrew culture and society. Your time line should include at least six dates with a brief explanation for each date.

THE EVOLUTION OF THE JEWISH FAITH

Although the ancient Israelites may not have established a vast empire or left a great deal of monumental architecture, their spiritual ideas have profoundly influenced much of Western culture, and continue to exert tremendous force on the modern world. Central

Rites of Passage
Sons and Daughters of the Commandment

The term Bar Mitzvah means literally "son of the commandment." *Bar* means "son" in Aramaic (at one time, a common Near Eastern language), and *Mitzvah* means "commandment." *Bat* means "daughter" in Hebrew and Aramaic. Under Jewish Law, children are not held responsible for observing all the commandments (613 of them) until a certain age. At some point, likely between 516 BCE and 70 CE, age thirteen plus a day was deemed the age that a Jewish boy becomes Bar Mitzvah, and a full member of his community.

It is not known exactly why thirteen was picked as the age for conferring some serious adult responsibilities. Possibly, the age was picked because Abraham was believed to have rejected idols and begun his journey with God at the age of thirteen; or perhaps, it was because Moses was said to have made thirteen copies of the Torah. Thirteen may have just seemed like the appropriate age for a coming-of-age observance. Many other cultures and civilizations have ceremonies that recognize adolescence as a gateway to adulthood. Eventually, it was written into the *Talmud* (Jewish Laws) that "… At age thirteen, one becomes subject to the commandments." Interestingly, Bar Mitzvah is not mentioned in the Torah, which actually suggests 20 as the age when adult obligations begin.

To become Bar Mitzvah, no ceremony is really needed and no ceremony is mentioned in the Talmud. It is simply the age that confers the status. After becoming Bar Mitzvah, certain obligations and privileges are assumed. These include:

- responsibility for observing the 613 *mitzvot* (commandments)
- observance of fast days (for example, Yom Kippur)

Boys may read from the Torah once they are Bar Mitzvah.

- status in the count for a *minyan* (the quorum of ten required for community prayer)
- eligibility for *aliyot* (being called upon to read from the Torah)
- the right to take part in religious services

When becoming Bar Mitzvah, the celebrant not only enters a new phase in the life cycle, but also adds to the strength of the community, and this could be another reason for the relatively young age of thirteen. It came to be celebrated in a ceremony (along with birth, marriage, and death) during which the thirteen-year-old blesses and, perhaps, reads from the Torah. Eventually, a celebratory meal was also added.

Bat Mitzvah ceremonies are a much more modern development, although according to Jewish Law, girls mature faster than boys and are responsible for their actions at the age of twelve. Since women did not lead religious ceremonies in traditional Orthodox communities, a girl's Bat Mitzvah often went unacknowledged, except by family and by her being subject to most of the commandments. Different communities adapted different habits when it came time for a girl to become Bat Mitzvah. The first recorded public Bat Mitzvah ceremony, where a girl read from the Torah, did not occur until the early 1920s. Today it is a much more common practice.

Activities

1. Make two lists — one with the reasons twelve and thirteen are suitable ages for the responsibility of becoming Bat/Bar Mitzvah, and one with reasons why the age may not be suitable.

2. Considering your life today, your beliefs and society's needs, design a ceremony to celebrate the passage from child to adult. Include a visual to help illustrate what the ceremony would be like.

to understanding the development of the Jewish faith is the concept of the Covenant. The Covenant was a formal agreement between the Hebrews and their god, Yahweh, that was first made at the time of Abraham and later renewed under Moses. According to this contract, the Hebrews were to worship Yahweh as their only god, and they, in turn, were to be Yahweh's chosen people and promised the land of Canaan.

Initially, Yahweh was likely just one god among many that were worshipped in the Near East. As the main god of the Hebrews, Yahweh would have faced competition from other gods such as Baal, Enlil, Marduk, and Amon-Re. Over time, the Hebrews came to regard Yahweh as the only true God, thus laying the foundations for a monotheistic (one god) religion. Yahweh, as he appears in the Old Testament, is an all-powerful and all-knowing god who created the world and then stood outside of it. He is, at times, portrayed as a jealous, vindictive, and intolerant god, but despite his often harsh nature, Yahweh was a god for everyone; a god who cared for all classes, and was not too aloof to care for the individual. The Hebrews believed that their god intervened in human affairs and forgave those who truly regretted their wrongs.

What made the Jewish faith stand apart from other faiths at the time of Moses was that it was a religion of the people. It was deeply and passionately felt from within, not imposed from above. It must be remembered that leaders such as Moses were not kings and, therefore, could not force the people to obey laws. These men of ordinary status were able to exert tremendous influence on the ethical behaviour of a society — an influence that has lasted for over 3000 years.

Critical to the success and development of Judaism was the passion of the prophets who emerged throughout Israel's history. A theme common to all the prophets was the corruption of society and God's forgiveness if people repented their sins. The prophets declared that God would prove his love for his people by providing a Messiah (a person with divine power) to lead the nation of Israel. From about 200 BCE on, Jewish thought maintained that a king would someday appear to lead the people of Israel and restore their power and glory.

History Continues to Unfold

Despite the dispersion of the Jewish people throughout Europe and around the world that began with the **Diaspora** in 70 CE, Jewish culture and religious beliefs have influenced all the ancient cultures of the Near East. Many of the traditions of the Israelites live on today — not only among the Jews, but also among several other major religions. It has been said that without Moses, there could have been no Jesus or Muhammad. To what degree this is true is difficult to say, but it is certain that three of the world's most dominant religions — Judaism, Christianity, and Islam — all find their spiritual roots in the beliefs of the ancient Israelites.

Current Research and Interpretations
Recent archaeological finds off the coast of Egypt should keep archaeologists and historians busy for years. For the first time there is physical evidence of the existence of three lost cities know only through the writings of Ancient Greek historians. Herakleion, once a busy commercial centre has been found beneath 20 to 30 feet of water — an entire city, frozen in time since the seventh century.

Chapter Review

Chapter Summary

In this chapter, we have seen:

- how a common religious belief, the accepted leadership of the Pharaoh, and a general respect for tradition and laws led to stability in ancient Egypt
- that Akhenaton's attempt at rapid and radical religious change was rejected by Egypt and had little lasting effect
- that women in ancient Egypt enjoyed a level of freedom and equality not shared by women in most other ancient civilizations
- that certain individuals in both ancient Egypt and Israel made significant contributions to the development of legal, political, and military traditions in their respective societies

Reviewing the Significance of Key People, Concepts, and Events (Knowledge/Understanding)

1. Understanding the history of ancient Egypt and the Israelites requires a knowledge of the following concepts and events, and an understanding of their significance in the development of society in both Egyptian and Israel. In your notes, identify and explain the historical significance of three from each column.

People	Concepts/Structures	Events
Akhenaton	Ma'at	Hyksos invasion
Hatshepsut	Amon-Re	Diaspora
Moses	Instructions in Wisdom	
Ramses II	hieroglyphics	
Tutankhamun	Ten Commandments	
Tuthmosis III	Temple of Jerusalem	

2. Geography was one of the major factors that shaped Egyptian society. Re-create the following chart. Be sure to explain clearly how each of the geographical features influenced the development of Egyptian society.

Once you have completed your chart, transfer two central facts about the relationship between Egyptian geography and society to the graphic organizer "Geography's Influence" in your *World History Handbook*.

Geographic Feature	Description	Influence on Society
Nile River		
Nile Delta		
Faiyum		
deserts		

3. Explain how each of the following tended to reinforce stability and continuity in ancient Egyptian society: art, education, careers, the yearly cycle of the Nile, the rule of the Pharaoh.

Record at least three of these ideas in your *World History Handbook* booklet, on the "Forces That Reinforce Stability and Continuity" organizer.

Doing History: Thinking About the Past (Thinking/Inquiry)

1. In two paragraphs, compare the economic, social, and political roles women played in Egyptian society (both commoners and the nobility) with the roles of women in Canadian society today. Transfer three of the most important ideas about women's roles in Egyptian society to the graphic organizer "Women's Roles in Society" in your *World History Handbook*. Finish and defend this statement in two paragraphs:

The two most important factors in the rise and dominance of ancient Egypt as a major cultural, military, and economic force in the Near East were...

Transfer these two central reasons to the graphic organizer "Why Some Societies Rose to Dominance" in your *World History Handbook*.

Applying Your Learning (Application)

1. On a map of the Mediterranean, indicate the flow of trade goods to and from Egypt. Your map must be visually appealing, use arrows to indicate the flow of goods, be properly labelled, and incorporate relevant pictures.

2. Create a 12-month calendar that highlights one of the Egyptian gods for every three months. Provide a colourful depiction of the god and a one-paragraph description of the god's place/role in the Egyptian pantheon.

Communicating Your Learning (Communication)

1. Write two biographical sketches to be included in the *Who's Who of Ancient Egypt*. The first is to be on a Pharaoh of your choice. The biography should include the approximate time the person lived, his or her major achievements, and any other relevant information. The second biography is to be a fictional character based on the life of a typical commoner. Describe this person's daily life, home, dress, and diet.

2. In two paragraphs, clearly explain the connection between (a) Egyptian religion and the concept of the afterlife and (b) mummification and Egyptian burial practices.

Unit Review

Grading the Civilizations

1. In Chapter One, the essential elements of a civilization were outlined and you were asked to rank in order of importance each of the elements. Now that you have had an opportunity to study a civilization in depth, apply your ranking to see how it measures up. Below are three broad categories under which the elements could be clustered. For each of the categories, provide a letter grade (from A+ to F) and an anecdotal comment of three to five sentences to support the grade. A fuller assessment of the civilization selected can be completed using your *World History Handbook*.

	Letter Grade	Comments
The Place of People • level of equality • just laws • distribution of wealth • overall quality of life		
Organization of Society • democratic • effective government • meets needs of society • provides security and stability for society		
Lasting Legacy • ideas • works of art • architecture • innovations/inventions • literature		

The Role of Individuals in History

1. Historians often grapple with whether history is shaped by individuals, or whether individuals are a product of their age and are shaped by history. Would the history of ancient Mesopotamia have been different if Hammurabi had not lived? Did Imhotep change the direction of Egyptian history? Below is a list of people drawn from this unit. Select any two. For each, identify his or her role in society, major accomplishments, sphere of greatest impact (e.g., art, ideas, religion, politics), and why you believe he or she shaped or was shaped by history. You may want to do additional research on the two individuals you select.

| Sargon | Assurnasirpal II | Imhotep | Akhenaton | Ramses II |
| Hammurabi | Menes | Hatshepsut | Tutankhamun | Moses |

Understanding Chronology

1. The study of history, whether the recent or distant past, relies on a sound understanding of the order in which events occurred. Without a clear understanding of how history has unfolded, it is difficult to see the relationship between earlier events and later developments. The following questions help to illustrate the importance of understanding the chronology of history:

   a) Why is it misleading to discuss Egyptian pyramids and King Tut at the same time?

   b) What is the relationship between the Neolithic Revolution and the Urban Revolution?

   c) Why would reversing the chronological order of the lives and actions of Moses and David make the history of the Israelites unintelligible?

   d) Assume you are an Egyptologist in search of the tombs of two Pharaohs. How would knowing when they ruled help you to know where to begin your search?

Cause and Effect in History

1. History often involves the study of cause and effect. We sometimes find that one cause has several effects, or that several causes led to one effect. Complete the Cause and Effect diagram your teacher provides for you. Once you have completed the diagram, use one as a guide to writing a paragraph on the issue addressed.

UNIT TWO

The Mediterranean

chapter 3
Greece in the Heroic Age

chapter 4
Classical Greece

chapter 5
The Roman Republic

chapter 6
The Roman Empire

This beaten gold death mask is from a Mycenaean royal tomb, ca. 1500 BCE.

O n a peninsula in southern Europe, in a land of limited natural resources, a people of astounding ingenuity arose some 3000 years ago. The ancient Greeks gave the world some of the most magnificent works of art, architecture, and intellectual thought. They also invented a democratic system of government to which we still look for inspiration today.

On a peninsula directly across from Greece, the centre of the greatest empire the ancient world had ever seen emerged from its beginnings on the banks of the Tiber River. The Roman Empire at its height would stretch from Britain in the north to Asia Minor, and across North Africa. Borrowing and adapting ideas from all over their vast empire, the Romans proved to be a very practical people. Paved roads criss-crossed their territory, fresh water flowed through aqueducts, and huge amphitheatres displayed gladiatorial games to quench the public's insatiable thirst for blood.

UNIT EXPECTATIONS

In this unit, you will:

O assess the contributions of Athens and Rome to the development of modern Western ideas of citizenship

O evaluate critically the role of significant artists, philosophers, and political theorists from ancient Greece and Rome

O demonstrate an under-standing of the factors that influenced the development of various forms of leadership and government in ancient Greece and Rome

O formulate significant questions for research and inquiry, drawing on examples from the study of Greco-Roman history

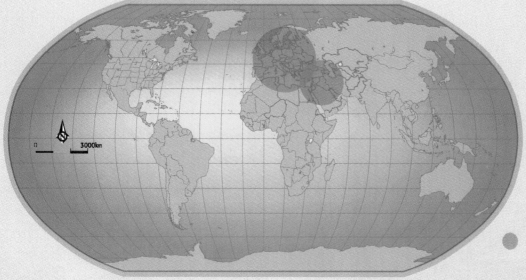

The Greek and Roman World

CHAPTER THREE

Greece in the Heroic Age

CHAPTER EXPECTATIONS

By the end of this chapter, you will be able to:

- *identify major changes in early Greek history including the introduction of bronze and the development of writing*

- *analyze diverse forms of government employed by the ancient Greeks including monarchy, dictatorship, and democracy*

- *assess the contribution of Athens to the development of modern Western ideas of citizenship and the rights of the individual*

- *explain the reaction of the ancient Greeks to outside influences such as the invasion of the Persians and trade with Egypt*

The Lions Gate entrance to the fortress at Mycenae, ca. 1500-1300 BCE.

The person many people call the "Father of History" was a Greek named Herodotus of Halicarnassus. In the fifth century BCE he wrote a book describing the conflict between two great civilizations: the Greeks and the Persians. The outcome of this conflict was crucial to the development of early European history and culture. Herodotus described the conflict as a struggle between West and East, between Europe and Asia, between the Greeks and what he called "barbarians," by which he merely meant foreigners. Herodotus wrote,

> These are the Researches [Histories] of Herodotus of Halicarnassus set down to preserve the memory of the past, and to prevent the great and wonderful achievements of the Greeks and the "Barbarians" from losing their glory, and in particular, to show how the two peoples came into conflict.

Herodotus *Histories* I.i

We now know that there were in fact two other civilizations that had thrived in the area of Greece well before the time of Herodotus (ca. 480–429 BCE). We call these two earlier peoples Minoan and Mycenaean, since we are still not sure what they called themselves. Differences between the cultures of the Minoans, Mycenaeans, and later Greeks are clear and easy to distinguish. But while differences caused by changes in the environment, opportunities for trade, and threats from more highly developed neighbours are to be expected over a 1500-year period, threads of continuity remained. The Minoans influenced Mycenaean art, technical crafts, writing, and religion. The Mycenaeans in turn passed on their language, legends, and some aspects of their religion to the Greeks of the Classical Age.

KEY WORDS

democracy

ostracism

sanctuary

trireme

tyrant

metic

polis

KEY PEOPLE

Herodotus

Solon

Peisistratus

Cleisthenes

helots

Lycurgus

Sappho

VOICES FROM THE PAST

Good habits are man's finest friend, and bad are his worst enemy.
Hesiod *Works and Days* 470–472

TIME LINE: GREECE IN THE HEROIC AGE

	ca. 7000 BCE	Earliest known people on Crete arrive
Neolithic farming villages develop on mainland Greece and Crete	ca. 7000 BCE	
	ca. 3200 BCE	Bronze introduced to the Minoans
Early Minoan period on Crete; Early Helladic period in mainland Greece	ca. 3000–2100 BCE	
	ca. 1900 BCE	Linear A script is developed by the Minoans
Minoan palaces destroyed and rebuilt	ca. 1750 BCE	
	ca. 1680 BCE	Wealthy and powerful Mycenaean states emerge in mainland Greece
Massive volcanic eruption destroys the island of Thera	ca. 1628 BCE	
	ca. 1500 BCE	Destruction of Minoan palaces, perhaps due to Mycenaean invasion
Trojan War and the decline of Mycenaean civilization	ca. 1200 BCE	
	ca. 1100–800 BCE	Greek Dark Ages
Archaic Period, Greek colonization begins	ca. 800 BCE	
	776 BCE	First Olympic Games held
Solon's reforms lay the foundations for Athenian democracy	594 BCE	
	508 BCE	Cleisthenes's reforms establish world's first democratic government
Ionian revolt leads to new Greek-Persian conflict	499–494 BCE	
	490 BCE	Persian attack on Athens beaten back in Battle of Marathon
Persia's second and final attempt to invade mainland Greece ends in failure	480–479 BCE	

THE EARLIEST CIVILIZATION IN EUROPE: THE MINOANS

Crete is a land of abundant agricultural wealth. The people of ancient Crete, whom we call Minoans, were highly proficient navigators. This navigational skill in combination with the island's agricultural bounty led the Minoans to become the first Europeans to acquire some of the facets of civilization. By about 1900 BCE, the Minoans had developed a form of writing, a palace-led social organization, advanced metal-working skills, and sophisticated artistic expression.

Crete is an island about 200 km long and divided into regions by tall mountain ranges. It enjoys a very pleasant, semi-tropical climate. When the first settlers made their way to the island from Asia Minor in the seventh millennium (7000–6000 BCE), they found a fertile, inviting home. Over the centuries, the settlers spread across the island, building small villages, growing grain, raising sheep and goats, hunting and fishing, and occasionally trading with neighbours on their own and nearby islands.

Innovations: The Introduction of Bronze

After more than 3000 years of this Neolithic farming life, several new elements were introduced to the culture. One of the most important was the use of metal to make better tools and weapons. The metal of greatest importance was bronze, an alloy of about nine parts copper to one part tin. Its introduction had as profound an impact on Crete as it did elsewhere in the ancient world, and the arrival of bronze on the island marks the Early Minoan period (ca. 3000–2100 BCE).

The copper used on Crete may have come first from the small island of Kythnos to the north, but it was especially plentiful at Lavrion near Athens on the mainland. On the eastern island of Cyprus, copper was plentiful, but tin was much rarer and therefore more expensive, perhaps coming from the mountains of southern Turkey. Separately, tools made of these metals were not much better than tools made of stone, but combined, they produced a tough but malleable metal with a reasonably low melting point, ideal for producing sharp knives and spear points, tough saws, hard chisels and many other implements.

How did the Minoans pay for bronze? Crete had no other valuable products to exchange except agricultural goods. It is likely that a new market developed, even if only on a small scale, involving surplus production of food or linen and wool clothing. Sailors, traders, merchants, and metal workers reaped profits for their work in the exchange system. There is certainly evidence of a great increase in the population of the island, and of better use of the land for agriculture: ploughing heavier soils, making cheese from milk, and planting grape vines. The farmers of Crete also planted olive trees to produce one of the most important staples of Mediterranean life: olive oil.

The process was slow, but over a thousand years, these changes brought about a society with more diverse skills and occupations, some accumulation of wealth, and greater contacts with peoples outside Crete. However, this development was interrupted toward the end of the third millennium (ca. 2300–2100 BCE), perhaps because of problems elsewhere in the eastern Mediterranean. It is not yet understood why settlements were abandoned and trading contacts severed.

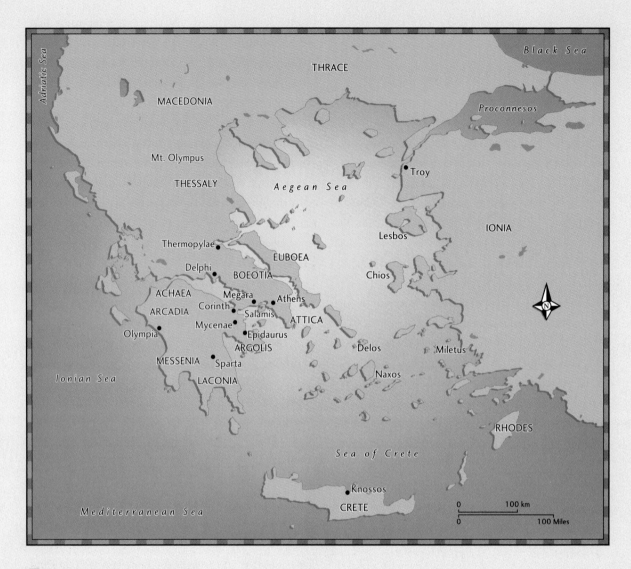

■ The Ancient Greek World

1. Does the geography of Greece give any clues about why, historically, it was difficult for the Greeks to unite?

2. If you were heading an army in Asia sent to invade Athens, what might your strategy be?

http://www.mcgrawhill.ca/links/echoes

WEB CONNECTION

Go to the site above to find out more about Minoan civilization.

TIME FRAMES
MINOAN AGES

Early Minoan ca. 3200–2100 BCE

Middle Minoan ca. 2100–1700 BCE

Late Minoan ca. 1700–1100 BCE

These chronological divisions were established by archaeologist Sir Arthur Evans, and were meant to parallel the division of Egyptian history into Old, Middle, and New Kingdoms. The date of the change from Middle to Late Minoan has been adjusted in recent years, based on a re-dating of the volcanic eruption on the island of Thera, and new thinking on the dates of certain Egyptian Dynasties.

Cross-cultural Influences and the Minoans

At the beginning of the Middle Minoan period, ca. 2100 BCE, a recovery occurred, with new population growth helped in part by immigration. Very quickly, life on Crete began to flourish in completely new ways. Foreign trade with the Near East increased as it stabilized following a period of turmoil. There were new burial customs, impressive buildings, higher levels of artisanship, and a system of writing. There were now sacred grounds called **sanctuaries**

built on hilltops. This was where temples, sacrificial altars and other forms or architecture were built in honour of the gods. Very clearly, some families on the island were accumulating substantial wealth. Archaeological evidence shows that these newly wealthy people found ways to enjoy their riches. They built bigger and finer houses — some on the scale of palaces — where possessions could be stored and administered. They had fine jewelry and clothing and enjoyed works of art and luxury imported products, many of which came from Egypt or elsewhere in the Middle East. To keep track of their property, the wealthy first developed a method of marking ownership with seals, then a system of record keeping using hieroglyphic characters, perhaps borrowed from Egypt. Eventually the Minoans developed a script of their own, which we call Linear A. By about 1900 BCE, civilization had appeared on the threshold of Europe.

Politics and the Palaces

The largest and most important palace on Crete was always at Knossos. It was also the earliest, along with the palaces of Phaestus and Mallia. These were certainly centres of political power. Knossos must have been home to the most powerful monarch on the island, king or queen, with other royal families ruling from other palaces. Power was partly exercised by controlling certain goods and products, so the palaces were also centres of exchange for the Minoan economy. The large storerooms for agricultural produce and for items of prestige created in the palace workshops are evidence of the role of the palace in the local economy.

The palaces were the most impressive buildings constructed by the Minoans. Dozens of interconnecting rectangular rooms on two, three, or more storeys were grouped around a large open courtyard in the centre of the palace. There were areas for administration, residences, religious purposes, storage, and workshops. The finest rooms were decorated with colourful wall frescoes depicting processions of gift bearers, scenes of nature, lively ceremonies, or charging bulls. Fine building skills can be seen in the masonry reinforced by wooden beams to protect it from earthquakes, in the deep light wells (like elevator shafts) to bring air and light to the lower storeys, and in the advanced plumbing.

A restored passageway in the Palace of Minos at Knossos. Note the painting on the back wall.

All these palaces were destroyed around 1750 BCE, possibly as a result of a massive earthquake. Earthquakes and volcanoes are common in the Aegean region, but are rarely strong enough to cause such widespread destruction. Nevertheless, a little more than a century later, the volcano on the tiny island of Thera, to the north of Crete, erupted with cataclysmic results.

The Eruption of Thera

The beautiful island of Thera exploded in a tremendous eruption, dated by tree rings to around 1628 BCE. This explosion enlarged an existing caldera from earlier volcanic activity. The sea poured in and caused even more turmoil when it met the red-hot lava. A small, thriving town was buried by the ash that rained down on the south coast of the island. In 1967, the Greek archaeologist Spyridon Marinatos came upon this town, which had been wonderfully preserved. Unlike the later volcanic eruption at Pompeii, the people of Thera had had sufficient time to save themselves, but had to leave behind many of their possessions. The vibrant wall paintings are only the most famous legacy left to us by this culture. Remarkably, this devastating eruption seems to have had little long-term effect on Minoan culture on Crete, only about 120 km away.

EXTERNAL FORCES

The new palaces were rebuilt almost immediately after their destruction in 1750 BCE. They were virtually identical to those that had been destroyed, with no sign of major changes to their structure or decoration, and were as large and as fine as ever. Minoan life continued for another 250 years, reaching new heights of wealth and vigour. Then, around 1490 BCE, the palaces were destroyed again — except for the one at Knossos. This time, the cause was probably not a natural disaster. It might have had something to do with the Mycenaean warriors who began to arrive on Crete.

There is considerable evidence to suggest that Mycenaean lords took over the rule of Crete, with Knossos as their administrative centre, ca. 1500 BCE. The most convincing evidence for this is the use of a new language, which we call Linear B, that was being written on clay tablets to keep track of palace goods. This form of writing was derived from Linear A (the Minoan script), but recorded the language of the early Greek-speaking Mycenaeans, not the non-Greek language of the Minoans. This discovery was made when a young Englishman, Michael Ventris, deciphered Linear B in 1952.

How and why the Mycenaeans invaded Crete is impossible to say. The Minoans might have been weakened by fighting among themselves, or perhaps by natural disasters. Whatever the cause, they could not hold back the newcomers. The palace at Knossos seems to have been taken intact and for about 80 years served as a main administrative centre. Many distinctive features of Minoan culture disappeared, such as buildings with central courts, art forms depicting scenes from nature, finely carved stone vases, and the Linear A script. Graves near Knossos contain the bodies and weapons of some of these new overlords. Eventually, the palace at Knossos was also destroyed, this time by a great fire. Whether the fire was an accident or was caused by an attack is not known, but the Mycenaean lords did not rebuild Knossos. Life on the island began reverting to its simpler past, and the finest accomplishments of the Minoans quietly disappeared.

The Myth of the Minotaur

Later Greeks had several myths about the Minoans, some of which may hold a kernel of truth. The most famous is the myth of Theseus and the Minotaur. The wife of King Minos of Knossos gave birth to a monster called the Minotaur, who was half man and half bull. The bloodthirsty Minotaur was imprisoned in a maze-like structure built by Daedalus, the court inventor. The Greeks called this the Labyrinth. Since the Minotaur's diet included young unmarried men and women, every year King Minos forced the people of Athens to select 14 of its finest youth as a sacrifice. This horrific practice would have continued annually but for the young hero, Theseus, who

volunteered to go to Knossos as part of the sacrifice. With the help of King Minos's daughter, Ariadne, Theseus killed the Minotaur, found his way out of the Labyrinth by following a string he trailed behind himself, and saved the youth of Athens.

A bronze figure of the mythical Minotaur, half man, half bull, and said to have lived in the Labyrinth at the palace of King Minos at Knossos.

This tale of human sacrifice seems out of character for the Minoans, who loved to show peaceful scenes of nature in their art. Nevertheless, in a few of the wall paintings and seal stones preserved at Knossos there are depictions of what looks like a very dangerous sport or ritual. Young men and women are shown leaping over the backs and long, pointed horns of charging bulls.

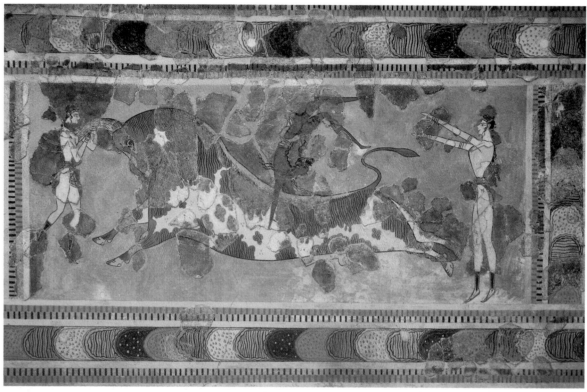

Young Minoan girls and boys jumping the bulls at Knossos. Can you think of any modern day activities similar to this?

Sometimes these acrobats are successful but some are gored and severely injured. Perhaps there is an echo of the Minotaur myth in these scenes. This idea is strengthened by the fact that the palace of Knossos itself could well be compared to a maze, given its complex plan of rooms and corridors.

Review...Recall...Reflect

1. How did the introduction of bronze change Minoan society?

2. Describe the Middle Minoan period.

3. What explanations have been suggested to account for the decline of the Minoan civilization?

THE EARLIEST GREEKS: THE MYCENAEANS

Mainland Greece developed in the same way as Crete, and at about the same pace, down to around 2000 BCE. Neolithic farming villages were scattered in the narrow valleys of Greece from ca. 6500 BCE to 3000 BCE. Then, as elsewhere around the Aegean, bronze came into common use, people learned to exploit natural resources more effectively, contacts with other regions increased, and life slowly changed. A new era began, now called the Early Helladic period, to distinguish this culture from the Early Minoan. Archaeologists have excavated several large, carefully planned houses that show the increased wealth of the Early Helladic people at this time. Then, toward the end of the third millennium, development was interrupted by episodes of destruction and signs of depopulation, a pattern widely found around the eastern Mediterranean, including Crete. Why this happened is not well known, but in mainland Greece, one cause might have been invasions of various peoples that began some time after ca. 2300 BCE. By ca. 2000 BCE, most vestiges of the prosperous Early Helladic culture were gone and a simpler, less wealthy farming-herding culture (called Middle Helladic) had taken its place. Meanwhile, in sharp contrast to mainland Greece, the Minoans on Crete had recovered from their late third-millennium disasters and begun reaching new heights of prosperity, including the construction of huge palaces for their monarchs.

There is no evidence that the invaders of mainland Greece at the end of the third millennium spoke Greek. The Greek language might have developed after their arrival as the language of the invaders mixed with that of the indigenous peoples. What we do know is that the Mycenaeans, the descendants of these Middle Helladic peoples, did speak an early form of Greek.

TIME FRAMES
THE BRONZE AGE IN MAINLAND GREECE

Early Helladic ca. 3000–2000 BCE
Middle Helladic ca. 2000–1680 BCE
Mycenaean ca. 1680–1060 BCE
Sub-Mycenaean ca. 1060–1025 BCE

During the seventeenth and sixteenth centuries BCE (1700–1500 BCE), a surprising change occurred in Greece, or so it seems from the evidence first revealed by archaeologist Heinrich Schliemann

(1822–1890). Powerful and wealthy chiefdoms sprang up and consolidated control of the small farming villages of the previous few centuries. What caused this rapid and important transformation is still not well understood. Most archaeologists now call this new culture Mycenaean, after its largest political centre, Mycenae. By the fourteenth century BCE, these chiefdoms had been further transformed into well-defined states ruled by kings with administrative centres (in palaces), a writing system for record keeping, and state institutions including a state religion.

The Mycenaeans were remarkable builders. To construct these burial places, called *tholos* tombs, stones weighing as much as 100 t had to be moved into place. Later Greeks believed that only the legendary one-eyed giants called the Cyclopes could have lifted these stones.

Schliemann did not know what he had found when he uncovered the fabulously wealthy graves at Mycenae in the fall of 1876. He thought he had discovered the burials of King Agamemnon and his family. He then declared that the epic poems of Homer, the *Iliad* and the *Odyssey*, were based in history. The two poems describe the adventures of Greek heroes who fought in the Trojan War around 1200 BCE, about 450 years before Homer's own time. Agamemnon of Mycenae, the leader of the Greek army at Troy, returned home from the war successfully, only to be murdered by his wife Clytemnestra.

WEB CONNECTION

http://www.mcgrawhill.ca/links/echoes

Go to the site above to find out more about Mycenaean civilization.

The Legend of the Trojan War

Sing of the building of the horse of wood, which Epeius made with Athena's help, the horse which once Odysseus led up into the citadel as a thing of guile, when he had filled it with the men who sacked Troy.

Homer *Odyssey* VIII.492–495

The Trojan War itself, despite Homer's long descriptions, is still a vaguely understood event in Mycenaean history, if it was an event at all, and not pure legend. Excavations at Troy show that a city there was destroyed in a battle ca. 1240 BCE. At that time, the city was really just a fortified town, only 2 ha in area, with a rather poor standard of living. No wonder some scholars have suggested that the Trojan War was merely a dispute over fishing rights or control over shipping, and not the great conflict of West versus East, as later Greeks believed.

Schliemann could not have known that the graves he had found actually belonged to a royal family of Mycenae, which predated the legendary Trojan War by 300–400 years. The wonderful gold funeral masks, inlaid bronze daggers, and other exquisite objects of gold, silver, ivory, and faience are stunning testimony of a wealthy and powerful royalty or nobility living in Greece ca. 1650–1550 BCE.

Mycenaean rulers were similar to feudal lords, each governing his own wide area of central or southern Greece from a well-fortified palace. All of them might have owed some allegiance to the king of Mycenae. Indications from the tombs and the walls at Mycenae certainly point to it being the most powerful of the Mycenaean states. The wealth of these kings probably came from trade, particularly in metals like gold or tin. We know from the Linear

Scripts & Symbols λ μ ν ο π θ υ ρ σ τ υ ϖ ω ξ ψ ζ α β χ ε δ φ γ

The Mycenaeans developed their script, Linear B, by borrowing from the Minoan Linear A, and making changes so that the two scripts could be distinguished. Of the 89 syllabograms (signs representing syllables composed of a consonant and a vowel) used in Linear B, 73 of them have predecessors in the Linear A script. The syllabograms in Linear B, however, were simplified and made more regular in writing. The Mycenaeans also adopted a different system for expressing numbers.

In the Field...

Heinrich Schliemann: Hero or Fraud?

There is a lot that can be said about Heinrich Schliemann, both good and bad. Much of what we know about him comes from his own writing, including an autobiography, at least 18 diaries, and close to 60 000 letters. Unfortunately, modern scholars have found many irregularities in Schliemann's writings, some trivial embellishments, but many outright lies.

After leaving home at age 14, Heinrich Schliemann first apprenticed as a grocer, but soon left to work in Amsterdam and St. Petersburg. He had an amazing facility with languages and became fluent in Dutch, English, French, Russian, and both ancient and modern Greek. Schliemann worked as a trader and a banker, and also as a war profiteer, a black market dealer, and a smuggler. He later worked in the United States briefly, but left under suspicion of unscrupulous business practices. Schliemann made a fortune no matter what he did. In 1867, he retired from business, a very wealthy man.

Heinrich Schliemann (1822-1890)

As a child, Schliemann became fascinated with the ancient city of Troy. Later, his fascination turned to obsession, specifically with proving that the Trojan War, as told by Homer in his epic poems the *Iliad* and the *Odyssey*, was a historical fact. This obsession led to an interest in archaeology. Ultimately, Schliemann wanted to prove scientifically that Troy and the Trojan War were not just the stuff of myth and legend.

Unfortunately, in his zeal to prove the links between literature, history, and scientific fact, Schliemann tainted his discoveries by combining treasures from various sites to support his research. Archaeologists today agree that Schliemann did find the location of ancient Troy, but his falsifications cast a shadow over his considerable contributions to the field of archaeology.

The tinge of scandal that surrounded Schliemann and his discoveries did not end there. Schliemann smuggled much of what he found out of Turkey, and eventually donated the treasure to Germany in 1880. At the end of World War II, the Russian army confiscated the treasure and it was not seen or heard of again until 1991, when Russian art historians made it public again.

After his death on 26 December 1890, Heinrich Schliemann's body was buried in a huge ornate mausoleum he had built for himself at the entrance to the first cemetery in Athens. On the front of the mausoleum there is a large carved bust of Schliemann. The inscription above the entrance reads, in Greek, "For the hero Schliemann."

This cup is typical of the treasures Schliemann found in the tombs of Mycenae. It is solid gold, decorated with figures of young hunters chasing wild bulls. Found in a tholos tomb near Sparta, it dates to ca. 1500 BCE.

Activities

1. Turkey would like to gather all the artifacts removed from Troy and create a museum near the actual site. The Turks believe that the items would be more valuable placed in the context of their original location. Support or reject this idea. Write a response as if it were from an historian in Russia, Germany, or Turkey.

2. Explain why it is or is not important to know the details of an historian's life and work before you assess that individual's version of history.

B tablets that the palaces acted as redistribution centres, taking in commodities from the areas under their control, storing them, and then sending them (or products made at the palace workshops — pottery, weapons, etc.) to places within the kingdom and beyond.

Minoan Influence on Mycenae

In their first two centuries, the Mycenaeans were very strongly influenced by the older Minoan civilization to the south. Minoan culture is reflected in Mycenaean wall painting, styles of dress, certain types of vases, seal carving, and even in some religious ideas. Both Minoans and Mycenaeans left clay figurines representing worshippers and human-shaped gods in their sanctuaries. Both cultures seemed to have practised animal sacrifice and the pouring of libations (small quantities of wine) into the ground, and both kept cult areas (smaller sacred areas) within the palace. The names of some of the Mycenaean gods are known from the Linear B tablets, and are the same as later Classical Greek gods, including Poseidon, Athena, and Dionysos. Zeus, the most powerful of the Greek gods, was actually thought to have been raised on the island of Crete. After the Minoan palaces were destroyed and Mycenaeans apparently took control of Crete, Minoan influence on Mycenaean culture diminished significantly.

The End of the Mycenaean World

The archaeological evidence shows that the first widespread destruction of Mycenae occurred around 1250 BCE. In order to protect water supplies, workshops, and storage areas from further destruction, the rulers extended the fortification walls. But around 1200 BCE, another series of disasters brought an end to the centralized administration, including the use of writing, and caused great depopulation in some areas. People continued to live at Mycenae, Tiryns, and Athens, but the monumental palaces fell into disuse. There was certainly a long process of decline, when the political and economic structure was weakened. Scholars continue to debate the causes of this decline, focusing on three main reasons: natural catastrophes (probably earthquakes), foreign attacks, and internal strife, or a combination of these factors. Clearly, the Mycenaean world had come to an end, leaving many impressive ruins and a deep-seated memory of a glorious past.

The Dark Ages

There was a period of recuperation lasting about 350 years, during which various groups of Greek-speaking peoples from the north settled in the Peloponnese (the Greek peninsula), established new homes, built new sanctuaries for their gods, farmed their new land, and built secure communities. But beyond vague notions of what life was like based on sparse archaeological finds, or what political changes were occurring, we know very little about this period. The collapse of the Mycenaean civilization took with it both the wealth and the writing used to keep track of that wealth. There are absolutely no written documents from this 350-year period and later Greeks did not preserve anything about this part of the past in their collective memory. For this reason, the period is called the Dark Ages of Greece. The Greeks did remember their distant, Mycenaean past as an age of heroes and supermen, like Herakles, Hector, Jason, and Achilles. Minstrels wandered from village to village, finding the houses of local nobles and singing their tales of past glory and brave adventures. In return, they would get a bed for the

A Greek black-figure vase (ca. 550 BCE) showing two heroes of the Trojan War, Achilles and Ajax, playing a board game.

these mountains are more like partitions than real barriers. They trap the fall and winter rains, provide pasturage for animals, yield highly prized marble, but otherwise keep the nation separated into small communities. Many of these isolated communities quite naturally grew and developed into what the Greeks called a *polis*, an independent city-state.

While the mountains hindered communication and transportation between city-states, the sea was a special blessing — a vast blue highway linking all parts of the country. This highway, however, extended well beyond the bounds of the Greek nation, stretching hundreds of kilometres in all directions to join the Greeks to all the other nations of the Mediterranean. Since at least 7000 BCE, geography has forced the people of Greece to become fine sailors. Greek sailors brought home ideas and wealth from abroad and this gave their culture a special advantage in antiquity.

THE ARCHAIC PERIOD

Several significant developments mark the end of the Dark Ages in Greece and point to a great new culture. First was the appearance of a new national literature, epitomized by Homer's work. This not only provided Greeks with a glorious past, whether real or imagined, but also gave them a common view of their gods, almost like a national religion. Second was the resurgence of trade as the Greeks again regularly plied the waters beyond the Aegean Sea. Their first destinations were in the eastern Mediterranean, probably to exchange food or metal for manufactured goods. But more important than the objects they bought were the skills and ideas they soon acquired: shipbuilding and metal-working techniques, better knowledge of geography and navigation, artistic and religious ideas, and not least,

night, a meal, and a small gift. By the second half of the eighth century, the handing down and constant enhancing of these tales provided Homer with the details he used to compose the *Iliad* and the *Odyssey*.

Geography and the Greek City-State

In what kind of land did the Greeks make their home? Flying into Athens today, a visitor is struck by three things: the tall grey mountains, the clear blue sky, and the deep blue sea. The mountains are everywhere, isolating one valley from another, one small cultivable area from its neighbour, and reducing the habitable land by well over half. But an alphabet. The alphabet we use today for English and many other languages came from the Greeks by way of the Romans. The Greeks themselves learned it from the Phoenicians, a seafaring people who lived in the region of present-day Lebanon. The new script had only 27 letters, and was easy enough for almost anyone to learn.

Soon after their voyages to the east began, the Greeks also began sailing westward, establishing contacts and settlements in Italy. They now had access to the iron and other metals found to the north of Rome, where a people known as the Etruscans were beginning to flourish. This led to the third development, colonization. Trading expeditions soon brought news to Greeks at home about the rich agricultural lands in Italy, Sicily, and other locations on the coasts of the Mediterranean. Since pressures to find better land were building in Greece, the trickle of groups emigrating from the Aegean soon became a flood. Hundreds of new Greek settlements were established abroad over a 200-year period, making much of the Mediterranean and Black Sea coasts an extension of the Greek homeland. While these settlements are often called colonies, for the most part, they were new, independent Greek city-states.

A fourth development, though minor at first, later became more important. The first Olympic Games in honour of the god Zeus were held in 776 BCE. This is the first firm date we have in Greek history, the starting point from which later Greeks marked their own past. The Olympic festival was one of four Panhellenic ("all Greece") games that drew competitors and spectators from every corner of the Greek world. Since the prizes at these prestigious festivals were treasured crowns of sacred tree branches, they were called Crown Games. There were some 300 other local athletic games around Greece where winners received very valuable rewards. These were called Prize Games. The Olympic Games continued until 393 CE when the Roman emperor Theodosius I, a Christian, ordered all pagan sanctuaries closed.

Colonization

Towns in Greece wanting to establish new settlements abroad often consulted the oracle of Apollo at Delphi, a sacred place where priestesses or priests could answer questions put to the god about the new territory (or anything else). Then with the oracle's blessing, a group of several hundred men equipped with ships and all the tools and equipment they would need (at great expense) and promises of further help, would sail away in excitement and anticipation. Whether women and children went on these expeditions or came later, we do not know. We do know that many Greek men took native wives in their new homes, but many more probably brought their Greek wives with them.

The Panhellenic Games

Games	Site	Frequency	God	Crown
Olympic	Olympia	every 4 years	Zeus	olive wreath
Pythia	Delphi	every 4 years	Apollo	laurel wreath
Isthmian	Isthmia	every 2 years	Poseidon	pine wreath
Nemean	Nemea	every 2 years	Zeus	wild celery wreath

The sanctuary of Apollo at Delphi, where people came to consult the greatest of the Greek oracles.

Below is an inscription discovered in Cyrene, Libya, that preserves the original foundation agreement between the colonists of Cyrene and their mother city, Thera. In this case, famine was forcing the mother city to send some of its hungry citizens away. Part of the agreement reads:

Agreement of the Founders
Decided by the assembly. Since Apollo has given a
spontaneous prophesy to Battus and the Theraeans
ordering them to colonize Cyrene, the Theraeans
resolve that Battus be sent to Libya as leader and
king: that the Theraeans sail as his companions:
that they sail on fair and equal terms, according to
family; that one son be conscripted from each
family; that those who sail be in the prime of life;

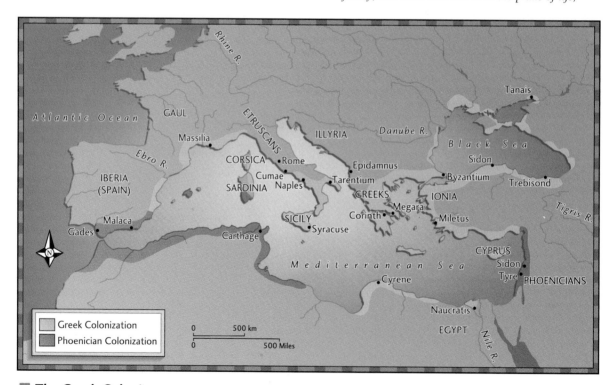

◼ The Greek Colonies

Greek city-states were established far away from the homeland. Why were so many Greeks willing to take their chances in new territories?

and that, of the rest of the Theraeans, any free man who wishes may sail. ... But he who is unwilling to sail when the city sends him shall be liable to punishment by death and his goods shall be confiscated. And he who receives or protects another, even if it be a father his son or brother, shall suffer the same penalty as the man unwilling to sail ...

Once colonists had arrived at their destination, they had to choose the best location for their new home, usually a harbour site. Besides the endless work of dividing the land, planting the first crops, and building their homes, settlers also had to contend with the native peoples whose land they were taking. The colonists of Cyrene, for example, were often helped by the native Libyans, but there were also bitter wars. In one battle, says Herodotus, the Libyans killed 7000 Greeks. The number of dead sounds unbelievably high but it points out the seriousness of the problem of conflict between Greek colonists and the natives of the lands they colonized.

Review...Recall...Reflect

1. Describe the political organization of Mycenaean society.

2. How did the Minoans influence Mycenaean culture and society?

3. List the four developments that marked Greece's emergence from the Dark Ages.

GOVERNMENT IN GREECE
The Age of Tyrants

Democracy is just one of many political systems developed by humankind to govern its communities. The Greeks were the first people to invent a formal democratic system in which citizens governed *themselves* through voting. The word democracy comes from two Greek words, *demos* meaning "the people" and *kratos* meaning "the rule" or "power." But democracy was not invented easily — it was arrived at after a long, painful process. Other systems of government had been tried and failed.

The early Greek states were usually focused around the main town in a valley area. The normal system of rule was government by a king, and each king acted as the chief judge, leading administrator, military leader, and at times, priest of the state cult (religion). These kings, however, did not have absolute power, nor was their power automatically passed on to their heirs. A king's authority was limited by the rights and powers of a small, close-knit group of aristocrats who acted as his counsellors.

During the Dark Ages, many of the kings lost some or all of their powers to other members of the local aristocracy. Arbitrary rule by aristocratic families replaced the monarchy in some Greek states. But arbitrary administration of unwritten laws was just one concern. The power held by some aristocrats and not by others provoked dissent, as did the lack of a voice in government for wealthy men of non-aristocratic background. Poorer Greeks suffered loss of land, debts, and even enslavement for debt at the hands of wealthy nobles. However, the aristocrats could keep their power as long as they continued to be the military backbone of the state. Down to the early seventh century BCE, fighting depended on

Heavily armed hoplites and their flute-boy going into battle. The detailed figures on this vase made in Corinth ca. 650 BCE are only 0.05 m high.

heavily armed individual warriors backed up by their lightly armed supporters. Only wealthy aristocrats could afford the arms and armour needed for this style of warfare.

This all changed in the period ca. 675–650 BCE, as a new style of warfare was introduced, one that depended on the unified movement of larger numbers of warriors, called *hoplites*. These were heavily armed men with large round shields, shin protectors (greaves), helmets, body armour, and spears, which they thrust rather than threw. By standing side by side, six to ten lines deep, and maintaining their places in the lines, these warriors could easily defeat the old style of fighting. Large numbers of warriors were crucial to preventing the hoplite lines from being surrounded and attacked from behind. But there simply were not enough aristocrats to fill the new battle lines. Consequently, any citizen who could afford the armour eventually came to stand shoulder to shoulder with the aristocrats. The strategic importance of these new soldiers was probably one factor that led to their demand for more political power.

People in control of a government usually do not surrender their power willingly. In the richer Greek states near the Isthmus of Corinth, a man of noble blood named Cypselus was excluded from the ruling circle of nobles at Corinth, despite his ability and great ambition. He gathered a military force composed of other discontented citizens and in 657 BCE defeated and forced the ruling clan of nobles into exile. Cypselus took control of the government and began to rule for the benefit of the middle class people who had supported him. The Greeks called such a person, one who had seized power unconstitutionally (for good or bad), a *tyrannos* or **tyrant**.

FOUNDATIONS OF DEMOCRATIC RULE
Solon and Peisistratus

Athens avoided tyranny for many years, first, by giving in to demands for a written code of law, and second, by appointing a special magistrate called an *archon* to try to solve the continuing problems between aristocrats and common citizens. The law code, written by Draco in 620 BCE was significant because it recognized that once laws were written down, they could be criticized and changed. The archon appointed in 594 BCE was **Solon**, who brought in a number of economic and social reforms. These included changes in the law code that helped relieve the debt and land problems of the poor. Solon also abolished the practice of selling debtors into slavery.

Solon's political reforms were an important step on the road to democracy. The most significant reform allowed all wealthy men, aristocrat or not, to run for the highest government offices. Solon also created a new institution called the Council of 400. One hundred citizens from each of the four traditional tribes of Athens were elected annually and met regularly to prepare legislation to be voted on by the entire Citizen Assembly. The Council probably also acted as a court of appeal for judgments of the archons.

Many adults living in Athens, or in any Greek *polis* for that matter, still had no political power at all. This included women, since citizenship ultimately derived from the ability to fight in the army; the large slave population, which had no personal rights whatsoever; and foreigners, who rarely acquired citizenship because normally it was only bestowed by birth.

One man who eventually did become tyrant of Athens was **Peisistratus**, a noble famous for his generalship, and very ambitious. He actually made three tries for tyrant's rule, interspersed with periods of exile. On the second try (ca. 555 BCE), he boldly decided to have a handsome woman named Phye dress up like the goddess Athena, with armour and spear, and ride through the streets of Athens in a chariot proclaiming that she, the goddess herself, had come to restore Peisistratus to power! On his third attempt (ca. 546 BCE), Peisistratus defeated his opponents in battle and took the city. He ruled until his death in 527 BCE, when power was handed over to his son, Hippias.

Cleisthenes Establishes Democracy

Hippias continued the tyranny in Athens after his father's death, but eventually lost support. In 510 BCE, the army of Sparta, Athens's most powerful adversary, besieged Athens and forced an end to the tyranny of Hippias. He and his family surrendered and were forced into exile and the tyranny ended. Athens again had to find new political solutions to her problems of government.

The solution this time was proposed by **Cleisthenes**, a member of another noble family, in 508–507 BCE. Cleisthenes's novel approach set aside the ancient division of Athenian citizens into four tribes based on clan relationships and created an equitable division of citizens into ten new tribes, each with members from all parts of the city-state. Cleisthenes also replaced the old Council of 400 with a new Council of 500, with 50 members elected from each tribe. Not only did these 50 members take part in meetings of the full Council, for one tenth of the year, they also acted as the executive committee of the Council. Each tribe also elected a general (*strategos*) who would lead the city in all its military affairs. By 487 BCE, it was recognized that only the generals had to be highly qualified elected officials. In truly democratic fashion, the other offices came to be filled by drawing lots every year. Any fit citizen could now hold these high offices.

Another novel measure was introduced in these democratic reforms — the practice called **ostracism**. This measure was meant to rid Athens of any citizen who might want to become a tyrant. Ostracism allowed the city to send any citizen and his family into exile for a period of ten years. Every year around

These pieces of pottery are ostraka. They were used to decide whether a person should be banished from Athens. Can you read any of the names of the people being judged?

Athenian Democracy

Before Solon

Government Institution	Eligibility	Duties
Magistrates (elected annually):		
basileus	aristocrats	chief religious officer
polemarch	aristocrats	chief army officer
archon	aristocrats	chief civil administrator and judge
six *thesmothetai*	aristocrats	lesser judges
Council (*Areopagus*)	ex-magistrates	advised *archons*, acted as "guardians of the law," passed legislation, served as criminal court
Assembly	all male citizens	approved motions of war

Solon's Reforms

Government Institution	Eligibility	Duties
Magistrates (elected annually):	based on wealth, not birth	
basileus		chief religious officer
polemarch		chief army officer
archon		chief civil administrator and judge
six *thesmothetai*		lesser judges
Council (*Areopagus*)	ex-magistrates	advised *archons*, acted as "guardians of the law," passed legislation, served as criminal court
Council of 400 (elected annually)	members of top three classes based on wealth	deliberated and proposed legislation, acted as court of appeal
Assembly	all male citizens	approved motions of war, approved legislation

Cleisthenes's Reforms and Later

Government Institution	Eligibility	Duties
Magistrates (chosen annually by lots)	all male citizens over 30 years of age	
basileus		chief religious officer
polemarch		chief army officer
archon		chief civil administrator and judge
six *thesmothetai*		lesser judges
Council (*Areopagus*)	ex-magistrates	acted as criminal court
Council of 500 (elected annually)	all male citizens over 30 years of age	administered government boards, proposed legislation, oversaw finances, acted as law court
Assembly	all male citizens over 18 years of age	elected generals (*strategoi*), debated and passed legislation, acted as treason court, approved ostracism votes

January (the middle of the Athenian calendar year), the Assembly voted on whether an ostracism was needed that year. For the ostracism procedure, a minimum of 6000 votes needed to be cast, and the person whose name appeared most often on the *ostraka* (pieces of broken pottery used as ballots) was sent into exile. The first ostracism occurred in 487 BCE and the last was held 70 years later.

Slaves in Greek Society

For those who had once been free, slavery was generally regarded as a wretched, degrading state. Conditions varied greatly — household slaves of the wealthy were the best off, while leased slaves working in state mines were probably the worst. In any case, slavery was common and totally accepted throughout the Greek world. Legally, slaves were simply property; they might be treated humanely or cruelly, depending on their owners. At the master's discretion, they were allowed to marry, have a home, and keep their children. Slaves were certainly an important part of the economy, filling virtually every occupation except government and military positions.

Athens was a major slave-owning state, obtaining new slaves in markets where foreign war captives or Greeks captured by pirates were for sale. Educated guesses suggest no more than one third (60 000 to 80 000) of the total population of Attica (greater Athens) in the fifth century BCE were slaves, of which the majority worked in manufacturing. For example, we learn from the fourth-century BCE orator Demosthenes that his father left him an estate that included a knife- and sword-making workshop with 32 skilled slaves, and a couch-frame-making workshop with 20 slaves. According to Thucydides, more than 20 000 slaves, of whom the majority were crafts workers, deserted Athens during the darkest part of the Peloponnesian War (412–404 BCE).

In 414 BCE, Cephisodorus, a *metic* (foreign resident) from Piraeus, had his 16 confiscated slaves sold for prices ranging from 72 drachmas for a boy, to 301 drachmas for a skilled man (1 drachma was a day's wage for a skilled worker at this time). These slaves included five Thracians, three Carians, two Syrians, two Illyrians, and one each from Colchis, Scythia, Lydia, and Malta.

Inscriptions in Athens dating between 349 and 320 BCE list 135 slaves (79 males, 56 females) who received their freedom (manumission). The men, where known, paid an average of 178 drachmas to be freed, while the women paid 180 drachmas on average. The occupations of these slaves were also given:

	Men	Women
Farmworkers	12	0
Crafts	26	48
Transport	10	0
Retail	21	7
Miscellaneous	10	1

Among the men in crafts, there was a bronze-smith, an ironworker, three goldsmiths, nine leather cutters, a pail maker, a glue boiler, and a sofa maker. Of the 48 women in crafts, 40 were wool workers. Retail workers included sellers of bread, pickled meats, incense, sesame seeds, fish, wool, rope, and cooked foods. Slaves did virtually every form of work needed for life to go on normally in Athens.

Lycurgus and Spartan Society

Of the more than 300 Greek city-states, Athens and Sparta were the most powerful. However, that is where any similarity between these two rivals ends. Spartans were foremost known as warriors, and despite their relatively small numbers, perhaps

5000 full Spartan warriors in good times, they enjoyed a position of leadership in Greece for some three centuries.

When other city-states were suffering from lack of land in the eighth century BCE and sending excess population overseas to settle, the Spartans took a different course. In a long war, Sparta defeated its neighbours to the west and thereby captured more needed territory. The conquered people joined the large and sometimes rebellious population of Spartan *helots*, the state slaves who worked the land.

The political, social, and military systems of Sparta were attributed in antiquity to one great legislator named **Lycurgus**. So much is credited to Lycurgus, but so little is known, that he has become an almost mythic figure. He may have lived in the early seventh century BCE and is supposed to have laid down the tough military training program that allowed Sparta to produce the best soldiers in the Greek world. At the same time, he proposed a constitution that guaranteed all Spartan citizens — meaning only adult males born to citizen parents — a minimum level of political equality. There were still rich and poor Spartans, aristocrats and ordinary people, but all who were "equals" (*homoioi*) could vote in the Assembly, have a share of Spartan land, and benefit from the work of the enslaved helots.

THE Past AT PLAY

A woman of royal blood from Sparta (Athens's chief rival city-state), named Kyniska, was the first woman to win a prize at the ancient Olympic Games. Married women could be neither competitors nor spectators at the Olympics: they were banned from Olympia during the games on pain of death. But Kyniska, who owned a four-horse chariot team, entered it and won twice (ca. 396 and 392 BCE). Though she was never able to see her team win, nor to accept the wreath in person, she saw to it that a statue of herself was erected at Olympia, like a true winner.

Sheltered family life for Spartan citizen boys ended at the age of seven when military training and rugged barracks life began. Spartiate boys learned to

Spartan Government

Government institution	Eligibility	Duties
kings (two, for life)	the two royal families	chief magistrates, army leaders
Assembly (no limit to numbers)	all Spartiate citizens over 30 years of age	approved legislation, elected Ephors and Elders
Ephorate (five Ephors elected annually)	Elders elected by the Assembly	acted as magistrates and judges, presided over Council and Assembly, supervised the state education system
Council of Elders (28 male citizens, elected for life)	aristocrats over 60 years of age, elected by the Assembly	advised kings, proposed legislation, acted as judges

withstand pain without complaint, be unquestioningly obedient to leaders, cunning when necessary, and above all, never to admit defeat. Though military service continued, only at age 30 did Spartan men become full citizens, able to vote in the Assembly, hold political office, marry, have a house, and receive an estate worked by helots.

The Spartan government was unusual in that it had two kings who ruled equally. This system provided a strong check on the powers of the monarchy since one king could oppose the other. Advising the kings was a Council of Elders, 28 men over the age of 60 who belonged to the Spartan aristocracy. Only this body could present legislation to the Assembly for approval. The Assembly could not initiate legislation, nor could it even discuss the legislation. The Council of Elders would explain the legislation to the Assembly and even give opposing views, but then the Assembly had to vote in favour or against it. Its decision was final. As a kind of advocate for the common citizens, a new institution, the *Ephorate*, was created; it soon took a leading role in running Spartan affairs. The Ephorate consisted of five men called *Ephors* who were elected by the Assembly to hold office for one year. The Ephors presided over the Council and Assembly, but were not part of either of those bodies.

The Spartan system of government was conservative in order to prevent revolt by the helots. Babies who were not healthy were abandoned at birth. Boys were sometimes brutally beaten and whipped. Interestingly though, Spartan women enjoyed more freedom and privileges than women anywhere else in Greece. As girls, they were encouraged to take part in sports to develop healthy bodies so they could have healthy children. They were given training in music and dance, like the boys, and when they reached adulthood, had both property and marriage rights. Other Greeks admired Spartan women, both for their independence and because they were said to be the most beautiful in all Greece.

THE PERSIAN WARS: GREECE UNITES IN CONFLICT

The Greeks took longer to recover from the serious political and economic turmoil at the end of the second millennium than their Near Eastern neighbours the Assyrians, Phoenicians, Babylonians, and Egyptians, all of whom quickly began accumulating wealth and territory. After centuries of great wars, it was the Persians, along with their close neighbours, the Medes, who emerged as the most powerful empire. By the sixth century BCE, the Persians threatened the Greek homeland itself. Somehow, the fiercely independent Greek city-states needed to find a way to cooperate to beat back the menace from the east.

Compared with the huge empires of the Near East, particularly Persia, Greek city-states were tiny. Even a coalition that included every Greek town would only equal a fraction of this eastern power. The fact that the Greek states were weakened by fighting amongst themselves and rarely agreed on anything long enough to act together, made defense against a mighty empire appear impossible. On the positive side, Greek soldiers were tough, their battle tactics and weapons inferior to none, and when they were finally ready to cooperate, they found good leaders.

The empire of the Persians and Medes had expanded northward toward the eastern Greek (or Ionian) cities in the early sixth century BCE, but was stopped by the wealthy power of the Lydians in west-central Asia Minor. While the Lydians acted as a buffer, keeping the Medes and Persians away from the Aegean for another 40 years, eventually the

Lydians themselves took over the eastern Greek cities, which were unable to unite even to resist a foreign invader. King Croesus of Lydia, for example, was famed for his generosity to Greek sanctuaries:

> Croesus now attempted to win the favour of the Delphian Apollo by a magnificent sacrifice. ... he melted down an enormous quantity of gold into one hundred and seventeen ingots about eighteen inches long, nine inches wide, and three inches thick; four of the ingots were of refined gold weighing approximately a hundred and forty-two pounds each: the rest were alloyed and weighed about a hundred and fourteen pounds. He also caused the image of a lion to be made of refined gold, in weight some five hundred and seventy pounds.

Herodotus *Histories* I.50–51

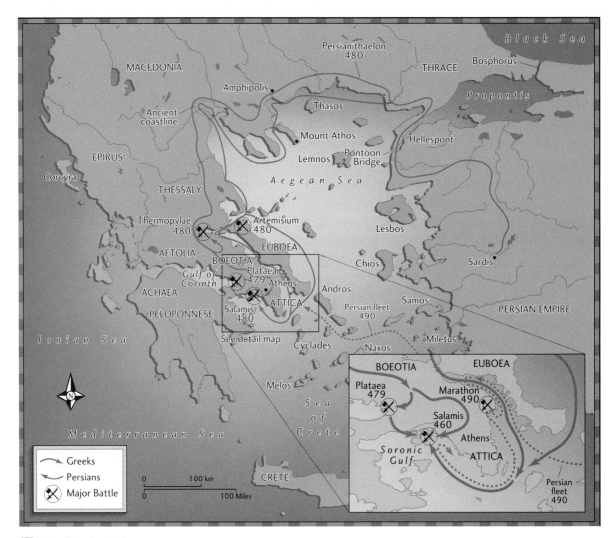

■ The Persian Wars

The Persian Wars were perhaps the only cause that forced the Greek city-states to unite and fight a common enemy. What factors made it so difficult for the Greek city-states to work together?

In 559 BCE, a great king and general rose to the throne of Persia — Cyrus the Great. Cyrus gained power over the Medes as well, and continued to expand the Persian Empire, which already stretched across Asia in the east to the shores of the Mediterranean in the west. A chance to expand further occurred when Croesus of Lydia decided to attack Cyrus across the old boundary between their empires about 546 BCE. We are told that the oracle at Delphi proclaimed that if Croesus crossed the Halys River, he would destroy a mighty empire. Little did Croesus know that it would be his own!

The fall of Sardis, capital of Lydia, brought the Ionian Greek states face to face with the "barbarian" Persians. Unable to secure favourable peace terms, the Greeks tried to fight, but again were unable to cooperate among themselves long enough to achieve any success. The Ionian states then surrendered to the Persians and accepted a fate that meant a greater loss of freedom and forced service in the Persian army. When the Greek governor of Miletus, Aristagoras, finally stirred up a revolt among the Ionians in 499 BCE, a call for help from the Greeks across the Aegean brought only 20 warships from Athens and five from Eretria (a city to the north-east). A naval battle off Miletus in 494 BCE ended the revolt. The Persians destroyed the city, killed many of the men, and sent the rest of the population into exile.

The Battle of Marathon

In 490 BCE, Darius, now King of Persia, sent a fleet with about 20 000 soldiers to punish Athens and Eretria for helping in the Ionian Revolt. After first burning and plundering Eretria, the Persian fleet sailed south to the eastern coast of Attica where a sheltered beach and small plain provided a perfect base for the Persian army. The plain was called Marathon.

The Athenians sent a professional messenger ("all-day runner") to Sparta, 250 km away, pleading for help. He returned about four days later saying that the Spartans would only come after the full moon, still a week or more away. So the Athenian citizen army of 9000 warriors went alone to Marathon to meet the Persians. Eventually, the only help to arrive was less than a thousand soldiers from Plataea, a close neighbour to the north.

After much debate, Miltiades, one of the Athenian generals, convinced his fellow commanders to attack, and thus won the Athenians everlasting glory. The Greeks in their heavy armour charged the Persians on the run and cut them down as they fled to their ships. Herodotus says 6400 Persians were killed but only 192 Athenians. Archaeological excavation of the burial mound of the Plataean dead has yielded less than a dozen bodies, including a young boy, perhaps their piper. The Persian threat had been beaten back, but its empire was far from destroyed.

Ancient ODDITIES

Writers after Herodotus maintained that the messenger who ran to Sparta and back before the battle of Marathon was the same runner who brought the news of victory from Marathon to Athens. He is supposed to have arrived at the Council House, spoken the words, "We have won! Rejoice!" and then dropped dead. This was the inspiration for the modern marathon race created by Pierre de Coubertin for the first modern Olympic Games in 1896. Herodotus, who could never resist a good story, never mentioned any of these events. So the truth is, there probably never really was an ancient Marathon run.

Thermopylae: Greek Cooperation Defeats Persia

The victory at Marathon provided the mainland Greeks with a ten-year break from further Persian attacks. Then in 480 BCE, Xerxes, the Persian king who succeeded Darius, crossed the Hellespont (the narrow strait between the Greek mainland and Asia Minor). Xerxes did this by having twin bridges constructed of boats held together by cables made of linen and papyrus as thick as a human torso! Herodotus says that the Persian infantry alone numbered 1.7 million soldiers, and that with the fleet, cavalry, and other contingents and attendants, over five million people were in the expedition. As is common with ancient writers, these figures are no doubt vastly exaggerated — Xerxes's army probably consisted of about 200 000 soldiers, still an immense force for the time.

The Greeks had done little to prepare themselves for this latest Persian attack, and many of them intended simply to accept Persian domination without resistance. Athens, at least, had used the money from a rich new strike of silver at its mines near Laurion to build a strong fleet of 200 ships, and gathered with Sparta for a congress at Corinth to plan their defence against the Persian invaders. In the end, the strategic decision was made to defend a narrow pass in central Greece called Thermopylae (the Hot Gates) through which the Persians had to pass.

A small force of 4000 soldiers led by King Leonidas of Sparta and his bodyguard of 300 was sent to hold the pass until the full Greek army arrived. This small force was backed by the Greek fleet waiting just offshore. The Spartan stand was heroic but a local Greek shepherd betrayed them by showing Xerxes a mountain path around Thermopylae. Leonidas and about a thousand soldiers who refused to escape the Persian trap died fighting bravely. The epitaph at the site where the Spartans died read, "Go tell at Sparta, thou that passest by, that here obedient to her word, we lie." The Persian army poured southward through Boeotia to Athens and took revenge on the city for its defeat at Marathon.

This relief sculpture shows Greeks battling Persians. The Persians are the ones wearing the baggy pants, which the Greeks thought were "womanish".

Salamis and Plataea

The combined Greek fleet of over 300 **triremes** (fast Greek ships with three levels of rowers) remained at Salamis, a large island just off the coast of Attica to the west of Athens. After much delay, about 600 Persian ships were enticed into the straits where they were attacked by the swift, well-crewed Greek ships. Xerxes could only watch in despair from his throne set high on a hill above the action. Aeschylus, a Greek playwright who probably fought at Salamis, puts these words into the mouth of a Persian messenger in one of his plays:

> First, then, the torrent of our Persian fleet bore up; but when the press of shipping jammed there in the strait, then none could help another, but our ships fouled each other with their rams, and sheared away each other's banks of oars. But the Greek ships, skillfully handled, kept the outer station, and struck in; till hulls rolled over, and the sea itself was hidden, strewn with their wreckage, dyed with blood of men. The dead lay thick on all the reefs and beaches, and flight broke out, all order lost; and all our eastern ships rowed hard to get away.

Aeschylus The Persians 412–423

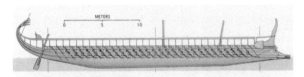

Swift Greek triremes like this won the battle at Salamis in 480 BCE.

The battle was a severe loss for the Persians. Xerxes himself escaped from Greece but he left behind his army under the general Mardonius.

In the new year (479 BCE), Mardonius took up a position on the southern edge of the Boeotian plain near the town of Plataea. Here, the united army of the Greek city-states, led by the Spartans, met the barbarians in all-out battle. The Greeks were victorious. Mardonius was killed, a vast amount of Persian wealth and luxury goods was captured, and the remnants of the great invasion force hastily retreated from Greece. After Plataea, the Greek navy attacked the Persians again in Asia Minor and freed the Ionian Greeks.

Review…Recall…Reflect

1. Explain the relationship between warfare and the development of democracy in Greece.

2. Describe the political reforms introduced by Solon and Cleisthenes.

3. What was the greatest challenge faced by the Greeks in preparing for the Persian invasion? What were the keys to their successful defence?

EARLY GREEK ART: CROSS-CULTURAL INFLUENCES

The great wars against Persia highlight the differences between the civilization developing in Greece and the older civilizations of the East. The Greeks beat back the Eastern threat to their freedom and won the opportunity to develop their own culture, accepting outside influences only if they appealed to Greek taste. This paid great dividends in the coming centuries, as the greatest Greek artists, writers, philosophers, and scientists began to explore their world in new ways and to new heights. But the Greeks were not ready to move forward until after they had absorbed many important ideas and influences from the East, Egypt, and other regions during the eighth and seventh centuries BCE. At this earlier time, Greek representational art (art that attempts to depict the world as it appears), for example, was so far behind that of the East that it was easily influenced by forms of Eastern art — scenes of people, animals, and mythical creatures like griffins and sphinxes. This period in Greek art is actually called Orientalizing because of the strong Eastern influence.

For Greek art, the opening up of Egypt to Greek merchants and travellers was very important. In Egypt, the Greeks observed monumental statues carved in

The enormous temple of Artemis at Ephesus was built and rebuilt from the 6th to the 4th centuries BCE. At least twice the size of the Parthenon, Ephesus had some 110 columns.

A life-size Greek kouros sculpture, ca. 540 BCE. The word "kouros" means male youth. Does this remind you of any sculpture you have seen earlier?

fine, hard stone and soon imitated these in the finest white marble of their homeland. Greek architects learned how to build great temples in stone after viewing the marvels of Karnak, Luxor, and Memphis. Greek artists began to appreciate the fine skills of drawing and the use of colour after seeing wall paintings adorning buildings and tombs all along the Nile. Likewise, metal-working skills, glass making, and other important crafts were picked up very quickly and brought back to Greece. In every case, the Greeks were not simply imitators. They did not merely

Current Research and Interpretations

Scholars today are still addressing important gaps in our understanding of the 2000 years of Bronze Age history. We still do not know how the Minoans ruled themselves or what bull-leaping really meant to them. As Greeks emerged from the Dark Ages, was it Phoenician trading in Greece or Greeks visiting Phoenicia that first opened doors to the East? Scholars still know very little about Homer, the Spartan Lycurgus, the poetess Sappho, or Thales of Miletus.

acquire skills, they also adapted them and applied them to their own needs and tastes. This is one of the keys to the greatness of Greek art and civilization.

We can see some of the great strides made in Greek art from the Dark Ages to the Persian Wars by looking at temple architecture. Temples changed from modest wood and clay "houses" for cult statues to grand marble showcases for Greek treasures, such as the temple of Artemis at Ephesus. This **sanctuary** was one of the largest in all the Greek world — the temple alone occupied an area almost the size of a football field — and was home to hundreds of marble sculptures of people, gods, and animals.

Sculpture was transformed from rather abstract figurines in bronze or clay to natural-looking, life-size statues in marble, bronze, or even a combination of gold and ivory. Vase painting also shows a similar transformation, changing from little black stickfigures to wonderfully fluid, idealized characters against a black, red, or white background.

Greek philosophy and science also took their first tentative steps during the Archaic Period. Thinkers from Miletus, like the astronomer Thales, were the first to ask, "How did the world originate?" and not be satisfied with the answer, "The gods created it." They wanted to know exactly how the Earth was formed and from what. They proposed theories about the world's origin, suggesting that all things had been formed from basic elements such as moisture or air or fire, through various fundamental processes, like condensation and vaporization. These ideas are no longer accepted, but it is significant that the development of philosophy (from the Greek *phileo*, "to love," and *sophia*, "wisdom") and a type of systematic science began in Greece.

Greek literature passed from the age of epic poems like the *Iliad* and *Odyssey* of Homer to an age of lyric poetry in dozens of forms. Drinking songs, war songs, poems sung by choruses or by a single person, love poems, and poems in praise of athletic victories are just a few of the new themes that appeared.

One of the lyric poets was a woman named **Sappho** of Lesbos, who was admired by some Greeks as much as Homer. This is remarkable, given women's generally lowly status in Greek society. Even those belonging to wealthier citizen families enjoyed few freedoms; they were married to men chosen for them, had no right to vote or possess property, and could not go to public places unaccompanied.

Besides lyric poetry, the very first dramatic plays were written in Athens just before the Persian Wars. They were performed in honour of the god Dionysos, god of wine and fertility.

History Continues to Unfold

By the end of the fifth century BCE, the Greeks were poised to enter their greatest adventure yet. The Persian threat had been beaten back and the way was clear for the Athenians to build their empire and create unprecedented heights of cultural and political achievement. The level of civilization to come in the Classical Period of Greek history would be looked back on by people and empires to come as a golden age.

Chapter Review

Chapter Summary

In this chapter, we have seen:

- how interaction between Greece and other societies sometimes led to conflict and other times led to cultural change
- that several factors including the introduction of bronze, development of writing, and the evolution of democratic government contributed to change in ancient Greece
- the critical role played by individuals such as Solon, Cleisthenes, and Herodotus in Greek history
- that over time the ancient Greeks adopted several different forms of leadership

Reviewing the Significance of Key People, Concepts, and Events (Knowledge/Understanding)

1. Understanding the early history of ancient Greece requires a knowledge of the following people, concepts, and events, and an awareness of their significance in the development of the Greek city-states. In your notes, identify and explain the historical significance of three from each column.

People	Concepts/Places	Events
Minoans	Crete	Olympic Games
Herodotus	Knossos	Battle of Marathon
Homer	*Iliad* and *Odyssey*	Battle of Salamis
Solon	Linear A script	Battle of Thermopylae
Sappho	Mycenae	

2. List the four developments in Greek society and culture between 2100 BCE and 500 BCE that you believe were the most significant in leading to a complex, advanced civilization.

3. How did the Persian invasions contribute to advances in Greek art, architecture, literature, and philosophy?

Doing History: Thinking About the Past (Thinking/Inquiry)

1. Throughout history there have been several key developments in technology that have led to profound changes in a society. Explain why the introduction of bronze to Crete should be considered one of these major changes in Greek history.

Connecting to the *World History Handbook*: Once you have completed your answer, transfer the main ideas to the graphic organizer "Change in History: Technological Developments" in your *World History Handbook*.

2. Was the development of Athenian democracy the product of historical trends and events or the result of the work of a few brilliant individuals? Explain your answer in a clearly argued and well-supported paragraph.

Applying Your Learning (Application)

1. Using a Venn diagram, compare the similarities and differences between Athenian democracy and Canada's current political system. Based on your comparison, do you feel the Athenian system of democracy could work for a country like Canada or is it limited to use in city-states? Explain your answer.

   Connecting to the *World History Handbook*: Once you have completed your Venn diagram, transfer some of the most important aspects of Athenian democracy to the graphic organizer "Political Organization" in your *World History Handbook*.

2. Create a diorama that demonstrates the reaction of Greek artists to their exposure to external influences. Through research, locate examples of Egyptian sculpture and Greek sculpture from the Archaic Period to about 500 BCE. Arrange the pictures of Egyptian and Greek sculpture in such a way as to show a progression in Greek art.

Communicating Your Learning (Communication)

1. Select either Athens or Sparta to defend in a debate over which had the superior political and social organization. Prepare three arguments you can use in the debate.

2. Write a front-page news article reporting on the second Persian invasion of Greece under Xerxes in 480 BCE. Your news article should have a headline, a concise report on the events unfolding at the time, and some background information to explain the factors that influenced the relationship between the Greeks and the Persians, dating back to 499 BCE.

Classical Greece

By the end of this chapter, you will be able to:

- explain how Greek culture and the political empire of Philip and Alexander came to dominate much of the ancient world

- identify the major changes in history defined by the Classical Moment and the Hellenistic Age

- demonstrate an understanding of how Alexander's military genius and political leadership formed the basis of his authority

- describe the role of women in ancient Greek society

In Greek, this figure is called Nike, victory. She was very popular in both Greek and Roman art, where she was Victoria. This version (ca. 150 BCE) was originally on a huge sculpture of the prow of a ship, as a naval victory monument.

Change in a society occurs at different rates. Sometimes it is so rapid and total that we call it revolutionary; other times it is so slow, extending over decades or even centuries, that it is hardly noticeable. From time to time, change occurs quickly in one or two aspects of life but not in others. If this change happens in the intellectual life of a society, it can appear to later times as a flash of brilliance. Classical Greece of the fifth and fourth centuries BCE was just such a revolution in intellectual life. The period that followed the Classical Age, from the death of **Alexander the Great** to the rise of Augustus in Rome, we call Hellenistic. This period rivalled the Classical Age, and the Romans were captivated by the wonders of Greek culture wherever they encountered them. Classical Greece was where the foundations of Western civilization were built.

This chapter will look at some of the great accomplishments of the Greeks, of people like Socrates, Pheidias, Sophocles, Plato, Aristotle, and Archimedes. It will also trace the troubled political events of the age that led to a weakening of the Greek states and eventually to their defeat by Rome. Alexander had quickly conquered the vast regions of the Near East held by Persia, and Greek culture spread throughout his newly acquired territories. Certainly, there were people whose lives were hardly affected by developments around them — shepherds, farmers, merchants, and dutiful mothers and fathers caring for their families. But eventually, even these ordinary people would have been touched by the rapid change.

KEY WORDS

Doric
Ionic
oligarchy
rhetoric
plague
sophist
gymnasium
dendrochronology

KEY PEOPLE

Pericles
Alcibiades
Socrates
Pheidias
Plato
Philip the Great
Alexander the Great
Aristotle
Archimedes
Hippocrates

VOICES FROM THE PAST

Nothing can be more absurd than the practice that prevails in our country of men and women not following the same pursuits with all their strengths and with one mind, for thus, the state instead of being whole is reduced to half.

Plato, *The Laws*

TIME LINE: CLASSICAL GREECE

	467 BCE	The Delian League decisively defeats the Persian fleet
The Treasury of the Delian League is moved to Athens, signalling the beginning of an Athenian empire	454 BCE	
	445 BCE	Athens and Sparta sign a peace treaty
In Athens, the Parthenon is completed	438 BCE	
	431 BCE	The Peloponnesian War begins, and continues for 27 years
Plague strikes Athens killing thousands, including Pericles	430 BCE	
	399 BCE	Socrates is found guilty of corrupting the youth of Athens and ordered to commit suicide
Philip of Macedon completes his conquest of southern Greek city-states. Shortly after, he is assassinated.	338 BCE	
	331 BCE	Carrying on Philip's military conquests, Alexander the Great defeats the Persians
Alexander the Great dies at the young age of 33. His vast empire splinters into three large parts.	323 BCE	
	148 BCE	Macedonia becomes a province of the Roman Republic
Ptolemaic Egypt comes under the control of the Roman Empire	31 BCE	

ATHENS BUILDS AN EMPIRE

The Greeks repulsed the mighty Persian invasion of 480–479 BCE and took a small piece of land along the coast of Asia Minor from Persia's huge empire. As the Persians were expected to attack again, at least to recover their lost territory, the Greeks discussed a permanent alliance to continue fighting them. Sparta refused to participate in affairs outside the Peloponnese, and so Athens needed a strong fleet and leaders with vision. Aristeides, acting for Athens, helped organize the Delian League to defend the Greek states should Persia attack again. Each state signed a defence treaty with Athens and agreed to pay an annual tribute toward maintaining a common fleet. Aristeides was the first to calculate how much tribute each member of the League should pay, and his fairness earned him the name, "Aristeides the Just." Athens provided all the officials and commanders of the League, and swore not to interfere in the internal affairs of its allies. The treasury and meetings were held at the great sanctuary of Apollo on the island of Delos, hence the name Delian League.

This League was originally a voluntary association but soon became a forced union. Some states that did not want to join were compelled to enter the alliance while others that wanted to drop out when the Persian threat receded were forced to remain and pay their share. Kimon, the son of Miltiades, who won the Battle of Marathon, moulded the League into an effective force to fight the Persians. As the fleet's commander, Kimon beat the Persians decisively in 467 BCE to keep them from any further attacks in the Aegean Sea. After this success, the League, led by young **Pericles** of Athens, felt strong enough to try to free the Greeks on the island of Cyprus and help in a new revolt against the Persians

in Egypt. The Egyptian expedition ca. 450 BCE turned into a catastrophe when a Persian force trapped the Greek fleet in one branch of the Nile River and wiped it out. Fearing a Persian reprisal by sea, in 454 BCE, Pericles moved the League's treasury from the island of Delos back to Athens. This was taken as final proof that the League had now become an empire controlled by Athens.

■ **The Athenian Empire**

1. **Find Delos on the map.**

2. **What was the effect of moving the treasury of the Delian League from Delos to Athens?**

Pericles and Democracy

The city of Athens, just one of more than 300 Greek city-states, enjoyed its greatest period of wealth and power — 30 years — under the guidance of Pericles. To us today, the term democracy means an opportunity to elect politicians who share our views and to voice opinions through the media and public meetings. In the Athens of Pericles's day, democracy meant far more. Every citizen could speak and vote on every piece of legislation in the Assembly. Every citizen had an equal chance to hold public office, with the exception of offices such as army general, which were elected positions. All law cases were decided by a majority vote of citizen juries of between 201 and 1501 people. The law and the government were firmly in the hands of the citizens. Pericles proclaimed, "We judge the man who takes no part at all [in public affairs] a useless, not just a quiet person. "

Pericles himself was elected annually to the Board of Generals in Athens and so maintained his leading position in the city. The other civic offices, even the archonships, were only one-year positions and candidates were selected by lottery from a list proposed by the tribes. The introduction of pay for serving on the Council of 500, on juries, and in the various civic offices, allowed even the poorest citizen to take time away from his work. Paid civil service was a radical departure from the earlier system of government.

In his funeral oration for the Athenian dead at the beginning of the Peloponnesian War, Pericles declared:

> Our constitution is called a democracy, because power is in the hands not of a minority but of the whole people. When it is a question of settling private disputes, everyone is equal before the law; when it is a question of putting one person before another in positions of public responsibility, what counts is not membership of a particular class, but the actual ability which a man possesses. No one, so long as he has it in him to be of service to the state, is kept in political obscurity because of poverty.
>
> Thucydides *The Peloponnesian War* II.37

There were far more opportunities for citizens to participate in political affairs in ancient Athens than in our modern democracies. There was no pay for attending the Assembly until the fourth century BCE, so at this time many poor people could not afford to attend. Women, slaves, and foreign residents could still not hold citizenship, and Pericles himself

Pericles of Athens. What might have happened to the Athenian Empire had Pericles not died from the plague of 430 BCE?

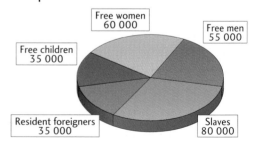

Population of Athens ca. 430 BCE

Free women
60 000

Free men
55 000

Free children
35 000

Resident foreigners
35 000

Slaves
80 000

Total population = approx. 150 000
What if there had been no slaves in Athens?

introduced a law that limited citizenship to only those men whose parents had been born of citizen fathers.

Rivalry between Sparta and Athens

While he held office as general, Kimon had acted to defuse the long-standing rivalry between Sparta and Athens, the two main powers in Greece. Things had changed when Sparta asked Athens for help during a dangerous **Helot** revolt in 462 BCE. Kimon convinced the Athenians to send soldiers to help Sparta, but when they arrived, Sparta refused their help and sent the Athenians home. This insult led to Kimon's ostracism the following year, and the quick rise of Pericles to political prominence.

During the 450s BCE, under the leadership of Pericles, Athens tried to build a land empire in central Greece that truly was a threat to Sparta's traditional power base. Although it did not last long, the attempt by Athens increased tensions between the two states. To try to ease the increasingly bitter rivalry, Athens and Sparta signed a 30-year peace treaty in 445 BCE, agreeing to stay out of each other's internal affairs. Sparta still led the Peloponnesian League, which included some members or allies in central Greece, while Athens held tight rein on the many coastal and island states of her empire in the Aegean. Despite the peace treaty, the rivalry between Athens and Sparta continued, leading them into all-out war.

There were basic differences between Sparta and Athens. Sparta was a land power, with a conservative, oligarchic government, backward in terms of trade, wealth, and recent advances in Greek culture such as **rhetoric**, philosophy, and literature. It sought leadership among Greek states simply in order to protect itself and its narrow interests, rather than out of a desire for wealth, power, or expansion. Athens was the opposite. A sea power governed by a radical democracy, Athens was at the forefront of advances in culture. It was a progressive, wealthy, trading nation. Athens maintained and tried to expand its empire for the sake of the power and income it provided. These differences alone caused suspicion and dislike between the two states, but it was the other states, especially Corinth, that finally pushed the two toward war.

THE PELOPONNESIAN WAR

Corinth was a rich trading city like Athens, but it belonged to Sparta's Peloponnesian League and so remained quite independent. Athens kept Corinth's merchants away from the profitable trade of the Aegean area and provoked Megara, another state, by likewise excluding her from ports of the Athenian Empire. When Athens began to interfere with Corinth's colonies, it was accused of breaking its peace treaty with Sparta and provoked the so-called Peloponnesian War. This was the longest, most bitter and costly war the Greeks ever fought. Almost every city-state aligned itself with one side or the other. At the outset, Athens seemed the strongest of the combatants and the best prepared for war.

Pericles knew that Attica (greater Athens) could be invaded yearly by the more powerful land army of the Spartans. He therefore arranged for food to be imported and for the people to take refuge behind the Long Walls connecting the seaport of Piraeus with Athens whenever Attica was attacked. The Athenian fleet was strong and could raid the coast of the Peloponnese at will, and there was a big surplus in Athen's treasury. Prospects for victory looked good.

What Pericles could not have foreseen was the **plague** that struck Athens in 430 BCE, the second year of the Peloponnesian War. Athenians had

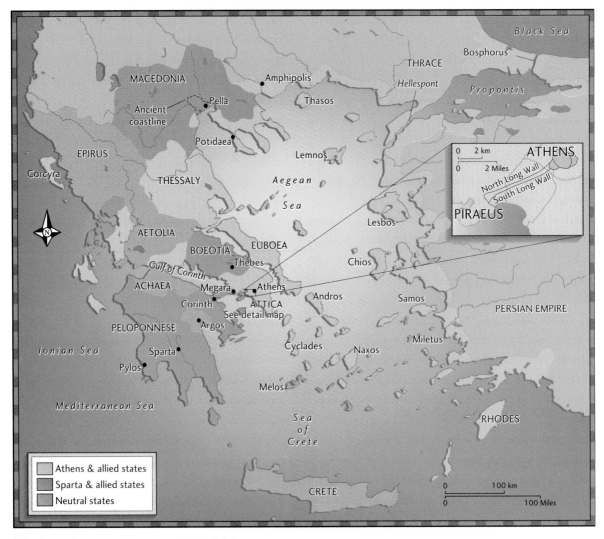

■ The Peloponnesian War, 431–404 BCE

1. How did the city of Corinth figure in the war?

2. Why do you think Athens went ahead with its plan to conquer Syracuse?

sought refuge between the Long Walls when Sparta invaded that year, and in the cramped, unsanitary conditions, a horrible disease struck. Thucydides, who wrote a history of this war, caught the plague himself but survived. He left a detailed description of its terrible symptoms. In two years, perhaps a third of the Athenians died, including their great leader Pericles. With Pericles out of the picture, the two opponents were now on more equal ground.

The conflict lasted for 27 years. First one side gained a strategic victory, then the other. After 300 Spartiates were trapped and captured alive off the coast of the Peloponnese, Sparta wanted peace. Then Sparta successfully attacked Athens's allies in the North Aegean, and Athens wanted peace. Finally, King Brasidas of Sparta, and Cleon, the leader of the radical democrats in Athens, were killed in battle at Amphipolis in the North Aegean. This provoked a brief peace in 421 BCE.

Athens found a new leader who pushed for further hostilities. He was **Alcibiades**, the nephew and ward of Pericles. In 418 BCE, Athens put together an alliance to fight Sparta on land; the attack was not very successful. In 416 BCE, Athens attacked Melos, killing or enslaving its population and bringing this island into the Athenian Empire. Sparta was on the point of attacking Athens again.

At this critical point, Athens foolishly decided to try to conquer Syracuse, the most powerful city on the distant island of Sicily. This two-year campaign (415–413 BCE) required huge quantities of ships, manpower, and money to undertake. It was a total disaster. Alcibiades strongly supported the expedition and could have saved it, but having been charged with a school boy prank at a drinking party, he was forced to flee to Sparta for several years. When he finally returned to Athens to help its sinking cause in 411 BCE, he was able to turn the war effort around for a short time. When he went into exile again for losing a small naval engagement, Athens could find no other general to take his place.

By 408 BCE, the Persians had begun supporting the Spartans, providing ships to fight the Athenians. The Spartan general, Lysander, developed more effective ways to combat the Athenian fleet. Athens became desperate as its money for new ships dwindled and losses at sea continued. After one Athenian victory at sea in 406 BCE, a storm suddenly blew up and prevented the Athenians from picking up 2000 men drifting away from their wrecked triremes. Athens recalled its ten commanders to stand trial for this added loss. Only six of them dared to return for the trial, including Pericles, the son of the great Athenian leader of the same name. All six were found guilty and executed.

The decisive, final battle occurred in 405 BCE at Aegospotami in the Hellespont area. Athens put one last fleet on the water, depending on it for victory. After days of manoeuvring against the Peloponnesian fleet without a battle, the Athenian sailors beached their ships to collect food for their lunch as they had on previous days. The Peloponnesians caught them off guard, burned or captured their ships, and rounded up the sailors. The end had come. Just as the Athenians had killed all the men of Melos in 416 BCE and enslaved their women and children, now they could expect the same treatment.

Sparta's allies, Thebes and Corinth, forcefully encouraged Sparta to do exactly as Athens had done to Melos. What a tragic loss it would have been for Greece. In the end, Sparta spared Athens. As punishment, Athens was required to tear down its Long Walls, surrender all but 12 ships of its fleet, take back its political exiles, and acknowledge Spartan leadership in matters of peace and war.

This loss of freedom was just the beginning of dark days for the Athenians. Thirty men, backed by a Spartan garrison, were granted the authority to rule in Athens. These men, who came to be known as the 30 Tyrants, unleashed a reign of terror during which many people were declared outlaws and killed. Over the course of eight months, 1500 men died. Finally, the city was retaken by exiles favouring democracy. The bloodbath came to an end in 403 BCE, after which Athens then began a remarkably swift recovery, but it was never again a great power.

Thucydides

Thucydides, writer of the remarkable history of the Peloponnesian War, was old enough to recall and record the war's events right from the outbreak of the hostilities; he also fought in the war as an Athenian commander. His refusal to help the Athenians near Amphipolis in 424 BCE proved to be a disaster for his military career, but a blessing for future generations. Rather than fight, he chose to go into exile instead, and from that neutral vantage point he had a better perspective on all the events of the war. Though he lived to see the end of the Peloponnesian War, his book ends in mid-sentence in the year 411 BCE, seven years from the war's end. It is possible that another Greek historian edited and prepared his account for publication.

The introduction to *The Peloponnesian War* tells us much about Thucydides and his goals.

> I lived through the whole of it, being of an age to understand what was happening, and I put my mind to the subject so as to get an accurate view of it. It happened, too, that I was banished from my country for twenty years after my command at Amphipolis; I saw what was being done on both sides, particularly on the Peloponnesian side, because of my exile, and this leisure gave me rather exceptional facilities for looking into things.
>
> Thucydides *The Peloponnesian War* 1.1; V.26

[THE CLASSICAL MOMENT
Literature

Fifth-century BCE Athens was the focal point of the brief age of brilliance sometimes referred to as the Classical Moment. With Pericles as leader and people like the playwright Sophocles and the sculptor Pheidias expressing Greek ideals in artistic forms, Athenian society reached a cultural peak. It was a period of optimism, when the Greeks believed that their world could be made better, and that troubles they faced could be overcome. In *Antigone*, Sophocles wrote this hymn to humankind:

> There are many wonders, but none more wondrous than man
>
> Across the white-capped sea in the storms of winter this creature makes his way on through the billowing waves. And earth, the oldest of the gods, the undecaying and unwearied one, he wears away with constant ploughing, back and forth, year after year, turning the soil with horses he has bred ...
>
> Language, thought swift as the wind, and the patterns of city life he has taught himself, and escape from the shafts of storms, and the shelter—piercing frosts of clear days. He can cope with everything, never unprepared whatever the future brings. Only from death does he fail to contrive escape. Even for diseases thought hopeless he has figured out cures. Clever, with ingenuity and skill beyond imagining, He veers now toward evil, now toward good ...
>
> *Antigone* 1.332–368

Other playwrights, such as Aeschylus and Euripides, hoped to improve their world by examining serious issues like the basis of justice, and the status of women in Greek society. The comic playwright Aristophanes also aimed to change his world — by making fun of it. In *Lysistrata*, he turns the world upside down by having Greek women go on strike — they refuse to have sexual relations with their husbands in order to force the men to end their destructive war:

> When the War began, like the prudent, dutiful wives that we are, we tolerated you men, and endured your actions in silence. (Small wonder

— you wouldn't let us say boo.) You were not precisely the answer to a matron's prayer — we knew you too well, and found out more. Too many times, as we sat in the house, we'd hear that you'd done it again — manhandled another affair of state with your usual staggering incompetence. Then, we'd ask you, brightly, "How was the Assembly today, dear? Anything in the minutes about Peace? " And my husband would give his stock reply.

"What's that to you? Shut up!" And I did...

But this time was really too much: ...

We women met in immediate convention and passed a unanimous resolution: To work in concert for safety and Peace in Greece. We have valuable advice to impart, and if you can possibly deign to emulate our silence, and take your turn as audience, we'll rectify you — we'll straighten you out and set you right.

Aristophanes *Lysistrata* l.507–528

Architecture

The most celebrated of all Greek buildings ever constructed is the Parthenon, built in Periclean Athens as a showpiece of Athenian wealth and

The Parthenon. Try to imagine this temple as it and most other Greek buildings actually appeared: with sculptural decoration brightly painted in blue, red, and yellow.

The Acropolis at Athens. These buildings were constructed over a period from 447–405 BCE. The word "acropolis" means "high city."

power. It dominated all of Athens from its perch high on the Acropolis. Designed by **Pheidias** and the architect Ictinus, this temple to Athena is a marvel of skill and beauty, inspired in part by the Greek victories over the Persians.

The construction of the Parthenon would not have been possible without masonry and sculpture techniques Greeks had learned 200 years earlier in Egypt. Each block of this huge temple was carved with incredible accuracy, using only hand tools.

It is the Parthenon's sculpture, however, that is its most striking feature. Though some remains in Athens, most of the sculpture from around the temple is now kept in the British Museum in London. The figures show the ideal forms of human beauty, serenely calm and unaffected by the momentary events of the world around them. Represented in the sculpture are mythological battles such as the Battle of the Gods and the Giants. The Birth of Athena, the goddess to whom

This sculpture of mounted Athenian warriors was on one side of the Parthenon as a frieze, a decorative panel above the columns.

the temple is dedicated is also portrayed. The Greeks chose not to represent the real battle with the Persians because they believed that such pride (*hubris*) in their own victory would surely be punished by the gods.

Housed in the great *cella* (centre room) of the Parthenon was a towering statue of the warrior goddess Athena, made by the artist Pheidias. It was over 12 m high and made of ivory and gold plates set on a wooden frame. A reflecting pool sat in front of it. One can only imagine the awe that it inspired. Such magnificent works of art were not cheap and it was the revenue from Athens's Empire, a forced federation, that paid for much of this beauty.

The reflecting pool in front of the ivory and gold sculpture of Athena would have both multiplied the visual impact and protected the ivory from drying out.

Review...Recall...Reflect

1. Explain how the Delian League came to be the basis of the Athenian Empire.

2. List three significant innovations of Athenian democracy.

3. Describe the sculptures that adorned the Parthenon and explain why they are considered a brilliant example of Greek sculpture.

THE ROAD TO PERSIA: ALEXANDER THE GREAT

As a result of the Peloponnesian War, Sparta, with Persian support, tried to dominate the other Greek city-states as Athens had done. In reaction to this, new alliances were made against Sparta. Corinth, for example, joined with its old rival Athens to prevent Spartan interference. For a brief time (371–362 BCE), Thebes, another city-state, defeated the Spartans and assumed Greek leadership. It was able to achieve this because of changes in military tactics, including the use of a very deep formation of men (called a *phalanx*) who used longer than normal spears to punch holes through enemy lines. Theban dominance ended with the death of its best general, Epaminondas. The careful balance of power between the leading Greek city-states was soon to be upset by a new force from the north, the kingdom of Macedonia.

Philip of Macedon

The broad plains and hill country of the North Aegean were home to a people considered backward cousins of the Greeks. The Macedonians spoke a Greek dialect, but they were farmers and shepherds, not craftspeople and traders. They were behind their southern cousins in wealth and culture. In the fourth century BCE, several kings rose to unite the Macedonians and bring them success in battle against their enemy neighbours. The key figure in this success was Philip the Great. As a hostage in Thebes for three years, he had learned the new battle tactics of the Thebans. He created a professional army with a strong cavalry and more flexible units on the battlefield. As a result, Philip was able not only to unite his country, but also to defeat the southern Greeks at the Battle of Chaeronaea in

338 BCE. For the first time, all mainland Greeks were joined together under the rule of a single leader. It is likely that this ruthless, ambitious monarch planned to turn the combined Greek forces against their old enemy, Persia, but before he could launch such an expedition, he was assassinated by one of his own officers at a wedding celebration.

In one of the most exciting discoveries in Greek archaeology this century, a royal burial chamber was excavated at Vergina in northern Greece. The outside facade had a painting of a lion hunt with figures identified as Philip the Great and a young Alexander. Inside the vaulted chamber were found silver drinking cups, bronze armour, and a heavy gold box containing a beautiful golden wreath of oak leaves. Wrapped in a purple and gold cloth were the burnt bones of a man whom many believe was Philip the Great himself. Many others now think this tomb actually belonged to Philip's son, Philip III Arrhidaeus, the half brother of Alexander.

Philip the Great of Macedon, as reconstructed from fragments of a skull found in the tomb at Vergina. Philip was known to have lost an eye in battle.

Alexander the Great

After Philip's death, rule fell to his 20-year old son Alexander. He was a student of Aristotle and one of the most successful military leaders the world has known. He took his father's experienced, professional army, his own genius for finding the weaknesses of his enemies, and Philip's ambitious plans for conquest, and in 334 BCE set out against the Persians. He never returned to Europe. Intentionally or not, he conquered the entire Near East as far as India, in a gruelling, decade-long campaign.

How could such a young man with a relatively small army of 35 000 foot soldiers defeat the Persian Empire? The Macedonian army now represented the ultimate in improved Greek warfare. The Macedonians were led by seasoned commanders and all were devoted to Alexander. The Persian army, though much larger, was made up of many different subject peoples. Darius, the Persian king, was a despot who ruled by force, and once Alexander defeated the Persian foot soldiers, the rest of the Persian troops lost their eagerness to fight. The battle of Gaugamela on 1 October 331 BCE, was the final blow against the Persians, whose land and wealth fell into Alexander's hands. Even this, however, did not satisfy Alexander. He forced his weary army eastward against several great kingdoms, reaching all the way to the Indus River valley before turning back, disappointed that he had not reached the eastern ocean.

This mosaic, found at Pompeii, is believed to be a copy of a lost painting. It shows Alexander the Great (on the left) in battle with King Darius of Persia, wearing a gold headress. The Battle at Gaugamela in 331 BCE may be the event portrayed.

Alexander had dreamed of conquering the entire world as far as the Indian Ocean, but finally faced the fact that he now had to govern what he had won. Though as a boy, Alexander had been tutored by Aristotle, as an adult, his ideas about how to make a better empire out of all these foreign peoples were probably his own. He tried to make Greek culture and language a kind of common, uniting force. At the same time, he respected the customs and laws of the peoples he had conquered and encouraged their leaders to help him rule the various parts of his empire. This was a wise decision on Alexander's part, since each nationality had its own culture and might have rebelled if forced to adopt Greek customs completely.

Perhaps Alexander's great experiment would have worked, but he died of an illness just short of his thirty-third birthday. The empire that he fought so hard to create soon split apart as each of his best generals grabbed a large piece of its territory for himself.

[THE HELLENISTIC AGE

The death of Alexander in 323 BCE marks the end of an era. It separates what historians call the Classical Age (480–323 BCE) from the Hellenistic Age (323–31 BCE). Greek culture began to travel from its home in the Aegean and, through conquest, became the common culture of all countries in the Near East. Teachers, soldiers, craftsmen, artists, writers, and

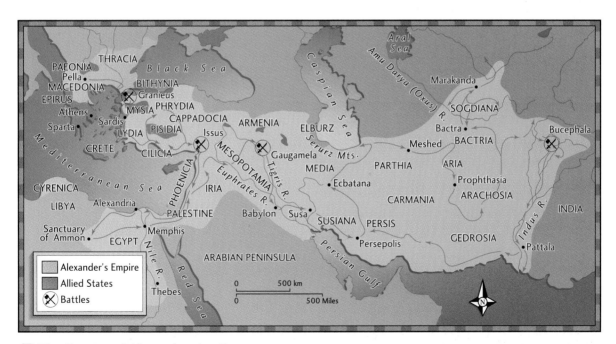

■ **The Empire of Alexander the Great**

1. **Alexander the Great tried to make the Greek language a uniting force in his vast empire. Do you think language can be a uniting force for so many people of different cultures?**

2. **What are some of the civilizations Alexander encountered?**

The History of the Imagination: Myths and Legends

Legends of Alexander the Great — Did you hear the one about …?

Legends often provide interesting clues in the detective work of piecing together history. Not wholly invented, legends usually grow around a real person who is larger than life, a hero like Alexander the Great. Since the hero is already braver, stronger, or somehow greater than average, legends tend to highlight these qualities. Though legends show plenty of imagination, at the heart, there is always some historic truth.

Several legends are attached to the life of Alexander:

- On the day of Alexander's birth, several extraordinary events occurred: there was a solar eclipse; the temple of Artemis at Ephesus caught fire; and an eagle, the bird of Zeus, sat on the roof of the building where Alexander was born. These were all taken to be signs of Alexander's future greatness.

- Also on the day of Alexander's birth, his father, King Philip, was told of two other happy events: one of his generals had won a great victory, and one of his horses won a race at the Olympic Games.

- While in the midst of his conquest of Persia, Alexander stopped at a place called Gordian. He was shown a famous wagon roped to a yoke pole by a mysterious knot. None of the ends of the rope were visible. Alexander was told that whoever was able to unravel the knot would conquer the world. At first Alexander was puzzled, but then he drew out his sword, cut through the knot, and fulfilled the prophecy his own way!

- While visiting Corinth, Alexander learned that the philosopher Diogenes was nearby. On his visit, Alexander was constantly surrounded by crowds of well-wishers, yet Diogenes did not seek him out like the others. So Alexander decided to seek out Diogenes and found him lying in the sun. Alexander stood over him and asked if there was anything he would like Alexander to do. Diogenes replied, "Stand a little out of my sun. " Impressed by this attitude, Alexander said: "Verily, if I were not Alexander, I would be Diogenes. "

Activities

1. What qualities of Alexander do these legends highlight?

2. Explain how legends still have a place in our lives today.

merchants flooded out of Greece into the newly conquered lands to take advantage of the many opportunities for fame and fortune in the Near East. Greek culture was so attractive that it significantly influenced every local society it met, especially the better-educated, urban populations of the Near East. Even when the Romans in turn conquered this area, Greek culture and language remained the common unifier until the coming of the Arabs, and much later, the Turks. Alexander founded more than 70 new cities, many of them named Alexandria. In these, and in the older cities of the Near East, we find typical Greek buildings: gymnasiums, theatres, stadiums, market buildings (the *stoa*), libraries, and temples. Everywhere, Greek became the language of the educated class, and Greek art and literature were appreciated as models of perfection to be imitated.

Alexander's empire was divided into three kingdoms. One of Alexander's generals, Seleucus, took over the Asiatic part of his empire and established the Seleucid dynasty. Another general, Ptolemy, established the Ptolemaic dynasty in the African portion of Alexander's empire (Egypt and eastern Libya), the last ruler of which was the famous queen, Cleopatra. Another Macedonian general, Antigonus, was able to snatch the European portion, including Greece and Macedonia, and founded the Antigonid dynasty. Smaller kingdoms like Pergamon and Rhodes became involved in the feuds between the Hellenistic kingdoms. The results of these conflicts are part of the history of Rome, since Rome eventually conquered Pergamon and Rhodes and made them part of its empire by 31 BCE. Macedonia itself was humiliated and made a Roman province by 148 BCE.

In the midst of this turbulent new era, most Greeks could find some degree of stability in the continuing role of the *polis*, their city. Most city-states maintained independence in their internal affairs, so the councils and assemblies continued to meet, local laws were passed, taxes were collected, and elections were held to fill the traditional offices. Democracy was the normal method of government on this level, but it was expensive to run a democracy. Gradually, wealthier citizens increased their power and the average citizen lost interest in participating in government when the individual polis was no longer threatened by neighbours. One means by which the small city-states could counter the influence of the great powers like Macedonia and Pergamon was to form leagues. Two in particular, the Aetolian and the Achaean Leagues, expanded their memberships beyond the regions of Central Greece and the Northern Peloponnese. Citizens of each league, or their representatives in the case of the Achaean League, met in large assemblies twice a year and decided matters of foreign policy and the military. In the end, however, none of the leagues could match the power of Rome.

Citizens, Slaves, and Foreigners

Demetrius of Phaleron was appointed governor of Athens in 317 BCE. Shortly afterward, he took a census and learned that there were 21 000 citizens (counting men only) in the city, 10 000 *metics* (resident foreigners), and 400 000 slaves (including those who worked in the mines). Even if the number of slaves is exaggerated, the ratio of slaves to free men was unusually high. This was partly because of the number of people captured during the wars of Alexander and his successors, and partly because slave dealers were rescuing abandoned newborn babies. Athens was not a typical Greek city, but it does give us some idea of the rights that different classes of people had.

This vase painting shows slaves working in a Greek mine. What must life for these men have been like?

Only men could be citizens, a legacy of their role in ancient warfare and law making. Women could not vote, hold office, or own property, but had protection within the family structure. Metics were obliged to pay taxes and contribute in other ways to the city, but like women, could not vote, hold office, or own land. Slaves had no rights. Some were fortunate enough to gain their freedom from generous owners. To abuse, assault, or even kill a slave was not a crime, though it may have been frowned upon. For most slaves life must have been miserable. We learn from the plays of Menander, however, that slaves did find ways to co-exist with their masters. In the difficult conditions of the ancient world where the survival of the individual, the family, and the community was regularly threatened, the rights of the individual depended strictly on his or her importance to the community.

GREEK CULTURE
Philosophy

Before the time of Socrates, Greek philosophy was often only concerned with scientific inquiry, such as the nature and origin of the universe. Thales of Miletus may have been influenced by Babylonian wise men when he predicted an eclipse around 585 BCE, or turned his thoughts to the problem of the beginnings of life. Another question addressed by early Greek thinkers concerned what we can really know for certain, when all the information about our world comes to us through our senses, which can be deceived. One noteworthy idea to come from this inquiry was the theory that all matter is made up of tiny, indivisible particles called atoms. Greeks of course never realized just how tiny atoms really are.

The foundations of Greek society were shaken by philosophers questioning traditional beliefs. Men called sophists sold their services as teachers for wealthy youths, training them in public speaking (rhetoric) and logic. One such sophist, Protagoras of Abdera, tried to throw out all the previous standards of judging what is right and wrong, good and bad, ugly and beautiful. He argued that people are the measure of all things — meaning that human beings themselves set all such standards for judgement. Into this climate of distrust of wise men, there appeared a greater genius — **Socrates**.

"Ugly in body, but magnetic in mind; convivial and erotic, yet Spartan in habits and of enormous physical endurance," is one scholar's description of Socrates. This true "lover of wisdom " left behind nothing in writing, but through Plato, his disciple, we learn that Socrates believed it was the duty of every person to care for one's inner being (soul), that is, the moral and intellectual personality, in order to

Socrates was accused of corrupting the youth of Athens and trying to introduce new gods. He was forced to commit suicide by drinking hemlock, a poison.

make it as good as possible. His method of inquiry, which came to be called the Socratic method, was to ask people simple questions about their beliefs, then to probe deeper and deeper into their assumptions, often making them look foolish as they recognized their errors. Socrates' impact on later philosophy has been profound, but in his own day he was often ridiculed. In the end, he was tried and forced to commit suicide by his own city.

> That was the end, Echecrates, of our friend, the man who of all men of his time whom we have known was, we may say, the best — yes, and what is more, the wisest and the most just.
>
> Plato *The Phaedo* 118

The most famous of Socrates' followers was **Plato**. Plato set up his own school, called the Academy,

beside the *Academus* gymnasium just outside Athens. Here, he taught philosophy to advanced students. Plato wrote many works, called *Dialogues*, with Socrates as the main character. In these he sought to explain concepts such as love, beauty, justice, and what he called "the Good. " The concept of the Good had a strong impact on later Christian thinking since it was similar to the Christian idea of God.

Aristotle was a student at Plato's Academy. After Plato's death, Aristotle started his own school, the *Lyceum*, where he organized his students to carry out research in many fields of scientific learning. Aristotle himself made many important advances in biology, zoology, astronomy, meteorology, psychology, political science, ethics, and rhetoric. He also made great contributions to philosophy. He opposed some of Plato's ideas about the nature of true knowledge, and the relationship between the world of the intellect and the world of the senses. Besides these schools there were dozens of others, including those of the Cynics, the Stoics, and the Epicureans, some of which especially influenced the Romans.

The Past
AT PLAY

Among the most popular games enjoyed by the Ancient Greeks were marbles, and an after-dinner game called *kottabos*. In this game, no doubt often played after consumption of considerable quantities of wine (always mixed with water), players reclining on couches in a circle tried to throw the last drops of liquid in their cups into a large vessel in the centre of the circle, without spilling any on the floor!

This is a sculpture of a wounded Amazon, one of a tribe of women warriors said by the ancient Greeks to live at the edge of the known world. Despite being wounded, her expression is calm and serene.

Art and Architecture

If you look at examples of Egyptian painting, you will see that they are really coloured drawings. A figure is drawn and then colours are added, like in a colouring book. Greek artists were the first to learn how to show three dimensions on a flat surface by using different shades of colour to give the illusion of depth. They also used techniques such as foreshortening (making near objects look bigger than distant ones) so as to produce images that looked real. Unfortunately, most Greek paintings are

This bronze sculpture of the god Zeus throwing a thunder bolt was cast ca. 460 BCE. Note the balance and proportions of this figure. Does his face match his body?

lost, but we can read stories about how painters painted grapes that looked so real that birds tried to eat them. Greek painters aimed at producing not only real-looking pictures, but also ideal images. These images reflected a Greek concept of the ideal, or most beautiful, human form — youth, harmonious proportions, and calm expression. When the Greeks depicted the gods, they showed them as ideal human figures, though often larger than life.

The same was true of sculptors. The Greeks concentrated on creating statues of nude young men, and over time observed each detail and proportion of the body. Sculptors wanted to make the statues appear natural but also conforming to certain rules about how an ideal figure should look. This concentration on detail and proportion resulted in statues that were almost lifelike. In the Classical period, the sculptors, like the painters, usually portrayed men and women in their ideal state — in the prime of life, in the most beautiful or handsome pose.

In the Hellenistic period, Greek architecture was refined by elaborating on existing styles rather than by using new methods or materials. More public money was devoted to non-religious buildings such as theatres, stadiums, gymnasiums, and stoas (long colonnaded buildings, often with stores and public facilities, like ancient shopping malls). Private architecture also began to develop as rich individuals decided to use buildings to display their wealth, most notably in the construction of tombs. The most famous such tomb was built at

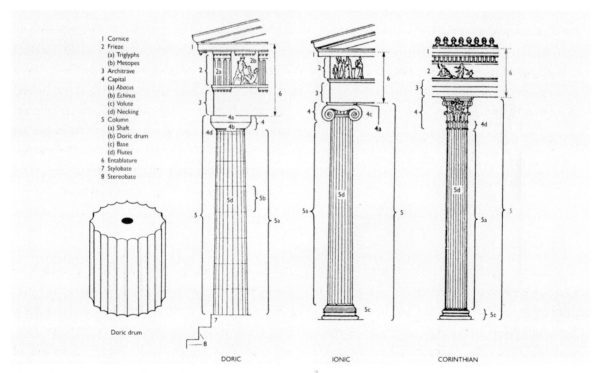

The Greeks developed three different orders, or styles, of architecture. The **Doric** and **Ionic** orders came first, and were used from the sixth century BCE on. The most ornate order, the Corinthian, was first used in Greece in the fifth century BCE, but was further developed and used more extensively by the Romans. Each order consisted of several distinct features and rules of proportion. More than one order of architecture was often used in one building.

Halicarnassus around 353 BCE by King Mausolus (from which we get the word "mausoleum") and his sister Queen Artemisia. Because of the novelty of the design, and the fame of the artists who decorated the building with sculpture, this building was later named one of the wonders of the ancient world. By the time of Alexander the Great, the Greeks had learned how to build arches and vaults out of stone, but it was the Romans who really took advantage of these new devices for spanning open spaces in their architecture.

Review...Recall...Reflect

1. Describe three ways in which the literature, art, and architecture of Classical Greece celebrated and glorified humanity.

2. For centuries, Greek city-states remained apart. How was Philip of Macedon able to unite mainland Greece? How was his son Alexander able to carry on after his father's death to build an enormous empire?

3. Describe what happened to Athenian democracy that tended to undermine the ideals upon which the government was built.

Medicine

Greek medical facilities, the equivalent of our hospitals, were located at sanctuaries of the healing god Asclepius. Compared to the worship of the other gods, worship of Asclepius began very late in Greece, around 500 BCE. The Asclepian sanctuaries were usually located well away from the noise and dust of the city, near a source of clean, cool spring water.

The oldest Asclepian sanctuary was at Epidaurus, and from there the cult spread to Corinth, Athens, Cyrene in Libya, the island of Cos, and many other places. At these sanctuaries, Greek doctors learned their skills in the use of potions, ointments, healthy diets and exercise, and surgery. A device to remove barbed arrows (like the one that went into the eye of Philip the Great) was one of the Greek surgical inventions. The usual cure for disease was to sleep in a special hall at a sanctuary and wait for a dream about the god to work a cure. This was probably combined with proper medical practices.

The most famous Greek physician was Hippocrates whose oath about caring for the sick is still repeated by newly graduated doctors even today. Hippocrates worked at the Asclepian sanctuary at Cos at the same time that Socrates lived in Athens. Hippocrates was the first to study how parts of the body work in relation to the body as a whole.

There was a great deal of superstition and religion mixed with the practice of ancient medicine, but cleanliness, healthy food, rest, and a number of good, naturally occurring drugs helped the healing process. There are many records of cures left at sanctuaries; some are unbelievable, bordering on miraculous, but a good portion of the inscriptions, and the hundreds of clay body parts dedicated in thanks to the god, suggest good success.

Sexuality

While some societies have abhorred, ridiculed, or even attacked homosexuality, that was not the case among the Greeks. On the contrary, it was quite a conspicuous part of Greek life. The Greeks were ready to respond favourably to the open expression of homosexual desire whether in words and behaviour, or in literature and the visual arts. Many vase paintings, for example, depict homosexual courtship and love. For the most part, these represent relationships

Daily Life in Classical Athens

The great majority of Greeks were farmers. A small plot of land, perhaps five hectares or so, would yield olives for oil, grain for bread and porridge, enough grapes for a year's supply of wine, and several fig trees. Pasturage for sheep and goats gave the people a small supply of meat, usually eaten only at festival times, and cheese, another staple. Most people lived close enough to the sea that they could get fresh fish occasionally, though salted fish was common too. Meat could also be found by hunting wild game, especially hares. Cattle were only killed on very special occasions, such as the 100 bulls sacrificed at the Olympic Games. Sausage making was popular to preserve meat. The Greeks also grew vegetables such as cabbage, beans, squash, and onions. Garlic was a favourite seasoning, and honey provided sweetness.

A typical day for an Athenian citizen might include waking early in the morning, leaving his daughters and wife at home, and then taking his son to the gymnasium for classes in music, literature (Homer, of course), and wrestling. Our citizen, whom we'll call Nikias, walks behind his son, nimbly stepping around donkey droppings in the narrow street. Above his head, he hears the sweet singing of his neighbour's daughter, Melosa, who won the weaving contest at Athena's great festival two years ago. An old slave woman hurries past — probably a midwife rushing to attend the birth of a baby.

Just as when he was a boy, Nikias's son learns Homer's two great epics, the *Iliad* and the *Odyssey* as both a history lesson and a way of learning about the Greek gods and heroes. Competing in sports at the gymnasium prepares his son to be a soldier, should Athens need him to defend her people and interests. Loyalty to his polis begins with these lessons at the gym. Nikias stays for an hour to chat with friends and argue with some loud young men who are constantly criticizing Athenian customs. He also stops to admire Kallias, practising the *pankration*, a sport combining wrestling and boxing. Kallias won this event at the seventy-seventh Olympiad, though he broke three of his fingers. Nikias leaves the gymnasium and strolls past a city fountain where four women are filling their water pots and putting them on their heads to take home. He knows they will not talk to him out of modesty, but he sees at least one of them remove the cloak from her face so passing young men can see her.

Nikias walks down to the Agora (the local mall) and directs the slave who has come with him to do the household errands. The slave buys some wool for the women at home to spin and weave into clothes, checks the vegetable sellers' tables, bargains for a fresh fish at the stalls near the Great Drain, and argues with the sandal maker, whose work for Nikias has again fallen apart. Everywhere vendors shout out their prices and bargains, and people carry baskets full of goods from place to place. The noises suddenly die down for a moment while a funeral procession passes, led by a group of mourning women who are shrieking out their grief, pulling at their hair and scratching their faces.

Nikias has his own business to conduct. His farm on the slopes of Mt. Hymettus had a good crop of olives, so he needs two dozen large transport amphoras, pots made for shipping olive oil. He also needs a new krater, a big vase for mixing wine and water (usually one part wine with six parts water) for an upcoming party with his drinking pals. Nikias chooses one with an exciting scene of Greeks fighting Trojans to remind his friends of Greece's great victories over the Persians in recent years. He also buys a little white jug for perfumed olive oil. Nikias will place this on the grave of his older son, who died fighting last year near the island of Aegina.

The draft of a new law about payment for jury duty, just posted on the base of the heroes' statues, is being discussed outside the Council House, and a fierce argument is raging inside. Nikias listens intently and decides how he will vote when the law is presented to the Assembly. Nearby, one of the open-air courts is busy with a trial for slander, and a jury of 501 old men listens as the defendant, with his crying wife beside him and his two ragged children, proclaims his innocence. Nikias knows the man is guilty, but he is good at pleading his case.

It is early afternoon and the sun is hot. Time to return home for a cool drink and a light lunch brought to him by a slave boy who works around the house. Nikias's wife and daughters have been taking turns spinning wool for a new cloak for his son, and washing their dresses for the upcoming festival of Demeter at Eleusis. His older daughter will begin her initiation into the mysteries of the Demeter sanctuary this year. There is time for a long afternoon nap before Nikias rides out to his farm to check on the sausages being made from two pigs killed the day before yesterday. Nikias will take some dried sage and thyme along for seasoning. Dinner will not be until very late, when the temperature cools.

After exercising, athletes cleaned away sweat and dirt by rubbing olive oil on their bodies and scraping the oil and dirt off with a tool called a strigil — once held in this young man's right hand. Nikias's son would have groomed himself this way after exercising in the gymnasium.

between older men and youths. This was particularly common in aristocratic circles. Homosexuality is also a common theme in Greek poetry, and Plato treats it on a philosophical level when he discusses the concepts of ideal beauty and love.

The finest unit of warriors in the Theban army, during its period of dominance in the fourth century BCE, was called the Sacred Band. The Sacred Band was made up entirely of pairs of homosexual lovers. It was believed, and indeed proved correct, that a warrior would fight more fiercely if standing in battle beside his beloved. At the battle of Chaeronea in 338 BCE, when Philip the Great of Macedon crushed the Greek army opposing his rule over mainland Greece, the entire Sacred Band of Thebes died fighting.

Female homosexuality was much less common but can be found in the poetry of Sappho (ca. 600 BCE), a woman poet who ran a finishing school for aristocratic girls on the island of Lesbos. Her poetry was regarded as among the finest of her age. A common theme was her love for certain of her students. It is because of the poetry of Sappho that the island of Lesbos gave its name to female homosexuality (lesbianism).

Science and Technology

Greek mathematics reached very advanced levels, especially by the Hellenistic Age. Best known are the works of **Pythagoras** and Euclid in geometry, but algebra and even trigonometry were also well developed. In the field of science, biology progressed particularly well, especially through the efforts of Aristotle. The Greeks did not know the scientific method, and while they observed natural phenomena carefully, they were not at all good at carrying out accurate experiments to test their theories.

The Greeks did develop a number of more complicated devices based on simple machines such as the pulley, the lever, and the plane. Clock-like mechanisms with complex gears, perhaps to measure astronomical data, have been found, as have large siege machines for hurling various projectiles against an enemy. The famous mathematician and inventor Archimedes, who lived in the third century BCE on the island of Syracuse, developed a device we call the Archimedean screw, which is still used today to draw water up out of streams to irrigate fields.

The Role of Women

The subject of women's roles in Greek society has received a great deal of attention in recent years. It is a topic that depends on very sparse evidence, since most of the archaeological and historical writings were produced by Greek men. Governments were run by men, temples were built by men, writers and artists were men almost exclusively. An exception was Sappho, of course, who was famous for her beautiful lyric verses.

Scripts & Symbols λ μ ν ο π θ υ ρ σ τ υ ϖ ω ξ ψ ζ α β χ ε δ φ γ

There are many names, common and uncommon that are directly derived from Greek words or characters: George, Jason, Homer, Irene, Hector, Helen, Penelope, Theodore, Alexandra, Alexander, Cleo, Christopher, and many more.

In Athens, women of citizen families led very sheltered lives. They closely oversaw the running of their own households, but rarely ventured out in public, even to shop. Their skills in the production of textiles were admired, but cloth was woven just to fill household needs, not for commercial purposes.

In religion, women had a significant public part to play. In Athens, more than 40 priesthoods were held by women, and some festivals and rituals were led only by women, such as the *Thesmophoria* festival of Demeter, goddess of fertility and agriculture. Another example of a festival dominated by women occurred at the sanctuary of Artemis at Brauron, located about 30 km outside Athens on the east coast of Attica. Here Artemis was worshipped as the goddess of childbirth, and especially of happy deliveries. She was linked to the bear (though the reason why is no longer known) so her young worshippers, unmarried girls, dressed as "little bears" (*arctoi*) in the rites performed in her honour. This was a rite of initiation that preceded puberty and was meant to guarantee a fertile marriage and safe childbirth. Childbearing was probably the single most important aspect of a Greek woman's life.

A woman in Greek society fulfilled her role in life almost entirely as a wife and mother, hidden in the home. She was, however, free to visit neighbours and participate in religious festivals, marriages, and funerals. Occasionally, women played a part in public life, as wife or mother of a ruler, but otherwise they did not participate in political life, either to hold office or even to vote. Women in most city-states could not even own property, and had to have a male guardian in legal matters. One exception to this was in Sparta. Though a Spartiate woman was still required to have a guardian, usually the woman's father before she married, and her husband afterward, she could own property. Women received their share of the family estate in the form of a dowry

when they married, and this returned with them to their family in the event of divorce or widowhood.

Some ancient authors leave the impression that Greek men were nervously fearful of women and that they regarded the female character as unpredictable and mysterious. Other authors regarded women with a more liberal attitude. Herodotus described their influence in many historical events. It was mostly through the imagination of Greek men that women made a contribution to the literature and art of this civilization. The Athenian playwrights gave women important and sometimes powerful roles in their dramas.

Sometime not long after 400 BCE, attitudes toward women and their role in society began to change. For example, statues of nude women first appeared at this time. Women were also allowed to participate in important athletic competitions (though the Olympics were never opened to them) and they began to acquire a stronger role in public life. Women like Cleopatra, ruler of Hellenistic Egypt, were still an exception, however, in terms of political power.

Greek Religion

The Greeks had many special days when they celebrated and honoured the gods, days that occurred at irregular intervals (remember, there was no such thing as a weekend). But Greeks did not wait for a holy day to pay their respects to their deities. There were altars, shrines, temples, and statues of the gods everywhere in towns and in the countryside. If a person felt the need for help in a certain aspect of life, they might give a small gift and say a little prayer at the appropriate god's shrine. There were gods of birth, death, and the Underworld; gods for women, the weather, and wine; gods of war, peace, victory, and healing; in

God	Concept or Entity
Zeus	The sky; king of the gods
Hera	Marriage; wife of Zeus
Apollo	Music, plagues, healing
Artemis	Goddess of the hunt; childbirth
Hephaestus	Crafts, especially metal-smithing
Hermes	Messenger of the gods; god of thieves
Athena	Wisdom, guardianship, invention
Ares	War
Demeter	Agriculture
Poseidon	Brother of Zeus; god of the sea and horses
Aphrodite	Love, beauty
Hestia	Hearth, home
Dionysus	Wine, fertility
Hades	God of the Underworld

The Aphrodite of Cnidus, the first known Greek female nude statue. This change in artistic attitude came with a somewhat greater freedom for women in the fourth century BCE.

short, there were gods for all aspects and stages of life. There were also more important gods, most of whom were thought to reside on Mt. Olympus. It was to these gods that the Greeks built their beautiful temples and sanctuaries.

All the gods were thought to have human forms and characters. This is an important idea to understand, since it explains the Greek attitude toward the gods. People honoured the gods with festivals, and offered sacrifices of honey-cakes, terracotta figurines, or sacrificed animals. In exchange, they expected the gods' blessings, or at least to avoid the gods' punishments.

Myths and Legends

In order to explain the many rites and cults, stories were told about significant events in the lives of the different gods. These stories, which we now regard as myths, were firmly believed by most Greeks. Myths had the weight of tradition behind them, and the support of great poets like Homer and Hesiod. Many stories, creations of fertile imaginations, arose as late as the sixth century BCE. They

then became fixed and written down, less easy to change or embellish.

There were also several cycles of stories, what we might call legends, surrounding great heroes of the past and the foes they fought: Herakles, Jason and the Argonauts, Perseus and the Gorgon, Theseus and the Minotaur, and great warriors such as Ajax, Achilles, and Hector. These heroes accomplished superhuman deeds, often with the direct help of the gods who were their patrons and sometimes even their parents. Such legends helped explain the tradition of a glorious past, the remains of which could still be seen in places like Mycenae,

Tiryns, and Knossos. The belief in the greatness of these heroes and their connection with the gods was so strong that many cities had hero shrines where people could worship a local hero and ask for help in their lives.

Temples, Oracles, and Curses

Temples were built as houses for the gods. The richer the city, the greater the temples. Temples were symbols of the wealth and power of the community and of its protecting patron deity. Temples themselves, however, were not places of worship. Virtually all rituals took place around altars outside the temples. In fact, in most sanctuaries there was only an altar and no temple at all.

The Greeks believed strongly that the gods communicated with them; this might take place through the songs of birds, the rustling of leaves, the entrails of animals, or the voice of a special person like a prophet. The sanctuary of Apollo at Delphi became famous because the oracle (prophet) there was regarded as reliable. Apollo spoke answers to inquiries through his priestess, an old woman called the Pythia.

It was also possible for people to address their concerns to the gods. The normal way was through prayers accompanied by gifts, but in popular black magic and sorcery, it was also possible to cast spells and put curses on people. A curse on an enemy might be invoked by scratching the enemy's name and the desired curse on a sheet of lead, often scrambling up the letters, then folding up the sheet and driving a bronze nail through it. This could then be buried in a grave or in a sanctuary to the goddess Persephone, who dwelt in the Underworld for three months of the year.

Festivals

Most festivals included a procession of priests, worshippers, sacred objects, and animals for sacrifice. The more popular festivals had competitions in poetry, music, dance, and athletics, with valuable prizes for the winners. The Olympic Games, held at Olympia, in the Peloponnese, were part of a five-day festival in honour of Zeus. Athletic contests were held on the second and fourth days of this festival as well as on the afternoon of the third day. The first, third, and fifth days were otherwise given over to processions, sacrifices, and prayers to Zeus. No music or poetry contest interfered with the athletic games here, and although the reward at Olympia was a simple wreath, the home city of a winner usually gave its winners prizes equal to tens of thousands of dollars.

Religion and Political Life

The Greeks were generally quite tolerant of the religious beliefs of others, probably because Greek religion did not have rigid rules. So, for example, the sophists in fifth-century Athens could discuss their serious doubts about the existence or knowability of the gods. The Greeks could also be deadly serious about religion, especially at times when they thought their city was being threatened or the gods were angry with them. In 414 BCE, in the dark days of the Peloponnesian War and its aftermath, a number of wealthy young men of Athens were tried and executed on the charge of impiety. Protagoras the sophist is said to have fled Athens after being convicted on a charge of atheism in 411 BCE. Socrates was executed (by drinking poison) in 399 BCE on twin charges of corrupting the youth of

Athens and introducing new gods. The concept of separation of church and state was unknown in the ancient Greek world, so the temples and cults were readily supported with public money. Since political leaders were often also religious leaders, threats to religion might also be regarded as threats to the state.

Ancient
ODDITIES

At the festival of Zeus in Athens, a very peculiar ritual known as the *Bouphonia* (from the Greek word for ox or cow) was performed. An ox would be killed, then the person who had done the deed would drop the axe and run away. The axe was put on trial and convicted, then thrown into the sea. At the culmination of this mysterious and odd ritual, the hide of the animal was stuffed with grasses, and the dummy ox was yoked to a plough!

Trade and Coinage

In Greece, trade over any great distance or in any bulk product was carried out by ship since overland travel by pack animal was difficult and expensive. It seems probable that Phoenician ships first visited Greek shores during the Dark Ages for trading purposes. These encounters may have encouraged Greeks to make voyages in their own ships, perhaps built especially for the purpose, though more likely used for fishing or island raiding. As underwater archaeological expeditions have revealed, these ships were small, able to accommodate a crew of four or five and a capacity of several tonnes.

Profits from a successful voyage could be substantial, as much as two or three times the cost of the cargo. However, these voyages were not without risks, from storms and pirates, as well as the great cost of hiring a ship to carry the cargo. A normal venture began when a merchant borrowed money from a banker at a rate of 25 to 60 percent for the term of the voyage. The money would be used to purchase a cargo. The merchant would then make a contract with a shipowner for space on his ship to carry the cargo, for example, copper ingots from Cyprus, back to Piraeus (the main port for Athens). The shipowner presumably would have a contract with another merchant to carry a cargo outbound from Athens, for example, olive oil and fine pottery, to Cyprus. The first merchant would accompany the ship in order to make the best deal possible for the copper. In Piraeus, he then had to find a buyer for his cargo, pay the shipowner, and pay his banker with the necessary interest. If demand for copper were high, as in wartime when armour was needed, the merchant could make a considerable profit.

The most common trade goods shipped to and from Greece included:
- grain from south Asia, Sicily, or Egypt in exchange for Greek olive oil and wine
- luxury goods like glass, alabaster, perfumes, and ivory from Phoenicia and Egypt in exchange for Greek silver or white marble
- timber and pitch for shipbuilding from the North Aegean in exchange for Greek olive oil and finished goods like pottery, furniture, jewelry, or textiles

Clearly, Greek merchants and sailors travelled to every corner of the Mediterranean and far inland from its ports in order to find trade opportunities and satisfy their natural curiosity about the world. These traders, together with Greek mercenaries, were no doubt the major force for spreading Greek culture abroad before the time of Alexander. These same traders, on their return to their homeland, brought back the natural resources, goods, and most importantly, the ideas that they acquired in distant places. Many foreigners in turn came to visit and live in Greece, either freely as traders or as ambassadors, or in captivity as slaves.

For centuries, trade depended on a system of bartering where traders made deals to exchange so much of one product for so much of another — there was no money involved because money did not exist yet. Two hundred kilograms of salt might be traded for 150 kg of grain, and so on. Days might be spent arguing over amounts and types of compensation. Eventually, traders recognized that small amounts of precious metals might be conveniently accepted almost anywhere in exchange for most products used in daily life. Precious metals like copper, bronze, silver, electrum (an alloy of silver and gold), and even pure gold, could be carried in small chunks, weighed by the traders and used as a form of exchange.

Chunks of different sizes always had to be weighed against different standards, which was awkward, and there were widely varying standards of purity for metals, or percentages of metals in alloys. To bring some uniformity to this process, beginning in the eighth and seventh centuries BCE, the chunks of precious metal were stamped with a symbol indicating their weight and purity. The stamps of certain traders came to be trusted more than others. Eventually, the uncertainty of this state of affairs was resolved when governments began stamping their own metal chunks, and so put the reputation of the state or monarch behind the quality of the metal and its standard of weight. This was the first coinage of the Western world.

The first mints, dating to the seventh century BCE, were in Lydia and the East Greek states, but coinage quickly spread to the trading cities of Athens, Corinth, Aegina, and Chalcis in the Western

A silver "owl of Athens." The goddess Athena was associated with the owl. The letters on this coin spell "Athe...."

Aegean. Silver became the most commonly used metal. By the time of the Athenian Empire in the fifth century BCE, the so-called owls of Athens — coins with an owl on one side and the head of Athena on the other — became the most common coinage in the Mediterranean area.

Review...Recall...Reflect

1. Briefly describe how daily life in rural areas differed from life in the cities in ancient Greece. Your response should compare daily routines.

2. Describe the relationship between religion, superstition, and medicine in ancient Greece. Would you have been comfortable visiting a sanctuary of Asclepius if you were feeling ill? Explain your answer.

3. Explain the origins of coinage in ancient Greece by tracing developments from the barter system to the creation of the first mints in the seventh century BCE.

THE GREATNESS OF THE GREEKS

Why were the Greeks able to accomplish so much during the Classical Age? The answer to this question is not such a mystery. The system of farming, with slaves and tenants doing the work, and the mercantile interests of many Greeks, produced both wealth and leisure time. This in turn gave freedom and time to many individuals for other areas of human interest — literature, philosophy, music, and art. As a consequence, a very large portion of the male population of Greece had the freedom and encouragement to exercise their natural talents and curiosity. Imagine what might have been accomplished had all Greeks — men and women, slaves, and foreigners — been given the same opportunities!

It is hard to imagine Western civilization without its foundations in ancient Greece:

- **Thought**: When it came time to build on the accomplishment of other cultures, the Greeks used careful, rational thought, to which they added their natural curiosity. This use of logical thinking may partly be credited to the political system. In small city-states, power derived from being persuasive in public argument, and persuasiveness depends in part on rational, logical thought.
- **Language**: Thousands of words used in English and other European languages are derived from ancient Greek, for example: technology, history, evangelist, cyberspace, titan, euthanasia, genetics, photography, economy, and microscope.
- **Politics**: The study of government was first begun by Plato and Aristotle. The very word "politics " is derived from ancient Greek, from polis, the word for a Greek city-state. Many of the words we use to describe our various

political systems also come from Greek words: democracy, monarchy, tyranny, aristocracy, and so on. The concept of democracy took its first breath in ancient Greece, albeit in a somewhat different, more limited form compared to what we know today.

- **Philosophy**: It has been said that all later philosophy is merely footnotes to Plato. This is an exaggeration, of course, but it points clearly to the importance of Plato and other Greek philosophers. Not only did these thinkers give rise to the field of philosophy as we know it, but they also introduced many of the philosophical questions that have occupied human minds since.
- **Art and Architecture**: Beginning in the fifteenth century CE in Europe, both sculptors and painters were strongly influenced by Classical art. Using Greek art as a model, problems in creating the human figure were solved, and techniques in foreshortening, light and colour, and perspective were employed just as the ancient Greeks had done. In architecture of the eighteenth and nineteenth centuries, there was a strong revival of Classical art called Neo-classicism. The architectural styles of government buildings, banks, art museums, train stations, and stately mansions imitated those of Classical Greece.
- **Myth and Literature**: Besides the myths and literature of the ancient Greeks that we still read today, there are a great many allusions to Greek myth and literature in our modern world. Sports teams are called Trojans, Spartans, or Argonauts; adventurous travels are called odysseys; and the space program that landed the first human on the moon was called Apollo.

History Continues to Unfold

Thousands of scholars in universities around the world still study the ancient Greeks, mostly through the written works they have left us: books, plays, letters, poems, inscriptions, and graffiti. The ancient Greeks also speak to us through the archaeological remains of their cities, cemeteries, sanctuaries, and ships. Where once we focused on the accomplishments of the most famous Greeks, the most important wars, or the most magnificent temples and statues, there has been a shift toward the study of the lives of the common Greek man, woman, or child, and their daily lives. What was the life of a Spartan boy really like? What supports did Athenian women find as they became wives and mothers? How did the playwright Euripides reach the emotions of his audience? What ran through the mind of a Greek attending an animal sacrifice at a religious festival? Women's lives especially have been looked at more closely so we can appreciate their role in the success of this society. There are thousands of questions yet to ask, even as hundreds of questions are answered each year.

Current Research and Interpretations

Herodotus was dubbed the "Father of History " by the ancient Roman writer Cicero. Herodotus's immediate successor, Thucydides, set the standard for historical research that has lasted through to today. The Greeks were the first to treat the writing of history not simply as the recording of events, but as the rational explanation of those events, an approach that remains one of the primary goals of historians working today.

Chapter Review

Chapter Summary

In this chapter, we have seen:

- the importance of trade in the economy of ancient Greece
- how individuals such as Socrates, Sappho, Pheidias, and Plato made important contributions to the development of intellectual thought, artistic expression, and political traditions
- how a variety of factors led Sparta and Athens to develop very different forms of social organization
- how conflict between city-states led to instability and change while the unity of the Greeks brought about by Philip of Macedon ushered in a era of peace and stability within Greece

Reviewing the Significance of Key People, Concepts, and Events (Knowledge/Understanding)

1. Understanding the history of Classical and Hellenistic Greece requires a knowledge of the following concepts and events, and an understanding of their significance in the development of both Greek and later Western society. In your notes, identify and explain the historical significance of three from each column.

   Concepts
   Delian League
   Peloponnesian League
   Parthenon
   Hellenistic Age

   Events
   Peloponnesian War
   Battle of Aegospotami
   Classical Moment

2. Classical and Hellenistic Greece made many significant contributions to the development of artistic forms. Make a chart with the headings Painting, Sculpture and Architecture, and list Greek accomplishments under each heading.

3. Carefully review the section on "Daily Life," and based on the discussion there, complete the chart below in your notes.

Members of Greek Society	Social, Economic, and Political Roles in Greek Society
Women	
Men	
Children	
Boys	
Girls	
Slaves	

Doing History: Thinking About the Past (Thinking/Inquiry)

1. The civilization of ancient Greece profoundly influenced later Western societies. Select and explain three major changes that took place in ancient Greece that have continued to influence Western society.

2. Although the ancient Greeks had no fixed theology or set of rules, religion still played a significant role in the governing of Greek city-states. In a paragraph, explain the relationship between religion and politics in ancient Greece.

   Connecting to the *World History Handbook*: Once you have completed your paragraph, transfer some of the main ideas to the graphic organizer "Religion's Influence on Political Structures" in your *World History Handbook*.

Applying Your Learning (Application)

1. Complete a Venn diagram to illustrate the features of Athenian democracy that were similar to and different from our democratic system today.

   Connecting to the *World History Handbook*: Once you have completed your Venn diagram, transfer the ways in which Athenian democracy contributed to the development of modern Western ideas of citizenship to the graphic organizer "The Development of Western Concept of Citizenship" in your *World History Handbook*.

2. The foundations of modern Western society lie in ancient Greek civilization. Complete the graphic organizer "Contributions of Ancient Greece to Modern Western Society" in your *World History Handbook*.

Communicating Your Learning (Communication)

1. Alexander the Great's victory over the much larger Persian army was in part a result of many improvements in Greek warfare. Complete the graphic organizer "Advances in Greek Warfare." Once you have completed this organizer, write one paragraph explaining how advances in warfare contributed to Alexander's victory.

2. Using the data found in the section "Citizens, Slaves, and Foreigners," construct a bar graph that illustrates the ratio of citizens to others living in Athens in the fourth century BCE. Once you have completed your bar graph, in a paragraph, explain the Athenian concept of citizenship and speculate as to why Athens placed restrictions on citizenship.

CHAPTER FIVE

The Rise of Rome

CHAPTER EXPECTATIONS

By the end of this chapter, you will be able to:

- explain the origins of the Punic Wars and Rome's need to expand

- demonstrate an understanding of the cause and effect relationship between reforms to the Roman army and the collapse of the Roman Republic

- demonstrate an understanding of the relationship between individuals, groups, and authority during the period from the founding of Rome to the end of the Republic

- describe the roles of different members of society during the period of the Roman Republic

Ancient Romans believed that their ancestors, Romulus and Remus, were kept alive with the help of a female wolf.

We study Roman civilization today for many reasons. The constitution of the Roman Republic, under development as early as 509 BCE, was a model for many present-day democracies. Roman architecture, which pioneered the use of concrete and its ability to span vast spaces, is still a major influence on how we construct buildings and cities. The Roman talent for administering a people while also allowing it to maintain a unique cultural identity could, perhaps, be a model for us today. We also study the Romans out of sheer fascination for one of the world's greatest empires.

Though the Romans were influenced by the Greeks, unlike their Athenian predecessors, they found ways to maintain long-term social stability. At the core of their being, the Romans had an unshakeable belief that it was their destiny to rule the known world, as Virgil put it, "to spare the conquered and put down the proud." By studying Roman civilization, we discover something about ourselves and our society. Will our civilization last as long as the Romans' did? Will our own increasingly globalized community be transformed beyond our ability to imagine its future shape, or recognize its roots?

KEY WORDS

republic

empire

aristocracy

tribune

patricians

plebeians

KEY PEOPLE

Romulus and Remus

Lucretia

Tarquin the Proud

Tiberius Gracchus

Gaius Gracchus

Marius

Julius Caesar

VOICES FROM THE PAST

The more laws, the less justice.
Cicero, *De Officiis*

TIME LINE: THE RISE OF ROME

	ca. 1000 BCE	Etruscans emerge as a distinctive culture in Italy
Mythological founding of Rome	753 BCE	
	509 BCE	Last Etruscan king is deposed and Roman Republic begins
Council of Plebeians is established to give the people a voice	494 BCE	
	450 BCE	The Twelve Tables codify Roman law
Rome is sacked by the Gauls	390 BCE	
	264 BCE	The First Punic War begins
The Second Punic War begins	218 BCE	
	146 BCE	Carthage is destroyed in the Third (and final) Punic War
	133 BCE	Tiberius Gracchus introduces land reforms to help the poor
Gaius Gracchus is killed for attempting to introduce radical social reforms	121 BCE	
	100 BCE	Gaius Marius creates Rome's first standing army
Slave revolt led by Spartacus is put down	71 BCE	
	60 BCE	First Triumvirate seizes control of the Roman government
Julius Caesar becomes dictator of Rome ending Republican government	46 BCE	
	45 BCE	The Julian calendar is introduced
Julius Caesar is assassinated and civil war ensues	44 BCE	

GEOGRAPHY: THE ITALIAN PENINSULA

The Italian Peninsula lies in the geographic centre of the Mediterranean basin, surrounded on three sides by what the Romans called *Mare Nostrum*, "Our Sea." The land is separated from the rest of Europe by the Alps, a rugged mountain chain that provides the people of northern Italy with a formidable protective barrier. The peninsula is approximately 1000 km long and 200 km wide and is itself divided along most of its length by the Apennine Mountains. This diagonal barrier, no higher than about 3000 m, to this day remains difficult to penetrate, and in Roman times, served to make internal communication difficult.

Although the Romans preferred to travel by boat, there were few rivers that were easily navigable for most of their length. The most important were the Po River, which for many centuries acted as a

border between the civilized inhabitants of Italy and their wilder neighbours to the north, and the Tiber River in central Italy. The story of Rome is the story of the growth, expansion, and influence of a small settlement in the Tiber River Valley, about 20 km from the Tyrrhenian Sea.

Although there were few good harbours and the Romans were unadventurous sailors, coastal trade was brisk. To the southeast were the ports of Brindisi and Taranto. To the northeast were the two ports of Genoa and La Spezia. The later Roman navies were stationed in the Bay of Naples south of Rome and in the north on the estuary of the Po, at Ravenna. An artificial, commercial port was built at Ostia at the mouth of the Tiber to supply the city of Rome. The word "port," in fact, comes from the Roman name for this place, *Portus*.

While the Italian Peninsula was generally fertile along the narrow coastal plains and in river valleys, an expanding urban population led to an increased reliance on grain imported from Sicily and Egypt. From the height of the Roman Empire to its ultimate collapse in the sixth century CE, the urban population of Rome was dependent on foreign imports.

The climate of the peninsula is relatively mild. In winter and summer, temperatures along the coasts are moderated by the proximity of the seas, although greater extremes of cold and heat are felt farther inland. In the summer months, the heat is intensified by a dry, southerly breeze that rolls away the clouds to allow the sun's uninterrupted glare. In winter, from October to March, the wind's direction is reversed, bringing cold fronts in from the European continent and making the seas unsuitable for sailing. The relatively mild climate, general agricultural prosperity, seclusion from the rest of Europe, and central position in the Mediterranean world, were all important factors in the rise of Rome.

■ **The Italian Peninsula**

What geographical features protected Rome from surrounding territories?

THE ETRUSCANS: FORERUNNERS OF THE ROMANS

Before Rome developed into a great urban community on the banks of the Tiber River, a sophisticated people inhabited north-central Italy. These were the Etruscans, who controlled territory roughly from the Po River to Cumae on the northern edge of the Bay of Naples. To the northeast, the power of the Etruscan civilization, though not its influence, was limited by the Apennine Mountains. Even though the Etruscan language has never been convincingly deciphered, enough is known about these people to form a relatively clear picture of how they contributed to the rise of Rome and to distinctive aspects of Roman culture.

■ **Etruscan Italy ca. 1000 BCE**

How might the Etruscans and early Romans have come into contact with each other?

Much of what we know about the Etruscans comes from their burial customs. The Etruscans buried their dead in tombs hollowed out of the ground or under great mounds of earth called *tumuli.* Usually, the interiors of these tombs were made to resemble the houses of the living. The life of the Etruscans is reflected in the relief sculptures cut into the rock walls of the chambers and in the frescoes showing banquets, gladiatorial combat, chariot races, and other everyday activities.

Much of what we know about the Etruscan civilization comes from the tombs of the wealthy. Like these Etruscan party-goers, the Romans also ate and drank while relaxing on couches.

The Etruscans were probably native to Italy and descended from earlier peoples. They were skilled artisans and accomplished traders. Only two other civilizations were competing in the Mediterranean world at the height of the Etruscan culture: the Greek city-states, especially the colonies of Sicily and Magna Graecia (southern Italy from Taranto up the west coast as far as Naples), and the Carthaginians in Tunisia (North Africa). Various complex arrangements kept Greek traders dominant in the south, while in the north, the Etruscan and Carthaginian fleets cooperated to their mutual advantage.

The Etruscan Monarchy: Kings of Rome, 753–509 BCE

According to the historian Livy (Titus Livius, 59 BCE–12 CE), there were seven kings of Rome. The first was Romulus (753–715 BCE), who was allegedly the son of Mars, the god of war, and a priestess named Rhea Silvia. The founding myth tells us that the death of Romulus and his twin brother Remus was ordered by their cruel uncle Amulius, who wanted them thrown into the Tiber River. Thanks to some kind servants, the basket containing the twins eventually came to shore near an area known as the *Palatine*, later recognized as one of the Seven Hills of Rome, and future residence of the emperors (Palatine comes from the word for palace). There, the twin boys were nurtured by a female wolf (or she-wolf) until they were discovered and raised by a shepherd. Various versions of the myth relate that once the boys attained manhood there was a bitter dispute between them over who had the authority to found the city. Romulus was favoured to be the founder and when Remus challenged Romulus, Remus was killed. So Rome, a city destined for greatness, had its origins in bloodshed.

In time, the Etruscans expanded their power southward and took control over the Romans. The first Etruscan king of Rome was L. Tarquinius Priscus (616–579 BCE), who cleared the site for the great temple of *Jupiter Optimus Maximus* (Jupiter Best and Greatest) on another of Rome's seven hills, the *Capitoline*. In later years, one of the features of civilized living in any Roman town was the central focus provided by its *capitolium*, the temple dedicated to Jupiter, the Father of the Gods. Tarquinius Priscus is also reputed to have built the *cloaca maxima* (great sewer), whose outflow into the Tiber can still be seen today draining the valley between the Palatine and Aventine hills. The second Etruscan king was Servius Tullius (579–534 BCE), said to have continued the program of urban renewal begun by his predecessor.

The last Etruscan king of Rome, Tarquin the Proud, was expelled by a popular rebellion in 509 BCE. In fact, the rebellion had been sparked because the king's son Sextus raped a virtuous aristocratic woman named Lucretia, who subsequently committed suicide. With the removal of the last king, the way was clear for Rome to form a democratic republic. The Etruscans, on the other hand, could not resist the pressure of the increasingly dominant Romans. Eventually, after the Roman

For artists of the seventeenth and eighteenth centuries, the infamous rape of the noble Roman woman Lucretia was a dramatic and challenging subject. This painting is by the French painter Simon Vouet.

capture of Veii in 396 BCE, the military power of the Etruscans collapsed. Those who lived near the city of Rome were absorbed into the new Republic, while those resident in cities a little further away saw their influence (if not their personal status) greatly diminish.

Etruscan Influence on Roman Life

There is a remarkable continuity between the Etruscan and Roman worlds. Several elements characteristic of Roman life including numerals, a fondness for blood sports, a belief in Hades and the underworld gods, augury (foretelling the future through the appearance of natural phenomena), and excessive superstition were all inherited by the Romans from the Etruscans. The Romans also adopted some elements of Etruscan political affairs. For example, the high magistrates of the Roman Republic used the purple robes and ivory thrones of the Etruscan kings (*lucumones*) as well as their symbols of authority over life and death called the *fasces*. The fasces was an axe bound into a bundle of wooden rods; when magistrates were present, it was carried by an escort of officials known as *lictors*.

Review...Recall...Reflect

1. How have the burial tombs of the Etruscans helped to shed light on their lives?

2. In your own words, recount the mythological founding of Rome.

3. How did the Etruscans influence Roman society?

THE ROMAN REPUBLIC

The Roman Republic (*Res Publica*, public matter) was a result of the people's discontent with the tyrannical, domineering attitudes of the Etruscan kings. However, up to 27 BCE, much of the subsequent internal history of the state of Rome can be traced by following the relationship that existed between an overbearing, landowning aristocracy, known as the patricians, and the often landless poor, the plebeians.

The Roman Republic was known to its citizens as the *Senatus Populusque Romanus* (SPQR, the Senate and People of Rome). As the name implies, there was a constant tension between the senatorial aristocracy and the people. Nowhere was this tension and the state's efforts to accommodate it more evident than in the system of government that developed as Rome achieved political maturity.

The Arch of Titus in Rome was built to commemorate the Emperor Titus's victory in Judea in 70 CE. The inscription above the arch opening reads: "The Senate and the People of Rome dedicate the arch to divine Titus ...."

Assemblies

The Roman Republican government was composed of several assemblies from which magistrates were drawn. Before the expulsion of Tarquin the Proud in 509 BCE, the kings of Rome had been advised and supported by a council made up of the men who controlled the most land. This body was known as the *Senate* and continued to be important throughout the history of the Roman Republic.

The *Comitia Centuriata* (Assembly of Centuries) was an important assembly of male citizens segregated into five electoral classes according to wealth. The wealthiest landowners were the first to vote and the *proletarii* (those who owned no land), were the last. The Comitia Centuriata passed laws presented to it by the annually elected senior magistrates. This assembly also included the *Comitia Curiata*, another assembly of the 30 divisions of citizens from the three clans: the Ramnes, Luceres, and Tities. The main function of the Comitia Curiata seems to have been to attend the inauguration of the king during the period of Etruscan rule. During the Roman period, it confirmed a magistrate's right to exercise the authority already granted to him by the Comitia Centuriata.

The *Comitia Tributa* (Assembly of Tribes) was an assembly that consisted of all the enfranchised people (those who had a right to vote) in the city who belonged to tribes, at least nominally. This assembly could pass laws on behalf of all the people including the aristocrats who owned land and the mass of ordinary folk.

Finally, the *Concilium Plebis* (Plebeian Tribal Council) was a tribal assembly much like the Comitia Tributa with the exception that aristocrats could not be members. It passed *plebiscita* (plebiscites), votes that had the force of law.

Magistrates

After Tarquin's removal, two men from the Senate were elected by the members of the Comitia Centuriata to become *consuls*, the chief magistrates of the Roman state. Consuls were elected annually; with the other lesser magistrates (discussed below), one colleague could *veto* (Latin for "I forbid") the decisions of the other, thereby acting as a check against abuse of power.

In addition to the regular, annual *cursus honorum* — the magistracies held consecutively — there was the extraordinary position of *dictator*. A dictator was appointed by the consuls for a specified period, originally six months. Such appointments were made in times of crisis, especially during wars.

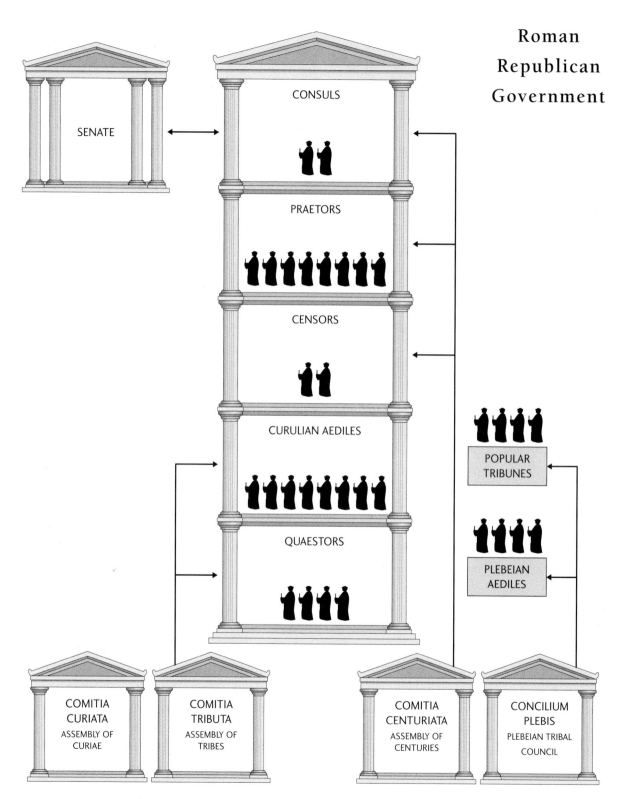

Roman Republican Government

SENATE

CONSULS

PRAETORS

CENSORS

CURULIAN AEDILES

QUAESTORS

POPULAR TRIBUNES

PLEBEIAN AEDILES

COMITIA CURIATA
ASSEMBLY OF CURIAE

COMITIA TRIBUTA
ASSEMBLY OF TRIBES

COMITIA CENTURIATA
ASSEMBLY OF CENTURIES

CONCILIUM PLEBIS
PLEBEIAN TRIBAL COUNCIL

Also elected annually by the Comitia Centuriata were the *praetors*. After the consuls, these officers were the next most powerful men in the state. Originally, there was only one, a patrician responsible for the administration of justice in Rome itself. After a short while, however, another was added whose primary responsibility became relations between Roman citizens and non-Romans. As Rome conquered foreign territories, more praetors were added. The number of praetors was increased to four in 227 BCE upon the conquest of Sicily and Sardinia, and then to six in 197 BCE, when Rome acquired Spain. Eventually, the power of the patricians was eroded to the point where the number of praetors grew so large that the position was no longer something special, and even plebeians won the right to stand for election.

The position of *censor* was established in the mid-fourth century BCE. Two censors were elected by the Comitia Centuriata to hold office together for five years. As former consuls, the major task facing these men was to draw up revised lists of citizens (the *census*). As Rome became more powerful, Roman citizenship became more attractive.

The person seated at the table and writing is a scribe. He is recording the census while the war god Mars looks on at the right.

The modern meaning of censor is derived from a secondary responsibility of the Roman officials, which was to oversee public morality.

Next down the ladder of elected officials in the Roman Republic were the *Curulian aediles* who were elected by the Comitia Tributa. Originally, there were two such officials. Their initial function was to assist the consuls. Later, their number was increased and they became responsible for such things as the maintenance of roads in the city, public executions, water, and official standards of measure.

The last of the originally patrician officers were the *quaestors*. They were elected annually by the Comitia Tributa and were charged with administering financial matters, always considered a rather sordid business. At first, there were two quaestors, but as the area of Roman influence expanded, more positions were added.

The People and Their Representatives

For all the continuing attempts to control tensions and curb individual abuse of power, the division of patricians and plebeians remained a division between rich and poor, between those with power and influence and those without. Early in the fifth century (494 BCE), in an attempt to correct that imbalance, the *Concilium Plebis* (Plebeian Tribal Council) was established and membership was restricted to non-senatorial males. Two *plebeian tribunes*, who were given sacred immunity (like that of foreign diplomats today), were elected annually by the Concilium Plebis. The plebeian tribunes had the authority to veto decisions made by the consuls. Gradually, the number of plebeian tribunes was increased to ten. In time, they came to be very powerful interpreters of the people's wishes. This became especially true later in the fifth century BCE when decisions made by the Concilium Plebis no longer needed the Senate's approval.

Growth and Maturity of the Republic

For the next 400 years, the Roman Republic underwent great expansion and faced extreme danger. First, the Gauls (a Celtic people of Europe north of the Alps), crossed the mountains into Italy, forced to do so by an increasing population. Their leader Brennus is remembered at the Brenner Pass, one of the most important road and rail links today between Italy and the rest of Europe. Although Rome was besieged and sacked by the Gauls in 390 BCE, the city recovered and struck back. The Gauls were defeated and dispersed. This action marked Rome's first major expansion to the far north of the Italian Peninsula, a move that had more to do with responding to external military pressure than with economic need.

By the second century BCE, Sicily was fast becoming Rome's breadbasket, supplying the many thousands of tonnes of grain required annually to feed the city's inhabitants. Approximately half of the grain was handed out to the people by the state, while the other half remained in the hands of entrepreneurs (*negotiatores*). There was also a constant and ever increasing need for cooking oil; southern Spain eventually became an important source of that essential commodity. This inevitably led to clashes with the Carthaginians, who were at that time the greatest maritime power in the western Mediterranean.

The Carthaginians were quite different from the Romans. In times of crisis, their gods demanded the sacrifice of infant sons. The Carthaginians came originally from Phoenecia (what is now Lebanon) and settled in North Africa. Above all, they were traders. Throughout much of their conflict with the Romans, from 264 BCE until the time of the final destruction of Carthage in 146 BCE, they maintained a commercial empire and effectively had control over Sicily and the Iberian Peninsula (present-day Spain and Portugal).

At the same time that Rome was in conflict with Carthage, it was also expanding its dominion into the eastern Mediterranean, taking control of eastern Greek cities. In Italy, spurred on in part by a constantly growing need for wine, produce, leather, and woollen goods, the Romans had already subdued many rival city-states and tribes, created towns that would support their interests, and encouraged other towns to prosper. Finally, and importantly, the great increase in military activity led to a massive increase in the trade in arms and armour.

EXTERNAL FORCES: THE PUNIC WARS, 264-146 BCE

There were three fateful clashes between Rome and the Carthaginians, called the Punic Wars (the word "Punic" is derived from the Latin word meaning Phoenician). Undoubtedly, the most dangerous time for Rome after the defeat of the invading Gauls, was the Second Punic War (218–202 BCE). The Carthaginian military leader at this time was Hannibal, the son of Hamilcar Barca, who had done much to help restore Carthage after its first defeat by the Romans in the First Punic War (264–261 BCE). Hannibal now ruled the Iberian Peninsula as if it were his private kingdom.

 http://www.mcgrawhill.ca/links/echoes

Go to the web site above to find out more about Hannibal.

In 218 BCE, Hannibal left Spain and led a land-based attack on the Romans by crossing the Alps, a feat still marvelled at today. Hannibal started from Spain with 35 000–40 000 troops and 37 elephants; by the time he arrived in northern Italy, only about 26 000 soldiers and one elephant had survived the crossing. It is likely that Hannibal's military skill was poor and that the Alpine barrier was much more formidable than he had been led to believe. For all Hannibal's losses, however, he engaged in four great battles over the next two years. These battles were astounding for the number of Roman losses. On 2 August 216 BCE, for example, at Cannae in southern Italy, over 50 000 soldiers from a Roman army of 86 000 were annihilated in one day.

Hannibal managed to conquer most of the Italian Peninsula. Fourteen years later, through patient guerilla warfare, the Romans eventually drove Hannibal out of Italy. The final Roman victory came at the Battle of Zama (202 BCE) in Tunisia, North Africa, under the leadership of the Roman general Publius Cornelius Scipio. For this victory, Scipio was given the honorary title Scipio Africanus. The Roman state had learned that it now had the potential to be the pre-eminent power in the Mediterranean world, and not merely a powerful city in the Italian Peninsula.

For their defeat at Zama, the Carthaginians paid a heavy toll to Rome: they were obliged to pay huge war reparations, forfeit their commercial empire, and dismantle their once powerful navy. Within 50 years, however, the Carthaginians were again on the rise, and when a neighbouring kingdom in North Africa became fearful, it appealed to Rome for help.

Rome then waged war against Carthage for the last time. Remembering their incredible losses at Cannae and elsewhere, the Romans utterly destroyed the city of Carthage. Thanks to a historian named Polybius, who was present at the destruction of Carthage, we have a record of the words spoken by the commanding Roman general, Publius Scipio Aemilianus, grandson of Scipio Africanus: "We have made a desert and called it peace."

Hannibal, one of Rome's most formidable adversaries

Eastern Expansion and its Consequences

The Greek world in the eastern Mediterranean also experienced the power of the Republic's armies. After the death of Alexander the Great in 323 BCE, there were squabbles among the inheritors of his empire: the kingdoms of Antigonus (Greece and Macedonia), Seleucus (Asia Minor), and Ptolemy (Egypt and eastern Libya). Added to this explosive mixture were the pirates in the Adriatic Sea. All of this put Roman trading and maritime commerce at risk.

The Romans had no particular desire to become embroiled in the politics of the Greek world. The state had its hands full with Carthage. Nevertheless, matters came to a head when a senatorial deputation that arrived in Corinth in 147 BCE was treated badly, and Rome could not tolerate the insults of the Greeks. In 146 BCE, an attack was mounted against Corinth — the city was razed and plundered. Romans would later equate the destruction of that wealthy city and the theft of its treasures in fine art and opulent furnishings with the beginning of decadence and a love of luxury in their own city.

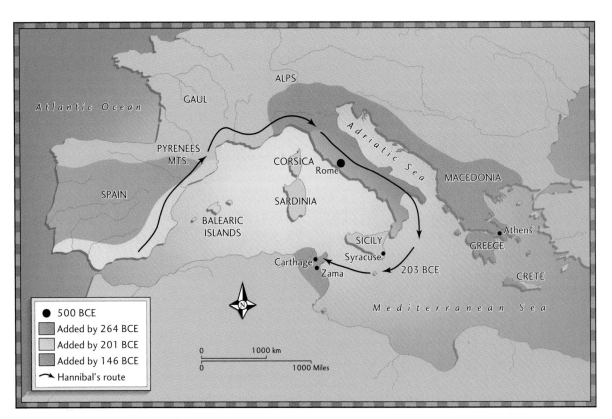

■ **Roman Territory 500-146 BCE**

1. **During which period of time did Rome expand the most?**

2. **Which of the regions conquered by Alexander were affected by Roman expansion?**

A Typical Roman Settlement

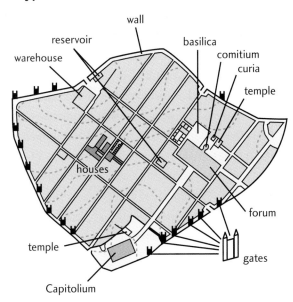

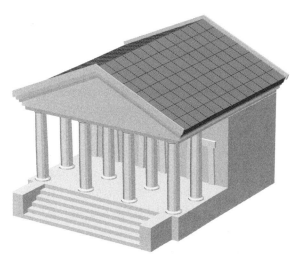

With each new settlement, came a new government, modelled on that of Rome, the mother city. With a new government, came the need for buildings to accommodate the public functions and services the government maintained. Public buildings would also follow models found in Rome. The essential public buildings of a typical Roman settlement are outlined below.

Forum (Town Square): The less official heart of a town. Like the Forum Romanum in Rome itself, it was a place for making business deals, meeting people, settling legal matters, buying and selling, and even such entertainment as staging plays or gladiator fights.

Basilica (Covered Hall): This was essentially a covered forum and had the same purpose — shops, businesses, and legal functions.

Curia (Senate House): Leading citizens of the settlement would meet in the curia to discuss important issues.

Comitium (Assembly Place): This was a circular area where the popular assembly and citizenry would meet and vote.

Capitolium (Capitol): This was a temple dedicated to Jupiter, the chief god of the Roman state. Like the Temple of Jupiter Optimus Maximus in Rome, the Capitolium was placed on a high podium fronting onto the forum. Inside it was divided into three cellae (sanctuaries) for the cult statues of Jupiter, Juno, and Minerva. There were also other temples dedicated to lesser deities.

For many, the capture of Corinth marked the loss of innocence and the passing of old Roman virtue. Today, we do not see this as a loss of innocence so much as the natural outcome of Roman imperialism and the inevitable influence of a relatively advanced culture on its conquerors.

Expansion and Colonization in Italy

As an important step in the Romanization of the Italian Peninsula, and a model for the subsequent domination of the rest of Europe, *coloniae* (colonies) were created in strategic places where there was no existing population. These colonies were composed of full Roman citizens who could be counted on to support the interests of the Roman regime. As often as not, the inhabitants of the colonies were recently discharged soldiers or members of the urban poor who had exchanged their impoverished occupation for a tract of land and the benefits of a rural existence. After the construction of the first paved road leading out of Rome, the *Via Appia* (Appian Way), colonies were planted throughout the Italian Peninsula south of the Po River during the third century BCE. Examples were Cosa in the northwest and Venusium (modern Venosa) in the wild interior of southern Italy, a colony that became an important Roman presence during the conquest of southern Italy and the subsequent opposition to Hannibal in 216 BCE.

Conflict at Home: Dissatisfaction in the Republic

There was a widening gulf between the landowning rich and the urban poor, who had no means to support themselves. A reformer named Tiberius Gracchus, elected tribune of the people in 133 BCE, thought he knew how to solve the problems of the urban poor. Earlier, much of the public land had been seized quite illegally by richer members of the Roman populace, so Tiberius set about redistributing land. A Land Commission was set up to distribute ten hectare plots.

Tiberius Gracchus, however, overstepped his authority. He announced that he would seek re-election as tribune, which was unheard of. His action instigated a riot by the angry, landowning senators in Rome. Some 300 people were killed, among them Tiberius himself. Nevertheless, the Land Commission continued to function and about 80 000 people from the city were resettled.

Tiberius's brother, Gaius Gracchus, was elected tribune in 123 BCE. He too was a zealous reformer and believed he had the answer to the problems of the conflicting interests of the population. First, to satisfy the urban poor, he instituted a free, monthly supply of grain. Second, in an attempt to meet the needs of the landless poor and not offend the Senate, he proposed new colonies at Capua, Taranto, and Carthage, cities that had been destroyed during the Punic Wars and so were available for resettlement. Lastly, he proposed a package of moderate compromises to give some rights to the non-Roman population. All Roman citizens were offended by this either on moral or religious grounds, or because they feared the loss of their privileges. Given this almost unanimous opposition, Gaius Gracchus made no progress with his proposals and succeeded only in incurring the wrath of the public. He was declared a public enemy in 121 BCE, and along with 3000 of his supporters, was attacked by a mob and killed.

The attempts made by the Gracchus brothers to bring greater political harmony to the Roman state had come to nothing. Eventually, over the course of the next hundred years, the state's inability to bridge the gulf between rich and poor and to come to grips with the Republic's new-found wealth and increasing commercialism led to its downfall.

Citizenship in Italy

In the aftermath of the failed attempts at reform, the free population of the Italian, non-Roman communities (which were located throughout the peninsula, especially to the south of the Po River) felt increasingly isolated from decisions affecting their welfare. Eventually, their resentment of Rome came to a boil. It was not that the Italians, as they called themselves, wanted to replace Rome but rather what they wanted was a share of the privileges that came with Roman citizenship.

The privileges of citizenship were significant. For example, a full Roman citizen was protected in Roman civil law from the arbitrary exercise of power by a Roman magistrate. A child born to a Roman citizen was also a Roman citizen if the father had the legal right (*conubium*) to marry the mother. Roman citizens enjoyed a favourable tax status and, with expansion overseas, were exempted from paying tribute in Italy. Finally, and high on the list of privileges, was the fact that any slave freed by a full Roman citizen was himself automatically a Roman citizen, although always dependent by law on his benefactor.

A bitter Social War broke out in 90 BCE. The Romans retained the upper hand and suppressed the uprising of the non-Roman Italians in 89 BCE. At the same time, they made several concessions. Later, after Julius Caesar's invasion of Italy south of the Rubicon in 49 BCE, the whole Italian Peninsula would gain full Roman citizenship and, under the Emperor Caracalla in 212 CE, all free males within the Empire were granted citizenship. By that time, however, provincial Roman citizens had lost their tax exemptions.

REPUBLICAN LAW AND LEGISLATION

Rome was among the very few societies in the ancient world to develop laws that were codified (officially written down) and analyzed in detail by professional jurists. The history of Roman law begins very early in the Republic, with the Twelve Tables in 450 BCE (which consisted of only a few sentences), and reaches its maturity with the legislation of the Emperor Justinian in 528–534 CE, the *Corpus Juris Civilis*, with over a million words! Latin was the language of law throughout the Roman world, even in the Greek-speaking east. The

judicial history of the Republic can be divided into two periods: a relatively primitive period ending in the third century BCE, and the later Republican period when a legal profession evolved, beginning around 200 BCE and ending with the victory of Augustus in 31 CE. Similarly, historians of Roman law identify two major legal divisions, not originally distinguishable: civil law and criminal law. To a great degree, Roman criminal law, in which the community acted for the sake of the public interest, sprung from an original tradition of the taking of private revenge. Theft, for example, was originally a private matter for civil action and only much later became the subject of criminal prosecution. Also, whereas in our society the law does not distinguish between the status of the individuals (rich or poor, male or female), a fundamental aspect of Roman law made that distinction. For example, there was not only a distinction between free people and slaves, there were also categories of free people, who were treated differently according to their status.

The Twelve Tables

According to tradition, pressure by the ordinary people led to the appointment of a board of ten men with consular power in 451 BCE, established for the writing down of statutes. This was to break the monopolization of the law by the patricians and priestly elite. Ten tables were compiled, with two added the following year. The tables originally included a law banning marriage between patricians and plebeians, but it was quickly struck down in 445 BCE. Most of the contents of the Twelve Tables, not formally abolished until the sixth century CE, were related to civil matters. Essentially, the Twelve Tables formed a list of basic legal procedures and appropriate punishments.

Excerpts from the Twelve Tables

Table IV. Paternal Power

1. A notably deformed child shall be killed immediately.

Table V. Inheritance and Guardianship

1. Women, even though they are of full age, because of their levity [lightness] of mind shall be under guardianship ...

Review...Recall...Reflect

1. How did the structure of the Roman Republican government attempt to balance power between the patricians and the plebeians?

2. List three reasons Rome sought to establish colonies throughout the Mediterranean.

3. What reforms did the Gracchus brothers attempt to implement? Why were they unsuccessful?

THE DECLINE OF THE ROMAN REPUBLIC

Military Reform and the Rise of Roman Generals

The formation of the Roman citizen army can be attributed to Gaius Marius (ca. 155–86 BCE) in 100 BCE. Throughout all of previous Roman history, soldiers had been farmers who tilled their fields, sowed their grain, and then went off to war when necessary. The campaigning season ended in the fall, always in time for the soldiers to return home to gather their harvest.

Seasonal campaigning had become a problem by Marius's time. Now, there were not as many citizen soldiers who owned land left in Rome. Grain, therefore, was becoming scarcer. The scarcer the grain, the more essential it was for the soldiers who did own land to return to their fields in the fall. At the same time, there were now many landless people normally resident in the city and these people had less reason to return home in the fall.

Marius realized the size of the problem and created a standing army. A standing army is a permanent force, not one recruited only to meet a particular need. Marius also gave his soldiers a fixed term of service — 16 years in the ranks and four years as a *veteranus* (reserve soldier) — with the possibility of being called up if needed. After his term of service, the soldier retired with a pension, a gratuity (fixed sum of money), or a plot of land — and he was now allowed to marry.

The new conditions of service, including regular pay, the provision of food, and clothing allowances, were only part of the more sweeping rearrangements that now affected "Marius's Mules," as the men were called. (This name came about because each man had to carry a standard, minimum amount of equipment when on the march.) Soldiers now served in re-formed legions and, with a new *aquila* (the eagle insignia), began to develop a fierce pride in belonging to a particular unit.

The legion was now a heavy infantry unit of about 6000 men, broken into smaller subdivisions called *cohorts*. There were ten cohorts to a legion with the first and most experienced cohort having a double complement of soldiers. Each cohort had approximately 480 men. These units were further divided into six smaller and more manageable units called *centuries* with 80 men to a century; each century reported to a *centurion*, the equivalent of a sergeant. The ultimate division was the *contubernium* of eight men sharing one tent. There were ten contubernia to a century and two centuries to a maniple.

The Structure of a Roman Legion

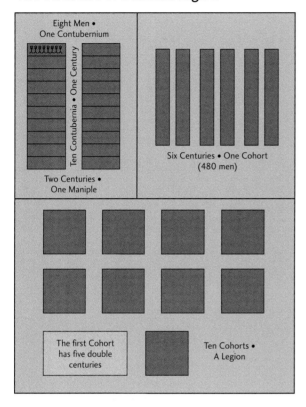

The result of these complicated arrangements was that a recruit would begin his service in the most junior century of the most junior cohort of a legion. As he gained experience, the soldier could work his way through the ranks to the *primus pilus*, the centurion commanding the first century of the first cohort. Another advantage of this arrangement was that the legion, with its smaller divisions, was easily deployed. The major drawback of the military hierarchy was that ordinary soldiers looked to their generals rather than to the state for security and pensions. By the first century BCE, these were "Sulla's legions" or "Marius's legions," not Rome's legions.

From Pompey to Caesar

By now, Romans understood that any man backed by either a powerful army or a band of ruthless, armed thugs could usurp the constitutional government. In quick succession, three men — Pompey the Great (Gnaeus Pompeius Magnus, 106–48 BCE), Crassus (Marcus Licinius Crassus, 115–53 BCE), and Julius Caesar (Gaius Julius Caesar, 100–44 BCE) — came to power. These men were all military adventurers who cared nothing for the Republican constitution by which they had prospered. According to their own private arrangement, they split the government of Rome among themselves in 60 BCE and formed the First Triumvirate, the Rule of the Three Men.

Caesar had the armies of Northern Italy. He set about gaining military glory by subjugating the entire population of what is now southern Germany, France, Switzerland, and parts of Austria. Crassus first did his part in Italy by crushing the bloody slave rebellion led by Spartacus in 71 BCE. Six thousand of this ex-gladiator's followers were crucified in a line flanking the Via Appia. Crassus then went off to campaign in Persia (modern-day Iran) against the Parthians. Pompey was already covered in glory from his vanquishing of the pirates in the Mediterranean Sea (67 BCE).

Still, no private arrangement could outlive ambition. Crassus was defeated by the Parthians at Carrhae and killed in 53 BCE. Pompey, having become the fervent guardian of senatorial privilege, came to oppose Caesar and agreed with a senatorial demand in 50 BCE that Caesar disband his army. Caesar realized that disbanding his army would leave him defenceless and would amount to suicide. He committed an illegal act, and in January 49 BCE crossed the stream known as the Rubicon with his army and therefore entered Italian territory. Pompey hurried to the defence of the constitutional, senatorial government but was beaten back on all fronts. He was forced to retreat to Alexandria in Egypt, where his army was defeated and he was decapitated.

In 46 BCE, Julius Caesar, the last surviving member of the Triumvirate, had himself appointed dictator for ten years. In 45 BCE, the appointment was extended to life. In the same year, he became *Pontifex Maximus* (Chief Priest) and assumed virtually all responsibility for decision making. Caesar was now behaving more like a king than a guardian of the Republic. He was even offered a

golden crown by a young supporter named Marc Antony (Marcus Antonius, 93–30 BCE). Caesar's glory was short-lived. On 15 March 44 BCE, a day known as the Ides of March, several self-proclaimed defenders of liberty — Brutus, Cassius, and other senate conspirators — converged on the dictator in Pompey's theatre and stabbed him to death.

DAILY LIFE IN THE REPUBLIC

Beliefs

During the 500 years since the fall of the Etruscan monarchy, the Roman people had developed superstitions, institutions, and modes of living. These practices and beliefs helped them, even in difficult times, to maintain a distinct identity and a cultural integrity. The Romans were among the most superstitious people the world had seen to that point. They essentially adopted the entire pantheon of Greek Olympian gods and created a remarkable synthesis of Greek, Roman, and Etruscan deities. In addition to the major gods, the Romans also believed in minor deities, werewolves, and all forms of magic. From the Etruscans, the Romans inherited the dark arts of laying curses, casting spells, and foretelling the future. Indeed, all public acts, including military operations and elections, were preceded by the taking of auspices (signs or omens from nature) to determine whether or not the gods approved. From their contacts with the East, the Romans also absorbed astrology and a belief in the signs of the zodiac.

The official religions came under the supervision of the Pontifex Maximus and were administered by several different colleges of priests who were all members of the senatorial elite. Naturally, the

As Pontifex Maximus, Julius Caesar introduced what would be his most famous and lasting reform on 1 January 45 BCE — the Julian Calendar. This was meant to bring the civil year into line with the solar year, which were approximately three months out of synchronicity. This calendar was used for some 15 centuries, until the reforms of Pope Gregory XII in February 1582. Even today, members of certain eastern European and Greek Christian faiths adhere to the Julian Calendar to determine the dates of their religious feast days.

Pontifex Maximus was a man of great political influence, one of the duties of which was to be in charge of the Roman calendar. This originally was simply an ordering of the months and days when the various deities were to be honoured.

Do ut des — "I give so that you might give" — was an elementary principle in Roman religion. This means honouring and placating gods, or seeking their help in times of crisis, through animal sacrifice. A particular favourite was known as *suovetaurilia*, the simultaneous sacrifice of a pig, sheep, and ox.

Principal Deities of the Roman World

Apollo — Son of Jupiter; god of poetry and peace
Bacchus — God of wine and ecstasy
Diana — Goddess of hunting and fertility
Janus — God of beginnings and endings. January became the first month of the year in 153 BCE.
Jupiter — Father of the gods and chief deity
Juno — Wife of Jupiter and goddess of marriage
Mars — God of war
Venus — Goddess of love
Mercury — God of liars and thieves; messenger of the gods
Minerva — Goddess of wisdom

Family Life and Morality

The Roman Republic was based on the family unit, the building block of society. The head of the household, the male *paterfamilias*, originally held complete power over his wife, children, and slaves. This included the legal right to abuse or even to kill. He was endowed, above all, with *potestas*, legally recognized and absolute power. He also was expected to maintain a public appearance marked by *gravitas* (conservatism) and *dignitas* (dignified status), and usually, *severitas* (the ability not to shrink from harsh justice).

Inheritance of property was the most important element in Republican life. The state consisted of families that were linked to each other in *gentes* (clans). Anything that endangered the integrity of the family was met with the harshest punishment.

Since inheritance was through the male line, adoption was a regular feature of society. On occasion, younger men even adopted older men. Affection was personal; adoption was not. Men whose wives repeatedly gave birth to daughters (a state of affairs believed to be the woman's fault) could divorce and remarry at will. Julius Caesar, who had several wives, was obliged to adopt in his will the young Octavian (the future Emperor Augustus), the son of his niece Atia.

Even though marriage was entered into as a duty rather than as an expression of love, often with neither partner having freedom of choice, marital harmony and the development of spousal affection was the norm for Roman couples. Children, especially male children, were cared for well. Of

The marriage of this Roman-Egyptian couple was probably arranged by their parents.

Rites of Passage

Portraits for Posterity: Death, Art and Ancestors

The Romans followed an ancient practice of creating wax death masks of the just deceased. At the funeral of a prominent, usually male, family member, the masks of the deceased, sometimes coloured to look like flesh, were paraded along with the funeral procession. Often the masks would be worn by family members who were most like the deceased in size and build. The family then kept the masks as we would a photo, a portrait-like remembrance of the departed. The masks were highly prized links to venerable ancestors, often preserved in special shrines or family altars. The masks would sometimes be brought out for other family funerals, out of respect for all the ancestors.

Early in the first century BCE, the respectful record was transformed into a more permanent, and ultimately artistic, display of ancient lineage. The most noble families of Rome started to have their death masks duplicated in marble. The busts and statues that were carved were done in a style known as verism (from the Latin for truth), a realistic style that showed the subject with all the wrinkles, furrows, and imperfections that come with age and experience.

The statue shown here is of a Roman patrician carrying the heads of his ancestors, probably his father and grandfather. All three seem to have been captured at about the same age. It is difficult to imagine better examples of what Romans meant by *paterfamilias* and the public appearance of *gravitas, dignitas, and severitas*. Notice that all three men appear distinguished, authoritative, and wise. This is partially due to the realistic sculpting of their receding hairlines, prominent cheekbones, furrows, and the set of the mouth. These characteristics were accentuated in the portrait heads out of respect and admiration for the ancestors.

Members of the Roman patrician class were the only ones allowed to display figures of their ancestors at funerals. How do people today commemorate members of their family?

Activities

1. If you were to have a portrait done for posterity, how would you like to be portrayed? What pose would capture your personality?

2. Pick a character trait that society admires today. Create a collage to illustrate that trait.

course, as in any society where inheritance of property is paramount, the legitimacy of offspring was of equal concern. A newborn infant had to be recognized by its father. Often, if an infant was not recognized by its father, it would be exposed, or abandoned, in a public place. A childless person could then take the infant for his or her own. Otherwise, the baby would be left to die.

Education

Male and female children of elite Republican families were raised together until puberty, usually by a nurse and family tutor. From approximately age seven to 11, children learned to read and write Latin; some were even taught Greek. Then, from about age 12 to 15, both boys and girls were given a liberal education in language and literature; girls always received instruction at home, while boys could be taught in public. At age 16, boys normally went on to study rhetoric (logical and persuasive argument) at public lectures. During the Republic, students kept regular hours of instruction, had vacations, and did homework. We even know the names of some schoolteachers (*grammatici*), such as Orbilius, the harsh taskmaster of the famous poet Horace. At the onset of manhood, a youth was introduced to public life. He was formally led to the Forum Romanum dressed in the toga of manhood. After this ceremony, the youth was expected to pursue a career in the law courts or army.

Young men were expected to serve the interests of state first and themselves last, in accordance with the interests of the dominant elite. These included the continuation of the clan, material and financial comfort, and the attainment of *gloria*. In such an exclusive system, children of the poorer sectors of society received no education at all.

In addition to language and literature, girls were instructed in the arts of singing and dancing, and in the crafts of spinning and weaving, thought to exemplify old Republican virtues. These virtues are honoured on an old Republican gravestone that reads, "*casa fuit; domum servavit; lanam fecit*" (she was chaste; she kept the house; she worked the wool). This system of education ensured the stability of the social order in Rome by teaching the children of the upper classes about their privileges and responsibilities to the state.

The Role of Women

Girls were usually educated in the home or sent to elementary school until they were married. Upon marriage, Roman women gained an independence that their earlier Greek sisters would have envied. Apart from the duty to bear children, marriage brought the ability to leave the house to go shopping, attend to business, and accompany one's husband to dinner. The normal age of marriage seems to have been about 15. There were two forms of marriage: the most ancient transferred the authority of the father to the husband. This marriage *in manum* (into the power) was conducted according to ancient rituals, of which the most common was a symbolic sale wherein the father sold the daughter to the bridegroom.

The other form of marriage came to be the most popular by the end of the Republic. This was *usus* (cohabitation). A couple stated their intention to live together in a married state and as long as they lived together, they were married. Divorce was simple: all one partner had to do was send a messenger to the other telling him or her to take their belongings away. In this form of marriage, *sine manu* (without power), the woman remained legally subject to her father as long as he was alive.

Continuing the family line was the main purpose of marriage. At about 15 years of age, a girl could expect a fairly rapid introduction to her responsibilities. Children as young as 12 suffered the risks of carrying babies in their immature bodies. Since male children were preferred, a woman could expect multiple pregnancies until she delivered a boy who was likely to survive. During the early Empire, families with three or more children were rewarded by the state.

This wall painting from Pompeii (ca. 20 BCE) shows a woman pouring perfume from a tiny pot. How does this painting differ from the figures on Greek vases you have seen?

Women could own property and engage in business activities. Occasionally, they even sponsored public buildings and were important people in their own right. During the Republic and much of the history of the Roman Empire, though excluded from the male political sphere, women exercised great influence.

Latin Language and Literature

Language

The Romans spoke Latin, the language of their neighbours to the south, in modern-day Lazio. As the Romans became dominant, the other local languages of the Italian Peninsula, such as Etruscan, soon died out. Only the Greek cities in southern Italy retained much of their own language. From the early years of the Republic, we have only a very few small scraps of Latin, usually on gravestones or other inscriptions. The Latin of those early centuries seems to have been rough and unsophisticated.

The favourite writing materials were papyrus, made from an Egyptian reed plant that grew in the Nile Delta swamplands, and later, parchment, the skin of goat or sheep (*membrana*). Papyrus was sold either in long rolls of 20 sheets that were sun-dried then glued together, or as individual sheets. For less formal writing, such as messages, wax tablets (*tabelli*) were used. The writer would scratch a message on the wax with a sharpened writing implement called a *stylus*. Once the message had been received and read, the recipient would scrape the wax smooth and write a return message.

For writing on papyrus or parchment, pens dipped in ink were used. The pens could be made of copper alloy, though often they were simply sharpened reeds or goose quills. The ink was made from several substances such as soot, resin, and the excretions of squid or cuttlefish. Care had to be taken not to dilute the ink too much, which would make it too faint to read. Writing errors could easily be erased with a clean, wet sponge.

Literature

In Republican literature, Ennius (239–169 BCE) stands out for his attempt to provide a year-by-year account of Rome's developing power. This account, the *Annales*, was in verse because in the earlier stages of the development of a literature, when there is a heavier reliance on memory than the written record, verse (which is easier to remember than prose) was more commonly used.

There are many people, mostly men, known to us by name through large or small fragments of their work. From the period before 133 BCE, two writers of comedy are known to us: Titus Maccius Plautus (?–184 BCE) — more commonly known as Plautus — and Publius Terentius Afer (195–159 BCE) — more commonly known as Terence. We are fortunate to have many complete plays by them. Peopled by stock characters such as love-sick youths, cunning slaves, prostitutes, and grasping old men, these plays have had an enormous influence on the development of Western drama, including the works of Shakespeare. Since plays were not considered good for public morality, there was no permanent theatre in Rome until Pompey the Great had his stone theatre built in 55 BCE.

In the first century BCE, literacy in Latin and Greek became common among the elite. All sorts of people committed their thoughts to writing, such as the philosopher Lucretius (T. Lucretius Carus, 94–55 BCE), who wrote *On the Nature of Things*, an epic poem describing his theories on existence and ethical behaviour.

Cicero (Marcus Tullius Cicero, 106–43 BCE), one of the most famous Romans, was a prolific philosopher, writer, consul, and staunch defender of the Republic. As an orator, Cicero defended notable Romans and prosecuted others in the courts. As a defender of the idea of constitutional government, Cicero was bitterly opposed to Marc Antony, whom he attacked in his published speeches, the *Philippics*. Eventually, in 43 BCE, he was killed by Marc Antony for his outspokenness.

Known to both Cicero and Julius Caesar was the poet Catullus (Gaius Valerius Catullus, ca. 84–47 BCE). Catullus was known for his lampooning and abusive attacks, and although some of his poetry would be considered obscene even today, on the whole, it is entertaining and skillfully created. For example:

> I hate and I love
> well, why do I, you probably ask
> I don't know, but I know it's happening
> and it hurts.

Latin, for the next thousand years and more, was first and foremost the language of the Roman government and the legal system. After the Empire had transformed into a number of successor kingdoms in the mid-sixth century CE, Latin continued to spread and was confirmed as the international language of the Christian church, of education, and of scholarship (e.g., Isaac Newton's *Principia Mathematica*, 1687). Latin still has a strong presence in the language of medicine and law, and is still taught and studied in most universities of the Western world.

WEB CONNECTION

http://www.mcgrawhill.ca/links/echoes

Go to the web site above to find out more about the writings of Cicero.

Pushing the Boundaries: Developments in Science and Technology

Concrete: Bigger, Better Buildings

Although the Roman Empire itself fell apart, many of its feats of engineering and architecture did not. For that, we can thank concrete, a Roman invention that altered forever the way we approach both the design and construction of large architectural structures. Concrete is strong, versatile, waterproof, and fire-resistant. While the formulas for mixing different types of concrete have changed somewhat over the centuries, we apply the same basic techniques in concrete construction today as the Romans did when they invented it around the third century BCE.

The idea of concrete emerged as a result of a few different factors. Ancient Romans had a deep appreciation for all things Greek, so many of their structures were similar to, or elaborations of, Greek architecture. Their pursuit of Greek style, however, was limited by resources. The beautiful marble used in Greek construction was not as easily available in the area around Rome. Importing materials was costly and time-consuming. Somehow, the Romans discovered that they could make economical use of a mixture of materials close at hand: lime, mortar, gravel, and rubble. With these materials, solid, strong but not very attractive walls and arches could be constructed and then covered with decorative brick, stone, marble, tile, or plaster. Originally, these facings probably also served as a frame for the first crude versions of concrete.

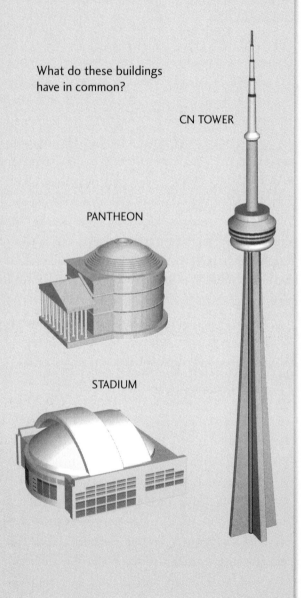

What do these buildings have in common?

CN TOWER

PANTHEON

STADIUM

The real breakthrough in concrete came when the Romans realized that adding volcanic ash (pozzolana) to lime and sand created superior concrete that would even set under water. Imagine the possibilities for sewers, bridges, and aqueducts. Once the Romans had settled on this formula, their architecture seemed to know no limits. In terms of mass, for example, the Colosseum in Rome is one of the largest single buildings anywhere. With its concrete core and kilometres of vaulted corridors, it could hold more than 50 000 spectators in its day. The lofty dome of the Pantheon, measuring 43.2 m in diameter and 43.2 m high, remained unsurpassed until the nineteenth century. The dome remains an inspiration for engineers and architects even today.

Activities

1. Think of the advantages of concrete building construction. Are there any disadvantages to the use of concrete?

2. List famous buildings or buildings in your city that seem inspired by the Roman style of large-scale concrete structures.

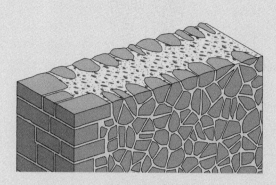

OPUS INCERTUM

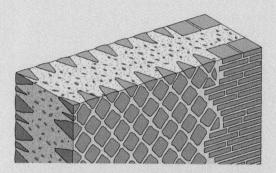

OPUS RETICULATUM

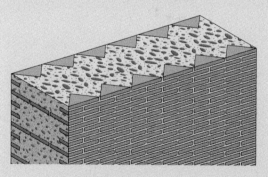

OPUS TESTACEUM

These techniques of facing or framing concrete had a number of advantages: they utilized materials at hand and had unprecedented strength. The materials were a lot less expensive than marble, and relatively unskilled labourers could handle the work.

ROMAN REPUBLICAN ART AND ARCHITECTURE

Rome was born with no strong art tradition of its own. Roman art in the early years was heavily influenced by the Etruscans until Rome's expansion into the Greek-speaking areas of Sicily and southern Italy. This contact brought a huge rise in interest in Greek sculpture and many statues were imported to the capital. The Roman appetite for all forms of Greek art — architecture, sculpture, paintings, silver plate — increased even more with conquests in Greece itself, and particularly with the capture of Corinth in 146 BCE.

Conquering generals could acquire art by plunder, but it had to be bought by the elite in Rome. In the second century BCE, to serve a booming market, there was not only a huge influx of all forms of art, but also the immigration of large numbers of Greek artists themselves. We know several artists by name: the Athenian painter Metrodoros, Demetrios the Alexandrian who painted maps, and the southern Italian sculptor Pasiteles. At the same time, in Athens and elsewhere, workshops were set up to create sculptures of mythological subjects based on earlier Greek models. These sculptural stories were imported by wealthy Romans and displayed in their gardens or reception areas (*atria*) of their homes.

In architecture, more than in the other arts, there was a fusion of the Roman and Greek cultures. The Greek style of peripteral temple (columns all around) was fused with the Italic tradition of a front-facing temple on a high podium. But while the style and structure of buildings in Rome owe a great deal to Greece, it was the Romans alone who gave the world one profoundly significant architectural gift — concrete.

This large wall painting is from the villa of Livia, wife of the Emperor Augustus. As if through a window, it shows a beautiful garden all around the room, with many identifiable plant and animal species.

THE END OF THE ROMAN REPUBLIC

The Roman Republic, a bold experiment begun in 509 BCE, eventually collapsed. At the outset, when the Etruscan monarchy was overthrown, true democracy had seemed possible. This possibility seemed to be strengthened by the fact that Rome's dealings with its neighbours had been generally fair, if often harsh. Strong divisions between the landowning and commercial elites, and the army reforms of Marius led to factional strife with the people supporting particular army chiefs, like Sulla, Pompey, or Caesar. In the Rome of the first few centuries BCE, if you were poor and without personal means of livelihood, you either starved or were reduced to slavery, or worse.

Under the Empire, things would get only slightly better for most Romans, who were tired of bloody civil wars. Augustus, the first emperor, consolidated his stranglehold on political and military power and claimed that he had restored the Republic. In reality, he was just the first in a long line of emperors that lasted until at least 476 CE. These emperors were in fact monarchs who relied on military power, moral authority, or perceived divine will to make their control of the known world legitimate. Whether or not Augustus and his successors were good emperors, their rule was absolute.

Review...Recall...Reflect

1. How did the rise of strong generals contribute to the demise of the Roman Republic?

2. How did life during the Roman Republic differ for males and females? Compare education, rights within marriage, and duties in the home.

3. Why is Roman architecture said to be a fusion of Greek style and Roman innovation?

History Continues to Unfold

Until fairly recently, much of the story of the Etruscan monarchy and the early Roman Republic supplied by the ancient historian Livy was more or less accepted as fact, or at least as a useful model given that there was no other. However, it is becoming increasingly clear that Livy's account is a less than reliable discussion of early Rome. There are no written records of any sort from earlier than the third century BCE, and even the date of the founding of Rome — 753 BCE — is a product of the first-century BCE. Archaeology is the most important key to understanding the remote past, and it is now clear that Roman society is much older and more complex than Livy led us to believe. A current trend in scholarship is to concentrate less on wars and alliances and more on social history, on how the ancient Roman people lived.

Current Research and Interpretations

Research into numismatics (coins), while still concentrating on the development and types of coinage, is now more about how a monetary economy, influenced by complex external realities, affected the Roman Republic and people's daily lives. Another, perhaps greater research effort is under way to understand ancient religious practices and the quite alien religious experience felt by the early Romans. Finally, in the field of Latin literature, much work is now being done on how it was affected by influences and models in the Greek world.

Chapter Review

Chapter Summary

In this chapter, we have seen:

- how ancient Rome developed a form of Republican government in an attempt to balance the needs of the patricians and the plebeians
- how the codifying of Roman laws in the Twelve Tables helped provide stability and continuity in Roman society
- the contribution the Roman Republic made to the development of the modern Western idea of citizenship
- that Rome experienced several different types of political leadership including monarchy, dictatorship, and democracy

Reviewing the Significance of Key People, Concepts, and Events (Knowledge/Understanding)

1. Understanding the early history of ancient Rome requires a knowledge of the following people, concepts, and events, and an understanding of their significance in the development of the Roman Republic. In your notes, identify and explain the historical significance of two from each column.

People	Concepts	Events
Etruscans	plebeians and patricians	Punic Wars
Romulus and Remus	SPQR	Battle of Zama
Tarquin the Proud	the Twelve Tables	
Hannibal	the First Triumvirate	
Scipio Africanus	the Appian Way	
Gracchus Brothers	Senate	
Julius Caesar		

2. How did Rome's location in the Italian Peninsula help to assure its dominance, first in Italy, and later throughout the Mediterranean?

3. Rome experienced many changes between its legendary founding in 753 BCE and the collapse of the Roman Republic. List three forces that tended to reinforce stability and continuity during the same period.

Doing History: Thinking About the Past (Thinking/Inquiry)

1. Explain how relations between Rome and other societies in the Mediterranean were shaped by trade and economic interchange. Consider the causes of the Punic Wars and the expansion of Rome.

   Connecting to the *World History Handbook*: Once you have completed your answer, transfer the main ideas to the graphic organizer "Relationships Between Societies" in your *World History Handbook*.

3. Between the founding of Rome in 753 BCE and the end of the Roman Republic, Rome experienced several different forms of government. For each of the following explain the basis of their authority: Etruscan Monarchy, Consuls of the Republic, the Gracchus Brothers, the First Triumvirate, and Julius Caesar.

Applying Your Learning (Application)

1. The role of women in Canada today is drastically different from that of the women of ancient Rome. Outline how the life of a typical teenage girl in Canada today differs from that of a Roman girl of the same age during the period of the Roman Republic.

   Connecting to the *World History Handbook*: Once you have completed your comparison, transfer some of the most important differences to the graphic organizer "Role of Women in Society" in your *World History Handbook*.

2. Imagine you have the opportunity to interview Hannibal, the great Carthaginian leader, following his daring journey through the Alps. Prepare four questions for Hannibal on his military strategies, his opinion of the Roman army, and his decision to cross the Alps. Give his possible responses to these questions.

Communicating Your Learning (Communication)

1. Roman culture and society were shaped by the influx of goods and ideas from many cultures. On a map of the Mediterranean, identify the goods and ideas that flowed into Rome from the surrounding cultures. Using broad arrows and labels, indicate what was imported (foods, art, ideas, etc.) and the origins of the goods or ideas.

2. Prepare a political cartoon that demonstrates your understanding of the role of the First Triumvirate in bringing about political change during the final years of the Roman Republic. Be sure your cartoon clearly expresses a point of view.

The Roman Empire

By the end of this chapter, you will be able to:

- *explain how ancient Rome was able to establish its dominance throughout the Mediterranean*

- *describe how the Pax Romana helped to create a sense of stability and continuity in ancient times*

- *demonstrate an understanding of the role of Jesus in the development of world religious traditions*

- *assess the form of economic organization that existed throughout the Roman world*

The four Emperors of the Roman Empire, ca. 305 CE, shown in carved porphyry, a hard stone from Egypt. The rulers are shown embracing to convey the ideas of unity and harmony within the empire.

The militaristic and imperialistic attitudes of the late Republican leaders continued in their successors. Indeed, the values of the high Roman Empire were very much the same as those of the Republic. While there was a slowly increasing respect for the rule of law, how a man retained ultimate power over his extended family (*patria potestas*) remained essentially as it had been during the Republic. Only in the later Empire were there attempts to change Roman society's structures and values. These attempts were largely the result of the adoption of Christianity as the official state religion by Constantine the Great in the early fourth century CE. In the closing decades of the first century BCE, the rule of the generals continued, characterized by personal loyalties to army commanders such as Pompey and Caesar.

Roman peace (Pax Romana) would last more than 200 years, until invading tribes began challenging Roman supremacy in Europe and North Africa. From the north came Goths, Visigoths, Vandals, and Huns, weakening the already divided Empire. By 293 CE, it was possible for an emperor who had never been to Rome to break the rule of the Roman Empire in two, and two again, as four men were needed to do the job. In the end, the Western Roman Empire did not fall so much as disappear. The Eastern Empire, with fewer pressures from outside, a new religion to inspire it, and the reassertion of Roman Law, was transformed into the civilization of Byzantium.

KEY WORDS

Principate

The Diaspora

manumission

barbarian

KEY PEOPLE

Augustus

Virgil

Nero

Hadrian

Jesus

Julia Domna

Diocletian

Constantine

Visigoths

Theoderic the Great

VOICES FROM THE PAST

Carpe diem, quam minimum credula postero

(Seize the day, put no trust in tomorrow)
Horace, *Odes*

TIME LINE: THE ROMAN EMPIRE

	15 March 44 BCE	Assassination of Julius Caesar
Second Triumvirate is formed, consisting of Marc Antony, Octavian (later Augustus), and Lepidus	43 BCE	
	30 BCE	Antony and Cleopatra commit suicide, leaving Octavian as sole ruler of the Roman world
Octavian adopts the semi-divine name Augustus	27 BCE	
	14 CE	Death of Augustus
Jesus is crucified	30 CE	
	64 CE	The Great Fire of Rome destroys much of the city
In response to Jewish uprisings, the Romans destroy the Temple in Jerusalem	70 CE	
	79 CE	Volcanic eruption of Mount Vesuvius buries Pompeii and Herculaneum
Emperor Titus opens the Roman Colosseum	80 CE	
	98–117 CE	Under Emperor Trajan, the Roman Empire expands to its greatest extent
Emperor Caracalla extends citizenship to all free men in the Roman Empire	212 CE	
	293 CE	Emperor Diocletian divides the Empire into two parts, East and West
Sunday is formally made a day of worship by Emperor Constantine I	321 CE	
	325 CE	Constantine I outlaws gladiator battles
Emperor Theodosius bans all pagan worship	391 CE	
	451 CE	Under Attila, Huns attack the Roman Empire, invading Italy in 452 CE
End of the Roman Empire in the West	476 CE	
	493 CE	Theoderic the Great becomes the first Gothic ruler of the Italian Peninsula

FROM REPUBLIC TO EMPIRE

After the assassination of Julius Caesar on 15 March 44 BCE, the Roman Republic was ravaged by civil war. A great power struggle ensued involving Caesar's adopted son Octavian, Marc Antony (Marcus Antonius), and a third powerful man named Lepidus (M. Lepidus). The struggle was quickly resolved and in November 43 BCE, these men formed another alliance called the Second Triumvirate. To further complicate matters, a son of Pompey the Great, Sextus Pompey (Sextus Pompeius), now essentially ruled the waters of the western Mediterranean Sea.

In 40 BCE, at Brindisi in southern Italy, the Triumvirate divided the Republic among themselves: Antony took the east, Octavian the west, and Lepidus took Africa. The pact was sealed with the marriage of Octavian's sister to Marc Antony. Within five years, the Second Triumvirate was renewed, although by this time, Lepidus had been pushed out of power and given the position of *Pontifex Maximus* (Chief Priest). In fact, Lepidus went into internal exile south of Rome and did not even properly perform the functions of his office.

Antony and Cleopatra

In 36 BCE, Octavian's admiral, Marcus Agrippa, defeated Sextus Pompey in a naval battle. In the same year, Marc Antony met, fell in love with, and married the ruler of Egypt, Cleopatra, a descendant of Ptolemy and former lover of Julius Caesar, with whom she had a child named Caesarion (Ptolemy Caesar). Marc Antony and Cleopatra, by all accounts, were motivated by sheer romantic love, despite the fact that Marc Antony already had a Roman wife.

Queen Cleopatra, who ruled Egypt from 51 BCE, was the last monarch of the last dynasty of Egypt, the Ptolemaic. She committed suicide in 31 BCE after she and her Roman lover Marc Antony were defeated by Octavian at the Battle of Actium.

By 34 BCE, Marc Antony and Cleopatra had guardianship of Caesarion and three children of their own (a girl and two boys). Together, this infatuated and politically unrealistic pair unilaterally divided the rule of the Roman East between themselves and their children. This division was more theoretical than real — the children were very young and the inhabitants and kings of the Eastern world had not been consulted. On 2 September 31 BCE, Octavian, with Agrippa as admiral, defeated the combined forces of Antony and Cleopatra at the Battle of Actium off the west coast of the Peloponnese. Within the year, Antony and Cleopatra had committed suicide and Caesarion, who posed a political threat, was put to death. The civil wars were over and Octavian was master of the Roman world.

The Age of Augustus

In an ingenious act, Octavian announced to the Senate in January 27 BCE that he was formally returning the Republic to the control of the Senate and the Roman people. For this, he was awarded the semi-divine name **Augustus**. He also redistributed all the provinces, keeping those with large armies for himself, and allowing the Senate to retain control over those with less military might. Augustus maintained Egypt as his personal domain.

Augustus tightened his grip on the Roman world. In 23 BCE, he increased his powers by becoming Tribune of the People, thus bridging respect for the rights of the ordinary Roman and the aristocratic, senatorial control of the late Republic. Augustus again expanded his powers in 12 BCE, when he assumed the position of Pontifex Maximus after the death of Lepidus. Unlike Lepidus, Augustus took this role very seriously, taking advantage of the importance of religion to the Romans. With decision-making power in all of Rome's religious matters, Augustus cleverly portrayed himself as quasi-divine — a descendant of Venus herself. Abroad and even in Italy, he linked the worship of Rome as a spiritual entity with a concept of his own supernatural being. In Italy, Julius Caesar (Augustus's adoptive father) was deified. In the

The exotic landscape and wildlife along the Nile River were popular subjects for Roman paintings and mosaics, like this one from the first century BCE. Augustus himself took a personal interest in Egypt. What makes scenes like this valuable to us as more than art?

This sculpture identifies Augustus in his role of Pontifex Maximus, the chief priest of Rome. Wearing his toga draped over his head like this indicates his priestly function.

Greek world, Augustus was worshipped as the new Zeus. Now, the power of Augustus was enhanced by the almost godlike aura he created around himself. The Roman Empire was born and Augustus, in no uncertain terms, was the first Roman Emperor.

The Principate

From 30 BCE until his death in August 14 CE (the month was named for him while he was still alive),

the Emperor Augustus was the undisputed ruler of the Roman world. What is remarkable about the early Empire is the skill with which Augustus expanded his authority within the spheres of his influence and power. He took great pains not to cause disaffection. He did not, for example, gain the reputation for arrogance and bizarre behaviour that marked the reigns of his immediate successors Tiberius (14–37 CE), Caligula (37–41 CE), and Nero (54–66 CE). In fact, the only title Augustus was happy with was *Princeps,* which referred to his claim that he was *primus inter pares* (first among equals). So, we refer to the Augustan period as the **Principate**.

This careful management of the Roman world, probably begun through an instinct for survival, was all-encompassing. The benefits of Augustan peace were celebrated everywhere in the literature and fine arts of the period. Just to make sure that no one missed the message, in Rome alone, Augustus, or members of his family, rebuilt 82 temples (by his own reckoning) and created many new public facilities. In the art of civil administration, Augustus made a career in provincial government or in the army a desirable and patriotic calling. He maintained a professional civil service in Rome, and instituted the *vigiles,* a combined police force and squad of paid firefighters (fires were an ongoing problem in Rome).

Augustus created a society in which material prosperity, the arts, religion, and a common sense of "Romanity" flourished. This was not mere propaganda, although Augustus did prove himself to be a consummate public relations person. Two factors above all contributed to the ultimate success of the Principate: the people's ardent desire for peace after years of brutal civil wars, and the fact that the supreme ruler of the Roman world had a very long life — Augustus managed to outlive most of his heirs and all of his rivals.

The Administration of the Provinces

Originally, the word *provincia* referred to an area of responsibility in which a magistrate had power (*imperium*). Most often, that power was related to waging war. By the late Republic, fighting was not the only activity for which the appointed magistrate was responsible. The term *provincia* then came simply to be applied to geographical areas for which magistrates were responsible. Given Rome's military history, it is not surprising that the first overseas provinces governed by magistrates sent from Rome were territories taken from the Carthaginians in the

First and Second Punic Wars: Sicily, Sardinia, and Corsica. Later, when Rome acquired Asia in 133 BCE, civilian matters in provincial administration came to be of at least equal significance. Thus, the provincial governor, usually an ex-consul or ex-praetor, commanded not only the occupying army, but also a bureaucracy of financial and other assistants, for whom taxation was a very important function.

The Arts in the Age of Augustus

Augustus, unlike previous rulers, knew the power of the arts as a tool for political propaganda. State-sponsored architecture and sculpture created throughout the Roman Empire began conveying the power and legitimacy of the emperor in a visual language the people understood.

This is all that remains of the Temple of Mars Ultor, Mars the Avenger. It was meant to show reverence for Julius Caesar, who by the time the temple was dedicated, in the late first century BCE, had been declared a god by the Senate.

Art and Architecture

During the Principate of Augustus, and indeed throughout the first and second centuries of our era, the visual arts — architecture, wall painting, mosaics, and sculpture — all flourished. In addition

Here, Augustus is shown in his role as a Roman general. Though this sculpture was probably carved after his death, it nevertheless shows Augustus as a handsome, young man. The fact that he is barefoot symbolizes that he is a hero.

All of the ideas and themes displayed on this political monument, the Ara Pacis, or Altar of Augustan Peace, were meant to show the peace and prosperity brought about by the rule of Augustus.

to the multitude of temples Augustus had built in Rome alone, he completed the Forum Romanum of Julius Caesar and built an even more magnificent forum — the Forum of Augutus, named after himself. It featured the imposing marble Temple of Mars the Avenger (*Mars Ultor*).

On his wife Livia's birthday in 9 BCE, Augustus also dedicated the splendid marble Altar of Augustan Peace (*Ara Pacis*). This masterpiece of political art has been restored and can still be seen today in Rome. On two sides of the altar, we see a procession of the family of Augustus — women, men, and children — including some members who were not even in Rome at the time. On the front, we see sculptural reliefs of episodes from the early history of Rome: Aeneas and symbolic figures of Mother Earth and the winds. These scenes assured viewers that the Emperor Augustus could trace his family back to the very beginning of the history of Rome. The altar was decorated heavily with symbols of the bounty and fertility brought by the peace of Augustus: fruit and flowers from every season, children, animals, and wheat.

Wall painting also developed and thrived during the first century CE. At first, painting on plaster simply imitated masonry. Later, this gave way to the representation of fantastic architectural scenes, impressionistic sacred landscapes, marine scenes, and mythological narratives.

Mosaics began as monochromatic (one-colour) compositions, but soon became like multicoloured carpets. These prized status symbols were made of thousands of tiny *tesserae* (cubes of glass), and usually had an intricate geometric border around a central scene, often from Greek myth or daily life.

The Roman taste in sculpture continued to favour the Classical Greek style, often merely imitating fifth-century BCE sculptors such as Praxiteles or Polyclitus. Relief sculpture, on the other hand, did begin to develop into distinctly Roman styles, especially on triumphal arches, columns, and other political monuments. A visual language of symbols, figures, and ornaments eventually celebrated, and often described in detail, the victories of the great conquering emperors such as Titus, Hadrian, and Constantine.

This panel from one side of the Altar of Augustan Peace shows a Mother Earth figure with other symbols of fertility and plenty.

Literature

Literature also flourished. It was during this time that many of the most important and enduring works of Classical literature were produced. Augustus knew that literature also had the power to solidify his rule and **Virgil** (Publius Vergilius Maro, 70–19 BCE) helped by giving Rome its founding epic, the *Aeneid*. This poem describes how the hero Aeneas escaped after the Trojan War and ultimately arrived in Italy. All members of the family of Julius Caesar, including his adopted son Augustus, are said to be descended from Aeneas and his son Iulus. This curious mixture of legends also makes Romulus and Remus direct descendants of Aeneas.

The poet Horace (Quintus Horatius Flaccus, 65–8 BCE) used his gifts to applaud the benefits of peace, Augustan rule, and Roman supremacy. Though an advocate for Augustus, Horace took pains never to appear enslaved by Augustan ideals. Works by Horace include his *Odes*, written around 15 BCE.

Ovid (Publius Ovidius Naso, 43 BCE–19 CE) was a poet and famous wit who wrote a well-crafted parody called *The Art of Love*. When it was not well received by Augustus (known to be a bit prudish), he wrote another piece called *The Remedy of Love*. For these poems, and for an unspecified crime that probably involved Augustus's notoriously adulterous daughter Julia, Ovid was banished from Rome. Ovid's most famous work is the *Metamorphoses*, a fascinating and entertaining collection of Roman myths and legends.

In the first century CE, there were also great scholars such as Pliny the Elder (Caius Plinius Secundus, 23–79 CE), who wrote many works, including the 37-volume *Natural History*. He actually died while trying to rescue people fleeing the eruption of Mount Vesuvius, which buried the city of Pompeii in 79 CE. Pliny the Elder's last hours were recorded by his nephew and adopted son Pliny the Younger (Caius Plinius Caecilius Secundus, 61–112 CE), who also compiled a highly prized nine-volume set of personal correspondence.

The Successors of Augustus

The first to inherit the Roman Empire created by Augustus was his adopted son Tiberius, in 14 CE. The rule of Tiberius became increasingly harsh, and he eventually went into semi-retirement on the pleasant island of Capri in the Bay of Naples. In his absence, two praetorian prefects (commanders of his Imperial bodyguard) ruled Rome in succession.

Following Tiberius, in 37 CE, came the Emperor Gaius Caligula. At first, Caligula's rule was benevolent, but it soon became marked by cruelty and vice. It is said that he had so little respect for the Senate that he made his favourite horse, Incitatus, a member. Caligula cared little for the sanctity of marriage and openly engaged in several adulterous and incestuous affairs. He was murdered in January 41 CE by a group of senatorial conspirators and a member of the Praetorian Guard named Cassius Caerea, whom Caligula had constantly taunted about his homosexuality.

Although his family thought he was an imbecile, Claudius (41–54 CE), the next emperor, eventually proved to be an able administrator. It was under his rule that the lasting conquest of Britain got under way around 43 CE. Claudius, who was not so able in love, received the Senate's approval to marry his much younger first cousin Agrippina, who already had a son named **Nero**. Nero was emperor from 54 to 68 CE. After about six years, in 61 CE, he tired of his mother and had her killed. After this, he became more and more unpopular, and it was even rumoured that he had started the Great Fire of Rome in 64 CE. Nero himself tried to blame the Christians for the fire and ordered many of them to be tied to poles in the grounds of his

In this portrait of Nero, a cruel emperor who ruled Rome from 54-68 CE, the artist has combined features that were associated with portraits of both Alexander the Great and Augustus. Why would Nero have wanted this done?

gigantic palace near the Colosseum. These unfortunate people were then covered with pitch and set on fire to light the emperor's night-time party.

Nero was assassinated in 68 CE, leaving no heirs. Several people tried to rule, including Galba, Otho, and Vitellius. In 69 CE, Vespasian (Titus Flavius Vespasianus, 69–79 CE) finally managed to seize power. Vespasian ruled wisely and well for the ten years before his death, after which there was a smooth transfer of power to his son Titus (79–81 CE). Titus's rule was brief but benevolent: when Mount Vesuvius erupted in August 79 CE, obliterating the towns on the Bay of Naples, Titus sent emergency aid to the devastated residents.

Vespasian's younger son Domitian (81–96 CE) followed his elder brother to power. An autocratic man, he was infamous for his persecution of both Jews and Christians. Domitian was murdered in 96 CE by a conspiracy involving his wife and, probably, his immediate successor Nerva (96–98 CE).

Before his rule began in 98 CE, Trajan (Marcus Ulpius Traianus, 98–117 CE) spent several decades refining his abilities as a soldier and provincial administrator in the Iberian Peninsula (Spain and Portugal), the Rhineland (Germany), and in what is today Hungary. In the early years of his reign, Trajan generously endowed the city of Rome with buildings and monuments, including his famous column celebrating successive victories over the Dacians in a remarkable spiral relief sculpture (Dacia is modern Romania north of the Danube). Trajan paid particular attention to the territories outside Italy, and expanded the borders of the Empire in virtually every direction — to the north in modern Romania, to the east across the Arabian desert and Mesopotamia, and to the west in Britain. He was so convinced that the health of the provinces was fundamental to the well-being of Rome itself that he spent 13 of the 21 years of his rule beyond the borders of Italy. Trajan was an able administrator who set the stage for his ward, adopted son, and successor Hadrian.

The column of Trajan (29.7 m high) is actually an extremely valuable primary source of historical information. This "documentary" of Trajans's war with the Dacians (a Germanic people) carries some 2500 carved figures of Roman and Dacian soldiers doing everything from unloading supplies (shown here) to executing prisoners.

Hadrian (Publius Aelius Hadrianus, 117–138 CE) was one of the truly great Roman emperors. Like his adoptive father, he was born in Spain and spent many years as a soldier and administrator in the provinces. He, more than any previous emperor and most of his successors, consolidated Roman rule throughout the known world. He achieved this by travelling and by taking a personal interest in his subjects. Hadrian's first great journey (121–125 CE) took him all over the Empire. During his second journey (128–134 CE), he played the part of imperial benefactor, founding cities and restoring buildings. The Jews of Jerusalem were less appreciative of Hadrian's attention; after a brief but ferocious rebellion in 132 CE, they were suppressed in 135 CE.

The Pantheon, finished by the Emperor Hadrian in 128 CE, still inspires architects today. Can you think of any buildings you have seen that have similar features?

 The
Past
AT PLAY

Although Roman children are only barely visible in the historical and archaeological records, there are some tantalizing glimpses of what they did at play. Children played a variety of ball games, including one much like modern soccer. Children also had dolls whose limbs were articulated like toys today. There was a game of knucklebones, the equivalent of our game of jacks, and many board games, including one called "Soldiers" (*Ludus latrunculorum*).

Hadrian's Masterpiece: The Pantheon

Hadrian was incurably curious and a lover of all things Greek. The most famous and enduring monuments to his reign are his magnificent villa at Tivoli outside Rome, Hadrian's Wall in northern Britain, and the Pantheon in Rome.

The Pantheon is a circular temple, built in 25–23 BCE by Augustus's general Agrippa, and totally rebuilt by Hadrian around 126–128 CE. It stands out in

The interior of the Pantheon was lit only by an opening in the ceiling called the oculus. There were statues of all the Roman gods amid columns and a floor made of multicoloured marble. The height of the dome was the same as the diameter of the temple floor.

history as one of the most architecturally influential buildings in the Western world, certainly as important, if not more so, as the Parthenon in Athens. The Pantheon, with its impressive dome, has inspired modern architects of every generation. The survival of this amazing structure is due entirely to the fact that it was converted to a Christian church in 608 CE.

Review...Recall...Reflect

1. Explain the role of each member of the Second Triumvirate, and what happened to him.

2. How did the arts (literature, art, and architecture) help to glorify and legitimize Augustus's position of authority as emperor of Rome?

3. Among the other Roman emperors you have read about, whom would you rate as the best and worst successors to Augustus? For each, provide a brief justification for your selection.

BUILDINGS AND PUBLIC WORKS IN THE EMPIRE

A people can be described as a coherent community when the majority speak the same language, are subject to the same laws and worship the same gods. To qualify as a civilization, the core of the society should also be centred in a city or urban development. In Roman society, there were plenty of communal activities. In fourth-century CE tourist guides to Rome, we learn that there were, among other structures, 11 public and 856 private baths, 37 gates, eight bridges, two capitols, two large markets (*macella*), 254 mills, 1352 fountains, ten basilicas, 28 libraries, two amphitheatres, two circuses, two *naumachiae* (artificial lakes for mock sea battles), and four gladiatorial barracks.

Thermae (Baths)

Heated bath complexes were, perhaps, the greatest of all Roman contributions to the art of living. These were not the simple bathtubs of modern times, but rather, elaborately built structures for steaming (like a sauna), relaxing, or taking an ice-cold plunge. Above all, these large public establishments were a place for socializing. This was a form of relaxation enjoyed by poor and rich, men and women alike.

Aqueducts and Water Supply

The ancient Romans used an enormous amount of water. To supply both safe, clean water for drinking, baths, and other uses, systems of aqueducts were built to transport water in every part of the Roman Empire. In fact, the most famous fountain in the Western world, the Fontana di Trevi (Trevi Fountain) in Rome, is at the outlet of an aqueduct (the Aqua Virgo) inaugurated by Augustus's favourite general, Agrippa, in July 19 CE.

To begin with, a source of water had to be found on a hillside, where the flow was fairly constant and the slope was steep enough that the water could flow

Aqueducts like this, the Pont du Gard in France, carried fresh water to people all over the Roman Empire. This stone and concrete structure is still standing today at 49.3 m high.

A Typical Roman Bath Complex, ca. 100 CE.

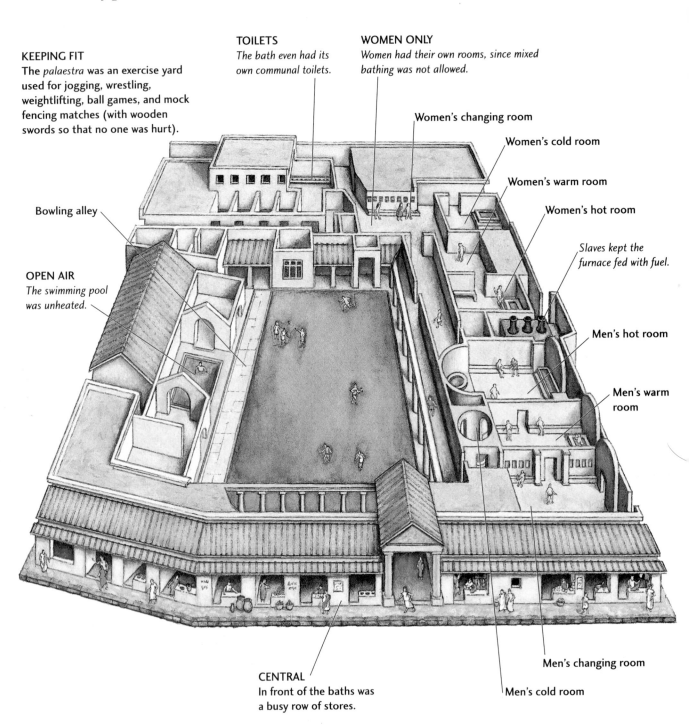

KEEPING FIT
The *palaestra* was an exercise yard used for jogging, wrestling, weightlifting, ball games, and mock fencing matches (with wooden swords so that no one was hurt).

TOILETS
The bath even had its own communal toilets.

WOMEN ONLY
Women had their own rooms, since mixed bathing was not allowed.

Women's changing room

Women's cold room

Women's warm room

Women's hot room

Slaves kept the furnace fed with fuel.

Bowling alley

OPEN AIR
The swimming pool was unheated.

Men's hot room

Men's warm room

Men's changing room

Men's cold room

CENTRAL
In front of the baths was a busy row of stores.

to its destination, needing only the force of gravity. Water was usually allowed to collect in a settling tank, so the flow of water could be regulated to some extent. Channels carrying water were lined with waterproof concrete and covered to prevent contamination or, better still, placed in tunnels through the hill so that the aqueduct would be less vulnerable.

Aqueducts carrying water over a series of arches are among the most spectacular surviving remains from Roman times. Occasionally, aqueducts were very high. The aqueduct at Segovia in Spain is a double series of arches 50 m high, and the Pont du Gard at Nîmes in France is a series of triple arches almost 55 m high.

Theatres

Permanent theatres were a relatively late Roman development — the first stone theatre in Rome (Pompey's Theatre) was not built until 55 BCE. Theatres were normally built on the Greek model: they were semicircular with a dance floor (*orchestra*), a stage, and a backdrop (*skene*). Behind the backdrop would be changing rooms and space to store props. As the Greek concept of an independent chorus became less influential, the orchestra diminished in size and the stage became more prominent.

Amphitheatres

The first stone amphitheatre in Rome was not constructed until 29 BCE although Pompeii had one about 50 years earlier. The most famous amphitheatre — an elliptical space surrounded by tiers of seats — is undoubtedly the Flavian Amphitheatre, or Colosseum, dedicated in Rome in 80 CE by the Emperor Titus (79–81 CE). The Colosseum is so named because a colossal statue of the Emperor Nero (54–68 CE)

stood nearby. There were 80 entrances, of which 76 were public. There were four seating areas, which could accommodate about 50 000 spectators. Tickets were inscribed with the entrance numbers on them. The sexes were segregated, with women and slaves restricted to the fourth and uppermost level. An eyewitness account of the Colosseum's inaugural games tells us that they lasted 100 days and that some 9000 animals were killed in wild beast hunts. An untold number of convicted criminals were also executed as part of the public entertainment, and gladiatorial combat took place in the afternoon.

In addition to seating 50 000 people, the Colosseum in Rome had a retractable roof called the *velarium*, which could provide shade and protection from the rain for the wealthier citizens. The velarium was made of cloth, like a sail, and was raised and lowered by ropes and pulleys handled by sailors who were stationed nearby.

Gladiators

From the first gladiatorial contest in 264 BCE until they were banned by the Emperor Constantine I in 325 CE, pairs of gladiators fought each other for public amusement in theatres, amphitheatres, the circus, even the Roman Forum. There were formal rules and, as in hockey or baseball today, even music to introduce the various forms of combat. Since it was expensive to train

This fourth-century CE mosaic picture shows several gladiators with their weapons and armour.

a gladiator, fights to the death were relatively rare. A cheaper way to satisfy the blood lust of the Roman spectators was simply to slit the throats of condemned criminals. Gladiatorial fighting was immensely cruel and marks the moral low point of Roman society.

Circus

A Roman circus was not a three-ring show under a big top; it was a long racetrack with starting gates at one end and a central area that chariots raced around, with turning posts at either end. Races were popular, in part because the seating was mixed, unlike in the theatres and amphitheatres. In every part of the Roman Empire, in any city of importance, there were circuses and chariot racing. The teams of charioteers were usually divided into four competing factions: the Greens, Whites, Blues, and Reds. Fan support for these factions was intense and sometimes violent. The charioteers, who had adoring fans like rock stars do today, were not expected merely to race. They also had to perform tricks, like climbing out of the chariot onto the backs of the horses running at full speed. The Circus Maximus in Rome was

probably the most famous. Built of stone, with tiers of seats along either long side, it was approximately 200 m wide by 600 m long (the same as two football fields) and could hold some 200 000 spectators.

The Private House: Pompeii and Herculaneum

Though there were variations throughout the Empire, the Roman house is best known to us through the ruins at Pompeii. Pompeii, in the Bay of Naples, is the most extensive and best preserved of all Roman towns in Italy. In its day, Pompeii was a relatively prosperous, middle-sized town that made good use of its location at the mouth of the Arno River between the west coast and the fertile slopes of Mount Vesuvius.

On 24 August 79 CE, Mount Vesuvius, continental Europe's only active volcano, erupted with enormous force. While Herculaneum, a town just a few kilometres to the north, was overwhelmed by a fast-moving flow of super-heated mud, Pompeii was quickly covered with a gentle but dense blanket of volcanic ash. The town was initially rediscovered in

Houses of the wealthier Romans always had an area called the atrium, a space open to the sky, often with a fountain. This is a patrician home in Pompeii.

On either side of the atrium, there were usually small rooms, probably bedrooms (*cubicula*). At the far end of the atrium was a reception area (*tablinum*) open to the atrium on one side, and separated from the garden on the other side by a moveable wooden screen. The garden was open to the elements in the centre, and surrounded on four sides by a covered colonnade. This area was a regular feature of the house and used for relaxation and recreation. At Pompeii, the Italian authorities have tried to reconstruct one of the formal gardens. Shrubs have been planted that are thought to resemble plants obliterated when Mount Vesuvius erupted.

For the poor and most ordinary people, home was an apartment or room in a tenement house called an *insula*. These buildings could be up to five storeys high with large windows for light and air. Living conditions could be very poor, with no private bathrooms and very little light at night. There was also a

1748, but systematic excavations did not begin until 1861; four fifths of the town is now uncovered. The excavations, which continue, have revealed all the usual types of buildings in Roman towns, including spectacularly well-preserved remains of private houses.

A long and deep entrance of varying dimensions (*vestibulum*) seems to have been standard. This opened into an *atrium,* a rectangular area surrounded by a sloping roof along the sides and open to the sky in the centre. Rainwater dripped from the roof into a waterproof, concrete tank (*impluvium*) set into the floor of the atrium. The water was piped away and saved in an underground cistern for household use.

Tenement housing such as this in Ostia, near Rome, was for the poorer people. These houses could be as tall as five storeys, with some rooms having no windows at all. If there was running water, it was only on the ground floor.

constant danger of fire because so much of the building was made of wood, and running water was only available at the ground-floor level, if at all.

BELIEFS

By the middle of the second century CE, the Roman Empire had reached its greatest expanse. It stretched from the lowlands of Scotland to southern Egypt, from what today is Romania to Morocco. It is hardly surprising that Rome and other major cities throughout the Empire became centres in which many different religions and beliefs could be found.

The Cult of Isis

According to Egyptian religion, Isis was the wife of Osiris and mother of the god Horus. The worship of Isis, though occasionally subject to state-sanctioned persecutions, eventually came to be one of the most popular religions throughout the Roman Empire.

In Roman Italy, there were elaborate rituals in honour of Isis. At Pompeii, for example, she had a temple complete with a cistern for holding sacred water from the Nile River. Isis could take many forms and appear as any number of deities. To judge from the archaeological evidence such as sculptural reliefs, gravestones, and carved gems, her worship was indeed widespread. There are many symbols known to be associated with her worship, particularly the *sistrum*, a form of hand-held tambourine.

Mithraism

Mithras, a Persian deity, was especially popular among the soldiers and merchants during the fourth century CE. They were converted to this faith as they travelled across the Empire, at first mostly in the Far East. The titles of Mithras included Lord of Light, God of Truth, Saviour from Death, and Giver of Bliss. An initiate had to pass through mysterious rituals, including a form of baptism, and the eating of a ceremonial meal.

At the heart of the worship of Mithras was the ritual killing of a bull. This act signified a spiritual victory of life over death, of good over evil. In Roman art, Mithras is often shown as a young man wrestling and killing a wild bull.

WEB CONNECTION

http://www.mcgrawhill.ca/links/echoes

Go to the site above to find out more about religions in ancient Rome.

Christianity

Christianity is, arguably, the most significant legacy of the Roman Empire to the Western world. Despite its various forms — there were many sects in the ancient world, just as there are today — certain beliefs are held by all Christians.

Christianity has its basis in Judaism, a form of Near Eastern monotheism that holds that the record of the religion (the *Torah*) was written under direct, divine inspiration. The laws of Judaism are believed by the devout to have been delivered by God to Moses on Mount Sinai in Israel. Around 30 CE in Palestine, a charismatic teacher named **Jesus** made his way toward Jerusalem, the centre of the Jewish faith. All that we know about the life and death, and teachings of Jesus is recounted in the *New Testament*. We are told that Jesus taught a new idea — that the prophecies of the Torah were not to be fulfilled at some indefinite time in the future but were unfolding in the present. The followers of Jesus believed he was the son of God and could forgive their sins if they believed in him and were repentant. The miracles Jesus is said to have performed were signs of his divinity, and that the kingdom of God was at hand. For the Jewish leaders at the time, the actions and teachings of Jesus were radical — only God could forgive sins.

When Jesus arrived in Jerusalem with a band of followers (the Apostles), he challenged the most powerful people in the Jewish hierarchy, the Sadducees. While in Jerusalem, Jesus was betrayed by one of his close followers, arrested by the Sadducees, and accused of a variety of crimes. The Sadducees did not have the authority to inflict punishment themselves, as this responsibility was held by the Roman provincial prefect and procurator (financial officer), who at the time was Pontius Pilate. Pilate was at first unwilling to become involved in a religious matter, but eventually condemned Jesus to crucifixion because he would not deny that he was king of the Jews, a direct challenge to Roman imperial power. Three days after his death and burial, some of his followers maintained that they had seen Jesus alive again (an event referred to as the Resurrection).

Jesus' surviving believers started spreading the word about their master and came into direct conflict with the official Jewish religious hierarchy. This conflict and the sudden conversion of Paul of Tarsus (St. Paul), the main opponent of the Christians, eventually led to the demise of the old pagan gods and the growth of the new faith.

Christianity, the belief in Jesus as a saviour for the oppressed Jews, was initially a relatively minor Hebrew sect. The next step in its transformation into an independent religion took place some two decades after his crucifixion, when former worshippers of pagan Roman gods were allowed into the faith. Now, the conversion of people other than Jews spread very quickly. The attraction of the new religion seems to have been its belief in equality. No matter what one's station in life, slave or noble, everyone could achieve salvation and a better life in the world to come.

Generally, the Roman state tolerated the new faith, with notable exceptions such as the Emperor Nero, who blamed the Christians for the Great Fire in Rome. Elements of worship, such as the ritual consumption of bread and wine representing the body and blood of Jesus, were also misinterpreted by the uninitiated pagan Romans as evidence of cannibalism and even infanticide.

The Spread of Christianity

The positive promise of life after death, the sense of equality the new faith offered, and the sheer morality of new converts to the religion provide only a partial answer to the question of why Christianity spread so quickly. One of the other most important contributing factors was, of course, that the religion was eventually adopted by the Emperor Constantine I in the early fourth century CE.

Christianity was practised by converts intent on behaving compassionately toward all people. They combined this conduct with the missionary zeal that characterizes all converts to a new and persuasive faith. For the Christians, religion provided a focus for their lives. For the pagans, whose deities were generally disinterested in the human condition, religion was not a great driving force.

The new religion's adherents were protective of their faith. More importantly, they were organized as no other religion had been organized before in the

Biography

Tacitus: Roman Historian

We know little of the life of the most influential Roman historian, Publius Cornelius Tacitus – even his first name is not certain. From his own writings, we do know that he was born around 55 CE from Celtic ancestors in northern Italy, and it seems that his father was the financial administrator for the province of Gallia Belgica (now north-central France).

Tacitus's career began under the emperor Vespasian (69–79 CE) and continued to advance under his sons, Titus (79–81 CE) and Domitian (81-96 CE). During Domitian's autocratic reign, Tacitus was elected Praetor for 88 CE and, having married the daughter of the general Agricola, was absent from Rome from 89 to 93, when he was governing a province. He returned to Rome for the last three years of Domitian's increasingly intolerable reign. In 97 CE, Tacitus held the consulship — still a very prestigious office. After that, we know very little about Tacitus, except that around 113 CE, he was the governor of the rich province of Asia (modern Turkey) and that he died just after 117 CE.

Tacitus wrote several lesser works: a dialogue on the decline of rhetoric, a sympathetic biography of his father-in-law (how a good man can prosper under a bad emperor), and an ethnography of Germany beyond the Empire. His major historical works, however, were the Histories, which were completely published by 109 CE (12 books) and the Annals (18 books), which were his latest work, and which covered the period from the death of Augustus to the death of Nero (14–68 CE).

The Emperor Tiberius, the subject of Tacitus's Annals, ruled Rome from 14 to 37 CE.

Tacitus was greatly appreciated in antiquity but has been valued differently in more modern times. Sometimes he has been considered a liar, but more often — especially since the recent discovery of an important Senatorial inscription in Spain — a reliable source for much of the first century CE. There are problems, however. He wrote from a Republican perspective, and his villains are too villainous. He is also too cynical about human nature. Tacitus nevertheless composed his historical works as impartially as he could, without, in his own words, "partisanship or bias." He believed that a historian's job is to get as close to objective truth as possible. Tacitus thus set the standard for historical research and writing for the rest of the Western Roman Empire, until its collapse in 476 CE.

Activities

1. Find a work by Tacitus such as the *Histories* or the *Annals* and briefly describe the contents of one of the books it contains.

2. Try to find the name of one other Roman historian, and give the title of one of his works and when it was written.

Greco-Roman world, with the exception perhaps of the quasi-religious worship of the emperor. The Christian religion had a defined bureaucratic structure with church elders and bishops. There was a well-understood hierarchy; the bishops of such cosmopolitan cities as Rome, Antioch, or Carthage had clear precedence over others from smaller, less cosmopolitan centres.

The Christians also had a coherent body of holy writings that they coupled with common rituals. No matter where you came from, as a Christian, you could feel fellowship. While worship in the pre-Christian world was fragmented and offered no universally accepted rites, scriptures, or structure, the Christian Church was an effectively organized bureaucracy. This bureaucracy had great influence and held several empire-wide councils. So pervasive was the Church's influence, that its temporal power (power on Earth) eventually challenged the secular administration of later Roman emperors. Perhaps it was this very success in spreading its message as an organized faith that brought about the great persecutions of the Christian Church in the third century CE.

The Jewish Diaspora

The Diaspora (dispersion) of the Jews began in 586 BCE, when Nebuchadnezzar captured the inhabitants of Jerusalem and sent them into exile. There then followed many years of movement and settlement around the eastern Mediterranean. While the Hellenistic city of Alexandria became the most important city of the Diaspora, by the second century CE, there were Jewish communities in most major European and Mediterranean cities. Between the second and fourth centuries CE, Rome itself had some 11 synagogues.

The Jews of the Diaspora spoke Greek but maintained the religious practices of the Jews in Jerusalem — among them, observance of the Sabbath, male circumcision, and avoidance of non-kosher foods (foods prohibited by Jewish law). Until 70 CE, all adult Jewish men also paid a tax to the Temple in Jerusalem. The collection of this tax, and its delivery to the Temple, was upheld by the Roman authorities. After the destruction of the Temple in 70 CE, the tax was extended to all Jews, including women and children, and paid to the new resident of the Temple, Jupiter Capitolinus. This small tax, just two drachmas, was at least implicit recognition of Jewish communities by the Roman state. Although there were periodic expulsions from the city of Rome (e.g., 139 BCE and 19 CE, during the reign of Claudius) when the authorities were afraid of non-Roman practices, for the most part, the Jews were tolerated. Over time, however, this state of affairs changed. In Alexandria, where the Jews had long been accepted, the privileges accorded the citizens of Alexandria were redefined after the Roman conquest of Egypt, and the Jewish population was excluded. When a grandson of Herod the Great visited Alexandria in 38 CE, synagogues were set on fire, shops were looted, and the Jews were confined to a *ghetto* (separate place where Jews had to live).

Conditions for the Jews changed yet again after the rebellions of the early second century CE, when the Jews of the Diaspora lived in harmony with their fellow citizens. Later, in the fourth and fifth centuries CE, when the Christian emperors placed restrictions on the Jews, the synagogues continued to function.

THE EMPIRE AT ITS HEIGHT

Pax Romana

To a large extent today, our identity — the sense of who we are — is tied up in a national or ethnic identity. We are Canadian, American, Japanese, French, and so on. In the ancient world, however, there was no system of nation states. A sense of community came from belonging to a certain culture. This way of seeing oneself was especially true in the second century CE, and in the peaceful years of the reigns of Hadrian and Antoninus Pius (117–161 CE). The provinces were secure and interconnected by a network of well-maintained roads and trade routes. Cities, even as remote as Volubilis in what is now Morocco, were flourishing, and everywhere there was a remarkably uniform air of Romanity.

Daily Life: Education and Status

For the elite citizen, the same laws applied and daily life continued much as it did during the Republic. The household, for example — the *familia* — which included the slaves, continued to be subject to male authority, and the education of children remained firmly based on rhetoric and the study of earlier Greek and Latin scholars. The elite also continued their disdain for manual labour, perhaps best shown by the fact that, with only very few exceptions, the architects and artists of the Roman world remain anonymous. There was one particularly noteworthy social change that affected both men and women equally: the use of public bathing facilities increased.

The Role of Women

The role and status of women did not change much between the Republic and the Empire; women's major function in the patriarchal Roman society remained primarily to produce legitimate male heirs who could inherit the family estate. However, that role did not stop women from playing an active and influential part in society. Eumachia, for example, was a public priestess at Pompeii, and patroness of the Guild of Fullers (launderers and makers of cloth). Wealthy women also erected major buildings in their home cities all over the Empire. A few, like **Julia Domna**, became formidable empresses.

Julia Domna was born in Syria and became the wife of the Emperor Septimius Severus in 187 CE. After her husband's death, she unsuccessfully supported her younger son Geta in his bid to become emperor. And even when Geta was removed from office, Julia Domna played such an influential role in the politics and administration of the Empire that she was given the title "Mother of the Senate and of the Fatherland." She took her own life after her elder son, the Emperor Caracalla, was murdered in 217 CE.

Roman society under the Empire was never egalitarian (fair to everyone). The poorer people had no access to a formal education, and one's status

Julia Domna, who was born in Syria, was the talented and powerful wife of Septimius Severus, emperor of Rome from 193 to 211 CE.

Roman and Native Law

Throughout the Empire, there existed a mixture of Roman and native law and traditions. For example, after the destruction of the Temple in Jerusalem in 70 CE, Jews were still recognized as a discrete people with their own laws and traditions. Similarly, Greek justice systems continued to be in effect in Syria, and local Spanish traditions were still upheld even after the Iberian Peninsula fell under Roman control. Of course, the residents of the provinces were expected to have some familiarity with the basic procedures of Roman law, but generally, they were not expected to be thoroughly conversant with its substance.

Citizenship

Emperors used the gift of citizenship as a reward for loyalty in times of crisis, for services rendered, or, sometimes, as a demonstration of imperial favour. The higher status was not bestowed automatically, but had to be requested. At some point in his reign, it seems that Claudius (41–54 CE) began giving Roman citizenship to the non-Roman soldiers in the auxiliary cohorts and to their wives and children, after the soldiers' discharge from military service. This was probably as much driven by a need to recruit soldiers as it was by the Emperor's desire to spread Roman citizenship throughout the Empire.

In 212 CE, Caracalla extended citizenship to all free Roman men throughout the Empire. Native law, however, continued to form the essential skeleton of the administration of justice. It was also acknowledged that an emperor need not be of Italian birth. Indeed, both Trajan and Hadrian were Spanish, and Septimius Severus, Caracalla's father, was African. Roman citizens were Roman citizens no matter where they lived.

before the law changed according to birth and wealth. By the second century CE, the *honestiores* (senators, magistrates, soldiers, and veterans) were legally protected; if they suffered some crime or injustice, the degree of outrage varied according to the injured party's status. Similarly, if one of the honestiores was found guilty of a crime, punishment was more lenient and not designed to humiliate. The *humiliores* (ordinary people), on the other hand, were subject to torture, death, or even enslavement. The society of the Roman Empire became increasingly rigid and controlled. Within about a century of the death of Marcus Aurelius (180 CE), a man was legally bound, on pain of death, to inherit his father's craft or profession.

Ancient

Slavery

In Rome, slaves constituted an estimated one third of the population. Only two things maintained control of such a huge group of people: the occasional affection of a master for a slave, and fear. If a master were murdered by one of his slaves, the entire slave household would be executed.

Throughout the Republic and the Empire, the Romans employed slaves in almost every aspect of human activity. There was never any development within the institution or any real recognition of human rights (an unknown concept in ancient Rome). There were slaves who were trained as gladiators, as were Spartacus and his followers. Slaves powered cranes and construction machinery. There were educated slaves used for dictation, for teaching free youth, or grooming the mistress's hair. In Rome, public slaves would act as executioners or be used to clear away the corpses of their less-fortunate fellows from the Colosseum. Even once the terrible ordeal of public auction had passed, the fate of a slave was grim, no matter how liberated the owner; torture was a standard way of finding out whether a slave's master had been up to no good.

The lowest order of slaves included those who worked on their masters' estates outside Rome; the most favoured slaves were those who worked indoors in Rome. A youthful slave (male or female) could also be expected to satisfy the master's or mistress's sexual desires. Sometimes slaves, especially those among the more favoured groups, could achieve **manumission** — eventual release from their servitude — by either buying freedom at a mutually acceptable price or being released according to the terms of a deceased owner's will.

Trade and Commerce

Under the orderly Empire, from the Far East, China, and India came silk and all kinds of spices. *Negotiatores* and *mercatores* (merchants) were exchanging all sorts of goods by the mid-third century CE, including amber from the Baltic coast and woollen cloaks from Britain.

After the grain bought by Imperial agents for distribution free of charge to the urban population of Rome, the most widely traded commodities were probably wine and olive oil. These were transported in *amphorae*. Amphorae were heavy pottery containers that were found all over the Roman world. Their distinctive shapes are often good indicators of their date and place of origin. Once these amphorae were emptied of their original contents, they could be put to any number of secondary uses. Often, they were broken accidentally. Today, a hill of shattered amphora sherds is still found on the banks of the Tiber River in Rome near the site of ancient warehouses.

Coinage

Roman coinage has a long history that spans both the Republic and the Empire. Before approximately 290 BCE, bronze coins had spread throughout the Italian Peninsula, and by 241 BCE, the typical Republican bronze coin (the head of Janus on one side, the prow of a ship on the other) had become well established. The worth of the coins was their face value.

At the time of the Punic Wars, the silver *denarius* was introduced, valued at ten *asses* (one *as* being the worth of the previous bronze coinage). Gold issues (*aurei*) were also produced, worth 2060 asses. The denarial standard continued through the end of the Republic. Money, so called because coins at Rome were minted in the Temple of Juno Moneta, was produced in the first century CE, often under the supervision of magistrates.

This gold coin shows the head of Cleopatra, the last queen of Egypt. It was issued in the first century BCE by Marc Antony, her political partner and lover.

After several important reforms by the Emperor Augustus, the value of Roman coinage was debased even further. In 215 CE, Caracalla issued the *antoninianus*, which soon replaced the denarius. Also in the third century CE, the solid-gold *aureus* became only a plated coin with a value that bore no relation to the weight of its precious metal. The value of the aureus continued to decline even further when, in about 309 CE, Constantine the Great introduced a lighter aureus. This was called the *solidus* and was, above all else, the coin of tax payment.

THE BEGINNING OF THE END

The Empire from Antoninus Pius to Diocletian

During the latter half of the second century CE and for much of the early third century, the Roman world remained secure and free from threat. There was a succession of emperors, both good and bad. Antoninus Pius (138–161 CE) was the respected successor to Hadrian, and Marcus Aurelius (161–180 CE) was also much admired. Next, there was Commodus (180–193 CE), who liked to see himself as another Hercules. Then came the first emperor from the province of Africa, Septimius Severus (193–211 CE), followed by his son Caracalla (188–217 CE), who gave citizenship to all free Roman males in 212 CE. This policy had more to do with increasing tax revenue than with benefiting the new citizens. Partisan strife and self-interest on the part of the military then gave rise to a further eleven "legitimate" emperors before **Diocletian** (Gaius Aurelius Valerius Diocletianus) was promoted to Emperor in 284 CE by his fellow soldiers in the Praetorian Guard.

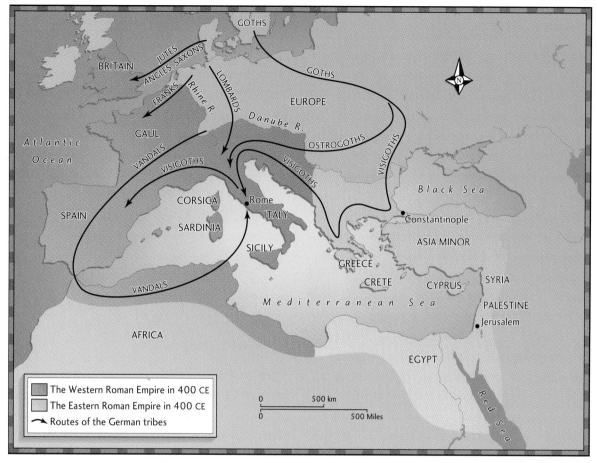

The map shows Western Roman Empire in 400 CE, Eastern Roman Empire in 400 CE, and Routes of the German tribes, with labels including GOTHS, JUTES, ANGLES, SAXONS, FRANKS, LOMBARDS, VANDALS, VISIGOTHS, OSTROGOTHS, BRITAIN, EUROPE, GAUL, SPAIN, ITALY, GREECE, ASIA MINOR, SYRIA, PALESTINE, EGYPT, AFRICA, Rome, Constantinople, Jerusalem, Atlantic Ocean, Mediterranean Sea, Black Sea, Red Sea, Corsica, Sardinia, Sicily, Crete, Cyprus, Rhine R., Danube R.

The Western Roman Empire in 400 CE
The Eastern Roman Empire in 400 CE
Routes of the German tribes

0   500 km
0   500 Miles

The End of the Roman Empire

1. The Roman Empire was attacked in places far from Rome. Which provinces fell to the Saxons?

2. What geographical factors would have protected the Eastern Roman Empire in the fifth century CE?

Diocletian's Reforms of the Army and the State

In 293 CE, without ever having visited the city of Rome, Diocletian instituted the first and, ultimately, most fateful of his reforms: he divided the rule of the Empire into two parts, the East and the West. Consequently, there were now two senior emperors called *Augusti,* who were assisted by two junior emperors, called *Caesares.* Although the Eastern and Western halves interacted closely, the split was permanent. In time, the Western part of the Empire lost its Roman nature, while the Eastern part developed into the fascinating world we call Byzantium. Diocletian also reformed the imperial bureaucracy, reordered the administration of the provinces, and completed the military reforms begun by his predecessors.

From now on, there were standing armies spread along the frontiers, and mobile units were distributed throughout the provinces ready to quell internal disturbances and lend support at the frontiers. Cavalry units also became as important as the infantry, and there was a continued and significant recruitment of non-Roman, Germanic immigrants.

After Diocletian was made emperor in 284 CE, he also began the last and most destructive attempt to eradicate the Christian faith. Churches were dismantled and the holy writings (scriptures) were burned. People were obliged to sacrifice to Diocletian or die. To some, martyrdom — willingly suffering torture and death rather than renouncing their faith — was the only option. Eventually, this active persecution of Christians came to an end after Diocletian's abdication and retirement.

Diocletian was never able to overcome the ravages of skyrocketing inflation, despite issuing a famous edict in 301 CE that established maximum prices and wages, and instituted a complex series of taxes. After he visited Rome in 303 CE, Diocletian suffered a stroke and on 1 May 305 CE, both he and the Western Emperor Maximian abdicated. Diocletian retired to live out the rest of his days peacefully at his palace at Split, Croatia. He continued to remain faithful to the old Roman gods and to oppose the rise of Christianity.

Constantine the Great

In a struggle for control of the Italian Peninsula, Diocletian's successor, the Caesar **Constantine** (Flavius Valerius Constantinus, 306–337 CE) had to defeat another Caesar named Maxentius. They fought the decisive battle at the Milvian Bridge outside Rome in 312 CE. Constantine was victorious; a contemporary account of his success attributes it in part to the active intervention of the Christian God. Certainly, that was Constantine's claim. After his own conversion, as the first Christian emperor, Constantine issued the Edict of Milan (also called the Edict of Toleration) in 313 CE, freeing Christians in the Roman Empire from persecution.

Constantinople

After his conversion, Constantine the Great favoured Christian communities everywhere. By his establishment of Byzantium (Istanbul in modern Turkey) as the major seat of Roman government, Constantine changed the course of Western civilization. In 359 CE, the revitalized city, New Rome, known as Constantine's City, or Constantinople, was

Scripts & Symbols λ μ ν ο π θ υ ρ σ τ υ ϖ ω ξ ψ ζ α β χ ε δ φ γ

I	II	III	IV	V	VI	VII	VIII	IX	X
1	2	3	4	5	6	7	8	9	10

Roman numerals are still widely used today: on clock faces, for book chapter numbers, and especially for formal functions such as names of sovereigns, as in Queen Elizabeth II, and popes, as in Pope John Paul I. This is most likely because of the historic influence of Rome on Europe for so many centuries.

given constitutional authority equal to that of Rome. The vision of a new, Christian Roman Empire was captured in the Church of Holy Wisdom (Santa Sophia or *Hagia Sophia*) in Constantinople, first dedicated in 360 CE. Setting aside all precedents, this was where Constantine and all his successors were buried. The magnificent building that survives today is used as a mosque and a museum. It was built on the site of the earlier church and consecrated by the Emperor Justinian in 537 CE. Ironically, it was the Christian armies of the Fourth Crusade that broke in and vandalized the church on 13 April 1204.

These are fragments of a colossal statue of Constantine the Great, carved ca. 313 CE. The sculpture showed the emperor seated, with one hand pointing to the sky. The head alone measures 2.6 m high. Do you think a monument like this would be effective propaganda today? Looking at the face of Constantine, what kind of message would you get?

Review... Recall... Reflect

1. Provide two examples that illustrate how the society of the Roman Empire was not egalitarian.

2. Describe the various roles fulfilled by slaves in the Roman Empire, and explain why slavery could have contributed to technological stagnation.

3. By the time of the rule of Diocletian, factors that would contribute to the fall of the Western Roman Empire were already evident. Describe the two factors you believe were the most significant.

The End of the West

The last phase of the Western Empire, the period of transition between the Roman world and the Medieval Age, was marked by successive incursions of **barbarians** from the north. There were the Goths (**Visigoths** and Ostrogoths), Alans, Franks, Suebi, Vandals, and Huns. The last years of the Western Roman Empire primarily involved the movements of these Germanic peoples and the efforts of the Roman emperors to accommodate and settle them. Many of the barbarian groups that entered the Empire actually did so at the explicit invitation of the Roman emperors themselves.

Theodosius the Great

After Constantine's death in 337 CE, there was a period of about 40 years when a series of emperors, both Eastern and Western Augusti, did battle and attempted to rule the now Christian Roman Empire. In 379 CE, the Emperor Theodosius emerged and ruled with restraint and wisdom. Despite incessant court intrigue, he was able to deal effectively with the barbarian menace and even employed Visigoths as mercenary soldiers.

http://www.mcgrawhill.ca/links/echoes

WEB CONNECTION

Go to the site above to find out more about the Germanic tribes of Europe.

Theodosius was also a devout Christian and a zealous believer in the Nicene Creed, a statement of beliefs composed by a consensus of bishops at Nicaea (now in Turkey) in 325 CE. It is still proclaimed in some Christian churches today. In 391 CE, in one of the most radical changes the Roman world had ever seen, Theodosius banned all pagan worship and ordered the pagan temples closed. In 393 CE, he even abolished the Olympic Games because they honoured a pagan god.

The Visigoths

When Theodosius died in 395 CE, his sons took over the reins of government — Arcadius (to 408 CE) in the East and Honorius (to 423 CE) in the West. A new Visigothic leader had been elected and the restraints on the Visigoths and their Eastern masters were lost. The new leader, Alaric, was persuaded to attack the power of the West and its current champion, Stilicho. Stilicho was a Vandal by birth but had become thoroughly Roman. Essentially, he ruled the West for the boy-emperor Honorius.

Stilicho defeated the Visigoths in 401 CE with the help of the Alans, whom he allowed to settle in northern Italy. Soon he was courting Alaric to help stave off famine in the peninsula. Alaric agreed but demanded a huge payment. In the meantime, Stilicho was branded an outlaw and beheaded in August 408 CE.

When Alaric realized that payment for his assistance was not forthcoming, he laid siege to Rome, and captured and sacked it in August 410 CE. Though Rome was ravaged, the Western Imperial court was protected by the marshes of the Po River estuary in northeastern Italy at Ravenna. Nevertheless, the impact of the event resounded all over the Mediterranean world.

After Alaric's death, the Visigoths moved through Spain and Portugal, destroying the power of the Alans. They then pressed on to southern France, where they settled in 418 CE with the blessing of the Western imperial administration. The Visigoths' capital was established at Toulouse. The Visigoths were so removed from Rome that they did not attempt to subjugate the Romans. Rather, they worked out an elaborate and effective way of sharing the land. They also established a code of law that allowed them to be judged by their own standards while leaving the Romans their own system of justice.

The Huns

The Alans, defeated by the Visigoths, joined forces with the Vandals and settled around Carthage (modern Tunisia). In Europe, the first half of the fifth century CE was a time of disintegration and transformation of the Western Empire into a series of successor kingdoms. To the north, the Saxons and Franks overran the British provinces, and Alammani settled south of the Rhine River. Other permanent incursions had been made by the Burgundians and the Suebi. Next came the Huns. They made their first advance into Roman territory under Attila in 451 CE, and were repulsed in what is today central France. The following year, 452 CE, they invaded Italy and were forced to withdraw, but not after causing massive devastation. Attila died in 453 CE.

The Final Years

The Western Roman Empire continued to survive, after a fashion, with its share of heroines and heroes. Galla Placidia, a formidable empress, had been obliged to marry the Visigoth, Athaulf, Alaric's brother. Restored to the throne in 416 CE, she was able to keep the West tottering on until her death at Ravenna in 450 CE. Flavius Aîtius, a Roman general with a Germanic wife, was victorious against the Burgundians at Worms and Attila in France. Although a man of great ability, he could do little against Attila's advance into Italy. He was assassinated in 454 CE.

In 476 CE, some 1200 years after the founding of Rome, the Western Empire came to an end. In that year, the general Odoacer deposed the ineffective Romulus Augustulus. Odoacer's reign was short-lived; he was replaced at Ravenna in 493 CE by **Theoderic the Great**. Theoderic ruled as the Italian Peninsula's first Gothic king until his death in 526 CE.

The Western Roman Empire had endured for almost 500 years and displayed a remarkable continuity of administrative practices during its first three centuries. Until the Emperor Diocletian, the administrative norms devised by Augustus and enhanced by his immediate successors essentially remained the same. Even Diocletian's economic and military reforms did not substantially change the ideological underpinnings of the Empire. In fact, the major ideological changes that did occur only did so as a result of the adoption of Christianity as the state religion.

History Continues to Unfold

Students of Roman civilization are left with the question: Why did the Western Roman Empire collapse? Not surprisingly, there are many reasons. We can point to the overwhelming pressures placed on the frontiers by the movements of the Germanic people. Crippling inflation occurred in the later years when the price of gold skyrocketed 600 percent. Rather than stabilize the economy, Diocletian's edict on prices had the opposite effect and drove the economy underground. Recently, it has also been suggested that slavery was a major factor in the Western Empire's collapse, since it contributed to technological stagnation.

The effect of Christianity, a new religion, also should not be underestimated. The abolition of the old Roman gods and, with them, the idea of an eternal Rome eroded the people's belief in the supremacy of the Roman ideal.

In the East, the Roman Empire centred in Constantinople did not fall. It was slowly transformed into the courtly and prosperous society we call Byzantium, which did not end until 1453.

Current Research and Interpretations

In addition to a recent flurry of research activity into the buildings and monuments of Rome itself, there is currently more interest in the countryside and the economies of outlying rural regions. There is also a deeper appreciation of the ideologies of the Roman world — how the cult of the Roman emperor, for example, affected the individual's sense of what it was to be Roman. Finally, scholars are still meditating on why the Western Empire came to an end — a rupture in society as great as any — while the Eastern Empire carried on successfully for almost another thousand years.

Chapter Review

Chapter Summary

In this chapter, we have seen:

- that accepted leadership of the emperors, the Justinian law code, and compatible religious beliefs were key factors in the stability of the Roman empire
- that the gradual process of change introduced by Augustus was more effective than the rapid and radical change attempted by Julius Caesar
- how the Roman concept of citizenship and the rights of the individual differed significantly from ours, yet nonetheless laid the foundations for the evolution of Western ideas
- how religions increasingly came to play a vital role in the administration and functioning of the later Roman Empire

Reviewing the Significance of Key People, Concepts, and Events (Knowledge/Understanding)

1. Understanding the history of the Roman Empire requires a knowledge of the following concepts and events, and an understanding of their significance in the development of both Roman and later Western society. In your notes, identify and explain the historical significance of three items from each column.

Concepts/Places	Events
Principate	eruption of Mount Vesuvius
aqueducts	crucifixion of Jesus
Colosseum	Jewish Diaspora
Circus Maximus	Edict of Toleration
Pax Romana	invasion of the Goths

2. Create a mini time line that traces events from the assassination of Julius Caesar to Augustus becoming the first Roman Emperor. Be sure to include both military and political developments.

3. Explain how slavery had an impact on the economic structure of the Roman Empire.

Doing History: Thinking About the Past (Thinking/Inquiry)

1. Julius Caesar attempted to seize control and radically alter the functioning of the Roman Republic in a rapid series of bold moves. By contrast, Augustus used planned and gradual change to establish his authority and solidify his power. Provide a few examples of gradual, planned change by Augustus. Explain why his approach was or was not more effective than rapid, radical change.

2. In a clear paragraph, explain why the Pantheon is considered one of the most architecturally influential buildings in the Western world.

Applying Your Learning (Application)

1. In Chapter Four, a description of a day in the life of a typical Greek family is provided. Create a similar description of a typical Roman family, drawing on evidence found in this chapter and additional research if required.

2. Construct a model or prepare a detailed sketch of either a public or private building from ancient Rome. Supplement what you have learned about these buildings from this chapter by doing some additional research. Use any material you want to construct your model. Prepare an informative but concise viewer's guide for your model. Your viewer's guide should explain the purpose, design, and construction of the building.

Communicating Your Learning (Communication)

1. Create a map that shows how external influences had an impact on the Roman Empire during the fourth and fifth centuries CE. Your map should show where groups originated and what parts of the Roman Empire they invaded.

   Connecting to the *World History Handbook*: To prepare for your map, complete the Roman section of the graphic organizer, "Response to External Influences" in your *World History Handbook*.

2. In a paragraph, explain why it is accurate to say that the wealth of the Roman Empire largely depended on an economy based on trade. Comment on the importance of roads, coinage, foreign trade, and trade within the Empire.

   Connecting to the *World History Handbook*: To lay the foundations for your paragraph, first complete the section on Rome on the graphic organizer "Economic Organization" in your *World History Handbook*.

Unit Review

Grading the Civilizations

1. In Chapter One, the essential elements of a civilization were outlined and you were asked to rank in order of importance each of the elements. Now that you have had an opportunity to study the civilizations of Greece and Rome in depth, apply your ranking to see how they measure up. Below are three broad categories under which the elements could be clustered. For each of the categories, provide a letter grade (from A+ to F) and an anecdotal comment of three to five sentences to support the grade. A fuller assessment of these civilizations can be completed using your *World History Handbook*.

	Letter Grade	Comments
The Place of People • level of equality • just laws • distribution of wealth • overall quality of life		
Organization of Society • democratic • effective government • meets needs of society • provides security and stability for society		
Lasting Legacy • ideas • works of art • architecture • innovations/inventions • literature		

The Role of Individuals in History

1. Historians often grapple with whether history is shaped by individuals, or if individuals are products of their age and thus shaped by history. Would the history of ancient Greece have been different if Pericles had not lived? Did Augustus change the direction of Roman history? Below is a list of people mentioned in this unit. Select any two. For each, identify his or her role in society, major accomplishments, sphere of greatest impact (e.g., art, ideas, religion, politics), and why you believe the person shaped or was shaped by history. You may want to do additional research on the two individuals you select.

Herodotus	Alexander the Great	Hadrian
Homer	Aristotle	Jesus
Solon	Tarquin the Proud	Spartacus
Cleisthenes	Hannibal	Diocletian
Pericles	Gracchus Brothers	Constantine the Great
Socrates	Julius Caesar	Theodosius the Great
Plato	Augustus	
Philip of Macedon	Nero	

Understanding Chronology

1. The study of history, whether the recent or distant past, relies on a sound understanding of the order in which events occurred. Without a clear understanding of how history has unfolded, it is difficult to see the relationship between earlier events and developments. The following questions help to illustrate the importance of understanding the chronology of history:

a) For many years, the explosion that destroyed the island of Thera was believed to have occurred around 1500 BCE. It is now known that the volcanic eruption occurred in approximately 1628 BCE. What are the implications of this new date for our understanding of what happened to Minoan civilization?

b) How was the development of the Athenian Empire a product of the successful repulsion of the Persian invasions?

c) How is the expansion of Rome connected to the Punic Wars?

d) Put the reign of the following emperors in the proper chronological order, and explain why studying the emperors in sequence is important in understanding the spread of Christianity: Theodosius the Great, Constantine the Great, Diocletian.

Cause and Effect in History

1. History involves the study of cause and effect. We often find that one cause has several effects, or that several causes lead to one effect. Complete the cause and effect diagrams provided by your teacher. Once you have completed both diagrams, use one as a guide to writing a paragraph on the issue addressed.

UNIT THREE

The Islamic Middle East and Africa

chapter 7
The Islamic Middle East

chapter 8
African Kingdoms

This is a small bronze statue of the Princess-priestess Takushit from the the Kingdom of Kush, in North Africa ca. 715 BCE. She is covered with symbols of gods and other Kushitic hieroglyphs.

Chapter Seven in this unit examines Islamic culture and society from Muhammad's epiphany and journey to Mecca, through to the expansion of the Islamic Empire at the beginning of the sixteenth century. By examining both the foundations of the Muslim faith and the political structure of Islamic societies, we gain a clearer understanding of the relationship between religion and government. Similarly, understanding the Islamic faith is essential to the study of Islamic art, science, and literature.

Chapter Eight surveys several of the historic and significant African kingdoms. The chapter introduces important cities, leaders, and innovations. A constant theme is the importance of trading networks that brought goods into Africa and carried African goods to Europe, the Middle East, and India. This chapter serves as an introduction to the study of African history by providing an overview of important peoples and kingdoms.

UNIT EXPECTATIONS

In this unit, you will:

O **analyze the interaction between Islamic and African societies and societies in Europe and India up to the sixteenth century**

O **evaluate the contributions of selected individuals or groups in the development of Islamic and African art, ideas, and religious traditions**

O **demonstrate an understanding of the steps in the process of historical interpretation and analysis**

O **draw conclusions based on effective evaluation of sources, analysis of information, and awareness of diverse historical interpretations**

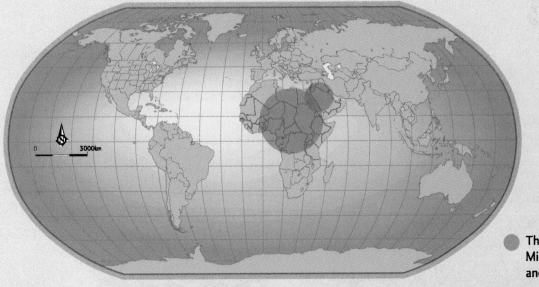

3000km

● The Islamic Middle East and Africa

CHAPTER SEVEN

The Islamic Middle East

By the end of this chapter, you will be able to:

- *demonstrate an understanding of the development of different forms of communities within the Islamic world between 620 and 1600*

- *analyze factors such as education, government, and Islamic traditions that contributed to the maintenance of stability and continuity in Middle Eastern societies*

- *evaluate the contributions of individuals such as Muhammad and groups such as the Sufis to the development of Islamic intellectual and religious traditions*

- *evaluate the influence of religion on the political structures of the Islamic world*

The tugra of the Sultan Suleyman (1550-1560). This was the Sultan's official monogram, used on documents, coins, and building inscriptions. The name of Suleyman and his father are written, with the words "the victorious."

In the 900 years from the seventh to the sixteenth centuries CE, Islam was born and grew to become the dominant religion of the Middle East. Islam formed the basis for both political organization and high culture: classical forms of Islamic philosophy, law, art, and architecture date from this time. Although today Islam is a world religion and the majority of Muslims live outside of the Middle East, the Middle Eastern legacy remains important for Muslims everywhere. The rise and development of Islam has been neither static nor uniform, and because of its potential for growth and change, Islam continues as a vibrant force in the twenty-first century.

Once the Western Roman Empire had disappeared, two great religious traditions would flourish in Eastern Europe and the Middle East. Christianity had been the first to emerge, in the early years of the first century CE. Eastern Europe would become the Christian, Byzantine Empire, while in the Middle East, a new faith, born in one man's vision, would take hold and dominate the region from the seventh century to this day.

KEY WORDS

cosmopolitan

prophet

polytheism

patronage

martyrdom

assimilation

pilgrimage

mosque

KEY PEOPLE

Muhammad

Muslims

Sunni

Shi'i

Sufis

Saladin

Khadija

VOICES FROM THE PAST

There is only one God and Muhammad is His messenger.

The Qur'an

TIME LINE: THE ISLAMIC MIDDLE EAST

	610	Muhammad founds the Islamic religion
Muhammad and his followers are forced to leave Mecca and flee to Medina	**622**	
	651	The *Qur'an* is compiled as the sacred book of Islam
Umayyads move the Muslim capital from Medina to Damascus	**661**	
	713	Islam spreads to India
Abbasids move the Muslim capital from Damascus to Baghdad	**762**	
	969	Fatimid dynasty of Egypt founds the city of Cairo and the University of al-Azhar
First of several Crusades of European Christians to recapture the Holy Land	**1096**	
	1258	Mongol warriors capture and sack Baghdad, ending the Abbasid dynasty
Constantinople becomes part of the Ottoman Empire	**1453**	
	1492	Granada, the last Muslim area of Spain, falls to Christians, beginning a period of religious intolerance, and the Spanish Inquisition
Safavid dynasty in Persia is established	**1501**	

GEOGRAPHY AND TRADE

A clue to understanding the importance of geography and trade in the history of the Middle East is found in the name "Middle East." The region is a kind of middle world, situated at the junction of three continents: Africa, Asia, and Europe. This central location made the Middle East a major crossroads of international trade. Middle Eastern merchants travelled far and wide carrying the luxury goods of different regions to markets elsewhere. The Middle East was a link between the two trading worlds of the Mediterranean Sea and the Indian Ocean, as well as a bridge between the Mediterranean world and sub-Saharan Africa. Cities such as Fez, Istanbul, Cairo, Damascus, Aleppo, Baghdad, Shiraz, and Samarkand were all great mercantile centres.

These trade and commercial links allowed the centres of Middle Eastern civilization to be in constant communication with one another. They underlay the **cosmopolitan** world of Islam in antiquity, and formed the material foundation of Islamic civilization. During the formative period of Islamic culture, the Middle East was an urban and mercantile world. Islamic law, philosophy, architecture, literature, and science — all the elements of Islamic civilization — were developed in the great cities of the Middle East.

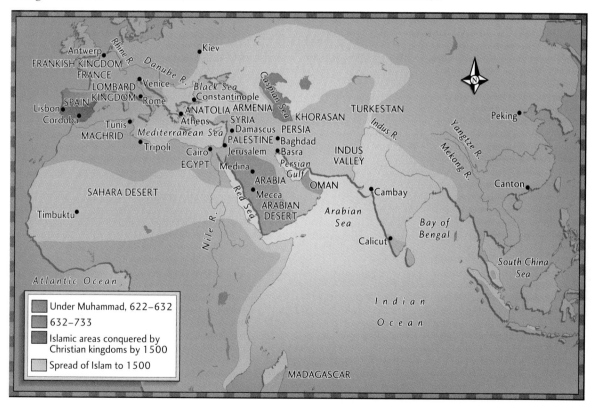

Legend:
- Under Muhammad, 622–632
- 632–733
- Islamic areas conquered by Christian kingdoms by 1500
- Spread of Islam to 1500

■ The Spread of Islam to the Sixteenth Century

1. By what means would Islam have spread to regions far from the Middle East, such as India and Africa?

2. Under whose leadership did the Islamic world expand the most?

Although luxury trade criss-crossed the Middle East, the region was not an integrated market. Each region usually had to produce its own food, cloth, and tools. Peasants, townspeople, and pastoral nomads (peoples who move from place to place with their grazing animals such as sheep and goats) were linked together in regional economies centred on major towns and cities. An example of a regional economy is Damascus in Syria. Located on the edge of the desert, the oasis of Damascus is vast. The city's hinterland embraced over 100 villages, from which it obtained food and raw materials for its craft industries. The products of these industries were, in turn, sold to the villagers. Pastoral nomads traded wool and dairy products to townspeople and peasants in exchange for manufactured goods and food. Merchants based in Damascus often acted as go-betweens in these transactions, and they organized long-distance trade in luxury items as well. This pattern of interrelationships between peasants, townspeople, and pastoral nomads was duplicated across the Middle East wherever large towns and cities were found.

MUHAMMAD AND ISLAM

In ancient times, the arid Arabian Peninsula was not as politically and culturally developed as the established states and civilizations of Byzantium (the Eastern Roman Empire), Persia (present-day Iran), and Abyssinia (present-day Ethiopia). Each of these empires subjected the fringes of Arabia to pressures and influences, but Arabian lands and peoples did not loom large in imperial affairs. It is, therefore, remarkable that a new religion, one that changed world history, was founded in Arabia in the seventh century.

The religion was Islam and **Muhammad** was its **prophet**. Muhammad was a merchant from Mecca, a town in western Arabia that benefited from changes in the east-west trade routes in the sixth century. The Fertile Crescent lands of Iraq and Syria had been wracked by a series of Byzantine-Persian wars that had left both empires exhausted. Because of trading links, the people of Mecca were aware of events and ideas in Byzantium, Persia, and Abyssinia. In his early career as a merchant, Muhammad is said to have travelled to Byzantine Syria and had conversations with Christian monks. Though most inhabitants of Arabia were animists (believers that natural objects have souls) or polytheists (believers in multiple gods), both Jewish and Christian communities were present in the more settled regions of the Arabian Peninsula.

Muhammad's life was radically altered in 610 when he is said to have received the first of a series of divine revelations. After a period of self-doubt and introspection, Muhammad accepted his role as a prophet of God and began to build a community of followers. His message was Islam ("submission" to God) and those who accepted it were **Muslims** ("those who submit" to God). Muhammad and his followers believed that these divine messages were identical to the prophecies that God had earlier sent to Abraham (Ibrahim), Moses (Musa), and Jesus (Issa). But because Jews and Christians had misunderstood or corrupted these messages, God was now retransmitting them through His final prophet, Muhammad.

Islam was strictly monotheistic, so Muhammad's message conflicted with the animism and **polytheism** widespread among Arabians. Islam stressed the unity and transcendence of God, and on these points it was critical of Christianity. According to the Islamic message, the Christian belief in the Trinity (three persons in one God: Father, Son, and Holy Spirit) denied the unity of God. The Christian doctrine of incarnation (that God became human in Jesus Christ) denied the transcendence of God.

The early revelations transmitted by Muhammad emphasized principles of faith and conduct. As the community of Muslims grew, the later revelations spelled out rules for believers to follow. After Muhammad's death in 632, the revelations he had transmitted were compiled into Islam's holy book, the *Qur'an*. Muslims believe that the *Qur'an* is the literal Word of God, rather than (as in Judaism and Christianity) scripture inspired by God. For Muslims, Muhammad did not interpret God's Word, but rather, he transmitted it.

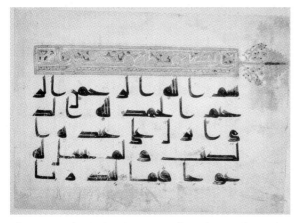

This is a page from a Qur'an written in the ninth or tenth century. The page is made of velum, specially prepared animal skin. The story, written in Arabic script, is about seven righteous men in the days before the coming of the Prophet Muhammad.

The wealthy mercantile establishment of Mecca opposed Muhammad. They resented Islam's sympathy for the poor and the powerless. This establishment also feared that Islamic monotheism would threaten Mecca's position as a polytheistic regional pilgrimage centre. So in 622, due to the persecution they faced, Muhammad and his followers decided to flee from Mecca to the town of Medina, a religiously and tribally mixed town, whose citizens asked Muhammad to arbitrate their internal disputes. This emigration is the event from which the Muslim calendar is dated. At Medina, Muhammad established an Islamic city-state, and now with a political base, the community of Muslims continued to grow. By the time of his death in 632, Muhammad had brought into the fold of Islam not only his former adversaries at Mecca, but also most of the pastoral nomadic tribes of Arabia. Muhammad's success is attributable to the power of his message, to his personal charisma, and to his remarkable qualities of leadership and integrity. Later generations of Muslims would seek to model their lives on his.

Islam makes five basic demands on believers.

The Five Demands of Islam

To recite the creed: "I witness that there is only one God and Muhammad is His messenger."
To pray facing Mecca five times each day.
To fast during daylight hours during the month of Ramadan.
To give alms.
To make the pilgrimage to Mecca at least once.

Sometimes a sixth duty is added: the obligation to wage holy struggle, *jihad,* to defend the interests of the Muslim community.

Islam is both a personal and a social religion. On the one hand, Muslims are expected to have personal faith in God and to express this faith through prayer, fasting, alms giving, and pilgrimage. On the other hand, Muslims believe that through the *Qur'an,* God has laid down rules and principles for community life. The Islamic city-state at Medina established during the lifetime of Muhammad is regarded as a norm to be imitated. Muslims must implement Islamic ideals not in personal isolation but in a community organized in accordance with God's laws. These laws, eventually compiled by Muslim legal scholars, seek to implement Islamic principles of fairness, social responsibility, and justice.

Diversity and Dissension

After Muhammad's death, no successor had his personal religious authority. Moreover, as the Muslim community grew and became geographically and culturally diverse, it was natural that disagreements should emerge over how to properly understand and implement the principles of the *Qur'an*. Islam soon came to reflect the diversity of its following.

Probably the most important aspect of Islamic diversity is the distinction between **Sunni** Islam and **Shi'i** Islam. The origin of the Sunni and Shi'i division was a political quarrel over who should succeed Muhammad as leader of the Muslim community. The majority — the Sunnis —favoured an elective principle for choosing Muhammad's successor. The minority — the Shi'is — believed leadership of the community rightfully belonged to the prophet's family, beginning with his cousin and son-in-law Ali.

The Muslim majority argued that the rules for proper individual and social behaviour were to be found in the *Qur'an* and in the precedent of Muhammad's own conduct: in Arabic, his *sunna*. Therefore, in order to establish guidelines for a good Muslim life, one should study the *Qur'an* and the sunna, and from these sources deduce religious law. Adherents of this methodology were called Sunnis.

While Shi'is also agreed that the *Qur'an* and the sunna were the bases of Islamic law, they disagreed with Sunnis as to the content of the sunna, that is, what Muhammad actually said and did. For instance, Shi'is believed that Muhammad had designated Ali as his successor, a contention that Sunnis rejected. Shi'is also argued that Muhammad's legitimate successors — namely Ali and his descendants — had special insights into the faith that allowed them greater latitude in the interpretation of scripture and law. So, ultimate authority in interpreting the faith resided not with the community as a whole (the Sunni position), but with Ali and his successors, called *imams*. According to Shi'i belief, the rightful imam remains present in the world but has been hidden from humanity since the ninth century. Therefore, learned scholars acting in the imam's absence must interpret Islamic doctrine for the faithful until the imam's reappearance at the end of time.

Scripts & Symbols λ μ ν ο π θ υ ρ σ τ υ ϖ ω ξ ψ ζ α β χ ε δ φ γ

Calligraphy is the highest form of art in the Islamic world. Since it is used to record the teachings of the Qur'an, it has a sacred function. The ornate Arabic script is based on the earliest known alphabet, the North Semitic, which developed around 1700 BCE. So vital is the art of calligraphy to Islam that the Qur'an itself has a chapter entitled "The Pen."

The broad outlines of Islamic law developed and took shape during the early Middle Ages. These rules spelled out Muslim expectations for social behaviour, marriage, divorce, inheritance, economic life, and criminal penalties. In fact, religious law was rarely used for criminal cases, which were handled, instead, through state courts that ruled according to customary, or common, law. However, personal status (marriage, divorce, inheritance, property — what is usually referred to as civil law) was mostly regulated by religious codes. Muslim religious scholars argued that the criterion for judging whether a government was Islamic was the ruler's enforcement of religious codes where applicable. Today, Muslim religious law is a basis of civil law in most Muslim countries, and in some countries (e.g., Saudi Arabia), it is also the basis of criminal law.

As far as the medieval religious scholars were concerned, religious law was the practical expression of Islam. Obedience to religious law was the mark of a good Muslim. But the legal-minded scholars were challenged by the **Sufi** mystics. These mystics argued that direct inner experience of God was equally, if not more, important than outward conformity to religious law.

Sufis were significant in both Sunnism and Shi'ism — they humanized and personalized religion, making it accessible and meaningful to people in their daily lives. Sufis favoured trance-inducing ceremonies culminating in the direct experience of God. They promoted veneration of saints and enjoyed reputations as living saints and miracle workers. Religious scholars frowned on Sufi populism, but Sufism was essential to the spread of Islam.

The people doing this whirling dance are called dervishes. They are members of certain Sufi Muslim orders who dance and spin in order to attain unity with God. As the dance goes on, the right hand faces upward to heaven and the left hand faces the earth.

Islamic Philosophy

Alongside the religious scholars and the mystics, were the Muslim philosophers. The first centuries of Islam saw a flowering of Islamic philosophy as Islam became a cosmopolitan and universal civilization. This civilization did not displace but absorbed and transformed pre-Islamic traditions and cultures such as the Hellenistic Greek legacy, particularly the works of Aristotle and Plato. Like medieval Christian philosophers, Muslims sought to demonstrate their faith through philosophy. Their challenge was to demonstrate the compatibility of faith and reason, to demonstrate that philosophical categories could explain rationally what religion taught through faith (the existence of God).

WEB CONNECTION http://www.mcgrawhill.ca/links/echoes

For more information about different groups in Islam, go to the site above.

Given the defensive mood of the late-medieval Islamic world, brought about in part by the Crusades and the ongoing Christian reconquest of Spain, royal **patronage** for philosophers dried up and religious scholars tightened their grip on intellectual life. By the time of the Mongol conquests in the thirteenth century, the philosophical tradition had fallen out of favour in most Muslim centres of learning. Nevertheless, by then Arabic philosophical treatises had been translated into Latin and helped to fuel the revival of philosophical studies in the West. In the Muslim world, philosophy continued to be taught in Shi'i schools, and its legacy lived on in dissident Iranian religious thought of the early modern period.

THE GROWTH OF EMPIRE
The Islamic Conquests

By the time of Muhammad's death, Islam prevailed in most of the Arabian Peninsula. Under the caliphs (Muhammad's successors), the Islamic world expanded. Arabian tribes, forbidden by Islam from raiding other Islamic communities, turned their energies outward against the weakened Persian and Byzantine Empires. Within 20 years of Muhammad's death, Egypt, the Fertile Crescent, and the Iranian Plateau had been brought under the rule of Arab Muslims. Later, the Islamic conquests were extended westward into North Africa and Spain, and eastward into Central Asia and India.

The Umayyad Caliphate

The Umayyad dynasty of caliphs was established in 661. The Umayyads were a prominent aristocratic family from Mecca who had opposed Muhammad through most of his career as a prophet. But once the Meccans had agreed to accept Islam, the talented Umayyads emerged as important leaders of the Islamic conquests. The Umayyads established themselves at the city of Damascus, which became their capital. Under the Umayyad caliphs (661–750), the Islamic political system operated like an Arab kingdom. Muslim Arabs were the privileged rulers, and their old tribal ties and affiliations continued to determine alliances and shape conflicts. Under Umayyad rule, Muslim Arabs were governors of the various provinces, were exempt from taxes, and shared the income of taxation among themselves. Eventually, the Umayyad caliphs consciously "Arabized" the administrative system left behind by the Byzantines and Persians, requiring that official business be conducted and recorded in Arabic. Arabs could act as a privileged elite under the Umayyads because in these early days of Islamic rule, most Muslims were Arabs. The subject populations of Egypt, the Fertile Crescent, and Persia at first retained their former religions and only gradually converted to Islam.

The site of the Great Mosque at Damascus (built 705-715) has been sacred for many centuries. It was first the site of a pagan Roman temple, then a church dedicated to St. John the Baptist. The mosque was a project of al-Walid, of the Umayyad dynasty.

Although the Umayyads established the Arab kingdom on a firm institutional footing, their policies gave rise to increasing opposition within the Muslim community itself. Dissident groups — including Shi'i partisans of Ali and his descendants, non-Arab Muslims, and Arab tribal opponents of the Umayyads — rallied behind an opposition movement led by the Abbasid family who were descended from one of Muhammad's uncles. The Abbasid-led movement overthrew the Umayyads in 750 and established the Abbasid caliphate at Baghdad in Iraq, near the old Persian capital of Ctesiphon. Once in power, the Abbasids expelled their uncompromising Shi'i followers and claimed legitimacy as the upholders of true Islam, which they said the Umayyads had betrayed.

The Abbasid Caliphate

The Abbasid caliphate (750–1258) marked the height of the Islamic Empire. In the Abbasids' view, all Muslims, whatever their linguistic or ethnic background, should be able to identify with the Abbasid caliphate. To bolster their religious credentials, the Abbasids lavishly patronized the emerging Islamic religious establishment. The Abbasids also adopted Persian imperial forms of government and administration. Echoing pre-Islamic Persian kings, the Abbasid caliph claimed to be the shadow of God on Earth. Arab tribesmen ceased to be the backbone of the caliph's military, and were replaced by standing armies of mercenaries and Turkish slave-soldiers recruited from Central Asia.

The Abbasid rulers used their wealth to support a vast bureaucratic and military establishment to patronize the arts, construct public works, and indulge in lavish living.

During the first century of their rule, the Abbasid caliphs used central government to run their far-flung empire, which extended from North Africa in the west to Central Asia and parts of India in the east. The political authority of the Abbasid caliphs began to decline, however, in the last half of the ninth century. Provincial governors became more autonomous and acquired increasing political power and taxation revenue. Eventually, the caliphs' effective authority was reduced to a small area around Baghdad itself. Indeed, during some periods, the caliphs were little more than tools of short-lived local dynasties. This reduction of power is not surprising given the uneven population distribution in the Middle East, and the frequent difficulties of communication between one region and another. From an Islamic empire, the Abbasid caliphate gradually became a kind of Islamic commonwealth.

As Abbasid power waned, most of the Islamic dynasties, states, and principalities continued to recognize the caliphs as theoretical leaders of the Islamic world. The major exception was the Fatimid dynasty of Egypt (969–1171), which established a Shi'i counter-caliphate, claiming that the Abbasids were illegitimate. The economic and demographic base of Egypt sustained the Fatimids and permitted them to build an empire encompassing Syria and much of North Africa. The Fatimids were unable to extend their rule permanently to other parts of the Islamic world, however. Eventually, the Fatimid dynasty collapsed and Egypt reverted to Sunni rule. Nevertheless, the Fatimids left a considerable legacy, including the city of Cairo, founded in 969, and the mosque-university of al-Azhar, the oldest institution of higher learning in the world.

The mosque of Ahmad Ibn Tulun is the oldest in Cairo, Egypt. Built in 876-879, it may have been inspired in part by the ziggurats of ancient Babylon. Do you see any similarities?

Crusader and Mongol Threats

The Crusades

The struggle between the Fatimids and the Sunni dynasties (who continued to recognize the authority of the Abbasids of Baghdad) was typical of the political fragmentation of the Islamic world on the eve of the Crusades. The Crusades were launched in 1096 by relatively small numbers of Frankish (West Germanic) knights who had been inspired by the pope to regain the Holy Land (Palestine, as it was then called) for Christendom. European Christendom was emerging from the Dark Ages, and the popes of Rome saw the recovery from the Muslims of Christian holy places in Palestine as a way to increase support for the papacy. Only the internal divisions of the Islamic world at the time made a Frankish conquest of coastal Syria, including Palestine, feasible. Although they conquered Jerusalem, the Crusaders' political control of the Syrian and Palestinian coast was always tenuous. Once Egypt and Syria had been reunited after 1171 under the Sunni Muslim warrior **Saladin**, the Crusaders lost Jerusalem and subsequently were destroyed in the thirteenth century. The Crusades loom large in the Western imagination, but they were a relatively small episode in the sweep of Islamic history. With the exception of Jerusalem, no major Islamic centres were lost to the Crusaders. The net effect of the Crusades was to accelerate the conversion of Middle Eastern Christians to Islam. The Crusaders' atrocities (such as their massacre of Muslims and Jews in conquered Jerusalem) cast Christianity in a bad light and intensified militancy among Muslims, who previously had no particular problems with local Christians.

A more successful Crusade was the Christian reconquest of Spain. Muslim rule of Spain was firmly established by the eighth century, when a fugitive Umayyad prince fleeing the Abbasids established an Umayyad dynasty at Cordoba. Spain subsequently became an important centre of Islamic-Arab civilization, in contrast to the barbarism that prevailed elsewhere in Europe. But by the eleventh century, Muslim rule in Spain was weakening, and Christian rulers began their takeover of the peninsula in 1085. The last Muslim principality in Spain — Granada — fell in 1492. Christian rule was characterized by religious intolerance, particularly, fierce persecution of the conquered Muslim and Jewish communities. Muslims and Jews who refused to convert to Catholicism were finally expelled from Spain in the sixteenth century and took refuge in the various lands of the Islamic Middle East.

The great Sunni Muslim warrior Saladin (1137-1193)

The Mongols

The Crusades touched the Islamic heartland, but were eventually repelled. But a third, nearly lethal threat to medieval Islam came not from the west but from the east, from the steppes of Mongolia. There the Mongols — horse-mounted warriors — were united under the leadership of Chingghis Khan in the late twelfth century. Within a short time, they had conquered Central Asia, and after a breathing spell, they continued their westward advance into Persia and Iraq. The Mongols terrified settled populations into surrendering without resistance. Chingghis Khan and his lieutenants were merciless toward populations that resisted them. Fortunately, many local rulers wisely declared their allegiance to the Mongols and became loyal vassals, sparing their lands from destruction.

The last Abbasid caliph, however, chose to make a heroic stand with humiliating results. Mongol warriors sacked and captured Baghdad in 1258, thereby ending the Abbasid dynasty. Legend has it that the Mongols were superstitious enough not to lay hands on the caliph directly, so they wrapped him in a rug and beat him to death. Little was left of the legendary Abbasid capital, its libraries, and its cultural riches once the Mongols were finished robbing, looting, and burning. The destruction of the Mongols was finally halted in 1260 in Palestine by Egyptian-based Turkish slave-soldiers called Mamluks (1250–1517). This victory saved medieval Cairo from Baghdad's fate.

With the destruction of the Abbasid caliphate, by default, Cairo became the major centre of Islamic civilization and learning for nearly the next two centuries. Nevertheless, with the exception of Iraq, Muslim countries conquered by the Mongols eventually recovered, particularly Iran. Mongol rulers of Persia (known as the Il-Khans) eventually

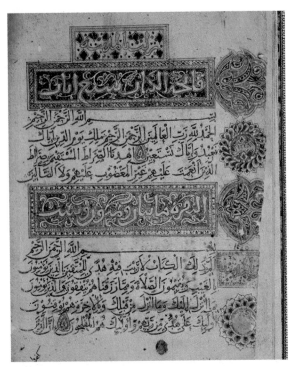

This page from the Qur'an was created in Baghdad ca. 1000-1001. This is the Naskhi script, which at the time was becoming the normal script of the educated classes. Its quickness and clarity also made Naskhi useful for books of instruction.

converted to Islam and embraced the high culture and civilization that their predecessors had tried to destroy. The conversion of the Il-Khans and the resurrection of urban civilization in Persia testify to the strength of Islamic urbanism. The Il-Khans patronized a revival of Islamic arts and learning before their own dynasty ended in 1350.

Review...Recall...Reflect...

1. Explain why Islam is said to be both a personal and a social religion.

2. What impact did the Crusades have on the Middle East and Islamic society?

3. Why were the Mongols more successful in their conquests than the Christian Crusaders?

Bureaucratic-Patrimonial States

From the Il-Khans onward, Muslim rulers and the political thinkers they employed developed the theory and practice of the bureaucratic-patrimonial state. According to this theory, the entire state apparatus, including soldiers and bureaucrats, was the patrimony or personal property of the ruler (sultan, shah, or padishah). In fact, servants of the state were legally slaves of the ruler, but this was a slavery of high status. The ruler and his slaves were actually the ruling class, legally separated from the rest of society, called "the ruled." The role of the ruled was to pay taxes and obey the rulers. The rulers, in turn, were to collect and spend the taxes, and offer the administration of justice in return.

The political resilience of the Islamic Middle East is demonstrated by the emergence in the early sixteenth century of two powerful bureaucratic-patrimonial states, one based in the old Byzantine lands of southeastern Europe and Anatolia, and the other in the Iranian Plateau. Beginning in the eleventh century, Byzantine Anatolia was conquered by Muslim Turks whose language and religion were eventually adopted by most of the formerly Christian, Greek-speaking population. In the thirteenth century, one Turkish dynasty, the Ottomans, became especially prominent and eventually ousted their Turkish rivals from Anatolia, and the Christian rulers from southeastern Europe (the Balkans). The Byzantine capital Constantinople (now Istanbul) became part of the Ottoman Empire in 1453. By the sixteenth century, the Ottomans had extended their conquests to include the Fertile Crescent, Egypt, and North Africa, and possessed the most powerful land army in Europe. They remained a great European power until the eighteenth century.

The term "checkmate," familiar to most of us through the game of chess, comes from the Persian *shah-mat*, meaning "the king is at a loss." If your opponent in chess says "checkmate," it means that he or she has captured your king and won the game. This is one of the many words that entered our English vocabulary from the Islamic world.

Ottoman society was multi-ethnic, multilingual, and multi-religious. The bureaucratic-patrimonial political formula of rulers and ruled worked well for a time. The Ottomans permitted internal self-government in the various religious, linguistic, ethnic, and tribal communities as long as they recognized Ottoman authority and paid taxes.

This sixteenth-century painting shows Suleyman the Magnificent, a great Ottoman ruler, in battle. Which figure is Suleyman?

Around the same time as the Ottomans were consolidating their power in Anatolia and southeastern Europe, the Iranian Plateau was reunified under a single, Persian-based dynasty for the first time since the Muslim conquest. In 1501, the Safavids, leaders of a messianic religious and political movement, claimed the kingship of Persia and proclaimed Shi'i Islam to be the state religion to distinguish themselves from their rivals, the Sunni Ottomans. Until this time, Persia had been a predominantly Sunni country, but by the seventeenth century, Shi'ism had triumphed at the grass-roots level and the Sunnis had become a minority.

The Safavids turned Persia into a powerful bureaucratic-patrimonial state. Like the Ottomans at Istanbul, the Safavids embellished their capital of Isfahan with architectural monuments that still delight the eye. The Safavid dynasty collapsed in the eighteenth century.

SOCIAL HISTORY
Social Structure

The social structure of the Islamic Middle East varied depending on the physical environments in which people lived. There were basically five different types: river basins, mountain regions, steppes, desert regions, and urban regions.

River Basins

River basins were home to peasant societies where the principal elements in the social structure were peasants and landlords. Peasants lived in villages and paid tribute to the landlords, as representatives of the state. These areas were the most productive of the Islamic Middle East, and their populations were heavily exploited by states and landlords. The resources of river-basin agriculture allowed Egypt and Mesopotamia to be distinct and often rival bases of state power, both before and during the Islamic period.

Mountain Regions

Mountains offered refuge from exploitation by states and from attacks by pastoral nomads. Mountain peasants (such as those in North Africa and the lands of modern Turkey, Syria, Lebanon, the Palestinian West Bank, and parts of Iran) were politically organized in clan and kinship groups. Because mountain agriculture yielded smaller harvests than river-basin agriculture, central governments were often content to accept tribute from mountain peasants rather than mount costly military expeditions to subjugate them directly. Therefore, in the mountain regions the principal classes were clan chieftains and peasant cultivators. Mountain peasants reared livestock as well, moving their flocks up and down the slopes with the changing seasons. Mountain chieftains were not as rich as the river-basin landlords, and the peasants were not as miserable and exploited as their counterparts in the river basins. The Christian Maronites and the Shi'i Druze and Alawis of present-day Lebanon and Syria are historically mountain-peasant communities. The Berbers of North Africa and the Kurds of modern Iraq, Iran, and Turkey are other examples of mountain peoples who remained aloof from the great empires of the cities and plains, cooperating with these empires when it suited their interests and opposing them when it did not.

Steppes

Steppes were the domain of peasants and landlords when states were strong, and of pastoral nomads when states were weak. Compared with river-basin land, steppe land is useful mainly for rainfall agricul-ture. Settled peasants in steppes were by definition exploited, either by state-supported landlords or by pastoral nomads demanding tribute, whereas pastoral nomadic society tended to be more egalitarian. Noble families, who often possessed more wealth than their fellow tribespeople, were expected to spread the wealth through gestures of hospitality and generosity. Clan and kinship solidarity was necessary for the survival and well-being of pastoral nomads, and this checked the development of extremes of wealth and poverty. Although pastoral nomads often entered into relationships with state authorities and urban merchants (regarding protection of overland trade, for instance), these relationships were between equals, since urban interests prior to the twentieth century had no way of forcing the highly mobile and warlike pastoral nomads to submit to urban interests. Today, Middle Eastern states have either suppressed and impoverished former pastoral nomads (e.g., in Syria and Iran), or built state structures in alliance with them (e.g., in Jordan and Saudi Arabia).

Desert Regions

Deserts are incapable of supporting large populations. Their importance was derived from scattered oases where settled cultivation was possible (typically date palms), and which also served as stopping points on caravan trade routes. In the desert, pastoral nomads reigned supreme — they controlled caravan transport trade (from which they profited), and taxed oases within their tribal domains. Oasis cultivators were, in this sense, subject to the pastoral nomads, but exploitation was often softened by real or fictitious kinship ties with their pastoral nomadic overlords.

Urban Regions

Cities of the Middle East were usually located in areas of river-basin agriculture (e.g., Cairo and

Baghdad) or well-watered regions surrounded by steppe or desert trade routes (e.g., Damascus, Aleppo, and Samarkand). The major cities of the Islamic Middle East were dependent on a combination of factors for their existence: location, administration, manufacturing, and trade. The populations of major cities followed a hierarchy of power and wealth, from top to bottom: soldiers and bureaucrats; merchants, landowners, and religious scholars; artisans and manufacturers; and simple labourers.

Merchants, landowners, and religious scholars often acted as mediators between non-Arab and non-Persian military rulers and the Arabic and Persian-speaking civil populations. Artisans and manufacturers were numerous in most cities, and served local and regional markets. Their skilfully made products brought fame to their cities: Damascus, for its distinctive types of cloth and steel — both called damask; Mosul (Iraq), for its muslin cloth; and Fustat (Old Cairo), for fustian cloth. Of the simple labourers who engaged in various menial and unskilled trades but formed most of the population of cities, little trace remains in the written records of the time.

Role of Women

In the predominantly pastoral nomadic society of Arabia, women were considered subordinate to men, but, nevertheless, played important public roles. Their advice and counsel was sought in political matters, and they were respected for the composition and recital of poetry (the major cultural pastime of pre-Islamic Arabia). Likewise, women could assume positions of religious leadership; the name of a local prophetess is recorded in the historical chronicles. Arabian women were neither segregated from men nor were they veiled. In some tribes, polyandry (marriage to more than one husband at a time) was permitted. However, the overall subordination of women to men was deeply ingrained. Women could counsel tribal leaders but were not themselves leaders, and in times of extreme difficulty, tribes practised female infanticide as a form of population control.

Muhammad's revelations corrected abuses and made adjustments without radically altering the existing society. The *Qur'an* outlawed female infanticide and guaranteed women and girls a share in the inheritance of deceased husbands and fathers. It also outlawed practices such as polyandry, which would create doubts about paternity. In most other respects, the *Qur'an* left the status quo alone. Consequently, women were able to play significant public roles in the early decades of the Islamic community.

The first convert to Islam was Muhammad's wealthy and respected first wife, **Khadija**. She gave him critical support during the early years of his prophetic career in hostile Mecca. Islam's first **martyrdom** was that of Sumayya bint Khubbat, a slave woman who was killed for her beliefs, and two of the first four caliphs were converted to Islam by their female relatives. Women also took part in the political and military battles of the early Islamic community, including Muhammad's youngest wife, Ayisha, who was a leader of the opposition to Ali when he claimed leadership of the Islamic community after Muhammad's death. Another woman, Hind bint Utba, was prominent in the Meccan opposition to Muhammad, but like other Meccans, she eventually embraced Islam.

The Muslim conquests of the Middle East (Egypt, the Fertile Crescent, Persia) gradually led to a change in Islamic customs. For many centuries, women in the societies of Byzantium and Persia had been limited to household and child-rearing duties, with emphasis on sexual segregation and veiling where practical (especially among the urban upper classes).

As the Arab Muslim conquerors of Damascus and Baghdad began the **assimilation** (a minority's gradual adoption of the customs and attitudes of the majority) of the culture of the Middle East, they introduced these restrictive practices into their own society. When Islamic law was consolidated under the Abbasids, it incorporated this pre-Islamic heritage. With regard to women, Islamic law downplayed Arabian practices (suitable for a pastoral nomadic society) in favour of traditions that now became sanctified by Islam. On the other hand, specific *Qur'anic* guarantees of women's property and material rights were retained in the compilations of Islamic law. So, in the synthesis that Islamic law represented, women's status was lower than it had been in Arabia at the time of the early Muslim community, but better than it had been in the pre-Islamic Middle East.

After the first Islamic century, the public role of women in Islamic life largely ceased. Politics, war, and intellectual and cultural life were virtually monopolized by men, with a few remarkable exceptions. Two contrasting examples are the mystic Rabi'a al-Adawiyya of Iraq (d. 801), who wrote religious verse, and Shajar al-Durr (d. 1257), who briefly ruled Egypt in her own right. Among her exploits was the assassination of her Mamluk husband. This deed outraged her mother-in-law, whose slave girls subsequently murdered Shajar al-Durr. In recognition of Shajar al-Durr's singularity and colourful career, there is today a street named after her in Cairo.

The general absence of women from public life belies their importance in society. Apart from their role as bearers and nurturers of children, women were critical in economic life as well. Among the literate and wealthy classes, property rights guaranteed by the *Qur'an* gave ambitious women opportunities to manage their property from behind the scenes through trusted male kinsmen or agents. Peasant women laboured in the fields alongside men, and pastoral nomadic women cared for the livestock on which their communities' survival depended. Preparation and processing of foods and animal products for home use and for sale typically were women's responsibilities.

Sexual segregation allowed the development of specialized trades among women who served other women as peddlers, healers, and prayer-leaders. Moreover, in Middle Eastern societies, where the extended family, or clan, was an important economic, social, and even political unit, women had considerable influence on the shape of relationships within and between clans through their women's networks. The difficulty for the historian is that these kinds of networks are not recorded in the medieval chronicles and biographical dictionaries — all, of course, written by men.

On the whole, the Islamic Middle East was a male-dominated society in which patriarchy was legitimized by male religious scholars' interpretations of Islam. For instance, while most Muslim women of Muhammad's day did not veil their faces, religious scholars subsequently interpreted *Qur'anic* demands for female modesty as requiring head-to-toe veiling. Patriarchy was built into the Middle Eastern social structure, and not until this structure began to change radically in the nineteenth and twentieth centuries did reformists challenge patriarchy in the Muslim world (the same is true of the West). Nowadays, although some Middle Eastern women have broken with Islam entirely, Muslim feminists more commonly appeal to the *Qur'an* and early Islamic practice in their campaigns for women's rights.

Customs and Festivals

Festivals in the Islamic Middle East included those that were strictly religious and followed the Muslim lunar calendar (determined by the phases of the moon), and local festivals of pre-Islamic origin that followed the solar calendar (determined by the position of Earth around the sun).

The greatest Islamic feasts were (and still are) those marking the end of the fasting month of Ramadan, and the end of the annual **pilgrimage** to Mecca. Every devout Muslim aspires to make the pilgrimage in his or her lifetime. The ceremony itself was and remains extremely important for fostering a sense of shared Muslim community. Pilgrimage to

The people in this mid-thirteenth century painting are celebrating the end of Ramadan, one of the most important religious observances in Islam.

the sacred enclosure in Mecca actually predates Islam. Muslims believe that God's first prophet, Abraham, founded the sacred enclosure, and that by destroying polytheism, Muhammad returned the enclosure to its original purpose. The pilgrimage ceremony itself lasts for a number of days, and involves an ordered sequence of rituals and ceremonies. In the days before modern communication, this trip could entail considerable hardship and danger.

Eid al-Fitr, the feast to mark the end of the Ramadan fast, was a joyous occasion. People who had endured a month of rigorous daytime fasting were now free to eat special meals and celebrate in the company of family and friends. The religious purpose of fasting in Islam was (and still is) to bring believers close to God and to remind them of the sacrifices that faith demands.

The second major Muslim holiday, Eid al-Adha, or Bayram, (the Feast of the Sacrifice), marked the end of the annual Mecca pilgrimage. Traditionally, families sacrificed sheep to mark the occasion, and wealthy people were obliged to distribute the meat of their animals to the poor. Like the feast marking the end of Ramadan, Eid al-Adha was an occasion for community and family celebrations and gatherings.

Local secular feasts are also important in the Middle East. The best known are in Egypt and Iran, two countries with ancient civilizations that assimilated Islam at least as much as Islam assimilated them. Both Egyptians and Iranians celebrate spring festivals around the time of the vernal equinox. The vernal equinox is the new year according to the traditional Iranian solar calendar. Iranians also mark the winter solstice, customarily by staying up well into the long night socializing and reciting poetry.

Biography
Khadija

Khadija, Muhammad's wealthy and respected first wife, is a good example of a woman who played a significant role in her community. Uncovering details about her life is somewhat challenging for Western learners, however, since very little about her life has been translated into English. As is often the case in history, there are descrepancies about some details. For example, Khadija is said to have been born in 565, but her age in the year of her death in 623 varies from 58 to 65.

Khadija, Mohammad's respected and highly successful first wife, made a fortune in the caravan trade.

Khadija's father was a successful businessman and merchant of considerable wealth. Khadija was quite an astute businesswoman herself. After her father's death, she managed her affairs in such a successful manner that it was said that when her tribe gathered all their trade caravans together to start a trip, Khadija's caravan was the size of all the other caravans put together.

By the time she was 20, Khadija had been orphaned, married twice, widowed twice, and was the mother of at least three young sons. (There is some question about the number of children, especially daughters, that Khadija had by her first two husbands.) Although she was a much sought after bride, she was not anxious to be widowed for a third time, so Khadija remained a single working mother for quite a few years.

Within her community, Khadija earned two nicknames: Ameerat-Quraysh (Princess of Quraysh) and El-Tahira (The Pure One). These names reflected the respect she had earned within her community, both as a businessperson and as a decent citizen. Khadija was famous for providing food and clothing to the poor and financial assistance to needy relatives. (In the days of clans and tribes, those who counted themselves as relatives were numerous.)

Khadija hired Muhammad to act as her agent on a trade caravan to Syria. He was a distant cousin and came highly recommended as trustworthy. Muhammad was younger than Khadija (how much varies from one source to another), but Khadija came to respect and admire him so thoroughly that she decided to set aside her reservations about a third marriage. Khadija took the initiative and sent an emissary to ask Muhammad if he would marry her. He was willing.

Their marriage was a happy one, and when Muhammad was perplexed by the holy words and visions that were revealed to him, he sought the advice and comfort of his wife. There was an old saying that, "Islam did not rise except through Ali's sword and Khadija's wealth," but this does not accurately portray either Islam or Khadija's role as Muhammad's wife. Her support of him was complete. In fact, it was Khadija who told Muhammad that he was the long-awaited Prophet, and she staked everything she had on it.

Activities

1. Describe Khadija in your own words.

2. Write an imaginary diary entry Khadija might have made when she was considering asking Muhammad to take her as his wife.

Education

Education was highly important to Middle Eastern Muslims, Christians, and Jews. Each of these faiths was based on revealed scripture, and each developed laws or guidelines for living according to God's will. God's will could only be fathomed through a careful and knowledgeable reading and interpretation of the sacred texts. In the specific case of Islam, a class of learned men known as *ulama* developed as specialists in the sciences needed to understand and apply religious law. These sciences included Arabic grammar, criticism, and the study of laws.

By the ninth century, law schools had been established as places where students and teachers met. The relationship between student and teacher was highly personal, and both ulama and their students travelled far and wide within the Islamic world to learn from noted scholars in other cities. This exchange of people and ideas contributed to the unity of Islamic high culture despite linguistic, cultural, and geographic diversity. In the tenth and eleventh centuries, these law schools became more institutionalized and took the form of state-supported *madrasas*. These madrasas offered formal legal instruction to students who were able to live and study there on bursaries. Graduates of the madrasas would themselves become teachers or state administrators. Over the centuries, madrasas also served as centres for religious propaganda and political action, but usually retained a strong religious identity.

Cross-Cultural Influences

The high culture of medieval Islam reflected many cultural influences: Byzantine, Egyptian, Persian, and Indian. Although Arabia was materially impoverished, by Muhammad's time, the Arabic language was a highly developed literary vehicle. Literary Persian, for its part, was temporarily submerged by the Arab conquests, but re-emerged as a medium of poetry, literature, and government administration beginning in the ninth century. From that point on, however, Persian was written in Arabic script and borrowed heavily from Arabic vocabulary. Somewhat later, with the establishment of the Ottoman and other Turkish-speaking dynasties, literary Turkish adopted the Arabic alphabet and numerous Arabic and Persian words.

By and large, medieval Muslims had little to learn from their European contemporaries. In Umayyad and Abbasid times, Europe was in the throes of the Dark Ages. Even when European high civilization began to revive in the eleventh century, it lagged far behind that of the Islamic world in most respects. Cross-cultural borrowing between Muslims and Christians in the Middle Ages flowed from the Middle East to Europe, not the other way around. The debt of Europe to Middle Eastern intellectual achievements did not stop there. Algebra, a word of Arabic derivation, was a Middle Eastern invention. Arabic numerals using zeros invented in India, were passed to Europe via the Middle East, replacing clumsy Roman numerals. Words such as "sofa," "ottoman," and "mattress," along with "admiral," "arsenal," and "barbican" indicate the European debt to the Middle East for both creature comforts and warfare. Likewise, words such as "sherbet," "orange," "yogurt," and "coffee" reveal the culinary aspects of Europe borrowing from the Middle East.

Islamic civilization was itself a synthesis of many cultural traditions. The self-confidence of Muslims in this period encouraged an attitude of openness toward other cultures, in the knowledge that they could be assimilated and Islamized. Self-confidence and openness combined to create a flourishing culture from the ninth to eleventh centuries.

THE ARTS

Literature

Literary expression in the Islamic Middle East took many forms, especially poetry. Arabic poetry predates the Islamic era, and had a well-established tradition. Other forms of literary expression included chronicles of the exploits of kings and leaders, biographical dictionaries, literature, humorous stories, folk tales, and epics. The chronicles and biographical dictionaries are our main source of raw material for writing about Islamic history.

The tremendous literary output (and scientific achievements) of the Islamic Middle East were made possible through royal patronage. The decentralization of the Abbasid caliphate from the tenth century onward actually worked to the advantage of literary production as each ruler in the Islamic common-wealth surrounded himself with poets, writers, and scientists to enhance his prestige. This cultural environment was reminiscent of the later Italian Renaissance, when the fragmentation of Italy into prosperous city-states provided a multitude of opportunities for artists to find patrons.

Architecture

The monuments of Islamic religious architecture today include some of the most famous buildings in the world, such as the Great Mosque in Granada, Spain (now a Catholic cathedral) and the Taj Mahal in India. The characteristic building was the **mosque**, with a basic floor plan that allowed worshippers to fulfill the various rituals of ablution (cleansing) and prayer. Atop this floor plan, however, a variety of architectural styles was displayed. Usually, mosques were surmounted by domes, and had a colonnaded courtyard and distinctive minarets (prayer towers). Pictorial representations were usually avoided in favour of abstract geometric patterns (arabesques) and *Qur'anic* calligraphy.

The earliest example of monumental Islamic architecture is the Dome of the Rock in Jerusalem, built by the Umayyad caliphs in the early eighth century. The Umayyad Mosque in Damascus also dates from this time, and both illustrate how Roman-Byzantine forms were assimilated into Muslim architecture. The locations of these mosques are also significant. The site on which the Dome of the Rock was built was originally the site of the Jewish Temple destroyed by Rome in 70 CE. Later, a Christian church was constructed there. The site of the Umayyad Mosque in Damascus originally

This is the interior of the Dome of the Rock, the earliest (seventh century) monumental architecture of Islam. The site in Jerusalem is sacred to Jews because it is believed to be where God prevented Abraham from sacrificing his son Isaac, and to Muslim tradition because it is where Muhammad ascended to heaven.

The History of the Imagination: Myths and Legends

The Arabian Nights

More than likely, you are familiar with at least one of the world-famous stories called the *Arabian Nights*. This collection of folk tales has been popular in the Islamic world for centuries. English and French translations have been available for nearly 300 years. You might remember *Aladdin*, *Sindbad the Sailor*, or *Ali Baba and the Forty Thieves* as favourite bedtime stories, movies, cartoons, or books.

One of the most interesting of the *Arabian Nights* collection is the first story, for it serves as the pretext for all the other stories. Also known as *One Thousand and One Nights*, the stories are presented as a framed narrative. The tales could be totally unrelated, except that they are all being told by one person to another. The relationship between the narrator and the listener provides the framework that allows the stories to unfold. In the first story, entitled "The Stories Begin," we meet the narrator and her audience:

> There was once a revered Sultan named Schahriah who discovered that his most beloved and pampered wife had deceived him completely. He not only ordered her execution, but also took an oath to marry a new wife each day and have her executed the next morning before she could deceive him too. This course of action did not make him popular, but no one knew how to stop him.
>
> Eventually, Scheherazade, the beautiful and clever daughter of the Sultan's close adviser, convinced her father to present her as a bride. Her father was against it, but Scheherazade had a plan and her father trusted her to know what she was doing.
>
> Before being presented to the Sultan, Scheherazade tells her sister, Dinarzade, that she will beg the Sultan to allow Dinarzade to sleep in the bridal rooms that night, since it is to be her last night. An hour before dawn, Dinarzade should wake Scheherazade and say, "My sister, if you are not asleep, I beg you, before the sun rises, to tell me one of your charming stories."
>
> Luckily, the Sultan allowed Dinarzade to sleep in the room and she followed her sister's instructions. Scheherazade then asked her husband's permission to tell her sister a story and the Sultan agreed. Wisely, she began a suspenseful tale, then stopped, forcing Schahriah to choose between her

execution that morning or hearing the rest of the story that night. So, Scheherazade holds off the execution one night at a time and stops the slaughter of others, for at least one thousand and one nights.

There is no one credited author for the stories. Most were probably part of the oral tradition, some of Arab origin, but some from much farther afield. Did you know, for example, that *Aladdin* was originally a Chinese folk tale? Eventually, someone gathered the stories and created the framework.

Although few of the stories are connected to the plight of Schahriah and Scheherazade ("Aladdin" and "Sindbad," for example), many do repeat certain notions. These include: some women are unfaithful, but not all; some oaths can be broken with dignity; death is not the only effective punishment; and others. More than anything, though, the stories are full of entertaining magic.

This a twentieth-century artist's conception of the harem of Sultan Schahriah.

Activities

1. Tell one of the *Arabian Nights* tales in your own words. Explain the main points and the lessons that can be learned.

2. Compare a modern version of one of the *Arabian Nights* tales with an older print version. For example, compare Disney's animated *Aladdin* movie with an older print version. Or, compare a video game with its source story. Explain your reaction to each version.

housed a pagan temple during Roman times, and later, a church dedicated to St. John the Baptist. Inside the mosque today is a shrine venerated by Muslims that is said to contain the head of St. John.

The mosaic work on both buildings is derived from Byzantine art. Interestingly, the mosaics in Damascus include exceptional pictorial representations of Paradise, complete with cities, flowing rivers, trees, and gardens, but no animal or human figures. Another notable early mosque is that of the Abbasid governor Ibn Tulun (d. 884) in Cairo. It is the best-preserved example of monumental Abbasid architecture, since hardly a trace remains of the Abbasids in Baghdad itself due to the Mongol conquest. The layout and design of the Ibn Tulun Mosque clearly reflect the influence of pre-Islamic Mesopotamian architecture, especially the ziggurat-style minarets. Later, the Ottomans embellished their capital at Istanbul with beautiful mosques whose characteristic domes owe a debt to imperial Byzantine architecture. On a visit to Istanbul, one can compare Emperor Justinian's sixth-century cathedral of Hagia Sofia with Sultan Ahmet's nearby Blue Mosque of 1000 years later.

Hagia Sophia, Istanbul. This is the church built by the Eastern Roman Emperor Justinian in the sixth century. It is now used as a mosque, as the minarets, the tall prayer towers, tell us.

WEB CONNECTION
http://www.mcgrawhill.ca/links/echoes
For more information about Islamic architecture, go to the site above.

Domestic architecture varied from place to place depending on climate and available building materials. Generally speaking, one- and two-storey houses were oriented inward around a paved courtyard. This inward orientation allowed extended families to retain their privacy, while at the same time giving them a large pleasant interior domain in which to go about their daily business. Architectural and artistic embellishments were inside the courtyards, rather than facing the streets outside. The houses were arranged so that the head of the household could receive visitors without the visitors violating the privacy of the family quarters.

The majority of houses in any city sheltered the poor, where privacy was hard to maintain. Typically, families shared a common courtyard. The architecture of the poor has not survived, but a few examples of middle- and upper-class houses have been restored and are open to the public in cities such as Cairo, Damascus, and Aleppo. The most luxurious houses had elaborate stone and inlay work around their courtyards, decorated ceilings, running fountains in the rooms, and fountains and fruit trees in the open courtyards.

The Caravanserai

Along with mosques, another characteristic Middle Eastern building was the *caravanserai*. This building, familiar in major cities, combined the functions of a wholesale market and a hotel for visiting merchants. Particular caravanserais often were identified with distinct trades or nationalities, such as the silk caravanserai or the Venetian caravanserai. Characteristically, a caravanserai was a two-storey structure surrounding a central square or rectangular courtyard. Pack animals and goods would be kept on the ground level, and travellers' quarters were on the upper level. In addition to these urban establishments, more modest caravanserais — the medieval equivalent of motels — were also located along major trade routes. Today, in countries like Turkey and Syria, caravanserais are being restored and preserved as museums (or even converted into modern hotels).

This thirteenth-century caravanserai is on the road to Aksaray in modern Turkey. Travellers and traders would have stopped here to refresh themselves on their long journeys.

Urban caravanserais were usually part of a large central market complex, called *souk* in Arabic and *bazaar* in Persian and Turkish. The central markets were often covered to provide protection from the elements. Different areas of the bazaar would be identified with specific trades: gold shops, copper shops, spice shops, woodworking, and fabric shops. A town's major mosque was usually located near the central market, and smaller neighbourhood markets were in residential quarters. Today, the bazaars and souks of Istanbul, Tehran, Fez, Cairo, and Aleppo are among the busiest and best known of the Middle East.

Painting

With the exception of the Umayyad period, pictorial representation in the Islamic Middle East was confined to manuscript illumination (illustrations). Arabesque abstracts and calligraphy decorated religious buildings. The paintings of the Islamic world are primarily human miniatures, and although Islam prohibited the representation of human figures in sacred art, there were no such restrictions on worldly arts and letters. The art of manuscript illumination can be traced at least as far back as the Abbasid period, even though relatively few examples of these manuscripts survive. Much more numerous are the manuscripts from the post-Mongol period produced through court patronage in Persia and India and in Ottoman Istanbul. The illuminations illustrated epic poems, historical chronicles, and scientific treatises. Subtle but distinctive differences can be seen in the art of miniature decoration in different regions of the Islamic world. Ottoman miniatures tended to be simpler and less sophisticated than the elaborate miniatures produced under the Persian rulers. By the same token, however, Ottoman painting was more realistic than the dreamlike atmosphere evoked by Persian miniatures. Miniatures produced in India under the Persian-speaking Mogul dynasty were similar to, yet distinguished from, Persian miniatures.

[SCIENCE AND TECHNOLOGY

Building on the legacy of Hellenistic and Indian learning, Muslim scientists added much to the fund of general human knowledge. The secret of their

Pushing the Boundaries: Developments in Science and Technology

Algebra: Another Islamic Innovation

Does the name Muhammad ibn Musa al-Khwarizmi (ca. 750–850) ring a bell? Many students around the world do not realize how indebted they are to Muslim scholars of the medieval Islamic world, scholars like al-Khwarizmi. They forget there was a time when cultural and intellectual influence flowed from the Middle East to Europe, not the other way around.

This is the Mosque al-Azhar in Cairo, Egypt, the oldest university in the world. Al-Khwarizmi and Omar Khayyam are part of the Islamic scholarly tradition that has flourished here since 970, when the mosque was built by the Fatimid dynasty.

While the rest of Europe muddled through what used to be called the Dark Ages, Islamic scholars both preserved ancient sciences, in Arabic translations, and made their own significant and lasting contributions. Muhammad al-Khwarizmi is a good example of a man who did both. A scholar with the Bait al-Hikmah institute (also known as the House of Wisdom), he put forward what is considered to be the first great advance in arithmetic — the introduction of Arabic numerals — the nine symbols and a zero that we still use today. He introduced these symbols in *The Book of Addition and Subtraction According to the Hindu Calculation*. It survives today in Latin translation, and is thought to be the oldest known mathematics text. Although the concept of numerals was borrowed, al-Khwarizmi set it down, demonstrated its usefulness, and popularized it.

The word "algebra" comes from the title of another book by al-Khwarizmi: *The Book of Restoring and Balancing*. The Arabic word for restoring is *al-jabr*. This new concept of algebra would develop over centuries with input from many other Muslim scholars. A notable contribution came from Omar Khayyam, a man remembered more today as a poet, although he was also a mathematician. As a student of algebra, he developed the solution of cubic equations.

Activities

1. Mathematics is not the only field that benefited from significant contributions made by Muslim scholars. Report on a contribution to another field during this time period. Consider history, philosophy, sciences, medicine, architecture, or music.

achievements, apart from having wealthy royal patrons willing to support scientific work, was their use of the scientific method. According to the scientific method, generalizations require testing and experimentation before they can be accepted, and they are always subject to change should new evidence come to light. Rather than blindly accepting the conclusions of earlier authorities, no matter how eminent, Muslim scientists tested such conclusions and discarded them if they were found to be unsound. For instance, the scientist known to the West as Alhazen, who studied optics in Cairo during the Fatimid period, refused to accept Euclid and Ptolemy's theory that the eye emits visual rays. Instead he conducted experiments and advanced the theory that vision is due to the impact of light rays.

Algebra, trigonometry, and geometry were all invented or developed by Muslim mathematicians. Chemistry (or alchemy, a word of Arabic derivation) was likewise an invention of Muslim scientists. From the ninth century, Muslim astronomers made exact measurements of celestial movements, developed astronomical tables and calendars, and estimated the circumference of Earth, which they assumed was round.

Growing political insecurity in the Islamic world, combined with a decline in its material fortunes after Mongol invasion, brought original scientific inquiry to an abrupt halt. Muslim rulers were no longer willing or able to lavish sums on experimental research with no direct military applications. So while the sixteenth-century Ottoman Empire kept abreast of developments in military technology, the spirit of scientific inquiry was no longer encouraged. Religious orthodoxy also dampened speculative inquiry. The Muslim scientific legacy was transmitted to Europeans primarily via translations of Arabic scientific treatises from Spain.

This page from *A Book of Fixed Stars* dates from 1009-1010. It shows the constellation Andromeda. This book borrowed from both Egyptian and Chinese scholars.

Review... Recall... Reflect...

1. Explain how education in Islamic societies helped to maintain stability and promoted continuity.

2. List three ways that Islamic culture influenced Western societies.

3. Explain how Islamic architecture, including the caravanserai, reflected the society of the Middle East.

Islam Today

Islam today is the world's second-largest and fastest-growing religion (after Christianity). This growth is due not only to population increases in countries with Muslim majorities (extending in an arc from

West Africa to Southeast Asia), but also to continuing conversions. The basic Islamic message is simple: there is one God and Muhammad is His messenger. The culture of Islam is a source of inspiration and pride for all Muslims. The cultural legacy of the Islamic Middle East is a powerful tool for newly independent peoples seeking to establish equality with the West, which dominated them for the last 400 years.

This is particularly true of the Middle East, where political nationalism has taken root in the last century. Arab, Iranian, and Turkish nationalists, as well as other mainly Muslim Middle Eastern peoples such as the Kurds, take pride in their shared language, history, territory, and culture. For nationalists, the historical memory of the Islamic Middle East is mainly cultural and linguistic. For those seeking to revive the faith, the religious significance of history is uppermost. Both these groups look to the history of the Islamic Middle East for lessons, inspiration, and guidance as they confront the many challenges facing Muslim peoples in the twenty-first century. Events that happened a thousand years ago are still fresh in people's minds today.

History Continues to Unfold

Research into medieval Islamic history continues to unfold in two directions. First, there is the discovery and study of new sources. Despite the long history of Islamic studies in Western universities, a significant number of medieval Arabic and Muslim manuscripts have yet to be carefully reviewed. Scholars have focused on manuscripts that discuss law, war, politics, theology, and philosophy, and have tended to neglect other types of writing such as manuals on dream interpretation. But these neglected manuscripts can tell us a great deal about how

mediaeval authors viewed the world and the influences they felt. Studying previously neglected sources can also help us to understand today how people in the past shared, adapted, and altered their culture and values.

History also unfolds as we ask new questions. Every generation of students has a set of questions that are important to them, and a perspective that may be different from that of generations that came before. The writing of history is constantly changing, not because the events of the past have changed, but because our understanding of these events, their connections and their significance changes. For example, 30 years ago, it would have been difficult, if not impossible, to write the section of this chapter that discusses women. We can do so now only because the growth of feminism in the 1960s and 1970s created the field of women's studies, and researchers turned to the sources to ask questions about the role and status of women in the medieval Middle East. Sources that previous generations consulted to find out about wars, battles, and dynasties can now be re-examined to see what they can tell us about human sexuality.

Beyond this, debates continue about issues that used to be considered settled. One of the fiercest debates going on now concerns how much we really can know about the life of Muhammad and the early Islamic community. Once, it was common to say that Islam (unlike Christianity) was born in the "full light of history." Now, however, the reliability of Islamic source materials on Muhammad's life is hotly disputed. Everyone acknowledges that the earliest Muslim history was written many years after the fact and that it is a crystallization of oral tradition (just like the Christian Gospels). One group of scholars believes that these early sources tell a coherent story, while others argue that the earliest Muslim sources are so biased by the authors' views that they cannot be regarded as truly historical accounts. This ongoing discussion provides fertile ground for new ideas about how Middle Eastern history was written and the different viewpoints and interests that helped to create it.

In the end, that is what history is all about: not learning and memorizing a set of stale and static facts, but a dynamic process of exploring the past and trying to make sense of it. By looking at the past this way, we gaze into a mirror, hoping to arrive at a better understanding of the human condition, with all of its doubts and tragedies, and joys and triumphs.

Current Research and Interpretations

One of the greatest gaps in our knowledge of the medieval Middle East is popular history — the history of common people. Most historical records were left to us by literate elites — teachers, administrators, dynastic chroniclers, and so forth. The views and voices of common people (the great majority of the population, after all) are not often heard. Fortunately, the development of the field of social history since the 1960s has encouraged attempts to get at the history of common people, in at least some times and in some places, where source materials are available.

Chapter Review

Chapter Summary

In this chapter, we have seen:

- the effects of isolation on communities in areas such as the desert and mountain regions
- the effects of religious training in Islamic schools on the stability of Islamic society
- that the basis of authority in Islamic societies is inextricably tied to religion
- that women, despite many restrictions, exerted considerable influence in the political and social life of Islamic societies

Reviewing the Significance of Key People, Concepts, and Events (Knowledge/Understanding)

1. Understanding the early history of the Islamic world requires a knowledge of the following people, concepts, and events, and an understanding of their significance in the development of Islamic society. In your notes, identify and explain the historical significance of seven from the lists below.

People	Concepts/Places	Events
Saladin	Islam	Crusades
	Qur'an	Mongolian invasion
	Dome of the Rock	Ramadan
	Mecca	caravanserai
	Umayyad caliphate	Ottoman Empire
	Abbasid caliphate	One Thousand and One Nights
	Fatimid dynasty	

2. Using a Venn diagram, illustrate how Islam and Christianity are similar and different.

3. Shortly after the death of Muhammad, the Islamic faith split into the Sunni and the Shi'i. Using a chart format, compare the differences between the two Islamic groups.

Doing History: Thinking About the Past (Thinking/Inquiry)

1. Historians often debate whether history is made by great people, or great people are made by history. Should Muhammad be considered a great historical figure who changed the course of history, or was he a product of his age, shaped by the forces around him? Using sound evidence, write a one-paragraph response that defends a clear position on this question.

2. Despite often facing restrictions in public life, Islamic women played a very important role in society, even to the point of influencing politics. Create and complete a chart with points under these two headings: "Status of Women in Islamic Society" and "Role of Women in Islamic Society."

Connecting to the *World History Handbook*: Once you have completed the chart, transfer some of the most important aspects of the role of women in Islamic societies to the graphic organizer "Role of Women in Society" in your *World History Handbook*.

Applying Your Learning (Application)

1. Create a suitable greeting card for one of the Islamic festivals or religious holidays. Make sure your greeting card clearly captures the importance of the tradition in Islamic society.

2. Within the Islamic Middle East there are several distinct physical environments from which unique societies emerged. Use the following matrix to analyze the factors that influenced a variety of forms of social structure throughout the Islamic world prior to the sixteenth century.

Physical Environment	Description of the Environment	Social Structure
River Basin		
Mountain Region		
Desert Region		
Steppes		
Urban Region		

Communicating Your Learning (Communication)

1. On a map of the world, show the factors that influenced the nature of the relationships between Islamic societies of the Middle East and other areas of the world. Use arrows and labels to indicate the flow of trade goods, ideas, beliefs, and invasions into and out of the Middle East. Use a variety of colours to differentiate the arrows clearly.

Connecting to the *World History Handbook*: Once you have completed your map, transfer the main ideas to the graphic organizer "Relationships Between Societies" in your *World History Handbook*.

2. Select an area of Islamic history that you would like to learn more about. Prepare five questions to guide your further research. Once you have created your questions, find three sources other than this textbook that could help you to answer your questions.

CHAPTER EIGHT

African Kingdoms

CHAPTER EXPECTATIONS

By the end of this chapter, you will be able to:

- analyze the interactions between African kingdoms and other civilizations prior to the sixteenth century

- identify forces that tended to promote and facilitate change among African civilizations

- assess the diverse forms of economic organization that existed in Africa prior to the sixteenth century

- evaluate the influence of religion on the political structures of African kingdoms

The Great Enclosure at Great Zimbabwe, built ca.1100.

For almost 2500 years — from about 850 BCE to 1600 CE — great cultures and civilizations thrived throughout Africa. With the exception of ancient Egypt, however, most Westerners are unaware of them. Past African civilizations are seldom studied in schools, or discussed in the media.

Many Westerners still cling to outdated stereotypes of Africa, including the view that African societies possessed no history or civilization before European contact. These ideas have formed the bases of many myths, misunderstandings, and racial prejudice. Such myths were invented by Europeans simply to justify colonization, slavery, and belief in their racial superiority. Although most of these myths have been disproved by modern scientists and historians, they often persist in the media with little regard for the feelings of African and African-Canadian communities.

Since the 1950s, however, the situation has changed dramatically as independent African states have emerged to become active members of the international community. An increasing number of historians have begun investigating African history with a more thorough, objective, and open-minded perspective. Consequently, the progress of modern research has not only brought to light Africa's extraordinary historical development, but also has started to lay to rest negative stereotypes of the continent and its people.

By examining the rise and development of ancient civilizations in Africa, we will discover how modern research has dispensed with the view that the peoples of Africa had no history of their own. We will shed light on the realities underlying the progress of society and civilization in Africa, and the continent's contributions to human achievement.

KEY WORDS

Meroë

saqia

Ge'ez

Swahili

Kilwa

Great Zimbabwe

Mutapa Empire

Ghana

Hajj

Songhay

KEY PEOPLE

Nubians

Kushites

Axumites

King Ezana

Soninke

Sundiata Keita

Malians

Mansa Musa

Sunni Ali

Askia Muhammad

VOICES FROM THE PAST

Semper aliquid novi Africam adferre.

"Africa always brings something new."

**Pliny the Elder,
Historia Naturalis,
Book 18:31**

TIME LINE: AFRICAN KINGDOMS

| | ca. 5000 BCE | Mande people begin migrating south as the Sahara Desert grows more inhospitable |

Permanent settlements begin to develop between the Niger and Senegal rivers — ca. 1000 BCE

ca. 800 BCE — Kingdom of Kush rises to dominance in northeast Africa

Kushites invent a 23-character alphabet — ca. 300 BCE

ca. 300 CE — Axumite Kingdom dominates trade in northeast Africa, the Kingdom of Axum becomes the world's first Christian state

Axumite armies invade and destroy the Kingdom of Kush — ca. 350 CE

ca. 400 CE — Axumites develop the Ge'ez writing system to suit their language

Arab and Persian settlers begin to arrive in East Africa, bringing the Islamic faith to the region — ca. 800

ca. 1000 — Great Zimbabwe begins to develop with the building of a great palace; Ghana is weakened by invasions from North African Muslims, leading to their defeat by the Kingdom of Mali

Kingdom of Mali is founded by Sundiata Keita — 1230

1324 — Malian leader Mansa Musa made his Hajj (religious pilgrimage) to Mecca accompanied by as many as 60 000 people

Portuguese begin to attack and destroy East African cities — ca. 1500

ANCIENT CIVILIZATIONS IN NORTHEAST AFRICA: THE KINGDOM OF KUSH

The earliest African civilizations developed along the Nile River in northeastern Africa. Each year, the Nile overflowed its banks and flooded the surrounding areas. As the flood waters receded, they deposited a rich black fertile soil on the nearby plains. This annual event created a narrow strip of habitable land between two generally uninhabitable deserts to the east and west. Stone Age farmers settled in this narrow fertile land abandoning their nomadic and hunter-gatherer way of life and establishing permanent farming villages. As these early agriculturalists produced more and more food, the number of people in the fertile areas increased. Villages became larger and grew into cities linked by trading routes and peopled by professionals such as artisans, priests, doctors, teachers, soldiers, and officials.

While this early Egyptian civilization was flourishing along the lower Nile, the Kushite civilization was growing along the Upper Nile. The ancient kingdom of Kush was located in Nubia, the northeastern region of present-day Sudan. Ancient Nubia is generally considered to encompass the region between Aswan (Egypt), at the first cataract (large waterfall) of the Nile, and Khartoum (Sudan), just south of the sixth cataract. The name Nubia is believed to have come from the ancient Egyptian word for gold (*nub*), as at the time, the region was famous for its abundant production of gold.

Geography

Although there is great diversity in its terrain, the region that was known as Nubia in ancient times is generally divided into two broad zones. The first is Lower Nubia, the northernmost portion that extends from the second to the first cataract. A lake formed by the Aswan Dam now covers this area. Before the construction of the Aswan Dam, most of the river flowed over sandstone and deposited fertile soil in some parts of the region, enabling it to enjoy a measure of prosperity. The region was significant as both a place for settlement and a point of contact between Nubia and Egypt.

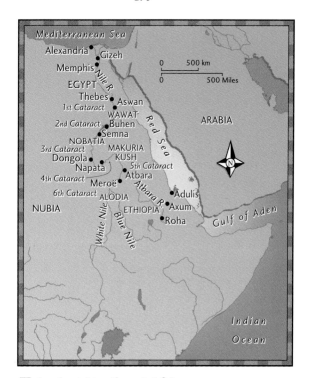

■ Ancient Northeast Africa

On a modern map of Africa, in what country will you find the ancient city of Atbara and the Nubian Desert? Spellings may vary from map to map.

The second zone, Upper Nubia, stretches south into Sudan and consists of different physiographic areas, including the barren rocks of Batn el Hajar, or Belly of Rock, the granite and clay plains of the Abri-Delgo Reach, and the flat plains of the Dongola

Reach. Of these areas, the Dongola Reach is the only one that receives an annual Nile flood similar to that of Lower Egypt. Because this area is the most fertile subdivision of Upper Nubia, it attracted the first Nubian settlements, including Kerma and Napata, the first capital cities of Kush.

Pyramids of Meroë, in the kingdom of Kush. How are these different from the Egyptian pyramids you have seen?

The Kingdom of Kush

Ancient Nubia's geographic location provided many unique advantages, including proximity to other ancient cultures. In the north were the civilizations of Egypt and the Mediterranean world. In addition, the Nile River — much of which runs parallel to the Red Sea — furnished waterways that made this region an important link between these civilizations and tropical Africa.

In the southern part of Nubia, the Blue Nile and its tributaries provided convenient access to the Ethiopian highlands, as well as to the Red Sea and Indian Ocean. In the west, Wadi al-Malik and Wadi

Huwar, which are now dry but had water in the past, offered Nubia an easy route to the Chad basin, and to the Niger Valley and West Africa. However, the land trade routes through Nubia were, undoubtedly, much older than those of the rivers.

Given their central location, it is not surprising that the ancient people of this region had ties linking them to civilizations both near and far. The region was an important corridor for trade between tropical Africa and the rest of the world, so **Nubians** had close and constant contact with their neighbours. Archaeological records indicate that ancient Nubia was a meeting place for different civilizations;

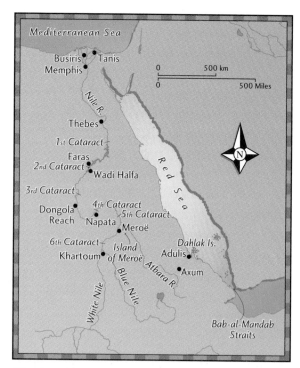

■ **The Nile Valley: Ancient Kush and Axum**

1 **What is a cataract? Try to locate the cataracts of the Nile River. How many are there?**

2. **On a map of modern Africa, in what country will you find the ancient city of Axum? Again, spelling may be slightly different from the ancient name.**

Egyptian and other Mediterranean influences are apparent in its art and architecture, while the influence of Central Africa is clearly evident in its material culture and languages. Despite these foreign influences, the ancient Nubians themselves exercised political dominance and cultural influence over other peoples during certain periods of their history. The Nubian civilization enjoyed a long period of power and prosperity during the Kingdom of Kush, which lasted from about 800 BCE to about 350 CE.

The Rise to Dominance of the Kushite Kingdom

Ancient Kush developed a complex writing system in the third century BCE, but because these writings have yet to be deciphered, we know little about the kingdom's early history. Nevertheless, we do know that the **Kushites** were rich, powerful, and influential, and that they had a close, ongoing relationship with ancient Egypt. This relationship included periods when each civilization became the colonial ruler of the other.

The ancient Kushites were agriculturalists and herders who traded with ancient Egypt and tropical Africa. Kush had a prosperous trade with ancient Egypt in gold, ivory, ebony, ostrich eggs and feathers, wild animals, and slaves. Sometime during the Egyptian New Kingdom, which lasted from 1580–1100 BCE, Egypt conquered Nubia. The strong Egyptian influence during this period is evident in Nubia's Egyptian-styled temples and pyramids; the Nubians even adopted Pharoanic titles and worshipped Pharoanic gods like Amon-Re and Isis.

These small statues, dated ca. 690–664 BCE, are called *shawabtis,* and they were buried in the tomb of the Nubian ruler Taharqa. Shawabtis were meant to serve the deceased in the afterlife.

Kush regained its independence when the New Kingdom collapsed in 1100 BCE. The Kushites moved their capital farther up the Nile, to Napata. Eventually, the Kushite King Piankhi invaded and conquered Egypt, and made Napata the seat of the Egyptian Empire. Kushite kings like Taharqa formed the twenty-fifth Egyptian Dynasty. Kushite rule of Egypt lasted for only a century; Kush lost Egypt to the Assyrians, whose superior iron weapons enabled them to expel the Kushites from Egypt. The Kushites then moved their capital farther south, from Napata to **Meroë** (mare-oh-ay), where their kingdom continued for another thousand years.

Located at the centre of trade routes, Meroë served as a centre for trade goods (e.g., gold, ivory, animal skins, perfumes, and slaves) from Africa to the Red Sea, the Middle East, and Europe. Meroë was also rich in iron ore, and its people were skilled ironworkers. Archaeologists have excavated great slag heaps as well as the furnaces where Kushite blacksmiths produced iron tools and weapons, clearly indicating that ancient Meroë had a booming iron industry. It is believed that the iron technology of the Kushites spread through trade to western and southern Africa. Finally, around 350 CE, the armies of King Ezana of Axum invaded and destroyed Meroë.

This gold cylinder from the ancient Kingdom of Kush (ca. 300 BCE) was used to hold scrolls of writing on papyrus.

Religious Beliefs

The official Kushite religion resembled that of the Egyptians, including all the major Egyptian gods. It was a polytheistic religion — one that encouraged the worship of many gods. Although the Kushites were devout followers of Amon, they later incorporated the worship of their own local gods, including the prominent war god Apedemak. Temple carvings always represent Apedemak with a lion's head, and historians believe that lions played an important role in his ceremonies. The Kushites also worshipped Sbomeker, who may have been both their creator-god and chief local god.

Arts and Architecture

Kushite cultural achievements included the magnificent architecture of their cities, as well as beautiful works of art. The great Nubian palaces and temples that have survived to this day testify to their architectural excellence. Not far from Meroë, at the site of Wad been Naqa, archaeologists discovered the ruins of two great palaces and a beehive-shaped structure that is thought to have been a storage house for grain.

Kushite artisans made very high-quality clay pottery — regarded as some of the finest in the ancient world. Kushite artisans frequently decorated their pottery with designs taken from the natural world. The Kushites were also jewelry makers, especially in gold and shells.

Science and Technology

Writing, great art, and architecture were not the only Kushite achievements. The Kushites may also have given humanity one of the first irrigation machines when they invented the *saqia*, a wooden wheel with earthen pots attached to bring up water from the Nile River. Farmers used oxen to turn the wheel that pulled the filled pots out of the river, and ultimately dumped the water into a reservoir. The reservoir was then used for irrigation. The saqia was a very important invention because it greatly simplified irrigation for Kushite farmers. Archaeologists have discovered saqia pots all over Nubia.

THE KINGDOM OF AXUM
Geography

The Axumite Kingdom was located on the northern end of the Ethiopian Highlands, close to the western shore of the Red Sea. Dry, hot plains lying along the African side and the South Arabian edge of the Red Sea border the highlands. Some places on the highlands themselves, however, have relatively pleasant environments. The varying elevation of the highlands causes variations in climate and vegetation. As the elevation increases, rainfall increases as temperature decreases. Because volcanic rocks formed the soils, they are more fertile here than in most other regions in Africa. Rainfall is also heavier and more reliable than in other northeastern African regions. As a result, most farmland is found in the Ethiopian Highlands. In most of these areas, farmers harvest two or three crops in a year; in other areas, they may even plant and harvest at the same time. It was in such places that the ancient **Axumites** built most of their cities, making use of the different environments and resources that were available. Archaeological and historical evidence shows that the first Axumite cities developed in the northern part of the Ethiopian Highlands.

Unlike other parts of eastern Africa, the Axumite Kingdom enjoyed many unique advantages due to its location — including its proximity to other ancient cultures. In the northwest, were the civilizations of Egypt and the Levant. The Red Sea, the Gulf of Aden, and the Mediterranean Sea all provided routes that facilitated commercial contacts between the civilizations of these regions and the Axumite Kingdom. In addition, the Axumites were strategically positioned, thanks to the inland trade routes that linked them to Nubia, the Horn of Africa, and the East African coast on the Indian Ocean.

The Growth of the Axumite Kingdom

The ancient kingdom of Ethiopia was named after its capital city, Axum. Little is known about the early history of the Axumites. From Roman and Greek sources, however, we know that an Axumite Kingdom was booming in the first century CE. At the time, the main city, Adulis, was one of the most important ports in Africa.

WEB CONNECTION

http://www.mcgrawhill.ca/links/echoes

Go to the web site above to find out more about the Kingdom of Kush.

Control of the Kushite trade routes was instrumental in dominance over the entire region of northeast Africa. Following the fall of the Kushite Kingdom, the Axumites took over these trade routes. Adulis was able to acquire much of the commercial role of Meroë. By 300 CE, almost all the goods coming in and out of northern Africa went through Axum. Archaeological and historical evidence indicate that the Axumite Kingdom had an extensive international trade with the Roman Empire, South Arabia, Nubia, Somalia, and India. Axum's imports included iron, precious metals, glass, fabrics, sugar cane, vegetable oil, aromatic substances, and spices. It exported African raw materials and luxury goods such as ivory, gold, rhinoceros horn, slaves, and live animals. Until the rise of Islam in the seventh century, the Axumites were the dominant trading power in the region.

Unlike Meroë, Axum minted its own money, which included fine gold coins. Axum was also a beautiful city, with large stone buildings and magnificent stone towers (stelae) that reached as high as 31 m. However, the purpose of these impressive stelae remains a mystery.

This stone tower, called a stele, measures 21 m high. It was erected in the fourth or fifth century CE in Axum (modern Ethiopia). The purpose of these monuments is not known.

Later, in the fourth century, **King Ezana** of Axum was converted to Christianity and declared his country a Christian state, the first Christian state in the world. King Ezana's conversion to Christianity influenced Ethiopian history well into the twentieth century.

Axum remained a powerful and prosperous kingdom until the rise of Islam in the seventh century. The Axumites maintained a friendly relationship with the Muslims for about a century, but in the eighth century, the Muslims finally destroyed the main port city Adulis, closing off the Mediterranean Sea and crippling the North African trade routes. After losing its prosperous trade networks, the Axumite Kingdom declined slowly until the Amhara Ethiopians, who believe they are the descendants of King Solomon and the old Axumite line of kings, took it over in the twelfth century.

Religion

The pre-Christian Axumite religion, which was derived from religions in southern Arabia, was polytheistic. The most important gods were Almouqah, the moon god, and the god of war, Mahrem. The Axumites believed that their gods controlled the Sun, Moon, and other elements of nature. They built impressive temples to please the gods, and the king — who also acted as the highest priest — offered sacrifices to the gods.

When Christianity became the official religion in the fourth century, the people of Axum worshipped one god. The Axumites glorified their new god with their art, literature, and a series of beautiful churches. Christian churches replaced the older temples. These early churches were each carved out of a single stone. The church called The Redeemer of the World, which still stands, is an excellent example of these single-stone churches.

Christianity not only formed the basis of Ethiopian national identity, but also helped Ethiopian kings stay in power both during the Axumite period and during the time of its Amharic successors. The Amharas considered themselves the only true Christians, identifying themselves closely with their church. In the past, the Ethiopian king headed the church. The king was both ultimate ruler and the highest priest. The Axumites considered the king to have divine powers, as indicated by the inscription of **King Ezana**: "King of kings, the son of the invincible god Ares."

People

The Ethiopian Highlands were not only attractive for settlement, they were also well positioned for contact with the outside world. Because the Highlands are close to southern Arabia and are accessible from the Red Sea, the first settlers were a mix of Kushitic-speaking Africans and Semitic-speaking South Arabians. These first settlers arrived in about 500 BCE. The South Arabian emigrants and the Kushitic-speaking Africans intermarried and exchanged customs. Out of this mix of cultures came the founders of the kingdom of Axum, with its unique written and spoken language, **Ge'ez**. The Axumites went on to create their own distinct civilization, the only one formed from a mixture of Semitic and African cultures.

This sculpture (45 cm) of an Axumite priest-king is dated to the fourth or fifth century BCE. He was a ruler of one of the early kingdoms that blended with the Kushites to form the later kingdom of Axum.

Review...Recall...Reflect

1. Explain why location was an important factor in the prosperity of the ancient Kingdom of Kush.

2. List and describe three areas in which Kushites were renowned for their skills.

3. List and describe three ways that the importance of Christianity was reflected in Axumite culture.

Writing

In addition to their achievements in religious architecture and the arts, the Axumite civilization also contributed intellectually to the art of writing. The Axumites developed a remarkable writing system for their Ge'ez language that contained vowel marks in each letter, and was written from left to right. In the fifth century CE, they replaced Greek with Ge'ez for writing church services, records, and manuscripts. One of these manuscripts was the Christian Bible — it had taken more than 200 years to translate the Bible into Ge'ez.

THE EAST AFRICAN CITY-STATES

As Axum declined, several trading cities and city-states with a unique Muslim African culture developed along the narrow East African coast that stretches from Somalia to Mozambique. We often refer to this culture as the Swahili Civilization, named after the modern inhabitants of the East African coast, many of whom speak **Swahili**. Swahili is a Bantu language rich in borrowed Arabic words, which originated on the coast as a trade language between foreign traders and the natives of the East African coast. Today, Swahili is the official language of Tanzania and Kenya, and it is spoken in much of eastern and some parts of central Africa.

These impressive East African cities began as small fishing and farming villages with wattle and daub (sticks and mud or clay) huts. Archaeologists have excavated many communities that flourished before the eighth century along the East African coast. The villages grew into towns and the towns into cities; by the tenth century, most of the coastal towns were very large and had houses of several storeys built from coral and cut stone.

Various names have been used to describe different parts and peoples of the East African coast. The Arabs and the Persians, for example, called the land between southern Somalia and northern Kenya the Land of the Zanj. The ancient Egyptians called Somalia the land of Punt. Azania was the name given to the East African coast by the Greeks. The medieval Arabs referred to the Somali people as Barbars (Berbers), while Portuguese explorers knew Africans as Moors.

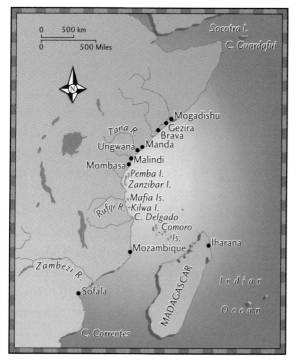

■ **Ancient Settlements on the East Coast of Africa**

Of the civilizations you have studied in this course, which ones were aware of the rich cities on the east coast of Africa? What did they call these places?

Geography

The East African coastal environment varies from open dry land with low rainfall in the north, to a tropical bushland with a moderate amount of rainfall in the south. The area from Raas Caluula to Warsheekh, in Somalia, is open land with few natural harbours, making it suitable for a nomadic way of life. From Warsheekh to Sofala, in Mozambique, the coast benefits from a reliable rainfall that increases southward, and the shore has more natural harbours. Often adjacent to this narrow, sandy coastal strip is a fertile plain where fresh water is available in many places. Because of its favourable environment and tropical climate, this part of the coast became attractive to early human settlement.

In general, the East African coastline is bordered with coral reefs that protect it from the ocean waves. There are also numerous offshore islands that spread out across this part of the Indian Ocean, providing more protection to the coast. These islands include Kilwa, Mafia, Zanzibar, Pemba, and the Bajuni Islands. The coast is frequently broken by a number of deep inlets or valleys, which provide natural harbours.

The shores that are more protected were ideal for use by the local sailboats, or dhows, as they are called locally. The dhows would sail from the ocean at high tide to anchor at the shore; as the tide receded, they came to rest on the shore where they were — and still are today — unloaded by hand.

The Monsoon Trade Winds

The reliable cycle of the monsoon winds, which blow across the ocean, was a major factor in the development of the Indian Ocean trade network that linked East Africa with India, Ceylon (Sri Lanka), the Persian Gulf, Egypt, and Arabia. The seasonal monsoon winds, which change direction every six months, helped merchants sail across the Indian Ocean. Every year, between November and March, these winds blow from the northeast; between April and September, they blow from the southwest. Sailors used these winds (and continue to do so today) to push their dhows from the East African coast to Southeast Asia and then back again. In other words, if you were the captain of an East African dhow and planned to sail from that region to India, you would leave in April before the monsoon winds died down in November. To return, you would leave when the winds changed, or end up waiting a whole year for the next monsoon to blow you back to the East African coast.

To this day, these boats called dhows are used to transport goods and food in East Africa. They have the advantage of being able to navigate both local coastal waters and the Indian Ocean.

The Rise of the East African City-States

The earliest historical document describing international trade in East Africa is the *Periplus of the Erythraean Sea,* written about 100 CE by an Egyptian-Greek merchant. This document provides a wealth of information about the inhabitants of the East African coast, their international trade, their way of life, and the products they exported. It also describes a number of thriving commercial towns on the East African coast. No central government existed in the region, and each town was independent politically as well as economically, and controlled by a chief. Among the major city-states mentioned in the document are Kilwa, Dar es Salaam, Mogadishu (Muqdisha), Malindi, and Mombasa. The most important exports from the East African coast were gold, iron, ivory, rhinoceros horn, leopard skins, and gums; these were exchanged for copper, tin, silver jewelry, fabrics, sugar, and oil.

Although ancient Egyptian, Phoenician, Greek, Roman, and Indian traders occasionally reached the East African coast in ancient times, it was not until the eighth century that the region became fully involved in international trade. With the rise and expansion of the Islamic Empire in the Middle East, trade expanded on the East African coast. From the eighth century, earlier settlements expanded and many new ones developed. The expansion of trade in this period is evident from imported Islamic objects such as pottery, glass vessels, and glass beads found all along the East African coast.

In about the ninth century, however, commercial contacts along the coast gained a new dimension — Arab and Persian travellers sought a permanent settlement on the East African coast. The movement of these immigrants was the result of religious, economic, and political factors. Some of the immigrants wanted to "spread the word" about their religion, Islam; some were seeking economic opportunities; others left their homes in the Middle East for fear of political and religious persecution.

As trade flourished along the coast, great wealth concentrated in the hands of local rulers and a few families, who then used their wealth to consolidate power and develop institutions of authority. Each town had its own chief with a council of elders. As ruling families adopted the universal values of Islam, factional policies gave way, to some degree, to a centralized authority. Rulers were able to exercise broader powers, manage large-scale trade systems, and control basic resources.

Kilwa Kisiwani

"Kilwa is one of the most beautiful and well-constructed towns in the world." These are the words of the famous North African traveller Ibn Battuta, who visited **Kilwa** in 1331. During Ibn Battuta's time, Kilwa, located in what is now Tanzania, was the most prosperous city-state on the East African coast. It controlled the coastal and Indian Ocean trade for many centuries. Kilwa's fortunes grew greatly in the thirteenth century, when the city gained control over the export of gold and ivory from the southern town of Sofala. During this time, local rulers and merchants profited from this trade and became extremely wealthy.

The Great Mosque at Kilwa was built by twelfth- and fifteenth-century sultans. The columns of the mosque, which are made of coral and concrete, once supported a great domed ceiling. Muslims controlled Kilwa's trade.

Architectural achievements in Kilwa included new palaces, a major expansion of the Great Mosque, and the common use of large stone houses, which, along with widespread use of expensive imported Chinese ceramics, attest to Kilwa's increased prosperity. However, it was not the only town on the East African coast that impressed foreign visitors. Ibn Battuta also described Mogadishu (Muqdisha), the present capital of Somalia, as a "very large town." As in Kilwa, the houses in Mogadishu were built of stone and were four or five storeys high.

Ibn Battuta commented on the diet of the Mogadishans, mentioning a variety of foods, including rice, chicken, vegetables, mangoes, bananas, and other fruits. The Mogadishans also consumed hundreds of camels and cattle every day. Ibn Battuta also described the city's traditional textile industry, which continues even today.

Thriving commerce continued in Kilwa, Zanzibar, Mogadishu, and the other city-states until the Portuguese attacked and looted them, one after the other, at the beginning of the sixteenth century. The trading cities of East Africa were unable to defend themselves against Portuguese ships and cannon attacks. In 1505, the Portuguese attacked Kilwa and Mombasa. The following year, they destroyed the Somali city of Brava. A captain of one of the ships that attacked Brava described the Portuguese brutality:

> The Portuguese flotilla arrived at a city called Brava, and had entered it by force of arms killing many Moors and stealing great wealth which its owners disdained to save, thinking only of defending themselves; nor their women, who were left there with great wealth and elegance, with seven or eight bangles on each arm, and as many on the legs, very thick and valuable. This

gave occasion to great cruelty because the men, more blinded by greed than inspired by mercy, and not to waste time, cut off their arms, legs and ears, where they carried the jewelry, without any thought of pity.

The Portuguese intended to control the Indian Ocean trade and to impose an annual gold tribute on the cities of the Swahilis. Though they tried for a very long time to dominate the Indian Ocean trade network, they had neither the ships nor the men to sustain control over such a vast region. This weakness enabled some Swahili groups to regain control of their cities at the end of the sixteenth century. Yet, the cities never regained the economic power and prosperity they had enjoyed before the Portuguese came.

The People

Historians do not know who the original inhabitants of the East African coast were, but it is believed that they may have been hunters and gatherers who spoke a language belonging to the Khoisan language family. Over time, these people were joined by three different groups who came to settle the East African coast. First came Kushitic-speaking herders; then Nilotic-speaking herders and farmers; and, finally, Bantu-speaking farmers. The original coastal people eventually adopted the Bantu language and culture.

Beginning in the ninth century, new immigrants from Arabia, Persia, and India settled on the East African coast. Wherever they settled, they intermarried with the coastal Bantus, who ultimately adopted Islam as their religion. The Bantus also adopted many words from these new settlers, especially from Arabic. Out of this mix eventually evolved what we now know as the Swahili civilization. The term "Swahili" is plural for the Arabic word *Sahil,* which means "coastal people."

This minaret (Islamic prayer tower) is on Lamu Island off the coast of Kenya. The island was a centre for the trade in ivory and mangrove tree poles used in house construction.

Review...Recall...Reflect

1. What evidence suggests that trade was central to the economy of East African states?

2. How did the arrival of Islam alter East African states?

3. Why was Kilwa described as one of the most beautiful towns in the world?

CIVILIZATIONS IN CENTRAL AFRICA
The Founders of Great Zimbabwe

Farther to the south and inland from the coastal Swahili city-states is an archaeological region known as **Great Zimbabwe**, which is presently occupied by the Shona people. *Zimbabwe* is a Shona word meaning "stone building" or "sacred house." Because its name was given to the country in which it is situated, Great Zimbabwe is one of the best-known archaeological sites in Africa. What is left of this once-powerful and prosperous state are massive stone ruins scattered across a high plateau in modern Zimbabwe. Among the ruins are huge blocks of stones so precisely carved that they were joined without the use of mortar. Other ruins include a great palace, a huge tower, high walls, steps, and walkways. These and other archaeological finds tell us that the site of Great Zimbabwe was settled at different times between the eleventh and fifteenth centuries.

When Europeans first visited these ruins in the nineteenth century, they refused to accept that the structures were African creations. They firmly believed that Africans could not have possessed the advanced technology and skills required to build such mighty stone monuments. As a result, until recently, Western history attributed the construction of Great Zimbabwe to non-African foreigners such as the ancient Phoenicians, Egyptians, Persians, or Sumerians. Recently, however, archaeologists confirmed that the builders of the ruins were, in fact, the ancestors of the Shona people, a Bantu group.

Geography

The Great Zimbabwe ruins are located on a highland known as the Zimbabwe Plateau, which rises over 1000 m above sea level. The Zimbabwe Plateau is located between the Limpopo and Zambezi rivers. The Zambezi River borders the plateau on its north side; the Limpopo borders on the south. On the east, an escarpment slopes gently into the vast coastal plain of the Indian Ocean, and the Kalahari Desert borders the plateau on the west.

Geologically, the plateau varies from rounded hills of granite and flat plains to deep river valleys. The area is relatively cool, with a wet season from November to March and a dry season from April to October. During the winter months of the dry

The purpose of the conical tower of Great Zimbabwe is not known. On the interior, there is a chevron (>>>>) pattern decorating the walls. As with the walls of the enclosure, the flat stones were laid without mortar.

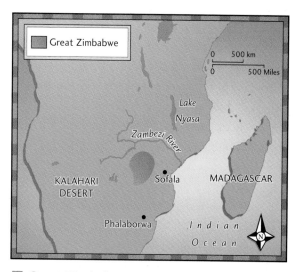

■ **Great Zimbabwe, ca. 1400**

How might traders have moved goods from Great Zimbabwe to the Indian Ocean?

This figure (40.5 cm) was carved out of soapstone (steatite) in Great Zimbabwe some time between 1200 and 1400. It was probably a votive offering to the gods in some sort of ritual.

season, the temperature can fall below freezing. In general, the plateau has fertile soil and a savannah woodland environment, dominated by shrubs and trees distributed among wide areas of grassland. Its combination of relatively fertile soil, abundant water, and good grazing and hunting grounds made the Zimbabwe Plateau desirable for early settlement. A further attraction was its strategic position on a major trading route linking the Shona with the port of Sofala on the Indian Ocean.

The Rise of the Mutapa Empire

Our knowledge of the Great Zimbabwe civilization comes not only from the archaeological evidence, but also from the oral traditions of the people currently living in the region. These unwritten stories, passed down from one generation to the next, have given us wonderful clues to the traditions of the early people

of Great Zimbabwe. Oral history tells us that, towards the end of the fifteenth century, the rulers of Zimbabwe's gold-producing regions broke away from Great Zimbabwe. One of these rulers was Mutota, who expanded his territory through military campaigns. Mutota eventually earned the title Mwene Mutapa, or Master Pillager. He created his own empire, which was called Mutapa or Monomutapa. The **Mutapa Empire**, which was centred on the northern part of the Zimbabwe Plateau, controlled a very large territory that extended from the Zambezi to the Limpopo River and covered wide stretches between the Kalahari Desert and the Indian Ocean.

The Mutapa Empire was a major source of ivory, gold, and copper. Because it served as a centre for local caravan trade and as an export outlet for local trading goods, the empire prospered from an international trade network linking it to the East African coast and to Asia. At the end of the sixteenth century, Portuguese traders made contact with the Mutapa Empire and established a friendly trading relationship. In 1570, however, the Portuguese attacked.

THE ROYAL KINGDOMS OF WEST AFRICA

West Africa is a vast geographic region including a broad spectrum of environments ranging from the Sahara Desert to tropical rain forest. It also comprises many peoples and cultures. For over a thousand years — from about 500 to 1600 CE — the region was home to many powerful and prosperous kingdoms. The best-known West African kingdoms are Ghana, Mali, and Songhay.

These three kingdoms were strategically positioned on the trans-Saharan trade network that linked West Africa to North Africa and the Middle East. They also had control of the Niger and Senegal rivers, which were natural waterways for trade. Ghana, Mali, and Songhay controlled the trade routes by collecting taxes on all merchandise transported through their territory. In turn, they exported ivory, gold, slaves, kola nuts, and other trade goods in exchange for salt, iron, copper, steel, dates, glass beads, and horses. While the kingdoms of West Africa prospered through agriculture and trade, they built many cosmopolitan cities, including Gao, Timbuktu (Tombouctou), and Jenne. For centuries, these cities served as important economic, religious, educational, political, and cultural centres.

Geography

West Africa covers the vast territory between the Sahara Desert in the north and the Gulf of Guinea in the south. From west to east, the region stretches from the Atlantic Ocean to near Lake Chad. The area ranges from desert in the north to rain forest in the south. In addition, the Futa Djalon Highlands give rise to several rivers, including the Senegal, Gambia, and Niger.

The Senegal and the Niger rivers are long, and have played a major role in the history of this region. The two rivers served not only as trade routes, but also made settled life possible. In early times, as today, farming villages were concentrated along the fertile banks of these rivers, as well as around Lake Chad. Over the ages in these areas, farmers have grown different kinds of cereal grains, beans, melons, rice, and yams. Historically, both men and women worked in the fields. Men prepared the land while women took part in weeding, threshing, planting, and transplanting the crops. As populations grew, some of these villages emerged as busy cities.

In general, we can divide the West African environment into two zones. The first is the savannah that lies between the Sahara Desert and the southern tropical rain forest. The vegetation in this zone varies with the amount and seasonal distribution of rainfall and the severity of the dry season. Rainfall increases southward from the northern edge down to the coast. In the rainier southern parts, tall trees and grasses grow. The northern part consists of almost treeless plains, with very short, widely spaced grasses, and much higher temperatures.

The second zone comprises the tropical rain forest and the Gulf of Guinea coast. It extends southward from the southern edge of the savannah to the Gulf of Guinea coastline. Because rainfall is very heavy throughout the year in the forest and along most of the coastal land, the region supports a large variety of trees, and forests are usually thick and dense.

The coastline of West Africa is also varied. In ancient times, much of the coast was inaccessible from the sea. There were few natural harbours since most of the coastline was exposed to massive waves and was bordered by mangrove swamps or inhospitable desert. The most formidable natural barrier, however, was the lack of seasonal winds that changed direction — as did the monsoons of East Africa. Along the West Coast, the winds have always blown from the north, which in times past, made only southward navigation possible. Ancient — and not-so-ancient — ships lacked the power to navigate northward against the winds. This changed in the fifteenth century, however, when the Portuguese developed the shipping technology and navigational skills needed for sailing across the oceans.

[THE RISE OF GHANA

Ghana was the first of the great West African kingdoms to attain power. The ancient kingdom of Ghana, not to be confused with the present state of Ghana, was located in the southeastern part of what

In the Field...

Gertrude Caton-Thompson and Great Zimbabwe: Pieces of a Puzzle

The story of archaeology in and about Africa is somewhat puzzling. The collection, arrangement, and interpretation of artifacts has been shaped, more than was usual, by hundreds of years of European settlement and by the colonial origins of the collectors.

Much myth and wishful thinking were added to the mix of colonial expansion. The ruins of Great Zimbabwe provide a good example of this. The earliest travels of Europeans down the coasts of Africa spawned all kinds of tales. In 1871, Carl Mauch, a German explorer, came across the ruins of Great Zimbabwe and declared that they were the legacy of King Solomon. In 1891, the Royal Geographic Society and the British Association for the Advancement of Science sent an archaeological expedition led by Theodore Bent. Bent rejected the Biblical connection, but created another myth by asserting that the site could only have been built by Arabs. The obvious simply did not occur to these

Shown here are the ruins of Great Zimbabwe, a civilization that flourished from the thirteenth to the fifteenth century. Great Zimbabwe became the centre of a huge Shona Empire that covered much of southern Africa.

early archaeologists: that the ruins were of an African civilization. Mauch and Bent both turned out to be wrong, but both could point to physical "evidence" to support their claims.

Eventually, the British Association for the Advancement of Science started to question earlier methods, so Great Zimbabwe was revisited. In 1910, David Randall-MacIver was the first to suggest that perhaps Africa had a history of its own and that Great Zimbabwe might have been built by an indigenous people. Then in the late 1920s, the Association sent Gertrude Caton-Thompson to Zimbabwe. She had built a reputation as an archaeologist in Egypt and was considered a pioneer in modern archaeological methods. Caton-Thompson spent two years painstakingly excavating and cataloguing. She concluded that Great Zimbabwe had to be of native African origin. Even Caton-Thompson was doubted, nevertheless, until radiocarbon dating in the late 1950s eliminated any possibility that the ruins were of non-African origin.

Gertrude Caton-Thompson continued a long and distinguished career as an archaeologist. Great Zimbabwe finally took its rightful place as a symbol of past achievement and freedom for Africans. The country of Zimbabwe took its name from this site when it achieved independence in 1980.

Activities

1. Explain in your own words how hundreds of years of colonization has tainted archaeology in Africa.

2. Class Experiment: Wrap a small personal memento in a newspaper. (It could be a key chain, a small ornament, hair clip, or costume jewelry.) Collect all the wrapped items, and then distribute them randomly. Each person in the class should make a small presentation on the object and who might own it. List the insights that this exercise gave you into the task of linking objects to their origin.

is modern Mauritania. The **Soninke**, a Mande-speaking group whose descendants still inhabit West Africa, built the ancient kingdom. Historians do not know exactly how or when the Soninke began their kingdom, though some believe that Ghana's roots may go back to about 300 CE.

The Soninke were the most northern of the Mande-speaking groups who had come from the Sahara Desert. Sometime between 5000 and 2500 BCE, when the desert became drier, the Mande people migrated from the desert southward into the West African savannah. Eventually, these people, attracted by the fertile lands between the Niger and the Senegal rivers, abandoned their nomadic way of life and settled down. The Mande first established farming villages; by 1000 BCE, they were growing some crops and keeping cattle and goats. Eventually, some of these villages developed into towns, which then grew into large urban centres.

The Soninke, in addition to being farmers, were successful traders. As the people became stronger, the kings of Ghana expanded the empire. Soon, the Soninke territory reached parts of what are now Guinea, Senegal, Mali, and Mauritania. The Soninke army was well organized and equipped with iron weapons, which gave it an advantage over opponents, who had only sticks, stones, and bones.

Unfortunately, we do not know exactly where the capital city of this important state was. However, an eleventh-century historian described the capital as a large city with 12 mosques. It consisted of two parts: Muslim traders occupied one part; the locals, along with their pagan king, inhabited the other. There were many other large trading towns in Ghana, and among them was Jenne, which in the eighth century had about 20 000 inhabitants. Nevertheless, most Soninke towns were much smaller, with fewer residents.

The prosperity of the kingdom of Ghana during the eighth century is attested to by an Arab geographer who referred to it as the "land of gold." Two centuries later, another Arab scholar placed it among the best of the Black kingdoms. Ancient Ghana remained a strong empire and trading power until the eleventh century, when the Almoravids, North African Muslim warriors, began a series of invasions. These led to the decline and breakup of the Ghanaian Empire in the thirteenth century, when the new kingdom of Mali conquered it.

Trade

Their success in trading enabled the Soninke to build the first state in West Africa. Archaeological artifacts indicate that the trans-Saharan trade that linked North Africa, the Sahara, and West Africa started in the third century. These artifacts include coins made in North Africa at that time.

The trans-Saharan trade, also known as the caravan trade, appears to have started at a regional level, with agricultural villages trading their surplus foods. Over time, the regional trade network expanded into the Sahara, the Mediterranean world, the Middle East, and the savannah and forest regions of West Africa. Each of these regions produced certain goods that were needed in one or more of the other regions. For example, salt was plentiful in the Sahara, but was badly needed in the savannah and forest regions of West Africa. Gold, on the other hand, was abundant in West Africa and needed in the Sahara, Mediterranean, and Middle East. From West Africa, caravans laden with gold, ivory, slaves, kola nuts, and other commodities moved across the Sahara Desert, and brought back salt, copper, dates, beads, steel, and horses.

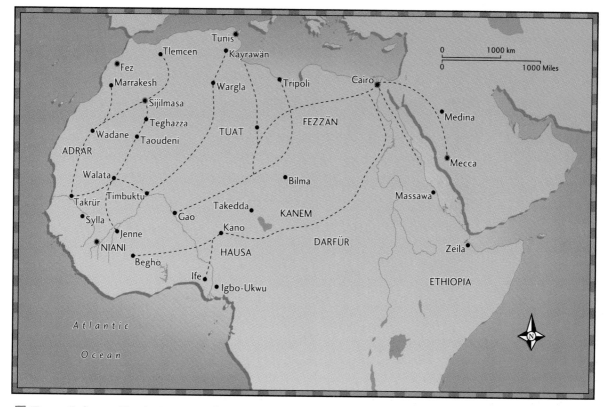

■ Trans-Saharan Trade Routes of the Fourteenth Century: Ghana and Mali

1. What is the distance from Cairo to Gao?

2. If you wanted to move goods from Gao to Igbo-Ukwu, what methods of transport might you choose?

As trans-Saharan long-distance trade grew and prospered, cities developed along the trade routes. Governments then arose to administer the cities and provide safety and security. Finally, the city governments developed into states and powerful kingdoms.

Ghana enjoyed a unique advantage due to its geographic location on the trans-Saharan trade route that ran between the Sahara and the forest regions of West Africa. Merchants from both regions had to come to, or pass through, Ghana to exchange goods. The kingdom of Ghana gained great wealth by collecting taxes on the goods passing through its territory.

Government

Ancient Ghana had a strong government that ruled over many lesser authorities or kingdoms. One king, who bore the title of "Ghana," headed the entire empire. The king was the ultimate ruler and judge. The Soninke also believed he possessed a divine power, so they feared him as well. When the Soninke approached their king, they showed respect by kneeling and showering dust on their heads.

The king also headed the army, and our eleventh-century historian wrote that the king had an army of 200 000, of whom 40 000 were well-trained cavalry. We are also given a detailed description of the court:

> When [the king] gives audience to his people, to listen to their complaints and set them to rights, he sits in a pavilion around which stand his horses caparisoned [richly ornamented] in cloth of gold; behind him stand ten pages holding shields and gold-mounted swords; and on his right hand are the sons of the princes of his empire, splendidly clad and with gold plaited [braided] into their hair. The governor of the city is seated on the ground in front of the king, and all around him are his viziers in the same position. The gate of the chamber is guarded by dogs of an excellent breed, that never leave the king's seat; they wear collars of gold and silver…

Although the king's authority was absolute, he relied on the assistance of a council of ministers and on the governor of the capital city. The majority of the council, which consisted of judges, governors, generals and counsellors, were Muslims.

As the empire of Ghana grew in wealth and territory, its system of government became more complex. Consequently, the king of Ghana had to appoint lesser kings or governors for distant provinces. From these far-off provinces, the central government received loyalty and a yearly tribute. Possibly to ensure their continued loyalty, the kings of Ghana demanded that the sons of each lesser king be sent to the royal court, where for most state occasions, they would sit next to the king.

Review…Recall…Reflect

1. How did racist assumptions prevent an accurate understanding of Great Zimbabwe?

2. Describe how the geography of West Africa created the conditions for settlement.

3. How did trade contribute to the development of Ghana as a dominant kingdom?

THE RISE OF THE MALI KINGDOM

With the decline of Ghana, the kingdom of Mali emerged as the most powerful state in West Africa. Between 1230 and 1235, **Sundiata Keita** founded the kingdom of Mali. Sundiata was a great warrior of the Mande-speaking Mandinka. He united his people and brought them a period of peace and prosperity. Sundiata made Niani the political and economic capital of his kingdom. Other important trading centres of the **Malians** were Gao and Timbuktu (Tombouctou).

After securing the West African gold fields, Sundiata started to re-establish the gold and salt trade, which had been disrupted by the long wars in Ghana. Eventually, Mali gained control of the gold trade. The Malian rulers expanded their trade routes farther north and east to Egypt and Tunisia, and south to what is now Ghana.

Sundiata also adopted a training program for agriculture, encouraging many of his soldiers to become farmers. Under his influence, the fertile land was planted with different grains, and with peanuts, onions, yams, cotton, rice, beans, and other products. As a result, Mali became an important agricultural country. Nevertheless, its economy was based on trade, and like Ghana, Mali became exceptionally rich by controlling the trade travelling in and out of its territory. Today, Mali is remembered for its wealth, stability, and intellectual achievements.

Mansa Musa

Probably the most famous ruler of the Malian Empire was **Mansa Musa**. He became the *mansa,* or king, of Mali in 1307 and ruled for 25 years. Although he was a dedicated Muslim, most of his subjects were not. Mansa Musa respected the faith of all of his subjects, allowing them to hold their religious ceremonies at his court. Under Musa's rule, trade in Mali increased remarkably, and many people converted to Islam.

When Mansa Musa came to the throne, Mali was already in control of the gold and salt trade routes. During his 25-year rule, he doubled the size of his territory by conquering neighbouring regions. Mansa Musa ruled one of the largest empires of the world at the time.

Mansa Musa was not just a successful conqueror; he was also an efficient administrator. He divided his empire into provinces and nominated a governor for each. The governor was in charge of the day-to-day management of his province. Mansa

In this portrait of Mansa Musa, set into a map of his kingdom, Mansa is holding a huge gold nugget. An Arab trader rides to meet and barter with him. The map was drawn in Spain in 1375.

Musa also appointed a royal tax collector and inspector for each of the major trading towns.

The Famous Hajj

For centuries, every capable Muslim has been required to visit once in his or her lifetime the holy cities of Mecca and Medina, Saudi Arabia, for **Hajj**, or pilgrimage. Fulfilling this religious obligation, Mansa Musa made his Hajj in 1324. The king's journey was an immense display of wealth and excessive generosity; it was long remembered and admired throughout Egypt and Arabia. Mansa Musa reputedly took with him as many as 60 000 people, including government officials, soldiers, doctors, advisers, friends, family members, and 500 slaves, each carrying a 2.5-kg staff of gold. In addition, a caravan of 100 camels, each loaded with 135 kg of gold, travelled with him. Another 100 camels carried food, clothing, and other supplies. This huge caravan arrived in Cairo after eight months of travel. During his stay, Mansa Musa was very generous to the people of Cairo, giving them many gifts of gold.

In fact, the king and his subjects spent or gave away so much gold that the price of gold in Cairo fell and did not fully recover for more than 12 years.

After three months, Mansa Musa left Cairo to continue his journey to Arabia. When he reached the holy city of Mecca, like other pilgrims, he visited and prayed in the Kaaba, the most sacred Muslim site. Altogether, the royal Hajj took more than a year. The most interesting aspect of this pilgrimage was its effect on the empire and Mansa Musa himself. The news of Mali's tremendous gold wealth became known throughout the Muslim world and Europe. Because of this, the empire began to appear on European maps. The news also attracted many European leaders who wanted African gold, since

Europe had just started using gold coins. At the same time, Mali established new diplomatic and trade agreements with other African countries, particularly Egypt and Morocco. These factors all contributed to Mali's international recognition and increased respect.

As for Mansa Musa, he did not return home as simply a renewed Muslim. He brought with him Muslim scholars and artists to improve education and help put into effect some of the new things he had seen on his journey. He invited these scholars to teach in Mali's educational centres and to build new mosques and palaces. Among them was al-Saheli, a Moorish scholar, poet, and architect who built several mosques and palaces in Mali, including the famous Sankara University mosque in Timbuktu (Tombouctou), which still stands. Timbuktu was one of the richest and most elegant towns in the world at the time, and a famous centre of learning and culture.

After Mansa Musa's death in 1337, Mali experienced a series of kings who could neither protect nor hold the vast empire together. Berber nomads, who had always wanted to gain control of the profitable trans-Saharan trade routes, captured some of the trading cities and threatened to seize Timbuktu. At the same time, people from the rain forest were attacking the empire from the south. Corruption and civil war had already weakened Mali.

As the central government weakened, distant states, including Songhay, began to rebel. By the middle of the fifteenth century, Mali had lost most of its northern states, along with its control of the trans-Saharan trade. This loss hastened its decline, and in time, Mali was replaced by a new power — the kingdom of **Songhay**.

THE SONGHAY EMPIRE
The Growth of Songhay

The last great West African kingdom was Songhay. The origins of the people of Songhay are unknown, but they claimed to be the original inhabitants of the middle Niger region. Nobody knows exactly where they came from, when they came, why they came, or how they rose to power. Archaeologists and historians are still trying to answer these questions.

The people of Songhay consisted of farmers, fishers, and traders who lived around the city of Gao

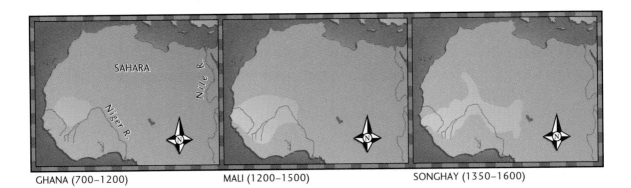

GHANA (700–1200) MALI (1200–1500) SONGHAY (1350–1600)

■ **Three Trading Empires of Ancient West Africa**
What geographic feature do these trading empires have in common? Why would it be important?

near the middle reaches of the Niger River. During Mansa Musa's reign, Mali ruled most of the Songhay kingdom, including the wealthy trading city of Gao. When Mansa Musa died, Songhay refused to pay taxes to the new ruler of Mali. In 1435, Gao declared independence. Mali tried to regain it, but the people of Songhay, under the leadership of Sunni Ali, defended their city, and soon after, Gao emerged as the capital of the new West African kingdom of Songhay.

WEB CONNECTION

http://www.mcgrawhill.ca/links/echoes

Go to the web site above to find out more about the African Kingdoms of Ghana and Mali.

Sunni Ali became king of Gao and the territories of the Songhay in about 1464. He was a clever king and brave warrior, who always fought and never lost. He was often on horseback, leading his powerful army, moving swiftly from one battlefield to the next, and often changing his place of residence. First, Sunni Ali turned his attention to Timbuktu, which was controlled by Berbers. Timbuktu and Jenne were essential for Songhay if it was to acquire the trans-Saharan trade that had made Ghana and Mali glorious empires. In 1468, Sunni Ali drove the Berbers out of Timbuktu and took the city without a fight. He killed most of its Muslim inhabitants. Unlike the leaders of Mali, Sunni Ali was not a devout Muslim, and he was in constant conflict with the leaders of the Muslim community.

With the capture of Timbuktu, Ali headed to Jenne, an important marketplace and gateway to the gold, ivory, and kola nut production of the forest regions of the south. Jenne had never been conquered, but Sunni Ali captured it after a seven-year

military blockade. By the end of the fifteenth century, he had secured most of the Middle Niger region.

When Sunni Ali died, his son Sunni Baru succeeded him. Like his father, Sunni Baru was unsympathetic to the Muslims. As a result, many Muslims, who were afraid of losing power, influence, and trade, joined forces to overthrow him. The leader of the Muslims, **Askia Muhammad**, overthrew Sunni Baru shortly after his first-year inauguration.

Unlike Sunni Ali and Sunni Baru, Askia Muhammad was a devout Muslim. He established a Muslim dynasty, declaring his country to be an Islamic state. He also encouraged many non-Muslims to convert. Like Mansa Musa, he made a Hajj to Mecca and Medina, which improved his country's relations with the Muslim world. Scholars, traders, and craftspeople from all over the Muslim world came to Songhay. Askia Muhammad built mosques and schools in many towns and cities.

As the number of Muslim traders increased, larger trading centres such as Timbuktu and Jenne prospered. In fact, Timbuktu was one of the wealthiest market centres in West Africa at the time. Culture and scholarly activities flourished as never before.

When Askia Muhammad returned from the Hajj, he continued the expansion of his empire until he created the largest state West Africa had ever seen. Askia Muhammad was a competent warrior and a remarkable administrator. Under his leadership, Songhay was, possibly, one of the most organized states in the world.

Government of Askia Muhammad

Askia Muhammad was an outstanding administrator and created an effective system for managing his vast empire. He divided it into provinces and appointed a governor for each. The governor had to report to the emperor directly. In addition, each town had a *Qadi*, an Islamic judge or legal expert, but Askia Muhammad was the highest judge in the country. He also assigned governors to major cities, and port masters, as well as customs authorities, for the cities of Gao and Kabara.

Although Askia's word was always final, a group of learned men advised him on all matters of government. For example, he had a distinguished council of judges to advise him on legal matters and to make sure Islamic law was applied fairly across the country. Under Askia's rule, Muslims and non-Muslims were treated equally before the law — no kind of injustice was accepted under his government.

Education

Qur'anic schools furnished many Muslims in Songhay an early basic education in religion, customs, and ethics. As in Muslim societies today, parents or close relatives were responsible for sending their youngsters to religious institutions to learn the holy *Qur'an*. Generally, children started Qur'anic schools before they were seven. In the early stage of their education, children learned how to read and write the holy scriptures, memorizing every lesson by heart. The teacher wrote a few verses from the *Qur'an* on a wooden tablet, which each student (individually or in groups) was required to memorize. When the student had learned the assigned verses, the tablet was washed for the next set of verses. This process was repeated until the student memorized the entire 30 chapters of the *Qur'an*. Students likely started with shorter and easier lessons and progressed to longer and harder ones.

As students became older and advanced in their Qur'anic studies, they started learning Arabic. The Arabic language was — and still is — important for Muslims because it is the original language of the holy *Qur'an*. To understand the meaning of the *Qur'an*, one must know the Arabic language. Some knowledge of Arabic also prepared students for higher religious training. Those who wanted to take religious careers, such as teaching or preaching the Islamic religion, were to go to mosque universities, like the Sankara mosque university in Timbuktu. There they learned various religious subjects, including Islamic law, Islamic justice, the prophet's traditions, language, literature, grammar, history, and logic.

The Decline and Fall of Songhay

Askia Muhammad reigned for 35 years. In 1528, when he was old and almost blind, one of his sons overthrew him. Songhay continued to flourish until about 1588, when the struggle for succession led to a civil war. The civil war weakened the state of Songhay, creating bloodshed and lawlessness. Furthermore, the civil war encouraged the Sultan of Morocco to invade Songhay.

In 1590, the Sultan of Morocco, who had always hoped to acquire the trans-Saharan trade routes and West African gold mines, sent 4000 soldiers to conquer Songhay. Their commander was Judas Pasta, a Muslim Spaniard employed by the Sultan. Most of Judas's soldiers were mercenaries (hired fighters) from Europe. There were only a few Moroccan soldiers.

About six months after it began its march, the Moroccan army crossed the desert, arriving in Songhay with only 1000 soldiers. Although larger than the invading Moroccan forces, the Songhay army was completely overwhelmed and defeated. Because their guns were superior to the spears and arrows of the disunited forces of Songhay, the Moroccan army won easily and captured most of Songhay.

Although the Moroccan army gained control of the trans-Saharan trade, it was unable to find the gold fields. The Moroccans were also unable to create a colony in Songhay. Many of the invading army became victims of diseases such as malaria and dysentery; many others remained in West Africa and married local women. Those who stayed in Songhay divided the country into smaller states and chiefdoms, where they became dictators, or *Arma*, as they were called locally. By the end of the seventeenth century, the descendants of the Arma had already been assimilated into the local population.

After the fall of Songhay, this part of West Africa never again united as one state. What was once a peaceful and prosperous land became a dangerous and poverty-stricken place. A contemporary West African historian wrote, "From that moment on, everything changed. Danger took the place of security, poverty of wealth. Peace gave way to distress, disasters and violence."

With the downfall of Songhay, the power of Islam decreased in the region, while the power of traditional religion flourished. In fact, many rural people — who had never been totally dependent on Songhay or any other state — continued to faithfully practise their traditional religion and customs.

History Continues to Unfold

African history is long, complex, and dynamic. The examples of ancient African civilizations discussed in this chapter make this abundantly clear. Modern research has discredited the old stereotypes and myths that, for hundreds of years, have obscured the real history of African civilization. Exciting new archaeological finds are announced almost every day. With every new find, and with more educated analyses of old finds, modern scientists are rediscovering the African past. For the African people and nations, this "rediscovery" of their glorious past is important, not only for strengthening their pride, but also for the knowledge, inspiration, and guidance it provides them as they face the many challenges of the twenty-first century.

Current Research and Interpretations

Scholars today, many of them Africans, are using various sources of knowledge to interpret and construct the African past. Among these are archaeological finds, local traditions, anthropology, linguistics, and old books and manuscripts. Our knowledge of African history is continually changing. As new evidence comes to light, our view of the continent's past changes as well.

Chapter Review

Chapter Summary

In this chapter, you have seen:

- that diverse forms of leadership governed African civilizations
- that, at times, dominant individuals in African civilizations were key factors in bringing about change
- how various African civilizations reacted to exposure to external influences
- that bias, prejudice, and stereotyping can contribute to a poor understanding of history

Reviewing the Significance of Key People, Concepts, and Events (Knowledge/Understanding)

1. Understanding the history of African kingdoms requires a knowledge of the following people and concepts, and an awareness of their significance in the development of African civilizations. In your notes, identify and explain the historical significance of three from each column.

People	*Concepts/Places*
Nubians	Kingdom of Kush
King Ezana	Kingdom of Axum
Sundiata Keita	Kingdom of Mali
Mansa Musa	Ge'ez
Askia Muhammad	Kilwa
	Great Zimbabwe
	Swahili
	Mutapa Empire
	Hajj

2. Copy and complete the following chart in your notes to summarize the main features of several of the major African civilizations discussed in this chapter. Based on the information you gather in this chart, provide one or more reasons why these kingdoms came to dominate their regions.

   Connecting to the *World History Handbook*: Once you have completed your chart, transfer the main ideas of why areas came to dominate to the graphic organizer "Why Some Societies Rose to Dominance" in your *World History Handbook*.

Civilization	*Type of Government*	*Major Cities*	*Religion*	*Source of Wealth*
Kush				
Axum				
Swahili				
Great Zimbabwe				
Mutapa				
Ghana				
Mali				
Songhay				

3. Using the information gathered for the chart above, write a paragraph that explains the influence of religion on the political structures of at least two African kingdoms or civilizations.

   Connecting to the *World History Handbook*: Once you have completed your paragraph, transfer the main ideas to the graphic organizer "Religion's Influence on Political Structures" in your *World History Handbook*.

Doing History: Thinking About the Past (Thinking/Inquiry)

1. Formulate five questions that could guide you in conducting further research on one or more of the kingdoms discussed in this chapter. These should be probing questions.

2. Identify two African kingdoms in which the introduction of a new religion (i.e., Christianity or Islam) altered the organization of society (politically or otherwise), and explain why you believe this was a positive or negative development.

Applying Your Learning (Application)

1. This chapter opens with the following sentence:
   "For almost 2500 years — from about 850 BCE to 1600 CE — great cultures and civilizations thrived throughout Africa. With the exception of ancient Egypt, however, most Westerners are unaware of them." Create a suitable poster that illustrates this claim visually, using images in the chapter and other research.

2. Write two diary entries from the perspective of a person living in one of the African kingdoms discussed in this chapter. The first entry should describe the first encounter with Portuguese traders, while the second should be set 50 years later and capture the impact of the Portuguese on the kingdom.

   Connecting to the *World History Handbook*: Once you have completed your diary entries, transfer a few of the main ideas to the graphic organizer "Forces That Promote Change" in your *World History Handbook*.

Communicating Your Learning (Communication)

1. On a map of Africa, Arabia, and Europe, label each of the kingdoms/civilizations referred to in this chapter. Using broad arrows, indicate the flow of trade goods — showing which goods flowed into and out of Africa. Use visuals to enhance the map.

2. In a paragraph, clearly describe two things you learned about African civilizations that most surprised or enlightened you. Explain your choice and defend the idea that all students should study African civilizations at some point in their education.

Unit Review

Grading the Civilizations

1. Chapter One outlined the essential elements of a civilization and asked you to rank the elements in order of importance. Now that you have studied a civilization in depth, apply your ranking and see how this civilization measures up. Below are three broad categories under which the elements could be clustered. For each of the categories, provide a letter grade (from A+ to F) and a comment of three to five sentences to support the grade. You can complete a fuller assessment of the civilization using your *World History Handbook*.

	Letter Grade	Comments
The Place of People • level of equality • just laws • distribution of wealth • overall quality of life		
Organization of Society • democratic • effective government • meets needs of society • provides security and stability for society		
Lasting Legacy • ideas • works of art • architecture • innovations/inventions • literature		

The Role of Individuals in History

1. Historians often grapple with whether history is shaped by individuals, or if individuals are products of their age and thus shaped by history. Would the history of ancient Mesopotamia have been different if there had been no Hammurabi? Did Imhotep change the direction of Egyptian history? Following is a list of people mentioned in this unit. Select any two. For each, identify his or her role in society, major accomplishments, sphere of greatest impact (e.g., art, ideas, religion, politics), and why you believe the person shaped or was shaped by history. You may want to do additional research on the two individuals you select.

Muhammad	Saladin	Askia Muhammad
Khadija	King Ezana	Sundiata Keita
Chingghis Khan	Mansa Musa	

Understanding Chronology

1. The study of history, whether the recent or distant past, relies on a sound understanding of the order in which events occurred. Without a clear understanding of how history unfolded, it is difficult to see the relationship between earlier events and later developments. The following questions help to illustrate the importance of chronology:

   a) How did developments in European technology have an impact on African history, and how does this highlight the importance of chronology in studying African history?

   b) How does the impact of the Islamic faith in African history highlight the importance of understanding chronology?

   c) Using the date 1250 CE, describe what was happening in the four regions of Africa discussed in Chapter Eight of this unit. Explain why this is a useful exercise in developing an understanding of African history.

Cause and Effect in History

1. History often involves the study of cause and effect. We often find that one cause has several effects, or that several causes lead to one effect. Complete the cause-and-effect diagrams provided by your teacher. Once you have completed both diagrams, use one as a guide in writing a paragraph on the issue addressed.

UNIT FOUR

Asia

chapter 9
India

chapter 10
China

chapter 11
Japan

Shiva, one of the most powerful Hindu gods, is the destructive force in the cosmic cycle of renewal and destruction. He is surrounded by fire, the destroyer of all things. This bronze image from southern India is dated to the eleventh century.

At about the same time as the Greco-Roman civilizations were flourishing in the Western world, rich, complex civilizations also emerged in Asia. Along the major river valleys, both Chinese and Indian cultures evolved into vast empires with extensive trading networks through which goods, ideas, belief systems, and innovations were exchanged. This exchange extended far beyond Asia, reaching into the Arab world, Africa, and throughout the Mediterranean. Asian civilizations contributed a great deal to the world, including major religions such as Hinduism and Buddhism, philosophies such as Confucianism and Daoism, innovations such as gunpowder and the wheelbarrow, and an array of commodities from spices and tea to silk.

UNIT EXPECTATIONS

In this unit, you will:

O demonstrate an understanding of the development of Asian communities from the earliest societies to the sixteenth century

O analyze the factors that contributed to change and continuity in Asian civilizations to the sixteenth century

O evaluate the contributions of selected individuals and groups to the development of artistic, intellectual, and religious traditions in Asian cultures

O demonstrate an understanding of the diversity and uniqueness of political structures in Asian cultures

O formulate significant questions for research and inquiry, drawing on examples from Asian history to the sixteenth century

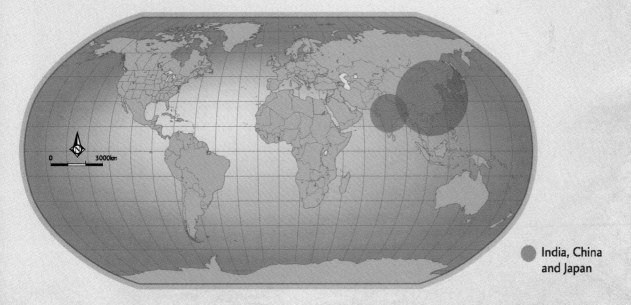

0   3000km

India, China and Japan

CHAPTER NINE

India

By the end of this chapter, you will be able to:

- explain how external influences shaped Indian culture

- identify forces in Indian history that tended to reinforce stability and continuity in society

- evaluate the contributions of certain individuals to the development of political, intellectual, and religious traditions in India

- evaluate the influence of religions such as Hinduism and Buddhism on the social and political structure of India

This sculpture of a nude girl dancing was found at Mohenjo-daro in the Indus Valley and dates to ca. 2300–1750 BCE.

During its five thousand years of history, India has had extensive contact with other great and powerful civilizations. In the very distant past, during the period of the Indus Valley civilization, India was exposed to ancient Mesopotamia. From the sixth century BCE on, it interacted with both ancient Iran and the Hellenistic world. Encounters with the Islamic world started in the eighth century CE, and, eventually, Europeans too came to know the Indian civilization. Throughout all this exposure to different cultures, political systems, and religions, however, India has preserved its essential unity. This is particularly true of India's major faith, Hinduism, the religion of eighty-five percent of its population. During the ancient and medieval periods, Cambodia and Indonesia also came to embrace Hinduism. Buddhism, on the other hand, originated in India but ultimately became a more dominant influence in East Asian and Southeast Asian countries such as China, Tibet, Korea, Japan, Vietnam, Thailand, and Indonesia than in its homeland.

After World War II, intensive archaeological research in Pakistan and India greatly increased our knowledge of the historical and geographical spread of the Indus Valley civilization. From west to east, the Indus civilization spanned 1600 km; from north to south, it stretched 1100 km. This is an area much greater than that occupied by ancient Egypt and Mesopotamia combined. Before the 1950s, archaeologists were unable to establish the origins of the Indus civilization and concluded that it was merely an extension of Mesopotamia. However, this hypothesis was unsatisfactory because of fundamental differences between the scripts, arts and crafts, and town planning of the Indus Valley and Mesopotamian civilizations.

KEY WORDS

Mohenjo-daro

Vedas

Upanishads

Gupta Empire

Delhi Sultanate

Hinduism

Bhagavad-Gita

KEY PEOPLE

Aryans

Brahmins

Ashoka

Kanishka

King Harsha

Chingghis Khan

Akbar

Gotama Buddha

VOICES FROM THE PAST

We meditate on the lovely light of the god, Savitri:

May it stimulate our thoughts!
The Rig-Veda (second millennium BCE)

TIME LINE: INDIA

	ca. 2500 BCE	India's first civilization, the Indus Valley civilization, emerges at Mohenjo-daro and Harappa
Indus Valley civilization begins to decline	ca. 1700 BCE	
	ca. 1500 BCE	Beginning of the Early Vedic Age
Beginning of the Late Vedic Age	ca. 1000 BCE	
	563 BCE	Gotama Buddha is born
Beginning of the Mauryan Empire	321 BCE	
	268 BCE	Reign of Ashoka begins, during which the social and ethical practices of Buddhism were brought into government
Beginning of the Gupta Empire, considered the golden age of ancient India	320 CE	
	650–1200	Age of Regional Kingdoms, during which there is little Indian unity
Period of the Delhi Sultanate	1206–1526	
	1526	Beginning of the Mughal Empire, during which Islam flourished in India

THE ORIGIN OF THE INDUS VALLEY CIVILIZATION

The idea that the Indus Valley was the origin of a unique civilization was a result of excavations conducted in Pakistan, about 150 km northwest of the ancient city of **Mohenjo-daro**. The excavation confirmed a change from nomadic herders to settled agriculturalists that led to the growth of large villages and wealthy towns. Artifacts included a lifelike sculpture of a man's head, small, delicately designed figurines of men and women, and terra cotta seals with engraved animal symbols. These discoveries revealed the beginnings of the Indus civilization phase. At Amri, a site situated southwest of

This is the excavated site of the ancient city of Mohenjo-daro. Note the closely arranged and regularly shaped dwellings. Does this site make it look like the city was planned this way?

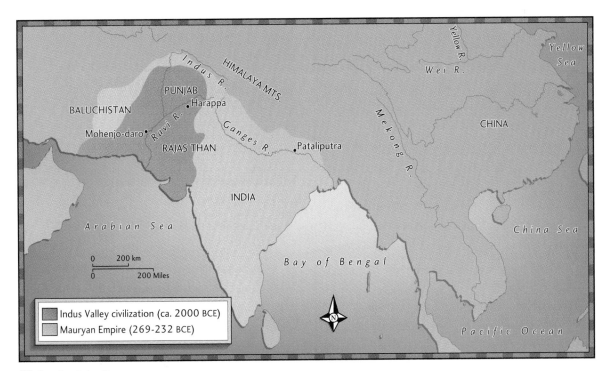

■ Ancient India

Ancient India from the Indus Valley civilization to the height of the Mauryan Empire. Which geographical feature(s) was essential for the growth of the Indus Valley civilization?

Mohenjo-daro, and excavated between 1958 and 1969, pottery, terra-cotta figurines, and seal markings clearly show a transition from a pre- to an early Indus Valley period. One of the most remarkable aspects of these Indus Valley cities was their town planning — with streets and buildings carefully aligned in straight rows.

The Rise and Fall of the Indus Culture

Much of what we know of the culture of the Indus civilization comes from seals. The writing of the Indus people is preserved on square and rectangular seals cut out of a soft stone called steatite (soapstone). Brief glimpses of legends are carved on these seals, although very little information is given. The script on the seals, which were used for stamping on clay, remained unchanged for over 800 years. This is in sharp contrast to ancient Sumerian and Egyptian writing, where changes in the script indicated the changing dynasties. Despite intensive efforts, including extensive use of computer technology, Indus script has yet to be deciphered.

The pictures carved on the seals are regarded as masterpieces of miniature art. Particularly interesting are the beautiful renderings of the humped bull and rhinoceros. The seals provide a useful clue to our understanding of the religion of the Indus civilization, since many of the religious signs found on them reappear as sacred objects and symbols in later Indian religions such as Hinduism and Buddhism. The seals depict a number of animals — tigers, water buffalo, deer and chimeras. Chimeras were fantastic, hybrid animals that were part bull and part elephant, part goat and part fish, or sometimes a combination of three or four animals, including humans. There are scenes of animal sacrifices, the worship of the

Stone seals such as these are an important source of information about the Indus Valley culture, especially their religion. Note the figure in a familiar yoga position, ca. 2500–1500 BCE.

sacred pipal (fig tree), the bull, and the Indian god Shiva. Gods who are part animal and part human, the yogic (meditative) position of the gods, and the swastika sign are common features of later Indian religions also depicted on the seals.

One of the puzzling features of the Indus Valley civilization is that the culture remained unchanged for at least 700 years. This is evident in the technology used throughout the civilization. For example, the pottery forms and techniques, bronze tools such as the adze, and Indus script show no variation from the earliest to the latest strata excavated.

The cities that came into their own around 2500 BCE began to decline at around 1700 BCE, becoming vast slums. Recurring floods, foreign invasions, changes in climate, geological changes at the mouth of the Indus River, population growth, and disease are all cited as possible causes of the decline. Recent analysis indicates that the city phase of the civilization — shown in structural differences, trade, writing, and specialized skills for producing goods — eventually disappeared and Indus society gradually merged into other cultures.

The Vedic Age

With the decline of the Indus civilization, came the arrival of the Aryan peoples, who cultivated and opened up new regions to the east of the Indus River. The name "Aryan" is used for both a group of Indo-European languages and certain Asian peoples. The Indo-Aryan language group dates back to about 1500 BCE, and includes the ancient language called Sanskrit, and modern Hindi. In Sanskrit, the term *arya* (which means "relatives," "nobles," or "honourable persons") referred to a group of people in ancient India. Among the **Aryans** were **Brahmins**, members of the higher class in Hindu society. Brahmins followed traditional religious practices and used Sanscrit.

Other peoples who referred to themselves as Aryans were the Iranians, including the Persian family of rulers known as the Achaemenids. The Indo-Iranians settled about 1500 BCE in what are now Afghanistan, northern India, Iran, and Pakistan. The name "Iran" comes from the word "Aryan."

Although several scholars hold the Aryans responsible for the destruction of the Indus cities, recent work suggests that by the time Aryan tribes migrated to India, the cities were already in decline. The waves of Aryan immigrants on horseback and on horse-drawn, spoke-wheel chariots, spread to the regions covered by the upper Indus River system and the River Saraswati, and later to the east in the land between the rivers Jamuna and Ganges.

TIME FRAMES
INDIAN HISTORICAL PERIODS

Indus Civilization ca. 2500–1500 BCE

Early Vedic Age ca. 1500–1000 BCE

Late Vedic Age ca. 1000–500 BCE

Mauryan Empire 321–184 BCE

Formative Period 184–409 CE

Gupta Empire 320–650 CE

Age of Regional Kingdoms 650–1206

The Delhi Sultanate 1206–1526

Mughal Empire 1560–1707

The earliest existing literature of the Aryans are the **Vedas**, which are about 3000 years old. These are Hinduism's oldest sacred books, and are still revered by Hindus today. Hinduism, the major religion of modern India, is one of the oldest living religions in the world — its roots date to prehistoric times in India. The Vedas were probably composed beginning about 1400 BCE, and include the basis of the doctrines about Hindu divinities. They also give philosophical ideas about the nature of Brahman, Hinduism's supreme divine being. The Sanskrit word *veda* means "knowledge." There are four Vedas. They are — beginning with the oldest — *Rig-Veda, Samaveda, Yajurveda,* and the *Atharvaveda.*

These collections of mainly verse texts provided the forms for public worship of the holiest rites of the early religion. Two later texts are connected to the Vedas. The first of these, the *Brahmanas*, are long essays that explain the mythological and religious meaning of the rites. After the *Brahmanas*, came philosophical works called the **Upanishads**. Indian philosophy developed from the *Upanishads* and their search for unity in existence.

Because Hindu law permitted only certain persons to hear the Vedas recited, the works became surrounded by mystery. Yet, ideas presented in the Vedas spread throughout Indian culture.

Early Vedic Society

The Aryans were semi-nomadic peoples. During the Early Vedic Age (1500–1000 BCE), they travelled in their chariots, with herds of cattle, which they considered their wealth and means of exchange. Using the descriptions provided in the Vedas, a present-day carpenter could build a passable replica of the Aryan chariot, and a brick-layer could replicate the elaborate sacrificial platforms the Vedic Aryans used to worship and offer sacrifices to their gods. We do not know what the Aryan houses looked liked because they lived in semi-permanent, makeshift settlements.

Natural elements and philosophical ideas have been associated with the ancient Indo-European divinities (gods and godlike beings) — for example, the god Indra (rain and thunder), Agni (fire), Mitra (the moon), Aditi (mother of worlds), and Varuna (infinite space). Ancient and modern Hindu philosophers, however, do not regard the divinities as just symbols — they view the gods' existence as a truth that is actually experienced. On the other hand, many Western researchers believe that the main Indo-European divinities were representations of the caste (class) system shared by some Aryan peoples. In ancient India, the gods Mitra and Varuna represented the Brahmin castes — the highest class in Hindu society, made up of priests and scholars. The god Indra represented the warrior castes, which ranked below the Brahmins. The Ashvin twins stood for still lower castes — farmers and herders. The relation between these divinities reveals what the Aryans considered proper behaviour among the castes. The warrior god, Indra, is described as pot-bellied with a tawny beard. He likes to drink and fight the enemies of the Aryans, destroying their fortifications. Later Vedic texts place the Aryan settlements on the upper Ganges River regions (the land between the Indus and the Ganges). By this time, the Aryans have made the transition from a semi-nomadic life to a peasant society, calling their newly occupied territory the *aryavarta* (the "region of the Aryans"). During this period, new regions came under extensive cultivation, with fields plowed by teams of animals of up to twelve oxen. Wheat, barley, and rice became the staple foods of the people, and in about 1000 BCE, these Indians started using iron as well as copper tools.

During this period, the magic and sacrifices carried out by the Brahmins became the central focus of Aryan religion. The Brahmins maintained that the cosmos was controlled by sacrifice and that they, with their superior knowledge of sacrifices, could thus control the cosmos. The Brahmins even claimed that they were the gods on Earth.

Late Vedic Society

By the Late Vedic Age (ca. 1000–500 BCE), states with kings as rulers began forming, gradually undermining the tribal and clannish political organization of the Early Vedic Age. The fundamentals of mystical thought found in the *Rig-Veda* are abundant in the later texts. These texts culminated in the emergence of Indian philosophy and mysticism recorded in the *Upanishads*. These texts focus on philosophical questions, such as what happens after a person dies, and the search for individual salvation. They explain the identity of the individual soul (*atman*) in relation to the soul of the universe (*brahman*), along with other states that ultimately lead to total happiness.

This small (7.6 cm high) sculpture of a bearded man, perhaps a ruler, was found in a house in the excavations at Mohenjo-daro.

Review...Recall...Reflect

1. What is the importance of seals to glimpsing life during the Indus Valley Civilization?

2. What did archaeological research after World War II reveal about the size and origins of the Indus Valley Civilization?

3. What contributions did the Aryans make to Indian civilization?

THE POLITICAL HISTORY OF ANCIENT INDIA

The period between the Late Vedic Age and the founding of Buddhism (ca. fifth century BCE) saw a shift in the main centres of Indian civilization to the central and eastern plains of the Ganges. Buddhist texts mention sixteen geographic and cultural regions from the northwest to the northeast and central India. Several kingdoms of the region were engaged in territorial wars, and by the time of Gotama Buddha (ca. 563–483 BCE), two kingdoms, the Magadha and the Kosala, emerged as the wealthiest and most powerful rival states. In time, the kingdom of Magadha, under the Maurya dynasty, would become India's first empire.

Mauryan Empire

Magadha emerged as the dominant state during and immediately after the Buddha's death. The Mauryan Empire of the Magadha (ca. 321–184 BCE) gave India political and cultural unity. Chandragupta, a member of the Maurya clan, became the founder of the empire in about 321 BCE. During the reign of Chandragupta, a man named Megasthenes visited Pataliputra, the capital of Maurya, and described what he saw in a book entitled *India*. The eyewitness accounts of Megasthenes, who was the ambassador of one of the Hellenistic rulers of Syria, are still an important primary source for the study of the Mauryan Empire. At Pataliputra, Megasthenes saw the emperor's palace, which had 80 pillars; the walled city, which had 570 towers and 64 gates; and the ditch filled with water that surrounded the walled city. The city had a circumference of about 33 km, and judging by this description, Pataliputra was twice as large as the city of Rome was during the second century CE.

Megasthenes observed seven levels of Indian society: philosophers, farmers, herders, soldiers, traders and artisans, inspectors and spies, and advisors and officers of the emperor. Surprised to find that there was no slavery, he wrote, "All Indians are free and not one of them is a slave." Megasthenes also praised the treatment given to foreigners living in Pataliputra. If a foreigner died in the city, the officers of the state would set aside his or her property in trust, inform the next of kin, and turn over the property to them.

Also to Megasthenes's surprise, the Indians carried on their business and legal transactions honestly. This was in sharp contrast to the practices of the Greek states, where legal quibbles, litigation, and frauds were frequent occurrences. He also relates that Chandragupta was constantly guarded by Amazon women with drawn swords.

The Reign of Ashoka

Ashoka (268–233 BCE), the grandson of Chandragupta, inherited his grandfather's bureaucratic government. In time, Ashoka had a crisis of conscience during one of his wars of conquest in which hundreds of thousands of people were killed, or wounded, or taken from their homes. Deeply touched by this misery, Ashoka declared that he would change his policy of outright conquest by war and, instead, practise the social and ethical teachings of Buddhism. Public announcements from Ashoka have been found inscribed on huge rocks and stone pillars. In these inscriptions, Ashoka asked his people to treat each other with justice and mercy — to tolerate all peoples and beliefs, and not to hurt people and animals unless it was unavoidable.

On great pillars such as this (just over 2 m high), Ashoka recorded Buddhist principles as well as his political and legal policies.

Ashoka asserted that he was like a father to his people and would care for them as he would his own children. Included in Ashoka's policy was a command to respect one's father and mother, relatives, teachers, and philosophers. He instituted free medical treatment for people and animals throughout his empire. He also built rest houses and hospitals that were supplied with medicinal plants. He planted trees for shade, and had wells dug to provide water. In a remarkable confession, Ashoka explained how hundreds of animals were killed daily for food in his kitchen; so, in compassion for the animals, he became a vegetarian.

Ashoka appointed special commissioners of justice who toured the countryside teaching the people to follow a path of righteousness and look to the needs of religious mendicants (beggars). Some scholars say that Ashoka used Buddhist social ethics to bind the people to a common purpose, raise the ethical and moral standards of his subjects, and promote internal harmony in his vast empire. Others point out that he ruled his empire with a firm hand and never let go of control. Despite his determination to stop wars of aggression, he did not reduce his army. Though he gave three days' respite to people condemned to death, he did not reduce their sentences. Ashoka's royal proclamations clearly indicated that a strong bureaucracy firmly controlled his empire.

The policy procliamed by Ashoka became the norm for subsequent dynastic rulers of ancient and medieval India. The inscriptions of the kings of ancient India who succeeded Ashoka proclaimed that they cared for widows and orphans; instituted free hospitals for cattle and people; built rest houses with free food; constructed canals and irrigation ditches throughout their kingdoms; and supported the Brahmins, the Buddhists, and other religious sects. There can be little doubt that Ashoka's policy had a lasting effect on Indian political behaviour. Because of his righteous policies, in inscriptions Ashoka referred to himself as "beloved of the gods."

The Formative Period

The Mauryan Empire deteriorated gradually after Ashoka's death, and by 184 BCE, rule passed into the hands of various regional powers in the northwest, south, and northeast. In central India and the south-west and southeast coastal areas, the Shatavahana kings ruled from the first century BCE to the beginning of the third century CE. Their empire extended from the east coast to the west coast, and their control facilitated international trade connections with countries to the west and east. The Shatavahana were the strongest military presence in central and south India; however, they had to contend with the Shaka in the west. The relationship between the two powers was not always hostile and they often established links through marriage.

Both the Shakas and the Shatavahanas practised Hinduism and Buddhism with equal passion. Although the Shakas were originally a foreign presence in India, they had become Hindus and used Sanskrit, the Indian language of the elite, for record keeping. The Shaka rule lasted until 409 CE, when they were conquered by the Gupta emperor Chandragupta II.

Northern India: The Age of the Kushans

The conquest of northern India from the first to the third century CE was the work of the Kushans, a dynasty that united the tribes of central Asia and established rule over the Shakas and the people of the Punjab. **Kanishka**, their greatest king, replaced the Shaka rulers in 78 CE. Like Ashoka, Kanishka adopted Buddhism as a state religion. The Kushan kings frequently adopted the Persian title "King of Kings" and the Chinese title "Son of God" in their inscriptions and coins. This was the introduction of divine kingship in India. By assuming such titles, the Kushan kings were legitimizing their rule over minor kings and chiefs in newly conquered territories.

The great Asiatic trade routes crossed territories held by the Kushans in Bactriana and northwestern

India. Through the Shaka chiefs, the Kushans held control over trade from the north to the west coast of India, and to Rome and the Mediterranean. Control over international land and sea trade routes made the Kushan kings wealthy and powerful. They were the first Indian kings to introduce gold coins and, according to some scholars, they did this by melting down Roman coins.

WEB CONNECTION

http://www.mcgrawhill.ca/links/echoes

Go to the site above to find out more about the early history of India.

Stupas can be found where ever Buddhism is practiced. This is the gate to the Great Stupa in Madhya Pradesh, India. It was built ca. 90 BCE. Note the characteristic dome shape of the stupa behind the gate.

In the tradition of Indian kings, the Kushan kings practised various religions. They were followers of Buddhism, but gave respect to the Hindu gods Shiva and Vishnu and the Persian cult of Mithras. King Kanishka has been ranked with Ashoka as a great Buddhist ruler. Kanishka held the fourth Buddhist Council (Ashoka had convened the third), and according to Buddhist tradition, at the end of the fourth council, all the Buddhist texts were to be re-edited and transcribed onto copper plates. These plates were deposited in the stupa (Sanskrit *stupah,* "summit") at Purushapura (modern Peshawar in Pakistan). A stupa is a dome-shaped monument that houses Buddhist relics, commemorates an important Buddhist event, or marks a sacred spot. A Chinese monk who visited this stupa in the fourth century CE recorded that it was 213 m high and a wonder of the age.

The Kushans also patronized and encouraged the arts and sciences, including Buddhist art forms that incorporated elements of Greek and Roman arts. The famous Buddhist philosopher, poet, and writer Ashvaghosha was in Kanishka's court, as was the physician Caraka, who wrote a brilliant book on Indian medicine. This book remains one of the foundations of India's indigenous system of medicine known as *Ayurveda.*

During what was considered a dark age in Indian history, the Mauryan Empire declined and finally disintegrated. For nearly five centuries — from 184 BCE to 320 CE — short-lived kingdoms rose and fell. Only the Kushans, Shatavahanas, and Shakas managed to maintain kingdoms for substantial periods of time. The year 320 CE saw the beginning of the next great Indian dynasty, the **Gupta Empire**.

The Gupta Empire

The imperial Gupta period is regarded as the golden age of ancient India; it lasted for two hundred years. The first king of the Gupta dynasty, Chandragupta I,

The artistic accomplishments of the Gupta Empire can be seen in the spectacular Ajanta Caves, built ca. 450–500 CE northeast of Bombay. The architectural interiors of the caves in this Buddhist monastic complex are decorated with paintings and sculpture of the life of the Buddha. The painting shown here is of a Padmapani, a "lotus bearer."

began his reign in 320 CE. His son Samudragupta (335–375 CE) was a great conqueror who brought much of northern India under his control. His invasion of southern India was even more interesting in that he did not actually take over the south, but instead collected tribute.

Samudragupta's son Chandragupta II reigned from 375–415 CE. It was he who defeated the Shakas in central and western India in 409 CE. Chandragupta II is one of the few kings of ancient India whose memory is preserved in both literary and folk traditions. Later Sanskrit literature preserves many tales about a great and wise king called Vikramaditya who ruled with justice and was a great patron of Indian art and literature. Vikramaditya is identified with Chandragupta II.

A Chinese monk, Fa Xian (fa shen), who visited northern India during the Gupta period (390 CE) observed:

> The climate of this country is warm and equable, without frost or snow. The people are very well off, without tax or official restrictions. Only those who till the royal lands return a portion of profit to the king. If they desire to go, they go; if they like to stop, they stop... The king governs without the use of capital punishment; criminals are fined according to circumstances, lightly or heavily. Even in cases of repeated rebellion, they only cut off the right hand.

Fa Xian's account reflects the relatively mild manner with which the Guptas administered their empire. The Gupta Empire diminished in size after the death of King Skandagupta in 467 CE, but continued until around 520.

The decline of the Gupta Empire was hastened by attacks from the Hunas, central Asian nomads. From the beginning of the sixth century, they controlled northwestern India for nearly fifty years. Hunas are held responsible for destroying the cities and trading centres of northwestern India. They quickened the formation of a number of competing regional kingdoms in the north that engaged in constant inter-tribal war. The Huna incursions into the Gupta Empire heralded the end of the Indian classical period and beginning of the medieval era.

King Harsha

One king who managed to sustain the glory of the Guptas was **King Harsha** (606–647). His empire stretched from the Punjab in the northwest to northern Orissa in the east, and from the Himalayas to the banks of the Narmada River. A Chinese scholar and monk, Hiuen Tsiang (yon chong) spent 13 years (630–643) in India during Harsha's reign. He returned to China with 20 horses carrying 657 Buddhist texts and 150 relics associated with the Buddha. He describes Harsha's rule as honest, with the people living together in harmony. Hiuen Tsiang wrote that in the trials of criminals, no torture was used. After the facts were brought to light, even the people who plotted against their superiors were put into prison without corporal punishment. Land tax was no more than one sixth of the owner's produce. Hiuen Tsiang compliments the people of northern India on their "explicit and correct speech, harmonious and elegant expression, and clear and distinct intonations" and notes that:

> The people, although hot-tempered, are upright and sincere. They never take anything wrongfully and often yielded to others more than fairness required. The people are honest and sincere. They are noble and gracious in appearance. They apply themselves much to learning.

Harsha devoted much of his spare time to constructing educational institutions and making provisions for highways. He built free rest houses, drink stalls, and planted fruit-bearing or shade trees for the people. He arranged philosophical debates among scholars and patronized the performance of plays with moral themes. Harsha himself wrote three plays in the ornate Sanskrit language. Hiuen Tsiang was also impressed by the free hospitals, which were supplied with food, drink, and physicians.

> Here come all poor or helpless patients suffering from all kinds of diseases. They are well taken care of and a physician attends them. Food and medicine is provided according to their needs.

They are made quite comfortable. When they are well, they may go away.

Another eyewitness account of Harsha states that "he forgot sleep and food in his devotion to good works." Harsha, like king Ashoka before him, is in many ways an archetypal king of ancient India who was literate, and considered it his duty to support religious institutions and build hospitals as part of his social responsibility as a ruler. The king in his inscriptions pledged to maintain order in society and to rule his subjects by the principles of justice and righteousness.

Government Under King Harsha

Harsha spent one fourth of his state income on charity. He held five yearly assemblies to listen to debates among various religious orders of the time, including both Buddhism and Hinduism. At the end of the debates, he gave away his accumulated personal fortune to charity. At one such assembly, Harsha distributed so much wealth that he was left with only the clothes on his back — his royal robes. Those, too, he then gave away. His sister, who was sitting next to him, had to give the king her shawl to cover his body. In keeping with the spirit of ancient Indian kings, he was tolerant of different religions and gave equal patronage to each. He was a Hindu, a devotee of the god Shiva, but his sister and brother were converts to Buddhism.

Harsha was the most powerful ruler of northern India, having conquered the whole of northern and central India with an enormous army that included 5000 elephants, 20 000 cavalry, and 50 000 infantry. In 630, Harsha eventually suffered defeat at the hands of Pulakeshin II, a ruler of the Chalukya dynasty of southern India. The people of the country ruled by Pulakeshin are described by Hiuen Tsiang:

They are all very tall and with a stern, vindictive character. To their benefactor they are grateful; to their foes they are relentless. If a general loses a battle, they do not inflict punishment but present him with a woman's clothes, and so he is driven to seek death for himself...

The Regional Kingdoms

The focus of Indian history from 650 to 1200 shifts from a single empire to regional kingdoms in the north and south. Many of the northern dynasties were short-lived; more stable dynasties were found in the southern peninsula. From the seventh to the fourteenth century, India experienced several important and lasting dynasties in the south, such as the Cholas.

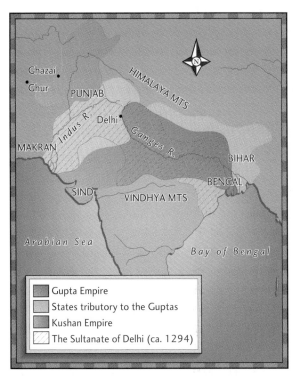

■ The Gupta Empire and Delhi Sultanate

What were the advantages and disadvantages of having Delhi as the capital of the Delhi Sultanate?

From 897 to 1120, the Cholas were a formidable power. As a great maritime force, they had active trade and diplomatic contacts with China and other southeast Asian rulers, including those of Cambodia, Java, Sumatra, and Malaya. Their naval fleet successfully fought and defeated the navy of the kings of Java and Sumatra (islands in what is now Indonesia).

❙ MUSLIM RULE IN INDIA

Muslims arrived on the Indian subcontinent in 712, when Arabs led by Muhammad ibn Qasim captured the coastal city of Debal, near modern-day Karachi in Pakistan. Muslim rule spread from the lower reaches of the Indus River to Multan in the Punjab. Although the Arabs tried to extend their territories toward the west and central India, they were defeated by powerful Hindu rulers in those regions. Arab territorial ambitions to the north were also contained. Muslims continued to settle along the west coast of India, where they set up trading colonies.

The next major Muslim inroad originated in northwestern Afghanistan, and led to permanent Muslim settlement in the north. The establishment of the Delhi Sultanate in 1206 meant the destruction of the Hindu rulers. A general named Qutub-ud-din, who had initiated the conquest of northern India from Afghanistan, became the first Delhi sultan. The **Delhi Sultanate** period lasted from 1206 to 1526. A number of Muslim dynasties made Delhi their capital, and consolidated their hold over the northern plain from the Sindh and Punjab to Bengal. During their height, the sultans penetrated south, central, and western India but could not control their southern possessions from Delhi.

From 1206 to 1296, the Delhi sultans consolidated their rule in the north and, more importantly, protected their northwestern frontiers from the

Mongols. The Mongols were united under the leadership of **Chingghis Khan** and his descendents, who had overrun much of Central Asia, Mongolia, and northern China. The Mongol raids had already destroyed important Islamic cultural centres in Syria and Iraq. Northern India, under the effective military leadership of the Delhi sultans, was able to contain the Mongol threat.

Muslim Conquests in Southern India

Alla-ud-din Khalji (1296–1320) was the first Delhi sultan bold enough to invade the rich kingdoms of southern India. He raided twice, and each time his army returned with their elephants, camels, and horses laden with gold and silver. Alla-ud-din paved the way for subsequent Islamic cultural and political entry into the south.

Alla-ud-din was noted for his talents as a great administrator. His revenue demands, constituting as much as half the produce of the predominantly Hindu peasants, was efficiently collected. With new access to the gold of the south and effective collection of land revenue, Alla-ud-din could maintain a well-paid standing army of 100 000 soldiers. This army was needed both for his own conquests and to protect the northwestern flank of the empire from the Mongols who increasingly threatened the Delhi rule.

Economic Policies of Alla-ud-din

Alla-ud-din also had to deal with discord within his own court. Through strong measures, such as banning public drinking and allowing social festivities among the nobles only with his permission, he controlled the nobility. Alla-ud-din established a deadly network of spies, who were so diligent in reporting conspiracies against the sultan that the nobles were afraid to speak to each other aloud in the open. Instead, they communicated by sign language.

To deal with short supplies of food and rampant inflation in Delhi and other cities of the north, Alla-ud-din introduced wage and price control — one of the earliest examples of economic control through government intervention. Alla-ud-din simply fixed the prices of all commodities, from slaves to horses. To prevent a shortage of food, he collected half of his taxes in grain, which was kept in state storehouses and redistributed to people at lower prices. State officials, backed by the secret police, hindered any cheating or dishonesty on the part of traders and merchants. If, for instance, a trader cheated when weighing goods, Alla-ud-din's officers would make up the loss by cutting an equal amount of flesh from the offender's body.

Sultan Muhamad bin Tughluq, who was a brilliant general and student of Islamic theology, built on the political and administrative infrastructure created by Alla-ud-din Khalji. Whereas Alla-ud-din was satisfied with merely raiding the south, Muhammad wanted to establish a permanent political presence in southern India. To that end — despite resistance from the bureaucrats — he built a new administrative centre at the city of Daulatabad in south-central India. During the last ten years of his reign, the southern part of Muhammad's empire began to disintegrate, and after his death, Sultanate rule continued only in the northern plains of India from 1351 to 1526.

POLITICAL UNION: THE MUGHAL EMPIRE

The political unification of northern India, from the Bay of Bengal to Kabul, and from the Himalayas to Gujarat and Malwa in central India, began with **Akbar**, the great Mughal emperor whose career spanned from 1560 to 1605. Akbar's religious policies helped his empire to overcome Islamic elitism. Prior to Akbar, Muslim rulers of India tended to regard non-Muslims in Muslim territory as second-class citizens who had to pay a poll tax (*ziziya*) to live in protective custody. Although the Muslim rulers were surrounded by Hindu tributary chiefs, none of them had appointed Hindus to the upper levels of the civil and military services.

Akbar treated Hindus as equal partners in his empire, giving the Hindu warrior classes in the north — known as the Rajputs — access to the inner circles of his court. He married women of royal Hindu families, but instead of converting them to Islam — according to the requirements of Muslim law — he allowed these women to remain practising Hindus. Akbar abolished the ziziya tax — another important signal to the Hindus that they were equal citizens of his empire — and abolished the taxes that Hindus had to pay when they went on pilgrimage to important centres such Benares (Varanasi). Some of the orthodox Muslim elite regarded Akbar's new policy toward the Hindus with severe misgivings, but were unable to change his policies.

Akbar enjoyed the religious discussions in the house of worship he had built for that purpose in his capital. Here he listened to Hindus, Muslims, Sikhs, and Christians explain the teachings of their faith and engage in interfaith dialogues. Eventually, Akbar started his own imperial cult, with a set of rituals borrowed from Islam and other religions. Those who joined his cult had to pledge to give up their faith, honour, property, and life to the service of Akbar, who regarded himself as an almost semi-divine being. Perhaps, this image was important to maintain control of his subjects, most of whom were Hindus. Some modern historians believe that Akbar had given up his faith and betrayed Islam.

Akbar also reorganized civil and military bureaucracy. The officers of his new imperial service were divided into 33 ranks, and were responsible directly to him for the administration of the vast empire. Akbar systematically surveyed the land under his control, over a ten-year period, and fixed the land revenue based on its average yield. The taxation system was fair and brought in a steady flow of income to the empire. Jahangir (1606–1627), his son, sustained Akbar's policies — he did not conquer additional territories, but consolidated the gains of his father. Jahangir was fond of the good life, and was noted for his drinking bouts, philosophical dialogues, and love of justice. His wife,

In this painting, completed in ca. 1605 as part of the Emperor's memoirs, Emperor Jahangir is the figure wearing a gold-coloured turban. How are you able to tell that he is the most important person in the picture?

Nur Jahan, a woman renowned for her beauty and wisdom, helped administer the empire to such an extent that she almost took over rule herself.

Sahajahan, Jahangir's son and successor, was a great general, prince, emperor, and builder. His masterpiece is the Taj Mahal, a monument he built to house the tomb of his second wife, Mumtaz Mahal, a Muslim Persian princess who was his constant comrade and counsellor. When Sahajahan died, he was buried next to his beloved wife. Sahajahan also built many impressive mosques, but his crowning achievement was an entirely new capital city in Delhi.

The last of the great Mughal emperors, Aurangjeb (1657–1707) was a puritanical ruler who regarded India as the land of Islam, and reversed the policies of his predecessors. Considering them sacred acts of a devoted Muslim, he reimposed the ziziya tax on Hindus, discriminated against them in his service, and gave orders to demolish Hindu temples. Aurangjeb spent the latter half of his career in the south, where he conquered new territories. With his death in 1707, the Mughal Empire collapsed.

The Taj Mahal, one of the most recognized architectural works in the world, truly was a labour of love. Emperor Sahajahan had it built to hold the tomb of his wife, Mumtaz.

Review...Recall...Reflect

1. Why is Kanishka considered the greatest king of the Kushans?

2. Explain why the Gupta period is often referred to as India's golden age?

3. Explain how many of the government policies implemented by Ashoka were inspired by Buddhism.

RELIGIOUS TRADITIONS OF ANCIENT INDIA

Hinduism

The features of classical **Hinduism** were consolidated and crystallized during the Gupta age. Hinduism is a complex set of religious ideologies and practices, the key features of which are the worship of God in the form of an image and the belief in rebirth. It is assumed that a person is born again and again, and that status and rank in this life depend on the good or evil actions one performed in past lives. This is known as the law of action, *karma*. If one violates the moral regulations (dharma) of society, and commits evil, then one will be born into a lower status in the next birth. Hinduism assumes that God comes down to earth periodically in various animal and human forms in order to save it from falling into total anarchy when the "law of fish" prevails. In this view of chaos, the big fish eats the smaller ones and evil triumphs.

The literature that has made the greatest impact on Hindu religious life is known as the *Puranas* ("ancient histories"). The eighteen *Puranas* describe the origin and exploits of Hindu gods and goddesses. They contain myths, philosophical debates, ritual prescriptions, and genealogies of northern dynasties up to the period of the Gupta kings.

Hindus worship their gods in the form of images made of stone, wood, or metal. The texts composed in the Gupta period describe the elaborate rituals followed by artists in making images of the gods. The texts also give detailed instructions for the priests on how, through ritual, to breathe life into an image by inviting the deity to reside inside it. The household and temple ceremonies involved in the worship of God existed prior to the Gupta Empire, but during this epoch rules were codified and standards established. Books from this period tell us the mode of worship of God in a Hindu temple: God, we are informed, is to be treated as the guest and lord of the house, to be awakened, bathed, fed, entertained, and worshipped by the devotee. Texts written during the Gupta Empire provide architectural plans for the different types of beautifully constructed Hindu temples housing images of gods and goddesses that became widespread from this time onward.

Important Hindu gods include Vishnu, Shiva, and Ganesh — seen here. Ganesh appears in the form of an elephant. This coloured stone image was made in the twelfth century in Mysore, India.

The Rig-Veda

The *Rig-Veda* is a Hindu text that deals with the origins of the gods and the universe. It was during the Vedic period that the Brahmins first articulated the theory of humans and the class system. According to a hymn in the *Rig-Veda* (tenth chapter) called the *Purusha,* the primeval man sacrificed himself and out of his head emerged the Brahmin, from his arms the Kshatriya, from his thighs the Vaishya, and from his feet the Shudra. Thus, the Brahmin is the thinker, Kshatriya the defender and protector of humanity, Vaishya the producer, and Shudra the labouring class. These classes apply to both men and woman of Hindu society.

The right to chant the Vedas was confined to three classes of Vedic society: Kshatriya the warrior; Brahmin the priest; and Vaishya the cultivator, cattle keeper, trader, and artisan. The Shudra, the fourth class — the workers, labourers, and servants — were considered low and impure, and were not allowed to speak the Vedas or even hear them chanted. One of the curses of a Brahmin lawgiver called Manu recommends unusually harsh treatment for the Shudra: "If a Shudra should hear the Vedas being chanted, then molten lead should be poured in his ears. If he should recite them, his tongue should be cut off." Although this edict was never implemented, it indicates how pure and sacred the Brahmins regarded the Vedas. Discrimination on the basis of birth into the Shudra class is an ongoing practice of the Brahmin class, and still part of Indian reality to this day.

Brahmin Life Rituals

The Brahmins acquired the exclusive privilege of consecrating rituals for the kings of ancient and medieval India from Vedic times. They thus became specialists in conducting elaborate sacrifices to the gods, often involving the killing of animals. Many of the sacrifices they performed were reserved for the warrior class, and were designed to ensure its success in war, long life, and happiness. The patrons, of course, paid the Brahmin fees for their services. The

Brahmins also received special concessions, such as land grants and properties, and in certain instances, they had immunity from paying taxes.

The Brahmins are the key players in the performance of Vedic rituals, which remain as valid today as they were during Vedic times. In fact, the Vedic Samskaras (pronounced *sum-scars*) — generally translated as "sacraments" — are life-cycle rituals that continue to be performed by Hindus all over the world. All sacraments require the presence of the sacred fire, which is set alight for the occasion by a Brahmin priest who also instructs the patron on the correct performance of the rituals.

In the sacrament of the birth of a male child — gender bias toward the male is obvious in this Vedic sacrament and others — the father holds the child near him and speaks in his ears the Vedic verses that wish him long life and intelligence. The father then feeds the child by touching his lips with his finger dipped in honey and butter. A "name giving" sacrament is performed on the tenth or twelfth day after the birth.

Upanayana is the name given to the initiation rite that a male child undergoes to study the Vedas, instructed by a Brahmin priest. At the completion of this sacrament, the male child becomes *dvija*, or "twice born." He is thus inducted as a full member into his community. The ceremony also signifies the child's formal entry into the world of education. A sacred thread woven in nine strands of munja grass (a tough fibre grass), cotton, or wool is ritually placed on the right shoulder of the child. He is duty bound to wear this thread on his body throughout his life, replacing it annually during the rainy season as it wears out. In the Vedic age, the young initiated male, while pursuing his studies, was instructed to lead an austere and celibate life — subsisting on food given by his extended family and the community. The child literally left his parents and lived in the house of a guru, or teacher.

The sacrament for the dead is called *an-te-sthi*, literally, "the last rite." Vedic Aryans practised cremation, as do modern Hindus. The sacred fire, lit amidst the chanting of the Vedas, is the ultimate consumer of the corpse. The death rite is incomplete without gathering the ashes of the dead person and immersing them in a river or the sea. The Vedic Aryans, like their modern Hindu counterparts, observed the remembrance and worship of the dead on the thirteenth day of cremation, and periodically thereafter every year on the death anniversary.

BUDDHISM

Gotama Buddha

Gotama Buddha (563–483 BCE) belonged to an aristocratic warrior clan, whose territory was located in the northeastern part of India near the foothills of the Himalayan Mountains. At the age of twenty-nine, Gotama left his wife and infant son to find true happiness and leave behind human suffering. He wandered for seven years in search of knowledge and was a disciple of the well-known philosophers of his time. Then one day, Gotama sought the truth by sitting under a tree and meditating. He supposedly saw the light of truth and became a buddha, an "awakened one."

After achieving the state of enlightenment, he gave his first sermon to the five monks who became his disciples. The sayings of the Buddha were collated and classified immediately after his death and further elaborated over the next one hundred years. The early Buddhist literature is vast, consisting of the Buddha's sayings and the rules of discipline that had to be followed by monks and nuns who accepted the Buddhist philosophy as the way to attain total freedom from suffering. Why did the Buddha's teachings hold such wide appeal? What was there in his teachings that many found relevant to their way of life and thinking?

The Buddha's Teachings

Gotama Buddha's basic teaching was the principle called the Four Noble Truths (in Sanskrit *arya-satya*, "noble truth"). They are: (1) all life centred around the self is suffering, (2) the cause of suffering is the mistaken belief that one's self is the centre of things and the most important thing, (3) there is a real freedom from this suffering, and (4) the path to that freedom consists of eight parts.

The first truth says that suffering (Sanskrit *duhkha*) is the central feature of all sentient (able to feel and perceive) beings' way of life. The second truth states that suffering is caused by ego-centred living and the longing for sensual pleasure — for wanting to be born, to die, and to be reborn. To Hindus and Buddhists, all sentient beings go through this cycle of life (*samsara*, literally "journeying") until they are liberated (become buddhas, "awakened ones"). The third truth states that suffering can be ended by getting rid of this longing. The fourth truth gives the Buddha's recipe for ending suffering.

This fourth Noble Truth is called the Eightfold Path (*ashtangika-marga*). It consists of:

(1) a realistic view of the world;

(2) realistic intentions;

(3) realistic speech,

(4) actions,

(5) livelihood,

(6) activities, and

(7) mindfulness; and

(8) realistic meditation.

Gotama Buddha advised all those seeking freedom from suffering to practise good will to all sentient

Rites of Passage
A Vedic Wedding

Vivaha, or "leading a bride to the bridegroom's place," the term used for the Vedic marriage ceremony, is the most important life-cycle ritual. The same term is used by modern Hindus, and the structure of the wedding ritual — as defined in Vedic and post-Vedic literature — remains to this day. The same mantras (chants) and steps of this ceremony from the Vedas are followed by the Brahmin priests. Three central sacraments lead to the completion of the Vedic marriage: The *panigrahana*, or "holding of the hands"; the *agniparinayana*, or "walking around the sacred fire"; and the *saptapadi*, or "seven steps."

In the "holding of the hands" step, the bride and groom jointly make offerings to the sacred fire. The groom, seated and facing his bride, holds her hands and recites the following Vedic mantras:

> *I take your hand in mine*
> *seeking happiness;*
> *I ask you to live with me*
> *as your husband*
> *till both of us with age*
> *grow old.*
> *Comprehend this*
> *when I say that*
> *the [Vedic] gods,*
> *Bhaga, Aryama, Savita, Purandhi*
> *have given you to me*
> *so that I may fulfill the*
> *dharma of the householder with you.*

In the "walking around the sacred fire," the groom leads the bride around the fire three times, keeping their right sides toward it and chanting the following verses:

A traditional Hindu wedding includes garlands of flowers and the sacred fire, seen above.

This is who I am [saying his name],
and you are you [saying his bride's name].
I am the heaven,
you are the earth. I am the music,
you are the poetry.
Let us be wed here.
Let us join together
and give birth to little ones.
Loving each other,
desirous of clean life,
with cheerful minds and hearts, thus may we live
through a hundred autumns.

The last "seven steps" ritual seals the wedding, after which there is no turning back. Leading the bride, the groom recites another mantra as they walk each of the seven steps.

The wedding sacrament — performed before the sacred fire — represents the strongly patriarchal nature of Hindu society. Its values stress a desire to continue the family line through a male heir. The man cannot, however, function alone. Although he is the "leader," the Vedic rituals stress the shared hopes and responsibilities of husband and wife.

Activities

1. How does the Hindu wedding differ from weddings in your religion or culture?

2. Why do you think the marriage ceremony is considered the most important life-cycle ritual?

beings; avoid lying, slandering, and gossiping; avoid occupations that harm sentient beings — such as butcher, hunter, weapons or narcotics dealer; become mindful of (pay attention to) their own body, feelings, thinking, and objects of thought; and concentrate by meditating on their breathing and thought processes.

One of the fundamental messages of the Buddha was that a person should actively cultivate an attitude of compassion, friendliness, and joy towards all sentient beings in the universe. Buddhism was part of the rationalist tradition of the age, which did not believe in a personal, all-powerful creator.

The Buddha's teachings were open to all classes of society, and so undermined class distinctions based

A statue of Buddha in a monastery in Ledakh, northern India. How would teachings of Buddha undermine a class structure?

on birth. The Buddha stressed the virtues of honest living, and is said to have given practical advice to his followers who were householders, possibly including advice on managing money in what was considered an ethically correct manner. The Buddha is reported to have once said: "The lay disciple with money obtained by hard work, gathered by strength of arm, earned by sweat, and legitimately acquired makes himself happy and cheerful, and he makes his parents, wife, children, slaves, and labourers happy."

For monks and nuns, however, the Buddha insisted that money is not conducive to happiness, and is an obstruction to true spiritual advancement. On one occasion, he said to the monks that the loss of such a thing as money is a trifling matter, whereas the loss of wisdom brings utter misery. For their survival, the monks had to depend solely on gifts (*dana*) from lay followers.

The Buddha appears to have had much to say about the political and social institutions created by people to safeguard their interests. When the world reached a stage of moral decay, strife, and insecurity in his opinion, there was a need to restore order out of anarchy. People assembled and elected the best person from among their group to protect their interests, and in return for these services, they would pay taxes. This is one of the earliest known examples of a social contract.

Kingship for the Buddha was a human institution created out of a collective human will. He told the story of a king whose wise minister advised that he should make his subjects prosperous and abolish criminal activities. According to the minister, the king should provide seeds to the farmers, capital to the traders, and suitable jobs to those who wanted to serve the state. In this manner, all the subjects would be happily occupied with their own duties, there would be no revolt, and the people would be glad to pay taxes. The Buddha was offering a solution to a very modern problem.

WEB CONNECTION

http://www.mcgrawhill.ca/links/echoes

Go to the site above to find out more about Buddhism.

Gotama Buddha's overriding concern for the welfare of humanity and his ideas on compassion, equality, social justice, and non-injury of all living beings were adopted by Indians and became a part of their humanist tradition. As Buddhism spread throughout Asia, this message of compassion, love, and respect for all living things became a part of Asia's heritage as well.

Cross-Cultural Interaction in India: Hindus and Muslims

The arrival of Islam to the Indian subcontinent in the eighth century led to the inevitable clash of two civilizations. Introduced into India was the cultural Islamic heritage of Arabia, Persia, and central Asia — with its distinct tradition of literature, languages, legal philosophy, and art. There were many important differences between Islamic culture and the traditional culture of Indian civilization.

Whereas Muslims believe in the conversion of others to their religion, Hinduism does not seek converts. Hindus worship images of gods and goddesses, while Muslims oppose the worship of images and associate such worship with the paganism of pre-Islamic Arabia. Whenever in a position to do so, Muslims consider it a sacred duty to destroy images and the temples that house them. Some scholars believe that the incompatibility of Hinduism and Islam was never resolved, and that the two went their separate ways with the creation of Pakistan as a sovereign Islamic state in 1947.

Civilizations tend to borrow traits of other civilizations with which they come to into contact. Before accepting those borrowed features, they try to locate similar ideas, or sets of ideas, within their own traditions. This process is called acculturation. For example, Hinduism in the medieval period actually incorporated many religious traditions similar to those of the Muslims by digging into its own Hindu tradition. One such tradition was the method of devotion — the worship and love of God by a devotee — known as *bhakti*. Bhakti doctrines emphasized direct access to God, rather than through an image. This negated the Brahmin role as intermediary between God and a person. The doctrine of bhakti became a central theme of Hindus in Muslim-dominated India.

EDUCATION IN ANCIENT INDIA: PROMOTING STABILITY

Beginning with the age of the Guptas, and extending into the ninth and tenth centuries, famous Buddhist universities flourished throughout India. Nalanda University in Bihar, northwestern India, was the most notable, with 30 000 students from Korea, China, central Asia, and all over India. Notable universities were also established at Vallabhi in Gujarat, western India, Kanchi in the south, and Kashmir in northern India. All were well maintained, with regular incomes from the ruling kings. Admission standards were very high. Since Nalanda was a Buddhist University, works belonging to the different Buddhist sects were taught as compulsory subjects. Other subjects included logic, grammar and philosophy, medicine, systems of philosophy, literature, and general knowledge. A Chinese monk who visited Nalanda university wrote: "The day is not sufficient for the asking and answering of profound questions. From morning till night, they engage in discussion; the old and the young mutually help one another."

The books taught included the *dharma shastras*, or "science of righteousness," which deal with social, legal, and religious behaviour. They contain civil and criminal procedures and a list of punishments for breaking the laws. Secular laws dealing with trade regulations, contracts, and debt also appear among the topics in the dharma shastras. The books are also regarded as an instruction manual for the correct social behaviour of all classes in society. Instructions cover the religious fasts, purification, foods, marriage, and the rules governing the conduct of social classes. Although the dharma shastra literature dates back to the first century CE, the majority of those texts known today were written during the Gupta Empire, beginning in the fourth century CE. The post-Gupta writers of medieval India merely commented on the dharma shastras written earlier. These commentaries offer insights into the historical changes brought about in the social, legal, and religious behaviour of Indians over the centuries.

Science and Technology

Ancient Indian scientists made contributions that were crucial to the development of virtually all branches of science and technology. Can you imagine life without the zero? An Indian scientist named Brahmagupta (598–660) gave us this most useful invention. Brahmagupta perfected the Indian decimal system for the notation of numerals, and developed a method of expressing tens and hundreds by position, using a special sign for zero. This method of expressing all numbers using just ten symbols is, perhaps, India's greatest legacy to the world. The same Brahmagupta also anticipated gravitational theory. He said: "Things fall to the ground not because of any inherent force within but because of the pull from the earth."

An earlier Indian scientist, Aryabhatta (476–520 CE) a mathematician and astronomer, computed the mathematical equation for pi (π), which was not derived in Europe until much later. Aryabhatta knew that the Earth's revolution (rotation on its axis) produced the apparent daily rising and setting of the Sun, planets, and stars. The trigonometric sine function, never mentioned by Greek mathematicians and astronomers, was used in India from the time of the Gupta period. A work on astronomy from that period entitled *Surya Siddhanta* actually provides a table of sine values.

THE Past AT PLAY

Akbar was a playful emperor. Across from his palace, he had a giant chessboard built, large enough to fill the squares with people dressed as knights, bishops, pawns, and queens. Watching from his balcony, Akbar would play the game with his nobles, and the live pieces changed positions at their commands. On another occasion, Akbar woke up the entire court in the middle of the night because he had a sudden urge to play polo.

TRADE

The period from 184 BCE to 320 CE saw tremendous growth in India's trading and commercial connections with western and eastern civilizations. Spices and silk were the main items of trade. The Roman senator

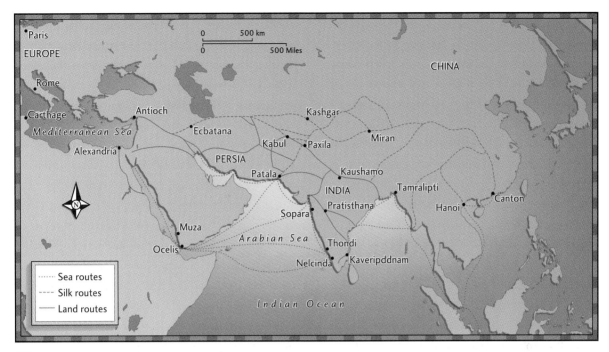

■ Ancient Trade Routes

Trace the journey from Canton to Ecbatana along the Silk Road. How far did traders travel by this route?

Pliny (ca. 77 CE) complained that Indian pepper drained the wealth of Rome: "There is not a year in which India does not attract a million sesterces [coins]." Greek sailors in the second century CE discovered the monsoon trade winds, which enabled them to reach India by sea, avoiding the time-consuming coastal route via the Persian Gulf. Merchants sailed from Egypt in July and arrived at Muzaris, in Kerala on the west coast of India, in 40 days. They stayed on the Kerala coast for about three months and then began the return voyage from Muzaris in December or January.

The Indian overland trade route was through Afghanistan to central Asia and across the Hindukush Mountains, where the route divided — one route going towards the east and China, and the other towards the west to the Mediterranean and

Rome. There were several Roman trading posts in southern India. Roman coins, bronze statues, and transport amphorae have been found in various archaeological excavations carried out in the twentieth century. Indian Tamil literature of the second century CE notes that in the thriving port of Mucharis (Roman Muzaris), "the beautiful and large ships of the Yavanas [Greeks and Romans] bringing gold, come splashing the white foam on the waters of Periyar [in Kerala] and return laden with pepper." The same literature describes the powerful Yavanas clad completely in armour and acting as bodyguards to the Tamil kings, and praises "the cool and fragrant wine brought by the Yavanas in their good ships."

Egyptians and Greeks were the principal carriers of overseas trade with India. The Greek word for rice, *oryza,* and the words for ginger, *zinziber* and cinnamon, *karpion,* closely resemble their Tamil equivalents *arisi, inchver,* and *karva,* respectively. Pliny, as stated earlier, referred to the great demand for pepper and ginger in Rome. An invader of Rome in 408 CE demanded and obtained, as part of a ransom, 1359 kg of pepper. We are told that the Kushan king Kanishka sent an Indian mission to the Roman Emperor Trajan on his accession, and that the emperor treated his Indian visitors with distinction, giving them senators' seats at the theatre.

INDIAN LITERATURE AND ART

Many of the Indian law books, the *dharma shastras,* laid down ethical and legal guidelines for the Hindus. Some of these were written in the second and third centuries CE, at a time when India was supposedly in a dark period. More importantly, India's two great epics were also composed during this period. The *Ramayana* is the story of Rama, a prince who was exiled by his father, Dasharatha. With his brother and his wife, Sita, Rama goes to the South in search of a livelihood. Sita is abducted by the demon king Ravana of Lanka. Rama wages a mighty war against Ravana with the aid of an army of monkeys, and rescues Sita, defeating and killing Ravana. Rama is the archetype of an ideal king who rules justly and wisely. The kingdom of Rama, the *Rama rajya,* is considered by Hindus a prototype of the golden age in which every man and woman lives happily under the protective custody of a wise ruler. Eventually, the hero Rama was elevated to the status of a god.

Another great epic tale is the *Mahabharata,* based on an actual battle fought in 850 BCE. The epic was recited orally for several centuries. The final, inflated version consists of 106 000 verses composed over a period of two hundred years, from 100 to 300 CE. The twenty-six books of the *Mahabharata* narrate the story of a great war fought between two rival segments of the Bharata clan. The five Pandava brothers, with their allies, collide with one hundred of the Kaurava brothers. Several sections of the *Mahabharata* deal with the ethics and morality of politics and social life. The revered Hindu religious text, the **Bhagavad-Gita**, is a poem within the *Mahabharata.*

A new Indian art style emerged in the brief Shunga period, which immediately followed the Mauryas. This period is noted for the creation of beautiful Buddhist monuments decorated with relief sculpture. In the Kushan period, Buddhist art in the northwest of India had been influenced by Graeco-Roman style. In central India and in the north, at Mathura, the Indian style continued and produced the classical Gupta style.

This sandstone sculpture of a preaching Buddha was created in the Gupta period, ca. 475 CE. On the base are shown some disciples and the Wheel of the Law of the Buddha.

SOCIAL STRUCTURES: DAILY LIFE IN ANCIENT INDIA

At age six, a young boy of the wealthier classes would receive a sacred thread in a ceremony that marked the beginning of his formal education. For the next decade, he would attend a well-equipped school, complete with a large underground exercise room. These schools, which were outside the city, were staffed by a large number of specialists paid by the king. Throughout their education, boys played, studied, and were guided by mentors selected by their parents. They were taught various arts (*kala*) and sciences (*shastras*). Training in the martial arts was also a part of the curriculum — including the use of weapons, hand-to-hand combat, giving and countering blows, and riding elephants and horses.

Girls of wealthy families received an education quite different from that of the boys. They were taught reading, writing, painting, and dancing by female tutors. The tutors were well-versed in legends and tales, and were proficient in the arts and sciences, as well as fluent in several languages and dialects.

The daily routine of a wealthy young man (*nagarika*) began in the morning with a series of exercises with wooden clubs, and yoga (Sanskrit *yogah*, "union" or "joining") to keep his body and mind alert. This routine was followed by an elaborate bath, after which fresh clothes fumigated with incense and a turban-like hat were put on. Before leaving the house to attend to business, young men ate a mixture of powdered, dry mango, camphor, and cloves to freshen their breath.

The daily schedule of men of the wealthy classes included looking after business interests, although much of this work was left to their business managers. Before the midday meal, men often played chess (which originated in India) or other board games. The midday meal may have consisted of game birds roasted on spits, wrapped in bitter leaves, and served with a sauce made of butter, mango juice, salt, and pepper. A soup prepared with beans, goat meat, fried eggplant, pieces of ginger, cumin spice, and lotus stalks fried in butter may also have been served. The meal would conclude with peaches and pears, when in season (both of these were introduced to India from China in the first century CE), or oranges, bananas, and mangoes. Churned buttermilk mixed with sugar, honey, and the essence of flowers would normally be drunk with the meal. On special occasions, Kapisha wine, from Afghanistan, was drunk. According to the Indian custom, men ate their lunch separate from women.

Often, a man of status possessed an art gallery that contained paintings to be admired by his friends. The men of the wealthy class were also trained in art and literature, and they displayed their knowlege in the company of friends by reading poems or plays they had composed. King Harsha wrote three plays, and the Emperor Samudragupta, who was an accomplished lute player, was referred to as the "king among poets." Occasionally, men would visit the *ganikas*, accomplished women entertainers who sang, danced, and engaged in literary conversations. Wealthy men and women enjoyed hosting dinner parties at which they would listen to music, make small talk, and sometimes sip imported Roman wines.

Life for the Common People of the Gupta Age

People of lesser means during the Gupta period lived on rice and rice preparations mixed with whatever else was available. More specifically, they consumed boiled rice with lentils, bean soup, and vegetables. Flattened, unleavened wheat bread cooked on a griddle — occasionally fried — was the staple food of northwestern India. Onions, garlic, and ginger were affordable items, as was a wide variety of vegetables, such as leafy greens, eggplant, gourds, and root vegetables.

Spices used to flavour food included dried ginger, cumin, turmeric, mustard, coriander, and black pepper. There was always spicy curry made with lentils. Even poor peasants consumed milk and milk products such as curd and buttermilk. Clarified butter (butter with the milk solids removed) was regarded as a luxury eaten by the rich; oils of sesame and mustard seed were used by the ordinary folk.

Inexpensive bananas and citrus fruits were available throughout the year, supplemented by seasonal Indian fruits such as jack fruit, jujube, and mangoes. Pork, regarded as inferior to goat, was eaten by commoners. Fish, too, formed part of the diet of the poor.

Basic education — reading, writing, and arithmetic — were available for all classes of society, including the poor. Children went to primary schools, referred to as *gurukulas*, literally "teacher's households," where they practised writing on wet clay or a sandy surface. Poor students would do household chores for their teacher in return for their lessons. Food was provided to the students by local householders or the teacher. Neighbourhood schools in villages, towns, and cities were sometimes attached to Hindu temples or Buddhist monastic establishments. Teachers were compensated by local kings, landlords, wealthy merchants, and guilds of artisans.

Higher education was reserved for the children of Brahmins and powerful warrior and commercial classes. By the Gupta era, the trade and crafts guilds were well-established, and young apprentices spent several years with a master to learn a craft. Sanskrit was not taught to the lower classes, whose language of instruction was the vernacular, or *pra-krit*. The literature of the Gupta age mentions women who could read and write, but in Sanskrit dramas, women always spoke pra-krit, not Sanskrit.

Ancient
ODDITIES

For security reasons, Emperor Chandragupta Maurya (fourth century BCE) frequently changed his sleeping quarters in the palace. Chandragupta proclaimed that he would reward handsomely any daredevil who could bypass the imperial guards and enter the royal bedchamber. The emperor was constantly guarded by strong, tall women with drawn swords.

Review...Recall...Reflect

1. Explain the role of the Hindu religion in Indian culture.

2. Why did the teachings of the Buddha have such great appeal for many Indians?

3. How did the education in Buddhist universities promote stability in ancient India?

India's Legacy

Modern India is the product of centuries of traditions as well as influences from many other cultures. In ancient times, its traditions were influenced by the Greeks; in late medieval times, by Muslims; and in modern times, by European Christians. While cross-cultural influences have been significant in the development of Indian culture, the core of India's cultural heritage, coming as it does from Vedic-Hindu, Buddhist, and other Indian religions, remains dynamic.

India's impact on other cultures of the world has been extensive. In the realm of agriculture, India introduced the world to cotton, which the ancient Greeks referred to as "wool that grows on trees." Sugar is also a product of India, and, in fact, its name derives from the ancient Indian Sanskrit word *sharkara*. However, many would say that India's greatest culinary gift to the world is spices: pepper, cinnamon, cloves, cardamom, and mace. Oranges, lemons, bananas, mangoes, and many other fruits are also of Indian origin.

Modern-day Hindus of India and those who settled throughout the world take pride in the historical and cultural continuity of their religion from the Vedic times. Despite regional variations in how they worship images of the gods, Hindus share the basic structure of worship: most worship and rituals are performed in the presence of fire and water. Hindu sacraments of the life cycle, derived from the Vedas, are also key features of Hindu philosophy. The Brahmins of Hinduism remain instrumental in maintaining this continuity, and are respected for their role as preservers of India's traditions.

History Continues to Unfold

After India's independence from British rule in 1947, Indian historians started vigorously reshaping the writing of the history of India. This meant rejecting British imperial historians' negative views of India's past. More recently, controversies have centred on the Aryans. A group of Hindu nationalist historians of northern India allege that the Aryans were the original inhabitants of India and the founders of the Indus civilization. But overwhelming archaeological and literary evidence indicate a central Asian origin of the Aryans. According to Hindu nationalists, the Aryans of the north were endowed with superior intellectual and physical traits, different from those of the Dravidians of southern India, who were overpowered by the Aryan culture of the north. The historians of the south resent this interpretation, and assert the Dravidians' equality with the Aryans. These debates emphasize the differences rather than similarities of the pan-Indian (all of India) Civilization.

For Hindu nationalist historians of India, who experienced a resurgence in the 1990s, India is the land of the Hindus. To them, non-Hindus — whether Christians, Muslims, or others — are outsiders who must accommodate the dominant Hindu cultural ethos or *Hindutva*. That ethos is left vaguely defined. Re-examining Indian medieval history dominated by the Muslim dynasties, these Hindu historians single out the anti-Hindu measures of some Muslim rulers, such as demolition of Hindu temples and forced conversion of Hindus to Islam.

Current Research and Interpretations

The existence of two views of medieval Indian history cannot be taken lightly. The exclusive Hindutva vision of India's past has generated inter-community tensions in present-day India. If Hindus, Muslims, Buddhists, Sikhs, and Christians are to coexist amicably in republican India, a view of their ancient and medieval past that promotes the spirit of community among them must prevail.

Chapter Review

Chapter Summary

In this chapter, we have seen:

- that religion had a significant influence on the political structures of ancient India
- that selected individuals made significant contributions to the military, political, religious, and intellectual traditions of ancient India
- how unique forces led to the development of the caste system in India
- that established religious traditions tended to reinforce stability in ancient India

Reviewing the Significance of Key People, Concepts, and Events (Knowledge/Understanding)

1. Understanding the history of India requires a knowledge of the following concepts and events, and an understanding of their significance in the development of Indian society. In your notes, identify and explain the historical significance of two or three from each column.

People	Concepts/Places	Events
Aryans	Mohenjo-daro	Vedic Age
Brahmins	*Upanishads*	Gupta Empire
	Bhagavad-Gita	Delhi Sultanate
		Hinduism

2. List and describe at least three of the samskaras still considered important to Hindus throughout the world.

3. Compare and contrast the Early and Late Vedic Ages by listing at least three key descriptors for each period in two columns labelled Early Vedic and Late Vedic.

Doing History: Thinking About the Past (Thinking/Inquiry)

1. Write a two-paragraph critique of the reign of Ashoka that assesses the degree to which he was able to transform Indian culture and society through his Buddhist-influenced policies.

2. To what degree, if any, did the differences between Hinduism and Islam make it difficult for the belief systems to coexist in India? To answer this question, develop a clear topic sentence and prepare at least three supporting arguments (using sound historical evidence) to support it.

Applying Your Learning (Application)

1. Create a visual depiction of the Brahmins' theory of the origins of classes in Indian society. Be sure to include the four classes, provide a clear definition for the role of each class in society, and creatively use the colour associated with each class.

2. Select any three of the philosophical traditions discussed in this chapter. For each, describe one idea you agree with, find intriguing, or reject. Explain the reason for your stance on each idea.

Communicating Your Learning (Communication)

1. Write a fictional diary account of a typical day in the life of a young girl in ancient India, and an entry for a young boy. The two entries should clearly indicate how life was similar and different for boys and girls in ancient India.

2. On a map of the ancient world, show the flow of trade into and out of India. Clearly indicate which goods came into India, which left India, and with whom trading was taking place. Based on your map, respond in a paragraph to the following question: "Was India the crucial trade link between the East and the West?"

China

By the end of this chapter, you will be able to:

- *explain the reaction of ancient China to exposure to external influences at different points in its history*

- *analyze the factors that contributed to the maintenance of stability and continuity during China's long history*

- *evaluate the contributions of selected individuals and groups to the development of legal, political, military, religious and intellectual traditions in ancient China*

- *demonstrate an understanding of the influence of women in the political and economic life of ancient China*

These Chinese women are using one of the oldest silk weaving methods, the backstrap loom. The figures decorate the top of a bronze vessel that was cast 4000 to 5000 years ago.

The Chinese, from earliest times, have called their land Zhongguo (pronounced *jong-gwo*), which means the "Middle Kingdom." This is because Chinese cosmology (the study of the nature of the universe) identifies five directions — north, south, east, west, and centre; the centre is the superior, most desirable of spaces. Throughout history, a sense of geographical, cultural, and political centrality informed the Chinese self-image and China's view of its place in the world.

In Chinese cosmology, the central position is also that of the father of a family, and throughout history, China took seriously its fatherly role of teaching, and punishing, its "children." Korea, Japan, and much of Indochina were eager students and drew much of their cultural inspiration from the Chinese example. China also gave to the rest of the world many of the formative inventions of human history: the compass, the crossbow, gunpowder, paper and printing, civil service examinations, paper money, silk, porcelain, tea, and many other things that are part of daily life today. Whatever our modern view of China's centrality, it is a fact that for most of the past two thousand years, China has been among the most advanced of all civilizations.

KEY WORDS

oracle bones

filial piety

Silk Road

Mandate of Heaven

Forbidden City

Buddhism

Hangzhou

ancestor veneration

xenophobic

KEY PEOPLE

Confucius

Lao Zi

Legalists

Han Fei Zi

Shi Huangdi

Wudi

Sui Wendi

Empress Wu

Khubilai Khan

Mongols

Chingghis Khan

VOICES FROM THE PAST

To go too far is the same as not to go far enough.
Confucius,
Analects,
Chapter 12, V. 7

TIME LINE: CHINA

	ca. 7000 BCE	Neolithic cultures appear along the Yellow River
Shang dynasty, the first Chinese civilization on the North China Plain	ca. 1600 BCE	
	ca. 1500 BCE	Earliest Chinese empire begins to take shape
The Zhou, a warlike people from Central Asia, conquer the Shang	ca. 1027 BCE	
	771 BCE	Invading nomads displace Zhou rulers, beginning 500 years of disunity
Mo Zi introduces Moism to China	470 BCE	
	221 BCE	Shi Huangdi reunites the provinces and establishes the Qin dynasty
Shi Huangdi has 460 Chinese philosophers buried alive and burns their books	213 BCE	
	207 BCE	The Han Dynasty, China expands its borders and trade
Wudi declares Confucianism the state religion, creates first university	124 BCE	
	First Century CE	Buddhism is introduced to China from India
Han dynasty collapses, nomads from the north seize control	220 CE	
	618	Tang dynasty begins China's Golden Age
Empress Wu becomes the only woman to rule China alone	690	
	752	Rebellion of An Lu-shan begins
Song dynasty brings a period sometimes called the Chinese Renaissance	960	
	1279	Song dynasty collapses under attacks from Mongols led by Khubilai Khan
Mongol rule in China ends, replaced by the Ming dynasty	1368	
	1405	Zheng He begins a series of seven great maritime expeditions
Portuguese pirates and traders first appear on China's south coast	1514	
	1600	Jesuits from Europe arrive in Beijing

PREHISTORY OF CHINA

Neolithic cultures developed along the Yellow River in North China from about 7000 BCE. Cultural mingling among these settlements gave rise to the development of a distinctive civilization. Chinese civilization began to leave its earliest records from about 1600 to 1500 BCE, a time when Mesopotamia, Egypt, and India were already well-established.

In the earliest times, the geographic area of Chinese culture consisted merely of a number of intensive farming communities scattered on the North China Plain, and it did not approach anything resembling its present geographical configuration until the first century BCE. As elsewhere, however, the physical environment provided challenges and opportunities for civilization to develop.

China today has a total land area of roughly 9 500 000 km², and its north-south extension (about 5500 km) includes agricultural zones from temperate to subtropical. Because of the wide range of crops they can produce, the Chinese have always considered themselves self-sufficient in food and other natural resources. Historically, they saw little need to trade with others, and tended to import only luxury goods.

In the earliest days, Chinese civilization was centred on the Yellow River; often called "China's Sorrow" because its floods have claimed millions of lives. The Chinese also say that their civilization is the gift of the Yellow River, since it also watered the North China Plain, a region of scarce rainfall, and made the cultivation of wheat, millet, and legumes possible. Along with pigs, chickens, and dogs, these foods formed the diet of the early Chinese.

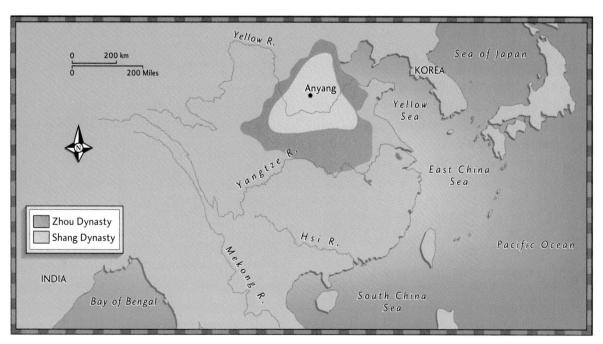

■ China Under the Shang and Zhou Dynasties

1. Why do the Chinese say that their civilization is the "gift of the Yellow River?"

2. What geographical features tend to isolate China from the rest of the world?

China's second major river, the Yangtze, is 5148 km long, (about 800 km longer than the Yellow). It was not fully developed as an agricultural region until long after settlement of the North China Plain, but it proved ideal for the intensive cultivation of rice, which became the staple food of the East Asian diet.

China is largely isolated from the rest of the world by high mountains, the deserts and steppes of central Asia, and by the great expanse of the Pacific Ocean. Internally, mountain ranges and river systems create provincial boundaries. Thus, in its formative years, Chinese civilization was largely isolated from the rest of the known world, and throughout its long history, China has been plagued by regionalism and provincial rivalries.

CHANGE AND CONTINUITY IN CHINA

Modern historians have tried to simplify China's complex history by defining a number of stages in the development of the civilization. Although no approach has been universally embraced, the following periods are widely accepted; each period had distinctive characteristics.

TIME FRAMES
PERIODS IN CHINESE HISTORY

The Formative Period 1600–1027 BCE

The Classical Age 1027–221 BCE

The First Empire 221 BCE–589 CE

The Second Empire 589–960

The Third Empire 960–1368

The Last Empire 1368–1911

Each period saw advances in the material aspects of Chinese civilization — standard of living, technological development, sophistication in the arts, and expansion of the economy. At the same time, the Chinese elite adhered to the Confucian value system, which prized stability over change, and balance and harmony over innovation. After Confucianism became the state ideology in 124 BCE, the Chinese created a number of institutions designed to foster stability. These were, most notably:

- a system of rulership headed by an emperor whose position was guaranteed by unchanging Heaven
- a civil service educated in a curriculum that was hardly altered over 2000 years
- an economy that encouraged agriculture and discouraged commerce and entrepreneurship
- a social system based on an ethic of authority and obedience, in which the places of old and young — man, woman, and child — were fixed and, in theory, perfectly in balance

These were the principal factors responsible for the unusual stability of dynastic China.

The Formative Period

The Chinese term for civilization means, literally, "to transform by writing." For the Chinese, the most important element of a civilization is writing, and China's first historical dynasty, the Shang (1600 – 1027 BCE), saw the creation of not only the written Chinese language, but also other marks of civilization. The development of cities, vocational specialization, complex social organization, and distinctive artistic endeavours such as the crafting of jade and bronze were also developed in the Formative Period.

This bronze wine bucket from the Shang period (ca. 1400-1100 BCE) was probably used in important ceremonies. At this time, China was unsurpassed in bronze making.

The Shang people occupied an area about the size of modern France on the North China Plain, and have left a rich archaeological record that has enabled scholars to reconstruct much of the history of the period. The most important of these archaeological remains are the superb bronze vessels inscribed with useful historical information, and more than 100 000 **oracle bones**. Usually tortoiseshells, or the scapular bones of cattle or sheep, these bones were used for divination (predicting the future). Using a sharp object, scribes scratched a question into the bone — for example, what would be the outcome of a military campaign? the next day's weather? the gender of the child of a pregnant queen? Small holes were then drilled into the bone. When it was held over a fire, the

Oracle bones like this were used by the Shang people to foretell the future. The scratches are the writing that spelled out the question to be answered.

bone cracked, and from the configuration of the cracks, priests interpreted and recorded an answer.

In Shang society, the king and his nobles lived in a series of walled capitals. Their houses were above the ground, while those of the commoners seem to have been below ground. The king, while never a god like the Egyptian Pharaoh, had priestly functions, and worshipped Shangdi (*shong-dee*), probably the ancestor of his family and the source of his power. This was likely the origin of ancestor veneration (showing reverence), which remains very important to this day in the lives of the Chinese people. Beneath the King was the nobility; followed by the social groupings of scribe-priest, farmer, artisan, merchant, and slave.

In this clearly delineated society, the order of the groupings was important. From the beginning of Chinese history, the ability to read and write has brought social status, and those who were educated were highly respected. Farmers were valued as primary producers. The artisans, who produced so much of the art found in museums today, were considered non-essential but useful to society. Merchants were seen as greedy and parasitical and were objects of contempt until modern times. These class divisions solidified over several centuries.

Slavery was legal in China until the twentieth century, but slaves — usually war captives and criminals — never seem to have made up more than two percent of the population. This proportion was tiny compared with the number of slaves in early Mediterranean civilizations.

Women occupied a relatively high position in Shang society, and at least in the early period, children probably took their surnames from their mothers. Young men often lived with their bride's family after marriage, and daughters were valued as much as sons. Over time, however, a distinct preference for male children developed because of males' greater economic value in agriculture, and because only males could perform ancestor veneration. Without a son, parents were doomed to a gloomy existence in the afterlife, and this gender preference is still strong in China today.

The Shang rulers exercised only loose political control over North China, and thus were easily overwhelmed in about 1027 BCE by a warlike people called the Zhou (*joe*), from Central Asia or northwest China. Before its fall, however, the Shang left a lasting mark on Chinese civilization — including their script, enduring religious and social values, and the artistic principles seen in Shang bronzes, ceramics, and jade.

THE CLASSICAL AGE

The Zhou period, which lasted until 256 BCE, can be divided into two segments. The first, called the Western Zhou, lasted until 771 BCE and kept much of the culture of the Shang. There were, however, changes in burial customs, military technology, and, more importantly, religion and politics.

In religion, Shangdi — the supreme deity of the Shang — was replaced by Tian, or "Heaven," and divination by oracle bones became much less frequent. Tian was not considered an anthropomorphic (in human form) god and was never represented in art. Instead, Tian was a divine force, a guardian of the Middle Kingdom (as the Chinese now began to refer to themselves) and its ruling family. Chinese rulers in the Zhou began to call themselves Son of Heaven, and later emperors used this term even into the twentieth century.

The Zhou established a decentralized political system of rule by lords, with vassals, fiefs, and investiture — a system of government similar to the feudal system that appeared in Europe almost 2000 years later. The differences, however, between Europe and China are as great as any similarities. This system did not last, and ended in 771 when invading nomads killed the Zhou ruler and his successor was forced to abandon the capital and flee to the east.

Warfare, Technology, and Politics in the Eastern Zhou

After fleeing to their new capital, Loyang, the Zhou court lost all real power and endured for another five centuries as merely the ritual and symbolic rulers of China. In fact, there was no real China during these centuries because no unified political system existed. Lords and their vassals began declaring themselves independent, leading to an age of extensive warfare, bloodshed, and violence, with hundreds of small domains struggling to survive. By the third century BCE, seven huge states had gobbled up all the rest, and in 221 BCE, one of these defeated its rivals and reunited the country.

At the beginning of the Eastern Zhou, China lagged behind the Mediterranean world in most material aspects of civilization. By the end of the period however, China had become, at least, its equal. Not surprisingly, progress was first seen in military technology. Better armour and weapons such as the crossbow appeared. Iron technology surpassed that of Persia, and the cumbersome Shang war chariots were gradually replaced by swift cavalry. Generals wrote some of the world's oldest manuals on military strategy and tactics, and one of these, Sun Zi's *Art of War* is still used in military academies throughout the world.

Rulers of competing Chinese states embarked upon programs to improve the livelihood of their people. They built walls, new dikes, irrigation works, and canals. Soybeans were cultivated and added protein to the diet, and new strains of wheat and rice were developed. Populations grew along with interstate trade, and some states even experimented with wage and price controls.

In the midst of violence and upheaval, few areas of daily life were unaffected. Music and poetry found new forms of expression, trousers began to replace the robe as everyday dress, and people cast off the "barbaric" use of knife and fork to eat with chopsticks. Above all, this period saw the greatest outpouring of original thought in Chinese history.

CONFUCIUS

China's classical age, the age of the "hundred schools of thought," occurred in the sixth and fifth centuries BCE, perhaps the most intellectually fertile period in the history of the world. Roughly contemporary with the great names in China are many of the seminal thinkers in other centres of civilization: Socrates, Plato, and Pythagoras in Greece; the Buddha in India; Zoroaster in Persia; and some of the greatest of the Hebrew prophets.

Confucius, known in China as Kong Fuzi, was China's most noted thinker during the Classical Age in China, the sixth–fifth centuries BCE. What other great thinkers do we know from this same historical period?

The first and greatest of the Chinese thinkers was a man known as Kong Fuzi ("Master Kong"), whose name was translated into Latin by the first Catholic missionaries as **Confucius**. Born in 551 BCE, he lived an unspectacular life, holding minor government offices in his native state. Confucius then travelled around, visiting many of the lords of other states and trying to convince them to adopt his principles. Failing at this, he returned to his homeland, where he taught until his death in 479 BCE. His words were recorded after his death by 72 close disciples, and these sayings exist today in a short collection of 497 verses called *The Analects*. This book became the guide to Chinese civilization.

According to Confucius, the solution to the evils of his time was for all people to practise the virtue of *ren* (pronounced *run*), which we translate as "humanity," "benevolence" — a kind of perfect virtue that combined courtesy, generosity, good faith, diligence, and kindness. "Love others," said Confucius, "and do not do unto others that which you would not have them do unto you." This passive version of the Golden Rule predates the words of Jesus of Nazareth by 500 years.

Confucius always said that he was simply a transmitter of the better ways of the past. New in his philosophy was that he offered a specific blueprint for the achievement of humanity. He believed that human beings were equal and alike at birth, and he went on to say that it was learning and practice that set them apart. In *The Analects*, Confucius defined how learning and practice could lead human beings to true humanity.

Learning, both formal and informal, was necessary to bring about a benevolent world. Education must be open to all, free of class distinctions. Teachers must respect their students, but at the same time, students were responsible for their own education. Confucius believed in a curriculum that included his-

tory, poetry, etiquette, music, and physical education. He said that we should never stop learning, and he admitted that his own education was incomplete until he reached the age of 70.

The Development of Chinese Writing.

Practice consisted of three major elements. The first was **filial piety**: young people must respect and obey all those older than themselves, especially in their own families. If a person learned to live in harmony, cooperation, and obedience within the family, he or she could help turn the whole world into a family. Confucius also believed that we become more experienced and wiser as we get older. He saw that wars were fought by passionate and ambitious young men who needed the wisdom and contemplation of the elderly to convince them that peace and harmony were preferable to war and strife.

The second element of practice was a doctrine called the "rectification of names." Confucius put it this way: "A father is a father, and a son is a son. A ruler is a ruler, and a subject is a subject." By this, he meant that in any society, there were universal definitions of what constitute good fathers and good sons, good rulers and good subjects. He believed that as people progressed through each stage of life, they should simply strive to be good at what they were, and not try to usurp the position above them. This would lead to the end of overambition and envy, of covetousness and competition. He probably also realized that it could lead to a static society, but he saw this as a good thing.

Confucius also insisted on the practice of courtesy, of observing the rules of etiquette and propriety in all our dealings with others. We expand our sense of goodness each time we perform even a small act of courtesy. This should do away with the need for laws and punishments in society.

Eighty generations of Chinese have followed Confucius and honoured him as their greatest teacher. Confucius defined the most distinctive hallmarks of Chinese civilization: filial piety, family-centred values, a thirst for education, a strong work ethic, and a belief in courtesy — not confrontation — to achieve final harmony in the family of humanity.

Other Systems of Thought in the Zhou Dynasty

To a large extent, the other systems of thought of this period arose as reactions to Confucius. Some disagreed with his philosophy, while others followed him but tried to answer questions he had not raised. His earliest opponent was a man called Mo Zi (*mo-tzy*) who lived from about 470 to 391 BCE. He criticized Confucian philosophy as being too idealistic and too secular. Although Confucius asked human beings to change their behaviour, Mo Zi said that Confucius offered no incentive to do so. Mo Zi believed that humans were motivated by selfishness, and that they would change for the better only if they could see benefit for themselves in it. In spite of his initial popularity, however, Mo Zi's influence lasted only a few centuries, unlike that of Confucius' second rival, the philosopher known simply as "The Old Master," or **Lao Zi**, the founder of Daoist philosophy (also written as Taoist).

Little is known of Lao Zi, and some scholars doubt his existence. His small book, entitled *The Way and the Power* (*Daodejing*), has been very influential

There are many deities in the Daoist pantheon. These are some that appeared on a wall painting in a Yuan dynasty temple.

Many will recognize this figure as the symbol of the principle of yin and yang, or Taiji, a central feature of Chinese cosmology and philosophy. The notion of the Taiji is that the universe functions through the constant interaction of two complementary forces, yin and yang. The basic idea is that situations are never simply black and white — in every yes there is a little no; in every male there is a little female; in every female, a little male; and so on.

in Chinese history, and has been translated into English more than 40 times. Lao Zi opposed Confucian doctrines of social responsibility. He believed in individual freedom and spontaneity, a flight from the cares of the world into a oneness with nature, or the Way (*dao*). For him, disorder and violence arose when human beings tampered with nature or tried to overcome it. He was, therefore, opposed to education, taxation, law, war, and any kind of government interference in the lives of the people. The best government, according to him, was one that existed but did not act. The only function of the ruler was to "empty the minds and fill the bellies" of his people.

Finally, Lao Zi realized that to get people to change their behaviour, he would have to change or even reverse their usual perceptions. He therefore filled his book with startling insights that might provoke people to think. He asked, "What is the most useful part of a cup? Not the handles or the bowl, but the empty space which can be filled." "Water is soft and rocks are hard," he observed, "Yet the water wears away the rock." "Men are strong, yet not so strong as the newborn babe whom no one would ever dare to harm. Men are powerful, yet women possess the greatest of power, that of giving birth to new life." Lao Zi's most important advice to the

world was his doctrine of *wu-wei*: "Do nothing and nothing will not be done."

WEB CONNECTION

http://www.mcgrawhill.ca/links/echoes

Go to the site above to find out more about Chinese religion and philosophy.

A group of philosophers then arrived and put an end to philosophical speculation. They believed that action, not "vain talk," would solve China's problems. Mostly hard-headed realists and practising politicians, they were known as the **Legalists**. They put forth a set of principles that would bring about the unification of China.

Review...Recall...Reflect

1. Explain in which ways Chinese civilization was a product of its geography.

2. How did Confucianism contribute to the stability of ancient China?

3. How did advances in military thought contribute to the development of Chinese civilization?

THE FIRST EMPIRE

Legalism was a philosophy concerned only with the power of the state and the elevation of its ruler. Unconcerned with ethics, morality, or human values, it had three guiding principles: anything done to strengthen the state was by definition good; the ruler must use devious methods to keep officials and other potential rivals from gaining power; the common people must be subjected to detailed, regular laws that embody harsh punishments and lavish rewards. Legalism insisted that offensive war was good, not only because it enriched the state with new territory, but also because it united the people against an external enemy and thus encouraged them to obey the ruler without question. Finally, Legalism stated that productive agriculture was the only valid occupation. All commerce and intellectual enterprise must be discouraged. Nothing could be permitted to interfere with the creation of a strong, rich state.

The most famous of the Legalist philosophers was a prince called **Han Fei Zi** (*hon fay tzy*), who tutored a young prince of one of the seven warring states and persuaded him that if he adopted his doctrines, the young man could become the first Emperor of China. The young prince learned his lessons well, and in 230 BCE began a series of massive and bloody military campaigns that destroyed the remaining six states. Although there were hundreds of thousands of casualties, his prime minister, Li Si (*lee suh*), later wrote that it had been "as easy as sweeping dust from the kitchen stove."

The First Emperor of China

China's first real dynasty began in 221 BCE, when the prince created a new title for himself — **Shi Huangdi** (*shih-hwong dee*), which means "the First Emperor." He called his dynasty the Qin (*chin*), from which we get our name for China. Shi Huangdi then transformed his country, and in ten short years created a legacy that would endure until the twentieth century.

Working closely with his prime minister, Li Si, the Emperor first seized all the land once held by the feudal nobility, and then divided China into 42 prefectures under magistrates that he appointed himself. This centralized the country. The Emperor then built a magnificent capital near present-day Xi'an (*shee-on*), and using 700 000 conscripted labourers, constructed a palace complex that covered about 70 square kilometres. The complex included 270 pavilions, meeting halls, and sleeping palaces where his many wives and concubines lived. Most of these structures were connected by covered walkways and secret passages so that the Emperor could conceal his movements from assassins.

Next, Shi Huangdi acted quickly to unify and standardize all the coinage, weights and measures, and even the size of chariots in his new empire. He outlawed all local customs, festivals, and folksongs as well as local religious practices. In 214 BCE, he ordered Li Si to produce China's first standard dictionary, and built a network of royal roads to distant regions of the country. Some of these roads even had express lanes. The Emperor also built canals that are still in use today.

Shi Huangdi believed in the principle that war enriched the state, so he sent out great armies, first against aboriginal peoples south of the Yangtze River, and then against a nomadic tribe called the Huns, who frequently raided and pillaged in North China. These expeditions were generally successful but were also costly, and the Emperor was determined to find a permanent solution to the problem of the northern border. Using hundreds of thousands of soldiers, mer-

Feature Study

In the Field...
A Work in Progress: The Tomb of Shi Huangdi

One of the top archaeological discoveries of the twentieth century was not uncovered by archaeologists. It was uncovered by workers digging a well in 1974. Imagine finding 8000 life size clay warriors, each one different from the other; then imagine hundreds of wooden chariots, each with its own life size charioteer and full-size horses. As dramatic as that sight must be, it is only a fraction of what has been found, and what is expected to be found, at the site of the tomb of China's first emperor, Shi Huangdi. The tomb is in Lintong county, Xi'an, Shaanxi province.

Archaeologists are still uncovering Shi Huangdi's underground army.

Since the first figure was uncovered, Chinese archaeologists have been working tirelessly to gently sift away the dirt from what is, in effect, an after-life city with everything an emperor would need on his way to the next world. Although most of the emperor's scholars were probably engaged in the search for eternal life, no chances were being taken — 720 000 slave labourers toiled for close to forty years to recreate what Han dynasty historian Sima Qian (145–90 BCE) reported was "everything in the world".

The thousands of individually shaped soldiers reflect the emperor's belief in an active army. This underground army was furnished with real weapons and a headquarters. Their discovery has helped war historians resolve questions about the formation of ranks, the use of weapons and military tactics during China's early dynastic history. Archaeologists were quite surprised to find that the weapons were all still sharp because a protective surface coating had been applied. Some looting likely took place around 206 BCE, but so far it seems that only weapons were taken. The menagerie of clay animals was left intact.

The best is probably yet to come, since the pyramid-like mound that is believed to cover the emperor's tomb is still unexcavated. If we trust Sima Qian, whose history has proven reliable, the tomb contains outer coffins made of copper, along with money, and other treasures. The royal tomb itself is presumed to be made of cast bronze and house a reconstruction of the kingdom of China. It is said that rivers and oceans were represented by mercury in order to appear to be flowing, and archaeological testing has confirmed that there is an unusually high mercury content in the soil.

When the tomb was eventually finished and the emperor's body interred, his concubines who had not had children were given the honour of accompanying the emperor to the next world, and were buried with him. It is also believed that anyone who had worked on the interior of the tomb was killed so as not to spread secrets. Deadly crossbow traps set off by trip wires were positioned to stop robbers, and those who set the traps were also slain.

Work at the site continues and, of course, the closer archaeologists get to the imperial tomb, the more exciting finds become. The artifacts that are closest to the tomb have greater significance or symbolic value since they were closest to the emperor. Opening the tomb is not something to be rushed, however. For now, the two square kilometre burial vault poses an archaeological challenge unlike any other. One of the curators of the museum at the site has been quoted as saying, "Until our generation, or the next generation, figures out a good plan, it's best to leave things alone."

The face of every soldier in Shi Huangdi's tomb is unique.

Activities

1. Conduct a search to see what the current status is at the site of the tomb of Shi Huangdi. What have been the most recent discoveries?

2. China has been careful to keep the dig very Chinese. Foreign archaeologists have been, for the most part, discouraged from joining the dig. Explain why China might prefer not to have outside help at this site.

chants, conscripts, and both male and female prisoners, he began the most ambitious building project of the ancient world — the Great Wall of China.

The Great Wall was not a new idea; several northern states had already built shorter walls. The Emperor joined and vastly extended these walls, so that the finished project reached, perhaps, 2000 km and crossed some of the most inhospitable terrain on earth — mountains, deserts, swamplands, and forests. Marauding barbarians often harassed the workers, and the number that were killed or died of exhaustion, exposure, or hunger is unknown. Many workers were buried inside the wall, so the Chinese sometimes refer to it as "the world's longest graveyard." Nonetheless, the Great Wall was a relatively effective defense mechanism, and defined China's northern territorial boundaries for centuries to come.

If Shi Huangdi had been a European monarch, his name would probably have been followed by

Emperor Shi Huangdi built the Great Wall to keep out raiders from the north in the late third century BCE. Why was it called the world's longest graveyard?

"the Great." Instead, Chinese historians have criticized him for his ruthlessness, massive conscription of labour, wars, harsh laws, and above all, for what they consider the worst of his crimes — the burning of the books. Li Si had complained that people were using the words of the wise and ancient philosophers to criticize the Emperor. To put a stop to this, in 213 BCE the Emperor decreed that only practical works on such subjects as agriculture, medicine, pharmacy, and divination were worth preserving. All other books were to be burned in public. When some scholars were slow to act, the Emperor made an example of them: 460 protestors were buried alive in the palace courtyards. There was no more resistance. This barbaric act ended the golden age of Chinese thought.

Two years later, the first Emperor died unexpectedly, leaving a country seething with discontent. His heir, the youngest of his more than 20 sons, was

This painting shows the first emperor, Shi Huangdi, ordering books to be burned and scholars who protested to be buried alive.

inexperienced, incompetent, and cruel. Rebellions broke out everywhere, and in 206 BCE, one of the rebels founded a new dynasty called the Han, which would last for the next 400 years.

The Han Dynasty

The Han dynasty was an almost exact parallel to the Roman Empire in the West, and the level of the two civilizations was similar. The Romans knew of China and called it "The Land of Silk." The Chinese called Rome "Great Qin", in recognition of the fact that it, too, was a great state, like their own first dynasty. The **Silk Road**, the world's first intercontinental trade route, linked the two empires.

China under the Han dynasty was vital and expansive. The population was somewhere between 50 and 60 million, and the peasantry, about 90 percent of the population, was generally prosperous. Under the remarkable emperor **Wudi** (*woo-dee*), who reigned from 140 to 87 BCE, China conquered Vietnam, Korea, much of Central Asia, and made its

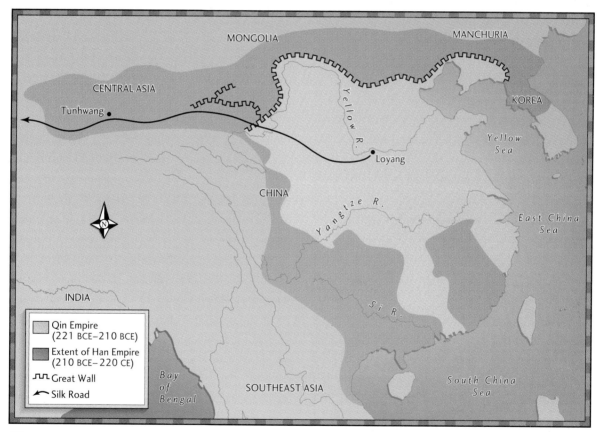

■ China in the Han and Qin Dynasties

1. The ancient Romans knew China as the Land of Silk. In what ways were the Roman Empire and China under the Han dynasty similar?

2. What factors allowed the rapid expansion of China under the Han dynasty?

earliest contacts with Japan. These states and many others along the Silk Road began to send regular tribute to China in acknowledgement of its leadership. The Chinese Emperor and his civilization gradually became dominant in East Asia.

Wudi made Confucianism the state religion, and China's first university (with a curriculum based on Confucian philosophy) was founded in 124 BCE. Officials were selected for public office by the world's first system of competitive examinations, a system brought to the West in the nineteenth century. The well-organized bureaucracy consisted of nine ministers who managed everything from tax collection to defense.

The Structure of Government

The Emperor was the supreme figure in the Chinese government. He was the father and mother of his people, the Son of Heaven, and the one person who kept the universe in balance. He made the laws (though he was above them himself), educated his people, and was responsible for their welfare. He, alone, could perform certain sacrifices such as the great annual ritual that asked Heaven to bless the earth, and each year he plowed the first furrow to produce a bountiful harvest.

The Emperor was not worshipped as a god nor did he rule by divine right. The source of his power was a political doctrine called the **Mandate of Heaven**. This doctrine stated that Heaven chose the ruler and Heaven could get rid of a bad ruler. If a ruler failed to do his job, Heaven would first warn him with omens and portents — floods, earthquakes, and strange phenomena like the birth of dragons or unicorns. If the ruler failed to heed the warnings and change his behaviour, the people, as representatives of Heaven, would rise up and depose him. The people of China therefore had a right of rebellion that existed nowhere else.

The Emperor presided over both an inner and outer court. The inner court consisted of four elements; the first was his wife, the Empress. She was responsible for running the palace and had few public functions. In fact, Chinese Empresses were not to be seen in public, though they often had great influence over their husbands and, especially, their sons. A Chinese boy — even if he became Emperor — always had to obey his mother. The second element was the harem, a group of 121 women who served the Emperor's personal needs. They entertained him, cooked his food, washed his clothes, and sometimes provided him with an heir. Third were the consort clans, the families of the palace women. The males of these families were often given high positions, and could help the emperor in his government. Finally, there were the eunuchs, men who worked in the harem and were castrated to prevent them from having sexual relations with the women. Their job was to guard and care for the needs of the women, perform the heavy work of the palace, and, sometimes, to advise the Emperor. Eunuchs were originally criminals or captives of war, but later, they were often volunteers. In the seventeenth century, more than 100 000 eunuchs lived in Beijing.

Education, the Examination System, and the Law

As in most pre-modern societies, the overwhelming majority of Chinese remained illiterate until the twentieth century. The elite, perhaps five to ten percent of the population, educated their sons and daughters together until the age of eight, when boys and girls were separated. Their mothers then instructed the girls in proper deportment and the household arts, while boys prepared to take the civil service examinations.

Many civil servants were needed to staff the complex and sophisticated Chinese government. These hopeful candidates were taking their civil service examinations in the second century BCE.

In its final form (in the fifteenth century), the examination system consisted of three levels — held each year in the prefecture, in the capital, and at the palace. Candidates were locked into cells for up to a week, where they answered written questions on the Confucian classics and on matters of current affairs. To pass, it was necessary to memorize the approximately 400 000 words that made up the classics, and boys often began their preparation at the age of two or three. Women and persons of low professions, such as merchants, were not allowed into the system. It remained in force until 1905, when it was abolished because protesters maintained that it had never tested scientific knowledge or any other "practical subjects".

Candidates successful in the exams entered a very sophisticated government. Below the Emperor was a group of chief ministers, three Departments, six Boards, and nine Courts. The ministers discussed policy with the Emperor, and the Departments implemented it after reviewing its practicality. The Departments — called the Secretariat, the Chancellery, and Department of State Affairs — also kept records and corresponded with the local magistrates. The Boards were in charge of such matters as taxation, defense, public works, and the civil service. The Courts handled less-important matters like foreign visitors and the regulation of clergy.

One of the Boards was in charge of justice and administering the Han law code, which became the model for all later codes and differed greatly from its Western equivalents. To begin with, Chinese law codes were detailed and specific, often following the statement of a law with a series of "What if?" questions. The law also treated people differently, even if they had committed the same offence. For instance, officials and women were treated more leniently than ordinary men. Penalties were much less severe than those in the West. Flogging, exile, and work camps were punishments for most offenses, and the death penalty was applied only for murder and high treason. No execution could take place until the Emperor reviewed the case. Chinese law also reversed the Western idea that a person was innocent until proven guilty. To them, the fact that a person was accused of anything at all was an upset in the cosmic balance, and the accused person was thrown into prison until proved innocent. Chinese prisons were terrible places; they were small and filthy, and only water was provided. Unless a prisoner's family brought food, the prisoner starved.

Although the Han law code exists today only in fragmentary form, most of its provisions were repeated when subsequent dynasties wrote their own codes. Law, therefore, was a source of continuity for over 2000 years. Since the Han Code became the model, and since it failed to embody such principles as "equality before the law," or "innocent until proven guilty," it hindered the development of human rights over the entire span of dynastic China.

The Decline of the Han

Wudi's capital of Chang'an (*chong-on*) rivalled Rome in size and population, but not in magnificence. The Chinese built in wood rather than stone, and had no concept of public space like the Colosseum or baths of Rome. The city, however, was a perfect grid, with the palace, or **Forbidden City**, at the north end, and the streets and avenues running in a north-south and east-west pattern. Great markets were built in the east and in the west. The government restricted merchants, controlled prices, and supervised the sale of everyday goods as well as exotic luxuries such as glass, amber, spices, and slaves from foreign lands. Chang'an, now called Xi'an, can be seen today, its walls still intact.

Before the end of Wudi's reign, his energetic policies put the government in a deficit position. Taxes were raised and one official complained that farmers did not have sufficient land to use a single hoe; they were forced to live on the "food of dogs and pigs." The peasants suffered and the gap between rich and poor grew wider and wider, as many independent peasants were forced to sell their land and become tenants or serfs. Great landlord families arose, and their power was so immense that they could corrupt the tax collectors and deny revenue to the impoverished government.

In 184 CE, great rebellions broke out in the northeast and southwest. Squeezed between these two forces, and betrayed by disloyal generals, the Han dynasty came crashing down. The last Han Emperor abdicated in 220 BCE.

The Period of Disunion

The final stage of the First Empire was a bleak one. China was divided into three kingdoms, then briefly reunited, before hordes of nomads swept in from the north and west. By 317 CE, nomads had taken control of the whole country north of the Yangtze River. These tribes, ancestors of the Mongols, the Manchus, and the Tibetans, held northern China in their grip for almost 300 years. In the south, at present-day Nanjing, a succession of weak, short-lived Chinese dynasties struggled to keep alive the culture of the Han. Some scholars regard these centuries as the Dark Ages of China.

The authority of the central government declined as great aristocratic clans set up independent domains. Peasants, who once worked their own land, fell into serfdom. The examination system disappeared, roads and canals fell into disrepair, and barter replaced coinage.

There were bright spots in this gloomy picture. Competition spurred technological advances in agriculture, with new plowing and irrigation techniques, terracing, and double crops of rice. New medical techniques appeared, such as inoculation and cataract surgery, and alchemy, chemistry, and the martial arts flourished. Figure painting and calligraphy surpassed the Han examples, and poetic expression became less Confucian and more free. The "barbarian" dynasties in the north experimented with new administrative techniques like peasant militia and equal land grants to the farming population.

Buddhism

Buddhism had been introduced into China from India in the first century CE. After initial setbacks due to Confucian opposition and the difficulties of translating Buddhist concepts from one language into another, the foreign religion spread rapidly. At this time, because people in China believed that human life was painful, the appeal of Buddhism was great. Buddhist temples, monasteries, and nunneries soon dotted the Chinese landscape. People flocked to hear sermons, and many wanted to be ordained. Pious Chinese made long pilgrimages to India to study, and returned to translate scriptures and write accounts of their travels. Chinese Buddhists began to become more independent, and even changed some of the original Indian teachings to suit the Chinese environment. The monasteries multiplied, and because so many travelling merchants stopped overnight and asked the monks to guard their valuables, these monasteries became the first banks and hotels in the country.

Magnificent art was created — depictions of heaven and hell, and great images of the Buddha in bronze, gold, and stone. Some were so large that 12 people could stand on the Buddha's outstretched finger. From China, Buddhism spread to Korea and Japan, and by the sixth century, more than half the world's population was Buddhist. Buddhism also acted as a cohesive factor, keeping the Chinese people together in a time of disunion. Along with Confucian family and state ethics, a common language, and the memory of Han dynasty glory, Buddhism helped to ensure that the Chinese Empire, unlike that of Rome, would endure and rise to even greater heights.

This image of Buddha Preaching was painted on silk. It measures 3.5 m high and was made in a monastery. This banner was probably sold to a wealthy pilgrim as an offering. A blank space was left at the bottom for the donor's name.

The Second Empire

In 589, a remarkable general called **Sui Wendi** (*sway won-dee*) conquered the last of the southern dynasties, reunited the country, and founded the Sui dynasty. Like the first Emperor of China, he was a vigorous ruler, restoring roads, canals, walls, and dikes, as well as the morale of the civil service. He rebuilt the schools and the examination system for choosing officials. He lowered taxes, and kept his government frugal and honest.

After the death of Sui Wendi, his son squandered not only the good will created by his father, but also the entire state treasury. He demanded such luxuries as a harem of more than 3000 women, and lavish canals where he sailed with his court on large pleasure boats. Worst of all, he undertook three unsuccessful campaigns to reconquer Korea. These campaigns caused hundreds of thousands of casualties, brought China to bankruptcy, and so angered the people that rebellions broke out again. The Emperor was killed by one of his own generals, and in 618, the Tang dynasty (*tong*) was established. It would last for almost 300 years.

THE GOLDEN AGE OF CHINA

The Tang was perhaps the brightest era in Chinese history. It was a confident and cosmopolitan time when culture flourished as never before. Under the Tang, China reached its greatest territorial extent, and its capital, Chang'an, was the greatest city in the world. With a population of over a million, at a time when Rome held only about 60 000, Chang'an was the cultural centre of Asia. Here lived thousands of Koreans, Indians, Syrians, and Arabians — foreign students, missionaries, entertainers, and merchants. In addition to the many Buddhist temples were churches of the Zoroastrians and Christians. There were floating restaurants, zoos, fairgrounds, frequent festivals, and sporting events. The women of the Tang — robed in low-cut, silken dresses, their hair piled high with golden and jewelled hairpins — competed in poetry contests, wine tastings, and even polo. They enjoyed a relatively high status during this period.

The second Tang Emperor, Taizong (627–649), is known not only for the great conquests he made in Central Asia, which extended China's power to the borders of Persia, but also for his contribution to the arts of peace. He restored the system of schools and universities, created a new law code, set up an office to compile the history of the preceding four centuries, redistributed land to the peasantry, consolidated a system of national defense, and put in place a system of taxation that was equitable to all. Above all, he listened to advice, consulting his ministers and through them, the common people on all important issues. His wife was a constant source of support and wise advice, but his son and successor was not a gifted ruler. He was, however, smart enough to place the fortunes of the dynasty in the hands of his own wife, known as the **Empress Wu**. She became the only female in Chinese history to usurp the throne and rule in her own right as Emperor. For almost 30 years, while her husband was alive, she ruled from "behind the screen," and in 690, on the death of her husband, she took the throne herself for 15 prosperous years. Capable, genuinely concerned about the common people, and at the same time astonishingly ruthless, she remains one of the most popular of China's historical rulers.

After her husband's death in 690, the Empress Wu was the sole ruler of China for fifteen prosperous years.

The Empress Wu's successor, Ming-huang, was called the Brilliant Emperor because he presided over an era of glittering culture, when literature, painting, architecture, textiles, and ceramics reached new heights. He composed and played music, some of which, like his "Pear Garden Suite," is still played today. One source tells us that he taught his horses to dance to his music.

Poetry was the glory of this age, and China's most famous poet, Bai Juyi (*by-joo-yee*), wrote a poem after Ming-huang's death in which he told the story of the Emperor's ill-fated love for the most famous beauty in China's long history. Her name was Yang Gueifei (*yong gwey-fey*), and her unparalleled beauty, as she danced in her "feathered-jacket and rainbow-skirt," led the Emperor to neglect the affairs of state and allow his government to fall into corruption and incompetence. This helped to bring about the rebellion of An Lu-shan (*on lew-shon*), which was perhaps the bloodiest rebellion in Chinese history.

The rebellion began in 752, and over the next decade, devastated the country and almost destroyed the Tang dynasty. The rebels, in fact, drove the unfortunate Emperor and the beauteous Yang Gueifei from the capital. When Ming-huang's troops refused to march any farther with the woman whom they blamed for their troubles, the Emperor was forced to put her to death.

The Tang dynasty survived for more than a century after this, but its glory days were over. Later generations called the early period the Golden Age of Chinese civilization because of its high culture, stable government, expansive foreign relations, and a degree of prosperity that permeated all levels of society. During the first half of the dynasty, every peasant household was granted a generous and equal amount of land. Nowhere else, and at no other time in history, did a government show such concern for its humblest subjects.

Perhaps expectations had been too high. After the great rebellion, China became regionalized, and local generals and warlords struggled for domination. The central government gradually lost control, and after 30 years of almost constant civil war beginning in 876, fell to one of its own generals in 907.

The Third Empire

The fall of the Tang was followed by a brief period of disunion in which five dynasties contended for power. In 960, the country was reunited and the Song dynasty was founded. Scholars often compare the Song with the Renaissance in Europe. It was a time when China's classical heritage was rediscovered and reinterpreted to become a vibrant and flourishing force. Song scholars began with the works of Confucius, blended them with the concepts of Daoism and Buddhism, and created a new ideology called Neo-Confucianism.

This ideology emphasized that "all under heaven" made up a family, and that in that family, the Emperor was the ideal father — compassionate but fair, and entitled to obedience. His government was to be staffed by virtuous men whose goodness was best recognized by education and success in the examination system. All individuals, female as well as male, had a duty to transform themselves and become the best they possibly could. This was accomplished by uniting knowledge and action.

The Song dynasty is notable for two other things: economic changes that were revolutionary, and artistic achievements that surpassed anything before or after in China. Industry, agriculture, and commerce formed the bases of the commercial revolution and of an economy that was the world's most advanced from the tenth to the eighteenth century.

Technology, Trade, and Fine Art in the Song

During the Song, important progress was made in shipbuilding, ceramics, and the production of coal and iron. The Chinese became the first people to use blast furnaces to smelt and carbonize iron for the production of steel. They discovered — perhaps by accident — the explosive power of gunpowder and used it for the mining of coal and iron, as well as weapons. They refined papermaking, and with their invention of block printing, revolutionized education by making books more widely available. Some cities, like Kaifeng, became manufacturing centres. Guilds, like trade unions, were formed for every profession from tea merchants to pickpockets.

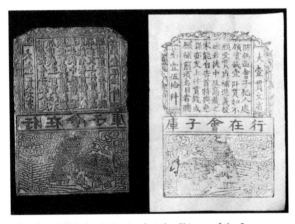

This sheet of block printing is what the Chinese of the Song period called "pocket money", ca. 1100. Paper money was printed by the Chinese long before it was used by Europeans. The intricate patterns are to help prevent counterfeiting

To feed the population, which had now reached 100 million, agriculture progressed rapidly. Advances in fertilizers and water control were made, and in the south, the sound ecological practice of crop rotation by sowing one crop of rice followed by one crop of beans or wheat was developed. The fertility of the soil was increased.

In commerce, the Song dynasty made its greatest advances after the loss of most of north China to the so-called Golden (Jin) Tartars in 1127. The Song had never been militarily strong, and the move of their capital south to the beautiful city of **Hangzhou** (hong-joe), sometimes called "China's Venice," was a wise one. By this time, perhaps two thirds of the population and wealth of the Chinese Empire was situated south of the Yangtze, and the loss of the rich agricultural north forced the southern Song court to turn to commerce for revenue. The so-called Southern Song dynasty became the "merchant" of the East Asian world. It was the first and last time that private capitalism was allowed to flourish without government interference. The medium of exchange for internal commerce was paper money, the "flying" cash first developed by the Chinese in

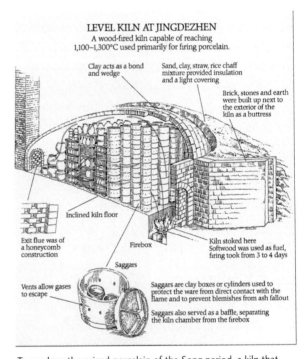

LEVEL KILN AT JINGDEZHEN
A wood-fired kiln capable of reaching 1,100–1,300°C used primarily for firing porcelain.

Clay acts as a bond and wedge

Sand, clay, straw, rice chaff mixture provided insulation and a light covering

Brick, stones and earth were built up next to the exterior of the kiln as a buttress

Inclined kiln floor

Exit flue was of a honeycomb construction

Firebox

Kiln stoked here Softwood was used as fuel, firing took from 3 to 4 days

Saggars

Vents allow gases to escape

Saggars are clay boxes or cylinders used to protect the ware from direct contact with the flame and to prevent blemishes from ash fallout
Saggars also served as a baffle, separating the kiln chamber from the firebox

To produce the prized porcelain of the Song period, a kiln that could reach and maintain a high temperature (1100-1300 degrees C) was needed. This kiln was used in the city of Jingdezhen, the renowned porcelain centre of China.

the middle of the ninth century. For the maritime trade, barter was still the rule.

This period was one of the rare times that the Chinese encouraged foreign trade, and the government derived much revenue from customs and transit duties. China imported only luxury goods such as textiles, spices, and some medicines, but exported silk, copper, and most particularly, porcelain, which only the Chinese knew how to make at this time.

Song porcelains — deep blue and green, translucent, eggshell-thin ceramics — have been found all along the coasts of Africa, India, and the Middle East, showing the vigour of sea trade in the twelfth century. Since the Chinese retained the secret of their white kaolin clay for the next five centuries, the words "porcelain" and "china" became synonyms in most European languages.

The carriers of this trade were Chinese ships, called junks. Some carried crews of 500 to 600. The junks were guided by the world's first magnetic compasses, and featured such innovations as watertight bulkheads, buoyancy chambers, bamboo fenders at the waterline, axial rudders in place of oars, scoops for taking samples off the sea floor, sounding lines, cargo compartments, and even firecrackers to frighten off pirates. This ocean-going trade gave rise to foreign communities in such cities as Canton (now Guangzhou), where Middle Eastern merchants were subject to their own laws, could worship as they chose, and were allowed to intermarry with the Chinese.

Above all, the Song represents the high point of Chinese visual arts. Prior to this period, paintings had been so formal that only the educated class could appreciate them and understand their symbolism. Scholars exchanged paintings only among themselves, and never signed their names since everyone in their circle knew the identity of the artist.

Now, artists became infused with a new, more accessible vision of the world. They also wanted to profit from their art. Landscape paintings, which everyone could appreciate, became the favourite subject. Artists also began to sign their works, especially when they painted for the newly rich merchants. The red ink seals on old Chinese paintings are the marks of the various owners. If we were to do this, it would be like signing our own name across the front of the Picasso hanging in the living room.

An example of fine porcelain, made in Jingdezhen ca. 1426.

DAILY LIFE IN THE CAPITAL

In 1271, the last decade of the Song, about 90 percent of the population of China was subsistence farmers. Their existence was precarious, and bad harvests often forced them to sell their daughters to tea houses or rent out their sons to wealthier neighbours for six years at a time as field hands. Life seemed easier in the large cities, and urbanization was a growing trend in the Song.

Marco Polo called the Song capital, Hangzhou, "the most noble city and the best that is in the world." Residences of the wealthy in Hangzhou were spacious, comfortable, and luxurious. Usually of a single storey, they were made of wood with brick floors, and had graceful, upswept tile roofs. Each one was a walled compound with many side buildings and pavilions for the household cooks, artisans, musicians, dancers, acrobats, tutors, astrologers, and even matchmakers. Gardening was a fine art, and there were elaborate rules for the placement of ponds, rare flowers, gnarled trees, grottoes, and curious rocks. Formal Chinese gardens avoided the symmetry of their European counterparts, and instead, tried to imitate nature with waterfalls and miniature hills.

Interior decor was simple, consisting of low tables and a few chairs, which had appeared in China only in the ninth century. There were curtained beds with rush mattresses, and pillows made of pottery. Since only the Emperor could use red lacquer, furniture was usually finished in black lacquer. Scrolls and landscape paintings hung on the walls, and the tables were decorated with antiques and flowers such as jasmine, peonies, chrysanthemums, and orchids. Incense and "mosquito smoke" freshened the air.

Outside the walls of each compound, the city was a colourful and bustling place, with men and

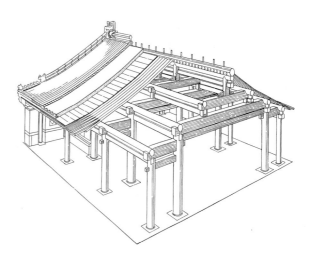

This architectural drawing shows the basic construction of a Chinese house such as might have been seen in the Song capital of Hangzhou.

women mingling freely in the streets. The women of the time wore their hair in a chignon (like a bun) with, sometimes, as many as a dozen metal and pearl hairpins. They wore white make-up, rouged their cheeks, and painted their fingernails pink. Their clothing was colourful. Bright red, green, and yellow silk dresses reached to the ground, and were worn under knee-length blouses and, occasionally, a jacket of gold brocade. Poorer women had to be content with drab pajama suits of hempen cloth.

Social custom confined women of the upper classes to the homes of their husbands, who were mostly government officials. They were further restricted by their physical lack of mobility due to the new practice of foot binding. These were called the women of the golden lotus, women whose feet had been tightly bound with bandages at the age of five or six, so that their feet always remained no more than 10 to 15 cm long. As the toes were bent under the ball of the foot, the pain must have been excruciating. It was a terrible price to pay for tiny feet, which in golden slippers, we are told, resembled the petals of a lotus. To Chinese men, tiny feet were beautiful and desirable, and in spite of frequent government prohibitions, the practice was not totally wiped out until 1949. Women whose feet were once bound, though rare, can still be found today.

The feet that fit into these shoes could not have been longer than about 14 cm. A mother would bind her daughter's feet to better the chances that the girl would find a husband.

The men of the Song added their own colour to the streets of Hangzhou. For them, clothing was a sign of social status. Men wore their hair long, bathed on every tenth day, and on their bath-day holiday, had their hair, face, and goatee oiled. Officials and wealthy men carried a parasol to shield their complexion from the sun, and wore black silk caps to distinguish them from the common people, who wore a sort of turban. They wore long silk robes with flowing sleeves in which they carried fans and wallets. Sometimes trousers were worn underneath. The essential article of male clothing was a very wide sash, almost like a girdle, with a decorative plaque on the front.

There were permanent fairgrounds in the capital filled with acrobats, trained animals, and storytellers who related in song and verse the myths of China — the tale of Pangu who grew so tall that his body pushed apart heaven and earth, or of Changwo, who stole the elixir of immortality from her husband and fled to the heavens, where she became "the lady in the moon." And there were fortune tellers — often blind — who foretold the future using astrology or by feeling the shape of the skull, facial features, or bones of the arm. These methods remain popular in China today.

Food and Medicine

Frequent famines in their history had taught the Chinese to use every edible food available, and waste nothing — from fish lips to bear paws. Scarcity of wood and charcoal had led to the invention of the wok, perhaps one of the world's most efficient cooking utensils. The search for a guaranteed recipe for long life led people to experiment with rare and unusual ingredients in their cuisine.

Ancient
ODDITIES

The Chinese used the saliva of swallows as the basic ingredient in bird's nest soup, and the fins of sharks were thought to ward off colds and other illnesses. Recipe books from the Song period are hard to decipher because the Chinese used poetic names for ingredients. A typical menu might be called "Dragon Fights the Phoenix in the Clouds." This probably meant a dish made with snake (dragon), chicken (phoenix), and snow-cloud mushrooms.

One Hangzhou source notes 200 dishes that might be served at a great banquet, and even tells us the correct order of service: There should be 41 dishes of shrimp, fish, snails, pork, goose, mutton, and pigeon — all fried, sautéed, grilled, and spitted or roasted in the oven. There should be 42 dishes based on fruits and nuts, and 20 based on vegetables alone.

There should be 9 rice dishes with different sauces, and 29 kinds of dried-fish dishes, with 17 different types of drinks — pear nectar, litchi juice, ginger juice, and uncounted types of wine.

If the people became ill because of overindulgence in food or wine, or other reasons, they could go to one of the branches of the School of Medicine established in Hangzhou in 1076. The school admitted 200 to 300 male and female students each year and treated mostly patients from the upper classes. Ordinary people tended to go to private doctors, or more accurately, to doctor families since doctors trained all their children in the healing arts.

In general, most illnesses were treated with herbs, and several prescriptions from the Song contain 25 different herbal ingredients. Massage and acupuncture, which had both been utilized for more than 2000 years, were frequently prescribed. Moxibustion, a process in which small stacks of medicinal herbs were placed on an acupuncture point and then burned, was common. Surgery was not. Some remedies, such as a cure for malaria that consisted of swallowing a particular fly found on the body of frogs, may seem fanciful to us, but many Chinese herbs have found their way into the pills we take today. Acupuncture is still widely used in anaesthesia and addiction treatment, and the Chinese holistic view of wellness has become quite popular today.

Beliefs

Religious life in Song China was so diversified that it is nearly impossible to describe. The Chinese were not a monotheistic people, and individual Chinese seldom gave their sole allegiance to any particular religion. As a result, their history is almost wholly free of religious wars, persecutions, and inquisitions. They tended to believe that there were many paths to salvation and many deities to worship. It was prudent to respect all deities, both to avoid calamity in this life and to ensure happiness in the next.

Chinese peasants, like most humans before the scientific revolution, lived in a world that we might

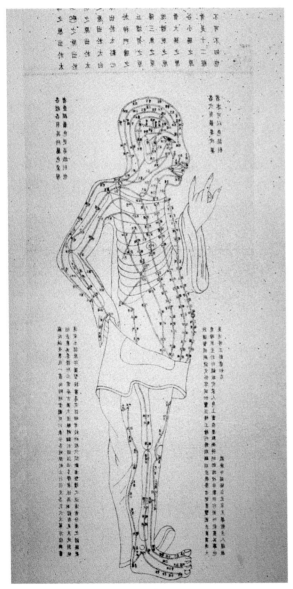
The parts of the body and their acupuncture points are shown in this chart. Part of traditional Chinese medicine, acupuncture is increasingly being used today by Westerners.

call superstitious. The educated class in China was well aware of these folk beliefs and tended to be skeptical of them. Even if they did not believe fully in such things as ghosts, spirits, and the power of magical objects to bring rain, they still painted fearsome gods on their doors to ward off evil, and made sure that graves faced the proper direction. Most saw no contradiction in attending services at the temples and shrines of the two organized religions, Buddhism and Daoism, and the next day, sacrificing a pig to the mischievous dragon who lived in the pool in their garden.

In China, however, there was one belief common to all classes — **ancestor veneration**. Any visitor to Hangzhou in the Song would be struck by the care taken of the dead. Throughout China, tablets inscribed with the names of the deceased were placed in each home. On special occasions, such as birthdays, the Festival of the Dead, and the New Year, families visited the grave sites, swept them, bowed before them, and burned images of money, food, houses, servants, and anything else that might be needed in the other world. The smoke carried these objects to their destination. Even today these practices continue, whether in Toronto, Vancouver, or in Beijing.

The Challenge of the Mongols

Hangzhou in 1271 was a fine, bustling city, but over it lay a shadow. That same year, far to the north, **Khubilai Khan** proclaimed that he was the rightful ruler of all China and sent his hordes southward to destroy the Song. In 1279, Hangzhou fell and Khubilai proclaimed a new dynasty, called the Yuan, which means "Beginning." One Chinese poet of the time visited the former palace of Hangzhou after the conquest and wrote:

The grass grows high round this old, old ruin,
Gone the guards, the gatekeepers
Gone the fallen towers, crumbling pavilions,
My soul destroyed.
Beneath the eaves of ancient halls,
Swallows dart.
But within,
Silence.

The Yuan dynasty was founded by the **Mongols**, a nomadic people whose disunity and internal quarrels had kept them from becoming a threat to their more civilized neighbours for many centuries. In the year 1206, however, a remarkable man called Temujin united the various tribes, proclaimed himself **Chingghis Khan** ("Universal" Khan), and set out to conquer the known world. He very nearly succeeded.

At that time, many of the peoples of Eurasia (Europe and Asia) were in a state of flux. Northern China and Tibet were in disorder. There were struggles in southern Russia and in the Turkish and Persian empires. Europe was gripped in the fervour

The feared Mongol warriors could shoot arrows and ride at the same time. Under Kubilai Khan and others, Mongols ruled China for almost a century.

of the Crusades, and Constantinople had just fallen. This unsettled situation made the Mongol conquest easier, but it is doubtful that any of the surrounding peoples could have resisted them anyway.

The Mongol armies were invincible. Each soldier, armoured in heavy leather, carried two bows capable of killing a person at 180 m. Each warrior had three horses, bred for speed and endurance, and changed mounts whenever one horse got tired. Mongol warriors could sleep on horseback, and could survive by drinking a mixture of horse blood and mare's milk. Consequently, they could cover great distances with incredible speed. In battle, they were utterly ruthless, taking prisoners only when they needed human shields for the next city they attacked. The Mongols poisoned wells, razed cities to the ground, and slaughtered even those who willingly surrendered.

When Chingghis died in 1227, most of Central Asia, Northern China, and all of Tibet were in his hands. His successors extended Mongol rule to Korea in 1231; Kiev, Moscow, and parts of Poland and Hungary in 1240; as well as Baghdad and the rest of the Middle East in 1251. Terrified Europeans had, for the most part, never seen an Asian person and they did not know who these warriors were. In their chronicles, they referred to Mongols as demon creatures unleashed by an angry God to punish their sinful world.

When at last, in 1279, the Mongols conquered Southern China, they found themselves in control of the greatest land empire in human history. Originally, they divided all their land into four parts with the capital in Mongolia, but in 1260, Khubilai Khan, Temujin's ablest grandson, realized that China was the richest part of his vast empire and moved the capital to Beijing.

The Chinese Response

The ordinary people of China felt very little impact from the conquest. After all, the Mongols never numbered more than 2.5 million, at a time when China's population had passed 100 million. The Mongols left local administrations in place, and ordinary peasants likely never even saw their conquerors.

The educated elite of society, on the other hand, were very much aware of the Mongol presence. Mongol rule was harsher than that of the Song, and court officials, for instance, were now subjected to cruel beatings. The taxes of officials and their families were raised and their salaries eroded by inflation. The Mongol rulers made clumsy attempts to discourage Confucian practices such as ancestor veneration, and to impose a crude form of Buddhism as the national religion. Worse than that, they blocked the road to official advancement by using Mongols and other foreigners in all the highest government posts. As Marco Polo, who served Khubilai from 1275 to 1292, said "The Great Khan rules Cathay [his term for China] not by hereditary right, but by conquest. Having no confidence in the native people, he has put all authority in the hands of Tartars, Saracens, and Christians..."

The Mongols set up a hierarchy of social classes with themselves at the top, applied different laws to the Chinese and to themselves, continued to wear leather and fur, to eat milk and cheese, to forbid intermarriage, and allowed their women far greater freedom than the Chinese thought proper. They even abolished the examination system for a time. Resentment grew among all the educated Chinese.

One unintended result of the exclusion of Chinese from official life was that scholars were forced to turn to other pursuits; thus two new art forms appeared. The first was the novel, and the second was the drama. In these works for the stage, plots were romantic or historical, costumes were lavish, and female roles were played by males just as in Shakespearean England. Today, we call this drama Peking Opera.

A final feature of the Mongol Empire was that many Chinese innovations now made their way to West Asia and from there to Europe. Caravans travelled regularly between Baghdad and Beijing, and ships sailed back and forth between the Persian Gulf and Canton (now Guangzhou). Through this trade, Russia, Persia, and Mesopotamia were introduced to Chinese gunpowder, printing, paper money, textiles, and porcelains, as well as iodine, inoculation, and even playing cards. The Chinese, in turn, assimilated aspects of mathematics, astronomy, and map making from the Arab-Turkish culture, but in general, showed little interest in the outside world. For Europeans, the greatest effect of the Mongol era was the transmission to Europe of the bubonic plague, or Black Death, which devastated an entire continent in the fourteenth century.

Mongol rule in China lasted less than a century, coming to an end in 1368 after a series of bloody rebellions. The Mongol leadership had exhausted itself in court intrigue and wars with Korea and other parts of its far-flung empire. Chinese resentment of their foreign overlords had remained strong, especially south of the Yangtze. There, secret societies had been formed to expel foreign rule. The leader of one of these societies, a peasant later called Emperor Taizu, emerged victorious among the rebel groups. He chose the name Ming (meaning "brilliant") for his new dynasty, and it would last until 1644. Together with the Qing (*ching*) dynasty, which ended in 1911, it constituted China's last empire.

THE LAST EMPIRE
Change and Continuity

Scholars view the 276 years of Ming rule as a time of peace, prosperity, and stability. It was an era when Chinese civilization seemed to have reached an equilibrium. As a result, the pace of change had slowed to a crawl.

Napoleon was later to say that "China slept" for several centuries, though that is not quite true. Some changes occurred: the village economy and internal trade networks continued to develop, Confucian philosophy was further refined, the examination system reached its final form, and scholarship progressed rapidly. Traditional arts and crafts were perfected, a new elite class emerged, and the position of the Emperor reached its final stage of development.

None of these changes, however, could match those that were taking place in Europe. Ming Emperors were on the throne when the travels of European explorers took them to the Americas and around the Cape of Good Hope. They still ruled when Europe was transformed by the Renaissance and Reformation. The Ming's successors, the Qing, remained oblivious to the European wars of religion, witch burnings, the formation of nation-states, and the various revolutions of the Western world — French, American, scientific, and industrial. If China did not sleep, it dozed, at least.

How might we account for this? There are three major reasons. First, the Chinese ruling group had seen too often that, in their own history, technological change had brought about social disruption in the form of urbanization, the weakening of the family, and even peasant uprisings. They preferred stability. Second, the Chinese of the Ming were proud of their victory over the Mongols. They came to

Pushing the Boundaries: Developments in Science and Technology

Fire Medicine: The Accidental Invention of Gunpowder

The invention of gunpowder is often called an accident, because its inventors were not trying to invent it. It was not a mindless accident though. The discovery came about as a result of scientific investigation, and in ancient China, science was not separate from culture. Part of the philosophy of Chinese culture was the notion of understanding through knowing, so investigations into all kinds of things were ongoing.

Sun Si Miao is recognized as the inventor of gunpowder. Like most Daoists around 700, he was an alchemist — he experimented and refined the mixture of many different materials. The alchemist's ultimate goal in China was an elixir of immortality (in Europe it was gold). Although no such elixir was ever found, many of the experimental combinations had other benefits.

Alchemy was practiced all over, so we could wonder why gunpowder was not discovered outside of China. Again, the answer relates to culture. In Europe, the leading scholars placed more emphasis on plant remedies and were actually afraid to use minerals as medicines. In China, however, minerals were used all the time, and experiments with the mixture of charcoal, sulfur and saltpeter were known to cause explosions. Sun Si Miao discovered that a fixed proportion of the three "medicines" was indeed highly flammable. Somewhat ironically, the search for the elixir of immortality created the prototype for gunpowder.

At first, gunpowder was rolled in paper, and later, it was placed in bamboo tubes. These devices were then used to scare off wild animals and a legendary unicorn that was supposed to appear at yearly intervals. The custom of setting off firecrackers at this new year interval is one that is with us still. Colour-luminescent chemicals were eventually added and cannons came to be used to shoot the firecrackers high in the air.

Perhaps not so worth celebrating is the discovery that gunpowder had other applications: cannons could be turned into weapons by placing small arrows or metal balls in them, along with the gunpowder. Grenades, bombs, signal rockets and flame throwers could also be manufactured. Eventually, the explosive qualities of gunpowder would also be used for more peaceful purposes such as building roads and mining.

About 400 years ago, the scholar Francis Bacon said there were three discoveries that "changed the whole face and state of things throughout the world." Gunpowder was one of them.

One of the happier and more peaceful uses of gunpowder.

Activities

1. The invention of gunpowder has had vast implications from its inception onwards. Design a graphic organizer to categorize the impact of gunpowder on humanity.

2. Write a paragraph about what might have happened had the Chinese not invented gunpowder.

believe that, since they had once again solved their own problems, they could continue to do so. The Chinese had used traditional ways to free themselves — not new solutions. Their own history held all the answers they needed, and they would change only within their own tradition.

Finally, the bitter experience of the Chinese with foreign rule led them to believe that they were better off without outside interference. What did they have to learn from anyone else? During the Ming and Qing, it seemed as if the Chinese had psychologically immunized themselves against foreign influence. There was no antagonism toward the rest of the world — only a growing sense of superiority. The Chinese became **xenophobic** (afraid of strangers).

On the Eve of Western Contact

The Ming dynasty had existed for almost 150 years before the first Europeans — Portuguese traders and pirates — made their presence felt on China's south coast in 1514. The objects of their desire — spices, silk, porcelain, and later, tea — were for them high-profit items, but they had nothing of similar value to offer the Chinese. For that reason, the Europeans simply took what they wanted, behaving with violence and greed in the Canton area, and earning the name *yangguei* or "ocean-devils."

It was only when the Jesuits arrived in Beijing in 1600 that educated Chinese began to have a more favourable impression of Westerners. The Jesuits were well-educated in Chinese literature and respectful of Chinese ways. Though they made few converts, they impressed the Chinese court with their mechanical clocks, their knowledge of astronomy, and their willingness to learn from a "superior" civilization.

THE Past AT PLAY

While the wealthy Chinese were raising and racing horses, and keeping small Pekinese lap dogs, a poorer child might keep a cricket as a pet, in a specially made cricket cage. The Chinese also enjoyed gambling, playing board games and a game called Mah-jongg, which used tiles with pictures on them similar to playing cards.

The Jesuits were more impressed with China than the Chinese were with them, and began to send back glowing reports to Europe. They had good reason to be impressed. The Ming was a prosperous, confident, and stable dynasty, and to the Jesuits, seemed an oasis of calm and wealth, compared with their own turbulent world.

The stability of the Ming is usually attributed to the course set by the first two Emperors, who between them ruled from 1368 to 1425. In the first place, they had fostered strong leadership. Abolishing the office of Chief Minister, as well as other ministries that had checked the Emperor's power, they created alternative offices, such as the grand secretaries who served the Emperor's whim and could be dismissed at any time. The Emperors forced their ministers to kowtow ("knock head" — like bowing) before them, and used eunuchs as secret service agents to keep files on officials, who thus seldom challenged the Emperors. Chinese historians deplore this emerging despotism, but cannot deny that it produced a unified command centre.

Secondly, the rulers were careful to ensure that their despotism had an impact on the officials, not on the people. The early Ming Emperors fostered the rise of a new ruling class, the gentry, who moderated the effects of absolute rule at the local level. The gentry, wealthy families who produced officials and held land, became the real rulers of China. They acted as an unpaid civil service — building schools, recruiting militia, repairing dikes and roads, setting up orphanages and homes for the aged, and settling disputes. They made their own lives models of Confucian rectitude, and living in the public eye, they encouraged the peasantry to follow their example. The gentry understood the people, and the people understood them. Orders from the capital in Beijing were often modified to fit local customs and conditions.

Finally, the second Emperor fostered a vision of Chinese pre-eminence in the world, which he symbolized by initiating a series of seven great maritime expeditions between 1405 and 1433. They made China, for a brief time, the greatest of the world's maritime powers. These expeditions, which sometimes included more than 300 ships and a total crew of over 30 000, plied the seas of Southeast Asia and extended Chinese influence into the Indian Ocean, along the east coast of Africa and into Arabia. More than 20 states and kingdoms now began to trade and offer tribute to China, but China seemed to be little impressed. The expeditions were stopped in 1433 for reasons we do not fully understand, though it is clear that they were expensive, and the commercial returns negligible. The missions were led by a great explorer called Zheng He (*jeng-huh*), but he was a eunuch, and jealous scholar-officials of the court were constantly undermining him. Finally, the Ming dynasty felt sufficiently confident in its power that it seemed unimportant to announce it abroad — it became even more introverted. What would have happened had the Chinese maintained their interest in the sea is one of the great "what ifs" of history.

As time went on, the Ming dynasty revelled in its wealth. In 1425, it is reported that the Emperor employed more than 6000 chefs in the palace and was a great patron of the famous blue-and-white porcelains that would later become the rage in Europe. The population of China was now approaching 150 million, literacy was spreading, and the Yangtze delta — with its manufactured goods of iron, ceramics, silk, cotton, indigo, sugar cane, and even woodblock prints — was, perhaps, the wealthiest area in the world. Drama and the novel continued to develop. On the eve of its first contact with the West, China was a civilization that was self-contained, inexperienced with Europe, and complacent in its success.

Review...Recall...Reflect

1. Describe life in the city of Hangzhou during the Song dynasty for both the elite and ordinary Chinese people.

2. Compare and contrast the impact of the Mongol invasion on the ordinary people and on the educated elite.

3. Why did the Chinese decide to stop their overseas exploration and close themselves off from the world? What had been the positive and negative results of trade with the West for both China and Europe?

The Chinese World View

The Chinese, even before Confucius, had seen themselves as the Middle Kingdom. Surrounding them, and positioned on a series of concentric circles, were all the other peoples known to them. The Chinese Emperor was at the very centre, the father of the human family. As Confucius said, "Within the four seas, all are brother and sister." This view of the world implied that, like a father, the Emperor would teach, educate, and when necessary, punish his "children." In turn, his children had a duty to learn. Therefore, the position of other countries on the circles were determined not by geography, but by culture. How closely did other civilizations resemble that of China? Korea, Vietnam, and Japan — which adopted and adapted aspects of Chinese culture early — were considered on the inner circle, even though they were geographically more distant from the Chinese capital than were some of the Central Asian nomads.

From the second century BCE onwards, Chinese Emperors had issued engraved seals, or chops, to neighbouring rulers. These seals confirmed the rulers as friends of China, and gave them permission to send delegations to the capital, where they offered tribute to the Emperor. The surrounding peoples valued this privilege, since the return gifts from the Emperor usually exceeded their own. More importantly, if these rulers did not offer tribute, they would not be permitted to trade with the Chinese. For more than 2000 years, tribute envoys came regularly to China. Special officials conducted them to

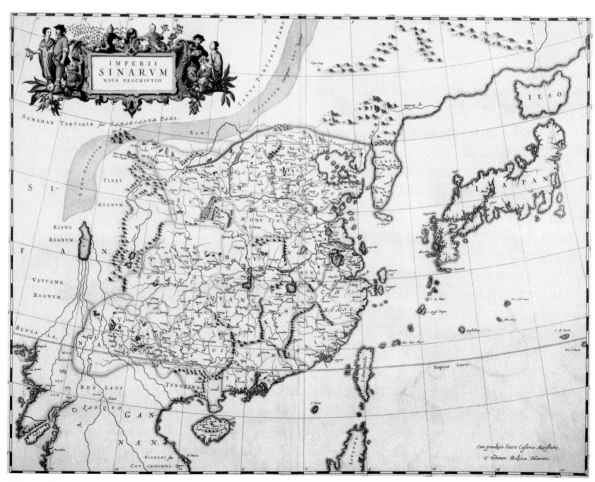

This map shows us how the Western world saw China about 150 years after the first Europeans made contact. How would the Chinese have seen Europe at this time? Would Europe be among the inner circles of the Chinese world view, or out on the edge, along with the other less cultured peoples?

the capital by prescribed routes so that they did not disturb the people. They lodged in fine hotels and awaited the pleasure of the Emperor. Ushered into his presence, they kowtowed before him, and presented their gifts. To kowtow, they had to kneel before the Emperor and bang their foreheads on the floor three times. The kowtow symbolized the submission of the envoys, their rulers, and their countries to the Chinese Emperor.

History Continues to Unfold

The most striking feature of the first three millennia of Chinese civilization is unity — unity in time, space, and the structures of life. Like the other ancient civilizations, China was invaded and even conquered several times. But unlike Mesopotamia, Egypt, India, Persia, and the Americas, China matured into a modern nation with its indigenous civilization intact. Only China defied what many historians identify as a rule of pre-modern history:

that large geographical and demographic entities are inherently unstable. Just as China endured through time, its spacial boundaries were established by the end of the first millennium and, thereafter, were never seriously violated.

These structures resulted from the imperial system, with its elaborate centralized bureaucracy. Over time, this system succeeded in fusing the regional and local diversities of a vast area into a single great tradition. The hallmarks of this tradition were a singular respect for learning and literacy, for familial rather than individual values, for honest agricultural labour, and for the combined spirituality of Confucianism, Daoism, and Buddhism.

China's complex sense of unity — along with its conviction of centrality — resulted in strong resistance to Western imperialism in the nineteenth century. It meant that China's process of modernization would be slow and often violent. It meant, too, that China would emerge at the dawn of the third millennium just as it had begun — as the Middle Kingdom.

Current Research and Interpretations

New archeological discoveries are revealing a higher level of civilization than earlier suspected for the first 1500 years of China's history. Studies of specific regions, especially in the South and coastal areas, are showing a cultural diversity probably as great as that of Europe. Long-neglected texts and other material evidence are proving that women at all levels of society were much more important and prominent than earlier depictions would have us believe. Finally, modern scholars have revealed a "civil society" in China, a network of informal organizations and social services that were independent of, and often more effective than, official mechanisms of government.

Chapter Review

Chapter Summary

In this chapter, we have seen:

- that China's longevity, lasting cultural influence, and complex social structure established it as one of the great civilizations of the ancient world
- how China's educational system played a vital role in maintaining stability in society through successive centuries
- that the Chinese "Mandate from Heaven" forged the basis of authority of the Emperor and provided a check on his use of power
- the effects of various innovations on the functioning of China's economic structure

Reviewing the Significance of Key People, Concepts, and Events (Knowledge/Understanding)

1. Understanding the history of ancient China requires a knowledge of the following concepts and people, and an understanding of their significance in the development of Chinese civilization. In your notes, identify and explain the historical significance of three from each column.

Concepts/Places	*People*
Legalism	Sun Zi
Daoism	Confucius
filial piety	Shi Huangdi
Great Wall of China	Wudi
Silk Road	Sui Wendi
Forbidden City	Empress Wu
Buddhism	Bai Juyi
ancestor veneration	Chingghis Khan
	Zheng He

2. For many of the world's early civilizations, geography played a key role in shaping the society. China was no exception. Create a mind map that illustrates the impact of at least three geographic features on the development of China's social and political stucture. Transfer the main ideas of your mind map to the graphic organizer "Geography's Influence" in your *World History Handbook*.

3. Copy and complete the following chart in your notes. This will provide you with a quick reference to the major dynasties of ancient China.

Dynasty	Time Period	Defining Features/Accomplishments
Shang		
Zhou		
Qin		
Han		
Tang		
Song		
Yuan		
Ming		

Doing History: Thinking About the Past (Thinking/Inquiry)

1. Imagine that you are a member of China's educated class and have studied Confucius. You have been given a copy of the *Daodejing* to read. In two paragraphs, explain how Confucianism and Daoism can coexist in your life, if that is possible.

2. China's political structure remained surprisingly intact for over two thousand years. To what degree can this stability be attributed to the organization of government and the checks on the power of those in authority. Respond in two to three paragraphs, using concrete evidence to support your answer.

Applying Your Learning (Application)

1. Create a series of five trading cards that feature the Movers and Shakers of Ancient China. On the front of each card, include a picture or sketch of the individual, her or his name, and when she or he lived. On the back, provide a short biography and a few critical pieces of information.

2. Prepare a "Guide for Young Women" in ancient China. In the guide, list the Dos and Don'ts for young women hoping to marry. Clearly identify how expectations differ for young women from various social classes.

Communicating Your Learning (Communication)

1. Create a diagram to illustrate the social hierarchy of ancient China. Include at least four different social groups. Create or select an illustration that reflects not only the position of each group, but also its level of prestige, or how others viewed it. Transfer some of the ideas in your diagram to the organizer "Forms of Social Organization" in your *World History Handbook*.

2. Imagine that you have been asked to write the official obituary for the Emperor Shi Huangdi. Prepare an appropriate statement in 200 to 300 words, tracing his rise to power and major accomplishments. Be sure to emphasize his best traits. In a separate, "secret" paragraph, record what you really feel about the Emperor, noting any events or actions you had to leave out of the official obituary.

CHAPTER ELEVEN

Japan

At the end of this chapter, you will be able to:

- *demonstrate an understanding of the effects of isolation on Japanese culture and society*

- *demonstrate an understanding of the roles of various emperors and shoguns in the process of change in Japanese history*

- *evaluate the role and importance of legends, myths, and traditions in the history and culture of Japan*

- *demonstrate an understanding of the factors that influenced the development of leadership and government at different points in the history of Japan*

Mt. Fuji is one of the most recognized landmarks of Japan. Here we see fishers working and boats sailing in an antique print.

In the middle of the sixteenth century, an Italian missionary wrote "The Japanese are like us in practically nothing… Their lives can be neither desired nor understood." This inability of Westerners to understand Japan is striking. It has been a prominent theme in cross-cultural studies from the time of the earliest contacts, and to some extent, remains with us today. Scholars are still puzzled by the origins of the Japanese people, their language, and their imperial family. They cannot fathom customs such as ritual bowing and the exquisite courtesy of daily life, the wood and rice-paper screens and straw sleeping mats in Japanese homes, or the elaborate kimono with its intricately folded sash and complex colour symbolism. The early European traders and missionaries simply recognized that Japan was the "most easterly of the east," and found it natural that it was also "the most exotic of the exotic."

The Japanese themselves have long emphasized their uniqueness. Their earliest book, the *Kojoki,* or *Record of Ancient Matters* (712 CE), tells of their divine origins: how the *kami* (*kah-mee*) who created their land also gave birth to the mountains, lakes, rivers, boulders and trees that dotted their landscape. Over time, shrines were built around these holy spaces, and with many thousands of such sites surrounding them, the Japanese considered their country a land of the divine.

Above all, the Japanese believed that their rulers were divine. The *Kojoki* relates that Japan's first emperor, **Jimmu**, was the great-grandson of Amaterasu (*ah-mah-teh-rah-soo*), the Goddess of the Sun. According to legend, he came to the throne in 660 BCE and the present emperor, Akihito (*ah-kee-hee-toh*), is numbered as the 125th of the same lineage. The Japanese claim an imperial house that extends in an unbroken line from Jimmu to the present day, and is thus the oldest ruling line in human history. Moreover, with Amaterasu as the mother of the imperial house, the Japanese have regarded themselves uniquely blessed. It is little wonder that they call their country Nihon (*nee-hawn*), which means "land of the Rising Sun."

KEY WORDS

Sun-line
Shinto
kami
Taiho Code
Nara
shogun
samurai
Zen Buddhism
Bushido Code

KEY PEOPLE

Jimmu
Jomon
Ainu
Pimiko
Prince Shotoku
Empress Suiko
Empress Koken
Fujiwara
Minamoto Yorimoto
Monk Saicho
Tomoe
St. Francis Xavier

VOICES FROM THE PAST

What is the sound of one hand clapping?
Zen koan
(riddle to assist
in meditation)

TIME LINE: JAPAN

	ca. 9500 BCE	Earliest archaeological remains date to 9500 BCE
Jimmu, great-grandson of the Goddess of the Sun, comes to the throne of Japan	ca. 6600 BCE	
	ca. 10 000 BCE	Jomon culture emerges in Japan; the Ainu begin to settle on Hokkaido
Yayoi people bring knowledge of rice cultivation, glass, and bronze to Japan	ca. 300 BCE	
	ca. 300 CE	Sun-line rises to political primacy with a unified government under an emperor
Buddhism arrives in Japan	552	
	ca. 600	Many elements of Chinese culture are imported to Japan
Taiho Code makes sweeping changes in law, taxation, education, and government	702	
	710	Japan's first city, Nara, is established
Kojoki, or *Record of Ancient Matters*, is the first Japanese book	712	
	794–1185	Heian period begins with the move of the court from Nara to Heian-kyo
Buddhist monasteries establish the first schools in Japan	ca. 800	
	1232	New law code establishes the power of the shogun
Khubilai Khan launches the first of two failed attempts to invade Japan	1274	
	1336	Ashikaga shogunate begins, bringing three centuries of bloodshed
Onin War begins a century of warfare within Japan	1467	
	1549	St. Francis Xavier, a Jesuit priest, travels to Japan and makes 150 converts
War of Unification creates the last shogunate, the Tokugawa; it lasts until 1867	1573–1600	

GEOGRAPHY OF JAPAN

Japan consists of more than 400 islands, but only the four largest are of historical importance. These are, from north to south, Hokkaido, Honshu (where one finds the major centres of population like Tokyo, Osaka, Nagoya, and Kyoto), Shikoku, and Kyushu. The islands were formed originally by violent volcanic activity on the sea bottom, and as a result, Japan is a mountainous land with numerous small rivers flowing directly to the sea.

In total land area, Japan is approximately 380 000 km² (smaller than Baffin Island). Today it supports a population of 125 million, about five times that of Canada. Only about one fifth of the land is sufficiently level to be cultivated, and as a result, Japanese agriculture is among the most intensive in the world. Japan has few natural resources and must import almost all its energy requirements such as oil, most of its minerals, and a good deal of its food.

At the same time, Japan's major islands have a temperate climate and abundant rainfall, with several climatic zones. They experience few extremes of temperature, and they have access to abundant fish and a wide range of vegetable crops. This gives Japan one of the world's healthiest diets, and the lifespan of the average Japanese person today is the longest in the world.

The Japanese islands lie at the extreme edge of the Eurasian (Europe and Asia) land mass and are, at their closest point, about 240 km from the Asian continent. People can swim the English Channel, but no one has ever been able to swim across the Sea of Japan. Ships that attempted the crossing — particularly before the invention of the compass — found it a dangerous and difficult undertaking, and shipwrecks cost many lives. As a result of this simple geographical fact, although Japan was deeply influenced by Chinese and Korean civilization, historical interaction was sometimes close but never continuous. Japan would borrow from these civilizations but always adapt what it borrowed to its own needs, in distinctive ways.

■ Ancient Japan

Which geographical features have tended to isolate Japan?

JAPANESE HISTORY: CHANGE AND CONTINUITY

Because of its geographical isolation, Japan exhibited an unusually high degree of continuity prior to the impact of Western imperialism in the nineteenth century. Blessed by the bounties of nature — a temperate climate, fertile plains, and a generous sea — the Japanese people suffered little from the sort of social disruption caused elsewhere by scarcity and overpopulation. Japan produced no revolutionary thinkers; the great catalysts of change were external influences — most notably the tidal wave of Chinese and Korean culture that flooded Japan in the sixth and seventh centuries. The failed Mongol invasions of the thirteenth century not only destroyed the Kamakura shogunate, but also gave the Japanese a sense of nationhood for the first time. It seems fair to say that Japan's development was evolutionary rather than revolutionary. The principal sources of stability were an unshakeable belief in the divinity of the emperor and his line, and the existence of a hereditary ruling class of aristocrats and warriors. This class enjoyed the support of both the throne and the established religions — Shinto and Buddhism. The warrior class alone monopolized the instruments of force so that conflict was confined within that class. The appearance of strife and violence in Japanese history is striking, but it conceals an underlying stability.

TIME FRAMES
JAPANESE HISTORICAL PERIODS

Formative Period (Jomon, Yayoi, and the Yamato States) ca. 10 000 BCE–710 CE
Nara Period 710–794
Heian Period 794–1185
Kamakura Shogunate 1185–1333
Ashikaga (Muromachi) Shogunate 1336–1573
Tokugawa Shogunate 1600–1867

THE GROWTH OF THE EMPIRE

The Formative Age

During the last ice age, which ended about 11 000 years ago, the Japanese islands were joined to the Asian mainland by a land bridge. Across this bridge came peoples from Korea and northeast Asia, and since Japan was geographically the end of the line, they settled there permanently. The earliest archaeological remains in Japan, consisting mostly of pottery, date from about 9500 BCE and are the earliest pottery remains in world history.

Over time, the first settlers were joined by peoples from South China or, perhaps, from the Polynesian Islands. In the space of thousands of years, these peoples blended together, creating a distinct culture, called the **Jomon**. This culture endured until about 300 BCE.

During this same period, another people came to Japan's northernmost island of Hokkaido. They were called the **Ainu** — a tall, fair-skinned people with facial hair. For many centuries, the Ainu remained distinct from the rest of the Japanese, but today their ranks have been thinned to less than 20 000 through intermarriage, and they are on the verge of disappearing. Their origin will always be a mystery. The Japanese are thus a people of mixed origin, but for most of their history, they have ignored this fact. They have, instead, emphasized their mythological beginnings, their divine descent, and their special place in the world.

The Earliest Civilizations

The Jomon were basically hunters, fishers, and gatherers. They took their name from a particular type of pottery decorated by pressing rope into wet clay. This pottery later came to include human figures with huge eyes, which some scholars regard as an attempt to depict "windows to the soul." The female figures are usually larger than the male, and this may indicate a form of female dominance in society.

Around the beginning of the third century BCE, Jomon culture began to blend with that of a new people called the Yayoi, who brought to Japan a knowledge of irrigated rice cultivation, bronze- and ironwork, glass, and mirrors. Most scholars believe that the Yayoi culture came to Japan from Korea, and when China conquered the Korean peninsula in 108 BCE, Korea became a bridge civilization joining China and Japan.

Crafters of the Jomon people — some of the earliest inhabitants of Japan — produced this decorative clay pot ca. 3000 BCE.

About 300 CE, the Japanese on the main island of Honshu began to join together to form a distinctive state. Since the Japanese at this time had no written language, historians are forced to rely on archaeological evidence, and on Chinese accounts, to gain knowledge of this early period.

The first Chinese account of Japan dates from 297 CE and tells of a land where the people went barefoot, ate raw vegetables, and bowed frequently to each other. The most intriguing part of the Chinese account, however, concerns Japanese politics. Japan was ruled not by a king, but by a queen. For some 70 or 80 years, male rule had led to wars and disturbances, so the people chose a woman called **Pimiko** as their ruler. She is said to have lived in a great fortified palace with 1000 women and only one man as servants, and to have had a prosperous rule. On her death, the succession passed to a male, but more violence followed. As a result, the people chose a female relative of Pimiko to rule again.

Japanese historians have always been skeptical of this account, because they have found the idea of female rule uncomfortable. Early in 1990, however, archaeologists discovered what seems to have been the fortress of Pimiko, at a small town called Yoshinogari in western Japan.

Beliefs and Rulers in the Yamato Period

Archaeology has also revealed a great deal about other aspects of life in early Japan. The royal tombs — great mounds laid out in the shape of keyholes — contain artifacts that suggest that in the Yamato period, the Japanese were a warlike people who fought on horseback. In and around these tombs, archeologists have found baked clay figures, called *haniwa,* which show the clothing, armour, and other paraphernalia of daily life in the period. Interestingly, the haniwa suggest that death was not considered a sad thing. Some haniwa seem to be dancing and singing, others are drinking sake (fermented-rice wine), and still others seem to be contentedly tending their fields.

Early Japan was an aristocratic society. Each region was dominated by a certain clan, called an *uji,* which worshipped a particular *kami* as their ancestor. Each owned a number of peasant retainers and slaves who farmed the land. In the warlike climate of the early Yamato period, and in a process that is not yet entirely understood, one of these clans was able

Haniwa figures, like this man — but also in the shape of warriors and animals — kept the dead company in tombs from 300 CE to ca. 550 CE. Thousands of figures could be found in a single tomb.

Shinto

Shinto means the "Way of the Deities," and is a unique Japanese blend of earlier cults of animism, shamanism, fertility rites, and nature worship. The deities of Shinto are called **kami** — not gods in the Western sense, but simply objects or personalities that are more highly placed, or that inspire awe. Kami could be mountains or lakes, caves or boulders, mythological figures, clan ancestors, and the emperor — even while he was alive. The kami were responsible for the good and bad fortune of human beings, but there was no guarantee that they would answer human prayers. People could only placate the kami with offerings of rice, cloth, cakes, and horses, and then could do no more than hope for the best. In the Yamato period, the Sun Goddess came to be considered the greatest of the kami. Her descendants, therefore, became the most important clan on Earth. It is interesting to note that the Sun Goddess was never depicted in art. Shinto shrines are empty; the presence of the deity is made more awesome by that very emptiness.

WEB CONNECTION

http://www.mcgrawhill.ca/links/echoes

Go to the site above to find out more about Shinto and other religions in Japan.

to assert its supremacy over all the others. This was achieved through diplomacy, marriage relationships, and, above all, by establishing the fact that the clan's ancestor, the Sun Goddess, was the greatest of all deities. This was the origin of the imperial **Sun-line** of Japan, which still rules today. The spiritual and temporal power of the Sun-line arose out of another major development of the Formative Period: the combining of diverse religious beliefs into Japan's native religion, called **Shinto**.

If the kami became unhappy, human beings suffered curses or pollution (*tsumi*). Pollution occurred for any number of reasons: wounding or being wounded, sickness, incest, snakebite, or any occurrence involving blood. Because human beings were seen to have no real control over their fate, and because good actions did not result in reward and bad actions were not necessarily punished, Shinto is called a "pre-moral" religion. Pollution was cured by a period of isolation accompanied by purifying rituals, which usually involved water. This may be the origin of the daily bath in Japan today.

Early Shinto ideas about death and the afterlife are difficult to know, because it was also a preliterate religion with no written scriptures or laws. At death, it seems that everyone, regardless of their moral conduct, went to the same place: a gloomy and shadowy underworld called *yomi*. There one lived on, in very much the same state as on the earth. Shinto offered no comfort or consolation in death, and no promise of paradise for those who had lived good lives. It might, therefore, be called a life-affirming religion, since it urged people to enjoy this world — to make the best of present existence. Shinto encouraged joy, but its failure to promise happiness after death meant that when Buddhism came to Japan and offered the consolation of salvation, it rapidly made many converts.

A shinto shrine at Nikko, Japan. The structure at the foreground is a torii gate, a common shinto symbol.

Shinto, however, did not disappear. Its greatest strength, the love, respect, and veneration of nature in a country of great natural beauty, could not be challenged. Where else would people erect a shrine to a single wave, to a perfect maple tree, or to an entire island, like Mayajima near Hiroshima, simply because of its beauty?

During the late Yamato period, which began with the introduction of Buddhism in 552, Shinto suffered a temporary setback. Some of its beliefs blended with those of the Buddhists, and it did not re-emerge as a distinct faith until the eighteenth and nineteenth centuries, when patriotic scholars portrayed it as the deepest expression of the Japanese soul. Shinto, with its many myths, was also the chief inspiration for the folk religion of Japan, which is seen today in seasonal customs and life-cycle rituals. At New Year, for instance, Japanese people place pine branches and straw ropes at their front door to symbolize the rebirth of nature and the purity of the household interior.

The Late Yamato and Nara Periods

Prior to 552, Japan was a primitive civilization with no unified identity, no system of writing, no distinct forms of artistic expression, no law code, and only the most rudimentary forms of political control. There was no capital city. Individual clan loyalties were strong, and although most Japanese accepted the need for societal hierarchy and hereditary authority in politics, a good deal of opposition to the growing authority of the Sun-line remained.

Even before 552, a few Japanese were becoming aware of the continental civilization of China and Korea. Some had learned to write Chinese and others had begun to study the Confucian classics. In 552, however, the king of Paekche, one of the three Korean kingdoms of the period, sent Japan a gift of Buddhist images and scriptures. This event marks the formal introduction of a new religion to Japan, and it threw the Japanese ruling class into turmoil. The Sun-line and their chief ally, the Soga clan, immediately championed the new faith and made the Buddha the chief kami of the Soga. Their more conservative enemies rejected the Buddha, but when the Soga defeated their rivals in war, the power of the new kami was proven. Cleverly asserting that only the Sun Goddess was superior to the Buddha, the Soga family then forged tight marriage alliances with the Sun-line and set out to reform Japan.

Review...Recall...Reflect

1. Explain how geography shaped early Japanese culture and society.

2. Outline how Japan developed from a series of clan-dominated regions to a unified country ruled by the Sun-line.

3. Why is the year 552 seen as one of the most important dates in Japanese history?

CHINESE INFLUENCE AND THE GREAT CHANGE

The architect of Japan's transformation was a man known as **Prince Shotoku** (574–622), whose face still appears on Japan's most common banknote. He never became emperor, but ruled as regent for his aunt, the **Empress Suiko** (*soo-ee-koh*), whose role in the reforms was likely as great as his own. Under Suiko and Shotoku, Chinese culture was imported with astonishing enthusiasm and swept like a great wave across the land.

Numerous missions, sometimes as large as 500 people, braved the dangerous crossing to China. Some Japanese remained for up to 30 years studying in China, but others returned swiftly with knowledge of Chinese science and technology, books and writing, clothing and customs, and above all, Chinese methods of government. In 604, Shotoku proclaimed his famous Constitution of 17 articles, which offered no specific laws or details of a new governmental structure, but proclaimed, instead, Japan's commitment to such Chinese ideas as a single supreme ruler, a civil service chosen by merit, centralized government, and roles for both Confucianism and Buddhism in Japanese state and society.

Shotoku died in 622, but not before his many other achievements, among which was the foundation of the exquisite Horyuji Temple near Nara — the world's oldest surviving wooden building. A power struggle followed Shotoku's death, but the reformers retained the upper hand and embarked on a second wave of reform starting in 645 called the Taika, or "Great Change." Over the next few decades, the supreme authority of the emperor, or *tenno*, was universally acknowledged, private land holding was abolished, and central authority was extended to the provinces. The first census was undertaken, and Chinese systems of taxation and law were introduced. Court ranks were reorganized, schools were founded, more Buddhist temples were set up, and finally, these and other reforms were made law in the **Taiho Code** of 702. Several of the reforms existed more on paper than in reality, but nevertheless, they provided Japan with the foundations for future rapid development.

The new law code, called the *ritsuryo* system, was particularly important since it served as the basis of political authority until Japan's first modern constitution was issued in 1889. Its civil and criminal provisions generally mimicked Chinese law, but in subsequent revisions, changes were made to reflect existing Japanese custom. After 820, for instance, the death penalty was never imposed because Buddhism prohibited the taking of life, and although Chinese law forbade females to inherit land, Japanese law permitted it. The law also became increasingly decentralized.

In 710, Empress Gemmyo established Japan's first city, which was also its first permanent capital. Prior to this, the capital had consisted of little more than a palace, which moved at each ruler's death to avoid lingering pollution. Now a whole new city, called **Nara** (*nah-rah*), was laid out as an exact small-scale replica of the Chinese capital. Its streets and avenues formed a rectangular checkerboard with the palace in the north. The many Buddhist temples and Shinto shrines, markets, and parks all imitated Chinese styles. Today, the only remaining examples of eighth-century Chinese architecture are found in Nara, not in China, because the Japanese reconstructed exact replicas of buildings when they were burned or otherwise destroyed.

Nara was not a happy place. The Chinese and Korean immigrants who flocked to the new city brought with them smallpox and measles, to which the Japanese had no immunity. From 735 onward, successive epidemics spread from Nara and killed, perhaps, 30 percent of the Japanese population. Fires often swept through large quarters of the city, razing the wooden buildings and causing great loss of life. The fragile tax base could not support reconstruction, and increasingly, could not even pay for basic services. Arrogant and unruly monks interfered in politics, and even though this period saw such cultural achievements as Japan's first literary works — the *Kojiki* and a collection of 4500 poems called the *Manyoshu* — life in Nara remained unstable.

An important reason for this instability was that throughout the Nara period, the Buddhist establishment became wealthier and more powerful. Devout emperors and empresses decreed that Buddhist monasteries, nunneries, and pagodas be set up in

The Hall of the Great Buddha at Nara is believed to be the largest surviving wooden structure in the world. It was built in 745 and is home to a 16-m tall bronze Buddha.

every province. They levied heavy taxes on the people to erect images such as the great statue of the Buddha at the Todaiji temple, said to be made from over half a million kilograms of metal. The Buddhists also built a fabulous treasure house for themselves — the famous Shosoin (*show-soh-een*) — containing a collection of over 10 000 objects from the eighth-century world. Still on view today are books and textiles; exquisite objects of gold, lacquer, and pearl; and weapons, screens, glass, and fine jewelry from such far-off places as Persia, India, Greece, Rome, and other outposts of the Silk Route.

In the end, Buddhism was the catalyst that brought the Nara period to a close. It is said that the formidable **Empress Koken** fell in love with a Buddhist monk. She abdicated the throne in 758 to be with him, but became unhappy with her successor and in 764, changed her name to Shotoku and again made herself empress. As she gave the monk more and more power and ever-higher titles, the court nobles and high officials feared that she might make him emperor and break the sacred chain of Sun-line descent. The empress died before realizing her plans, and the monk was immediately banished. As a result of this incident, no woman would rule Japan again until the seventeenth century.

The new emperor decided that he could not remain in a city where Buddhist clerics had become such a threat. The court left Nara, and in 794, designated a new site called Heian-kyo (hey-on-kyoh), or "City of Peace," and began once more to construct a model of the Chinese capital. Heian-kyo, known today as Kyoto, was the capital of Japan from 794 until 1868.

THE HEIAN PERIOD

Early Heian culture was eclectic. In 894, the Japanese court decided to ignore their former teacher, China, and for the rest of the period, sent no further missions. Instead, they integrated the ancient myths, folklore, and philosophy of China into their own civilization. The Heian also adopted China's rich heritage of religion, literature, and historical writing, along with its most up-to-date techniques in architecture, textiles, ceramics, and engineering. To each of these borrowings the Heian gave a distinctive twist, and once they had severed the continental contact, adapted what they had learned with increasing independence. By the end of the Heian period, Japan's resemblance to China was merely superficial.

Emperors, Aristocrats, and Common People

The emperors who ruled from Heian-kyo are not well-known, since throughout the period, they had little influence on policy and their power tended to become weaker and weaker. Finally, the emperors of the period were all married to wives from one aristocratic clan called the **Fujiwara** (foo-jee-wah-rah). As second only to the Sun-line, the Fujiwara had early asserted their right to provide royal brides, often marrying their mature daughters to boys who had not yet reached their teens. Because the emperors were so young, the fathers or uncles of these empresses created new offices for themselves — Regents and Chancellors — and issued their own orders in the name of the young emperor. Whenever an emperor showed signs of independence, he was encouraged to abdicate, and the cycle began anew. Sometimes, an emperor who had been forced to retire to a monastery formed a cloistered government and issued his own decrees. So, during the Heian period, policies originated from at least three or four sources, and since no one knew which ones to obey, politics became little more than an irrelevant annoyance to the courtiers and aristocrats in the capital. In the provinces, however, the lack of direction was to have severe consequences.

The Fujiwara were typical of many great families that had gradually evolved over the preceding centuries. They had initially risen to power through a combination of military strength and the possession of large tracts of land, and had used these to secure court rank and titles. By the Heian period, any clan holding rank and title had come to be included in the kuge (pronounced koo-geh), or aristocracy. The kuge was a totally closed class; its members married only other kuge, monopolized all government posts, and supported themselves by official salaries and revenues from their provincial estates. They made up less than one percent of Japan's total population, and, without exception, lived in the lofty isolation of the capital. Some scholars refer to the kuge as "Dwellers Among the Clouds."

Daily Life in Heian-kyo

Our picture of life in the capital comes from the voluminous literature of the period, written mostly by women. The aristocratic males engaged in a constant struggle to master classical Chinese, the only language of "respectable" literature. Few of them ever succeeded. Since Chinese was unsuitable for expressing either the grammar or nuances of Japanese, the results were stilted, artificial, and unclear. Women, on the other hand, were free to write in *kana* (*kah-nah*), a phonetic alphabet developed by the Japanese for the expression of their own language. Their poems, diaries, and pillow books — a form of literature in which women recorded at night their observations of the day's experiences — survive to this day. One of these literate women, Lady Murasaki Shikibu (*moo-rah-sah-kee shee-kee-boo*), was the author of the world's first novel.

This brilliant work, entitled the *Tale of Genji,* or the *Tale of the Shining Prince,* was written over the space of twenty years (1000–1020). The novel sweeps its readers across the whole landscape of Heian aristocratic life. *Genji* is one of the longest novels in world history, containing over 360 000 words and running to more than 1200 pages of small type in the best-known English translation by A. Waley. Its astonishing detail makes it an indispensable historical source, and today, educated Japanese know *Genji* just as well as educated Westerners know the Shakespearean plays.

What does *Genji* tell us about Heian Japan? To begin with, it describes the appearance of the people.

Both men and women wore heavy, light-coloured make-up, and sometimes, only a small goatee distinguished the male from the female face. For both sexes, make-up covered part of the lips since small mouths (and eyes) were considered a sign of beauty. Men powdered their faces, and women plucked their eyebrows and painted new ones higher up. Women rouged their cheeks and tiny mouths. They dyed their teeth black — another example of historical fashion harming women's health — using a tooth dye composed of a mixture of powdered iron, tea, and vinegar. A woman with white teeth, or "peeled caterpillars" as they are called in *Genji*, was an object of scorn. A woman's hair was her "crowning glory." Parted in the middle, and unadorned, it flowed to the ground, sometimes reaching 2 m.

The costume of Heian men was drab compared with that of women. Men wore a stiff black cap and a patterned, waist-length robe with voluminous sleeves over billowing trousers — the whole outfit dyed in shades of white, brown, or black. Women, on the other hand, wore long silken robes of gorgeous colours and intricate patterns. Sometimes, they wore as many as twelve of these robes, one on top of the other. A special feature of this costume was that each robe had shorter sleeves than the one beneath, so a rainbow of colours flashed when the arms moved.

Scripts & Symbols λ μ ν ο π θ υ ρ σ τ υ ϖ ω ξ ψ ζ α β χ ε δ φ γ

Historically, there have been three ways of writing in Japan. The kanji used by men in the Heian period consisted of Chinese characters and was very difficult to learn. Women during the Heian period wrote the more graceful native Japanese alphabet called hiragana, and this alphabet is used today. Finally, there is an alphabet called katakana, which is used to express the many foreign words in daily use in Japan, for example, ho-te-ru ("hotel").

A scene from the *Tale of Genji*, a novel of and about Heian aristocratic life ca. 1000.

The Cult of Beauty

The ability to appreciate beauty determined the divisions or gradations within the aristocracy. Rank and wealth played a part, but far more important were aesthetic sensibility and emotional depth. Social pressure to be considered a good person, a *ryo-min*, was enormous, and Heian literature is filled with stories of aristocrats driven to monasteries or nunneries because of social failure. Religion in the period was also influenced by the cult of beauty: Buddhist and Shinto sites were forced to compete in the elaborate embellishment of their architecture and gardens, and make their festivals ever more lavish and gaudy.

Homes in the Heian period were beautifully designed, but not very comfortable. They were generally built of wood, and most were raised about 30 cm off the ground to avoid dampness and humidity. Most had a small garden, with streams, moss-covered rocks, and small trees laid out to mimic a famous landscape from one of the beauty spots of Japan.

Furniture was almost non-existent — perhaps a chest or a low table, a decorative screen, or a charcoal heater; people generally lived on the floor and kept such things as clothing and bedding in cupboards built into the walls. Movable partitions created a bedroom, and people slept on straw mats, or *tatami* (*tah-tah-mee*), just as many Japanese do today.

Relations between men and women in Heian Japan suggest that women enjoyed a mixed sort of freedom. Custom forbade a woman to be seen by any male other than her husband or members of her immediate family, and women's clothing and long hair restricted their physical mobility. At the same time, however, the law guaranteed inheritance rights equal to those of men, prohibited physical abuse, and allowed women a degree of sexual freedom. Many women, married and unmarried, took lovers of their choice. Women were active in politics, often managed large estates, and above all, were the arbiters of taste.

Children of both genders were welcomed and indulged. It was universally believed that an ancestral spirit entered the baby's body at birth and caused the first cry, making the child human. This spirit was unstable, nevertheless, and many rituals were designed to prevent its departure from the child's body, which would cause death. Most important were the visits to a shrine at the ages of three, five, and seven, after which the spirit was "anchored" and childhood officially ended. This ritual, called Shichi-go-san (meaning "7-5-3"), is still performed today.

While the aristocrats of the capital savoured their cherry blossoms, the provinces were showing signs of restlessness. For a long time, the aristocrats had paid little attention to the administration of their provincial estates, and had failed to realize that in a land-poor country, possession of property was crucial. Their vassals had been fighting for years to protect the land of these aristocratic lords, and, in the process, had developed unique fighting skills. Out of this provincial conflict arose the Age of the **Samurai**. From the twelfth century onward, a new class, the warrior, or *bushi* (*boo-shee*), would dominate the history of Japan.

THE KAMAKURA SHOGUNATE

The Fujiwara clan had succeeded in dominating the imperial family for nearly three centuries, but having finally run out of daughters suitable for marriage, their power began to decline. At the same time, their provincial estates, or *shoen* (*show-en*), which had provided them and the other aristocrats revenue, were under constant threat from ambitious and greedy rivals. Provincial families were becoming ever more powerful and independent as they honed their fighting skills in frequent battles to protect their masters' land. Many began to wonder why they

The armour of a Japanese warrior.

Biography
Minamoto Yoritomo: The First Shogun

Shakespeare once wrote that some men are born great, some achieve greatness, and some have greatness thrust upon them. Minamoto Yoritomo seems to have been an example of all of these possibilities. When Yoritomo was born, in 1147, the Minamoto clan was a dominant military force who traced their descent to the emperor Seiwa. Their family name had already been forever immortalized by what many consider to be the world's first novel, *Tale of Genji*. (Genji is the Chinese version). The shogunate system that Yoritomo ultimately created would continue to straddle the military and imperial worlds of his youth for nearly 700 years.

By the time Yoritomo was 12 or 13 he had been orphaned as the result of his family's clash with another dominant military family, the Taira. Why the Taira clan did not also kill the Minamoto sons remains a mystery. Instead, Yoritomo was exiled to live in what was basically a house arrest situation, under the protection of a Taira family supporter. The Taira family and their supporters came to regret their small mercy in more ways than one. In his turn, Yoritomo would not make the same mistake of letting potential rivals live, no matter who they were.

It seems likely that Yoritomo was a charming young man. He had to flee the home of his first jailer, Ito Sukechika, when it became evident that Yoritomo had seduced one of the Ito daughters. Yoritomo was smart enough to flee to Hojo Tokimasa. Tokimasa was also allied with the Taira clan, although not very happily. Hojo had, in fact, been the one to arrange for Yoritomo's banishment with the Itos. Luckily, when Yoritomo also seduced one of Tokimasa's daughters, it coincided with Hojo family discontent with their subordination to the Taira clan. Tokimasa and Yoritomo formed an important alliance that helped lead to the defeat of the Taira family and started Yoritomo on his road to power. Eventually Yoritomo married Tokimasa's daughter, Masako.

With the support of the Hojo family, Yoritomo set about gathering support from other dominant families and samurai. Yoritomo was able to capitalize on his working knowledge of the discontent that had been festering for years in the areas remote from the imperial court in Kyoto. As it turned out, many of the noble families and some of the religious leaders were tired of the Taira clan domination. He was so successful that many members of the Taira family even joined forces with him.

In 1180 Yoritomo joined an imperial prince in attempting to put down a rebellion that had broken out in a variety of places. As the acknowledged leader of so many families, Yoritomo set up his own headquarters in Kamakura, just south of modern day Tokyo, and this was why the period became known as the Kamakura period. War raged for five years. In the process Yoritomo established several "boards", run by his supporters, who took over the bureaucratic and judicial duties of area after area, staying loyal to the emperor through the delivery of taxes collected. Yoritomo also found it necessary to order the death of a close cousin and one of his brothers, among other potential rivals.

When the Genji War ended in 1185, Yoritomo was the real leader of Japan, though he continued to present the appearance of loyalty to the emperor, and resisted any urge to usurp the throne. (In fact, he even tried to place two of his daughters in the emperor's harem, perhaps hoping one day to be the grandfather of an emperor.) Besides all bureaucratic and judicial matters, Yoritomo also set up the *Samurai - dokoro* — the office responsible for organizing all the affairs of the fighting men. This special office attending to the fighting ranks created a golden age for the samurai and a particularly loyal following for Yoritomo.

Minamoto Yoritomo, renowned samurai, was the first to receive the title of shogun, in 1192, during the Kamakura shogunate.

In 1192 Yoritomo named himself *Seii Taishogun*. This ancient and hereditary title asserted the shogun's right to act independently against any rebel. For the next several hundred years the emperors acted on the advice and the pleasure of the shoguns.

Minamoto Yoritomo died in 1199 as the result of a fall from his horse. Among other things, his administration is noted for developing an efficient system of roadways complete with post stops, rest stops and spare horses. This helped spread religion out from the noble class to the common people and aided trade. Trade guilds were formed and a successful mercantile economy started to grow.

Activities

1. Why do you think Yoritomo did not just usurp the throne and put himself in charge completely?

2. With a partner, prepare a dialogue that might have taken place between Yoritomo and one of his daughters as he tries to place them in the emperor's harem. Remember it is 12th century Japan.

should endanger themselves for the sake of a far-off overlord, and their ties of loyalty weakened considerably. In the capital, the aristocrats saw previous friends become enemies because of the scarcity of tax revenue, and they began to fight among themselves. The frightened emperor called in the leader of the most powerful of the provincial clans to restore order, but he, too, was ambitious, and in 1180, attempted to make his two-year-old nephew emperor. This sacrilege resulted in the outbreak of a bloody five-year war and the foundation of the Kamakura shogunate.

The victor in this war was a man named **Minamoto Yoritomo** (*mee-nah-moh-toh yoh-ree-toh-moh* — Japanese practice always puts the surname first). He was a relative of the emperor, a feared warrior, and a skilled administrator. After his victory, Minamoto realized that the capital administration was both decadent and incompetent, and that if he moved there, he and his followers might also become corrupt. At the same time, he was determined to become the real ruler of the country, and so he demanded from the emperor a special title. In 1192, he was made **shogun**, a title that simply means "general." Since his power base had always been in the east — at the small town of Kamakura, near Tokyo — Minamoto set up a national administration there, calling it a tent government, or *bakufu*. This is the term we translate as "shogunate."

For the next century and a half — until 1333, the bakufu governed Japan. Formal orders came from the powerless emperors in Kyoto, but only the instructions of the shogunate were acted on. Imperial prestige, nonetheless, legitimized the shogunate.

After his death, Minamoto's remarkable wife, Masako, held the regime together until 1203, when she finally lost patience with these two young men and decided to declare her father Shikken, or Regent, to rule for them. Henceforth, the real power resided in her family, the Hojo. The office of shogun now became like that of the emperor — a symbol.

A new law code was proclaimed in 1232, and it confirmed the entire chain of command, clarifying rights and duties at all levels of the administration. Interestingly, this code continued to give women more rights than they enjoyed elsewhere in the world. They retained equal inheritance rights, could divorce, and the penalty for adultery was milder than anywhere else, and applied equally to both genders. Elsewhere, the woman was more harshly punished than the man.

Kamakura Buddhism

In spite of its somewhat confusing command structure, the Kamakura administration remained efficient. The population grew, more cities appeared, internal trade expanded, and contacts were renewed with China, bringing new technology and ideas to Japan.

Buddhism flourished. Monasteries extended their land holdings, and often had to arm their monks to protect their property. New schools or sects of Buddhism appeared, being distinguished from earlier Buddhist forms by doctrines that were easier to understand and more appealing to the common people. In Japan's violent and militaristic society, they all emphasized the achievement of personal salvation.

The first of the new schools was called Pure Land, and it taught that the individual could achieve enlightenment by faith alone. Simply by repeatedly reciting the name of Amida Buddha one could achieve rebirth in the Pure Land of Heaven. The second school, called the Nichiren, was founded by a monk of that name in 1253. He claimed that his was the only true form of

These statues of Buddha were carved of wood some time during the Kamakura period, ca. 800-900. The Japanese brought the art of woodworking to great heights. Not only artworks but also buildings — including great temples and private homes — were made from cut, carved, and painted wood.

Buddhism, that salvation was to be achieved by veneration of the *Lotus Scripture,* and that those who rejected his teachings would be damned.

The third and ultimately the most important of the Kamakura schools was called **Zen Buddhism**, or the School of Meditation. Zen emphasized self-discipline, the idea that emotion was the source of action, and the practice of *zazen* — sitting in still-minded meditation until a sudden flash of intuition brought enlightenment. Zen became the favoured school of the samurai class. Since their world was filled with violence and sudden death, Zen provided both a technique for tranquility and composing the mind as well as a rationale for the sudden, spontaneous act of killing an enemy in battle. All schools of Buddhism forbade the taking of life, but through Zen, the belief gradually spread that the sword, not the person holding it, was the killer.

The Buddhist monasteries were Japan's first schools. The gifted **Monk Saicho** (767–822) pioneered a twelve-year curriculum, the first six years of which were "learning by hearing" and the last six, "learning by thinking." Private schools (*shigaku*) for the children of the nobility appeared in the Heian period, but a monk named Kukai founded the first short-lived school for commoners in 828. After that, schools appeared in most monasteries, emphasizing the ethics of Buddhism and Confucianism, and these still exist. From the Kamakura period onward, military houses established schools for members of their extended families, so education was a privilege of the elite. Literacy rates remained low until the sixteenth century, when monasteries set up *teraoka,* or temple schools, outside their precincts to teach reading, writing, and mathematics independent of Buddhist ethics.

Review...Recall...Reflect

1. Is the description of Nara as an unfortunate capital appropriate?

2. After several women ruled prior to the late eighth century, Japan had no female rulers for nearly a thousand years. Why was this the case?

3. Explain how the Kamakura shogunate shifted the real power in government away from the emperor to the shoguns.

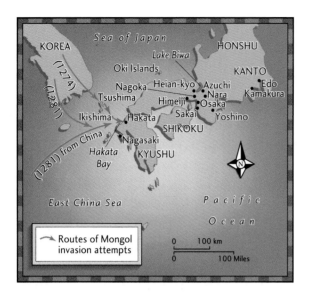

■ The Mongol Invasions of Japan

What made war with Japan so difficult for the Mongol invaders?

THE MONGOL INVASIONS: CHALLENGE AND RESPONSE

The Kamakura shogunate fell due more to external than internal factors. Early in the thirteenth century, the fearsome Mongols had burst forth from their Central Asian homeland, and had rapidly conquered much of the known world, including Japan's two closest neighbours, China and Korea. In 1268, Khubilai Khan, now the Emperor of China, sent a mission to Japan, and in a letter addressed to "the ruler of an insignificant country," ordered the Hojo Regents to offer formal submission to him. They refused. In 1274, Khubilai responded by sending an armada of 450 Korean ships, carrying 15 000 of his finest troops, to Japan's southern island of Kyushu.

The Japanese, though not entirely unprepared, were initially outmatched. The Mongols were master tacticians, fighting in coordinated formations. Their powerful crossbows made the Japanese bows look like toys, and they used catapults that hurled flaming explosives. The samurai had no defense but their swords and their courage. Nonetheless, the battles were inconclusive, and when fierce storms destroyed many of the Mongol ships, the invasion was aborted.

Khubilai, however, was unaccustomed to defeat, and he immediately sent more envoys to demand Japan's submission. The shogunate responded with the ultimate act of defiance. They beheaded the envoys, and then prepared for war.

Khubilai struck in the summer of 1281. He sent an armada of over a thousand ships carrying about 140 000 troops against Japan. This was the largest naval invasion force before the twentieth century. The Japanese were hopelessly outnumbered, and once the invaders had successfully landed their troops, the samurai seemed doomed to defeat. For almost two months, battles raged daily.

At the end of August 1281, a great typhoon with hurricane-force winds arose from nowhere. For two days, it battered the Mongol fleet as it lay at anchor. Most of the ships sank and the soldiers who fought to save them drowned. The remnants of the invading force, marooned on land, were slaughtered by the jubilant samurai. Victory was complete, and the good news swept the land. The typhoon was given the name *kamikaze*, or "divine wind," and was considered proof for all time that Japan was a Divine Land, protected by the gods.

Even as the country rejoiced, and as the shogunate basked in its victory, ominous signs of discontent began to appear. The samurai, who had fought so bravely, received no reward for their valour since no land had been confiscated and no booty seized. Thousands upon thousands of widows and orphans found themselves destitute, grieving their lost husbands and fathers who had left them without support and protection. As these loyal subjects departed empty-handed from Kamakura, they took their loyalty with them. The shogunate could no longer depend on its most loyal supporters.

The problems of the shogunate came to a head in 1318, when an unusually vigorous and ambitious emperor came to the throne in Kyoto. This man, Go-Daigo (*go dye-goh*), felt humiliated by the loss of imperial power, and immediately after his enthronement, took a number of steps designed to reassert the influence of the emperors over the shogunate. The Kamakura responded by demanding that he abdicate. When he refused to do so, they attacked him with a huge army commanded by one of their last loyal vassals, Ashikaga Takauji (*ah-shee-kah-gah tah-kah-oo-ji*). Ashikaga, however, switched sides. He turned his army around, and gathering support along the way, attacked the town of Kamakura and burned it to the ground.

Long and complicated negotiations with Go-Daigo convinced Ashikaga, however, that his own interests would not be served under an imperial regime, and once again, war broke out. By 1338, he had forced Go-Daigo into a final exile and proclaimed himself the new shogun, inaugurating a new era in Japanese feudalism. In this new shogunate, the old cult of beauty would blend with the brutality and sudden death of constant war, and with the profound peace of Zen Buddhism.

THE ASHIKAGA SHOGUNATE

The Ashikaga shogunate began bloodily, ended bloodily, and witnessed almost three centuries of bloodshed in-between. The Ashikaga shoguns, with little support from the emperors, lacked the legitimacy of their predecessors, and were forced to depend on raw force

to govern the country. The Ashikaga saw no need for the Sun-line to approve their actions.

The problems of the Ashikaga, from beginning to end, were rooted in the fact that their authority was not universally recognized as legitimate. Powerful local clans constantly conspired against them and against their own neighbours, seeking the slightest weakness so that they might annex their estates. The most successful of the warriors in this long struggle became *daimyo* (*dye-mee-oh*) — the supreme samurai lords of each principality — and as they gained ever-greater revenues, they asserted their independence from the shogun's administration. Great castles, more like fortresses, began to appear, many of them protected by moats, clever booby-traps, and nightingale floors that would sing at the approach of a ninja (invisible) assassin.

The Ashikaga shoguns took up residence in the old capital of Kyoto. They built their magnificent residences in a section of the city called Muromachi, so this is often called the Muromachi period. Outside the capital, violence was constant, but during the reigns of early shoguns such as Yoshimitsu (*yoh-shee-mit-soo*), who ruled from 1368 to 1408, and Yoshinori, who reigned from 1428 until his assassination in 1441, all seemed well. These early shoguns presided over an era that saw a second great flowering of culture, a growing feeling of nationhood among the Japanese, and most immediately, an understanding of what it meant to be a warrior.

Bushido, Warrior Ethics, and a Militarized Society

The class structure of the Ashikaga shogunate divided the people of Japan into four groups. On top was the warrior and then, in descending order: the merchant, the artisan, and the farmer.

This is a samurai trained in the art of invisibility, called *ninjutsu*. He is a ninja.

Not until the seventeenth century was this division formalized in law, but throughout the Kamakura and Ashikaga shogunates, class divisions hardened, the commoner's human rights declined, and the ethos of the warrior was more clearly defined.

The creed of the samurai, the **Bushido Code**, was composed of several elements. The first was the conviction that "death weighs no heavier than a feather" — the mark of the true warrior was that he would never retreat or surrender, no matter how great the odds against him. The samurai seemed almost to welcome death, and the most admired figures in Japanese history are those who went down trying. The second tenet of faith was that absolute, unconditional loyalty to one's superior was a necessity. Nothing took precedence over this — nothing.

The third element of the code was the importance of "face," a kind of pride that included a horror of bringing shame upon oneself or one's family. In the Ashikaga period, battles usually began with warriors facing each other to recite their family histories, dwelling on the brave exploits of their ancestors. Then, after an exchange of arrows, the warriors charged on horseback into battle, dismounting only to engage in hand-to-hand combat with worthy opponents. The samurai counted their victories by collecting the severed heads of the enemy. They burned incense in their helmets before a battle so that if their own heads became trophies, at least they would be fragrant.

The ultimate expression of face was ritual suicide. The Japanese call this act *seppuku*, or *hara-kiri*, which means "slitting the abdomen." Seppuku was undertaken to express shame, to show loyalty to one's lord, and sometimes, to admonish a lord to change his behaviour. It was a very painful way to die.

Bushido, meaning the "Way of the Warrior," had many other facets. A samurai was physically hardened from youth, forced to stand for hours under a freezing waterfall, to run for kilometres barefoot in the snow, and sometimes, to go for days without food. No hardship whatsoever could make the samurai complain. He was forced to be alert at all times by tutors who would try to sneak up on him and hit him with a heavy stick. He was taught to appreciate art, to dance and sing, to arrange flowers, and to paint. He was warned constantly to avoid a luxurious or soft life. And he was taught that his wife and children were expected to behave in the same way.

At the beginning of the feudal period in the twelfth century, there were also women samurai. The best-known of these was **Tomoe** (*toh-moh-eh*) of the Minamoto clan:

She was a woman fair of feature with long black hair and a light complexion. She was a rider without fear, and neither the wildest horse nor the roughest terrain could dismay her. So skilfully did she handle her bow and her sword that she was a match for a thousand warriors, and she could vanquish both gods and demons. Many times she took the field, faced her heavily armed foes, and won unparalleled fame as she fought the bravest of captains... And so, in this last battle, when all the others had been killed or had run away, she was one of the last seven. Into the fray rode Tomoe...

As time went on, however, female warriors like Tomoe became more rare and the general status of women declined. They came to be seen as too weak to defend property, and inheritance laws changed accordingly. Warriors spent more and more time fighting away from their homes, and their wives were confined to the tasks of child raising, housekeeping, and managing the estate. Women of the samurai class came to be used as pawns, hostages, or spies in the shifting alliances of the time, and so came, increasingly, to be considered as commodities. The Japanese never developed an ideal of courtly love as did the knights of Europe, and women were never placed on a pedestal. Instead, the masculine and militaristic spirit influenced the lower orders of society. Women were compelled to practise the strictest chastity before and after marriage, so samurai bloodlines would not be polluted and illegitimate sons not make claims on the estate. In this warrior society, only the priestesses and shamans, the courtesans, and those female entertainers who would later become the famous geisha (*gay-sha*) were able to enjoy any freedom. The Japanese woman, once equal, or even superior to the man, was forced into a subordinate position in society.

The samurai class, which represented three to five percent of the population at any given time, was easily distinguished from all other Japanese people. Samurai alone were permitted to carry two swords, and to wear silk clothing. Their manner of walking was a swagger, and they all wore a *kataginu* — a special type of jacket with protruding, stiffened shoulders over a skirt and trousers. On the jacket was a family crest. Warriors shaved the top of their heads, then gathered together the long hair from the back and sides, oiled it, and doubled it back over the crown, tying it tightly so that not a hair was out of place.

In battle, samurai wore several layers of undergarments and fitted over these an armour made of tiny scales of lacquered iron, which was strong, light, and flexible. It was considerably tougher than European chain mail and weighed less than 12 kg.

The samurai's most prized possession was his sword — many were given names, while others came to be venerated as kami. Swords were believed to have lives and spirits of their own, and warrior literature is filled with stories of them and their masters. The Japanese blade is probably the finest in world history. As early as the thirteenth century, each samurai sword was tested by the maker before delivery to the buyer. Sometimes, he placed the sword upright in a stream. If it failed to slice cleanly through a floating leaf, it was rejected.

Sword makers in Japan were greatly honoured and were serious about their craft. They fasted and purified themselves before beginning work on a blade. Wearing priestly white robes, they spent days melding together metals of varying hardness, heating them to white-hot temperatures, hammering them out, and folding each layer over and over again onto the next. The completed sword consisted of thousands — sometimes a million — layers of hard and soft metals. It would never break and would never become dull.

WARRIOR CULTURE

The accession of the third shogun, Yoshimitsu, in 1368, marked the beginning of a flash of glory in warrior culture that would long survive his 40-year reign. Under his watchful and discerning eye, a new set of aesthetic principles began to evolve and would remain important in Japanese culture until the present day.

http://www.mcgrawhill.ca/links/echoes

Go to the site above to find out more about samurai warriors.

Warrior culture in Japan was composed of three elements: the superb taste of the old Heian aristocrats, the vigour and power of the samurai, and the spirituality of Zen Buddhism. It had three major characteristics, and these are seen in all the arts, whether major or minor. The first of these was called *yugen,* and refers to a sense of sublime restraint, of symbolism, and the mystery that lies behind appearances. The new Noh theatre, which developed at this time under the famed dramatist Zeami, epitomized yugen — with its lack of sets, its gorgeous costumes, hidden orchestra, and the masks of the performers. Although the masks hid performers' emotions, a simple tilt of the head to catch the light in a different way could alter the overall mood of a scene. Noh actors, all male, were trained from earliest childhood in just how to tilt their heads.

The second characteristic was *wabi* (*wah-bee*). It, too, was a mysterious quality seen in such works as the superb ink and water (*suiboku*) paintings of the time, which sometimes consisted of little more than a perfect circle (*enso*) that embodied an ongoing Zen process begun by the monk-artist and continued in the mind of the viewer.

The final characteristic of Muromachi culture was *sabi* (*sah-bee*), the mystery of change and aging.

It took many years for a samurai to master swordsmanship. Some of the best swords became famous and were actually given names.

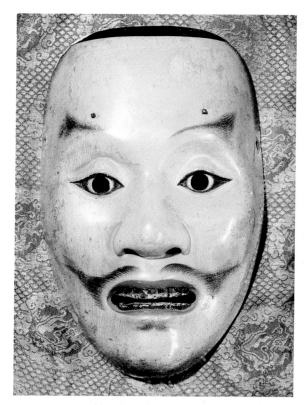

In the Noh theatre, a mask like this represented a warrior. Different masks and gestures were used for male and female characters, but men played all parts.

The best example, perhaps, is the art of flower arranging, *ikebana* (*ee-keh-bah-nah*), which means the art of "making flowers live." Seasonal flowers were arranged in a classic fashion, each stem in perfect proportion to the others and to the bowl holding the arrangement. Blossoms were matched by tint and size, and the symbolism of the various colours and lengths matched notions of "Heaven, Earth, and Humanity" or "Body, Heart, and Soul." Sabi entered the arrangement as the flowers withered and faded. The person who knew sabi understood that the arrangement was as beautiful on its last day as on its first. For the same reason, women and men in the warrior period did not try to disguise their true age with cosmetics and hair dyes.

All these features of aesthetics were combined in the tea ceremony, especially under *Sen-no-Rykyu*, its most celebrated practitioner. Tea had been introduced to Japan by the earliest Zen monks, probably as a drink designed to keep them awake during long hours of meditation. Gradually, tea came to be cultivated in amazing variety all over Japan, and the drinking of tea became a ritual, providing the warrior a temporary respite, a small pause in the serious business of killing.

A sixteenth century tea house in Kyoto. The objects for the tea ceremony would be brought in. Otherwise, there was little or no furniture.

WARRIOR CULTURE ON THE BRINK OF CHANGE

The reality of these centuries was not found only on blood-soaked battlefields. In the countryside, diligent peasants perfected the art of growing rice: pre-sprouting the kernel, creating special nursery-beds, and, later, transplanting the seedlings so that rice production grew enormously. These peasants developed new means of pest control, such as spraying seedlings with a mixture of whale oil and vinegar heated together, and rotated rice crops with wheat and barley. Plums, persimmons, oranges, pears, radishes, lotus, and indigo (used as a blue dye) all became commercial crops, and both hemp and silk were produced for clothing. Certain regions began to specialize in the manufacture of such products as *sake* (fermented-rice wine) tea, and paper. The Japanese showed little inventiveness, but refined and improved the various technologies that had earlier come from China and Korea. Japanese mining techniques were among the world's most advanced. Artisanship in textiles, lacquer, and ceramics equaled or surpassed that of China, and innovations in shipbuilding put the Japanese in the forefront of East Asian trade.

Lively commercial towns began to appear, especially where harbours were good, as overseas trade began once more to flourish. Early in the period, the Chinese severed all relations because of Japanese piracy, but in 1402, Yoshimitsu solved the problem by rounding up thousands of pirates and executing them. Now the Japanese began to import large quantities of copper coins, porcelains, paintings, books and medicine in exchange for their swords, folding fans, painted screens, and sulphur from volcanoes — from which the Chinese made gunpowder. Cities like Osaka, Sakai, Hakata, and Nagasaki were soon filled with merchants and tradespersons, and with great trading and manufacturing guilds (*za*), the distant ancestors of today's multinational corporations.

THE COMING OF THE EUROPEANS

Soon all pleasure disappeared from Japan. In 1467, the Onin (*oh-neen*) War broke out. Its immediate cause was a succession dispute in the shogunate, but other factors had been at work for a long time. The war lasted ten years and tore the country apart. When the war ended, almost sixty separate principalities had claimed independence, and as each one strove to conquer the others, fighting began anew. The next century in Japanese history is called the Sengoku Period, or the "Period of a Country at War," and it was in this chaotic world that the first Western explorers and missionaries appeared.

The first Europeans to reach Japan were the Portuguese, who found the Japanese friendly, civilized, and eager to acquire European knowledge of firearms and ships. The Japanese paid generously, in silver, to acquire Portuguese clothes and guns, as well as the silks and other luxury goods the explorers had acquired in China. One sea captain, Jorge Alvares, who visited Kagoshima in southern Kyushu in 1547, wrote with enthusiasm about all things Japanese, describing the beauty of the country and the abundance of exotic fruits and flowers. Alvares took some Japanese to Goa (in India) to meet the missionary St. Francis Xavier, and there, they became the first converts to Christianity. Xavier, intrigued by the accounts of Japan, travelled there in 1549 and in his first year, succeeded in baptizing 150 converts. Soon however, everywhere Xavier went, he encountered proud daimyo, the supreme samurai lords of each principality, who were more interested in having Portuguese ships protect their valuable cargoes from the China trade than in hearing about God, or *Deus*, as the missionaries called him. Regrettably for them, the word "deus" was rendered in Japanese as *dai-uso*, which meant "Great Lie."

The so-called Christian Century in Japan ended in failure. By about 1580, Japan was at a turning point. A few major daimyo had consolidated their power, and ruled domains as large and as populous as some European countries. A sense of nationhood was well-developed. All Japanese spoke the same language, practised the same customs, communicated freely with each other, held many of the same religious values, and the powerless emperors and shoguns were the symbols of unity.

Review...Recall...Reflect

1. How was Japan able to resist the massive seaborne invasion launched by the Mongols?

2. Explain why the Ashikaga shogunate represented the lowest and bleakest point for the Sun-line.

3. Why did the Japanese at first welcome Europeans and allow Christianity into Japan, and then later expel all foreigners and kill many of the Christian converts?

History Continues to Unfold

In 1573, the War of Unification began. Three great daimyo, each building upon the work of his predecessor, brought the country together, and in 1600, after the crucial Battle of Sekigahara, the ultimate victor, Tokugawa Ieyasu (*toh-koo-gah-wah ee-ei-yah-soo*), moved the seat of government to Edo (present-day Tokyo), and established the final Japanese shogunate, the Tokugawa. It would endure until 1867.

Ieyasu and his successors brought to the country an era of total peace and order. They soon expelled all foreigners from the land, and crucified thousands of native Christian converts who had rebelled in 1638. Thereafter, no foreigner — not even shipwrecked sailors — would be allowed to live on Japanese soil. This was the beginning of Japan's Seclusion Policy. The feudal system was frozen and samurai rule was confirmed both in law and custom.

Japan would remain isolated from the rest of the world for the next 250 years. Only when the American Commodore Matthew Perry's black ships appeared in Tokyo Bay in July 1853, would the Land of the Divine be catapulted into the modern world.

Current Research and Interpretations

There are three new trends among scholars of pre-modern Japanese history. First, there is a turning away from the previous assertion of Japanese uniqueness and a new emphasis on Japan as part of an "East Asian world." Second, is a wide and growing interest in what one scholar has called "unheeded voices, winked-at lives": women, peasants, merchants, and clerics are at last making their appearance on the historical stage and greatly modifying the previously dominant and elitist view of Japanese history. Finally, there is a realization that Buddhism, Shinto, and folk religion played a far greater role in Japanese daily life than was previously suspected.

Chapter Review

Chapter Summary

In this chapter, we have seen:

- that several factors in the development of Japanese societies led to a unique and distinct culture
- that several major changes, including the influence of the Chinese and changes in who held authority, took place through the course of Japanese history
- how isolation led to a homogenous population in Japan and restricted the influx of ideas, disease, and goods from outside
- that women's significant influence in the political life of Japan took many forms

Reviewing the Significance of Key People, Concepts, and Events (Knowledge/Understanding)

1. Understanding the long and rich history of ancient Japan requires a knowledge of the following concepts and events, and an understanding of their significance in the development of Japanese civilization. In your notes, identify and explain the historical significance of three from each column.

People	Concepts/Places
Jimmu	Shinto
Pimiko	Sun-line
Prince Shotoku	Nara
Empress Suiko	Cult of Beauty
Empress Koken	shogun
Murasaki Shikibu	samurai
Minamoto Yoritomo	Zen Buddhism
Tomoe	Bushido Code
St. Francis Xavier	

2. In many ways, geography defined the character of Japanese culture. From its temperate climate to the isolation of its islands, Japan developed a unique society in response to its geographic features. On the graphic organizer "Geography's Influence" in your *World History Handbook*, note three significant ways in which Japan's geography shaped its culture.

3. Copy and complete the following chart in your notes. This will provide you with a quick reference to the major periods in Japanese history.

Period	Years	Defining Features/Accomplishments
Formative Period		
Nara Period		
Heian Period		
Kamakura Shogunate		
Ashikaga Shogunate		
Tokugawa Shogunate		

Doing History: Thinking About the Past (Thinking/Inquiry)

1. To what degree was Shintoism a reflection of the close relationship between the Japanese and nature? Can elements of this close relationship with nature be seen throughout Japanese history? Respond to these questions by first formulating a clear and concise thesis, and then defending the thesis in two or three paragraphs. Transfer the most important ideas to the graphic organizer "Religion's Influence on Political Structures" in your *World History Handbook*.

2. In your opinion, did the Cult of Beauty reflect a highly advanced and complex civilization or an unhealthy obsession with appearance and an attempt to mask an essentially violent warrior culture? Formulate a clear and concise thesis, and then write two to three paragraphs in response to this question.

Applying Your Learning (Application)

1. By the fourteenth century, Japan was a land of striking contrasts. On the one hand, it was a violent culture whose warriors were highly trained and skilled in the art of killing. Yet at the same time, beauty was highly valued, and the arts were embraced by even the most militaristic in society. Prepare a poster/collage of images from Japan during the Ashikaga shogunate that reflects this dramatic contrast.

2. Imagine you are among the first Europeans to visit Japan during the sixteenth century. Write a diary entry explaining the three central elements of the Bushido Code, and explain your reaction as a Western observer to this code.

Communicating Your Learning (Communication)

1. Prepare a list of five questions you would ask a samurai. For each question, write a 50- to 75-word response you might receive from the samurai.

2. Create a line graph to illustrate the changing role of women in Japanese society. On the vertical axis, use a scale of 100, with 0 representing a total absence of rights or participation in society, and 100 representing full equality and participation in society. On the horizontal axis, plot a time line of Japanese history from 300 BCE to 1600 CE. Label the peaks and valleys, and provide brief notes where appropriate. Transfer the main ideas to the graphic organizer "Women's Roles in Society" in your *World History Handbook*.

Unit Review

Grading the Civilizations

1. In Chapter One, the essential elements of a civilization were outlined and you were asked to rank in order of importance each of the elements. Now that you have had an opportunity to study these civilizations in depth, apply your ranking to see how they measure up. Below are three broad categories under which the elements can be clustered. For each category, provide a letter grade (from A+ to F) and an anecdotal comment of three to five sentences to support the grade. You can complete a fuller assessment of the civilization selected using your *World History Handbook*.

	Letter Grade	Comments
The Place of People • level of equality • just laws • distribution of wealth • overall quality of life		
Organization of Society • democratic • effective government • meets needs of society • provides security and stability for society		
Lasting Legacy • ideas • works of art • architecture • innovations/inventions • literature		

The Role of Individuals in History

1. Historians often grapple with whether history is shaped by individuals, or if individuals are products of their age and thus shaped by history. Would the history of ancient Mesopotamia have been different if there had been no Hammurabi? Did Imhotep change the direction of Egyptian history? Below is a list of people mentioned in this unit. Select any two. For each, identify his or her role in society, major accomplishments, sphere of greatest impact (e.g., art, ideas, religion, politics), and why you believe the person shaped or was shaped by history. You may want to do additional research on the two individuals you select.

Buddha	Lao Zi	Pimiko
Ashoka	Shi Huangdi	Prince Shotoku
Kanishka	Wudi	Empress Suiko
King Harsha	Sui Wendi	Lady Murasaki Shikibu
Chingghis Khan	Empress Wu	Minamoto Yoritomo
Akbar	Khubilai Khan	
Confucius	Zheng He	

Understanding Chronology

1. The study of history relies on a sound understanding of the order in which events occurred. Without a clear understanding of how history has unfolded, it is difficult to see the relationships between earlier events and later developments. The following questions help to illustrate the importance of understanding the chronology:

   a) If you were studying the history of China and Japan, which would you study first? Why?

   b) How has the recent work done by archaeologists and historians altered the role the Aryan peoples were believed to have played in the decline of the Indus Valley civilization? How does this reflect the importance of understanding chronology in the study of history?

   c) The year 552 CE is seen as one of the most important dates in the history of Japan. Why is understanding the changes that occurred around this date crucial to understanding Japanese history?

Cause and Effect in History

1. History involves the study of cause and effect. We often find that one cause has several effects, or that several causes lead to one effect. Complete the cause and effect diagrams provided by your teacher. Once you have completed both diagrams, use one as a guide to writing a paragraph on the issue addressed.

UNIT FIVE

The Americas

chapter 12
The Maya

chapter 13
The Aztecs

chapter 14
The Inca

This figure of a Maya war captain in full regalia is from a procession scene found among the mural paintings at Bonampak, Chiapas, Mexico.

The three chapters in this unit explore in depth the Maya, Aztec, and Inca civilizations. In each chapter, the history of their rise to dominance is followed by an examination of the social, political, and religious structures that framed these civilizations. While each of the cultures was unique, they all faced a similar devastating fate: the arrival of Europeans. With no immunity to the diseases they brought, and unprepared for the greed and aggressiveness of the Spanish, the Maya, Aztecs, and Incas were all quickly overwhelmed. Yet, Maya and Incan culture survives throughout Central America and the Andes, and beneath Mexico City lies the remains of the once-great Aztec city, Tenochtitlán.

UNIT EXPECTATIONS:

In this unit, you will:

O come to understand the development of different forms of communities in the Americas to the sixteenth century

O identify forces that tend to promote and facilitate change and those that reinforce stability and continuity

O develop an understanding of the relationship between individuals, groups, and authority in different societies and periods to the sixteenth century

O analyze the development and diversity of social structures in various regions of the Americas

O draw conclusions based on effective evaluation of sources, analysis of information, and awareness of diverse historical interpretations

0   3000km

The Americas

CHAPTER TWELVE

The Maya

CHAPTER EXPECTATIONS

By the end of this chapter, you will be able to:

- identify the forces that led the Maya to choose their particular form of social organization

- identify the forces that tended to promote change, and those that tended to reinforce stability and continuity throughout Maya history

- demonstrate an understanding of the bases of authority in Maya society prior to the sixteenth century

- evaluate the influence of religion on the political structure of the ancient Maya

The pyramid of the Maya god Kulkulcan at Chichén Itzá (tenth–twelfth century). At the top is a temple to Quetzalcoatl, and to the left is the figure of a standard bearer.

M aya — mention the name and most people would imagine the ruined temples of a mysterious, lost civilization hidden in the jungles of Central America. This image arises from the popular media, not from historians and archaeologists. But too often, the studies carried out by archaeologists and other specialists have made the ancient Maya seem remote from today's world, and from the living Maya who carry the proud heritage of their ancestors. In this chapter, you will encounter a blend of information derived from archaeology, early Spanish records, and studies of the modern Maya. These will place the achievements of the people where they rightly belong: among the foremost in the story of humankind's great trek through the ages.

Many of the ancient cities of the Maya are enveloped in dense tropical forest, but the land in which they achieved so much — and where their descendants continue to dwell — is not all hot, green, and wet. Its diverse forms and resources shaped many different aspects of ancient Maya life.

KEY WORDS

Yucatán Peninsula

Chichén Itzá

Teotihuacán

Spanish Conquest

Cenote of Sacrifice

KEY PEOPLE

Maya

Spaniards

VOICES FROM THE PAST

Then the face of the sun was eaten; then the face of the sun was darkened; then its face was extinguished.

Maya inscription about a solar eclipse that occurred just before the Spaniards arrived.

TIME LINE: THE MAYA

	ca. 1700 BCE	First recognizable Maya culture emerges
Growth within Maya society and the development of government structures	ca. 800 BCE	
	ca. 1 CE	Maya city-states develop throughout the Maya highlands and lowlands
Classic Period begins with rapid growth of cities and large-scale public architecture	ca. 250 CE	
	ca. 300 CE	Development of a calendar, mathematics, and a writing system
Peak of building large-scale public architecture	ca. 550 CE	
	ca. 900–925	Decline of the Maya Classic Period
Christopher Columbus explores the Bay of Honduras	1502	
	1511	First documented meeting of Europeans and the Maya
First Spanish conflicts with the Maya	1521	
	1544	Spain controls the Yucatán, but never completely subdues the Maya people

GEOGRAPHY AND HISTORY OF THE MAYA WORLD

Geography

The **Maya** world can be divided into two general zones. The first, and less well-known archaeologically, is the highlands. The great granite and volcanic Sierra Madre mountains extend down the western side of the Mexican state of Chiapas, and through Guatemala into Honduras. In its plateaux, basins, and plains, the ancient Maya found rich land, abundant water, and many other natural resources. In such places, they concentrated their settlements, but they also made use of every part of the rugged land.

The second zone, the lowlands, consists of two parts. On the west, bordering the Pacific Ocean, lies a plain made fertile by erosion of the volcanic mountains behind it. The ancient population was large throughout the plain — an area that has still experienced little archaeological investigation. The rest of the lowland area, east of the mountains, is the most familiar part of the Maya lands. The vast Caribbean tropical lowlands of the **Yucatán Peninsula** (the modern Mexican states of Campeche, Yucatán, and Quintana Roo, and the country of Belize) and the Guatemalan Petén contain most of the famous ancient Maya cities, and have become centres for tourism. Here, more than anywhere else in the territory of the Maya, the land, forest cover, and resources vary tremendously. Surprisingly, one of the highly variable resources in this tropical setting is water.

Perhaps more than anything else, water supply dictated the locations of most Maya lowland communities. In the Guatemalan and southern Yucatán Peninsula rain forests, the river valleys are naturally attractive sources of water and rich agricultural soil in a region where most of the earth is thin and poor. The Maya made settlement possible throughout the forests by modifying natural sinkholes and building reservoirs where there was no surface water. They also employed many ingenious methods of irrigation and soil improvement. The situation was much more critical in the north, which has extremely poor soils and neither rivers nor the high rainfall of the south. Though its barrenness today is partly the result of eighteenth- and nineteenth-century cultivation, it has always been a sparsely forested place. In its eastern section, the

■ The Maya World

This map shows important sites of Maya Civilization. How did the availability of water affect the settlement pattern of the Maya?

Maya used natural and excavated caverns (*cenotes*) to reach the water table and thus make life bearable, but in the hilly west, no such solution was possible. The Maya found ways to live here, nevertheless, and developed as rich a culture as they enjoyed elsewhere.

TIME FRAMES
MAYA TIME PERIODS

Pre-Classic Period 600 BCE to 300 BCE

Classic Period 300 CE to 900 CE

Post-Classic Period 900 CE to 1300 CE

History of the Maya

The Maya did not, as far as we know, use their complex writing system to record history as it is defined today, or to set down the daily events of their lives. Furthermore, the history of their civilization had undergone a great deal of upheaval before the first Europeans arrived, and most of what remained disappeared quickly under Spanish rule. Without a written Maya record of past events, for information on every part of ancient Maya life we must depend on two sources: archaeological evidence and early Spanish colonial (sixteenth and seventeenth century) documents. Neither is in itself sufficient to give a clear picture of how the Maya lived, and the two often disagree. Furthermore, many aspects of a society's life are unlikely to be recorded by a conquering people. Just as many, or more, things leave no traces in the ground. As a result, there are holes in our knowledge of many features of Maya life. We do know about many things in the Maya past, nevertheless, and there are many more about which we can make intelligent guesses despite the years and cultural differences that separate their time from ours.

Archaeological work in the Maya world began a little more than a hundred years ago, when scholars set out to explore, record, and, sometimes, excavate sites in Mexico and Guatemala. After this period of initial exploration, which lasted until early in the twentieth century, came the first scientific excavations in the 1920s. Like the explorations before them, they concentrated on large and famous sites such as **Chichén Itzá** in northern Yucatán, Uaxactun in Guatemala, and, to a lesser extent, the sites of Palenque and Copán. The modern era of Maya archaeology began in the 1950s, and our understanding of ancient events in the Maya world has grown tremendously since then. Today, more archaeologists and historians are at work on the story of the ancient Maya than at any time in the past. Yet, we are losing irreplaceable information as each day passes — looters, who outnumber the archaeologists by as much as twenty to one, plunder sites in order to sell artifacts to collectors.

[THE GROWTH OF EMPIRE
Government and Law

The use of one name for all the people who lived in the Maya area suggests that the Maya were united under a single system of government. They never recognized themselves as one people, however, although there were many things besides language (Mayan) that bound them together. If you could ask an ancient Maya to identify the group to which he or she belonged, the answer would probably be the name of a city and the territory it controlled. Each major Maya settlement was a city-state with its own ruler who controlled many surrounding towns and villages and acknowledged no central, higher authority.

Even though the Maya had no king or emperor, our own experience leads us to expect that there would have been regional capital cities. In fact, at any given moment, some cities were more powerful politically — and, probably, militarily — than others. Alliances between communities also increased the focus of power, and at times, a single city's power extended over large areas and involved the subjugation of several other major city-states. Except for a brief period not long before the Spaniards arrived, at no time did a single city dominate the Maya world. The importance of cities grew and shrank as circumstances changed, and some places that were early great centres were abandoned just as others were gaining prominence. Many of the truly important discoveries about ancient Maya life have come from small, seemingly insignificant communities — sometimes on the fringes of the Maya land.

The sharing of language and religious beliefs, as well as a great many aspects of technology, gave all Maya city-states some similarity. It is very likely that the importance of religion in government made political organizations similar too, but we know very little about variations among Maya communities. A large part of the energy of every group went into communal work, especially building, which was controlled by the ruler, his courtiers, and other members of the elite. How far did such control extend? One thing is clear: the rulers of the city-states had far more power over their people than we would probably have found bearable had we been Maya.

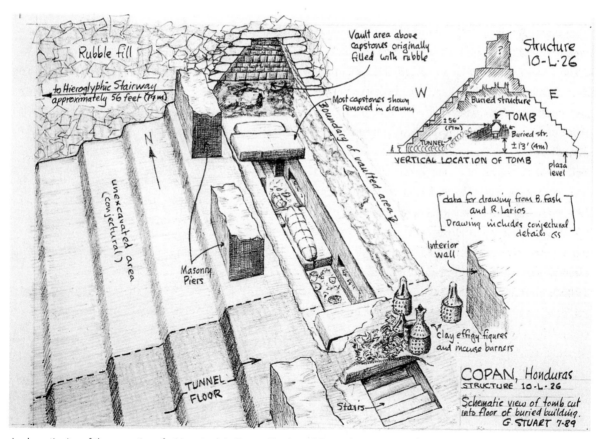

A schematic view of the excavation of a Maya tomb in Copán, Honduras. What is the main reason for making such a detailed and precise map of the area being uncovered?

The Rise to Dominance

The origins of Maya civilization lie hidden deep beneath the great ruined cities, and in tiny villages concealed by the forest. We do not know what led the first people to enter the area, probably long before the first recognizable Maya culture emerged about 1500 to 1700 BCE. Neither do we know where they came from, or what language they spoke. We can be sure, however, that the earliest settlers lived simply, probably by mixing agriculture with hunting and gathering. At this stage they possessed few, or none, of the attributes that their descendants developed into the greatest of the many high cultures in the ancient Americas.

As agricultural abilities improved and population grew, the Maya spread throughout the land — not as conquerors displacing earlier inhabitants, but rather, as the first to make use of a difficult and forbidding part of the world. With the spread, in what archaeologists call the Pre-Classic Period, came growth in community size: villages evolved into towns, then cities, and, finally, city-states. Development did not proceed at the same rate everywhere, but by about one CE most features of Maya society had appeared in the city-states throughout the region. By 250 to 300 CE, the time of greatest city growth, what archaeologists term the Classic Period had begun.

Religion was at the heart of the development of Maya communities, and the driving force behind every aspect of life. It was especially important in the growth of cities because, as religious practice became increasingly complex, the demand for temples and related buildings grew. In small villages, whether at the beginning of Maya prehistory or in later times, temporary or household shrines might have served the gods perfectly well, but as the population swelled and wealth was accumulated, the building of temples — first in wood and thatch, and then in stone — became an almost constant activity. Out of this activity, came cities with many great stone buildings at their core, and an increasing demand on the people for the labour to build and maintain them.

Together with the physical development of cities, came many changes in technology, including production of elaborate carved stone monuments (stelae) that showed rulers in elaborate costume, accompanied by texts that told of their lineage and accomplishments. Like the construction of civic buildings and the many other tasks that were central to Classic Maya life, the making of stelae required much time and effort. Labour demands on the people grew heavier as community size, temple size, and the general complexity of life increased during the Classic Period. It may be, in fact, that this huge need for labour, as much as anything else, brought the Classic Period to an end in the southern lowlands of Guatemala and Belize by about 900 to 925 CE.

What is usually called the "collapse" of the Classic Period is probably the most widely known episode in the Maya story. Foreign invasion, soil

Scripts & Symbols λ μ ν ο π θ υ ρ σ τ υ ϖ ω ξ ψ ζ α β χ ε δ φ γ

The longest Maya inscription is on the stairway of the pyramid at Copán. There are some 2500 carved hieroglyphs on the 63 stairs, many of which have yet to be deciphered.

Large carved stone figures such as these, at Palenque, adorned many Maya buildings. Such figures can also be valuable sources of information about their builders.

exhaustion, disease, and famine have all been suggested as causes. Most authorities now believe that although these might have contributed to the collapse in some places, the primary causes lay within Maya society itself. Top-heavy government, increasingly unbearable burdens on common people, and the growing isolation of rulers from those they governed very likely made Maya communities vulnerable to decay. Because there was no central government, there was no one date when all city-states died. The process was gradual, having started in some communities before 800 CE, for different reasons in each case. The ultimate result was general upheaval in politics and economy throughout the southern lowlands — only a very few communities managed to survive.

The fall of the great political and economic capital of **Teotihuacán**, in central Mexico, early in the eighth century likely helped set the stage for the Maya collapse. The event made life unstable over a very large region, and its shockwaves swept into the Maya area as well. At its strongest, Maya society, conservative and deeply religious as it was, might well have survived the unrest. In their weakened condition, however, most of the southern city-states fell into decline and were gradually abandoned.

The decline and fall did not occur in every Maya community. Life in the highlands and on the Pacific coast had followed different paths throughout the Classic Period, and continued to do so in the tenth century and afterward. In the northern part of the Yucatán Peninsula, and — we now know — in a few centres in the southern lowlands, life went on through all of what archaeologists call the Post-Classic period. Society changed in many ways, and technology — including the kinds and sizes of civic buildings constructed — changed as well. Yet, Maya religious beliefs and many other important aspects of their culture stayed largely intact.

The southern lowland communities that survived somehow managed to stay alive as islands of calm in a sea of trouble, while most of the great Classic centres fell into decay. Nevertheless, the archaeological record of life in these communities, as in city-states farther north, indicates that the Post-Classic period was not a time of decline and decadence. It was actually a rich and vibrant period with its own identity. People clung to the old while they moved toward the new, and probably enjoyed greater freedom and lower labour demands. The catastrophes of the tenth century altered people's lives everywhere in the Maya area, but in many cases, changes were very likely for the better rather than the worse.

The Classic collapse and the events of the following centuries meant that the **Spaniards** who arrived in the area in the 1520s and afterwards did not witness Maya culture in its most elaborate form. The early colonial documents tell us more about life in the Post-Classic period — as seen by Europeans whose aim was to impose their rule on the indigenous people — than they can tell us about what went before. Still, they show that the Maya culture encountered by the Spaniards, though less complex in some ways than in earlier times, was still as alive, evolving, and exciting as it had been centuries before.

❙ BELIEFS

Maya Mythology

Although the Maya built a vast and complex physical environment around themselves, they remained conscious of the natural world that lay beyond. As a result, much of their mythology focused on forces in nature, both positive and negative. Only a few tales from a once-rich mythology have survived intact from ancient times. Yet, a great many modern Maya continue to believe in the power of natural elements to help or harm, and can recite stories that are evidence of that power. Animals with human abilities appear in such stories, sometimes mingled with gods and bits of real history from the early years of the **Spanish Conquest**. Although, today the tales lie outside the Christianity introduced by the Spaniards, in times past, such stories were part of a formal religion that taught that the environment, whether on Earth, in the sea, or in the heavens, was the home of deities whose favour had to be constantly sought if communities were to survive.

Organized Religion

Religion was the main engine that drove Maya culture. It determined most of the shape of city centres and laid down the rules for much of what happened there. It lay behind the organization and control of

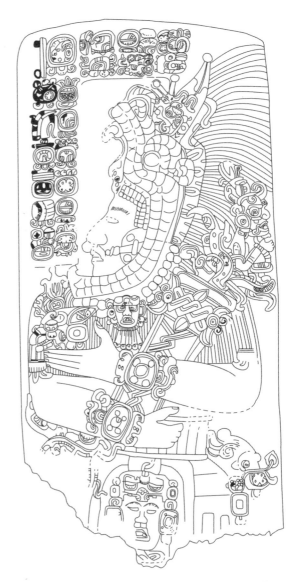

The stela drawn here is of a Maya ruler named "smoking shell." His serpent headdress is decorated with the faces of various gods. What other information might these sculptures provide?

The History of the Imagination: Myths and Legends

The Quiché Creation Myth

And the creation of all the four-footed animals and the birds being finished, they were told by the Creator and the Maker and the Forefathers: "Speak, cry, warble, call, speak each one according to your variety, each according to your kind." So was it said to the deer, the birds, pumas, jaguars, and serpents. . . but they could not make them speak like men; they only hissed and screamed and cackled; they were unable to make words, and each screamed in a different way. When the Creator and the Maker saw that it was impossible for them to talk to each other, they said: "It is impossible for them to say our names, the names of us, their Creators and Makers. This is not well," said the Forefathers to each other. Then they said to them: "Because it has not been possible for you to talk, you shall be changed. We have changed our minds: Your food, your pasture, your homes, and your nests you shall have; they shall be in the ravines and the woods, because it has not been possible for you to adore us or invoke us. There shall be those who adore us, we shall make other beings who shall be obedient."

Activities

1. What were the "other beings" the Creator and Maker decided to make?

2. Why and how do you think this myth might have been created?

Some of the creatures made by the Creator and Maker: a monkey, a jaguar, and others that appear to be combinations of animals.

labour for communal construction, and dictated smaller-scale alterations of houses as well. In the countryside, religion established the schedule for agricultural work and for rituals performed both in the villages and the fields. In every setting, religion spoke of a great variety of gods who needed appeasing. The gods ranged from Kinich Ahau, the sun god — one of the principal deities — to other heavenly figures such as Ix Chel (Venus). There were natural forces such as Chac, the rain god, and creatures of nature such as Balam the jaguar and Zotz the bat. Each had special powers, and there were special periods in which those powers became all-important.

All the gods were recognized throughout the Maya world, and some were worshipped everywhere, though probably not in quite the same way in all communities. Other gods were of limited importance overall, but might have served as the patron deities (guardian gods) for specific city-states, as the crocodile did for *Lamanai* (*Lama'an/ayin*, meaning "submerged crocodile") in Belize. The power of such deities may have risen and fallen as the fortunes of their special cities shifted, whereas that of the major gods remained perpetually great. Maya religion spoke in varying ways to the people in different times and places, but it always spoke of the gods in an elaborate framework of time.

Because the reckoning of time was critical to their religious practice, it has often been said that the Maya worshipped time. That characterization is often employed to portray the Maya as strange and very different from ourselves. Yet, if someone from another time and place were to compare an ancient Maya with a modern North American, whom would they see wearing a device that tells time to the second and gives the hour of the day in various cities around the world?

The Maya method of reckoning time, like many aspects of their religion, was so complex that it was understood by only a few people in each community. The existence of a calendar allowed priests, led by the ruler, to predict eclipses and other celestial events. In this way, it gave real authority to priests' warnings of doom, and to their orders for offerings of food and other things to prevent disaster. Because the Maya concept of time revolved around cycles, the calendar also made it possible to fix appropriate times for the temple rebuilding that was the greatest undertaking in Maya cities — and at the very core of religious belief and practice.

The Temple of the Sun at Palenque, shown here, includes a tower (on the right) that was used for making astronomical observations. Knowledge of astronomy was essential to the Maya reckoning of time.

Besides all its other functions, the calendar also set the times when the priests and the ruler offered up their own blood to the gods. Because the Sacred Well, or **Cenote of Sacrifice**, at the northern Yucatan site of Chichén Itzá is famous as a site of human sacrifice, most people believe that the practice was a major aspect of Maya religion. In fact, the offering of blood was the most important activity throughout ancient Maya times. Human sacrifice was rare or non-existent in most communities throughout the Classic Period, and only became common once the northern Yucatán Maya had come under Mexican influence in the Post-

Classic. Then people — old and young, male and female — were cast into the *cenote* (a natural cavern), with the intention that they act as messengers to the gods. Had the Maya of earlier times been able to witness such sacrifices, they would possibly have found them horrific, and concluded that their descendants had gone seriously wrong.

In addition to blood sacrifice, continual temple reconstruction was a mainstay of Maya religion. To the Maya, temples (and, perhaps, other civic buildings as well) seem to have been living things, with life cycles like those of human beings. The temples were avenues of communication with the gods, and if they were to serve this purpose, they had to be kept alive through periodic small changes or complete rebuilding over the existing structure. Because the midline of each temple was the main lifeline to the gods, rebuilding could not include a shift to a new spot, and, generally, could not involve complete destruction of the aging building. So, Maya temples had to grow on the same spots over time, both upward and outward. Each change made possible the ceremonies that permitted the ruler and priests to hear the voices of the gods, and thus to receive guidance that would keep the community alive; to be deaf to the voices was to invite disaster.

Temples served as great theatre settings for processions and ceremonies. Plazas in front of the buildings were places where commoners could witness such activities. The ceremonies were, like the buildings themselves, designed to be remote from the average person and to inspire awe and fear. In this respect, a temple and its accompanying plaza can be seen as very like the medieval cathedrals of Europe. Both were designed as an expression of belief, and raised to the heavens not only for the glory of a deity, but also to convey a clear message to the worshippers. Few witnesses of a ceremony on a

Maya temple could have failed to be convinced by the great show that the gods were all-powerful, all-seeing, and highly likely to stamp out the entire community unless kept well-fed and happy. The ability of the priests to speak to the gods and transmit their messages was obvious, and their knowledge of time and its measurement must have been awe-inspiring in itself.

Review...Recall...Reflect

1. Describe the two geographical zones of the Maya world.

2. Describe the political organization of the Maya world and the features that were common among those we call the Maya.

3. Explain two possible reasons for the end of the Maya Classic Period.

Morals and Values

The importance of religion in Maya life created very strong systems of morals and values. Spanish priests who wrote about Maya life judged things in European terms, and were mostly concerned with recording what they saw as pagan practices they felt had to be overcome by the spread of Christianity. A little of the Mayas' morality and some of their values do emerge from the pages of Spanish documents. In our eyes — and, probably, for the ancient Maya as well — the most important element in their moral and value systems was the view of their role in the world around them. This view seems to have been at the heart of Maya philosophy. It set the tone for much religious activity, and, probably, daily life as well. The Maya saw themselves as simply one part of a unified world, what we today would call a single ecosystem — they did not control nature, but, rather, dealt with the environment respectfully and atoned for wrongs committed. Respect and atonement were expressed in religious rituals that are still carried out in many parts of the Maya area. This philosophical viewpoint did not produce the sort of conservationist attitude held in our world today because, if one sinned against nature, it was possible to wipe away the sin through prayer and offering.

SOCIAL HISTORY OF THE MAYA
The Roles of Men and Women

Until about a quarter-century ago, most Maya archaeological work was undertaken by men, and men wrote most of the history of the Maya. Because of this, Maya society was interpreted as male-dominated. As a result, it is difficult to sort out information about men's and women's roles in Maya society, and only very recently have intensive and extensive studies of gender roles in ancient Maya life begun. Even so, most objects excavated by archaeologists indicate little about how they were used, let alone whether they were used by men or women. We must depend on studies of the modern Maya, and, to a lesser extent, early colonial records, for much of our basic understanding of gender roles.

Whenever we describe a culture as a whole, we must refer to norms — what most people do most of the time — rather than individual activity. Although we accept that most household tasks were performed by women, we must not rule out the possibility that Maya men occasionally used a stone *mano* (roller) and *metate* (slab) to grind corn. Such deviations from the norm are almost a certainty in any culture, and happen because the woman of the house is ill or absent from the home for some other reason.

Males who wrote about Maya history once saw only kings among the rulers, but we now know that city-states were ruled by women too. In one instance, at the site of Lamanai, succession from a male ruler to a female — or, perhaps, in the reverse order — is strongly suggested by tomb evidence. Very elaborate tombs of female rulers have been encountered at Caracol, in Belize, and at Copán, and there are portraits of women on monuments from a number of sites. There are no portraits and texts on stelae that provide information on the kings and queens below the level of ruler. Were most architects male or female, or did neither sex dominate the profession? Did merchants include both men and women, and if

This sculpture shows the wife of a Maya lord making a blood sacrifice by pricking her tongue. This practice was common among upper class Maya women.

so, did women travel as widely as men to sell their goods to distant buyers? Were feather workers female and jade carvers male, or the other way round? Perhaps, some answers to these questions about gender roles in Maya life will, eventually, come from study of hieroglyphic texts, but for many aspects of life at this level, the questions may never be answered.

Social Structure

Maya social organization was a tightly knit multi-layered system. Parts of the organization seem to have been what we would call castes, which is to say that membership in them was hereditary and movement out of them was difficult if not impossible. For others, there appears to have been more freedom, including the ability to improve one's lot in life and to move from one community to another.

At the top of the society was a large and complex elite that included the ruler, the royal family and retainers, courtiers, priests, and anyone else who could claim a link with the community's leader. Some professional people, such as architects, formed part of the elite, as did higher-level merchants and others whose skills were used in the service of the ruler, or in ways that earned them high status in the community. Below them lay a variety of other specialists, artisans, and craftspeople, and probably managers and bureaucrats, especially in the late centuries of the Classic Period. Where movement from one group to another was allowed, it may have been made possible by talent, contacts, or just hard work. It is simplest to view this assemblage of groups as a middle class because, in some ways, it resembles the middle class in our own society. Its divisions were, however, more rigidly defined than ours, and movement upward — either within or beyond a group — was difficult.

Finally, beneath the middle class was a lower class made up of all the providers of services needed to make a city run. The situation was rendered more complicated by the fact that labourers were brought in from surrounding communities to work on temples and other civic buildings. We are forced almost entirely to guess about their lives, because such people are virtually hidden in the archaeological record; very few lower-class houses, and no labourers' quarters, have been identified in Maya sites.

Social Customs and Festivals

Think back to the last non-religious festival you attended, and ask yourself what future archaeological evidence there would be of the event. The answer will, no doubt, be that most of what you experienced would be beyond an archaeologist's ability to recover from the ground. As a result, for the ancient Maya, we are forced to depend on depictions of festivals, and these are difficult to identify and interpret. There are quite a few scenes painted on Maya pottery vessels that have the look of festivals about them, and all are clearly religious or political.

As for customs, such as marriage ceremonies, we are unlikely to dig them up, or detect them in Maya art. The Maya are often portrayed as so bound up in religion that all customs were dictated by religious belief — all festivals were religious, all sports were dedicated to the gods, and all entertainment found at the festivals was of a religious nature. Excavations yield small pottery whistles — often in the shape of birds or other animals — that could have been used in religious activities, but also blown just for fun. Other musical instruments exist (including rasps, rattles, ocarinas, flutes, and conch-shell trumpets), and except for the trumpets — the shells were blown to summon the gods — all seem just as likely to have been for everyday entertainment as for ceremonies. It is undeniable that religious thinking was present everywhere in Maya life, but it could not have stifled all natural human impulses to lighten life with music, dance, song, and other activities that forgot the gods, if only for a few moments.

Review...Recall...Reflect

1. How were the lives of the Maya people affected by the decline of the Classic Period?

2. How is the importance of the natural world reflected in the beliefs of the Maya?

3. How did the Maya view of their relationship with the environment make them better caretakers of the earth than we generally have been?

Food and Drink

Accidents of preservation and studies of ancient pollen provide evidence of Maya vegetable foods, but we depend, for the most part, on animal bones from garbage heaps to tell us what the ancient Maya ate. We are still a long way from being able to describe or prepare a typical sixth-century Maya meal, though we know a bit more about food habits at the time of the Spanish Conquest. Except for items introduced by the Spanish or brought to the Maya area in more recent times, it is probably reasonable to take the food of the area today as a sample of what was enjoyed centuries ago.

The agricultural staples in the Maya diet were corn, beans of several varieties, and squashes that were probably eaten when very young but raised primarily for their seeds. Chilis — probably eaten with food, rather than cooked in it — flavoured the meal, and modern Maya cookery suggests that a

number of natural forest products spiced up the cook's work as well. Over 150 foods, including herbs and spices as well as important sources of nourishment, can be collected in the forests of the southern lowlands, and a smaller number come from the highland forests. These were probably always used to supplement agricultural produce, and they may have been of great importance in times of crop failure.

Corn preparation seems to have omitted the great Mexican and Central American food the tortilla until late in the Classic Period. It is difficult to imagine Maya cuisine without the tortilla, but corn can be made into many other nourishing dishes. The importance of the tortilla (for which the archaeological evidence is the *comal*, the clay griddle used to cook them) goes beyond its value as a bread. Treatment of the corn kernels with lime to produce a coarse flour adds calcium to the corn, which makes the combination of corn and beans an excellent source of complete protein, vital to health. In addition, the tortilla probably served in the past as it does today, as a container and a kind of spoon for many other foods.

The only domesticated food animal kept by the Maya was the ocellated turkey, a large bird quite different from the one we eat today. Deer were among the prized game, as were peccaries (small pigs) and armadillos, just as they are among the present-day Maya. Surprisingly though, the guinea pig-like agouti and paca, much enjoyed by Maya today, are not as evident in the ancient bone collections as one would expect. Some of the wild creatures that could have been eaten seem to have been generally avoided, presumably for religious reasons, but even the jaguar, very important in religion, may have been a food animal on rare occasions. Wherever possible, the Maya made as much use of fish and turtles as they do today, and there are even places where crocodile bones are common in garbage dumps. Lakes and rivers also yielded snails that were eaten in great quantities. Those who lived near bodies of water probably strengthened their economies by trading dried fish, turtle meat, and snails to other communities.

What did the Maya drink? Based on modern Maya life, we can be reasonably certain that various concoctions of ground corn sweetened with honey were used in ancient times. From Spanish records, as well as modern evidence, we also know that *balche*, a fermented drink made from honey and tree sap, was available for religious use, if not for everyday consumption. The Maya grew cacao, from which

This small terracotta figure (36.5 cm) found in a tomb appears to be of a drunken old man. He is clutching two bottles and looks unsteady on his feet. The Maya did prepare a fermented drink called *balche*.

they produced chocolate in a form that we would recognize, although it was far from the rich, sweet drink of today. Traces of cacao in cups and bowls, as well as ancient references to it written on the vessels, tell us how important chocolate was in Maya ceremonial life. Beyond this, cacao was used as an addition to other foods, and the beans came to be valued — at least in the centuries just before the Spaniards arrived — as currency for high-level trade. Cacao did not provide them with cups of hot chocolate on cool nights, but the ancient Maya did enjoy sweet drinks and foods, though with a sweet tooth far less developed than our own.

Although the range of ancient Maya foods was great, it would be wrong to conclude that all the foodstuffs appeared on every individual's plate. In Maya society, those of highest rank got the largest share of the most-desirable items. In some sites, refuse piles near the residences of rulers and other elite contain almost all the deer bone, all the large turtles, and much of the other favoured game. It has been suggested that the taller stature of most rulers is partly a reflection of better diet; whether this is true or not, it is clear that people with power lived better than those beneath them.

Cross-cultural Influences

It is highly probable that the Maya were borrowers from the beginning, and obtained their knowledge of the calendar — and at least part of their writing system — from earlier peoples on Mexico's Gulf Coast. Throughout their history, they maintained contact with other peoples, both to the north and to the south, exchanging ideas just as they traded material goods. It would be a mistake to think of the Maya as isolated by their environment, forbidding though the jungle and mountains may seem. In addition to moving goods into and out of the region, their far-flung trading networks also served as information networks, whether officially or simply because every traveller picked up gossip along the way.

MAYA LITERATURE AND ART

Literature

As the Western world understands the term, no literature is known to have existed in ancient Maya culture. The Maya produced many books, but the folded bark paper specimens that have survived are all religious and have to do with astronomical events, deities, and predictions of the future. We do know, however, that books or documents of other forms and materials were used by the Maya. There is also indirect evidence that both bark paper and a kind of parchment (animal skin) were used for other purposes. For example, in blood-offering rituals, paper strips soaked in blood were placed in bowls and burned. With so much paper in use, the possibility exists that someone set thoughts down in a form that we would identify as literary. One day, we may recover such a volume from an ancient tomb, or even a residence.

Although they are not literature as we would define it, the many texts that adorn monuments, buildings, jade and bone objects, and pottery form a very significant body of writing, much of it with some historic content. The Maya obviously thought of all types of record keeping as parts of a single process since they used the same word for writing, painting, and carving.

Architecture

Of all the objects created by the Maya, the largest and most striking are their buildings. Though damaged or reduced to ruins by the effects of tropical rains and forest growth, Maya buildings remain evidence of the ability of the ancient people to design, build, and maintain structures as complex as any in the ancient world. The buildings differ from site to site; the Temple of the Inscriptions at Palenque seems almost totally unlike Temple I at Tikal, which, in turn, is very different from Temple B-4 at Altun Ha. Regional and community differences of these sorts are what one would expect in a city-state system, and almost every site contains unique buildings as well. Yet, no matter how different from one another the temples, palaces, and other buildings may be, they all share many basic features.

WEB CONNECTION

http://www.mcgrawhill.ca/links/echoes

Go to the site above to find out more about Maya art and architecture.

Maya buildings seem curious to some because they do not reflect the jungle environment by copying natural forms in stone, or in some other way "fitting into" their setting. With a few exceptions, the great temples are tall, angular structures that seem almost to have been built in defiance of their surroundings. They were raised as links with the world of the supernatural, and, probably, also as representations of the sacred mountain, an important element in Maya beliefs. The Maya were not unique, there are few places in the world where the architecture physically mirrors the environment. The more important question is whether or not the buildings are a sensible response to their environment. For the Maya, the answer is partly yes and partly no.

Maya architecture began with houses that were built of poles and thatch, set atop very low platforms. These buildings, as well as the first communal structures, were standardized quite early, and were excellent responses to the environment in two important ways. First, they made use of renewable resources that occurred naturally near most communities. Second, they were cool, weatherproof (as long as the roof had the proper pitch), and if not shaded by nearby trees, they lasted many years with very little maintenance. All of these characteristics can be found in traditional Maya houses to this day.

Problems arose in the ancient cities only when builders moved from poles and thatch to stone and mortar, a change that may have begun not long after communal architecture first appeared. Excavations have produced no direct evidence of the shift from thatch to stone, but we can envision the move as an attempt to make important buildings more permanent. The new stone temples sometimes held the graves of rulers and, occasionally, of others of high rank, but their main purpose was to provide settings for ceremonies. In use, as well as in form and construction, Maya temples and their platforms, though some would call them pyramidal, were very different from the great pyramids of Egypt.

To create the new type of building, the Maya used the soft limestone that was found in many parts of their land and was relatively easy to quarry and shape. Where this material was unavailable, they made use of granite, slate, or even river rocks, but still kept much of the shape and size that marked work in limestone. The permanent architecture grew to be an essential part of Maya religious life and a very visible part of a city centre. More and more material — and, therefore, more and more workers — were required to meet community needs. This was just one of the ways in which stone architecture was a dangerous departure from the simpler style — it meant increasingly heavier labour demands on the people.

The stone buildings retained many of the ideas that went into thatched structures. Their rooms had ceilings that resembled the undersides of thatched roofs, and copied, in non-functional form, some of the roof bracing. Doorways in both types of structure were, generally, about the same width, and both were usually placed in the long walls. The building sat atop a platform, though much higher in stone than it had been in the simpler thatched structures. The main environmental problem created by stone buildings was that they used a non-renewable resource. Limestone not only made up the facings, but also was burned to the produce mortar and the plaster

A reconstruction of the Classic Period pyramid at Copán. Building and rebuilding religious and civic architecture eventually put enormous stress on the common people of cities and ceremonial centres.

that coated building surfaces. On the other hand, the platforms were a partial solution to another kind of environmental problem. Because they were built of stone mixed with refuse collected around the city, in many cases, they served the Maya as a sort of aboveground sanitary landfill.

Almost from the first, the architects who designed civic buildings and the builders who created them must have recognized some of the problems that the new architecture created. The civic buildings were waterproof as far as room interiors were concerned, but were subject to damage from heavy rains that frequently rendered stairs and other parts of the structures unusable. The soil in platforms worked like a sponge, taking up water during the rainy season and losing it at other times, so plaster surfaces cracked and once-level surfaces tilted dangerously. Though the rooms were cool shelters from the tropical sun, it was much harder to close them against the wind and rain than was the case with pole-and-thatch buildings. As a result, much more human time and energy were required to keep the buildings in reasonable condition so that they could continue to serve as sets for religious ceremonies. It is a wonder that the buildings have survived as well as they have in spite of the fact that they were never the best response to a tropical environment.

Sculpture

Because they are so awesome in both size and carving, stelae are the best known examples of Maya sculpture. Other large-scale sculptural work, both in stone and in plaster, adorns many buildings, especially in the northern Yucatán, at Palenque in Chiapas, and at Copán in Honduras. The most numerous sculptures are, however, small portable works in stone, primarily jade. Jade was especially significant to the Maya because its green colour was associated with water and living plants and, so, with fertility. Pendants, beads, and other ornaments of jade were part of the dress of rulers and priests, and were often buried with them. Most large sculpture, and almost all the small work, depicts rulers (as on the stelae), deities, or individuals who are probably rulers costumed as gods. Yet, among the small works in stone are such things as a simple carving of a porter bearing a burden with a tumpline (headband) and numerous representations of animals. The uses of stelae are clear: they commemorate rulers, as do many of the carvings on building facades. Most of the small

This stela from Palenque, ca. seventh century, shows a figure in a pose of humility.

carvings were also linked with royalty, but some, even those of jade on rare occasions, are found in middle-class graves, where their uses and meanings are much less clear.

Painting

Maya buildings were not gleaming white; the exteriors of most were brightly painted, sometimes entirely in red but frequently (especially in later centuries) in a great many colours. Most such painting has disappeared with time, as have murals that once adorned building interiors. Only the most fortunate circumstances, often the result of the covering of one building by a later one, have preserved paintings partly intact. The best-known murals, from Bonampak in Chiapas, were saved for us to study and admire by an even rarer event — the growth of a thin coating of mineral over their surfaces. Elsewhere, we have only traces to show what once was there; the greatest body of evidence of Maya painting is preserved on pottery.

Out of a tradition of monochrome (single-colour) pottery, the Maya evolved two- and then three-colour pottery painting, with the occasional use of additional colours. The basic palette of red and black on an orange ground was used to depict rulers, gods, nobles, priests, and animals, both fanciful and real, almost always in scenes without perspective. Though limited in the range of colours, the paintings are also our largest source of information on Maya clothing, of which only the tiniest bits of textile have survived. Pottery figures, often made as whistles when small, or as incense burners in larger sizes, also show costumes. Although the painting of standard bowls and other vessels can, at times, seem rather stiff, Maya vase painting at its finest displays a handling of body proportions and a delicacy of line that rivals the best products of any ancient culture.

Maya temples were the settings for great processions and ceremonies meant to inspire awe and fear. These figures are musicians from the murals at Bonampak.

MAYA SCIENCE AND TECHNOLOGY

Medicine

It is probable that the folk remedies used by the Maya today come down from ancient times, but, in most cases, knowledge of medicinal plants and their uses cannot be traced back even to the early Spanish colonial period. As in any society, illness and injury were common among the Maya, and evidence of increased anemia in some communities in colonial times suggests that health was worsened by Spanish arrival in more ways than through the introduction of disastrously infectious European diseases. Evidence of the healing of broken bones shows that many people survived serious trauma, but setting of fractures is not clearly documented. The healing may, however, tell us that the Maya middle class, or perhaps the elite, included medical practitioners, but no doctor's home or kit of instruments has yet been found. We do know that the Maya possessed surgical skills and good knowledge of human anatomy. We can be sure that, like information on plant remedies, such knowledge was put to good use and passed down from generation to generation.

Discoveries and Inventions

Though clearly adept at the use of many simple aids to human muscle power such as levers, inclined planes, rollers, and wedges, the Maya are not known to have invented any major technological devices. The principal inventions they produced lay, instead, in the intellectual sphere: a calendric system, mathematics, and writing.

We have seen how the calendar affected so much of Maya life, and how important cycles were to its workings. The system, which was based — as all calendars must be — on very long periods of astronomical observation, remains one of the enigmas of the Maya past. The tropical lowlands are not well-suited to astronomical work, and even the possibility that the calendar was introduced in its basic form from the Mexican Gulf Coast does not avoid this problem. Beyond this there is the question of how anyone, having observed the moon's short cycle and concluded that other cycles might exist in the heavens, could have persuaded others to work for the tremendously long time needed to prove the existence of cycles, and then use the information to create a calendar. That this happened is beyond question, but how it happened may forever remain a mystery.

Maya mathematics involved the use of a concept known only to the Muslim world at the time, the principle of zero. In addition to the symbol for zero, the system, which was based on multiples of 20, used a bar for five and a dot for one. This would have been an impossibly cumbersome arrangement had the system not also used positions in the recording of unit counts (such as those in the calendar). Without this positional feature, a Maya

This circular sculpture (diameter 55 cm) shows a Maya ball player and around him the signs for various days and 20-day periods.

scribe could scarcely have found a writing surface large enough to hold a number above 1000. Besides their appearance in the calendar, number notations were clearly applied to measurements for building plans and to the other uses numbers have in any society. So, a good many people who knew nothing of the calendar probably were able to use written numerals. No architectural or other everyday mathematical calculations have yet been identified, though bar-and-dot numbers appear in carvings on stone and bone, and on many pottery vessels.

The Writing System

To write their language, the Maya created a complex hieroglyphic system that remained almost entirely undeciphered from its first reporting in Spanish colonial times until the 1980s. We have come to understand the basic elements of the system and many of its structural and grammatical elements, even though many hieroglyphs cannot yet be read, and new ones are still being discovered. The hieroglyphs, which include day and month names that have been understood for many decades, number in the hundreds, so it was clear that the system could not be alphabetic. In fact, it is both ideographic — meaning the hieroglyphs can stand for complete ideas — and phonetic, which means that the symbols convey sounds. Some of the ideas are known, but it is the phonetic aspect of the system that makes deciphering possible. Most writing occurs on stelae, buildings, portable jade sculptures, and pottery vessels, as well as in the few remaining books. We are now able either to read these or, at least, understand their meaning with reasonable certainty.

Ability to decipher the texts has told us much about the relations among city-states, and has changed our understanding of the information on stelae, as well as the reason for erecting these monuments. We now also have a picture of the workings of dynastic succession among the Maya. Perhaps most important, is the realization that not all texts are religious or political. Before the hieroglyphs could be read, archaeologists assumed that Maya writing was purely ceremonial, but now we know otherwise.

WEB CONNECTION http://www.mcgrawhill.ca/links/echoes
Go to the site above to find out more about the Mayan system of writing.

Recent research into Maya pottery has revealed that plates and bowls can now tell us where they were made — and, often, for whom. Sometimes, the texts identify the vessel as a gift from one community to the leader of another, and sometimes they speak of the circumstances of the gift. Perhaps most interesting of all, many vessels identify the contents they were intended to hold: chocolate, in the case of deeper vessels, and tamales (as a ceremonial gift of food for a ruler or noble) in the case of plates. More than other texts, those on pottery vessels give the ancient Maya a real voice, and bring them alive in a way that no one could have anticipated. The most revealing of all the aspects of the pottery texts is that many of the artists signed their work. There are now more signed vessels known from the ancient Maya world than from the world of the ancient Greeks, and the presence of the signatures tells us much

An eighth century ceramic vase showing the figure of a man holding up a large snake. Such objects provide much information about Maya clothing and customs, and even artists' names.

Pushing the Boundaries: Developments in Science and Technology

Maya Mathematics

Although we take the principle of zero for granted today, it is a facet of mathematics that required both investigation and discovery. The Maya were among the first peoples to acquire this knowledge. While no mathematical calculations have been identified, we presume that Maya mathematics was used for measurements, on calendars and to keep track of transactions.

Zero was represented by a specific symbol and was certainly necessary as a placeholder. Maya math was a *vigesimal* system (based on multiples of 20). The symbol for 1 was a dot and the symbol for 5 was a bar. Now try to imagine writing the number 1001. Actually, the system also used positions to record unit counts so that large numbers could be written quite simply. Here's 1001:

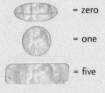

= zero

= one

= five

(2 units of 400)

(10 units of 20)

(1 unit of 1)

Here's another example, 411:

(1 unit of 400)

(0 units of 20)

(11 unit of 1)

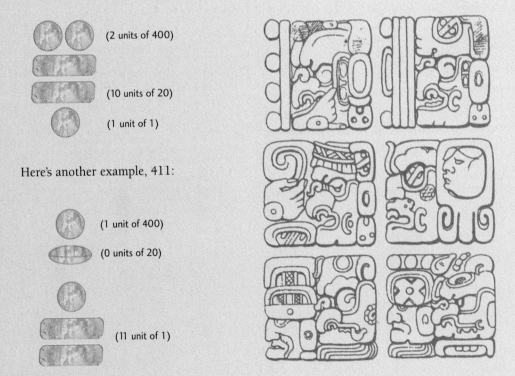

Five dots in any position convert to a bar in that same position, and four bars convert to a dot in the next higher position. The numbers can be read from top to bottom. The bottom symbol represents units of 1, the next symbol up represents units of 20, the symbol up from that is units of 400, and so on.

Here's one more example, 128:

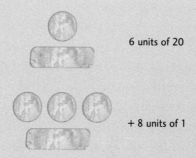

6 units of 20

+ 8 units of 1

Arithmetic was significant enough to the Maya that bar-and-dot numbers appear in stone and bone carvings and on pottery.

Activities

1. Measure your textbook and write the dimensions Maya-style.

2. Remembering that Maya writing was a hieroglyphic system, write your address as it could have appeared in the time of the ancient Maya.

about roles in Maya society. Instead of illiterate painters, the vessel artists emerge as people of high status — proud of their talent, and able to express that pride by including their signatures. To some, this suggests that the painters were nobles, as does the nature of some of the signatures, but it may also be that artists in ancient Maya times, like those of today, gained fame and standing in their communities through the ability to create beauty with a brush.

Review...Recall...Reflect

1. Why is it difficult to know, with certainty, the separate roles played by men and women in Maya society?

2. How did the diet of the elite of Maya society differ from that of the commoners?

3. Why was the development of stone architecture a dangerous departure from the earlier simple architecture?

THE MAYA ECONOMY
Trade Routes and Contacts

Natural resources varied greatly in the Maya area, and because of this, internal trade was the lifeblood of the society. Commodities such as dried fish and shellfish, shell for the manufacture of ornaments and tools, and stingray spines, coral, and sea fans for ceremonial use made their way from coastal communities, through the forest or up rivers, to inland centres. Down those same routes may have come hardwoods, pottery clays, obsidian (volcanic glass) obtained by inland communities through long-distance trade, and many other things unavailable on the coast. Often, we cannot be sure of

either the source or the direction from which an import came. Sometimes, however — as in the case of the goods from the ocean — the source can be pinpointed, and a specific route to inland centres can be suggested.

Countless examples exist of trade ties between Maya sites that involved very distinctive kinds of pottery, jades carved in specific regional styles, or even — at the level of ideas — architectural forms and techniques. Such evidence makes it clear that the land of the Maya must have hummed with activity — not only in each city-state, but also along endless trails travelled by porters (the Maya had no beasts of burden). To fuel this exchange, each community had to develop its own resources, both natural and human, to the fullest extent in order to provide materials and goods to pay for things that could not be obtained locally. Though the output of pottery at some sites reached very high levels, the Maya never adopted mass-production techniques. Their economy was based, from beginning to end, on small industries, organized and controlled at the first level by merchant-traders and, ultimately, by royalty.

The matter of trade in staple food supplies cannot be studied from the archaeological evidence, for nowhere do we have an entire community's foods preserved. We are unable to identify imported — as opposed to local — corn, beans, or squash seeds when, on rare occasions, such things occur in garbage deposits. The possibility exists that some areas, notably the Belize River Valley and some of the low-lying northern parts of the country, may have been "breadbaskets" that supplied both nearby and distant communities. Exploitation of most such areas depended on elaborate irrigation systems that required continual maintenance. Distribution of the products of intensive agriculture, on a large scale and over long distances, would have forced inter-city organization and regulation, which must have been disrupted by the Classic collapse. Thus, the survival of some communities in the midst of chaos is all the more remarkable.

History Continues to Unfold

The ancient Maya emerge as an outstanding example of the ability of a people to build a great, complex, and long-lived civilization in surroundings that hardly seem suited to the task. Yet, if we were to make the mistake of looking at the Maya in our society's terms, we would consider their civilization a failure. This is because we tend to emphasize growth as the only measure of success and see a static situation as the beginning of decline and imminent collapse. How else but as evidence of failure would we view the fact that many of the Maya's grandest cities were swallowed up by the jungle a thousand years ago? We may forget that before the collapse, during the Classic Period, the Maya dominated a very large territory for more than 2400 years. Moreover, pre-Hispanic Maya (before the Spanish arrived) society had survived upheaval and lived on until it was brought down by the Spanish over 3000 years after its first appearance on the human stage.

The domination of Maya life by the Spaniards, combined with the European accounts of the last 500 years, has led us to think of the Maya of colonial and later times as no more than a poor remnant of what once was. That picture has been unintentionally reinforced by archaeologists focusing on the great achievements of Classic times without attention to the continuity that marked Maya life up to the time of the Spanish Conquest and beyond. In weighing the modern Maya against their illustrious ancestors, we may forget that the story of Maya life is one of the great survival stories — both physical and cultural. The traceable record of that survival now comes near to spanning four millennia, and the record, in full, runs even farther back into the past. The same people remain on the land whose ancestors held it more than 3700 years ago; they speak languages closely related to those of ancient times, and they retain some beliefs and practices that shaped their ancestors' lives many generations ago. These facts add to the dignity that today's Maya people possess naturally by underlining their highly distinguished heritage and their strength in clinging to it.

Current Research and Interpretations

One of the recent sources of information about the Maya writing system is text on pottery vessels, which now number in the thousands. Once thought to be purely decorative, and to have been painted by illiterate artists, the texts can now be shown to contain as much information as those on monuments and elsewhere.

Chapter Review

Chapter Summary

In this chapter, we have seen:

- that the geography of the Maya highlands and lowlands were important factors in determining the nature of Maya society
- that their legal and political institutions contributed to a sense of continuity among the Maya
- how myths, legends, and traditions played an important role in Maya society
- that innovations such as writing and a calendric system had significant effects on the functioning of the Maya economy

Reviewing the Significance of Key People, Concepts, and Events (Knowledge/ Understanding)

1. Understanding the history of the Maya requires a knowledge of the following concepts and events, and an understanding of their significance in the development of Maya society. In your notes, identify and explain the historical significance of four.

    Concepts/Places
    Yucatán Peninsula
    Cenote of Sacrifice
    Chichén Itzá
    Teotihuacán
    Mayan

    Events
    Spanish Conquest

2. Maya civilization was very conservative, which meant a great deal of stability and continuity. Yet, significant changes did occur and are reflected in the differences between the Pre-Classic, Classic and Post-Classic eras. Copy and complete the chart below in your notes by listing factors for change and continuity in the appropriate columns.

	Change	*Continuity*
Pre-Classic		
Classic		
Post-Classic		

    Transfer one of the factors contributing to change and one of the factors contributing to continuity to the graphic organizers "Forces that Promote Change" and "Forces That Reinforce Stability and Continuity in your World" in your *World History Handbook*.

3. Describe how the Maya world was organized politically (i.e., Who had power at various levels? What was the relationship between cities?).

Doing History: Thinking About the Past (Thinking/Inquiry)

1. In a paragraph supported with historical evidence, respond to the statement: "If we ever hope to understand the nature of the Maya civilization, we must first understand the importance of the natural world in their belief system." Transfer two key phrases from your response to the graphic organizer "Geography's Influence" in your *World History Handbook*.

2. In virtually all civilizations, various innovations have had significant impact on the functioning of the economy. Can it be argued that the concept of time was one of the most important innovations of the Maya world to influence their economic system? Respond in a well-argued and factually supported paragraph. Transfer two of the arguments you use in your paragraph to the graphic organizer "Economic Influence of Innovation" in your *World History Handbook*.

Applying Your Learning (Application)

1. Assume you are a servant in the household of a member of the Maya nobility. You have been sent to the market to gather food for the evening meal. While you are there, you decide to pick up the items your own family will need for its evening meal. Prepare the two different lists you would make to run your errands.

2. Visually depict the Maya concept of time and our own concept of time.

Communicating Your Learning (Communication)

1. Make a diagram to illustrate the social hierarchy of the Maya world. Create or select an illustration that reflects not only the position of each group in society, but also how it was viewed. Transfer some of the ideas from your diagram to the organizer "Forms of Social Organization" in your *World History Handbook*.

2. Create a map of the Maya world that illustrates at least eight major sites, trade routes, and the nature of the goods exchanged. Use visuals to capture major features of the sites, the goods traded, and distinctive features of the Maya world (e.g., *cenotes*, rain forests).

CHAPTER THIRTEEN

The Aztecs

CHAPTER EXPECTATIONS

By the end of this chapter, you will be able to:

- evaluate the degree to which a society that practises human sacrifice can still be considered highly civilized

- identify the major changes that took place in the history of the Aztecs from their journey to the Valley of Mexico to the clash with the Spanish

- evaluate the role and importance of myths and legends in the rise and fall of Aztec civilization

- assess the role of trade and tribute in the economy of Central Mexico during the fifteenth century while the Aztecs were the dominant force

This large Aztec fan was used to signify rank, identifying ambassadors and messengers. It is made of wicker and feathers.

The conquest of Mexico on 8 November 1519, is a story of intrigue, deception, and death. In this chapter, we will describe Aztec civilization before it was shattered and altered forever by the Spanish soldiers and priests of that conquest. At the same time that the Aztecs became Christians and adopted aspects of European culture, the Spaniards in Mexico absorbed Aztec culture, married into Aztec families, and adopted and adapted Aztec foods and cooking techniques, child-rearing practices, crops, and customs. Christian saints and holidays merged with ancient traditions and celebrations. The result is modern Mexico, a true and vibrant blend of Old and New World patterns of culture. Although archaeology is contributing a great deal, especially in recent years, to our knowledge of ancient Mexico, it is largely through the eyes and pens of the Spaniards and Mexica (what the Aztecs called themselves) that the civilization of ancient Mexico is known to us today.

KEY WORDS

Tenochtitlán

chinampas

tribute

Teotihuacán

Tula

Aztlán

KEY PEOPLE

Mexica

Huitzilopochtli

Tlacaelel

Tezcatlipoca

Tlaloc

Quetzalcoatl

Montezuma II

Bernal Díaz del Castillo

Hernán Cortés

VOICES FROM THE PAST

Amid the jangle of bells bound to the ankle, the dust rises like smoke.
Aztec War Poem

TIME LINE: THE AZTECS

| | **ca. 750 CE** | Teotihuacán civilization comes to a sudden end, but leaves a rich legacy |

The Aztecs begin their journey from Aztlán south to the Valley of Mexico — **1111**

1150 — Tula civilization, ruled by the Toltecs, in decline

Aztecs visit the ruins of Tula on their journey southward — **1163**

ca. 1250 — The Aztecs arrive in the Valley of Mexico

The Aztecs found the city of Tenochtitlán in the Valley of Mexico — **1325**

1428 — Aztecs begin conquering cities in the Valley of Mexico

A devastating famine hits Central Mexico, weakening many cities — **1450**

1519–1521 — Invading Spaniards conquer the Aztecs

GEOGRAPHY OF THE AZTEC WORLD

The Valley of Mexico

Aztec civilization flourished in what is known as the Valley of Mexico, the home of modern Mexico City. The valley is one of a number of natural basins found in the mountainous region of central Mexico, a land of volcanoes and earthquakes. Approximately 7800 km^2 in area, the valley floor is almost 2500 m above sea level, and some of the mountains surrounding it rise to over 5000 m. In pre-Columbian times (before the arrival of Columbus), the valley floor was covered by a shallow system of lakes, and the Aztec capital of **Tenochtitlán** was situated on an island in one of the lakes, called Lake Texcoco.

The city had an organized system of canals, and lake-bottom sediments were scooped up along shorelines to form narrow plots or strips of cultivable land. The land rose above the level of the water in the lake, which at its deepest was only 2.2 m. These plots were called *chinampas* by the Aztecs, and are considered to be among their greatest achievements. Chinampas are still built and cultivated today in lake and swamp areas south of Mexico City. Because the roots of the plants always have access to moisture provided by the lake waters, chinampa cultivation is a kind of hydroponic agriculture. In addition to building and tending the chinampas themselves, Aztec farmers set plants to germinate on the surfaces of reed mats that they floated on the lake waters. When the seedlings were old enough, the plants on their reed rafts were pulled along by canoes to chinampas and replanted there. This is probably how the chinampas came to be called "floating gardens" by some of the Spanish settlers.

Chinampas were, and are, extremely productive. In Aztec times, as much as several crops a year could be grown with the use of seedbeds and crop rotation. The canals that drained the chinampas also served as access routes for canoe traffic. Tenochtitlán, its canals, and chinampas are now buried by modern-day Mexico City.

As one sixteenth-century Spanish friar stated, "There are very beautiful hills which surround the city like a wall." This wall of mountains ringing the Valley of Mexico had no natural outlet. When it rained, mountainside runoff and overflowing spring water collected in the lake; in fact, any changes in the pattern of rainfall in the past resulted in great variation in the size of the lake. Excessive water flow would occasionally raise the level of the lake to cover one-storey buildings in Tenochtitlán. During the winter dry period, however, rain seldom, if ever fell — total rainfall was, and still is, less than half that of the Maya Lowlands. Conditions could be quite arid, creating problems for Aztec farmers even though the soils were fertile. Although two maize (a type of corn) crops a year were possible at lower elevations, only one crop per year was normal in the Valley of

■ **The Aztec Empire of Meso-America**

How were the Maya Lowlands different from the Valley of Mexico?

Mexico. Loss of the yearly crop to arid conditions was devastating. If the rains did not come when expected — in May or June — but later, the maize would be planted late and might not mature before the onset of the frosts in November or October.

Central Mexico

There were zones outside the Valley of Mexico, particularly to the south and east, that were more temperate and tropical, where threats of drought or frost were minimal. The Aztec conquests of areas outside the valley were initially motivated, in part, by the need to ensure supplies of food such as maize. A devastating famine spread throughout central Mexico, beginning in the year 1 Rabbit, according to the Aztec calendar, or 1450, according to ours. Frosts destroyed crops in the valley, and this was followed by two years of severe drought. Temporary abandonment of the city occurred from 1454 to 1455. Some families were so desperate that they sold their children to people who lived in areas outside the valley, where maize was still successfully grown.

Why the Aztecs would want to take action to avoid such tragedies in the future is obvious, and one action they took was to conquer people in fertile areas outside the Valley of Mexico who could provide them with **tribute** in the form of food. Most of the tribute paid the Aztecs by conquered peoples was in the form of luxury goods, such as feathers and jade, or raw and manufactured materials, such as gold dust and cotton clothing. By 1519, the Aztecs and their allies had gained control of areas outside the valley, in which environmental conditions varied. The timing of maize harvesting also varied, and in some areas, more than one annual crop was produced. The conquered towns not too distant from the Valley of Mexico could then send tribute in the form of food to Tenochtitlán at different times of the year, and the Aztecs were able to store maize over a longer period. In this way, the effects of local agricultural disasters on the Aztecs and their allies were minimized, and the famine of 1 Rabbit would not be repeated.

Adapting to a Dry Environment

Arid and cool conditions challenged Aztec ingenuity. Coupled with the high elevation and physical constraints brought about by the mountains surrounding the valley, the dry, cool climate required management techniques that differed from what was suitable for the high temperatures and humidity of the Maya lowland forests. No two areas seem less alike than the Valley of Mexico and the Maya Lowlands. Though the Aztecs and Maya shared staple crops such as maize, beans, and squash, they grew different varieties, and there were crops and animals distinctive to each area. When we think of the Aztecs, we picture scrub- or desert-adapted plants and animals, such as cactus, rattlesnakes, coyotes, eagles, and rabbits. But we also think of lake-dwelling species — herons, frogs, salamanders, turtles, and reeds and rushes of all kinds. Two plants, nopal (a cactus) and maguey (a succulent also known as agave or century plant), were important to the Aztecs for several reasons. The nopal yields a tasty fruit called prickly pear. Maguey fibres were used to make cord and clothing, the thorns were used as needles, and the plants themselves formed ideal field boundaries. The leaves were roasted and eaten, and the juice of maguey, when fermented, produces the alcoholic drink called pulque. More familiar to Canadians is a refined and distilled form of pulque known as tequila.

Texcoco, the name of the lake surrounding the Aztec capital, produced an interesting and nutritious taste treat the Aztecs called *tecuitlatl*. You can find tecuitlatl, a form of algae, in your neighbourhood health food store as spirulina. A Spanish friar referred to tecuitlatl as "a very fine slime," which the Aztecs prepared and ate as a delicacy. It has a salty taste.

THE ORIGINS OF THE AZTECS

The Aztecs called themselves **Mexica**, but since the name Aztec is more familiar to us, it will be used here. The Aztecs were newcomers to the Valley of Mexico; numerous communities already dotted the area when the Aztects arrived. The people in these communities had a long and civilized history — they built monumental temples and public buildings, planned their cities, irrigated their fields, had state-administered tax and tribute systems, had extensive markets, and traded goods over long distances. They claimed that their traditions went back to the days of Teotihuacán, and they viewed the Aztecs as uncultured savages. It was not long, however, before the Aztecs became sufficiently cultured to view Teotihuacán as a model for their own particular destiny.

Teotihuacán and Tula

Teotihuacán, on the northeast shore of Lake Texcoco, was the centre of one of the greatest civilizations in the Americas. Its roots stretched back to 200 BCE, but it was at the height of its power between about 250 to 750 CE. Teotihuacán had a population of around 150 000 people, and covered more than 20 km^2. We do not know who these people were, what they called themselves, or the language they spoke. We do know from archaeological excavations, however, that Teotihuacán was a thriving city, and that its markets attracted merchants and their goods from all over Meso-America, including the Maya Lowlands. Despite its sudden demise in 750 CE, Teotihuacán provided a model of culture and behaviour that later peoples living around the lakes in the Valley of Mexico would claim to remember. Although Teotihuacán was in ruins when the Aztecs came to power, this "City of the Gods," as it was known to the Aztecs, contained the spirit of a glorious past that the Aztecs sought to capture.

Another past civilization the Aztecs wanted to emulate was the **Tula**, which flourished from 900 to 1150 CE. Although we do not know who built Teotihuacán, we do know that people called the Toltecs ruled Tula, which lies to the north of the Valley of Mexico. The area around Tula is arid and characterized today by the growth of mesquite, a scrubby bush that is well-adapted to semi-desert conditions. Recent research in environmental history has shown that before the Spaniards Conquest, the area around Tula was a settlers' paradise — wooded hills, bubbling springs, and fields coloured green with crops nourished by an extensive system of irrigation canals. What happened? The Spanish introduced animals unknown in the New World — grazing animals such as sheep and cattle — and in the area around Tula, it was, as one historian put it, a "plague of sheep." Sheep alone were not responsible for the extreme environmental degradation that took place, nevertheless. It was due chiefly to extensive mismanagement — the Spaniards' blindness to the delicate environmental balance achieved by the

Aztecs. The huge numbers of sheep that were eventually let loose on the land caused irreversible processes to be set in motion: vegetation was cropped to the ground, soils began to erode, nutrients washed away, and, after a time, only hardy species like mesquite could take root in the dry, thin soil.

WEB CONNECTION

http://www.mcgrawhill.ca/links/echoes

Go to the site above to find out more about the Toltec civilization.

An early Toltec sculpture showing Quetzalcoatl as the morning star emerging from a serpent's mouth.

The Aztecs considered the Toltecs rulers of a Golden Age. Aztec children would be told that the Toltecs had been the wisest of people, their houses the most beautiful, their craftspeople the most skilled, and their works the ultimate in perfection. Although Tula had fallen before the Aztecs rose to power, the memory of the Toltec Empire was far fresher than the memory of Teotihuacán, and Aztec nobles would come to claim descent from Toltec heroes.

The Arrival of the Aztecs

According to Aztec legends, their home was a place called **Aztlán**, the "Place of the Herons." No one knows exactly where Aztlán was located. Some say it was in the southwestern part of the present-day United States; others, that it was only 100 km northwest of Tenochtitlán. Since the journey from Aztlán to the Aztecs' final home in Lake Texcoco supposedly took 200 years, it is easier to imagine Aztlán lying at least as far as the northwestern part of Mexico. Wherever it was, the journey from Aztlán was an arduous one. According to Aztec histories, the journey began, in our calendar, in the year 1111. From their homeland, the Aztecs moved slowly southward, stopping in places for periods of time, building temples and ball courts, and then moving on. They spent time in the northern reaches of the Valley of Mexico, and are supposed to have visited the ruins of Tula. They celebrated an important new year's ceremony near Tula in 1163, and then proceeded southward. They arrived in the Valley of Mexico in the thirteenth century (probably by around 1250), but when they tried to settle among established peoples, they were driven away. One of the towns, called Culhuacán, finally accepted them, but with conditions.

The people of Culhuacán, the Culhua, saw themselves as direct inheritors of the high culture of the Toltecs at Tula. Tula fell because it was destroyed by Chichimec groups (predecessors of the Aztecs) who were migrating southward from the northern desert to escape conditions of drought and scarce game. The refugees in and around Tula fled southward to the Valley of Mexico, and established towns around the lakes. Culhuacán was one of these towns.

Therefore, the Culhua felt justified in setting conditions for the Aztecs. They allowed them to remain in the vicinity of Culhuacán if, and only, if the Aztecs worked the lands of their Culhua masters, and

lived in a place no one wanted: a dreary, snake-infested place just west of Culhuacán, called Tizapán. To the surprise of the Culhua, the Aztecs thrived in this environment. Grudgingly, the Culhua came to accept their presence, and soon the Aztecs were serving as mercenaries for their Culhua lords. The Aztecs were fierce warriors and struck terror in the hearts of their enemies. All might have been well but for a horrible incident in which the Aztecs struck terror in the hearts of their allies, too.

There came a time when the Aztecs went to the king of the Culhua and asked for his daughter — in some accounts she was a ruler in her own right — to be mistress of the Aztecs' principal god, **Huitzilopochtli**. The young woman was brought to the Aztec camp — and promptly sacrificed, apparently with the intent of provoking war. The Aztecs invited the Culhua king to attend the ceremony dedicating his daughter as a goddess, but when he found that she had been killed, not wedded, fighting broke out immediately and the Aztecs were defeated and forced to flee into the marshes around Lake Texcoco.

The Aztec chronicles recount that their god Huitzilopochtli had told them to settle where they saw an eagle perched on a prickly pear cactus. They wandered among the marshes until such a sign supposedly appeared to them, on an island in the lake. They named this island, their new home, Tenochtitlán. Another island, Tlatelolco, just north of Tenochtitlán, was also settled. Eventually, as swamps were drained and the land built up, the two islands became one. Tenochtitlán was founded in 1325.

For a time, the Aztecs served as mercenaries for mightier powers on the mainland — the Tepanecs of Azcapotzalco. Gradually, the Tepanecs — with Aztec help — began to conquer other cities in the Valley of Mexico; in the process, the Aztecs evolved from mercenaries of the Tepanecs to their

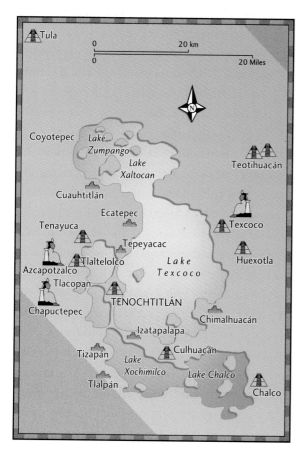

■ **The Valley of Mexico**

1. **Find Tenochtitlán and Tlatelolco on the map.**

2. **How were the Aztecs able to make these lands habitable?**

allies. As could probably be predicted, the Aztecs became increasingly powerful as they learned statecraft, as well as tribute administration, from the Tepanecs. Itzcoatl became the Aztec ruler in 1426. Under his leadership, and, partly, because the legitimate Tepanec ruler had been betrayed by his own people in a coup, the Aztecs turned against the Tepanecs, and two years later, with the help of new allies, brutally crushed Azcapotzalco. In the following years, the Aztecs cemented relationships with their two most powerful allies and formed what is known as the Triple Alliance. From this point on, the Aztec Empire was established, and for the next 90 years, until the arrival of the Spaniards, the Aztecs and their allies embarked on a program of military expansion that had never before been seen in Meso-America. By 1519, they ruled an empire of several million people who spoke a variety of languages, and their territory stretched from the Pacific Ocean to the Gulf of Mexico, and from central Mexico to Guatemala.

[RELIGION AND BELIEFS
Human Sacrifice

The Aztecs were a people of contradiction. Their empire rested on war and human sacrifice, yet they sought to capture in song and poetry the beauty of the world around them. As they saw it, the continual offering of blood through human sacrifice ensured the perpetuation of the universe. It is this aspect of their culture and tradition that we today find most difficult to understand, yet trying to explain it fascinates us. Spanish observers, even those most sympathetic to the Aztecs found the practice of human sacrifice revolting. According to one account:

. . .the men or women who were to be sacrificed to their gods were thrown on their backs and remained perfectly still. A priest then came out with a stone knife... and with this knife, he opened the part where the heart is and took out the heart, without the person who was being sacrificed uttering a word. . .

The Aztecs were unusual, even among Meso-American cultures, for the extent to which they carried out human sacrifice. Along with warfare, mass sacrifice was institutionalized as political policy. No one knows for certain how many humans met their deaths on the sacrificial block. The Spanish conqueror Hernán Cortés estimated that 50 people were killed at each temple every year. This would put the yearly estimate at approximately 20000 people. Tenochtitlán was certainly the site of the greatest numbers of sacrifices — as many as 800 victims may have been killed for one festival alone. One of the Spanish friars wrote that thousands of warriors were sacrificed at the consecration of the great temple of Huitzilopochtli. The skulls of victims were often displayed on what is called a skull rack. The largest skull rack stood in the plaza at the foot of what the Spaniards called the Templo Mayor, the major temple in Tenochtitlán. Here, the skulls were defleshed and displayed in rows. Two of Cortés's soldiers estimated that at least 136 000 skulls were displayed on this particular device; however, there is little doubt that this was an extreme exaggeration. The major temple at Tlatelolco, near Tenochtitlán, has been excavated, and exactly 170 skulls perforated for skull-rack display have been recovered. One reason for the discrepancy may be that many Spaniards exaggerated Aztec behaviour to justify the often-harsh Spanish treatment of the indigenous people.

Even 170 sacrifices may seem a large number to us, although if you had lived in Tenochtitlán, you would likely have drawn some comfort from the fact-that it was not the Aztecs, but their enemies, conquered in battle, who comprised the majority of the sacrificial victims. Also, one could ask what the real difference is between dying on the battlefield — which we may accept — and instead, being captured and dragged back to a temple to be killed there Aztec-style. Even so, how did the Aztecs come to terms with such practices when they produced not only warriors, but also poets and philosophers who wrote of matters such as the attainment of truth, the beauty of flowers, and the transitory nature of earthly things? The answer may lie, in part, in the Aztec concept of the universe.

One Aztec legend relates that the Fifth Sun, the world in which the Aztecs lived, was created at Teotihuacán (the Classic civilization in the Valley of Mexico) by the sacrifice of creator-gods. In order to create the sun and moon and set them in motion in the sky, these gods cast themselves into a Divine Fire. Thus, they set an example of sacrifice that humans were expected to follow. Another myth relates that the god Quetzalcoatl shed some of his blood to help restore life on Earth. The Aztecs viewed the shedding of blood as the ultimate gift to sustain life for the community. Aztec men and women could attain immortality in two ways, both

The Aztec sacrifice of the human heart. Two victims are shown in this illustration from a work by a Spanish historian. Note how the heart of one victim seems to be flying out of his chest. Can people who make human sacrifice be considered a civilization?

associated with bloodshed: for women, death in childbirth; for men, death on the battlefield.

Tlacaelel's Reforms

A single individual may have had much to do with encouraging the frequency of human sacrifice among the Aztecs. This individual, **Tlacaelel**, was the royal counsellor to Itzcoatl, the Aztec king who led the conquest of the Tepanecs in 1430. Tlacaelel was said to have persuaded the Aztec kings whom he served (there were two others after Itzcoatl) that they must make it their mission to extend the domain of their principal god, Huitzilopochtli, so that there would always he captives to sacrifice to the god. Tlacaelel's advice was heeded, and Tenochtitlán became the setting for the sacrifice of large numbers of captives from places as far away as Oaxaca, Chiapas, and Guatemala.

Tlacaelel is remembered for more than his ritual reforms, however. He revamped the Aztec judicial system, the army, and the organization of travelling merchants, the *pochtecas*, who often served the Aztec state as gatherers of information — an Aztec CSIS. Perhaps the most astounding reform was that Tlacaelel and Itzcoatl decided to change recorded Aztec history. Like the Maya, the Aztecs had a written language and recorded aspects of their history in books made of bark paper or deerskin that were folded, accordion-like. Tlacaelel concluded that the history that had so far been recorded did not serve the Aztec state, and he had the relevant books burned. In the new version of history, the Aztecs became descendants of the famous Toltecs. Huitzilopochtli was described as equal to older gods such as Quetzalcoatl, but perhaps most important, warfare was exalted to new heights, and the Aztecs (the "people of the Sun") were said to be destined to conquer all other nations.

They destroyed records carefully kept for decades by their historians and scribes in order to create a past that better suited the goal of the empire and the quest for captives for sacrifice.

Aztec Deities

What were the gods who demanded human sacrifice like? There were too many to describe here. When the Aztecs conquered other people, they assimilated their gods; as the empire grew, so did the pantheon. Basically, the gods can be divided into three groups. There are those associated with creation, those associated with rain and agricultural fertility, and those for whom the Aztecs fought in war.

In the first category are the Lord and Lady of Duality, often represented by a single deity with both male and female aspects. There was also **Tezcatlipoca**, the "Smoking Mirror." He was all-powerful and could see everything that happened in the world as reflected in his mirror. He was associated with the night, the jaguar, and sorcery. Tezcatlipoca was the source of all natural forces; human strength and weakness; wealth; happiness and sorrow. He is usually shown with two mirrors, one at his head and the other in the place of a foot bitten off by an earth monster. His body was black and his face yellow with black bands. Being a warrior, he carried a shield, an *atlatl* (dart thrower) and darts. Huehueteotl, the fire god, was also associated with creation. Every 52 years, the Aztecs celebrated a fire ceremony. All fires were extinguished and all household articles, such as statues and cooking implements, were discarded. When night fell, people climbed to the housetops. In the darkness, the priests held a ceremony at a nearby mountain peak in which a captive was sacrificed, and a new fire kindled in the chest cavity of the victim. If the fire remained lit, all would be well and the world and its people would exist for another 52 years. If the flame were to die (as it never seemed to), the world would end, darkness would come over the earth, and the celestial monsters would descend and devour all human beings.

Of the rain gods, **Tlaloc** is the best-known. He is always portrayed with a distinctive mask that makes him look as if he had a large curled moustache and wore goggles. Tlaloc caused the rain to fall and the crops to grow. There were also a number of goddesses associated with fertility. One of these, Tonantzin, merged after the Spanish Conquest with the image of the Virgin Mary. There was also Xipe Totec ("Our Lord, the Flayed One"), the god of vegetation and its renewal, who heralded the arrival of spring.

The warrior gods included Tonatiuh, a sun god well-known to many peoples in central Mexico. And, of course, there was Huitzilopochtli, the patron god of the Aztecs, who was also associated with the sun. All Aztec warriors were dedicated to the service of the sun, and supplied the sun with the blood of their captives.

Outside the three groups described above was **Quetzalcoatl** — the plumed, or feathered, serpent. Quetzalcoatl is a very old and much-revered Meso-American god. He is often shown as bearded, a sign that he was an ancient deity. He was worshipped in one form or another by the Maya and the Toltecs, and is believed to have been a creator-god who provided sustenance for humanity. He was also associated with the rain and the wind. Tezcatlipoca, the Smoking Mirror, was a capricious god who demanded warfare and human sacrifice. Quetzalcoatl was said to be a benevolent god who brought maize to humanity, as well as learning and the arts. He demanded of his people only the peaceful sacrifice of jade, snakes, and butterflies.

The terrifying earth goddess Coatlicue. She is also the mother of gods and men and patron of life and death. Her head was severed and two serpents emerged from her neck to form her face. The stone sculpture is 2.5 m high.

Review...Recall...Reflect

1. Describe how the arrival of the Spanish altered the natural environment around the ancient city of Tula.

2. Outline the events that took the Aztecs from Aztlán to become rulers of central Mexico.

3. Explain the connection between the widespread practice of human sacrifice and Aztec legends and religious beliefs.

SOCIAL HISTORY
Social Structure

The fundamental division of Aztec life was between nobles and commoners. Basically, there were — in descending order — rulers, chiefs, and nobles in the highest class. Intermediate positions were occupied by merchants and luxury artisans. The commoners were divided into free commoners — those in rural areas who worked the land of the nobles — and slaves.

All nobles considered themselves to be descended from Quetzalcoatl. The ruler wore the most intricately decorated cotton cloaks, and nobles beneath him wore cloaks suitable for their rank. Commoners could not wear cotton cloaks but were restricted to cloaks made of palm fibres. Commoners could not wear cloaks that reached below the knee, unless, as warriors, they had received leg wounds. Neither could commoners wear luxury ornaments; only nobles wore gold headbands with feathers, gold arm bands, lip plugs, ear or nose plugs, and ornaments set with precious stones. Only certain nobles had the right to wear sandals, and only the king and his second-in-command could wear sandals in the palace at Tenochtitlán. In addition, only nobles were allowed to build two-storey houses. Even without this restriction, it is doubtful that commoners could afford such houses. These status symbols make it clear that the nobles controlled most of the important economic resources of the empire, and through this economic power, they were able to acquire gold armbands and afford the labour it took to build large houses.

Strict legal codes governed behaviour, and punishments were more severe for the nobles. For example, drunkenness in public was considered a serious offense for all but the elderly. Commoners found inebriated had their heads shaven; nobles, however, were put to death (at least this was the law; how often it happened is not known). Judges who accepted bribes, favoured nobles over commoners in court, or used their offices for personal gain were severely punished.

Rulers (*tlatoque*)

The ruler of a city-state was called a *tlatoani*; the plural was *tlatoque*. These individuals controlled cities, towns, and subject communities. In addition to the supreme ruler in Tenochtitlán, there were others who held power over cities and towns throughout the empire. **Montezuma II**, for example, was the imperial Aztec tlatoani in Tenochtitlán at the time of the Spanish Conquest, but there were other lesser tlatoque of towns such as Texcoco who made their mark in Aztec history. Tlatoque controlled their own lands, managed labour and tribute, adjudicated disputes not resolved in lower courts, organized military activities, and sponsored certain religious celebrations.

Tlatoque lived the lifestyle of the rich and famous, which in ancient Mexico meant elegant dress, a large and pleasant house, and many servants and slaves. There were jugglers and acrobats to keep the household amused. Tlatoque gambled as well, both at the ball game — a spectator sport — and at the playing of board games such as *patolli*. They ate well: tortillas and tamales of all kinds, sauces of many colours and flavours, turkey, quail, venison, rabbit, lobster, fish, and fruits. They drank chocolate, the most highly valued beverage among the Aztecs, as it was among the Maya, and they smoked beautifully decorated cigars after meals. According to the Aztec nobles, tobacco was good for the digestion, and a meal without tobacco was not a real feast. Tobacco was accorded great of respect and had its place in Aztec custom.

Chiefs (*tetecuhtin*)

Tetecuhtin (the singular form was *tecuhtli*) formed the next lower rank of nobility. Tetecuhtin controlled more restricted areas and sets of activities than the rulers and received their titles through success in war. They could hold a political, military, or judicial office; owned and controlled agricultural lands; and were heads of houses to which lesser nobles were attached, as well as commoners. Tlacaelel, the counsellor to Itzcoatl, for example, would have had the status of a chief.

Nobles (*pipiltin*)

Pipiltin were the children of rulers and chiefs. They were attached to the chiefly house into which they were born, and had rights to lands and to the people who worked the land. They could, and did, succeed to the ranks of rulers or chiefs when positions were available. Otherwise, they often became tribute collectors. Although a *pilli* (singular form) was below the rank of a tecuhtli, the pilli's palace would be part of a large compound, with the houses set on platforms. The pilli would have been able to import a wide range of luxury goods from distant places.

The artisans of luxury goods, the toltecca, crafted objects such as this double-headed serpent made of pieces of turquoise. This ornament (43 cm) would have been worn on the chest of a high priest.

Luxury Artisans (*toltecca*)

Metalworkers, engravers, painters of codices (books), and feather workers formed, along with the merchants, a kind of middle class in Aztec society. The creations of these luxury artisans were highly esteemed, and were reserved for nobility. The artisans were organized into groups similar to the craft guilds of medieval Europe. They lived in their own residential sections of the city, known as *calpulli*; they controlled education within their ranks; they had their own deities and ceremonies, and maintained special relations with the state. Artists and craftspeople enjoyed positions of honour and respect.

Merchants (*pochteca*)

Trade in central Mexico at certain levels could be carried out by anyone, and regional merchants moved large quantities of goods within their home territories. It was the professional merchants, however, the famed *pochteca*, who dealt in large quantities of a wide range of goods on what is called an inter-regional scale — that is, throughout the territories of the Aztec Empire. They traded the luxury commodities destined for the noble class, and they carried out business in marketplaces and in neutral ports of trade that lay beyond the bounds of the empire. Identified by their trademark staff and fan, merchants also wore distinctive clothing and were restricted by law to a minimum of ostentation (display of wealth). They could not, in other words, imitate the nobles in their fancy dress — a rule established by one of the Aztec tlatoani advised by Tlacaelel.

Like the luxury artisans, the merchants enjoyed special privileges and status. Merchants also had their own guilds, residential areas, and were the only people allowed to create and enforce their own laws and codes. They had supreme authority over the greatest and most extensive market at Tlatelolco, just north of Tenochtitlán, where they enforced fair prices and ensured proper conduct in market dealings. Merchants travelled extensively to trade and discover new sources of raw materials or products valued by the Aztec nobility. Because their occupation so often took them outside central Mexico, they served as spies for the empire, particularly in areas that had not yet been brought under Aztec control, and they could actually declare war and conquer communities. Both men and women were merchants, and at the top of the merchant hierarchy were principal merchants called "fathers" and "mothers." Below the principal merchants were the slave dealers, the merchants who acted as spies and state agents, and the ordinary merchants.

Commoners (*macehualtin*)

These were the bulk of the Aztec population. The *macehualtin* worked the soil, fished the seas and rivers, and specialized in certain crafts. They also served as soldiers in the Aztec armies of conquest. They were certainly poorer than nobles, but resources varied among them. Their homes were not luxurious, they had few garments, and their meals consisted chiefly of vegetables with chili and tortillas with little to no meat. They worked the lands of others, but also had rights to work land for themselves. They were grouped into different wards, or neighbourhoods, based on family ties within a town or a city; each ward was called a *calpulli*. The calpulli was also a territorial and landholding unit through which land was given out to members for their use. Usually, the individual could not sell the plot he worked, but it would be passed on to his children. In some instances, though, land did seem to be possessed by the owner and could be sold with the permission of the calpulli council. Each calpulli had a temple where

members worshipped. Calpulli members were also expected to work land set aside especially for support of the temple.

Aztec women among the macehualtin would have made simple pottery such as this for household use.

Rural Tenants (*mayeque*)

Often described as serfs, the *mayeque* were attached to the private lands of the nobles, and they could not leave these lands. Unlike the commoners, or macehualtin, they were attached to individuals rather than units such as the calpulli. The macehualtin could leave the calpulli — in theory, at least — but the mayeque were forbidden to leave the land of their lords.

Slaves (*tlacotin*)

Commoners could become slaves for a variety of reasons. These included punishment for theft, gambling, or inability to pay off debts or tribute. On the whole, slaves were more common in urban areas than in the countryside. In fact, the greatest numbers of *tlacotin* were attached to households of nobles. The status of slave was acquired and not inherited. Children of slaves were born free. Slaves who were less than cooperative received public warnings before witnesses, and if this did not work, they were fitted with a wooden collar and sold in the marketplace. If they did not improve and were sold three times, they could then be sacrificed. Generally speaking, this was not common, and sacrificial slaves were usually supplied through tribute from the provinces and warfare.

Raising a Family

As in all societies, the prospect of the birth of children brought great joy, and banquets were held when conception had taken place. The expectant mother followed a number of rules to keep herself healthy and maximize the chances of a successful birth. Some advice is familiar to us, such as that pregnant women were not to lift heavy objects. Other advice seems strange: women were not to look at an eclipse of the sun or moon, not to sleep in the daytime, not to chew chicle (chewing gum), and not to look at anything red. Just as men gained honour on the battlefield, so women gained honour in bearing and raising children. If men lost their lives in battle, they were rewarded in the afterlife by following the sun in its rise to the zenith. Women who died in childbirth were revered as goddesses and believed to accompany the sun as it descended from its zenith and set in the west.

After a successful birth, the midwife cut the umbilical cord and buried the afterbirth in a corner of the house. The cord of a baby girl was buried near the hearth; a boy's umbilical cord was dried and later left on a field of battle to dedicate him to service in war. The midwife bathed and wrapped the infant, and sung a song praising the baby, welcoming it but also warning that life was not a good place but one of weeping, sorrow, and suffering. Despite the melancholy tones with which the infant was greeted,

Aztec parents believed that young children should be healthy, strong, and happy.

From the age of three, children were supervised by fathers in the case of boys, or mothers in the case of girls. When boys were ten or twelve, they went to school. Sons of commoners, merchants, and artisans attended the *telpochcalli* or House of Youth. Here they received religious training and were taught the arts of war. They were also expected to work on the lands set aside for the support of the school, and to collect fuel (wood) for the temple fires. They also spent time at home learning their father's craft. There was another school called the *calmecac*, or priests' house. This was a school of higher learning for the nobility, but some children of merchants and commoners were admitted. Here, in addition to basic education, students were prepared for careers as priests, public officials, and military leaders. Religious and philosophical doctrines were studied, as were calendrics (the study of the calendar), timekeeping, astrology, and history.

There were also schools for girls that taught temple maintenance, ritual duties, weaving and other tasks, preparation for household maintenance and marriage, and music, which was considered important in the education of all children. From the age of fourteen or so, boys and girls attended the House of Song to learn singing, dancing, and the playing of musical instruments. Instruction here was not simply for training in religious ritual and ceremony. The songs and poetic texts were ways in which knowledge and beliefs were transmitted from one generation to another, and much cultural information was bound up in them.

Men usually completed their education at the age of twenty or twenty-two; women, at sixteen or seventeen, at which time marriage was arranged by the parents. Matchmakers played a role in helping

Montezuma II, sometimes called Moctezuma, was the ninth and last real Aztec emperor of Mexico. Succeeding his uncle, Ahuitzotl, in 1502, Montezuma reigned over the vast Aztec Empire until his death in 1520. The arrival of the Spanish adventurer, Hernán Cortés, in 1519, meant the beginning of the end for both Montezuma and his empire.

An artist's interpretation of the meeting of Montezuma and Cortés. Do you think the artist was there?

Montezuma's reign was not that long ago, historically speaking, so you might think that there would be plenty of information about him. Remember, however, that history tends to be written and destroyed by the winners. Both the historic accounts that do exist and the relative paucity of Aztec information about Montezuma have to be considered in more than one light.

The surviving eyewitness accounts of the Aztec culture on the eve of its destruction were written by Spanish members of Cortés's party. These writers did not understand the Aztec language or their way of thinking. The Spanish were also totally repelled by the Aztec religion, which they believed to be inspired by the devil. Their interpretation of events must, therefore, be read with caution. Not only that, Aztec eyewitnesses became conquered people after Montezuma's death.

Besides the accounts of the lavishness of Montezuma's palace and court, we are told that Cortés was able to win over allies among the tribes that surrounded the capital city of Tenochtitlán. This has been interpreted to mean that Montezuma's reign was inadequate, yet historically, discontent in outlying areas is more common than not. Cortés also brought some powerful weapons with him, so the term "ally" should be used carefully.

The puzzling thing was Montezuma's apparent submission to the Spanish. Montezuma supposedly invited Cortés into the capital, thus guaranteeing its conquest. This seems odd, however, considering that Montezuma was the commander of the army and had organized several successful conquests of his own. What happened?

One explanation is that all Aztecs, including Montezuma, expected, and feared, the return of the bearded god, Quetzalcoatl, who would take over the empire. Did Montezuma welcome the bearded Cortés as a god? Perhaps the commander of the army really invited Cortés to the capital to trap him, to keep his enemy close, but the plan went wrong. Although Cortés was able to take Montezuma hostage, it is telling that he did not kill him for fear that the Aztecs would retaliate.

What happened next is difficult to explain. There was no huge uprising, but enough unrest erupted to make Cortés present Montezuma to his people. It is said that the Aztecs threw stones and arrows at their leader (not at the Spanish?) and Montezuma died three days later as a result of these wounds. Many Aztecs, however, believed that the Spanish murdered their emperor and did rebel, but it was too late. The Spanish were able to conquer the Aztec Empire completely by 1521, and change the course of history.

Activities

1. What do you learn about history making from this feature about Montezuma?

2. In groups of three or four, discuss experiences you have had where situations could have been interpreted in more than one way. Have you ever been in a situation that was misinterpreted? What do you think caused the misinterpretation and conclusion?

the families of the eligible girl and boy reach an agreement on consent to marriage. Soothsayers were consulted to help decide on a proper day for the ceremony, and the elaborate preparations took several days: cacao beans were ground, flowers were gathered, tobacco and smoking tubes were procured, pottery cups and baskets were bought, corn, tamales, and sauces were prepared. The bride was decorated with red feathers and dyes, and was carried to the groom's house after listening to advice from the elders. The bride and groom were married on a mat in front of the hearth. Various rituals took place, such as tying the couple together by their garments. The bride and groom were then led to a private room where they remained for four days — their honeymoon. The room was guarded by the matchmakers, who apparently drank pulque in quantity to pass the time. On the fifth day, more festivities took place.

The Aztec Household, Rules of Conduct, and Games

Once the household was established, the couple assumed the duties of life. The woman managed the household, developed her skills in food preparation and weaving, maintained household hygiene and

health, and was responsible for the early education of her daughters. Men administered the household property, advised and taught their sons, but were also required to fight on the battlefield and participate in community and temple activities. Commoner women could also participate in the market and buy and sell goods there. Noblewomen had servants do the shopping, and were encouraged to develop arts such as weaving.

Only noblemen were permitted to have more than one wife. Divorce was possible for anyone, but could be expensive as gifts had to be returned. Disputes over divorces or any other matters were settled according to an elaborate legal code, and a hierarchy of courts existed to settle cases. Punishments were generally severe. Death was the penalty for murder, rebellion, cross-dressing, and adultery. Thieves were made slaves after one offense; any further offence led to hanging.

The Aztecs enjoyed games and gambling. The principal spectator sport was the ball game, and wagers were made on the outcomes of games. The walls of the ball court were built of stone, and the playing field was shaped like an upper-case letter I. The object was to drive a rubber ball through a stone ring mounted vertically in the middle of the court walls. The ball could be hit with the hips, buttocks, or elbows — but not with the hands. Padded leather guards protected players' knees and hips. Professional ball players toured the country, exhibiting their skills; rulers and nobles maintained their own teams. Gambling was intense, and nobles wagered jewelry, cloaks, slaves, lands, and even houses.

Clothing

Most Aztec clothing was draped and not fitted. Men of all classes wore loincloths; these were cotton or

These figurines of Aztec gods and temples were used for worship in household shrines.

palm-fibre fabric, and were wrapped around the lower torso, passed between the legs, and tied in a large knot at the waist. Nobles' loincloths were elaborately ornamented with dyes, embroidery, feathered disks, or ocelot or coyote fur.

The hip cloth was another form of garment worn around the waist, but tied on one side and folded in such a way that a corner hung down at the sides or back. The most important status item for men was a cloak, or mantle, tied at one shoulder. Nobles could wear cotton cloaks, elaborately decorated, that hung below their knees. Commoners' cloaks were of maguey or other crude fibre, were plain, and, as noted earlier, could not hang below the knees unless the individual had leg wounds suffered in battle.

THE Past AT PLAY

A popular Aztec board game was called *patolli*. The board, similar to the better-known game of parchesi, had a criss-cross pattern along which pieces were moved. As with the ball game, betting could be fierce. Conquest accounts say that some people were addicted to the game. These individuals would walk around with mats under their arms and their own dice tied up in small cloths — ready to sit, play, and gamble at a moment's notice.

Warriors wore heavily padded cotton armour — a sleeveless garment that was pulled over the head, hugged the body, and reached to the top of the thigh. The padded cotton was very effective and was adopted by the Spanish soldiers in preference to their heavy, hot, metal armour. Nobles in battle wore special tunics with short skirts decorated with feathers. There was even a sort of body suit used as a warrior costume. It had fitted sleeves and trouser legs, and was constructed of cloth covered with feathers and made in a variety of colours and styles.

Women wore a mid-calf-length skirt secured at the waist. As with the men, noble women had the most magnificently embroidered and decorated clothing. In ritual contexts only, women wore a triangular slip-on garment, a bit like a poncho in shape, that hung on the shoulders and came down only as far as the chest. An example of similar s pecial-purpose ritual clothing for men was a short, fringed sleeveless jacket that tied in front, which Aztec priests sometimes wore.

The basic upper-body garment for women, worn over the skirt described above, was a kind of long tunic, or shift, that hung to just below the hips or top of the thighs. It is still worn today by women throughout Meso-America, and is generally known as a *huipil*. Aztec women embroidered the huipil borders with many colours, and worked feathers into decorative designs on the front in the area over the chest. Thread made from rabbit's fur was often used, which had a silk-like sheen and was supposed to hold dyes well.

Overall, clothing reflected the sharp stratification of Aztec society. Though the general garment styles were the same for different classes, the fabrics, specific lengths, and, especially, the ornamentation were different for each level of society. Not strictly part of the clothing, but certainly part of the costume, was face and body paint. Although serving women could rub their feet with a mixture of burned copal incense (copal is an aromatic resin) and dye, wearing elaborate face and body paint was a privilege of the nobility only.

Though nobles were permitted to wear more luxurious clothing than merchants or commoners, the most elaborate costumes were associated with rituals of religion and war. Clothing depicted on images of gods, and worn by priests who impersonated these gods, was very ornate and was sewn or decorated with the specific symbolism of the god. Among the nobility, those who had distinguished themselves in war displayed huge feather headdresses and elaborate costumes with ocelot skins or eagle feathers. These same nobles were the only ones who had the privilege of walking about the city carrying bunches of flowers.

Review...Recall...Reflect

1. Why were the legal codes governing behaviour more severe for Aztec nobility than for commoners?

2. Explain how the education of Aztec boys and girls differed.

3. How did clothing reflect the social hierarchy of Aztec society?

THE ARTS AND SCIENCES
Literature and Music

Aztec literature was preserved in both written and oral forms. Literary forms and rules were learned in childhood in both the calmecac, the schools where noble children were trained, and in the House of Song. Standardized songs and histories had to be memorized, as did religious songs and dances. People from all walks of life learned what they needed to participate in the various public ceremonies. There were also professional singers, who had to have clear voices and excellent oratory skills. These singers were employed by Aztec rulers to create songs and poems about the successes of

their reigns. Singers were also attached to temples to write songs to the gods.

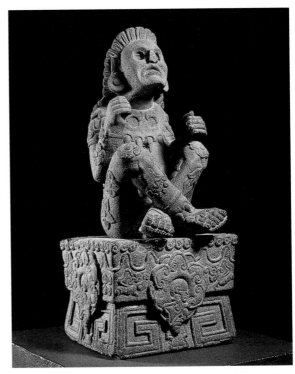

This is a sculpture of Xochipili, the Flower Prince, an Aztec god of music, dance, feasting, and other pleasant things.

The Aztecs valued oratory skills, and the good narrator was said to be a "speaker of joyful words," and to have "flowers on his lips." Lyric poetry was also highly valued. Through this form of expression, Aztec intellectuals contemplated the significance of human and godly actions, and expressed doubts and fears about the course of life and the world around them. Their religion did not make the meaning of life entirely clear for them, and poetry and song provided an outlet — as it does for us today — for emotional expressions of both doubt and joy about the human condition.

The Aztecs also wrote chronicles to record the history of their people. These focused on the adventures of heroes, the founding of cities, the lives of rulers, warfare, migration, and empire building. As noted previously, Aztec chronicles recorded the manipulation of history, as when Tlacaelel burned Aztec records to create a more glorious heritage for his people. Written records were important to the Aztecs not only in preserving their past, but also in passing on this information to future generations. The Aztecs used pictorial representations to express ideas (such as *mat*, "marriage") and not an alphabet.

Architecture

What remains of the great temples, palaces, houses, bridges, and streets of Tenochtitlán are today buried beneath the urban sprawl of Mexico City. Unfortunately, the Spaniards were not sufficiently interested in indigenous architectural styles to provide detailed and accurate architectural descriptions. Most of the monumental buildings were temples, and the Spaniards' abhorrence of Aztec ritual prevented them from recording information of any but the most general historical or architectural interest.

Similar to the architecture of the Maya, temples were built of masonry (stone) and stood atop terraced stone platforms — often referred to, in modern times, as pyramids. These had wide stairways leading from the base of the platform to the temple on top. The Aztec variation on this theme was the presence of double stairways leading to two temples atop a single platform. Palaces and other upper-class buildings stood on low platforms, and their rooms were spread out over one or, at most, two storeys. Commoners' houses were usually built at ground level. Depending on the raw materials available, these houses were built either of adobe (clay mud formed into bricks and sun-dried) or wooden poles with thatched roofs.

The fully restored Pyramid to Acatitlán, in Santa Cecilia, Mexico. The temple to the god was at the top.

Although the Spanish conquerors left no detailed accounts of Aztec buildings, they did describe their impressions of the Aztec capital when they gazed on the magnificent and orderly city for the first time. **Bernal Díaz del Castillo**, a soldier and historian in Cortés's army, has left us a description of the approach to the Aztec capital, when the Spaniards were walking along a wide road, or causeway, just outside the lakes area, and from which they could see Lake Texcoco and the cities built in its midst:

> Next morning, we came to a broad causeway, and continued our march... And when we saw all those cities and villages built in the water, and other great towns on dry land, and that straight and level causeway leading to Mexico, we were astounded. These great towns and temples and buildings rising from the water, all made of stone, seemed like an enchanted vision... Indeed, some of our soldiers asked whether it was not all a dream. Early next day we... followed the causeway... On the land side there were great cities, and on the lake many more. The lake was crowded with canoes. At intervals along the causeway there were many bridges, and before us was the great city of Mexico.

http://www.mcgrawhill.ca/links/echoes

Go to the site above to find out more about Aztec civilization.

To many people, this description makes the Aztec capital seem like Venice, with people bustling along in watercraft, and with picturesque bridges over the canals. Díaz del Castillo was describing his march along one of the main causeways leading to Tenochtitlán. In the centre of the city, he found a great plaza containing the major temple, markets, and other religious and political buildings. The four major causeways of the city radiated from this central hub, but other minor causeways ran from city to city. The causeways were roads that saw a great deal of traffic as people travelled between cities or brought trade goods in and out of the capital.

Unlike Venice, Tenochtitlán was laid out in a systematic pattern. Its rectangular grid made chinampa construction practical, and the orderly canals made possible a smooth flow of traffic since literally thousands of canoes entered the city every day. Therefore, Aztec urban planning accounted for not only population growth, but also traffic flow. The city depended for its survival on a massive influx of foods and other products; therefore, free flow of canoe traffic, as well as travel by land over the causeways, was essential. The Aztecs had no beasts of burden such as cattle or horses, nor did they use the wheel, so the roads leading into and out of Tenochtitlán would not have been worn down by horses, oxen, or carts — only people.

How did the Aztecs themselves describe their city? Not in architectural terms, but in language that, perhaps, gives us more, since it conveys the beauty symbolized for the Aztecs by Tenochtitlán:

> The city is spread out in circles of jade,
> radiating flashes of light like quetzal plumes.
> Beside it the lords are borne in boats;
> over them extends a flowery mist.

Sculpture

Aztec stoneworkers surpassed those of previous central Mexican civilizations in the quantity, quality, and range of sculpture production. When the Aztecs praised their best sculptors, however, they compared them to the earlier Toltec artists of Tula. Though the most famous Aztec sculptures, such as the Aztec calendar stone, are colossal, their repertoire also included miniature figures only 2 or 3 cm high: dogs, turtles, jaguars, monkeys, rabbits, eagles, grasshoppers, and, occasionally, even plants such as squashes. Skulls were also a popular sculptural image. Deities were frequently represented in stone, as were various architectural elements such as serpent heads that were placed at the bases of temples near stairways.

Human figures, usually standing images of commoners or warriors, were carved in stone and placed at the entrances of temples to serve as standard-bearers. Montezuma II apparently commissioned 14 sculptors to carve a monumental statue in his likeness. That sculptors often worked together suggests that they received a similar basic training, although it is not known whether they were organized into guilds in the way luxury artisans (such as feather workers or gem polishers) were. We do know that they tended to concentrate in cities, and it is in the cities, that we see the most monumental sculptures.

Monumental stone figures on the steps of the remains of the temple pyramid at Tenochtitlán.

Writing and Painting

The Aztecs had libraries that housed a number of different kinds of books and manuscripts. There were ritual records, almanacs that coordinated astronomical events with astrological predictions, calendrical records, tribute accounts, histories and genealogies of rulers, maps, and legal records. These were written on paper made from the bark of a fig tree, which was peeled off and soaked in water. Then, the bark fibres were scraped and separated, laid out in a criss-cross pattern on a board, and then pounded ferociously with a specially made stone to smooth and then fuse them into paper. Various materials, such as lime or white paint, could then be used to create a workable writing surface.

The symbols, or hieroglyphs, that the Aztec scribes used were painted in a variety of colours — usually red, yellow, green, and blue — and outlined in black. The Aztecs did not use symbols to represent the sounds of vowels or consonants the way we do. Most of their symbols were pictographic or ideographic. That is, a picture of a house would mean "house," or a picture of a flower would mean just

that. They also used shorthand symbols: footprints to represent travel, a squiggly line near people's mouths to represent speech, or a burning temple to mean "conquest." Some glyphs (carvings), mainly names, were phonetic, which means that they stood for sounds and not whole words or concepts.

In addition to the symbols and their meanings, the size of elements depicted was also important. Where people were drawn, the larger representations stood for more important people. Colours, too, were varied and transmitted critical information about the objects represented. For example, the four directions were symbolized by different colours: south by white or blue; east by yellow or red; north by red or black; west by blue-green or white.

Medicine

The Aztecs were actively involved in finding medical cures for a variety of illnesses and injuries. Physicians were expected to be good diagnosticians, to be familiar with remedies, to restore people to health, to set broken bones, and to administer drugs and potions. A number of herbs were used for poultices as well as internally, and different curers had different remedies, although some herbs were generally associated with certain cures. Sweat baths were popular and recommended for various illnesses, and were particularly important in problems of childbirth. Sweat baths were considered important in relaxing and soothing an individual during any sort of recovery.

When an illness was believed to have a supernatural cause, a shaman would attempt a cure that included medicinal herbs but also some form of ritual procedure or divination (calling on the supernatural for information). For example, by scattering corn kernels on a cotton cloak, a diviner would try to determine the cause of a person's illness. The cure might then involve the administration of herbs and potions, as well as a ritual, such as retrieving the patient's soul. Mirrors (of polished obsidian or hematite) were used to determine the extent of soul loss in a child: a blurred image meant that the case was severe, a clear image that recovery would take place soon.

Calendrics and Time

The Aztecs, like us, sought to keep track of time and did so by observing the night sky and counting the days until familiar planets and stars returned to the same locations. They did not, of course, wear wristwatches, but probably would have if given the opportunity. Unlike us, however, they believed that certain kinds of events recurred. For example, they believed that the universe had already undergone four time cycles in which a sun had been born in each. Their existence was part of the Fifth Sun; at the end of this Sun, they believed that the human race would perish. This belief in recurring cycles made it crucial to keep track of time in order to predict the future based on what had occurred in the past, and calendars were developed for just this purpose.

The Stone of the Sun, the Aztec calendar stone is a 20 tonne stone disk. Though buried in the fifteenth century by the Spaniards, it was rediscovered in the eighteenth century. It likely served as both a calendar and a history of the world.

The Solar Calendar

The solar year (365.25 days) was divided into 18 months of 20 days each. The Aztecs, who could only use markers on the horizon to track the sun, determined the time Earth and the sun took to return to the same position relative to each other. Since 18 x 20 = 360, the year was rounded out at the end with five days, which were viewed as unlucky.

Scripts & Symbols λ μ ν ο π θ υ ρ σ τ υ ϖ ω ξ ψ ζ α β χ ε δ φ γ

Aztec chronicle manuscripts had symbols that were recognizable to all people throughout the Aztec realm speaking different languages. The Spanish missionaries borrowed this imagery and used Aztec symbols and pictorial manuscript style to spread Christianity.

The Ritual Calendar

This calendar was not keyed into a solar year, but was simply a different time cycle not unlike our week of one to seven named days — but somewhat more complicated. Rather than what we have — only the numbers 1 to 7 that coincide with 7 day names — the Aztecs used a cycle of numbers 1 to 13 that coordinated with a series of 20 day names such as *Cipactli* (alligator) or *Tochtli* (rabbit). So, once the cycle of numbers with coordinated day names was completed, it was given a different name than it had the "week" before. (In our simpler system of weeks, day 1 is always Sunday.) This went on for 260 days (13 X 20) until the cycle repeated itself. For example, day 1 Alligator would recur once every 260 days.

Each solar year was named after the number and day name combination of the last day of the previous year. The great famine, for example, was said by the Aztecs to occur in the year known as 1 Rabbit. When the solar calendar and the ritual calendar were combined, the cycle repeated itself every 52 years. For example, the ninth day of the month *Quecholli* in the solar calendar — also 8 Wind in the ritual calendar — would not recur in this combination for 52 years.

AZTEC ECONOMICS
Tribute and Trade

Exchange in the Aztec Empire took three forms: tribute and taxation, state-sponsored foreign trade, and exchange in the marketplace.

The term "tribute" refers specifically to revenue demanded and collected by the dominant Aztec state from the regions it had conquered. State-sponsored trade involved specific transactions for the ruling powers in Tenochtitlán who would, on occasion, send out merchants (the pochteca) to neutral trade areas to acquire specific goods — usually luxury items. Most pochteca trade, however, was entrepreneurial and initiated by the pochteca for their own profit. Market exchange involved people at all levels who came to centralized markets to sell or buy goods and services. Markets served to integrate surplus production at local, regional, and state levels. Each conquered province of the Aztec Empire was required to pay tribute. People who lived close to the cities of Lake Texcoco gave foods and other supplies as tribute. For example, one province in a tropical area distant from the capital sent products not available in central Mexico:

9600 decorated cloaks	7 strings of jade
1600 women's tunics	40 lip plugs
1 warrior's costume and shield	16 000 rubber balls
1 feather standard	80 handfuls of quetzal feathers
1 gold diadem	24 little bunches of feathers
2 strings of gold beads	200 loads of cacao
100 pots of liquidambar (this is an aromatic resin)	

Tribute assigned to these provinces and cities was recorded in documents known as imperial tribute lists. These lists contained pictographs showing the nature and quantity of the sorts of tribute that the conquered territory was to provide to the Aztec capital.

The commoners assumed the heaviest burdens regarding tribute, since they tilled the fields in which food products and cotton were cultivated. Artisans, too, had to give part of their production in tribute payment. The nature of tribute was often indirect. For example, cotton was grown in lowland tropical areas, and travelling merchants purchased the raw product and carried it to highland areas, where no cotton was grown. Here, however, the raw cotton was turned into finished textiles, which, in turn, were given in imperial tribute. Therefore, whatever demands the Aztec state made on the highland manufacturers in turn affected the lowland producers.

Agriculture

Agriculture was the foundation of the Aztec Empire, and steady food supplies were essential in maintaining the Aztec state. Certain crops were grown throughout the empire, such as maize, beans, amaranth, chilis, and squashes. Tribute was coordinated with the times these crops ripened in each area to maximize stability. Other crops were grown only in tropical areas, such as cacao, vanilla, cotton, and varieties of fruit. These were accessible predominantly through tribute. Cacao and cotton (as woven cloaks) appear repeatedly on tribute lists. Cultivation of crops involved what is called swidden farming, or fallowing — a field was cleared of vegetation and cultivated for two or three years, and then allowed to rest so that the soil would recover lost fertility. More intensive cultivation took the form of irrigation agriculture and chinampa construction. Chinampas in Tenochtitlán ranged from 100 to 850 m^2 and were cultivated by up to 30 people. They produced corn, beans, chilis, amaranth, tomatoes, and flowers. Flowers were used in all religious festivals and political ceremonies and thus were always in great demand.

In addition to vegetable products, many animals were hunted to supplement the Aztec diet: deer, rabbits, hares, opposum, armadillos, pocket gophers, wild pigs, and tapirs. Bows and arrows as well as snares and traps were used. Many lake-dwelling creatures were also food for the table: turtles, salamanders, frogs, tadpoles, shellfish, and

The Great Temple at Tenochtitlán as painted by the Italian artist Fumagalli in the nineteenth century. This view provides some sense of the scale and natural setting of the Aztec capital. How can you tell that this painting was done after the Aztec civilization had passed?

waterfowl. The Aztecs domesticated only five animals: the turkey, the Muscovy duck, the dog, the bee, and the cochineal beetle (used to produce a dye). The dogs raised for food were a hairless variety, probably very much like the modern breed known as Mexican hairless.

Aside from the major groups of foods already listed, there were others used by the Aztecs that may seem strange and exotic to some of us: locusts, grubs, fish eggs, lizards, and tecuitlatl, the lake slime already described. Honey was used as a sweetener, and salt as a taste enhancer, but chili of all kinds was the universal seasoning. The Spaniards were amazed that the Aztecs could survive on so little food. The Aztecs imposed this regimen on themselves, and when children were quite young, they were encouraged not to be greedy but to eat sparingly.

Review...Recall...Reflect

1. Explain how the Aztec view of time differed from ours.

2. Explain the three ways that goods were exchanged within the Aztec Empire.

3. How was the city of Tenochtitlán like and unlike the Italian city of Venice?

Markets

The markets of central Mexico were an important part of the economy. The largest and most famous, and the one that impressed the Spaniards most when they arrived in the Aztec capital, was the market at Tlatelolco just north of Tenochtitlán. Hernán Cortés, in one of his letters to King Charles, estimated that 60 000 people traded at this market. Cortés recounts that every sort of merchandise in the land was found

here: ornaments of gold and silver, brass, copper, tin stones, shells, bones, and feathers. He also saw building materials such as lime, cut and uncut stone, mud bricks, tiles, and wood.

Cortés described streets of herbalists and apothecary shops where medicines were sold. In other zones of the market were barber shops, and shops where people stopped for food and drink. Porters were available to carry loads. There was firewood and charcoal for sale, as well as earthenware braziers, bedding and seats made of woven mats. All sorts of vegetables, syrups, and various alcoholic beverages were sold. Spun cotton in a great variety of colours was displayed, as were colour pigments for painters, deerskins dyed and undyed, and pottery of all shapes and sizes. Cortés also noted how well-run the markets were, because they were strictly regulated by judges. These judges were, of course, the powerful pochteca.

All goods were sold by count and volume but not by mass. Although the Aztecs had no monetary system — and no currency — there were items that had standardized values and were generally accepted in trade as a kind of money. The most widely used were cacao beans — money that really did grow on trees — but cloaks, quills filled with gold dust, and small copper axes were also used.

History Continues to Unfold

With the arrival of the Spaniards, the world of the Aztecs, the People of the Sun, came to an end. In the beginning, during the first encounters, the Europeans held Aztec achievements in awe. The conquistadors ("conquerors") married Aztec women, the priests were pleased by the Indians' reception of Christianity, and there was optimism about the creation of a New World culture that would surpass the old. But

These two oil paintings show the meeting of the Aztec King Montezuma and Hernán Cortés, in 1519. The event is interpreted here by a Spanish artist of the seventeenth century. What might have been his source of information? Having seen and read what you have about the Aztecs, do you think these paintings are accurate? What might have been different from what you see here?

prejudice soon set in, and greed reigned as Spaniards poured into Mexico bent on making fortunes by exploiting Aboriginal labour, and taking Aboriginal land. The most devastating consequence of the Spanish Conquest (1519–1521) was the radical depopulation that resulted from introduced diseases, forced labour, slavery, and demoralization. Not least important was the introduction of cattle, sheep, and goats, whose demands for grass and leaves had to be met, thus forever transforming the relationship between people and nature.

Montezuma, the Aztec king, is often said to have feared **Hernán Cortés** before the two ever met, because Montezuma thought Cortés was the ancient god-king Quetzalcoatl. This popular story is now known to have been invented by the Spaniards after the Conquest, perhaps to justify their actions. We leave the Aztecs, with a statement made by Hernán Cortés in one of his letters to the Spanish king that demonstrates the conflicting emotions the conquerors experienced about the people they were to overcome and the culture they were to destroy:

> Yet, so as not to tire Your Highness with the description of the things of this city... I will say only that these people live almost like those in Spain, and in as much harmony and order as there, and considering that they are barbarous and so far from the knowledge of God and cut off from all civilized nations, it is truly remarkable to see what they have achieved in all things.

Current Research and Interpretations

Estimates vary as to the population of central Mexico before the Spaniards arrived, but one source places it at 25 million just prior to the Conquest, with a decline of 95 percent by the end of the sixteenth century. Others maintain that the decline was not quite this severe. The New World was not free of disease prior to the Conquest, but major epidemics were unknown. People died by the hundreds, and then thousands, and neither the Aboriginal people nor the Europeans understood why. Eventually, after many died, some gained immunity and populations recovered, but in some areas it has taken until modern times to do so.

Chapter Review

Chapter Summary

In this chapter, we have seen:

- that the threat of a scarcity of resources was a crucial factor in the development of the Aztec social organization
- how the militaristic nature of Aztec society defined the bases of authority in the society
- that the Aztec superior military skills allowed them to dominate the Valley of Mexico during the fifteenth century
- that Aztec culture and society were shaped by external influences both from the past and from their contemporaries

Reviewing the Significance of Key People, Concepts, and Events (Knowledge/Understanding)

1. Understanding the history of the Aztec civilization requires a knowledge of the following concepts, and an understanding of their significance in the development of Aztec society. In your notes, identify and explain the historical significance of three from each column.

   Concepts
   Tenochtitlán
   chinampas
   Teotihuacán
   Tula
   Spanish Conquest

   People
   Tezcatlipoca
   Huitzilopochtli
   Tlaloc
   Montezuma

2. Prepare a chart in your notes like the one below to compare life among the Aztecs for the nobility and the commoners.

	Homes	Diet	Clothing	Laws
Nobility				
Commoners				

3. Explain the connection between religious prophecy and the rapid collapse of the Aztec Empire. Transfer the central idea of your response and the nature of the legend associated with this event to the graphic organizer "Myths, Legends, and Traditions" in your *World History Handbook*.

Doing History: Thinking About the Past (Thinking/Inquiry)

1. To a large degree, the prosperity of the Aztecs was dependent on nature. In a paragraph, assess how successful the Aztecs were at adapting to their natural environment. Be sure to discuss at least two specific examples in your answer.

2. List, in order of importance, the three major reasons the Aztecs were able to quickly build the dominant empire in central Mexico, and justify your ranking. Transfer each of these reasons to the graphic organizer "Why Some Societies Rose to Dominance" in your *World History Handbook*.

Applying Your Learning (Application)

1. On a map of central Mexico, depict pictorially the growth of the Aztec Empire, showing their conquests and the flow of tribute into the capital city, Tenochtitlán. The intent of this activity is to capture symbolically the growth of the empire, rather than to depict exactly where the goods came from.

2. Write an obituary for the Aztec leader Montezuma II, citing his contributions to the political and military life of the Aztecs and the circumstances of his death. You may need to do extra research to prepare his obituary.

Communicating Your Learning (Communication)

1. Create a diagram illustrating the social hierarchy of Aztec society. Include at least five people or groups. Transfer some of the ideas from your diagram to the organizer "Forms of Social Organization" in your *World History Handbook*.

2. Write a news story for the *Aztec Chronicle* explaining the events of 8 November 1519. Make sure your story has an effective title and follows the proper format for a newspaper article. You may want to read a recent account of an event in a local paper to review the key elements of a news story.

CHAPTER FOURTEEN

The Inca

By the end of this chapter, you will be able to:

- *describe the characteristics of Inca society that allowed stability through the Empire*

- *evaluate the effectiveness of different forms and processes of change as they relate to the expansion of the Inca Empire and the encounter between the Inca and the Spanish*

- *evaluate the role and importance of legends, myths, and traditions in Inca society*

- *evaluate the influence of religion on the political structure of the Inca Empire*

For the Incas, the llama was the most important of the sure-footed, camel-like anim native to the Andes Mountains. The Inca used llamas as pack animals and for sacrifi This figurine is silver, and made in the early fifteenth century.

The first encounter between the Inca Emperor Atawallpa and Francisco Pizarro, the leader of a small Spanish force of about 160 soldiers, came on 16 November 1532. This meeting has been described by several eyewitnesses, retold by Spanish historians who drew on this testimony, and later reinterpreted by indigenous chroniclers. Here is a summary account:

> Atawallpa crossed the plain in a slow procession from his encampment at the thermal baths toward the Inca administrative centre at Cajamarca [about 6 km]. Proceeding at this slow pace, Atawallpa seemed to hesitate in his intention to confront the Spaniards, deciding at one point to stop for the night, but Pizarro's emissaries urged him to continue. Pizarro waited impatiently in the walled plaza of the Inca centre, observing the approach of the Inca, accompanied by about 5000 troops armed only with small maces and slings. Atawallpa was carried in a litter lined with feathers and covered with plates of gold and silver, borne by 80 nobles dressed in blue tunics. Entering the compound, Atawallpa was met by a Spanish priest who spoke to him briefly and showed him a book. Atawallpa may have tossed down the book or allowed it to fall onto the ground. The priest shouted out that the Christians should attack these enemies of God, and the Spanish fell upon the Inca, firing two cannons as a signal to attack. Atawallpa's litter bearers struggled to save their emperor, but the goal of the Spanish attack, modelled on the success of Cortés, was to capture Atawallpa and use him as a hostage to extend their control over the empire. They did capture Atawallpa alive and then proceded to push the attack as the Incas took flight across the plain.

The accounts note that no Inca offered armed resistance to the attack. By early evening, 7000 Inca lay dead. Eventually, after extracting a huge ransom — more than 13 000 pounds of gold and 26 000 pounds of silver — the Spaniards executed Atawallpa on 26 July 1533.

While the outline of the story is clear, the details vary so widely that we will probably never know exactly what happened. These uncertainties illustrate the problems historians face in trying to reconstruct Inca history, if we interpret history as mainly an account of events. On the other hand, we can use information from the chronicles, together with archaeological information, to understand Inca culture and provide perspective on its development.

KEY WORDS

Cuzco

Quechua

tambos

wak'as

Tawantinsuyu

Sapa Inca

Qoya

ayllus

Machu Pichu

kipu

KEY PEOPLE

Manqu

Mama Waqu

Pacha Kutiq

Thupa Inca

Wayna Qhapaq

Atawallpa

Francisco Pizarro

Wira Qucha

Virgins of the Sun

mindalaes

mitmaq

VOICES FROM THE PAST

With the strings the whole kingdom was governed.
Felipe Guaman Poma ca. 1565, on the *kipu*

TIME LINE: THE INCA

	ca. 10 000 BCE	Andean area is first settled by tribes of hunters and gatherers
By this time, a variety of plants and animals have been domesticated	ca. 2500 BCE	
	ca. 1800 BCE	Increasing reliance on agriculture leads to the development of irrigation systems
Ideas from the Amazon, Andes, and coastal plain fuse into a common cosmology that influences all future cultural developments in the Andes	ca. 800–200 BCE	
	1438	Threats to the Inca city of Cuzco lead to the expansion of the Inca Empire as a defensive measure
Without naming an heir, Inca Emperor Wayna Qhapaq dies of smallpox brought by a Spanish adventurer.	1527	
	1532	First encounter between the Inca and Spaniards
Spaniards execute Atawallpa, the Inca Emperor, Inca Empire is on the verge of collapse	1533	

GEOGRAPHY OF THE INCA WORLD

The Inca Empire was the largest in the New World, stretching some 4000 km from north to south along the western edge of South America. The northern frontier was the area that now spans the Colombia-Ecuador border, while the southern frontier was in what is now central Chile. Because of the early impact of foreign diseases, the population of the empire is uncertain, but estimates range between six and twelve million people. Administering an empire

of this size would have been difficult in the best of circumstances, but the region's geography makes the Inca accomplishment even more impressive.

The backbone of the imperial territory was the Andean mountain chain, consisting of two or three parallel ranges separated by mountain basins. Mountain peaks rise to elevations of over 6000 m above sea level. On the slopes of the peaks, at elevations of about 4000 m above sea level, are rolling grasslands useful for herding the native Andean llamas and alpacas — animals related to the Old World camels. Below the grasslands are lands suitable for agriculture. Some plants, like beans, potatoes, and other Andean root vegetables, do well at altitudes over 3400 m above sea level. Other plants, such as maize (a type of corn), only grow at elevations below 3400 m and are confined to the inter-Andean mountain basins. Maize was an extremely important plant for the Inca and they called the area where it could be grown *quechua*. This was also the name of the people who lived in the region and came to be used by the Spaniards as the name for the language spoken by the Inca. Other plants, such as chili peppers, gourds, cotton, and most of the tropical fruits, only grew in the lowest areas of the inter-Andean basins, below about 2800 m.

The climate of the Andean highlands was generally warmer and wetter in the northern part of the empire — present-day Ecuador and northern Peru. It is much colder and dryer south of Lake Titicaca, on the Peru-Bolivia border. Because of this, it is easier to grow maize in the north, where it served as a staple food, but potatoes were the major staple throughout the Andes mountain chain. Some maize was consumed in the form of beer, as a ritual food. One indigenous chronicler noted that people in the north were fierce because they ate maize, while those in the south were gentler because they ate potatoes.

■ The Inca Empire

How do the sizes and populations of the Inca and Aztec Empires compare?

While maize would not normally grow at the high altitude of Lake Titicaca (3800 m), the massive quantity of water tends to moderate the climate around the lakeshore (similar to the lake effect on the Niagara Peninsula), so some maize could be grown on islands and peninsulas. The Inca exploited this geographical feature, which may partially account for Lake Titicaca's major importance in Inca mythology.

On either side of the Andes, the land descends quickly into warmer lowlands. For the most part, the empire's eastern frontier corresponded with the eastern slopes and foothills of the Andes. In northern Peru, the Inca incorporated into their empire the Chachapoyas region, a mountainous outlier of the Andes that extends into the Amazon basin. In the south, they expanded into the Bolivian lowlands, where they could grow maize, and northwestern Argentina, which was rich in metal ores. Generally, though, the Inca viewed the peoples of the eastern lowlands as savages. While the Inca considered the lowlanders inferior, some tribes exerted considerable military pressure on the southeastern frontier. The Inca also traded with the lowlanders for feathers to decorate their clothing, the hard wood of the chonta palm to make war clubs, and medicinal plants. In fact, the Amazonian peoples are still regarded as particularly knowledgeable about medicinal plants.

The Inca exerted direct control over the coastal strip bordering the Pacific Ocean in present-day Peru and Chile, but never fully controlled the coast of what is now Ecuador. The coastal plain of Ecuador is warm and wet, supporting tropical forest similar to that found on the eastern side of the Andes. The Inca were more interested in trade than control of this region. Trade along the coast of Ecuador was well-developed, using large balsa log sailing rafts for transport of goods. One of the main products the Inca were interested in was a type of seashell they called "thorny oyster," which they used as a sacred offering to mountain springs in order to attract rain.

The Inca were cautious with the people of the dry coastal plains of Peru and Chile, shown here.

The coast of Peru and Chile is a stark contrast to the Ecuadorian climate. Here the coastal plain is an extremely dry desert, periodically crossed by rivers flowing down from the Andes. The Inca were wary of the coastal people, especially those on the northern coast of Peru, where the Chimu kingdom had strongly resisted Inca conquest.

ORIGINS OF THE INCA

The Inca represent the culmination of thousands of years of cultural development in the Andes. The Andean area was first settled about 12 000 years ago by people practising a hunting and gathering lifestyle. By about 2500 BCE, a variety of plants and animals had been domesticated in different parts of the Andes: cotton on the Pacific coastal plain; potatoes, beans, llamas, alpacas, and guinea pigs in the highlands; chilis, coca, and manioc (cassava) in the tropical forest east of the Andes. While as yet not fully relying on agriculture, people began constructing monumental mounds on the coast and in the highlands. The mounds were built gradually, beginning with a small core, and then adding to the core periodically, for several centuries, until the mound reached its final form. These constructions represented a variety of architectural styles — some emphasized huge patios bounded by lateral mounds; others incorporated a sunken circular court into the patio. The focal building of others was a small room, with a ceremonial hearth in the centre, which probably functioned much like a sweat lodge. These different architectural traditions represent varying religious traditions, although, with our present knowledge, we cannot be sure of the belief systems. What is clear is that the construction of these mounds demonstrated the ability of the early cultures to coordinate large amounts of labour over many generations to produce an architectural form that embodied the community's beliefs.

By about 1800 BCE, increasing reliance on agriculture had led to the development of irrigation systems, at least on the coastal plain. Again, the construction and maintenance of irrigation canals, as well as the orderly distribution of water from the canals, implies a united and well-organized community. People could now rely on a broad range of plants and animals for their livelihood. On the coast, animal protein was provided by fish, shellfish, guinea pigs, and llamas. In the highlands, guinea pigs, llamas, and alpacas were the major source of protein. Potatoes and other root crops, maize, and several varieties of beans were grown in the highlands. On the coastal plain, maize, beans, squashes, tomatoes, peanuts, manioc, and a variety of fruits (the best-known in North America likely being the avocado) rounded out the diet. Everywhere, chilis and salt were used as condiments, and tobacco, coca, maize beer, and other mind-altering plant extracts were used for ritual purposes. Metals — first gold, then silver, copper, tin, and their alloys were used for both functional and decorative objects.

Between about 800 and 200 BCE, a major cultural synthesis took place. Ideas from the Amazon, Andes, and coastal plain were combined into a cosmology (model of the universe) that influenced all later cultural development in the Andres.

INCA HISTORY
Dynastic Origins

As with other aspects of Inca history, the details of Inca dynastic succession and expansion are described in quite different ways in the historical sources available to us. Some accounts, for example, attribute very long reigns to each of the Inca kings in an attempt to align Inca dynastic history with events in the Old World, such as the birth of Jesus. Others provide conflicting lists of the Inca rulers, their queens, their generals, and the territories they conquered. The overall outline of Inca history, however, can be gathered from these accounts.

In legend, **Manqu** is credited with founding the Inca dynasty. Founding ancestors were important figures in Andean mythology, and were thought of as emerging from the earth, springs, or caves in ancient times. In one version of the story, Manqu emerged from a cave along with three brothers and four sisters at a place called Pacarictambo ("origin place"), about 35 km south of Cuzco. They were given a gold staff and told to plunge it into the ground as they wandered from place to place. They were to settle where the staff disappeared deep into the ground. Along the way, one of the brothers was sent back to the cave to retrieve some things they had left there, but another brother sent a man along

Inca nobles paying homage to Manqu, founder of the Inca dynasty. From a book by an Andean historian.

with him to wall him into the cave. Another brother turned himself into a mountain, Wanakawri, that became one of the most sacred places in the empire. They found the land they were looking for at **Cuzco**, where the third brother turned himself into a stone. Since Cuzco was already occupied by people, one of the sisters, **Mama Waqu**, killed an inhabitant and cut him open. She pulled out his lungs and blew into them to inflate them. The people were so terrified by this that they ran away.

This story is significant for a number of reasons. It follows the general form of Andean origin myths. The ancestral heroes emerge from the ground and wander around the landscape, sometimes becoming part of the landscape, before arriving at the place

they settle. It is also common in Andean origin myths for the newcomers to have to defeat people who already occupied the area. It is unusual, however, for a woman to take the initiative in warfare and defeat a male opponent. While Manqu was legendary, the remaining Inca in the dynastic list were probably real people. The Spaniards were able to discover, and eventually destroy, mummified bodies that were believed to be the Inca kings.

The early Inca kings ruled only a small area around Cuzco itself. The title *sinchi*, which means "strong man" or "war leader," may imply that the earliest members of the dynasty did not have a hereditary right to rule, but only acquired authority in times of crisis. The title *qhapaq*, which has the connotations of "rich" and "lordly," suggests a hereditary nobility. The reigns of the early Inca kings are described as a time of shifting alliances and recurring warfare with their immediate neighbours.

This description must be understood in an Andean context. The lack of fortifications in the Cuzco area and the general uniformity in ceramic styles suggest a more stable situation than the chroniclers imply. Andean warfare rarely involved prolonged sieges, and, instead, usually consisted of a series of battles. Generally, the battles were not intended to destroy the other group, but only to establish a dominant-subordinate relationship that ranked the groups participating in the battle. The battles were also viewed in part as signs of which side the gods most favoured.

Growth of the Empire

Pacha Kutiq

About 1438 CE, a series of events led to Inca expansion out of the Cuzco area. Faced with an attack by the Chankas, longtime enemies of the Inca, the Inca king,

Wira Qucha, and his designated heir, Inca Urku, decided that Cuzco could not be successfully defended. They retreated to a fortress north of the city. Another son of the king, Kusi Yupanki, decided to stay and defend the city against the Chanka attack with the help of two experienced generals. On the eve of the Chanka attack, Kusi Yupanki had a vision of the creator god, who told him that he would be victorious. During a crucial moment in the battle, the very stones of the battlefield are said to have risen up to help the Inca contingent defeat the Chankas. Based on his success in this battle, and the obvious favour of the gods, Kusi Yupanki usurped the throne and changed his name to **Pacha Kutiq**. The term *pacha* signifies both "time" and "earth," while *kutiq* signifies a "change" or "turning." By taking on the name Pacha Kutiq, Kusi Yupanki was proclaiming a new world order.

The terraced buildings of the Citadel at Machu Pichu, built as a royal estate under Emperor Pacha Kutiq.

The new king began constructing that new order almost immediately by sending soldiers to the north under the command of a brother, Qhapaq Yupanki. Included in the force, were a large number of Chankas, now allied with the Inca. King Pacha Kutiq had instructed his brother not to go beyond a river called the Yanamayo. However, the Chankas fled, fearing betrayal and attack by the Inca. Qhapaq Yupanki pursued them, hoping to catch and reintegrate them into his force. The Chankas crossed the Yanamayo River, with Qhapaq Yupanki in pursuit, and disappeared into the Amazon jungle. Qhapaq Yupanki was now faced with a difficult decision: should he return to face Pacha Kutiq without the Chankas, having also disobeyed orders and crossed the Yanamayo? He decided to continue north, conquering all the way to Cajamarca in the northern highlands of Peru. Again, this conquest should be understood as simply a series of battles to establish the superior military strength of the Inca; it did not result in effective control of the vast territory or its population. Qhapaq Yupanki left part of his army in Cajamarca as a garrison force, and began the march back to Cuzco and the king.

Thupa Inca

Pacha Kutiq had Qhapaq Yupanki executed before he was able to return to Cuzco; an insubordinate and successful brother was a dangerous combination. Pacha Kutiq was faced with a garrison isolated hundreds of kilometres to the north and rebellious allies nearer home. He first fought a series of battles around Cuzco and in the Lake Titicaca basin to the south to bring the allies into line. He then sent his son and designated heir, **Thupa Inca**, north to relieve the garrison at Cajamarca.

Thupa Inca's expedition was probably the most important empire-building event in the history of the expansion of the Inca Empire. Again, the historical

Rites of Passage
Some Inca Rituals

Very little occurred in Inca society without some kind of ceremony or ritual sacrifice — even the daily rising of the sun. Priests lit fires early every morning and threw corn on them to toast, then urged the Sun to eat the corn and remember that they were the Sun's Children. Strict observance of the ritual was believed to ensure that the sun would rise again.

Once the Sun was up, only the most mundane matters were not subjected to divination. Divination is the attempt to foresee or predict the future by various means. Some forms of divination that you may have experienced or heard about are Tarot Cards and palm reading.

The Inca relied on divination to help deal with many concerns: all political and military actions, to appease the gods, to diagnose illness, even to uncover and judge crimes. One method of divination was to watch a spider wander — one direction or pattern meant one thing, the opposite direction something else. Another way of divining appropriate action was to assess the arrangement taken by coca leaves dropped in a shallow dish (like reading tea leaves). Serious divination required priests to interpret the inflated lungs of a pure white llama that had been sacrificed.

Much has been written about sacrifice in Meso-American cultures, but most of that was written by the Spanish conquerors, so it is difficult to know how much was misunderstood, fabricated, or an attempt to justify the Spaniards' own behaviour. Many rituals did involve some kind of sacrifice, especially if you count all the food, plant and drink sacrifices. There is some evidence that on the first day of every lunar month about 100 pure white llamas would be sacrificed in the main square. Clothing was also sacrificed, particularly finely woven tunics. Miniature articles of clothing might also be burned. The Inca ruler wore a new tunic every day and the old ones were ceremoniously burned.

Human sacrifice was for extreme situations only — perhaps there had been a drought, famine, virulent disease, or military defeat. Perhaps there were criminals and prisoners of war to sacrifice. In the scheme of things, it seems that humans had had only a small part to play in the Inca world vision. Appeasing the gods and preserving world order took precedence over everything else.

The Inca frequently sacrificed llamas, shown above in their Andean habitat.

Activities

1. Defend or reject the following statement: It is impossible for members of one society to truly comprehend the ritual practices of another society.

2. Describe rituals in your own everyday life. What makes them similar to or different from Inca rituals?

accounts are often contradictory. It is clear that Thupa Inca not only was able to relieve the garrison in Cajamarca, but also continued northward into Ecuador. In Ecuador, Thupa Inca descended to the coast and undertook a sea voyage on a balsa log sailing raft. One of these rafts was captured during Francisco Pizarro's second expedition southward along the coast; it was described as capable of carrying 30 t of cargo.

Thupa Inca then attacked the Chimu. The Chimu Kingdom controlled the entire north coast of Peru, extending almost from Lima to the Ecuadorian border. The Chimu presented both the greatest challenge to the expanding Inca Empire and the best model of successful large-scale administrative organization. After conquering the Chimu capital of Chan Chan, the Inca took the last independent Chimu king to Cuzco as a hostage, and appointed one of his sons to rule in Chan Chan as a puppet. They also removed thousands of skilled artisans, predominantly weavers and metalworkers, to Cuzco and other Inca centres.

Thupa Inca then turned his attention to the south coast of Peru, and then rounded out his career by conquering Bolivia and penetrating deep into Chile and the northwestern part of Argentina. Accounts suggest that some of the south-coast valleys fiercely resisted conquest. In one case, after Thupa Inca had been frustrated by the resistance offered by a coastal queen to his attempts to conquer the Cañete valley, the Inca queen took control and conquered her rival with a clever plan. On the other hand, testimony from the central highlands of Peru indicates that the Inca conquest sometimes took place without battles at all: the Inca would show up with a huge army and offer the local nobility the opportunity to join them. If the local rulers accepted, the Inca gave them gifts and confirmed them in their office. If they resisted, they would be conquered. There are even cases from northwestern Argentina of the local rulers inviting the Inca into their territories as allies against hostile tribes. In many cases, the rapidity of Thupa Inca's conquests was due, in part, to the lack of substantial resistance. Conquest was also facilitated by the fact that the areas he conquered shared in the Andean cultural tradition to varying degrees. That is, they already had similar economies and similar philosophies relating to religion, politics, and social organization.

Wayna Qhapaq

Thupa Inca's successor, Wayna Qhapaq, faced a different situation, and much of his career was spent fighting on the frontiers against unacculturated peoples. In the southeast, hostile tribes were a constant threat. In the far south, he was never able to make much progress against the Mapuche, who also resisted Spanish domination into the nineteenth century. In the north, he had more success in Ecuador, but this came at the cost of prolonged

---

Scripts & Symbols λ μ ν ο π θ υ ρ σ τ υ ϖ ω ξ ψ ζ α β χ ε δ φ γ

The Inca had no written language. Their spoken language was called Quechua *and many words have been translated from speech. The closest thing to a written record was the* kipu, *the device used to keep numerical calculations.*

Expansion of the Inca Empire

Map legend:
- Pacha Kutiq (1438–1471)
- Thupa Inca (1471–1493)
- Wayna Qhapaq (1493–1527)
- Inca Roads
- Modern political boundaries

warfare. Gradually, through force of arms, diplomacy, intermarriage with the local nobility, and the transformation of the local economies, Wayna Qhapaq was able to integrate central and northern Ecuador into the Inca Empire.

Wayna Qhapaq died from smallpox or measles in Ecuador. The disease had been brought into the empire by a Spanish sailor who landed on the Atlantic coast of Brazil and crossed the continent with members of a marauding tribe who were raiding the eastern frontier of the Inca Empire in Bolivia and northwestern Argentina. From the southeastern frontier of the empire, the disease spread to the

capital at Cuzco, and then to Quito, where Wayna Qhapaq had been fighting. As the disease spread throughout the empire, it devastated the population, noble and commoner alike, since the Aboriginal peoples had never developed resistance to these old-world diseases. Wayna Qhapaq died in 1527 without being able to properly designate an heir to the throne.

While Waskar, who was based in Cuzco, had the stronger claim to the throne, Wayna Qhapaq's other son, **Atawallpa**, had his father's experienced generals with him in Quito. With the aid of these generals, Atawallpa gradually was able to push back the army Waskar had sent to Ecuador. As his army moved south towards the capital, Atawallpa ruthlessly punished ethnic groups who had sided with Waskar. Arriving in Huamachuco in the northern highlands of Peru, he consulted the oracle Catequil, who predicted that he would come to a bad end because he was such a bloody tyrant. Angered, Atawallpa set up camp at the shrine of the oracle and put part of his army to work destroying it. He was there two months, while his generals defeated Waskar's army, captured Waskar, and massacred all the members of Waskar's family and faction in Cuzco.

It was also during this time that the Spaniard **Francisco Pizarro** landed in Peru. Atawallpa was aware of Pizarro's arrival and sent envoys to gather information about these strange people and their movements. Through his envoys, he instructed Pizarro to proceed to Cajamarca, just north of Huamachuco. Cajamarca was a major Inca administrative centre from which the emperor administered most of northern Peru. Just outside Cajamarca, across the flat plain of the Cajamarca valley, are natural hot springs that Atawallpa intended to visit to undergo purification rites. While Pizarro's troops climbed from the coast into the Andean mountains — complaining of the cold and altitude —

Atawallpa proceeded with much ceremony to Cajamarca and set up, with his army, an impressive tent camp at the hot springs.

Historians have no clear idea of Atawallpa's motives and plans: Was he simply planning to meet with Pizarro? Or, as some accounts suggest, was he secretly planning to surround and attack the Spanish force to capture them alive, castrate them, and use them as eunuchs to guard the houses of the "Chosen Women"? What is clear is that Atawallpa had shown himself, in a very short period, capable of dealing with crisis in an efficient and ruthless manner.

Review...Reflect...Recall

1. List and explain two reasons why Andean geography makes the Inca Empire an impressive accomplishment.

2. What evidence suggests that by 1800 BCE united and well organized communities had developed in the Andes?

3. What does the legend of Manqu reveal about Andean history and religion?

MILITARY HISTORY

Military tactics and logistics were gradually transformed during the Inca imperial expansion. Little is directly known about early Inca military history, but later observations, clues in the dynastic history, and **Quechua** (the Inca language) terminology relating to warfare give a reasonably detailed picture. Battles generally took place in open fields. The sling was the long-range weapon of choice and could propel a stone somewhat larger than an egg at least 50 m with good accuracy. The stones that were said to have risen up to aid Pacha Kutiq against the Chankas were probably sling stones. Bolas (short ropes with balls on both ends that were thrown) were also used at times to entwine the legs of the enemy, and this was the weapon used in Mama Waqu's legendary conquest of Cuzco. Maces (a type of club), with star-shaped or round stone heads, were the traditional short-range weapon. A sharp-edged wooden sword, made from the wood of a tropical forest palm, may not have been readily available to the Inca until the reigns of Pacha Kutiq or Thupa Inca. Similarly, during these later reigns, tropical forest bowmen were added to the Inca armies.

Tactics were relatively simple. The battle started with slingers and bowmen firing at long range. Then, the combatants closed in a rather chaotic hand-to-hand battle. There were no organized phalanxes, as among the Greeks and Romans. In fact, many Quechua terms relating to warfare connote one-on-one competition, either in war or in a game. One typical Inca tactic seems to have been to divide the force into three parts and engage the enemy in a pincer movement. The Inca also set grass fires to drive the enemy out of strong positions.

The earliest Inca armies probably consisted of volunteers, and were likely composed only of ethnic Incas or a few closely allied ethnic groups. During the initial period of expansion, in the reigns of Pacha Kutiq and Thupa Inca, the armies became more multi-ethnic. Each contingent was led by its own ethnic leaders, under the overall generalship of an Inca king or close relative. By the time of Wayna Qhapaq, the army had become more professionalized, probably the result of his prolonged campaigns on the frontiers. Generals were still high-ranking Inca nobles, but might not be close relatives of the emperor. Instead, they were his retainers, members of his court who owed him direct allegiance. Most of the troops continued to be draftees from the various ethnic groups, but a few ethnic groups now provided a core of shock troops.

The transport of food and other provisions of warfare certainly changed over time. There is no indication that the early battles relied on this support, and they may have been fought, in part, with the hope of plundering what was needed. Women usually accompanied the troops — a fact that shocked the Spaniards — but warfare and fertility were linked in the Inca mind. Women also supported the troops by serving as porters and even carrying the sling stones into battle. Thupa Inca likely had no support on his first expedition north into Ecuador and against the Chimu. Thupa Inca and Pacha Kutiq also issued orders to repair and maintain the highland road system, large sections of which probably already existed. The road system was crucial for the movement of troops to the frontiers, and it was probably also Thupa Inca who had the *tambos* (way stations and administrative centres) built at convenient marching intervals along the roads. The tambos became the focus of Inca administration in the provinces, as well as the bases for the armies.

This is a clay figure of an Inca porter carrying a jug on his back. This was how the Inca transported materials for military campaigns, to stock the tambos, and for everyday purposes.

The Spaniards were very impressed with the quantity and variety of material stockpiled in the tambos. There was everything from firewood to sandals, uniforms, blankets, tools, weapons, and food. Included in the food, were dried meat (our word "jerky" comes from the Quechua *ch'arki*) and quantities of corn and potatoes. While potatoes were the staple food in the highlands, the troops were supplied with large quantities of corn, both toasted kernels as a lightweight travelling ration, and, especially, maize beer. The tambos had areas in which the "Chosen Women" could brew the beer, and other areas where it was served in the form of ritual hospitality — the Inca leader providing a feast for his troops. Wayna Qhapaq made an important innovation in this regard by reorganizing corn production in the Cochabamba Valley, Bolivia, to better supply the army. By the time of Wayna Qhapaq's reign, there was also a well-designed set of frontier fortifications protecting the perimeter of the empire.

Warfare was always closely linked to religious beliefs. A myth told that people were once immortal, but the growth in population led to food scarcities. So, in exchange for the ability to procreate, they agreed to become mortal. In the Inca view, death begot life, and death in war was linked to this belief and thought to promote the regeneration of the world. In a related vein, warfare was considered a form of divination: success in war showed not only that the gods were on your side, but also that you were maintaining a proper relationship with the gods. Indigenous (native) chroniclers describe warfare as the conquest of the enemy's deities. The idols of the conquered ethnic groups were taken as hostages to Cuzco. The Incas carried their own idols into war.

One of their most important deities was the emperor himself, the Son of the Sun, who was often carried into battle on his litter. If the emperor could

The citadel at Cuzco, the capital of the Inca Empire.

not be present at the battle, he sent his own personal idol, his "brother," as a substitute. Success in battle was then linked directly to the power of the emperor and his ability to intercede with and defeat other deities. If he was successful, it showed that he had the divine right to rule. If he was unsuccessful, it showed that rebellious brothers or the leaders of other ethnic groups might be better able to maintain the proper balance between supernatural and natural forces.

INCA RELIGION
The Concept of Wak'as

Like other Andean peoples, the Inca believed that the world was inhabited by many different supernatural forces, which were referred to as *wak'as*. In general, the wak'as can be viewed as forces of regeneration, but there were many different kinds of wak'as. Some were connected to specific points on the landscape, such as mountains, springs, lakes, caves, and rock outcrops. Certain springs and caves were considered the places where the ancestors originally came out of the ground. Some rock outcrops were also explained as ancestors who had turned themselves into stone or as enemies that the ancestors had turned to stone. Some high

mountain peaks were thought to control the fertility of animals. Some springs were worshipped in order to attract rain. Wak'as related to the landscape usually had local or regional significance, but a few, Lake Titicaca for example, were important over very large areas. Other wak'as, such as strangely shaped fruits or oddly coloured stones, might be important to only a single household. The ancestors themselves were also considered to be wak'as, but were only significant to the people descended from them. Celestial phenomena, such as the sun, moon, lightning, and certain constellations, along with the earth and the ocean, were also wak'as, and were significant throughout the Andes, under different names. The wak'as were sometimes represented by human-made idols.

Ancient
ODDITIES

The reverence that the Incas had for their ancestors was so great that the bodies of the dead emperors were mummified. These bodies were brought out and paraded during major festivals, and the dead would feast and drink toasts with each other and with the living. The mummies themselves also owned large estates to support their cults.

The worship of wak'as entailed maintaining a proper relationship between the wak'as and people. Offerings were made to them, and they were treated with great respect, in the expectation that the wak'as would reciprocate and provide the people with life's necessities. In an agricultural society, this meant rain at the proper season, lack of killing frosts, reproduction of domesticated animals and plants, and human reproduction. In a world with so many different wak'as, maintaining a proper relationship with all of them was a complicated undertaking. If things were going well, one could assume that the wak'as were satisfied. When things went wrong, it was difficult to determine which of the wak'as might be dissatisfied. Partly for this reason, many different forms of divination (an attempt to predict the future or discover hidden knowledge by the observation of omens) were widely practised.

The Incas and the Wak'as

Inca religion was inclusive and the wak'as of conquered peoples were incorporated into its religious system. Some of these regional wak'as have already been mentioned: the origin place of the Incas at Pacarictambo, the hill called Wanakawri that one of Manqu's brothers turned himself into, and the stones that rose up to help Pacha Kutiq in his battle against the Chankas. The Inca emperors were considered to be wak'as themselves, and their role was to know all the wak'as, to mediate between them, and assure a proper relationship between all the wak'as and humanity.

As the empire expanded, one of Pacha Kutiq's first administrative acts was to organize the Cuzco regional wak'as into a coherent system. He conceived of the wak'as as being located along 41 or 42 lines, *ceques* in Quechua, that radiated in all directions from the centre of the city. The ceque system provided a sacred landscape that symbolically linked Cuzco, as the centre of power, to the rest of the empire.

Pacha Kutiq made other important innovations relating to religion. He may have instituted the worship of a creator-god for the first time. The Inca creator-god was called **Wira Qucha**. As part of his reconstruction of the capital, he also built the Temple of the Sun, the point from which the ceque lines radiated out into the empire. This was a

magnificent set of buildings inside a walled compound. The stones in the walls were beautifully laid, without using mortar between them. There were gold plates on some walls to reflect the sun, and in one part of the temple, was a ceremonial garden with all the plants and animals, including an image of a llama herder, all fashioned of gold.

Pacha Kutiq also instituted the Chosen Women, sometimes referred to as the **Virgins of the Sun**. These women (*aqlla* in Quechua) were selected at about age ten from all parts of the empire as the most beautiful and unblemished girls. They were placed in convent-like institutions where they were taught the skills that well-bred women should know, especially weaving and the preparation of ritual food, including maize beer. As they grew older, some became concubines of the Inca emperor, others were given by the emperor to favoured nobles and very successful warriors as either primary or secondary wives. Others remained in the Houses of the Chosen Women in perpetual chastity to serve the official religion, the cult of the sun. In all of this, Pacha Kutiq sought to firmly identify the Inca dynasty with the sun, one of the most powerful celestial wak'as.

This rock formation was considered a wak'a by the Inca. The zig zag channel and basin were for offerings of maize beer.

Thupa Inca also made innovations in the sphere of religion, though less comprehensive than those of his father. During his conquests on the coast of Peru, he encountered the shrine of Pachakamaq (Quechua for "world animator"). This shrine had been important, especially among the coastal peoples, for a thousand years. Pachakamaq was viewed, in part, as a creator-god, but his more immediate significance was as a powerful and respected oracle: people went to the shrine of Pachakamaq to put questions to the oracle. Like the oracle of Delphi in ancient Greece, the answers Pachakamaq gave, through his priests, were usually cryptic and ambiguous. Still, his track record over centuries must have been good enough to impress Thupa Inca, who formed an alliance with the oracle. As part of this alliance, Thupa Inca built shrines for the "sons," "wives," and "daughters" of Pachakamaq in a number of different places in the empire. Pachakamaq also provided a travelling oracle that accompanied Thupa Inca personally.

It has recently been proposed that Wayna Qhapaq established a similar relationship with the oracle, Catequil, whose main shrine was located near Huamachuco in the northern highlands of Peru. Wayna Qhapaq had passed through this area many times on his way to the campaigns in Ecuador, and established a special relationship with the region. While Catequil was not as famous as Pachakamaq, Wayna Qhapaq became a patron of his cult and spread it to Ecuador, where there are still at least seven places named after Catequil. Catequil was associated with the origin of the people of Huamachuco, but he was also a lightning deity and, in that capacity, was associated with abundant flows of water.

As with the Inca emperors themselves, the power of the wak'as, including oracles such as Catequil and Pachakamaq, was judged by their success. If the oracle's predictions were correct, they were respected and offerings were made to them. If their predictions were wrong, however, they could be punished by the Inca emperors, who were themselves wak'as.

SOCIAL HISTORY

Tawantinsuyu

The Inca's own name for their empire was **Tawantinsuyu**. This name is often translated as "the empire of the four quarters," but a stricter translation is more informative. *Tawa* is four and *suyu* are territorial divisions, while the term *ntin* indicates all four divisions taken together as a whole. The name reflects the Inca concern with divisions on the one hand, and wholeness on the other. This concern for defining complementary pairs is central to their religious, political, and social philosophies.

Government

The emperor was called the **Sapa Inca**, or "Unique Inca." The Sapa Inca was the head of the governmental, religious, and social hierarchies. He reigned along with his queen, the **Qoya**, who was, at

The Past AT PLAY

Inca children had few toys; one was a top that was spun by whipping it with a cord. Adults played a number of board games that used a five-pointed dice and beans as counters to move through the spaces on the board. The board games were often accompanied by gambling for small stakes, such as blankets and livestock.

least from the time of Thupa Inca, his full sister. The Qoya also exercised considerable power in her own sphere.

A close relative was appointed prefect for each of the four divisions, and these officials also formed a council of state to help the Sapa Inca administer the empire. Each province had an Inca official as governor, but much of the actual provincial administration was done by lords who belonged to the conquered ethnic groups. The Inca confirmed these lords in their offices, provided them with gifts, and sometimes formed marriage alliances with them. The provinces and the provincial nobility were structured by a decimal administrative system. Each province tended to have about 20 000 households, if it was divided into two halves, or 30 000 households, if it was divided into three parts. At the head of each group of 10 000 households (called a *hunu*), was a provincial noble. The hunus were divided into two halves, each with 5000 households (called *pichqa waranqas*) that were also led by nobles. These, in turn, were divided into five groups of 1000 households (called *waranqas*). The waranqas were divided into two groups of 500 households (called *pichqa pachacas*), and then five groups of 100 households (called *pachacas*). Leaders of groups at the pachaca level were still considered members of the nobility, though of lesser rank than the leaders of larger groups. The pachacas were subdivided into groups of fifty, ten, and five households, led by non-noble foremen. The terms used are the Quechua words for the numbers of households in each unit.

Age Grades

To keep an accurate census of the population, the Inca classed people into twelve census categories, often referred to as age grades. These categories were only partly defined by age, however, and were mainly an indication of the potential usefulness of the people to the state. There were parallel categories for men and women, each defined in part by the types of service the members of the age grade could perform. The most important category consisted of the able-bodied adults. Men of this category were eligible for service in the army and all other taxes, while women were described as wives of warriors and capable of weaving for the state. The Andean chronicler, Guaman Poma de Ayala, provides a list of the age grades, which emphasizes the particular jobs that people in each of the age grades, male and female, were expected to perform.

One of the notable aspects of the age grades is, again, the way in which males and females — from birth to death — were viewed as complementary to each other.

Households and Ayllus

The basic unit of social organization was the household. People only became full members of society when they married and set up a household. The basic household consisted of a husband and wife and their unmarried children. Wealthier households, such as those of the nobles, were larger.

Larger units were formed by members of the lineages, people who considered themselves descended from a common ancestor. The lineages, called **ayllus**, were another basic building block of Andean society, and contained varying numbers of households. Members of an ayllu held land in common, and each household was allotted a plot each year to work for its own subsistence. The allotments of land varied in size, depending on the number of members in the household. Members of an ayllu were supposed to marry people within their own ayllu, thus preserving the ayllu's land holdings. As with other aspects of Inca

Terrace systems such as this at Winay Wayna, near Machu Pichu, expanded the amount of land available for produce. Produce from these lands could be destined for religious or government use.

organization, the ayllus could be split into two halves for ceremonial purposes, or paired with a complementary ayllu to form larger units. The social boundaries of the ayllu were somewhat flexible, and depended on the particular context.

Land Tenure

The Inca divided lands into three major categories: land for the support of the state, land to support the state religion and the major wak'as, and land for the support of the ayllus.

As the Inca expanded, some lands were alienated from local control, and new lands were opened up through the construction of terrace systems and irrigation canals. The produce from these lands supported governmental activities, such as military operations, the bureaucracy, and labourers engaged in state-sponsored construction projects. The produce was kept in government storehouses that were distributed throughout the empire.

Other land was set aside to support the state religions, and the produce was stored in separate facilities. It was used to sponsor festivities related to the cult of the sun, to support the priests dedicated to the cult, and to support the Chosen Women. In addition to the official state religion, other major wak'as also had lands assigned to them that supported their cults, priests, and servants. Many of these cults predated the Inca expansion, and the Inca simply confirmed the land holdings. If the Inca favoured a particular cult, however, they might allocate new lands to it or, if they were annoyed by a wak'a, they could also take away the lands of that wak'a.

In the same way, the Inca confirmed the tenure of the ayllus lands. These lands were managed by the leaders of the ayllu, who decided what part should be left in fallow each year, allocated plots to individual households, and determined the crop rotation to be followed on the household plots.

Split Inheritance

From at least the time of Pacha Kutiq, the Inca emperors adopted a practice called split inheritance. Each Inca emperor founded his own descent group, to which all his sons and daughters belonged, except for the designated heir. The designated heir inherited the office of Sapa Inca, and, eventually, founded his own royal ayllu. The members of the royal ayllus inherited the lands of the deceased emperor and used them to support themselves as well as the cult of the mummy of the deceased emperor.

Each new emperor, then, had to accumulate his own royal estates to support himself and, eventually, the members of his descent group and the cult of his mummy. Many of these royal estates were located in the area immediately surrounding Cuzco. In fact, many of the sites that we most closely associate with the Inca, such as **Machu Pichu** and Chinchero, were the royal estates of the Inca emperors. Machu Pichu was one of the royal estates of Pacha Kutiq, and this explains its impressive terrace system, which

This is a drawing of Inca people parading the sacred mummy of a deceased emperor on a litter. Each new emperor had to support the cult of his predecessor.

produced food to support his court and later his royal ayllu.

Review...Recall...Reflect

1. Describe a typical Inca battle including the weapons and tactics used.

2. Explain the relationship between the Incas and the wak'as. How did this relationship differ for the rulers and the commoners?

3. Explain how land in the Inca Empire was divided. What was the purpose/function of dividing land in this way?

Occupational Specialization

For the most part, all people in the Inca Empire provided for their own subsistence by farming and herding. Indeed, the Inca encouraged self-sufficiency on the local level and, in times of peace, encouraged local groups to exploit lands in different elevational zones. Sometimes, these lands were located at a distance of several days' walk from the home communities. The home communities sent out a few members to herd llamas and alpacas on high-altitude grasslands or to exploit coca (a shrub whose leaves are used to produce cocaine) fields on the eastern or western slopes of the Andes. Some communities in the Lake Titicaca basin sent members all the way to the Pacific Ocean to bring back edible algae.

There were some exceptions, however. For example, people on the coast tended to specialize more and some were full-time artisans, fishers, and brewers, while others only farmed. In Ecuador, there were also full-time trade specialists who worked under the patronage of the local nobility and, later, under the patronage of the Inca. These traders, called *mindalaes*, travelled widely to accumulate and transport luxury items such as gold and cotton cloth, and used strings of shell beads, called *chaquira*, as a form of primitive currency. There are also reports of full-time traders based in the Chincha Valley on the south coast of Peru who travelled into the Titicaca basin to obtain copper, and to the coast of Ecuador to obtain thorny oyster shell.

The more common pattern in the highlands, however, was for craft specialists to be farmers, too. There are well-documented cases of the Inca moving potters, metalworkers, and weavers of high quality woollen tapestry cloth to new locations in the highlands, and providing them with fields to support themselves while also practising their crafts.

Taxation

In the Inca Empire, taxes were collected only in the form of labour. People never had to provide anything from their own lands or herds to the Inca state. The labour tax was levied on households, and took several different forms. One form of the labour tax related to agricultural production. People had to work the lands dedicated to the cult of the sun, the other major wak'as, the Inca state lands, and their own ayllu lands. At planting time, the Inca called out all the people and they came dressed in their best clothes, singing and dancing. Even the Sapa Inca (the emperor) himself and the nobles came out to work the lands. The Sapa Inca began the work by turning over a few bits of sod using the Andean foot plow, a specialized kind of digging stick. It had a bronze blade that could be pushed into the ground by exerting force with one foot on a horizontal bar attached to the vertical shaft; the blade was then twisted by hand, using another horizontal handle.

The Sapa Inca only worked a little while and then sat down to drink and feast, while the nobles and commoners continued the work. Gradually, in order of rank, the nobles also stopped to drink and feast, while the commoners finished the work. The fields of the state religion and wak'as were prepared first, then those of the state, and, finally, the people could work their own lands. Men and women worked together, with the men wielding the foot plows and the women breaking up the clods and planting the seed. While they were working, the owner of the field provided them with food and drink, whether from the religious stores, those of the state, or the household whose plot they were working. The communal atmosphere and feasting made the work more enjoyable, like a pioneer barn raising.

At harvest time, the same protocol was followed, and the people carried the produce to the appropriate storehouses. In the case of the state fields, especially, the produce might have to be carried several days' journey to the nearest administrative centre. On the other hand, since people only had to provide their labour, they were not held responsible for the success or failure of the crop.

A second labour tax, again levied on households, was the *mit'a*. The Quecha word *mit'a* means "working in turns," and only some households needed to perform the tax in any given year. The allocation of the tax by household was determined by the local

One type of labour tax was the working of land for various state purposes. These Inca are harvesting potatoes. Note the use of the Andean foot plow on the left.

nobility through the decimal administrative system. The Sapa Inca, or his officers, determined how many people were required from each province, and the levy would then be distributed proportionately across each division. The mit'a provided labour for many different purposes, including the draft for the army, work in mines, and construction and maintenance of roads, buildings, and the agricultural infrastructure. The amount of labour that could be raised by the mit'a was enormous; one account mentions that the Inca employed 20 000 labourers for 50 years to construct a single temple-fortress overlooking Cuzco. At times, women and older children could help the head of household complete his mit'a service. While serving the mit'a, people were supported from the state stores and provided with the necessary food, tools, and even clothing. For example, each soldier received two complete sets of clothing per turn. Some ethnic groups contributed only certain services to the mit'a. Another form of labour tax involved spinning and weaving. People were provided with llama and alpaca wool from the state herds, which they spun and wove into sets of clothing, bags to hold produce, and blankets.

The Tax-Exempt Classes

Some people were exempted from the ordinary mit'a. Artisans, for example, produced craft products for the state as their labour contribution. These artisans included specialized weavers who produced the finest cloth, and metalworkers who produced bronze tools and weapons, gold and silver ornaments, figurines, and drinking cups. Potters also created the enormous quantities of pottery in the standard Inca shapes and designs that were used in the state administrative centres. The state supplied

A wooden drinking vessel called a *kero*, showing a warrior with club and feather work shield. This might have been a gift of the state to a favoured warrior.

the raw materials and then redistributed the products as gifts to favoured nobles, warriors, and, at times, even the common people serving in the mit'a. These gifts were highly prized, and many colonial-period wills mention a tunic or drinking cup that was received as a gift from the Inca.

Colonists or Mitmaq

Another category of people were the *mitmaq*, who were colonists moved from one part of the empire to another for state purposes. There were large numbers of mitmaq; in some regions, almost half the population consisted of people moved by the state. Although Pacha Kutiq is credited with creating the first mitmaq, many more were created by Thupa Inca and Wayna Qhapaq. One role of the mitmaq was to aid in the pacification of newly conquered territories. Loyal subjects, often from the Cuzco area, were moved into newly conquered territories to teach the local people Inca customs and the Quechua language. They emigrated as ethnic communities, rather than as individuals, under the leadership of their own ethnic lords and given new lands in their new location. Moving people out of the Cuzco area also freed up lands there, which could be turned into royal estates. In turn, people from the conquered provinces could be moved onto the royal estates to work the estates. The Inca also moved artisans from one part of the empire to another to produce craft products for the state in areas in which the products were needed, or where raw materials were closer to hand. The mitmaq, then, might include garrison troops and artisans, and this category of people overlapped some of the categories mentioned above.

THE ARTS AND SCIENCES
Kipu

While the Inca did not have a writing system, they did develop a very effective method of record keeping using the *kipu*, or knotted string record. Kipu consist of a main cord that can have dozens, or even hundreds, of pendent cords attached to it. The pendent cords use knots in different positions to record numbers: the knots closest to the main cord record numbers in the thousands. Hundreds, tens, and units are recorded by knots progressively farther from the main cord. Each pendent cord represents a different category of thing. For example, in a census record, the first cord might represent adult married men, the most important category because they were the basis of the tax system. The next cord might represent married women, and subsequent cords would represent sons and daughters

of different ages, and people exempt from taxes. Periodically, there would be cords that sum the people in the previous categories.

The keepers of the kipu, the *kipukamayoq*, had to remember what each cord represented, but this was facilitated by always arranging the cords in a standard order, from the most important category to the least important. So in practice, as long as the kipukamayoa knew that the kipu represented the census for a particular province, he would be able to read off very easily the numbers of people in each of the age grade categories. In addition to census data, the kipu recorded such things as the contents of storerooms, the levy for a mit'a, and the numbers of llamas and alpacas in state herds (and whether they were males, females, juveniles, and so on). An

The kipu was an efficient way of recording information about numbers of livestock, quantities of agricultural produce, and the census. An Inca abacus did the counting.

indication of the accuracy and efficiency of the kipu is that they were commonly accepted as testimony in Spanish courts during the colonial period.

While the kipu were an efficient way of recording information, they were not useful for doing calculations. For this, the Inca developed an abacus consisting of a set of squares or boxes that could be simply marked out on the ground. While it is not entirely clear how the abacus worked, Spanish descriptions indicate that the accountant moved markers, beans, corn kernels, or stones from one square to another to do the calculation. They noted that the accountants worked rapidly — adding, subtracting, multiplying, dividing — and could do accounts from 1 to 100 000. Modern scholars have suggested, in detail, how this might have been done, using the abacus illustrated by the indigenous chronicler Guaman Poma de Ayala.

Calendrics

The Incas used both a lunar and a solar calendar. The lunar calendar marked out months of 29.5 days by observing the phases of the moon, and each lunar month was associated with a major religious festival in the capital. The twelve lunar months marked out a ritual calendar of 354 days.

The solar calendar was marked by the passage of the sun from solstice to solstice, allowing for the calculation of a 365-day year. The solstices were observed from the plaza in Cuzco as the sun rose and set on the horizon. Along the mountains surrounding Cuzco on the east and west, the Inca constructed towers to fix the solstices. It has also been suggested that one of the motives for conquest into Ecuador was to mark the zenith passage of the sun over the equator on the equinox. There is, in fact, a hill located almost exactly on the equator

with an Inca circular platform constructed on its summit that could have been used for this purpose. The solar calendar was used to fix the times for planting crops. It is unclear how the Inca might have synchronized the lunar and solar calendars, however.

Architecture and Stoneworking

The finest Inca architecture was constructed of precisely fitted stones in two different styles. One style employed brick-like square blocks, while the other used polygonal stones with a mass of up to 100 t. In either case, the joints between the stones were mortarless, and the stones were fitted so closely together that it is impossible to fit even a knife blade between them.

Although the Inca had bronze pry bars and chisels, they worked the stones by pecking them with other stones. Each stone was individually shaped by pounding with stone hammers of increasingly smaller size. As the stones were laid up, a bed was prepared on the stones already fitted into the wall that corresponded exactly to the bottom and one side of the next stone to be added.

Small stones could simply be carried into place, but the largest had to be hauled by teams of hundreds of men pulling them with ropes. Rollers may have been used to facilitate the hauling, and cobblestone roads were constructed to support the stones as they were pulled across the ground. As mentioned earlier, the mit'a were able to provide huge workforces to move the stones, and some accounts mention that special stonemasons were brought in from the Lake Titicaca basin to do the actual fitting.

Inca architecture usually consisted of separate buildings arranged around a central courtyard, and surrounded by a wall to form a compound, called a *kancha*. The layout of buildings in a kancha remained

In the Field...
John Topic

John is currently with the Department of Anthropology at Trent University, Peterborough. His area of expertise is Andean Archaeology and Ethnohistory. Dr Topic has worked in Peru since 1969. From 1981 to 1989, John worked in the northern highlands of Peru directing a large project that surveyed and excavated a number of sites near the modern town of Huamachuco. Since 1998, John has been involved in the study of the ancient oracle, Catequil. John's research has been supported by the Social Sciences and Humanities Research Council of Canada and the National Science Foundation (US).

John, what made you decide to become an archaeologist?

Well, I didn't start off wanting to become an archaeologist; I wanted to become a doctor. In university, I had to take physics, chemistry, and biology and then happened to get very interested in archaeology. As a matter of fact, when I switched majors, one of my professors was a medical doctor. I started off enjoying biological anthropology so much that in my third year, I went off to Peru with my professor to join him in his field work for the summer. That's how it all started for me, and I still try and go to Peru as often as possible in the summer for field work.

What are the more important skills a person must have, or learn, in order to become an archaeologist?

The skills are endless. There are the skills that one would first consider for an archaeologist: perseverance, patience, research skills. Then there are other skills that are not so evident. For example, as an archaeologist, it would be very advantageous to know a foreign language. This is so you are able to read all the documentation — both present and historical — and be as accurate as possible with your research. It would also be helpful to have a background in history or the arts. Biology and chemistry come into importance when you are taking samples or dating artifacts. Some of the best archaeologists are those who are the most inquisitive, have an open mind, and are willing to look at things from very different perspectives. Remember, the more questions that are asked, the more information will be gathered. Do you like hiking, camping, geography? All of these are important to an archaeologist, particularly during long treks to the sites or spending long days away from the comforts of home. So, as you can see, the more skills one has the better, and there is no one skill that is more important than another. One of the most famous archaeologists right now, Joan Gero, was a school teacher first. Her specialty is feminist archaeology — the study of the female arena — i.e., botanical (gathering) vs. male, i.e., bones (hunting).

To what sort of person would you recommend archaeology as a career?

Archaeology is for a variety of people and you don't have to decide to be an archaeologist when you're a very young person. Are you a relaxed person who likes to putter around? Then archaeology may be for you. Are you the kind of person who is very organized and likes everything in order? Archaeology is definitely for you. Are you persistent? Do you ask a lot of questions? Do you like walking down the street and looking at material things such as cars, houses, people's throwaways? Archaeology may well be a career for you. For example, one archaeologist, Bill Rathje, studies garbage dumps. Do you ever notice the garbage that people throw away and comment on it?

Are there ways to get involved in archaeology, other than by becoming an archaeologist?

Actually, archaeology is only one part of the whole field of anthropology. There are four areas in anthropology — biology, culture, linguistics, and anthropology — so, if you are interested in any of these areas, you can become involved. For example, the Ontario Archaeological Society is always looking for volunteers to join excavation digs in Ontario. There are chapters of the society in Toronto, London, and Ottawa. You may just want to learn about what's happening archaeologically. Well, then, you can go to hear talks, visit heritage interpretation areas such as St. Marie among the Hurons, Fort York, Québec City and find out what's going on. The museums and art galleries are always looking for volunteers and magazines are always looking for articles about aspects of archaeology. So, you don't have to be an archaeologist, you can just get involved as a citizen of your community.

What skills does one need to work at an archaeological site such as this, the ancient Inca royal estate at Machu Pichu?

essentially the same, whether the kancha represented the house of commoners, a palace, or even the temple of the Sun, the *Qorikancha* (golden enclosure).

In addition to architecture, the Inca shaped rock outcrops for ritual purposes, carving out basins for offerings of maize beer that connected to zigzag channels that represent the lightning deity. They also carved ledges into the outcrops. Often referred to as "thrones of the Inca," ledges were probably used as places to deposit offerings. Some of these carved rock outcrops are incredibly complex and quite large. The Inca also integrated architecture with the living rock, carving an outcrop to form part of a wall for a larger building.

The System of Roads

The Spaniards were very impressed with the Inca road system. Although much of this system predated the Inca, they maintained and expanded it into a system that incorporated more than 23 000 km of roads. Two main routes ran north-south, one along the coast and the other through the highlands, which were connected periodically by cross-routes. The roads were designed for foot traffic and llamas, which were employed in caravans to transport goods. At intervals of a day's march, were way stations with storage facilities where travellers could spend the night. Traffic along the roads was regulated by the state, and they were used mainly for state business. On flat stretches, the roads reached a width of 10 m, and were often marked by lines of stones. In isolated desert areas, roads were marked only by occasional piles of stones.

WEB CONNECTION

http://www.mcgrawhill.ca/links/echoes

Go to the site above to find out more about the Spanish Conquest of the Inca.

Inca stonework at Machu Pichu. The labourers needed to move stones into place were provided through the mit'a.

Bridges and causeways were built to span streams, rivers, and lakes. Small streams were bridged with logs set into stone abutments on either side of the stream bed. Marshy areas sometimes had stepping stones, and, at other times, causeways were built across them. In the Lake Titicaca basin, the Inca constructed a floating causeway supported by reed pontoons. Larger rivers were spanned by suspension bridges made of thick ropes woven from grass. These suspension bridges were strong enough to support the Spanish horsemen.

Roads enabled the troop movements crucial to the Inca military effort. They were also the means by which communication was maintained for administrative purposes. To facilitate communication, the Inca used young boys as runners. These runners stationed themselves along the roads in small huts at convenient intervals so that they could transmit messages in relay. As one runner approached the hut, the next was ready to take the message, often in the form of a kipu. The two boys briefly ran side by side to pass on the kipu and information about its contents; then the new runner raced to the next hut. In this way, messages could be transmitted at the rate of about 240 km per day. There are also reports that the runners carried fresh fish from the coast to Cuzco for the emperor's table in just two days.

Metallurgy

The Inca inherited a well-developed metallurgical tradition that included work in copper, silver, gold, tin, and — in Ecuador — platinum. While there were two types of bronze, one an arsenic-copper alloy and the other a tin-copper, the Inca promoted the tin-copper alloy. Bronze was the alloy of choice for utilitarian objects, while gold and silver were considered luxury goods, to be presented as gifts. A

The Inca developed high standards of metallurgy. This figurine of a noble is made of silver, stone, and pink shell. We know he is a noble by his stretched earlobes, created by wearing large ear-discs. Only nobles were allowed to do this.

wide variety of objects was produced in metal, ranging from ear ornaments, to figurines of people and llamas used as offerings, drinking cups, tools, pins to secure women's shawls, tweezers for plucking facial hair, mace heads, and so on. The Inca imposed highly standardized production and design on all arts, but these standards also reveal an interest in the technology itself. For example, the Inca cast bolas, "stones," from bronze using the lost-wax method. This method involves making a model of the object out of wax, which is then encased in a fire-resistant mould. When molten metal is introduced into the mould, the wax melts and runs off, and the mould is broken to release the bolas stone once it has hardened. A casting technology is usually used to mass-produce objects, but in this case, each bolas stone required a separate mould. This was an inefficient process, but the Inca were more interested in producing an object that was beautiful and functional, rather than in mass production.

Weaving

Weaving and the fibre arts are perhaps the epitome of Inca craft. Again, they had inherited a tradition that stretched back at least four thousand years, but they used this tradition in innovative ways to create beautiful and technologically sophisticated articles. These ranged from suspension bridges woven largely from grass, to tapestry tunics so fine that they were passed down from generation to generation, even in the colonial period, to the simple sophistication of the kipu. Even everyday articles such as slings were produced in complicated braids that cannot be duplicated today.

The Inca made three general qualities of cloth, the coarsest used only for blankets. They used the other two qualities, *awaska* and *qombi,* for ordinary and fine clothing respectively. While every household produced awaska, qombi was a much finer cloth, used only for the finest garments. These were not only different qualities of cloth, they were woven in quite different ways on different looms. Qombi was woven by specialist weavers and by the Chosen Women. The Inca gave this cloth to favoured subjects as one of the most valued of gifts. Qombi was also burned as an important offering. Whether awaska or qombi, the Inca did not just weave cloth to cut and sew into other artifacts; each piece was woven for a particular purpose. The Inca also made cloth covered in beautifully coloured feathers for ceremonial purposes.

WEB CONNECTION

http://www.mcgrawhill.ca/links/echoes

Go to the site above to find out more about the Inca Empire.

Inca clothing was woven of different qualities of cloth for different purposes. This intricately woven garment would have been made for a noble.

1. Explain three ways the Inca state organized and used labour to ensure self-sufficiency and the continued prosperity of the state.

2. Why were the Spaniards impressed by the Inca road system?

3. How did Inca metallurgy and weaving reflect their interest in producing goods that were both beautiful and functional?

History Continues to Unfold

Building on past civilizations of the Andes, in only 90 years or so — just three generations — the Inca were able to forge an empire that exceeded anything seen previously in the Andes, or anywhere else in the New World. Inca military accomplishments have been compared to the conquests of Alexander the Great. Administratively, they have been compared to the Romans.

While we may never completely understand the confrontation between Atawallpa and Francisco Pizarro in Cajamarca, we can better understand it with this perspective: Atawallpa had repeatedly demonstrated his superiority to his brother Waskar through a series of battles extending over several years. Atawallpa had also successfully punished Catequil, one of the most important wak'as in the empire. He instructed the strange foreigners to meet him in Cajamarca, and did nothing to impede their progress to the administrative centre. In fact, he gave them gifts and invited them to dine and drink with him, part of the Andean tradition of initiating relationships. Atawallpa's slow procession, with a huge entourage, across the plain at Cajamarca was the way an Inca emperor normally travelled. Atawallpa approached Pizarro, confident of his position in the world order he had so recently succeeded in establishing. He did not realize that he was approaching a man with a completely different conception of the world.

Current Research and Interpretations

The Inca Empire is fertile ground for further research. Because of the size of the Inca Empire and the fact that it incorporated different ethnic groups, investigators are looking at different political strategies in different regions. Also, Inca thought did not separate sacred from secular matters, so there is continuing work on how religious ideas affected Inca expansion.

Chapter Review

Chapter Summary

In this chapter, we have seen:

- that geographic factors and a desire for self-sufficiency influenced the development of Inca society
- that although the basis of Inca authority lay in military power, the justification of the leaders authority was closely tied to religious beliefs
- how the Inca organization of labour to serve the needs of the state tended to reinforce stability and continuity
- that several factors, including trade and economic interchange and proximity, defined the relationship between the Inca and the many different peoples they interacted with in South America

Reviewing the Significance of Key People, Concepts, and Events (Knowledge/Understanding)

1. Understanding the history of the Inca civilization requires a knowledge of the following concepts and people, and an understanding of their significance in the development of Inca society. In your notes identify and explain the historical significance of three from each column.

People	Concepts
Atawallpa	tambos
Francisco Pizarro	*wak'as*
Manqu	Sapa Inca
Pacha Kutiq	Qoya
Thupa Inca	*ayllus*
Virgins of the Sun	Machu Pichu

2. The Inca were able to establish a widespread empire in a very short time in part because it had characteristics common to stable societies. Complete the chart below in your notes to illustrate how these factors contributed to the success of the Inca

Characteristic	Inca example	How did this factor contribute to the rapid development of the Inca Empire?
accepted leadership		
tradition and law		
compatible religious beliefs		

3. Religion played a central role in many spheres of Inca life. Write a paragraph on the influence of religion on political and social structures in the Inca Empire.

Doing History: Thinking About the Past (Thinking/Inquiry)

1. In a paragraph supported with historical evidence and sound analysis, respond to this statement: "If we ever hope to understand the true nature of the Inca civilization, we must first come to understand the importance of the natural world in their belief system."

   Transfer two key phrases from your response to the graphic organizer "Geography's Influence" in your *World History Handbook*.

2. Historians have argued that aspects of Inca religion and society, such as maintaining land for ancestors, created an unsustainable empire that was, in part, responsible for the rapid collapse of the empire in the early sixteenth century. Agree or disagree with this thesis in a short essay of 500 to 700 words. Be sure to state clearly your position and support your argument with historical evidence from the chapter.

Applying Your Learning (Application)

1. Create a series of three Great Inca Leaders trading cards. Each card should have a picture or image of the individual on the front and biographical details on the back, including birthplace, year of birth, and major contributions to Inca culture and society. You may need to do some additional research beyond the information contained in this chapter. If you cannot locate an image of the leader(s) selected, create your own drawing for the front of the card.

2. Using the medium of your choice, create a model or drawing of one of the following Inca innovations or sites. You may find it helpful to consult other sources for images and more detailed descriptions of the item or site.

bolas	kipu	Inca roads system
Machu Pichu	Qombi	Inca mummy

Communicating Your Learning (Communication)

1. Make a diagram to illustrate the social divisions of Inca society. Create or select an illustration that reflects the role or type of work provided to the state by each social group. Transfer some of the ideas from your diagram to the organizer "Forms of Social Organization" in your *World History Handbook*.

2. Create a visual map of the Inca Empire that clearly shows the dominant physical features of the landscape and the forms of agriculture carried out in each of the areas and at each of the elevations.

Unit Review

Grading the Civilizations

1. In Chapter One, the essential elements of a civilization were outlined and you were asked to rank in order of importance each of the elements. Now that you have had an opportunity to study a civilization in depth, apply your ranking to see how it measures up. Below are three broad categories under which the elements could be clustered. For each of the categories, provide a letter grade (from A+ to F) and an anecdotal comment of three to five sentences to support the grade. A fuller assessment of the civilization selected can be completed using your *World History Handbook*.

	Letter Grade	Comments
The Place of People • level of equality • just laws • distribution of wealth • overall quality of life		
Organization of Society • democratic • effective government • meets needs of society • provides security and stability for society		
Lasting Legacy • ideas • works of art • architecture • innovations/inventions • literature		

The Role of Individuals in History

1. Historians often grapple with whether history is shaped by individuals, or whether individuals are a product of their age and are shaped by history. Would the history of the Aztecs have been different if Montezuma II had not lived? Did Pacha Kutiq change the direction of Inca history? Following is a list of people drawn from this unit. Select any two. For each, identify their role in society, major accomplishments, and sphere of greatest impact (e.g. art, ideas, religion, politics), and why you believe he or she shaped or was shaped by history. You may want to do additional research on the two individuals you select.

Atawallpa

Francisco Pizarro

Pacha Kutiq

Thupa Inca

Montezuma II

Hernán Cortés

Tlaloc

Understanding Chronology

1. The study of history, whether the recent or distant past, relies on a sound understanding of the order in which events occurred. Without a clear understanding of how history has unfolded, it is difficult to see the relationship between earlier events and developments. The following questions help to illustrate the importance of understanding the chronology of history:

a) Explain, in chronological order, the difference between the Pre-Classic, Classic and Post-Classic periods in Maya history.

b) How did the Aztec reckoning of time differ from the European concept of time? What challenges does this pose for students of Aztec history?

c) How did the Maya reckoning of time differ from the European concept of time? What challenges does this pose for students of Maya history?

d) Why would it be advisable for someone wanting to understand the development of Aztec culture and society to study the Toltecs, as well?

2. Would it be accurate to say that although the Inca Empire lasted only a century, the history of Inca culture goes back over one thousand years? Why? Why not?

Cause and Effect in History

1. History often involves the study of cause and effect. We find that one cause has several effects, or that several causes lead to one effect. Complete the Cause and Effect diagrams provided by your teacher, and use one as a guide to writing a paragraph on the issue addressed.

UNIT SIX

The Middle Ages

chapter 15
The Early Middle Ages

chapter 16
The High Middle Ages

chapter 17
The Late Middle Ages

The Granger Collection, New York.

This illustration from a fourteenth-century Italian manuscript shows one of the most enduring images of the Middle Ages: the chivalrous knight.

The decline of the Roman Empire in the late fifth century meant that Europe was no longer controlled by the Mediterranean basin. For much of the next thousand years, Northern Europe would dominate the political and cultural landscape of the continent. During this time, the Germanic tribes of Northern Europe developed new political structures that laid the foundations for later parliamentary democracies. Still, Roman influences remained strong. Even the name Middle Ages would be drawn from the Latin phrase *medium aevum*, which means "middle age" and is the source of the English word "medieval."

The first chapter of this unit examines the Early Middle Ages, when petty kingdoms took over from the unified Roman Empire. The second chapter focuses on the flowering of culture that occurred during the High Middle Ages. The final chapter considers the impact of great calamities — famine, plague, and war — and innovations, such as the printing press and gunpowder, and examines how these events helped bring about significant change during the Late Middle Ages.

UNIT EXPECTATIONS

In this unit, you will:

O analyze the interactions between medieval Europe and other societies

O analyze the factors that maintained continuity and contributed to change during the Middle Ages

O evaluate the contributions of various people and groups to the development of legal, political, and military traditions during the Middle Ages

O analyze the changing nature of the economic structure of Europe from Early to Late Middle Ages

O demonstrate an understanding of the steps in the process of historical interpretation and analysis

O communicate clear and concise opinions based on effective research

3000km

Europe

CHAPTER FIFTEEN

The Early Middle Ages

CHAPTER EXPECTATIONS

By the end of this chapter, you will be able to:

- *demonstrate an understanding of the characteristics of early medieval society*

- *analyze the factors that sparked change as the Romans withdrew from Western Europe, as well as the factors that contributed to continuity from the Roman period to the medieval world*

- *demonstrate an understanding of the relationship between individuals, groups, and authority in the Early Middle Ages*

- *analyze how new social structures emerged in Europe between 500 and 1000*

This bronze statue of Charlemagne, whose empire dominated Western Europe in the Early Middle Ages, was probably crafted more than 50 years after his death.

For centuries, scholars reserved special scorn for the period from 500 to 1000, often calling this era the Dark Ages. In 1788, for example, Edward Gibbon completed his master work titled *The History of the Decline and Fall of the Roman Empire*. Gibbon's famous book reflected the deeply ingrained bias, which persists even today, that the Roman Empire represented the highest cultural achievements — and that these achievements were destroyed by primitive barbarians. More than a century later, Charles Oman reinforced this idea in his book *The Dark Ages*, which portrayed the Early Middle Ages as a time when civilization collapsed.

People who embraced this idea of history viewed the Early Middle Ages as a time when the forces of darkness — the barbarians — overwhelmed the forces of light — the Romans. Today, however, historians are adjusting to new findings and new ways of understanding what happened in the Early Middle Ages. They see this period when the Roman emperors lost their grip on Western Europe as a time of change during which the foundations of contemporary society were laid.

University of Toronto historian Walter Goffart is one of those who contributed to this new understanding of the Early Middle Ages. In 1980, his book, *Barbarians and Romans, A.D. 418– 584: The Techniques of Accommodation*, redefined thinking about the relationship between the Roman Empire and the barbarians. It is now documented that, in return for military service, the Roman government granted barbarian mercenaries land within the Roman Empire where they settled and collected tax revenues. These mercenaries, who were paid for their services to the Roman Empire in Gaul and Italy, eventually became the new rulers in these regions.

KEY WORDS

pope
patriarch
heresy
paganism
Justinian's Code
warband
monasticism
Merovingian
Salic Law
Carolingian
Treaty of Verdun

KEY PEOPLE

Justinian the Great
Theodora
Clovis I
Charlemagne
Moors
Alfred the Great
Vikings

VOICES FROM THE PAST

History ... is indeed little more than the register of the crimes, follies, and misfortunes of mankind.
Edward Gibbon,
The History of the
Decline and Fall of
the Roman Empire,
1776–1788

TIME LINE: THE EARLY MIDDLE AGES

	507	Clovis I establishes the Merovingian Empire in present-day France
Legend suggests that King Arthur led Celtic Britons in a successful battle against Saxon invaders	516	
	529	St. Benedict founds a monastery at Monte Cassino, Italy
Justinian the Great brutally suppresses the Nika Riot	532	
	545	*Justinian's Code* is completed, providing a unified set of laws for the Byzantine Empire
The Moors, an Islamic people from North Africa, conquer southern Spain	711	
	751	The Carolingian Empire is founded when Pepin I ascends the throne with Pope Zacharias's blessing
Abd al-Rahman establishes Muslim state of Andalusia in Spain	752	
	790	The first recorded Viking attacks occur at monasteries in Ireland
Pope Leo III crowns Charlemagne Emperor of the Romans	800	
	841	The Vikings establish their first permanent settlement outside Scandinavia at Dublin, Ireland
The Treaty of Verdun divides the Carolingian Empire into three kingdoms	843	

FROM ROMAN EMPIRE TO EARLY MIDDLE AGES

As the Roman emperors gradually gave up control of their Western Empire and made Constantinople their new capital, they set the stage for a power shift in Western Europe. As a result of this shift, which took place over centuries, Western Europe was transformed from a backwater of the Roman Empire to the political, economic, and cultural centre of the continent. Though Rome was no longer the dominant political power in Western Europe, its influence remained strong in other areas of people's lives. The languages, laws, and cultures of the kingdoms and dynasties that rose to replace Rome often retained — or adopted — distinctively Latin features. In many ways, the people of Europe became more "Romanized" after Rome gave up control than they had ever been when their territory was ruled by the Romans.

The changes that occurred in Western Europe did not take place peacefully. The Early Middle Ages were marked by violent upheavals as various peoples formed alliances and fought to gain control of the territories that had once been part of the Western Roman Empire.

THE BYZANTINE EMPIRE

As the Early Middle Ages dawned in Western Europe, Eastern Europe was still firmly under the control of the Roman emperors. The political, military, economic, and cultural centre of the empire was Constantinople, the former city of Byzantium, which had been renamed by Constantine the Great in 330 CE.

Constantinople was located on the European side of the Bosporus, the narrow strait that separates the Black Sea and the Sea of Marmara. This city grew in importance through the Early Middle Ages, attracting an ethnically diverse population. By 1000, Constantinople's population was about 750 000, making it the largest city in the world west of China. Its strategic location on international trade routes and its natural harbour, one of the largest in the world, meant that it had become the commercial gateway between East and West. As a result, the Byzantine gold coin, called the bezant, was the main currency of international trade.

The provinces of the Eastern Roman Empire, which is often called the Byzantine Empire, were ruled on the Roman model. The emperor appointed military governors, who were supported by a sophisticated bureaucracy based in Constantinople and an imperial army made up mostly of mercenaries. The emperors imposed heavy taxes on all subjects, and the royal family, including officials, priests, and courtiers, benefited from taxes on trade as well as monopolies on certain industries.

TIME FRAMES
EARLY MIDDLE AGES ca. 500–1000

Some historians date the beginning of the Early Middle Ages to 476 CE, when the puppet Roman emperor Romulus Augustulus was deposed. Others say that the era began even earlier, with the sacking of Rome by the Visigoths in 410 CE. There is even less agreement about when the Early Middle Ages ended. Some historians maintain that the period ended as early as 800, while others believe that it stretched past 1000.

The Byzantine Empire and the Church

As a result of Constantine the Great's conversion to Christianity, Constantinople also became an important religious centre. By establishing a "second Rome," which was intended to be more spiritually exalted than Rome itself, however, Constantine laid the groundwork for religious conflict that would eventually split the Christian Church into two distinct branches.

At the heart of this conflict was the fact that Constantine — and the emperors who succeeded him — claimed to be the spiritual leader of the empire, as well as its political and military leader. Believing that they had been appointed by God as Christ's representative on earth, the Byzantine emperors ruled the Church with an iron hand. They appointed Church officials and issued decrees governing both Church administration and religious matters.

The two leading officials of the early Church were the bishops of Rome and Constantinople. The bishop of Rome came to be called the **pope**, while the bishop of Constantinople came to be called the **patriarch** of Constantinople. Both titles — pope and patriarch — derive from Greek words for father.

This photograph shows the walls of Constantinople today. Built in the fourth and fifth centuries to protect the capital of the Byzantine Empire from the barbarians, the walls of Constantinople were not stormed till 1203.

Because he was based in the Byzantine capital, the patriarch of Constantinople was firmly under the control of the emperor. For most of the Early Middle Ages, however, Rome was no longer part of the empire. This meant that the pope was able to function more independently than his counterpart in Constantinople.

Throughout the Early Middle Ages, the pope of Rome and the patriarch of Constantinople coexisted as Church leaders with powers that were equal — in theory. In fact, the two, and their followers, were locked in a nearly constant struggle for supremacy. Finally, in the eleventh century, their disagreements came to a head and led to a split that divided the Christian Church into two independent branches: the Eastern (Greek) Orthodox Church based in Constantinople and the Roman Catholic Church based in Rome.

As the influence of the Church grew, emperors who succeeded Constantine began to pass laws designed to persuade, then force, people to become Christians. At first, activities like magic, astrology, and soothsaying (which involves predicting the future), were declared illegal. In 380 CE, however, Emperor Theodorus introduced laws barring other religions. He issued decrees like the following, which banned **heresy** — the holding of beliefs that question or contradict the official religion:

> We command that those persons who follow this rule [belief in the single Deity of the Father, the Son, and the Holy Spirit] shall embrace the name of Catholic Christians. The rest, however, whom We adjudge demented and insane, shall sustain the infamy of heretical dogmas … and they shall be smitten first by divine vengeance and secondly by the retribution of Our own initiative, which We shall assume in accordance with the divine judgement.

At first, heretics faced heavy fines. The law was not entirely effective, however, and served more to drive other religions underground than to stamp them out. Subsequent laws decreed harsher and harsher penalties until, finally, the death penalty was imposed. Christianity, which had once been driven underground because of persecution, was now imposing the same conditions on others.

Only Jews were exempt from the laws against heresy, which were intended to ensure that all citizens of the Byzantine Empire became Catholics. As the military situation in the empire deteriorated, the emperor, as if trying to appease God, devoted more and more attention to passing laws governing religion.

Justinian the Great

One of the most influential Byzantine emperors was Justinian I, who ruled from 527 to 565. Often called **Justinian the Great**, this emperor considered himself a Roman and had one ambition: to reunite the Roman world — as a Christian Empire. To achieve this, he waged frequent wars and eventually reconquered areas around the Adriatic Sea, including the Italian Peninsula and Rome, Southern Spain, and North Africa, including Carthage.

Because Justinian believed strongly that his subjects should share his Christian beliefs, he suppressed all remnants of **paganism**. Pagan religions

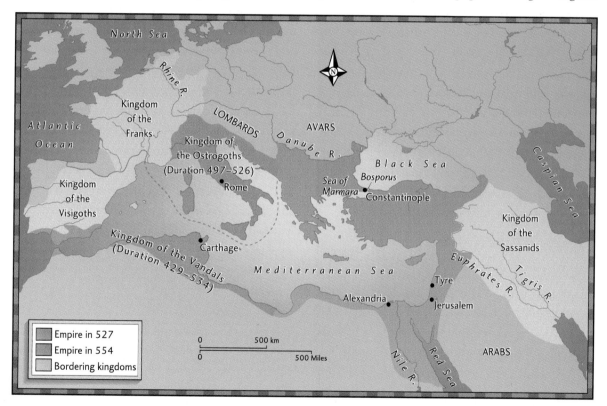

■ **Justinian's Conquests, 527–555**

1. **What barbarian groups did Justinian defeat in his quest to restore the glory of the Roman Empire?**

2. **What important factor might have facilitated Justinian's reconquest of the areas he had recaptured by 555?**

are usually characterized by a belief in many gods and the spirituality of nature. The word "pagan," however, was often used as a catch-all to describe anyone who was not Christian.

In his zeal to impose religious unity, Justinian continued to persecute Christians whose beliefs did not match his own. The Monophysites were one group whose beliefs were considered heretical. Orthodox Christians — those whose beliefs coincided with official doctrine — said that Christ was both human and divine or God-like. Monophysites, however, believed that Christ possessed a single divine nature.

The Arians were also branded heretics. Arians were followers of Arius, who argued against the Catholic doctrine that stated that God was the holy trinity, made up of God the Father, God the Son (Jesus Christ), and God the Holy Spirit. Arius said that Christ and the Holy Spirit were, in fact, secondary gods, who mediated between God the Father and the world. This theory challenged the Christian belief in a single god and seemed to reintroduce pagan ideas about many gods. Still, Arianism attracted many supporters, including many barbarians who may have been drawn by its echoes of pagan beliefs.

The Justinian Code

Justinian's commitment to unity — of his religion and of his empire — extended to the laws that governed people's behaviour. Under orders from Justinian, a committee of jurists worked for 16 years — from 529 to 545 — to clarify, codify, and eliminate contradictions from the many laws that had governed the Roman Empire. The result, titled *Corpus Juris Civilis* or the *Body of Civil Law*, is also known as *Codex Justinianeus* or *Justinian's Code*.

The codification of Roman law may have been this emperor's most enduring legacy. The principles of *Justinian's Code* defined things such as the property that people could own, how property could be passed on to heirs, and how disputes should be resolved. These principles formed the basis of civil law not only in the Byzantine Empire, but also in medieval Europe. Today, it continues to influence Western legal codes, including Canada's.

Justinian and Theodora

Though Justinian persecuted heretics, he ended up marrying a Monophysite. Theodora was, however, an exceptional woman. When the two met and fell in love, Justinian had not yet inherited the throne — and Theodora's religious beliefs were not the only thing that seemed to rule out marriage to a future emperor.

Theodora was a not a patrician and was, therefore, not considered a suitable wife for the heir to the throne of Byzantium. To overcome this obstacle, Justinian raised her to the rank of patrician. The two also faced another obstacle, however. At one time, Theodora had made her living as an actress. In Byzantium, the word "actress" was synonymous with "prostitute," and a law barred government officials from marrying actresses. To enable the two to marry, this law was changed.

Two years after they married, Justinian became emperor, and Theodora was proclaimed augusta. As empress, Theodora was active in all the affairs of the empire. In fact, she was so active that some people suggested that it was she, rather than Justinian, who really ran the empire. Theodora supported churches, orphanages, and public works. She also supported laws forbidding the sale of young girls and helped change divorce laws to protect women. Furthermore, she never abandoned her religious beliefs. She even established a Monophysite monastery in Constantinople as a haven for refugee bishops.

Theodora's influence on Justinian may have been most obvious during the notorious Nika Riot of 532. This rising started as a riot among fans at a chariot race in Constantinople's Hippodrome, where supporters of rival charioteers cheered on their favourites by yelling "Nika," which means "victory." Though the authorities put down the riot, the brutality of their actions united the fighting factions in anger at Justinian. The riot turned into a full-blown rebellion when the two factions were joined by others who were dissatisfied with the emperor. The rebels proclaimed a new emperor, and set the city ablaze. The situation was so dangerous that Justinian was ready to take the advice of his advisers and flee.

At this point, Theodora stepped in. In a fiery speech, she urged Justinian to stand his ground. According to the historian Procopius, she said, "For an emperor to become a fugitive is a thing not to be endured; the purple [of royalty] makes a fine winding sheet [a shroud or cloth used to wrap corpses for burial]." The empress's words strengthened her husband's resolve, and the rebellion was crushed when Justinian's forces herded 30 000 to 40 000 rebels into the Hippodrome and slaughtered them.

This mosaic depicts Theodora and her retinue. She is clad in purple, the colour of royalty, and is wearing costly jewels.

WEB CONNECTION

http://www.mcgrawhill.ca/links/echoes

Go to the site above to find out more about Justinian and Theodora.

The Byzantine Empire after Justinian

In Justinian's time, Latin was the official language of the Byzantine Empire. This changed after Justinian's death. Greek became the preferred language. This development meant that people in Eastern and Western Europe no longer shared a common language and emphasized the differences between the two regions.

Though Justinian had extended the reach of the Byzantine Empire, his gains were later reversed by the barbarian warbands of Western Europe and the Islamic dynasties who conquered vast territories that had once been part of the empire. As a result, Byzantium had shrunk to the size of modern Turkey and Greece by the early eighth century.

The Iconoclastic Controversy

One of the religious disputes that divided Christians in the eighth and ninth centuries arose over icons. These were portable images of Jesus, Mary, and the saints. Icons had become very popular with many people who believed that the images possessed spiritual powers. The practice of creating icons horrified other Christians who believed that it violated the Third Commandment, which forbade the creation and worship of "graven images" of anything in heaven or on Earth.

Those who opposed the use of icons were called iconoclasts, which means image destroyers. In 730, the emperor barred icons, harshly persecuted those who worshipped them, and ordered the destruction of an enormous number of sculptures, paintings, and other artifacts that represented an artistic heritage of more than 700 years.

This situation was reversed in 787, when the use of images was re-established. The iconoclasts triumphed again in 815, when image veneration was once again prohibited. Finally, in 843, icon veneration was restored for good. This event is still celebrated in the Eastern Orthodox Church.

WEB CONNECTION

http://www.mcgrawhill.ca/links/echoes

Go to the site above to find out more about the Iconoclastic Controversy.

WARRIORS AND WARBANDS

At the same time as the Byzantine Empire was flourishing in Eastern Europe, the Western European regions that had once been firmly under the control of Rome were entering a long period of change. One of the agents of this change was the barbarians, who were migrating into areas that had been given up by the Romans.

Until the Early Middle Ages, the might of the Roman legions had kept the barbarians at the fringes of Roman territory. Though barbarian bands had sometimes attacked the borders of the empire, at other times they had lived as peaceful neighbours and trading partners of the Romans. Indeed, they often forged alliances with the Romans to help protect the borders of the empire.

This situation changed when the Huns, a Mongol people from Asia, swept westward in the fourth century. When the Huns began invading territory just beyond the eastern fringes of the empire, the attacks created a domino effect. To escape the Huns, the barbarian tribes who lived in these areas started moving westward. Their migration, in turn, pushed the other tribes westward.

The barbarians are often divided into three main groups — Celtic, Germanic, and Slavic — based on the languages they spoke. Though the tribes within a particular group may have shared common language roots, little else united them. Some tribes formed alliances — with one another or with Rome — but these alliances shifted frequently. In addition, the distinctions between groups were often blurred as members of tribes migrating to new territory either assimilated into other tribes or were themselves assimilated.

Celtic Peoples

At the time of the Roman conquest, the Celts were the native peoples of Western Europe. They spoke Celtic languages and included
- Gauls, who inhabited present-day France and Belgium
- Britons, who lived in the present-day United Kingdom and Ireland and who gave their name to Britain
- Bretons, who lived in the Brittany Peninsula of present-day France

Over time, the Celts evolved into a **warband** society that sent out raiding parties to obtain loot. In *Lady with a Mead Cup: Ritual, Prophecy and Lordship in the European Warband from La Tène to the Viking Age,*

Michael Enright wrote that the Celtic warbands were made up of free men including the immediate kin group of the leader and others from the outside, who swear an oath of allegiance and military support in return for maintenance, gifts and plunder. Political and military leadership were the exclusive preserve of an equestrian nobility among whom weaker nobles paid allegiance and tribute to stronger ones. The same pattern applied all the way down the social pyramid.

Germanic Peoples

The Germanic peoples were the most numerous of the barbarians. Historians believe that they originated

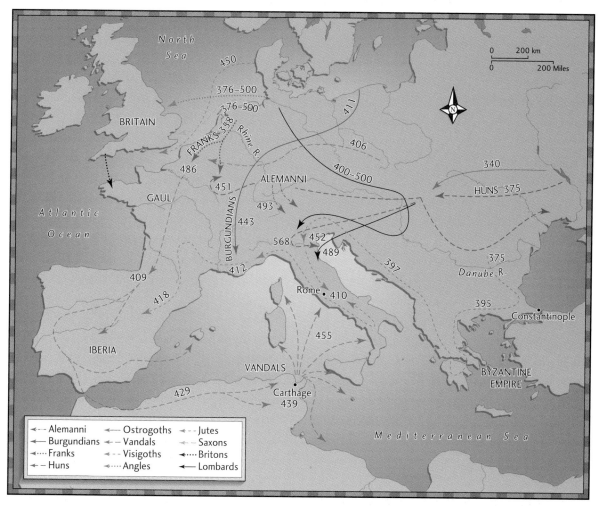

■ Migration of the Huns and Germanic Tribes

1. How did Constantinople's strategic location make it hard for barbarians to attack?

2. Which barbarian group came closest to attacking Constantinople?

3. Which barbarian groups made the longest migrations?

in Scandinavia and migrated southward to occupy the areas on the eastern fringes of the Roman Empire. Historians also believe that they adopted their war-band social structure from the Celts.

The Germanic peoples included the Goths, Franks, Vandals, Angles, Saxons, Jutes, Frisians, Burgundians, and Suebi. The Suebi were made up of various tribes including the Lombards and Alemmani, whose name lives today in the French and Spanish words for Germany: *Allemagne* and *Alemania*.

The Goths

The Goths separated into two distinct kingdoms: the Ostrogoths, or Eastern Goths, and the Visigoths, or Western Goths. The fate of the Goths is typical of that of many European peoples of the Early Middle Ages.

The Ostrogoth kingdom, which stretched from the Black Sea to the Baltic and included present-day Ukraine, was the most easterly territory held by a Germanic people. As a result, it was the first to be attacked by the Huns when they swept westward from Asia in the late fourth century. In response, many Ostrogoths fled westward. Others remained behind, living for more than a century under the domination of the Huns. During this time, the Huns, under the leadership of Attila, invaded the Italian Peninsula and sacked several cities. Finally, in 474, the Ostrogoths rebelled and overthrew their conquerors. Growing stronger, they successfully invaded the Italian peninsula in 493.

http://www.mcgrawhill.ca/links/echoes

WEB CONNECTION

Go to the site above to find out more about warriors and warbands of the Early Middle Ages.

In Italy, however, the Ostrogoths fell victim to Justinian the Great's dream of reuniting the Roman Empire. From 534 to 561, the Ostrogoths were locked in a bitter — and ultimately unsuccessful — war against Justinian's armies. This prolonged war spelled the end of the Ostrogoths, who disappeared from history. Historians believe that they were dispersed and assimilated into other tribes.

As they fled westward to escape the Huns, the Ostrogoths invaded present-day Romania, territory that was held by the Visigoths. Faced with this invasion by the Ostrogoths, the Visigoths, too, moved westward — across the Danube River into Roman territory.

Realizing that the empire's Danube frontier was under threat, the Romans allowed the Visigoths to settle on the western side of the river. In return, the Visigoths agreed to help protect this border. This arrangement was short-lived, however, because of the harsh conditions imposed by the Romans. In 378 CE the Visigoths rebelled and defeated a Roman army. Over the next 32 years, the Visigoths advanced farther and farther into Roman territory until they reached the heart of the empire. In 410 CE, led by Alaric, they sacked Rome.

After their success in Rome, the Visigoths moved into Southern Gaul and Spain. There, they often allied themselves with the Romans to fight other tribes, such as the Franks and the Huns. Though they were eventually driven out of Gaul, they remained in control of Spain until the Muslim conquest of 711, when they suffered the same fate as their Ostrogoth cousins. Assimilated into other groups, they disappeared from history.

Slavic Peoples

The Wends were the strongest of the Slavic tribes during the Early Middle Ages. They settled in an area that is now Eastern Germany.

THE CHURCH IN THE EARLY MIDDLE AGES

One of the most enduring legacies of the Roman era in Western Europe was the Christian Church. When Emperor Constantine converted to Christianity in 312 CE and extended tolerance to Christians in 313 CE, he set in motion a wave that would ripple across Europe to become one of the most important influences of the Early Middle Ages.

In Constantine's day, most Europeans, including most Romans, worshipped non-Christian gods. By the end of the Early Middle Ages, this had changed. Christianity dominated Western Europe and had extended into Scandinavia and Eastern Europe. The Christian Church had become an important political, economic, spiritual, and cultural force in Europe.

The Spread of Christianity

As the Christian Church extended its influence during the fifth century, it was granted favours by the Roman emperors. These favours enabled the Church to amass considerable land and wealth. In addition, Church lands were exempt from most taxes, and bishops and other clergy were immune to prosecution in secular courts; in fact, these church officials took on many of the functions of local magistrates and judges.

As the sixth century unfolded, the Church became even more powerful. Its members included the ruling classes of the Byzantine Empire and most of the barbarian kings who had taken over areas of Western Europe. Both the barbarian kings and the Church benefited from this arrangement. Entering an alliance with the Church and its powerful bishops helped the kings secure their claim to rule. The kings also looked to the Church to supply educated administrators to help run their kingdoms. In return, the Church received gifts,

One of the first great churches built to glorify the Christian God was the Hagia Sophia (Holy Wisdom) in Constantinople. Construction began in 532 during the rule of Justinian the Great. This is the church as it looks today. What architectural features show that Hagia Sophia became a mosque after the Turks took control of Constantinople?

including land, that contributed to its growing wealth. The Church was also able to call on the kings to enforce laws prohibiting other religions.

During this time, many people were converted to Christianity by force. When a Christian king successfully invaded a non-Christian neighbouring territory, the conquered people were usually required to become Christians.

Conversion did not always occur by force. Sometimes, it was a matter of social or political pressure. A community leader, for example, might decide that embracing Christianity would increase his influence, especially if those in power had already converted. Once the leader converted, his family, followers, servants, and slaves would follow. In early societies, religion was an important part of the fabric of everyday life. People who did not follow the religious practices of the majority placed themselves outside the network of kin and community, the only society in which they could make a living and raise a family.

The people who lived in areas ruled by the new kings may not have become Christians because of a deep belief in Christian principles, but they were required to adhere — at least outwardly — to Church practices. This situation was not much different from Roman times when conquered peoples had been required to accept the official Roman religion.

Because Rome was the home of the pope, who controlled the Western arm of the Church, Church leaders retained many of the customs and traditions of the Romans. As a result, Roman cultural influences, as well as traditions of law and government, spread across Europe along with Christianity.

Monasticism and Missionaries

Inspired by people such as Anthony the Hermit, a fourth-century monk who lived alone for 20 years in a cave in Egypt, some early Christians felt moved to express their faith in God by copying Anthony and becoming monks. Monks are men who give up their worldly possessions and withdraw from society in order to devote themselves to religious life. Many women also felt moved to live lives devoted to religious devotion and became nuns.

Though some monks chose to live alone, most formed communities with other people who shared their vision of a Christian life. These communities were called monasteries, a word that comes from the Greek *monachos*, which means living alone.

Monasticism was a central feature of the Middle Ages, and hundreds of monasteries were established between 400 and 700. Built at first as retreats from the world, many monasteries later became centres of education, literacy, and learning. This was very important at a time when few people could read or write.

Monastic life was usually governed by strict codes of behaviour. One of the most influential of these was the Rule of St. Benedict, often credited to Benedict of Nursia. As a young man, Benedict had retreated from Rome to live a monkish life in a hillside cave. Learning of Benedict's devotion to spirituality, a religious

This photograph shows the Abbey of Monte Cassino as it looks today. The monastery, which had stood on this site for more than 1400 years, was destroyed during a World War II battle. It was painstakingly reconstructed after the war.

community invited him to be its leader. This led to the founding of the famous monastery at Monte Cassino, Italy, in 529.

The Rule of St. Benedict required monks to serve a year's probation before being accepted as full members of a monastic community. After this, they were required to take solemn vows of obedience, chastity, poverty, and silence, though necessary conversation was allowed. Personal ownership of even the smallest items was forbidden, and strict rules governed daily activities. Every day, monks spent five to six hours in prayer, four hours reading spiritual writings, and another five hours at work, which might include labouring in the monastery's kitchen, garden, or fields.

Though this monastic code is called the Rule of St. Benedict, it was not recorded until years later. Historians agree that it was probably based on a variety of monastic traditions, including that of Monte Cassino. Some historians even question whether St. Benedict existed at all.

Cult of the Saints

In the Catholic Church, a saint is someone who has, among other things, performed miracles that are interpreted as evidence of a special relationship with God.

Canonization, the official process of declaring someone a saint, can take place only after the person's death.

During the Early Middle Ages, many devout men and women who had devoted their lives to Christianity and who had suffered for their faith were canonized by the Church. Anthony the Hermit, for example, whose influence led many early Christians to become monks, became St. Anthony after his death and Benedict of Nursia became St. Benedict.

Early saints such as St. Anthony and St. Benedict became icons of popular culture. At a time when the Christian God was feared as a God of vengeance, people often chose to pray to a saint instead. They hoped that the saint might intervene with God on their behalf. People also made pilgrimages to sites where the saints had lived or reportedly performed miracles. This promoted economic activity and the growth of towns.

St. Augustine

Augustine, considered one of the most influential thinkers of the Christian Church, was appointed bishop of Hippo in 396 CE, just as the power of the Western Roman Empire was declining. Hippo was located on the Mediterranean coast near Carthage in present-day Algeria.

A prolific writer, Augustine explained his theories in numerous sermons and writings. His most famous work is *Confessions*, which describes his spiritual journey from a worldly life to one devoted to religious thought. Augustine's ideas about ethics, self-knowledge, and the role of free will in people's lives influenced the Church's later teachings and helped shape the monastic tradition. Augustine was canonized after his death.

One of the most difficult issues Augustine faced as bishop was presented by the Donatists. The Donatists were North African Christians whose idea of the nature of God and Christ differed from orthodox views. The Donatists had resorted to violence to maintain their own church and clergy. After much soul-searching, Augustine decided to meet force with force and created a theological justification for using force against heretics. This theory was used by later writers as a rationale for a "just war."

Illuminated Manuscripts

Before the invention of the printing press, books were laboriously copied by hand, usually by nuns and monks. Because this process was expensive, only the very wealthy could afford books.

The Granger Collection, New York.

It probably took Irish monks several decades to complete the *Book of Kells*. This page is the beginning of the Gospel of St. Mark, from the New Testament of the Christian Bible.

During the Early Middle Ages, wealthy patrons began commissioning monasteries to create one-of-a-kind books of prayers or gospel readings. These manuscripts — a word borrowed from the Latin for "written by hand" — were written on vellum, which was created from the skin of animals such as calves, sheep, and goats. The pages were often decorated with elaborate lettering, borders, and pictures. Gold and silver, in both leaf and powder form, were often used for these decorations, giving the impression that the manuscript really had been "illuminated."

One of the most extraordinary illuminated manuscripts was the *Book of Kells*, created by Irish monks starting in about 730. Named after the monastery at Kells, where it was completed, this manuscript features ornately decorated paintings of religious figures, as well as abstract human and animal forms.

THE MEROVINGIANS

The name **Merovingian** comes from Merovech or Meroveus, the mythical leader of a tribe of Franks. Merovech, who gave his name to the first European dynasty after the Romans, may have been the grandfather King Clovis I, who founded the Merovingian dynasty.

Clovis I succeeded his father, Childeric I, as leader of the Salian Franks in about 481 CE, when he was about 15 years old. At the time, the Franks were a Germanic people who lived just beyond Rome's Rhine frontier. Though various Frankish tribes had tried to cross the Rhine River and settle in Roman territory in Northern Gaul, their attempts had been largely unsuccessful.

This changed under Clovis. He was able to take advantage of Rome's weakened Rhine defences when troops were withdrawn to fight other barbarian groups. Clovis was also able to unite the Frankish

Conquests of Clovis

1. Compare this map with the map showing the migrations of the Huns and Germanic tribes on page 501. Which tribes would Clovis and his armies have battled?

2. Compare this map with a map of present-day Europe. What present-day countries were once part of Clovis's kingdom?

tribes, in part by arranging the assassination of rival Frankish leaders.

By uniting the Franks, Clovis was able to muster a much larger fighting force than previous tribal leaders. This enabled him to gain a foothold in Northern Gaul. Clovis's army grew even stronger after he converted to Christianity, a move that won him the support of the Catholic bishops and may have attracted non-Frankish Christian soldiers to his cause.

Clovis went on to defeat a number of other Germanic tribes, enabling him to expand the borders of the kingdom he had inherited.

Merovingian Government

To rule their kingdom, which became known as Francia, the Merovingian kings adopted many of the governing techniques that had worked so successfully for the Romans. They often employed Gallo-Roman clerics who had been educated during the Roman occupation of Gaul. The kings issued decrees, made laws, and developed bureaucratic shortcuts called formularies. Formularies — from the word "formula" — were standard forms used to complete legal transactions such as land transfers.

Justice was administered by travelling judges and *rachimburgi*. Though the judges presided over the courts, they were administrators only. The rachimburgis' job was to "speak the law," which means that they were expected to know the law and pronounce on how it should be interpreted.

The laws were often a mixture of Germanic and Roman traditions. Clovis himself is thought to have written the **Salic Law**. This law code followed the Germanic tradition of assigning a specific financial value to everyone and everything. The wrongdoer was required to pay this amount to the victim or the victim's kin. Here are some of the laws that applied to murder (the denarius and solidus were Roman coins):

- If someone is proven to have killed a free Frank or barbarian who is living by Salic Law, let the offender be judged liable for 8000 denarii, which amount to 200 solidi.
- Should he kill a member of the king's retinue, let the offender be judged liable for 24 000 denarii, which amount to 600 solidi.
- If someone is proven to have killed a Roman, who is a companion of the king, let the offender be judged liable for 12 000 denarii, which amount to 300 solidi.

Salic Law included various trial options. Well-to-do, well-connected citizens could choose trial by oath, which allowed oath helpers — people of recognized position or status — to swear in defence of the accused. A more common option was trial by ordeal, in which guilt or innocence was decided by how — and whether — the accused survived a difficult physical test. Trial by ordeal was based on the belief that God would protect the innocent. An accused might be required to carry a red-hot piece of iron or stone, submerge a hand or limb in boiling water, or be victorious in a combat.

Merovingian Religion and Culture

As a result of Clovis's conversion to Christianity, the Merovingians founded many monasteries and religious establishments. This contributed to the spread of Christianity throughout Western Europe by helping to consolidate the power of the Church. The alliance with the powerful Merovingian rulers enabled the Church to expand its wealth and landholdings to a level that has never been matched.

The Merovingians were great builders of churches and palaces, employing many skilled stonecutters and masons. Objects found in Merovingian tombs reveal the skill of their metalworkers, which exceeded that of the Romans. They developed the art of *cloisonné* enamel, which involves separating colours with thin metal strips and is often used in creating jewelry. Merovingian artisans also produced fine glass and carvings of ivory.

The Decline of the Merovingians

Throughout most of their 300-year rule, the Merovingian monarchs were known as the long-haired kings because they retained the Germanic custom of wearing long hair and beards. Until the middle of the seventh century, they were active rulers who led their armies themselves. From the mid-seventh century onward, however, the dynasty began to decline as the later kings relaxed their grip on the kingdom. The monarchs became little more than figureheads as powerful officials and leading aristocratic families began to dominate the government.

Review...Recall...Reflect

1. How effective at spreading Christianity were the laws passed by the Byzantine emperors?

2. How did the Emperor Justinian bring unity to the Byzantine Empire?

3. How did the withdrawal of Roman forces from Western Europe contribute to the spread of Christianity in this area?

THE CAROLINGIANS

Charles Martel, a name that means Charles "the Hammer," was one of the aristocrats who came to dominate the government of Francia when the Frankish kingdom fell under the rule of a series of weak kings in the early eighth century. By winning a series of military victories, Martel eliminated all his rivals. By 719, he had become mayor, the most powerful position in the kingdom. Though the king still ruled in theory, Martel was the person who really wielded power.

Martel continued to solidify his claim to leadership with more military victories. The most important of these occurred in 732, when he drove back an Islamic force that was marching north from Spain. This victory was the first in a series of triumphs that not only pushed the Muslims south of the Pyrenees, the chain of mountains that separates modern-day France and Spain, but also firmly established Frankish control of Southern Gaul.

To reward his followers, Martel confiscated some of the lands that earlier kings and nobles had given to the Church. Though this action enraged some Church officials, it helped pave the way for Church reform. At the time, many Church officials in the Frankish kingdom had strayed from monastic principles and become quite worldly. The reformers opposed this trend. They wanted to restore spirituality to clerical life, hold regular meetings (called synods) to discuss religious matters, and eliminate pagan practices.

When Martel died in 741, his son, Pepin the Short, took over his father's office and allied himself with those who sought Church reform. Pepin's zeal for reform may have been inspired as much by self-interest as by a genuine desire to restore the spirituality of the clergy. By getting rid of Church officials who were actively involved in politics, Pepin eliminated one source of political opposition.

Pepin's drive for reform brought him into contact with an English monk named Boniface, who supported reform. Boniface, who was later canonized by the Church, had been chosen by the pope to work as a missionary in areas of present-day Germany. Pepin offered him protection, which boosted the success of Boniface's mission — and helped earn Pepin the gratitude of the pope. This collaboration with the Church was to provide Pepin with a very important stepping stone to power.

By 751, ten years after he took over from his father, Pepin clearly controlled the Frankish kingdom. Still, the Merovingian king Childeric III sat on the throne. Believing that this situation was unjust, Pepin sent an embassy to Pope Zacharias in Rome. He asked the pope to rule that the person who held the reins of power should also bear the title "king." Pope Zacharias supported Pepin's claim. With the power of the Church behind him, Pepin deposed Childeric and sent him to live in a monastery, thus removing the last of the Merovingian kings from the throne.

Pepin's ascent to the throne established the Church as the maker of kings. In 753, when Pope Zacharias wanted to regain territory in Italy that had been seized by the Lombards, he called on Pepin for help. Pepin vanquished the Lombards, seized the Lombard crown, and secured the territory that became known as the Papal States for the pope. His success established the **Carolingian** dynasty — named for Pepin's father Carolus Martellus, the Latin version of Charles Martel — as the protectors of the papacy, while establishing the pope and bishops as the makers of kings.

Charlemagne

On Pepin's death in 768, his kingdom was divided, according to ancient Frankish custom, between his two sons, Carloman and Charles. When Carloman died three years later, Charles took over the entire kingdom. This was the beginning of the reign that was destined to establish Charles, who became known as Charles the Great or **Charlemagne**, as the greatest of the Carolingian kings — and to change the political and cultural face of Europe.

Charlemagne was a tireless and remarkably successful military general. By 799, he had defeated the Saxons in Saxony, the Avars in Hungary, the Bretons in Brittany, the Bavarians in Bavaria, and various Slav peoples. In 800, he came to the aid of Pope Leo III, who had appealed for his help after being exiled by a group of Roman aristocrats. Charlemagne restored Leo to his position, then travelled to Rome. There, on Christmas Day, Leo placed a crown on Charlemagne's head and gave him the awe-inspiring title "Emperor of the Romans." Charlemagne's coronation in Rome cemented the relationship between the Frankish kings and the papacy. It also set the stage for Charlemagne to take his place in history as the first ruler of what would later become known as the Holy Roman Empire, a dynasty would continue for more than 700 years.

THE Past AT PLAY

Because Charlemagne loved to bathe and swim, his favourite residence was at Aachen, a city in present-day Germany. Aachen's thermal springs had made it a popular spa since Roman times.

According to Einhard, Charlemagne's biographer, the emperor was an extremely strong swimmer who loved to exercise in the water. Charlemagne often persuaded other people — his sons, friends, and sometimes even his attendants and bodyguards — to swim with him. "Sometimes a hundred men or more would be in the water together," wrote Einhard.

Carolingian Rule

One of Charlemagne's first concerns was to impose order on his empire in accordance with God's will. To achieve this, he took steps to ensure that clergy obeyed Church law, that monasteries conformed to the strict codes of conduct, and that people throughout his kingdom lived a Christian life.

Charlemagne also established schools to educate people and the clergy. By the time he ascended the throne, Latin was no longer the everyday language of Western Europe as it had been during Roman times. People's knowledge of Latin had deteriorated so much that they could no longer understand the Bible, which was written in Latin, or Church services, which were recited in Latin. As a result, Charlemagne ordered that Latin be standardized.

■ Charlemagne's Empire in About 800

1. **Which names derive from the barbarian tribes that invaded the area?**

2. **Notice the areas held by "tributary peoples." What strategic advantages might the tributary states offer the Carolingian Empire?**

Textbooks for teaching Latin were created, and new pronunciations were developed. The result of these reforms was that Latin as it had been spoken by the Romans virtually disappeared.

Manuals for preaching were also introduced. They required, among other things, that sermons be delivered in the language of the people. For the first time in Western Europe, Church and state united to bring Christianity to everyone under their control.

Literacy, liturgy, and scholarship flourished under the stewardship of Alcuin, an English theolo-

gian and Church reformer, at the palace school of Aix-la-Chapelle and at the monasteries of Tours, Metz, Saint-Denis, and Reims. In addition, a new form of handwriting called the Carolingian minuscule became the model for other medieval scripts until the invention of printing in the 1400s.

Charlemagne's focus on education had a number of benefits. It provided a pool of educated people who could help administer the empire. It also produced a precise written language — Latin — that could be understood by people everywhere in the multilingual empire. Finally, it produced a generation of scholars — poets, historians, critics, theologians, and philosophers — whose achievements began to rival those of the Roman period.

The Carolingians after Charlemagne

In accordance with Frankish custom, Charlemagne drew up a will that divided the empire among his three sons. When two of his sons died, however, Charlemagne bestowed the entire empire on his remaining son, Louis.

When Louis ascended the throne in 814, he continued the Church reforms begun by his father. He declared, for example, that all monks in the empire must follow the Rule of St. Benedict. His zeal earned him the name Louis the Pious.

Louis had three sons, and even before his death, the brothers began quarrelling over who would inherit the throne. When Louis died in 840 without specifying a successor, the strong empire that had been built by Charlemagne began to fall apart. For the next three years, the empire was plunged into bitter civil war as the three brothers and their followers fought to gain the upper hand. The Church, convinced of its role as a maker of kings, intensified the conflict by taking sides.

Finally, in 843, the feuding heirs settled their differences. They signed the **Treaty of Verdun**, which split the empire into three kingdoms: Francia Occidentalis (Western France) went to Charles the Bald; Francia Orientalis (Eastern France, which included much of present-day Germany) went to Louis the German; and

■ **Division of the Carolingian Empire, 843**

1. **Which kingdom would be most vulnerable to attack by outside invaders? Why?**

2. **Which kingdom would be most vulnerable to attack by other kingdoms? Why?**

Scripts & Symbols λ μ ν ο π θ υ ρ σ τ υ ϖ ω ξ ψ ζ α β χ ε δ φ γ

The Latin written alphabet used by the Romans included only capital letters. During Charlemagne's reign, a new form of handwriting was developed. Called Carolingian minuscule, in honour of the emperor who promoted it, it combined both capital and small letters in a single system. Carolingian minuscule greatly influenced later handwriting styles and was a forerunner of today's cursive writing, in which letters are joined in rounded, flowing strokes.

Carolingian minuscule

The History of the Imagination: Myths and Legends

Chanson de Roland: A Song of Deeds

When twelfth-century French nobles gathered to listen to troubadours singing *chansons de geste* (songs of deeds), one of their favourites was the *Chanson de Roland — Song of Roland*. Written in about 1100, this epic poem tells the highly romanticized tale of Charlemagne's battle against the Saracens at Roncesvalles.

The hero of the *Chanson de Roland* is Charlemagne's nephew, Roland. As the story unfolds, it is 778 and Charlemagne's army is making its way home through the Pyrenees after successfully fighting the Saracens in the Iberian Peninsula. Roland's treacherous stepfather, Ganelon, has arranged for his stepson to be placed in command of the rearguard. In a stunning betrayal, Ganelon plots with the Saracens to attack Roland's small force. Ganelon wants his stepson dead, and he gets his wish in the bloody battle that ensues. Though Roland and his troops fight fiercely, they are badly outnumbered, and Roland dies heroically. Afterward, Ganelon's treachery is revealed, and the poem ends with his trial and execution.

Like many legends, the tale told in the *Chanson de Roland* is based in fact. A Frankish historian, for example, recorded an account of the Battle of Roncesvalles. The poem, however, was written more than 300 years after this battle — and the poet clearly added many imaginative touches to his account.

According to histories written at the time, Charlemagne did lead an army over the Pyrenees into the Iberian Peninsula. The campaign, however, never amounted to much. On the homeward trek through the mountains, the rearguard was ambushed at a place called Roncesvalles — not by Saracens, but by a band of Basques. These native inhabitants of the region were seeking revenge for the havoc wreaked by Charlemagne's troops on their journey into the peninsula. Several Frankish nobles, including one named Hrudoland, were killed in the skirmish.

No one knows for certain who wrote the *Chanson de Roland*. The story concludes, however, with this line: "So ends the tale which Turold hath conceived." This clue has led historians to suggest that the poem was penned by a Norman poet named Turold. As Hrudoland was a lord of the Marches of Brittany in northwestern France, historians have also suggested that he was, in fact, the Roland of the poem. Perhaps Turold's purpose was to highlight the exploits of a fellow northerner.

Like all legends, the *Chanson de Roland* provides tantalizing clues for students of history. Because many legends are based on real characters and events, the stories are often historically significant. Legends use history to tell us something.

Since the twelfth century, pilgrims making their way from France to the holy shrine at Santiago de Compostela in northwestern Spain have passed the site of the Battle of Roncesvalles. This monument at the battle site commemorates Charlemagne.

Activities

1. Find a retelling of the *Chanson de Roland* and create a visual representation of one segment of the story. The representation could be realistic or abstract, collage-style or 3D.

2. We sometimes like to make our heroes even more heroic. Think of someone who is a hero to you. Create a cartoon that takes an episode or deed from your hero's life and makes it larger than life, or make up a story that you can tell, chanson-de-geste-style, about an episode from your hero's life.

Francia Media (Middle France, which was often called the Middle Kingdom and included the Italian provinces and Rome) went to the eldest brother, Lothair, who also inherited the title "emperor."

When Lothair died, he left the Middle Kingdom to his three sons, weakening the power of the Carolingian Empire even more and leaving it vulnerable to invasion by the Vikings from the north, Magyars from the east, and Saracens from the south.

Review...Recall...Reflect

1. What was the significance of the crowning of Charlemagne by the pope on Christmas Day, 800?

2. How do the art forms of the Early Middle Ages illustrate that the period was not a "dark" age?

3. Describe the nature of education in the Early Middle Ages, including who was educated, and what was studied.

IBERIA

The peninsula made up of present-day Spain and Portugal was called Iberia by the Romans. During the Roman period, large agricultural estates had been established there. By the time the Romans withdrew from the peninsula, the owners of these estates had grown wealthy and developed into a privileged class of *seniores*. The status of the seniores was built upon the labour of slaves and semi-free peasants.

Cities had also developed, and with them a middle class of urban dwellers who continued to be heavily influenced by Roman culture and customs long after the decline of the Roman Empire. One of the dominant features of this culture was its strong ties to the Church in Rome.

The Iberian Christian tradition was first threatened by invading Visigoths in 409 CE. The Visigoths established a capital at Toledo, from where they ruled most of the peninsula for about 300 years.

In the south, with the aid of Justinian's Byzantine armies, the Iberians threw off Visigothic domination and re-established their Roman-influenced culture. Still, conflict with the Visigoths, who were Arian Christians, continued. It ended only when the Visigothic king Reccared converted to Catholicism in 587 and allied the Visigoths with the Church.

The Visigothic kingdom started to collapse in 711, when Southern Spain was conquered by the **Moors**, an Islamic people from North Africa. At first,

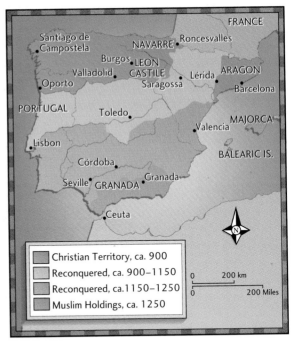

■ Christian Reconquest of Iberia, 900–1250

1. **Locate Toledo and Córdoba. Why would Abd al-Rhaman have preferred to establish a new capital at Córdoba?**

2. **What geographic advantages would have enabled Muslims to hang on to Granada?**

the Islamic conquerors did not interfere with the religious practices of the Iberian Christians. This changed in 756, however, when Abd al-Rahman took control and created the Muslim state of Andalusia, with Córdoba as his capital.

Surrounded on all sides by Catholic kingdoms, the Muslim caliphs of Andalusia zealously guarded their state's Islamic foundation and tried to suppress the Christian faith. From this religious struggle emerged the Mozarabs, urban Iberians who remained Christian but learned to speak Arabic and adopted many Islamic cultural traditions. In later centuries, Mozarabic cultural influences would spread to other Iberian kingdoms.

Under Charlemagne, Christian forces began reconquering the Iberian Peninsula from the Muslims, whom they called infidels. The word "infidel," which comes from Latin and means unfaithful, was used to describe those who did not believe in the Christian God.

Under various leaders over a period of centuries, Christian forces gradually fought their way south. At this time, three distinct Spanish kingdoms — Castile, Portugal, and Aragon — emerged. In 1085, King Alfonso VI of Castile captured Valencia and Toledo, with the help of the legendary Roderigo Díaz de Vivar, better known as El Cid. By 1212, the Muslim-controlled area of the Iberian Peninsula was reduced to the state of Grenada, which survived until 1492.

THE BRITISH ISLES

Northwestern Europe, including Northern Gaul and the British Isles, was never as important to the Romans as the Mediterranean. The Romans thought of the northern reaches of their empire as the fringes of civilization and considered this area useful only as a buffer against the barbarians beyond.

As a result, few of the Celtic-speaking people of Northwestern Europe, who were much less heavily Romanized than those who lived in the provinces of the Western Mediterranean, would have noticed Roman control. And when the Romans withdrew, life for the Northwestern Europeans did not change dramatically — at first.

Taking advantage of the withdrawal of Roman troops, however, Germanic tribes started to move into the area. As a result, large areas of the Northwestern Roman Empire became Germanic in language and culture. The westward migration of the Germanic peoples allowed peoples from territories farther to the east to move into Eastern Germany, Scandinavia, and the Slavic territories of present-day Eastern Europe.

Britain

The Early Middle Ages began in Britain when Roman rule collapsed in the fifth century and the southern sections of the island were invaded by Germanic peoples: Angles and Saxons, as well as some Jutes and Frisians. According to British tradition, the first Saxons were invited in as mercenaries by a British leader but rebelled and set up their own kingdom.

To escape the invasions, many native Britons fled west into present-day Cornwall and Wales or north into Scotland. There, they often made a stand. One of those who fought off the invaders was thought to have been the legendary King Arthur. The native Britons who fell under the rule of the invaders were often forced to work as slaves and servants, and adopted their conquerors' language and customs.

The Anglo-Saxons, as the invaders came to be known, established eight separate kingdoms. Each kingdom was ruled by an aristocracy of warriors headed by a king. The head of the dominant kingdom of the time was called the *bretwalda*, or British ruler.

The organization of local government in England today originated with the Anglo-Saxons. They divided their lands into units called hundreds and boroughs, which were administered by officials called reeves. The hundreds and boroughs were grouped into larger areas called shires, which were governed by shire reeves, a term that evolved into "sheriffs." This system of local government continued into the later medieval and modern periods.

The first bretwalda was King Ethelbert of Kent. During the 600s, the title shifted to the kings of Northumbria to the north, where learning and culture flourished in York. The rulers of the 700s were the kings of Mercia, the most noteworthy of whom was Offa. Offa's use of the title *rex Anglorum* — Latin for king of the Angles — suggests that the English of this period were one people under a single ruler. Indeed, the word "England" comes from the phrase "Angle Land."

After Offa's death, the power of Mercia declined, and Wessex dominated Southern England for the remainder of the Anglo-Saxon period.

Alfred the Great

In the ninth and tenth centuries, Vikings from Denmark and Norway frequently raided and invaded England. When the Danes conquered Northumbria and East Anglia, the area became known as the Danelaw. The Danes also threatened Mercia and Wessex until King **Alfred the Great**, who ruled Wessex from 871 to 899, beat them back.

Alfred built strong defences by constructing forts, building a fleet of ships of his own design, and requiring all free men to serve in the military. He also established an alliance with nearby Mercia by marrying a member of the Mercian royal family and brought the princes of Southern Wales under his authority.

■ **Kingdom of Alfred the Great, 886**

This map shows the kingdoms ruled by Alfred and the Danes.

1. **What geographic advantages would have helped the Vikings maintain control of the Danelaw?**

2. **What areas were still controlled by the native Celtic peoples of Britain? Why would it have been easier for them to hang on to these areas?**

Alfred's support for learning and Anglo-Saxon traditions played an important role in early English history. He assembled scholars and established a court school to educate and promote literacy among the nobility. He learned Latin and translated several Latin works into Old English (Anglo-Saxon), including Pope Gregory the Great's *Pastoral Care*, works by St. Augustine, and possibly Bede's *Anglo-Saxon Chronicle*.

Working from the strong base established by Alfred, his successors were able to recapture the Danelaw.

Conversion of the Anglo-Saxons

The Anglo-Saxon conversion to Christianity, which was initiated by the Roman Church in the late 500s, started with the rulers of the Anglo-Saxon kingdoms and their courts. From this beginning, the new religion trickled down to the people of the countryside. In the 600s, Celtic missionaries from Ireland and Wales joined other missionaries in spreading the Christian religion, especially in the north.

The Venerable Bede

Bede was the most illustrious scholar and teacher of medieval England. Born in Northumbria in 673, he entered the monastery of Wearmouth at the age of seven. He studied at this monastery and later at the nearby monastery of Jarrow. Ordained a deacon at 18 and a priest at 30, Bede mastered Greek, Latin, mathematics, astronomy, and music, and helped

This is part of a manuscript by the Venerable Bede.

make Wearmouth-Jarrow a great centre of learning.

Bede's *Ecclesiastical History of the English People,* which was completed in 731, dramatizes the conversion of the English people to Christianity. The work earned him the nickname "father of English history" and is the primary source of knowledge about the early Anglo-Saxons.

Ireland

Ireland escaped occupation by the Romans and Anglo-Saxons and remained relatively untouched by foreign influences until the Viking raids that began in the late 700s. Irish society was organized into clans and tribes under the authority of five provincial kings who were nominally ruled by the king of all Ireland at Tara.

In Ireland, literature and the arts were held in high esteem, and Ireland enjoyed a golden age of learning and culture. Every king and chieftain had his own poet, or druid, who preserved his people's oral traditions.

The conversion of the Irish to Christianity was spearheaded in the fifth century by Patrick, a missionary who was later canonized by the Church. Another important figure was Brigit of Kildare, who founded a monastery and was also declared a saint.

When a monastery was established in Ireland, the kin of the person who donated the land to the Church were granted certain rights in the monastery. This made a monastery a kind of family affair, and the abbot — the person in charge — was drawn from the family. This custom meant that, rather than creating retreats from the world, the Irish extended their kinship system into the monasteries. As a result, Irish monasteries became the focus of life in their communities: bases for missionary activity and centres for education in Latin, for book production, and for training clergy. Eventually, they also became important economic and political centres.

In the Field ...

Proof of Life: The Archaeological Search for Arthur

The mythical castle of Camelot forms an important part of the legend of King Arthur. Toward the end of the twelfth century, Camelot was mentioned by the French poet Chrétien de Troyes in his version of *Lancelot*. It was also mentioned by Thomas Malory in *Le Morte d'Arthur*, which was written in the late fifteenth century. And, in 1542, John Leland, a traveller and historian, wrote: "At the very south end of the church of South-Cadbyri standeth Camallate, sometime a famous town or castle.... The people can tell nothing there but that they have heard Arthur much resorted to Camalat."

Was Camelot mythical or real? This question has intrigued historians for centuries. If King Arthur's castle was real, where was it located? Some of the sites investigated have included Caerleon, Caerwent, Camelford, Carlisle, Castle Killibury, Slack, Stirling, and Winchester.

In recent decades, historians and archaeologists have focused on Cadbury Castle in Somerset as the most likely of the possible sites. Small excavations carried out at Cadbury in 1890 and 1913 showed that the area had been settled since before the Roman conquest. It was not until the mid-1950s, however, that serious research began.

Historians and archaeologists took an interest when a farmer ploughed up some flints and pot sherds on top of a large hill. These were examined by a local archaeologist, who showed them to C.A. Ralegh Radford, a professional archaeologist who had carried out previous Arthurian research. Radford's assessment of the sherds indicated that they had been owned in the late fifth century by someone of wealth and standing, someone who could afford luxury goods. Could that someone have been King Arthur?

To answer this question, the Camelot Research Committee was formed and serious excavations began at Cadbury in the mid-1960s. Under the direction of Leslie Alcock, these excavations turned up a wealth of information. Cadbury Castle was a late-fifth-century hill fort rather than a stone castle of the kind built in the later Middle Ages. Though it was a hill fort, the elaborate fortification consisted of a stone wall nearly five metres thick and a kilometre in length. Historians suggest that this kind of fortification could have been built only by a very important leader who was able to mobilize many labourers. Evidence of a large timber feasting hall, a possible kitchen, smaller buildings, and an unfinished church was also found within the fortification.

Was this earthen stronghold Arthur's headquarters? Though no one can be certain, Cadbury Castle dates from the right period and seems to have been custom made for an Arthur-like character and to have been used in the way Arthur might have used it. This may be as close as historians and archaeologists can come to confirming that this hill fort was, in fact, the site of the legendary Camelot.

These archaeologists participated in the preliminary excavations of the ruins of Cadbury Castle in Somerset, England.

Activities

1. List the kind of evidence that would be necessary to prove that King Arthur existed. Do you think the evidence proves — or disproves — Arthur's existence?

2. Conduct more research about King Arthur. Find two other theories about his existence.

The idea that monasteries might be centres for teaching and training missionaries and priests rather than simply retreats was carried to Britain and the rest of Europe in the sixth century by Columba and Columbanus, two Irish missionaries. Their efforts contributed to the spread of Christianity in Britain and the European countryside and resulted in their canonization by the Church.

THE VIKINGS

The first recorded Viking raids — on three monasteries in Ireland — took place in the 790s. Monasteries were a prime target of the attacks because they were known to contain significant riches. By the 800s, Viking raids were so frequent in England that monastic libraries had been almost completely destroyed and monasticism became virtually extinct. Though Irish monasteries also came under attack, they were not as severely damaged. The accounts left by the monks provide vivid account of the raids.

When the **Vikings** began to attack monasteries and settlements in the Carolingian Empire in the ninth century, people were surprised. Until then, Scandinavian merchants from Norway, Denmark, and Sweden had been their trading partners. In fact, the word "Viking" means men who go to trading places. The Vikings had brought furs, walrus ivory, amber, and slaves to Northwestern Europe in exchange for glass, pottery, metalwork, weapons such as swords, and coins.

No one is certain why the Vikings turned to piracy. Overpopulation, internal political battles, and a deteriorating climate and food supply have been cited as possible reasons. One theory suggests that the supply of silver from the Abbasid Empire in present-day Russia, which Vikings had brought to Francia to trade, was cut off because of political troubles among the Abbasids. When this lucrative trading material was no longer available, the Vikings became pirates in order to gain what they needed. The conspicuous wealth of the Carolingian Empire made it an obvious target.

The design of the Viking ships, probably developed for trade, made piracy possible. Viking longboats, usually propelled by oars and a square mainsail, could carry 30 or 40 warriors and their weapons. Yet the longboats' draft — the depth of their keel in the water — was shallow enough to allow them to sail up rivers, giving the Vikings access to both inland and coastal sites.

The earliest raids were relatively small and quick, never penetrating far inland. In the 830s, however, the Vikings began to organize large-scale raids, taking

Called the Gokstad ship because it was found at the Gokstad farm in Norway, this Viking longboat was probably built as a warship in about 890. Later, it became the burial chamber of a Viking chief. This ship, which is 24 m long, and two smaller boats were preserved in the chief's burial mound for nearly 1000 years. Where would the single mainsail have been mounted?

advantage of knowledge gained earlier and, in Francia, of the political troubles of Louis the Pious and his feuding sons. The Vikings wintered for the first time in Ireland in 840–841, where they founded permanent settlements, including Dublin. Later, they established settlements in Francia and England.

The civil war that followed the death of Louis the Pious led to an increase in Viking attacks, which culminated when the raiders threatened to invade Paris in 845. Only a payment of 7000 pounds of silver stopped them. From then on, Francia suffered the worst of the Viking raids.

Some historians say that the Vikings were as interested in trade and settlement as they were in war and looting. As proof of this theory, these historians cite the fact that the Vikings created permanent settlements in Ireland and elsewhere. In England and Francia, for example, tenth-century rulers successfully bought off raiders by offering them land. In England, the area controlled by the Vikings came to be called the Danelaw. In the Frankish kingdom, it came to be called Normandy, a word derived from Norsemen or Northmen, another name for the Vikings.

The Vikings settled in Normandy under the leadership of a chief named Rollo, who negotiated a treaty with the Frankish king Charles the Simple. In return for the right to settle in a large area of present-day Northern France, Rollo agreed to help protect Charles's territory from other raiders. Abandoning piracy for commerce, the Normans, as the Viking settlers in Normandy came to be known, adopted the customs, religion, and language of the Franks and grew wealthy from trade, collecting rents from the Church, and raiding other regions.

Other Vikings, meanwhile, began to turn their attention to lands farther west, across the Atlantic Ocean.

Review...Recall...Reflect

1. How was the political situation in the Iberian Peninsula unique in Europe in the Early Middle Ages?

2. Explain how the conversion of Ireland to Christianity affected England and Northern Europe.

3. Describe the impact of the Vikings on Europe before 1000.

SLAVES AND SERFS

Slavery was a common feature of the Early Middle Ages when invading tribes often enslaved people they had conquered. Though some tribes treated captives cruelly, others placed great trust in their slaves, treating them almost as family members. In some cases, captors offered to return their captives to their families in exchange for a ransom. If payment was not made, the captive became a slave.

In Southern Europe, non-Christians were often sold as slaves to Christians, who were forbidden to enslave other Christians. Muslims in Spain also purchased slaves from Europe because Islamic law prevented them from enslaving others. The Qur'an states that slaves are to be treated with kindness and compassion and that freeing slaves is an act of charity.

Over time, slavery became less attractive to many segments of European society. Rural slaves sometimes became serfs, who worked the land on which they lived for the benefit of its owner and provided labour for public works such as road building. In exchange, the serfs received a small wage and a share of the harvest. Urban slaves tended to do different kinds of work, acting more as servants or even administrators.

In some ways, little distinguished slavery from serfdom. Unlike slaves, serfs were not considered mere property. Still, they were considered part of the lord's estate and could be bought, sold, or exchanged for material goods or other serfs. At the same time, however, serfs could own property and support themselves and their family by their own labour. And the lord was legally obliged to protect them from external threats.

Though serfdom may have been an improvement over slavery, a serf's life was still miserable. They were often poorly nourished because they were responsible for finding their own food. And, like slaves, they worked the entire day without rest, leading lives of unrelieved drudgery.

THE ROLE OF WOMEN

Women of all classes of society played a more prominent role in the Early Middle Ages than they did in later medieval periods. Women — usually noblewomen — were active, for example, in the monastic movement, founding and running monasteries for women and sometimes for men too. They also acted as patrons, abbesses, and scholars, often copying and illuminating the manuscripts that are the hallmark of the Early Middle Ages.

Radegund was an early medieval woman who played an important role in the monastic movement. Born a princess of Thuringia, a kingdom located in present-day Germany, Radegund was taken prisoner by the Franks in the mid-500s. She married the Frankish king Clothar I and became Queen of the Franks.

While still queen, Radegund left the royal court to found a monastery at Poitiers, one of the first royal monasteries ever established. As abbess, she gathered many relics, which are remnants of the body or belongings of saints. Relics were very important to early Christians who believed that these artifacts possessed special spiritual power. Among the relics collected by Radegund was one that was said to be a fragment of the cross upon which Christ was crucified. After her death, Radegund was canonized by the Church.

In addition to the significant role they played in spreading Christianity, women could — and did — rule. Bathild was one of these. An Anglo-Saxon slave who grew up in the Frankish courts, Bathild caught the eye of the Merovingian king Clovis II. The two married and, when Clovis died in 657, Bathild was named regent, someone who is appointed to look after a kingdom in the absence of the monarch. In this case, the monarch-in-waiting was Bathild's son Childeric, who was too young to take over the throne. For the next ten years until Childeric was 15 years old, Bathild ruled as regent, playing an active role in the dangerous politics of the period.

When Childeric took the throne, Bathild retired to a monastery, where she devoted herself so completely to religious pursuits that she was canonized after her death.

In the Byzantine Empire, Irene became the first woman to rule in her own name. When Irene's husband, the Byzantine emperor Leo IV, died in 780, she became regent for their son, who was only ten years old. Irene did not shy away from doing everything possible to maintain her hold on power. Even when her son eventually took over the throne, becoming Emperor Constantine VI, Irene arranged to be appointed co-ruler.

When Constantine seemed to be plotting to get rid of her, Irene ordered him arrested and blinded. For the next five years, Irene ruled alone as emperor — not empress. Finally, she was herself deposed and sent into exile.

THE BIRTH OF MODERN LANGUAGES

The most significant phenomenon of the Early Middle Ages may have been the birth of modern languages, which were forged in the migration, resettlement, conflict, and change that took place during this period. By the tenth and eleventh centuries, Old English (Anglo-Saxon) had started to incorporate words borrowed from Latin, the language of the Church and scholars, and Old French, the language of the Normans. Similar changes were taking place in Old French, Old High German, and Old Norse. The roots of contemporary Spanish, Italian, and other Romance languages have also been traced to this period.

Though Latin remained the language of scholarship and the Church, people had started to write popular stories in the vernacular — the native language spoken by the people of a specific area. One of the most important poems in medieval literature and the first major poem written in the English vernacular is *Beowulf*. This epic of nearly 3200 lines relates the story of the young warrior named Beowulf and his victories over three monsters. Thought to be based on oral traditions that date back much farther than its eighth-century written form, the poem clearly reflects its roots in Norse and Germanic legends. The poem underlines the continuing power of pagan beliefs to capture the hearts and minds of a society that had become, to all intents and purposes, thoroughly Christian.

History Continues to Unfold

Clearly, European history was not as "dark" during the Early Middle Ages as some historians have painted it. The legacy of Rome remained alive in many areas, and various cultures flourished. The Carolingian Renaissance, though short-lived, was a remarkable achievement.

Though the Carolingian Empire was a crude affair compared with the Byzantine Empire or the caliphates of Baghdad or Spain, it represented an important transition. The political, social, and cultural focus of Europe had moved from the Mediterranean to the north, where kingdoms and great estates were being assembled. These units would become the driving forces behind the next stage of European history.

Current Research and Interpretations

The story of King Arthur is one of the most popular legends of all time. The earliest reference to Arthur occurs in a seventh-century Welsh poem that credits him with defeating the Saxons in 516. This claim is called into question, however, by an account of the battle written in 540. Arthur is not even mentioned. Still, writers and poets could not resist embellishing the legend, and tales of Arthur's exploits have captured imaginations ever since.

The real Arthur? Many historians now believe that he was a Welsh chieftain of the early 500s who won a battle against Saxon invaders. At the same time, research into the truth of the legend continues.

Chapter Review

Chapter Summary

In this chapter, we have seen:

- that early medieval societies embodied many traits of complex civilizations
- how the development of legal codes such as *Justinian's Code* and Salic Law contributed to a sense of stability and continuity
- how the spread of Christianity influenced the social and political structures of the Early Middle Ages
- how myths and legends have shaped popular views of the Early Middle Ages
- that women often exerted considerable influence over the political and spiritual life of the kingdoms and dynasties of the Early Middle Ages

Reviewing the Significance of Key People, Concepts, and Events (Knowledge and Understanding)

1. Understanding the history of the Early Middle Ages requires an understanding of the following concepts and events and their significance in the development of medieval society. In your notes, identify and explain the historical significance of three items from each column.

   Concepts
   Byzantine Empire
   heresy
   Justinian's Code
   monasticism
   Salic Law
   Carolingian dynasty

   Events
   Nika Riot
   Treaty of Verdun
   Viking raids

2. Though the decline of the Roman Empire brought about dramatic change in Europe, many things remained the same. In your notes, create a two-column chart. Title the first column "Change" and the second "Continuity." In the "Change" column, list four changes that occurred during the Early Middle Ages. In the "Continuity" column, list four things that stayed the same.

3. Though the Early Middle Ages is often considered a violent and chaotic era, the period produced many works of art and literature that clearly showed that it was a rich cultural age. In your notebook, create a three-column chart. Title the first column "Category," the second "Example," and the third "Description." Enter "Art" and "Literature" in the "Category" column and fill in the rest of the chart.

Doing History: Thinking About the Past (Thinking/Inquiry)

1. The spread of Christianity through Western Europe contributed to continuity between the Roman Empire and medieval Europe. In a clearly written and factually supported paragraph, explain this contribution.

2. For years, the period between 500 and 1000 was called the Dark Ages because people thought that civilization nearly disappeared. What evidence in this chapter suggests that this view is inaccurate and misleading? Answer this question in a clearly argued paragraph that cites sound historical evidence.

Applying Your Learning (Application)

1. On the Venn diagram provided by your teacher, compare Salic Law with contemporary Canadian law. Once you have completed the diagram, transfer its main ideas to the graphic organizer titled "The Development of Western Concepts of Citizenship" in your *World History Handbook*.

2. Many women played prominent political roles in the Early Middle Ages, either directly as rulers or indirectly as the wife of a ruler. Write an obituary for a woman who had political clout in the Early Middle Ages. Be sure to highlight her political influence.

Communicating Your Learning (Communication)

1. Create a cartoon or drawing to illustrate who had authority in early medieval societies and the basis of that authority. Transfer a few of the main ideas captured in your cartoon or drawing to the graphic organizer titled "Basis of Authority" in your *World History Handbook*.

2. Religion played a significant role in the Early Middle Ages. Choose one of the following pairs of characters and write an imaginary dialogue between the two. The dialogue should illustrate the influence of religion during the Early Middle Ages and be at least one page long.

   - Justinian the Great and Arius
   - Pope Leo III and Charlemagne at Charlemagne's coronation

   Once you have completed your dialogue, transfer some of the main ideas to the graphic organizer "Religion's Influence on Political Structures" in your *World History Handbook*.

CHAPTER SIXTEEN

The High Middle Ages

CHAPTER EXPECTATIONS

By the end of this chapter, you will be able to:

- *explain how Islamic culture affected medieval Europe as a result of the Crusades*

- *describe the role of guilds and universities in medieval education and understand their role in society*

- *assess the methods used by various members of medieval society to check the power of those with authority*

- *assess the nature of the economic system that developed during the High Middle Ages*

The graceful flying buttresses of Notre Dame de Paris make this cathedral one of the most recognizable monuments of the High Middle Ages. It was built at a time when the Christian religion was a pervasive influence in people's lives and Church officials were figures of authority who vied with monarchs for power.

The turn of the first millennium is often designated as the beginning of the High Middle Ages, a period that lasted from about 1000 to 1300. During this time, European society was dominated by leaders battling for land and power. Because this struggle was taking place in a society that was becoming more and more Christianized, historians now realize that to study medieval society is to encounter an authoritarian Christian state.

The Christian religion pervaded all aspects of people's lives. It provided the ritual and social underpinning of daily life from birth to death. For many Christians, spirituality was the most important consideration, and the teachings of the Church often governed their personal choices. Church leaders and, increasingly, the pope exercised absolute authority.

Like other world religions, however, Christianity was forced to respond to a wide range of political pressures and social changes. Expressions of Christian devotion evolved differently in different parts of Europe. The Eastern and Western Churches parted company soon after the beginning of the High Middle Ages. In addition, different interpretations of the Christian faith resulted in the emergence of new religious groups, some of whom would be labelled heretics. As a result, the High Middle Ages witnessed the militarization of the Church as the pope and Church leaders went to war against heretical movements both in Europe and farther afield.

KEY WORDS

Peace of God

Truce of God

primogeniture

feudalism

War of Investitures

Magna Carta

Crusade

guild

commune

chivalry

KEY PEOPLE

Pope Gregory VII

William the Conqueror

Thomas Becket

Thomas Aquinas

Marie de France

Francis of Assisi

béguines

VOICES FROM THE PAST

Law: an ordinance of reason for the common good, made by him who has care of the community.

Thomas Aquinas, *Summa Theologica*, 1273

TIME LINE: THE HIGH MIDDLE AGES

	987	Capetian dynasty begins
Peace of God begins effort to restore and sustain peace in Western Europe	989	
	1027	Truce of God marks further attempt to establish peace
Schism divides Christian Church into two independent branches	1054	
	1066	William the Conqueror successfully invades England
War of Investitures pits the pope against the Holy Roman Emperor	1075	
	1086	*Domesday Book* is compiled, providing detailed census of English properties
First Crusade to recapture the Holy Land is launched	1095	
	1122	Concordat of Worms ends War of Investitures
Thomas Becket is murdered in Canterbury Cathedral	1170	
	1215	Rebellious English nobility force King John to sign the Magna Carta
Crusaders surrender Acre, last Christian stronghold in the Holy Land	1291	

FROM EARLY TO HIGH MIDDLE AGES

By the late tenth century, the Carolingian rulers, like their Merovingian predecessors, had allowed power to slip into the hands of powerful nobles. Some of these nobles had become so powerful that they threatened the Carolingian rule.

Hugh Capet was one of these. By 985, he ruled Francia Occidentalis, the Western Kingdom, in all but title. When the king died in 987, Capet — with the backing of powerful Church officials — convinced the nobles that the rightful heir to the throne was unfit to rule. As a result, the nobles elected Capet king and started a new royal dynasty, the Capetians. For the next 300 years, Capetian monarchs would rule the area that came to be known as France.

At first, few would have predicted that the Capetian dynasty would last. The Western Kingdom was already in turmoil, and the Capetian takeover of the throne only made things worse. Feeling no loyalty to the new rulers, lesser lords and knights began to compete more fiercely — and violently — than ever for land, power, and influence.

To counter the threat presented by the armed warbands that were pillaging the countryside and disrupting people's lives, the Church stepped in. In 989, religious and secular leaders were called to a peace council at Charroux. This council and others that were held over the next several decades issued a series of decrees designed to protect the unarmed populace by limiting the private warfare that plagued the countryside.

Called the **Peace of God**, the decrees did not prohibit violence against armed men. Stealing church property and assaulting or robbing clerics, pilgrims, merchants, women, and peasants were, however, to be punished by excommunication from the Church.

Excommunication, which barred people from taking part in the Church ceremonies and rituals that formed such an important part of their social lives, was a serious punishment. It set those who had been excommunicated outside the community.

In an effort to expand this peace movement, the **Truce of God** was declared at a council held in 1027. The truce outlawed all fighting from Thursday to Monday morning, on important feast days, and during other religious periods such as Advent and Lent. A later council, held in 1054, proclaimed that "no Christian should kill another Christian, since whoever kills a Christian doubtless sheds the blood of Christ."

The truce also encouraged the idea that the only combat pleasing to God was that carried out in defence of Christendom. This created a paradox. Though the Peace of God and the Truce of God were designed to bring order and civility to society, this peace movement also contributed to the idea of the righteousness of holy war. In 1095, when Pope Urban II called on the knights of Western Europe to join the First Crusade in support of Christians in the East, it is not surprising that he spoke of renewing the Truce of God.

TIME FRAMES
HIGH MIDDLE AGES ca. 1000–1300

Though there is disagreement over when the Middle Ages began and when they ended, most historians agree that that the term "High Middle Ages" accurately describes the period between 1000 and 1300.

SOCIAL UPHEAVAL
AND REORGANIZATION

The turbulent transition between the Carolingian rulers and the new Capetian dynasty contributed to the disruption of European social organization in the tenth and eleventh centuries. To protect their territory, local lords in many regions began to build motte-and-bailey castles. These early castles were wood structures that were built on a motte, or mound, and protected by a timber palisade. The motte was surrounded by a ditch, which separated it from an outer compound called a bailey. A second palisade surrounded the bailey. A bridge allowed people to cross the ditch.

From these castles, local lords imposed their will on the people of the surrounding countryside. They also stopped attending the courts of their overlords, gatherings that until then had provided the political and judicial focus of the countryside. Members of the high nobility often found themselves forced to accommodate those who were, in theory, their subordinates.

To maintain their new-found power, many lords recognized the need to change their inheritance patterns. They began to abandon the Frankish custom of dividing their wealth among surviving family members. Instead, they introduced **primogeniture**, a system in which the eldest son inherited everything. Primogeniture would have important effects on future generations of disinherited younger sons — and on society in general.

For peasants, the new regime represented a step back. Until then, free peasants had existed. These new pressures gradually forced all farmers into a single class and treated them like serfs. The peasants were subject to the local lord's justice and to his demands to provide labour and payments, as well as lodging for his troops.

Even the Church did not escape the demands of the local lords, who often interpreted their rights over Church lands as a licence to plunder without fear of reprisal. New legal customs and traditions, often developed to meet local needs, were replacing the Carolingian system. As a result, disputes between local lords and monastic communities over property sometimes lasted for generations.

Medieval Society: More Than Feudalism

Though historians agree that a dramatic power shift occurred in Europe around the turn of the first millennium, they disagree over the degree of disruption caused by this shift. Still, it is now clear that the term "**feudalism**," which is often used to describe the social organization of the High Middle Ages, does not accurately or adequately describe this complex period.

In this eleventh-century illustration, vassals and clergy stand beside the throne of Otto the Great of Germany.

The word "feudalism" comes from *féodalité*, a term that was borrowed in the seventeenth century by French scholars from a Lombard source. The Lombard system, called *Libri Feudorum*, set out rules governing ownership of land that was called a *feudum* or fief. The property holders were called *vassi*, or vassals. As a result, French scholars and others defined "feudalism" as a system in which property, usually land, was granted by an overlord to a vassal in return for military and other services.

Some lords could — and did — claim that men who held fiefs must provide military service, attend their courts, pay them dues, and accept their judgment about who had the right to inherit the fief. Claims like these were not invariably accepted by the vassals, however, and often sparked bitter and violent disputes. As a result, relations between lords and vassals were often turbulent.

Some historians now suggest that the medieval social structure was made up of "three estates," a term coined by King Alfred the Great of England and used by later medieval writers. The word "estate" comes from the Old French word *estat*, which was, in turn, borrowed from the Latin word *status*. It means a class of society. The estates were thought to have been ordained by God. When referring to the three estates, Alfred was suggesting that members of society could be grouped into three classes: *oratores*, the Latin word for worshippers; *bellatores*, the Latin word for warriors; and *laboratores*, the Latin word for workers. The terms came to represent the clergy, nobles, and peasants.

Just as it would be a mistake to use the word "feudalism" to sum up medieval society, it would also be a mistake to present this society only in terms of these three social classes. The reality was more complex. Medieval people were classified in different ways for different purposes and could be members of a variety of overlapping social groups according to their estate or class, legal status, and gender. A man, for example, could be a vassal of the king or another lord. At the same time, he could be a lord over his own vassals. A woman who was born into a noble family belonged to the noble estate. At the same time, however, she was viewed by the Church as inherently inferior, had no distinct legal status, and probably laboured in the shadow of the men.

Medieval MISCELLANY

During the Early Middle Ages, people in Europe were usually identified by a single name. Those who shared the same name were often distinguished by nicknames, such as William the Conqueror or Geoffrey Plantagenet. Nicknames also identified physical characteristics, occupations (e.g., John the Miller or John the Cooper), or where people lived (e.g., John of the Wood probably lived near a forest). As the European population grew during the High Middle Ages, nicknames often evolved into last names. John the Miller, for example, became John Miller, John the Cooper became John Cooper, and John of the Wood became John Wood.

WARS AND CONFLICTS

War was an experience common to all Europeans during the High Middle Ages. The ruling elites of Western Europe launched campaign after campaign to expand the frontiers of their domains — to the east against the Slavs; to the south into Italy, Spain, and the Muslim territories in the Holy Lands; and to the north and west into England, Wales, and Ireland. Everywhere they went, lords built castles, both to show their power and to provide a haven to which they could retreat when they came under attack. Castles were the focal point around which military campaigns revolved.

These wars often included Church officials, who were as anxious as secular, or non-religious, leaders to establish and expand their power base. In addition to fighting one another, secular leaders were often in conflict with the Church. In 1054, the simmering conflict between the pope and the patriarch of Constantinople over who was in charge of Christendom came to a head. Each excommunicated the other. This led to a permanent schism, or division, between the Eastern (Greek) Orthodox Church, based in Constantinople, and the Roman Catholic Church, based in Rome.

War of Investitures

One of the most divisive power struggles between religious and secular leaders came to be known as the **War of Investitures**. It began in 1075 with a standoff between **Pope Gregory VII** and the Holy Roman Emperor Henry IV. At the time, secular leaders often chose important religious officials such as bishops and abbots. At investiture ceremonies, the monarch handed the bishop his staff and ring, the symbols of his religious power. This gave the impression that the secular leaders controlled the clergy.

This idea did not sit well with Pope Gregory, who declared that only the pope should invest, or ordain, bishops. When Henry IV challenged Gregory's edict, he was excommunicated. This action set off a civil war in some parts of Henry's empire as supporters of the two sides took up arms against each other. So powerful was the idea of excommunication, however, that Henry eventually gave in. According to legend, he was forced to do

penance by standing barefoot in the snow for three days before the pope would forgive him. Though Henry and Gregory did make peace, the break in the conflict was only temporary.

The investiture conflict lasted nearly 50 years, until long after the deaths of Henry and Gregory. It was finally settled in 1122 by the Concordat of Worms (Worms is a city in present-day Germany). There, the Holy Roman emperor and the pope reached a compromise. Bishops and abbots would be invested first as a vassal of the emperor; then, they would be handed the staff and ring by the pope.

Norman Conquests

After settling in Northern France in the tenth century, the Normans converted to Christianity and were assimilated into the local population through intermarriage. Still, continuing feuds plagued Normandy until the rise to power of Duke William, who united the duchy (the territory of a duke) and extended his influence into present-day Belgium by marrying Matilda, daughter of the count of Flanders.

When William's half-Norman cousin, King Edward the Confessor of England, died childless in 1066, Earl Harold of Wessex took over the country as King Harold II Godwinson. William, however, believed that his connection to Edward the Confessor gave him a better claim to the throne. He immediately started recruiting an army and building a fleet to carry this army north across the English Channel.

King Harold knew that a Norman invasion was coming and gathered an army to defend his kingdom. Suddenly, however, he found himself facing another threat. A large Viking force was poised to attack York, a stronghold in Northeast England. Quickly, Harold marched his army north, where he routed the Vikings at the Battle of Stamford Bridge on 25 September 1066.

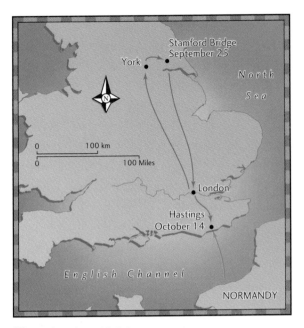

■ England in 1066

1. **What route did Duke William likely follow to England from Normandy?**

2 **What route did King Harold's forces likely follow south to London and then to Hastings?**

Meanwhile, William's fleet had crossed the English Channel and landed near Hastings in Southern England. King Harold marched the remnants of his army south, stopping briefly at London to gather reinforcements.

On 14 October 1066, the two forces met at the Battle of Hastings. In the battle, Harold was killed and his army was nearly wiped out. English soldiers who tried to escape were ridden down and killed by the Normans. William, Duke of Normandy, was crowned King William I of England — and became known as **William the Conqueror**.

What led to William's decisive victory? Some historians say that Harold's use of the time-honoured tactic of drawing his infantry into close formation and creating a defensive shield wall was his downfall. This strategy proved ineffective against William's army of infantry, archers, and cavalry. The Norman archers were also armed with crossbows, a relatively new weapon that was unknown in England.

The Norman victory in the Battle of Hastings is described in many sources of the period. Its most vivid portrayal may be in the famed Bayeux Tapestry. This embroidered tapestry, named after the French city where it is kept, is considered one of the most important documents of eleventh-century history and art. More than 69 m long and 50 cm wide, the tapestry depicts the Norman Conquest of England, concluding with the Battle of Hastings and the death of King Harold. An important source of information about the military equipment and tactics used during the Conquest, the tapestry also provides insights into eleventh-century culture, clothing, architecture, and ships.

After the Battle of Hastings, the Normans moved quickly to secure their hold on England. To strengthen his position, William started building castles. Over the next 20 years, the Normans may have built up to 500 castles in their newly conquered territory. The Norman rule of England, which lasted for 300 years, also left an indelible stamp on English culture and the English language.

Domesday Book

In 1086, King William decided to conduct a massive survey to find out the value of his conquest. The

The *Domesday Book* was written on parchment by a scribe in the *scriptorium*, a room set apart for writing, in England's Winchester Cathedral. Scriptoria were found throughout Europe until the twelfth century, when they evolved into universities.

This is one of the 72 scenes in the Bayeux Tapestry. King Harold's infantry is resisting the attack of the Norman cavalry. What information about the weapons used by the opposing forces does this scene provide?

results were recorded in what has come to be known as the *Domesday Book*. Modern historians owe William's surveyors an immense debt. Their meticulously detailed records make it possible to reconstruct English society at the time. Each district was required to provide an account, complete with current values, of all landowners and their properties, tenants, and livestock, as well as a list of natural resources such as water and timber. This information was used to determine what revenues were owed to the king.

Plantagenet Conflicts

The Norman rulers of England allied themselves with the Angevin rulers of France when Matilda, William the Conqueror's granddaughter, married Geoffrey IV of Anjou. Though neither Geoffrey nor Matilda ever ruled England, their son, who was already the Count of Anjou, took over the English throne in 1154 and became King Henry II.

Henry II was the first Plantagenet king of England. Plantagenet was the nickname sparked by Geoffrey IV's habit of either wearing a sprig of broom or planting broom, a kind of shrub, to improve hunting in his domain. *Planta* is Latin for "plant" and *genista* is Latin for "broom." Plantagenet kings ruled England until Richard II was deposed in 1399.

Struggles with the Church

Shortly after taking over the English throne, Henry II met a Church official named **Thomas Becket**. At first, the two were friends, and Becket seemed to support Henry's attempts to bring the Church under the control of the monarch. This changed in 1162, however, when Henry appointed Becket Archbishop of Canterbury.

To Henry's dismay, Becket took seriously his new responsibilities as the most important Church official in England. Becket refused to go along with the king's attempts to control the clergy. This shattered the friendship between the two men, who spent the next

The murder of Thomas Becket is commemorated in this stained glass window at Canterbury Cathedral.

eight years locked in a bitter power struggle. When Henry raged against Becket one day, some of the king's followers interpreted his displeasure as an order to assassinate the troublesome archbishop. On 29 December 1170, the assassins made their move, slaughtering Becket as he was conducting a service in Canterbury Cathedral.

The murder shocked the deeply religious people of England and Europe, and Becket was canonized soon afterward. Henry was forced to do public penance and give up his plans to subjugate the Church.

Struggles with the Nobles

The fifth and youngest son of King Henry II and his wife, Eleanor of Aquitaine, was nicknamed John Lackland because he lacked land. Unlike his broth-ers, John inherited no important fiefs from his father. John did, however, manage to outlive his four older brothers, one of whom was the popular King Richard the Lion-Heart. As a result, John inherited the throne of England in 1199.

King John immediately embarked on a series of ill-advised actions, which included extortion and other abuses. His excesses alienated the English nobles and triggered unrest throughout the king-dom. In 1215, angry nobles forced King John to place his seal upon the **Magna Carta**, or Great Charter, which limited the power of the king.

One of the most important documents in English history, the Magna Carta forms the founda-tion of English constitutional law and liberties and has been declared part of the Canadian Constitution.

The Magna Carta assumes that the king, like those he ruled, was subject to the law. To ensure that justice was applied fairly and equally under the law, all free men were entitled to be judged by their peers. This principle led, over time, to the system of trial by jury.

WEB CONNECTION

http://www.mcgrawhill.ca/links/echoes

Go to the site above to find out more about the Magna Carta.

Review...Recall...Reflect

1. Although the peace movement at the beginning of the High Middle Ages had little success in sustaining peace, it did have some important consequences for medieval Europe. Describe two of these consequences.

2. Why is it misleading to use the term "feudal" to sum up medieval society?

3. Describe the relationship between the Roman Catholic Church and the rulers of medieval Western European kingdoms.

[THE CRUSADES

When Pope Urban II launched the First **Crusade** in 1095, he started a tradition of Christian holy war that continued long after the Middle Ages. Urban wanted to help the Byzantine emperor, Alexius I Comnenus, drive Muslim Seljuk Turks out of Palestine, which they had conquered in a series of battles. Palestine, which includes much of present-day Israel and Syria, was called the Holy Land because it was where Jesus Christ

had lived. Christians did not want it to stay in the hands of Muslims, whom they regarded as infidels.

Reclaiming the Holy Land for Christianity was not Urban's only motive for declaring a holy war. By uniting the kings of Europe under a papal military banner, he hoped to end the divisive investiture controversy that had split Church and secular leaders — and to consolidate his own power. Not a single king joined the First Crusade, however.

Still, Urban's call for crusaders did appeal to the younger sons of nobles. Prevented from inheriting their father's property, many of them saw an expedition to the Holy Land as an opportunity to improve their lot in life by gaining land and plunder. As an added incentive, Urban promised that anyone who joined his Crusade would receive a special form of religious pardon called an indulgence. Crusaders who joined the holy war would be forgiven for all their sins, and if they died in battle, they would go straight to heaven.

Two holy men — Peter the Hermit and Walter the Penniless — began to spread word of Urban's call to arms among the peasants of Europe. Those who joined the "Peasants' Crusade" did not wait till they reached the Holy Land to launch attacks on people they viewed as heretics, however. Whenever they encountered a Jewish settlement, they attacked ruthlessly, destroying homes and killing anyone who had not already fled. Other Christians were not immune to attack, either. To feed themselves, the peasant crusaders looted the countryside as they passed through. When they finally reached the Holy Land, this band of peasants was ambushed and slaughtered by the Turks.

About 5000 lords, knights, priests, workers, and prostitutes sewed crosses on their garments to mark themselves as Crusaders. Once in the Holy Land, they captured Antioch, a city in present-day Syria, then went on to take Jerusalem in 1099, slaughtering thousands of Arabs and Jews. To administer their conquests, they set up three Crusader kingdoms: the Principality of Antioch, the County of Tripoli, and the Kingdom of Jerusalem.

In 1144, Bernard of Clairveaux, a monastic leader who was later canonized, managed to recruit two kings, Louis VII of France and Conrad III of Germany, to lead the Second Crusade. This Crusade ended in disaster, however, when the Crusaders were slaughtered in Turkey.

In 1187, Jerusalem was recaptured by the great Egyptian Arab warrior, Saladin. This sparked the Third Crusade, which was organized by the pope and led by the powerful kings of England, France, and Germany. The kings ended up bickering with one another rather than fighting the Arabs. As a result, they accomplished nothing. Over the next 200 years, five more Crusades were equally unsuccessful.

By 1291, the zeal of the Crusaders had faded. When it became clear that there would be no further help from Europe, they surrendered the port of Acre, their last foothold in the Holy Land, and returned home peacefully.

Other Holy Wars

Between 1209 and 1244, the papacy persuaded French nobles to launch a Crusade in southern France against a Christian sect known as Albigensians. The mission of this Crusade was to either convert or kill members of the sect, who were considered heretics. Another military campaign initiated by the papacy as a Crusade was the invasion of southern Italy by the French in the 1250s. The politically motivated invasion of the Christian kingdom of Aragon by King Philip III of France in 1285 was

This picture shows a group of Hungarians attacking members of the Peasants' Crusade in an attempt to reclaim their stolen property.

also called a Crusade. In the late thirteenth century, a group of German Crusaders known as the Teutonic Knights began a 150-year invasion of Eastern Europe that, at its height, reached as far as Lithuania.

Effect of the Crusades

From a military point of view, the Crusades were a failure. By channelling the attention of warring nobles into holy wars, however, the Crusades reduced the violence that had plagued Western Europe, and the papacy gained new prestige as the defender of Christendom. Venetian, Genoese, and other Italian merchants, shipbuilders, and fleet owners created thriving businesses out of transporting Crusaders and their supplies. Some French and German knights did carve out territories in the Mediterranean and Eastern Europe, and the Crusades also led to the founding of powerful orders of knights such as the Hospitaller Knights of St. John, the Knights of the Temple (Templars), and the Teutonic Knights.

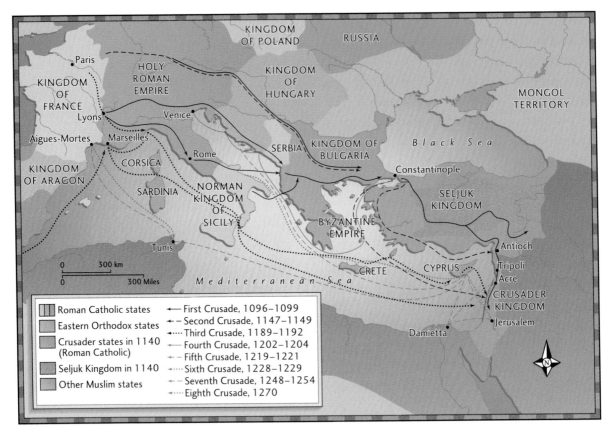

Legend:

Roman Catholic states	← First Crusade, 1096–1099
Eastern Orthodox states	←– Second Crusade, 1147–1149
Crusader states in 1140 (Roman Catholic)	←···· Third Crusade, 1189–1192
	← Fourth Crusade, 1202–1204
Seljuk Kingdom in 1140	←– Fifth Crusade, 1219–1221
Other Muslim states	←···· Sixth Crusade, 1228–1229
	←– Seventh Crusade, 1248–1254
	←···· Eighth Crusade, 1270

■ **Routes of the Crusades**

1. **How did the routes of the later Crusades differ from those of the first two Crusades?**

2. **What might be the advantages of each route?**

The most important effects of the Crusades, however, were unintended. Nearly 200 years of contact with Muslim civilization changed the European Crusaders in many ways. They learned to appreciate different foods, to bathe more regularly, and to value the fine goods that the Turks brought from Asia. They also returned home with new scientific and cultural knowledge. Starting in France in about 1140 and later in Spain, schools of Arabic language and Muslim thought were established, and Islamic learning became a vital part of the curriculum at the universities that were taking shape in Western Europe.

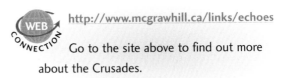

http://www.mcgrawhill.ca/links/echoes

Go to the site above to find out more about the Crusades.

NEW ECONOMIC GROWTH

During the Early Middle Ages, people had fled the large cities and trade centres that had been the prime

One important effect of the Crusades was to revolutionize mathematics in Western Europe by spreading the use of Arabic numerals. Until then, most traders, merchants, and others who worked with numbers had used Roman numerals. This made complex calculations difficult, because the Latin system did not use zero or placeholders. Only experts could multiply, divide, and figure out square roots.

Though Arabic numerals, which had developed from a system used by Hindus in India, were known in Europe in the tenth century, they came into common use a result of the Crusades — and are still used today.

Roman Numerals	I	II	III	IV	V	VI	VII	VIII	IX	X
Arabic Numerals	1	2	3	4	5	6	7	8	9	10

targets of marauding warbands. As a result, country villages and small towns dominated Western Europe. These self-contained rural communities practised subsistence agriculture, a system that involved growing just enough produce to feed the community. As secular and religious leaders gained a measure of control over the violence that plagued the countryside, conditions began to improve. Travel, for example, became safer, making the movement of merchandise and money more secure. This set the stage for the rise of towns and cities.

Towns and Cities

During the High Middle Ages, a new urban culture began to emerge in Western Europe. At the same time, the population was growing rapidly. This population growth is often attributed to a warming climate cycle, which lengthened growing seasons and increased the food supply. More and better food meant that people ate more and were, therefore, healthier. This led to higher fertility rates and gave infants a better chance of survival.

As a result, more and more people began to gather in towns, particularly those in Northern Italy. Feeding and housing Crusaders stimulated business. The Crusades also stimulated demand for trade goods from the Middle East and Asia. As the volume of trade increased, methods of payment developed to support these transactions. Instead of carrying sacks of silver, a method that was vulnerable to robbery, merchants carried letters of exchange, the forerunners of today's cheques. This change led to the development of banks in the commercially advanced towns of Northern Italy. Banks quickly began to play a role in financing international trade, often by raising investment capital through partnerships and business associations. These transactions were supported by a sophisticated legal system in which contracts were drawn up by public notaries, a new profession. New employment opportunities related to the explosion of trade sparked further population growth — and transformed villages into towns and towns into cities.

Still, the cities of Western Europe were small in comparison to centres like Constantinople. By 1300,

The town of Avila in present-day Spain is one of the finest examples of medieval town fortification. The walls are 12 m high and 3 m thick.

the population of cities like Paris and Rome stood at about 100 000. About 75 000 people lived in cities like London and Florence.

Walls were built around the cities to protect the inhabitants from war and marauders. An urban centre with a bishop's cathedral was officially a "city"; otherwise, it was a "borough" or "burg," a word that originally meant "fortress." As a borough grew under the protective walls of a lord's fortress and more people built houses and shops outside the original wall, another wall would be built. As a result, medieval cities grew in concentric circles.

Guilds and Communes

Self-governing **guilds** emerged during the eleventh and twelfth centuries, beginning in the towns of Northern Italy. These organizations of artisans, craftspeople, merchants, and other professionals were formed to ensure consistent standards of prac-

tice and to protect members from competition. They also established apprentice systems to train young people under master craftsmen.

Aristocratic guilds — for merchants, professionals, and certain highly trained artisans, such as goldsmiths, tanners, and so on — often controlled civic governments to the exclusion of the plebeian guilds, which were made up of semi-skilled craft workers. Sometimes, plebeian resentment of political dominance by the aristocratic guilds burst into open rebellion and rioting.

In urban centres, masters of the merchant guilds, usually the sons of wealthy families involved in trade, dominated the councils. These merchants patronized the arts and churches, and successfully negotiated with royal officials to win certain rights of self-government. Because of the guilds' close connections with wealthy nobles, monarchs often distrusted them and viewed them as possible threats to royal power.

One of the chief functions of guilds was to enforce standards. This illustration shows wool merchants using a balance to weigh fabric.

NEW LEARNING

From the late eleventh century to the end of the thirteenth century, Western Europe witnessed a flowering of learning and creativity. So dramatic was this new intellectual interest that some scholars call this period the Twelfth-Century Renaissance. "Renaissance" is French for "rebirth." When referring to a period in history, a renaissance is a time when ideas are reborn and rejuvenated.

During the Twelfth-Century Renaissance, European thinkers became reacquainted with Greek and Roman classics that had been lost after the withdrawal of the Roman Empire and the decline of classical education. These classics had been preserved and translated by Islamic scholars. In addition, philosophers such as St. Anselm, Peter Abelard, Albertus Magnus, and John Duns Scotus explored new ideas.

One of the foremost thinkers of the time was **Thomas Aquinas**, who lived from about 1225 to 1274. A Dominican friar who was later canonized, Aquinas wrote *Summa Theologica*. In this book, he argued that reason and science are compatible with revelation and faith. This was a radical position at the time. Aquinas used reason to prove that God exists and to argue that the principles of ethics and the laws of the state must conform to the universal principles of reason. Along with the writings of St. Augustine, *Summa Theologica* is often considered to be one of the Christianity's greatest theological works.

Some cities became so powerful that they actually gained independence from monarchs. These cities came to be called **communes**, a term that originally meant an association of people bound by oath to help and protect one another. Communes first appeared in Northern Italy. Local nobles were often accepted as overlords who received taxes and rent in exchange for protection and relative freedom, but the communes were unwilling to let the nobles interfere with their day-to-day commercial activities. Venice was one of the first and most successful communes.

As well as playing an important role in local government, guilds extended their influence into the social and religious aspects of urban life. Guildhalls were often centres of social activity, and guilds provided social welfare services to their members. Guilds also adopted patron saints, led processions, organized festivals, and staged mystery and miracle plays, which dramatized the life of Christ or the saints.

At the same time as cities were becoming the focus of economic activity, they were also becoming centres of learning. Universities grew out of the scriptoria, or writing rooms, of the Early Middle Ages. The first "university," a word borrowed from the Latin *universitas*, which means "all the world," was established at Bologna, in present-day Italy, in the late eleventh century. The University of Paris followed in about

1170 and Oxford University in England was well established by the late twelfth century. Students from all over Europe sought out teachers with the best reputations, and there was a keen exchange of ideas.

Though Latin continued to be the official language of high learning, new literary expression emerged in the vernacular languages of Europe. The French writers **Marie de France** and Chrétien de Troyes expressed the spirit of courtly love in prose and poetry. In 1285, Jean de Meun completed *The Romance of the Rose*. In the early 1200s, an anonymous German writer wrote *The Niebelung*, one of the most influential works of the period. Wolfram von Eschenbach produced the Arthurian tale *Parzival*, and Gottfried von Strassburg wrote the epic *Tristan*. The *Song of Roland*, mentioned in Chapter 15, was written at this time, and an anonymous twelfth-century Castilian poet penned *El Cid*, the story of Rodrigo Díaz, the folk hero and military leader who helped reclaim the Iberian Peninsula for Christianity. In addition, Snorri Sturluson wrote his Icelandic sagas.

Though young men could enrol in university, this form of education was not available to women. To earn a bachelor's degree, students studied the *trivium* — grammar, rhetoric, and logic — and the *quadrivium* — arithmetic, geometry, music, and astronomy.

NEW ART AND ARCHITECTURE

No facet of medieval society better reflects the emergence of European culture than the art and architecture of the High Middle Ages. The new prosperity of the twelfth century allowed for a huge investment of capital and labour in large-scale projects, such as the building of cathedrals. Between 1180 and 1270, 80 cathedrals, 500 abbey churches, and thousands of parish churches were built. More stone was quarried than for the pyramids of Egypt. The names of the artists who created these buildings are rarely known. Skilled artists and architects were simply regarded as superior craftspeople.

Gothic Architecture

Church construction shifted from the Romanesque style to what is now known as the Gothic style, a new design that originated in Northern France. Romanesque churches, with their rounded arches, were often cramped and dark. Their windows were small because their walls and columns had to be massive to carry the enormous weight of the entire building.

In addition to introducing pointed arches, designers of Gothic-style buildings increased the

Compare the appearance of the Romanesque church on the left with that of the Gothic cathedral on the right. What differences in design are evident?

size of the windows, reduced the number of structural supports, and opened up the interior to create a sensation of height and light. Towns began to compete with one another to see who could build the largest and most splendid churches. The cathedral in Chartres, for example, attained a height of 36.5 m, and in 1163, the people of Paris built Notre Dame de Paris, which rose to a height of 35 m.

The Gothic style was largely restricted to Northern Europe, however. In the Mediterranean regions, the rounded Romanesque arch continued to dominate.

Gothic architecture included a number of distinctive features.

Flying buttresses: A buttress is an exterior support, and flying buttresses may have been the most distinctive external feature of Gothic architecture. These graceful supports seem to "fly" because they

are partly detached from the wall they support. Still, they bear the weight of the structure and reduce the need for massive walls and thick pillars. They enabled medieval architects to design and build soaring cathedrals that were bathed in sunlight.

Piers: These internal columns share the job of supporting the massive overhead arches of the vaulted roof with the exterior flying buttresses.

Vaulted roofs: A vault is a series of parallel arches that form a roof of brick or stone. The great height of Gothic cathedrals was achieved by constructing ribs to direct the weight of the roof onto the piers and flying buttresses.

Stained glass: The flying buttresses that carried the weight of Gothic structures allowed the walls to contain less stone and more glass. The huge windows of

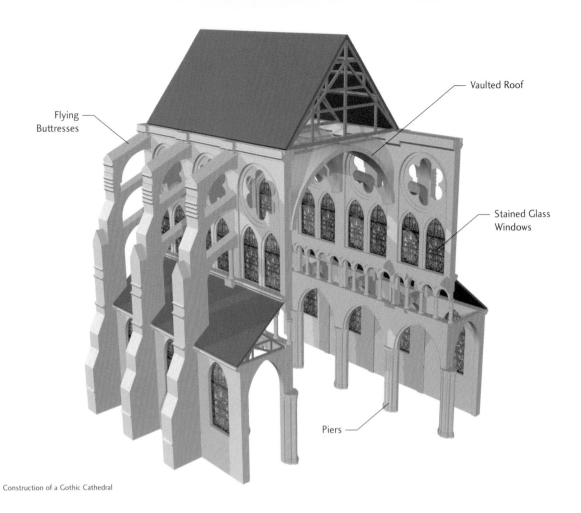

Construction of a Gothic Cathedral

Flying Buttresses

Vaulted Roof

Stained Glass Windows

Piers

stained glass flooded the interior of the church with a magical blend of light and colour. The art of creating stained-glass windows flourished along with Gothic architecture from the twelfth to sixteenth century. The windows often illustrated Biblical scenes, religious symbols, and pictures. Their purpose was to help the largely illiterate population recall Bible stories and lessons. The effect of light streaming through the coloured glass was designed to contribute to people's sense of the glory of God.

Sculpture

A renewed interest in sculpture developed as stone-masons began to adorn buildings with decorative

arcades, capitals, and doorways. They also carved gargoyles as decorative stone spouts at the ends of gutters. Shaped into bizarre and grotesque forms, these spouts were designed to shoot rainwater clear of the walls. As stone decoration became more extensive, the entire sides of buildings were sometimes decorated with symbols and statues intended to convey medieval beliefs and religious ideas. In many cases, these decorations have come to be considered great works of art.

Painting

Painters in the High Middle Ages also often worked at decorating churches and cathedrals. Bright murals and patterns were painted directly on the plaster of church walls and ceilings. Carved tombs and wooden sculptures were often painted as well. Over the centuries, many of these paintings were lost. As fashions changed, the plaster was often removed and the painting disappeared.

Review...Recall...Reflect

1. Why were the Crusades a military failure for the Europeans who set out to recapture the Holy Land?

2. List the three key factors that led to the rise of towns and cities in twelfth-century Europe.

3. Explain how guilds functioned and their role in the economy of the High Middle Ages.

NEW RELIGIOUS SPIRIT

Though the art and architecture of the High Middle Ages flourished as a result of increased economic stability, they also reflected the deeply religious nature of the people. Much of the artistic outpouring of this period was dedicated to the glory of God. The new religious spirit of the High Middle Ages is remarkable for both its intensity of feeling and its diversity of expression. Religious activity followed two main streams: the first involved correcting weaknesses and abuses in the Church; the second involved creating new forms of piety leading to a striving for greater holiness.

Church Reforms

Pope Gregory VII, who lived from 1020 to 1085, was the first in a succession of reform-minded popes in the High Middle Ages. Gregory believed that, as head of the Church, the pope deserved the allegiance of

kings and emperors and was zealous in his efforts to strengthen the papacy. As a result, he became embroiled in the War of Investitures. He also demanded that the clergy remain celibate and started codifying Church, or canon, law. He also conceived of a Crusade against the Muslim occupiers of the Holy Land that his successor, Pope Urban II, made a reality.

Carrying on the spirit of reform, Pope Innocent III, who took over from Urban, approved the work of two new religious orders, the Dominicans and Franciscans. Their mission was to preach against heresy, reinforce orthodox Christianity in the universities, and work with the new urban Christian community.

Innocent called upon French nobles to mount a Crusade against Albigensian heretics and advocated trying accused heretics in Church courts, a move that led to the formation of the papal inquisition. At the Fourth Lateran Council in 1215, Innocent confirmed a number of important policies that would profoundly affect medieval life. Forming new religious orders and canonizing saints now required papal permission. Jews were to be segregated and identified by a distinctive badge. In addition, marriage was declared a Church sacrament that could be reversed only with the permission of the pope. This made a divorce or annulment much harder to obtain.

Monasticism and Medieval Spirituality

Monasticism continued to be an important force during the High Middle Ages. To join the third estate of oratores, or clergy, and live a life devoted to God was considered a high calling. Monasteries continued to be richly endowed by kings and nobles and often managed agricultural estates, housed libraries and schools, developed medicines, and cared for the sick.

The degree to which monasteries observed the Rule of St. Benedict varied widely. Many of the older monasteries were closely bound to secular society, and their accumulated wealth embroiled the monks in earthly matters such as property disputes. Toward the end of the eleventh century, however, a new and more austere form of monasticism began to emerge. Like the early monks, members of these new monastic orders, such as the Cistercians, set themselves apart from the world. They also recommitted themselves to poverty and reintroduced manual labour to monastic life.

Later, mendicant, or begging, orders began to emerge. **Francis of Assisi**'s Franciscan Order, for example, was founded in 1209 to help meet the needs of urban Christians. Franciscan friars lived in houses set up in or near towns where they preached, performed works of charity, and took vows of poverty. The Rule of St. Francis was strict about what the friars could own, as this excerpt makes clear:

> The brothers shall possess nothing, neither a house, nor a place, nor anything. But, as pilgrims and strangers in this world, serving God in poverty and humility, they shall confidently seek alms, and not be ashamed, for the Lord made Himself poor in this world for us. This is the highest degree of that sublime poverty, which has made you, my dearly beloved brethren, heirs and kings of the Kingdom of Heaven; which has made you poor in goods but exalted in virtues.

Women and Monasticism

Women, too, continued to embrace monasticism, though they were excluded from positions of power within the Roman Catholic Church. Perhaps as a result of this, some women turned to mysticism, a form of intense spirituality that they believed opened direct channels of communication with God. Though many of these women worked within the Church, their mysticism enabled them to transcend the limitations placed on them by male Church officials.

Héloïse was one such woman. As a young woman, she was a brilliant scholar whose sex barred her from enrolling at a university. As a result, her family hired Peter Abelard, a theologian and philosopher, to teach her. Teacher and student fell in love and married after Héloïse secretly gave birth to a baby boy. When her family discovered what had happened, they were outraged and arranged for Abelard to be attacked and castrated. As a result, Abelard entered a monastery and Héloïse entered a convent. Despite their separation, the two stayed in touch by letter.

One of the most original minds of his day, Abelard continued teaching, and his work set the stage for the founding of the University of Paris.

This painting shows the pope confirming the Rule of St. Francis. Which monk is Francis of Assisi? What symbol indicates that he was later canonized by the Church?

Héloïse outlived Abelard by many years, dying in 1164 when she was in her 60s. By then, she had become the respected abbess of a famous religious house, corresponding on equal terms with abbots and prelates. She was buried beside Abelard.

Some women who did not want to join an established Church order turned instead to the béguine movement. This provided them with a way to devote their lives to spirituality and charitable works without being controlled by male Church officials. Béguines took no official vows and, though they promised to be chaste, they were also free to leave the community and marry. Béguine communities, called béguinages, represented a true alternative lifestyle for women and were a forerunner of contemporary feminism.

The first béguine communities appeared in Belgium in the late twelfth century and soon spread throughout Europe. The béguines generated a distinctive Christian literature of piety and mysticism. Mechtild of Magdeburg, for example, wrote *The Flowing Light of the Godhead*, a collection of mystical visions, letters, parables, reflections, allegories, prayers, criticism, and advice that also criticized the corruption of the Church.

WEB CONNECTION

http://www.mcgrawhill.ca/links/echoes

Go to the site above to find out more about Marguerite Porète and the béguines.

Another béguine, Marguerite Porète, was declared a heretic and burned at the stake in Paris in 1310 after her book, *The Mirror of Simple Souls*, was condemned by the local bishop. In 1311, fearing that béguinages had become breeding grounds for heretics, the Church ordered the communities to disband. Though this order was later reversed, the movement never returned to prominence. Still, some béguine communities continue to exist today, mostly in Belgium.

LIFE IN THE HIGH MIDDLE AGES

The seeds of the social organization of the High Middle Ages were sown in the warband societies of the Early Middle Ages. All people, whether peasants or royalty, expected to live in a society where roles were well defined. This did not mean that people could not step outside their roles, or that relationships were always simple and straightforward. It did, however, mean that daily life was often conducted according to rigid expectations.

The Knight

Knights as a distinct class of warrior emerged in the tenth century. A far cry from the mythical noble knights depicted in various legends, real medieval knights were little more than mercenary thugs. Taking advantage of the chaotic situation in Europe at the time, these independent warriors pursued personal gain through ruthless violence, making them a threat to both the peasants and the Church.

In an effort to control the indiscriminate violence and plundering inflicted by knights, medieval society developed a code of conduct, or **chivalry**, that established a standard for acceptable knightly behaviour. The Church also tried to curtail knights' destructive behaviour by sponsoring initiatives such as the Peace of God and the Truce of God. Church leaders hoped to redefine knights as protectors of the peasants who were a source of income for the Church through the tithes they paid. A tithe was like

Rites of Passage

The Apprenticeship of a Knight

In the Middle Ages, boys who were destined to become knights began their training early, usually when they were seven years old or even younger. Until they reached adolescence, these boys were called pages. Pages were assigned a variety of duties in a lord's household. It was also here that they received their education, consisting of instruction in reading and writing; music, manners, and religion; and hunting, fencing, wrestling, falconry, and riding horses.

When pages were about 14, they became squires in the service of a knight. Squires continued to hone their skill as warriors by helping their knight and practising with a knight's armour and weapons. This training was rigorous. Squires were expected to follow their knight everywhere. They slept on the floor beside the knight's bed, carved the knight's food at the dinner table, and followed the knight into battle.

In battle, a squire was expected to attend his knight by handing over his horse if needed and dragging the knight to safety if he was injured. Sometimes squires stepped into battle, but this was frowned upon. Knights did not think it honourable to fight mere squires.

After serving a knight for about seven years, a squire expected to be made a knight himself. Sometimes this promotion was a reward for a brave deed; more often, it was because the squire had mastered the necessary skills and proved himself useful and companionable in the household — and had the money to equip himself with a horse, arms, and armour.

For many years, becoming a knight involved a simple, secular ceremony known as dubbing. The squire knelt in front of the parrain — the knight dubbing him. The parrain struck the squire forcefully on the shoulder with either his hand or the flat of his sword, saying, "I dub you knight."

Over time, the ceremony became more formal and much more religious. It was preceded by a day and night of prayer, a purification bath, and a ritual beard shaving that indicated a desire to serve God. The squire dressed in white-and-red clothing to represent purity and blood shed in duty. A crowd might be invited to watch the ceremony, which was often followed by a tournament. Knights would come from great distances to enjoy the festivities, jousts, and combats.

After becoming a knight, a young man was free to go where he pleased, though most knights continued to serve under a lord. A knight errant was one who travelled from place to place, joining the fight for various causes. Several orders of knights were founded during the Middle Ages. These orders organized knights around specific purposes. The earliest orders were religious, but secular orders were also formed. Some of the secular orders continue to exist today.

Activities

1. Imagine that you are a squire in training. Write a note home to your family telling them about your day, how you feel, and your hopes and fears.

2. Think about a knight's training from age seven to 21. Create a chart comparing a knight's apprenticeship with your own schooling.

This highly romaticized picture of a dubbing ceremony was painted by Edmund Blair Leighton in 1901. What details contribute to the romantic image?

As armour became heavier and heavier through the Middle Ages, knights came to rely on staying mounted on their horses. When they were off their horses, the weight of their armour rendered them awkward and helpless.

The Granger Collection, New York.

a tax, except that it was paid to the Church. The required tithe was ten percent of a person's annual income or agricultural produce. The knights were also mobilized to take part in the Crusades, which redirected their violence against the Islamic world.

The Catalan poet Ramón Lull, a Christian mystic and missionary to the Muslims, wrote the first book on chivalry in the thirteenth century. This book set out rules to be followed by truly chivalrous knights, who were supposed to embody the virtues of justice, piety, and honour, as well as defend the Christian faith, the king, and the weak. Though this idealized view of knighthood took root in the High Middle Ages, it did not begin to blossom until the Late Middle Ages.

Courtly Entertainments

Fables were immensely popular in the courts of the nobles of the High Middle Ages. These stories, which were usually recited aloud rather than read silently from books, were satires of conventional society presented as fables about animals. Some historians believe that many of these anonymous tales were created by urban clergy who were critical of secular society.

Marie de France was the author of more than 100 fables. One of the most talented writers of the Middle Ages, this twelfth-century author was connected with the court of King Henry II and Eleanor of Aquitaine and was the first woman to write narrative verse in a

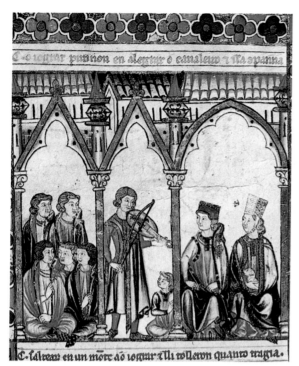

Troubadours were travelling minstrels who entertained noble courts by writing and performing ballads that focused on chivalrous values and the romance, heartbreak, and infidelity of courtly love. Though troubadours are usually depicted as male, the works of more than 20 female twelfth- and thirteenth-century troubadours have been preserved.

Western European vernacular language. At a time when most poets remained anonymous, Marie signed her tales of romance and adventure works with her first name.

Castles

Castles may be the most visible legacy of the High Middle Ages. Products of the violence and disunity that characterized medieval Europe, they are a reminder of the wealth and power enjoyed by a select few. As the High Middle Ages unfolded, the motte-and-bailey castles that had been characteristic of the beginning of the period gave way to castles built of stone.

Daily Life in a Castle

During the High Middle Ages, castles were increasingly viewed as homes as well as fortifications. By about 1300, living quarters had been moved to the upper floor of the keep, which was a castle's central stronghold, and had become much more comfortable. Timber floors were installed, and carpets covered walls, tables, benches, and, eventually, floors. A fireplace had replaced the central hearth, distributing heat more efficiently and safely. Near the kitchen, gardens were planted with fruit trees, vines, herbs, and flowers. Water carried by lead pipes was often available at a central place on each floor. The latrine or *garderobe*, usually placed as close as possible to the lord's bedchamber, extended beyond the castle wall so waste could drop to the moat below or be carried by a long shaft to a cesspit in the ground.

A typical day began when the servants arose at daybreak. Knights and men-at-arms relieved the night watch. Later, the servants wakened the lord and lady, who attended mass in the chapel before breakfast, which usually consisted of bread washed down with wine or ale. After breakfast, the castle residents went about their daily business. For the lord, this usually meant meeting various officials. The lady would oversee the castle's domestic affairs.

Dinner — the midday meal — was prepared and served according to strict rules. There was a correct way to do everything from laying the tablecloths to carving the meat. The conventions governed the order in which dishes were served, where dishes were placed, and even how many fingers were used to hold a joint of meat for the lord to carve. Dining was often a lively affair that included various forms of entertainment such as music, jokes, and storytelling.

The activity around the castle generally subsided in the early evening as most people went to bed shortly after dark.

Caerphilly Castle in Wales was built in the thirteenth century. Instead of a moat, it was surrounded by a lake. What features of this castle would have made it difficult to attack successfully?

Life in the Manor

Despite the growth of towns and cities, more than 90 percent of Europe's population lived in villages that were organized primarily to support a local king, noble, bishop, or knight. In these villages, peasants lived, worked, socialized, loved, married, gave birth, died, and were buried. The villages formed complete and permanent communities organized around agricultural production.

In England, these communities were called manors. In most villages, houses and a few shops were clustered around a crossroad near the manor house, a parish church, and a grinding mill, usually owned by the lord of the manor. Villagers shared a common pasture for cattle and sheep and worked farmland in the area around the village.

Originally, peasants could hold their small tenements, or plots of land, in much the same way as larger fiefs were held. By the eleventh century, how-ever, free tenants had become a small minority of the population. This was especially true in England after the Norman Conquest. The typical manorial tenant was a serf, whose family was legally bound to the lord of the manor.

Serfs' holdings were just large enough to support a family at a subsistence level in a normal season. The serfs' main obligation was to provide the labour and services required to make the lord's landholdings profitable. Fulfilling this obligation took most of their time, especially during ploughing and harvesting seasons. Only when their obligation to the lord had been met could serfs and their families work the land they rented from the lord.

The freedom of serfs was also limited in other ways. They had to use the lord's grain-grinding mill, attend the manorial court, and serve in various manorial offices if called upon. If their actions or those of their family or livestock affected the life of the manor, they could be fined. Holy days offered some relief from their day-to-day labours, but serfs' only prospect of real relief lay either in the hope that the lord might grant them manumission — freedom from their obligations — or in escape to a chartered town. Serfs who escaped to a town and lived there for a year and a day were considered legally free.

A serf's chief protection against arbitrary decisions by the lord or his agents lay in the traditions of the manor. Villages were close-knit, highly conservative communities made up of families who had lived there a long time, often many generations. People came together regularly at the manorial court, and they farmed together on fence-free fields. Everyone would suffer if people dealt unfairly with one another.

Unfortunately, few serfs shared in the prosperity of the High Middle Ages. Because the lord claimed any surplus crops, the serfs' diet, housing, and dress were no better than they had been during the Early Middle Ages. After the tenth century, the Church could also claim a portion of the serfs' produce through the tithe.

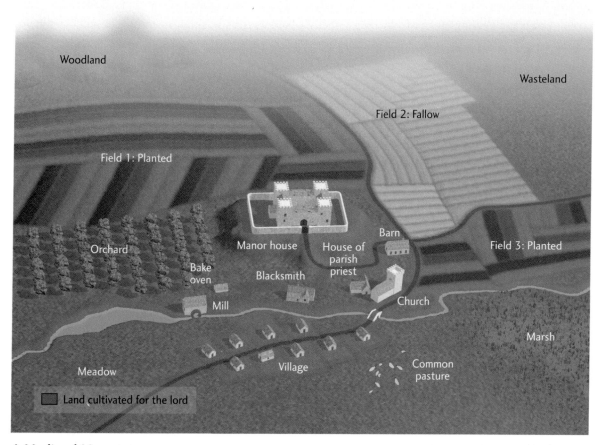

A Medieval Manor

Though peasants might own or rent the land they farmed, the lord retained some land — called the demesne — for his own use. In some villages, such as the one illustrated here, the lord's demesne was made up of strips of land alongside strips that were worked by peasants. In others, the lord might own one large tract, usually the most productive land in the village.

Birth, Marriage, and Death

At all levels of society, babies were born at home with the help of midwives. Because of the dangers of childbirth and the high death rate among newborns, babies were baptized immediately after birth. This sacrament admitted the child to the Christian Church and was thought to ensure the child a place in heaven should he or she die.

Though the primogeniture system of the High Middle Ages kept landholdings intact, it forced younger sons to leave home to earn a living. The younger sons of wealthy peasants might hope to be given a small landholding purchased by their father, but the sons of poor peasants were not so fortunate. If they did not want to remain dependent on their parents at home, their choices were limited. They could embrace the celibate life of a member of the clergy, or they could try to earn a living as a soldier or day labourer. With so few choices, many became vagabonds or slipped into a life of crime.

When peasants decided to marry, they usually exchanged vows at the door of the village church. Many peasants, however, chose to exchange their vows privately, a situation that remained a problem for the Church throughout the Middle Ages. These marriages, which were considered valid as long as both husband and wife gave their consent, were known to happen in the woods and in taverns, and usually took place without witnesses.

During the High Middle Ages, less than ten percent of children survived to the age of ten, and the life expectancy of a peasant was about 45 years. Violent and accidental deaths were common, and tuberculosis, pneumonia, typhoid fever, and heart attacks took a toll. Leprosy, a wasting disease that was incurable at the time, was widespread, and victims were isolated from society either individually or in colonies. Lepers were allowed to appear in public if they were covered by a sheet and clacked castanets as a warning.

WOMEN IN MEDIEVAL SOCIETY

The status of women actually declined as the High Middle Ages unfolded. The primogeniture system deprived women of the right to inherit family property, and they were explicitly barred from government, the priesthood, universities, and, except in certain circumstances, most professional guilds. Some scholars have suggested that women's role in the High Middle Ages was limited mainly to producing heirs and consummating political alliances through marriage. At one time, members of the clergy even suggested that there was no evil equal to women, who were a barrier to salvation because they lured men into committing sins of the flesh. Despite attitudes like these — and laws and customs that severely restricted what they could do — women of all classes played a vital role in the society of medieval Europe.

When considering attitudes toward women during the Middle Ages, it is important to remember the nature of the times. This was an age when power was determined by brute strength and was, therefore, concentrated in the hands of the militaristic aristocracy. It was also an age when the influence of the Church was everywhere. These two groups — clergy and aristocracy — presented contradictory stereotypes of women. While the clergy often portrayed women as temptresses, the romantic literature of the aristocracy placed women on pedestals. According to the romances, the ideal woman was a beautiful, intelligent, fair, and delicate damsel who was probably in need of rescue by a brave knight. Neither view acknowledged women as complete individuals. Instead, women were perceived as inferior simply because of their sex.

The Lady of the Manor

Even women born into noble families lived under the guardianship of men — first their father and then their husband. As a result, they were often pawns in the power struggles that dominated the times. A woman who had not married by the time her father died was made a ward of her father's lord. Though single women had some legal rights, including the right to own, inherit, and sell land, they lost many of these rights when they married. A husband could sell his wife's land without her consent, unless the land was part of her dowry. Only by being widowed could a woman escape male guardianship.

What features of her clothing indicate that this twelfth-century woman was a member of the nobility?

From Birth to Marriage

Babies born to nobles were often sent to wet nurses for as long as a year. A wet nurse, who either lived with the family or on her own, breastfed the baby, and provided the child's earliest instruction and care.

Childhood was brief for women in medieval Europe. Girls as young as five were often promised in marriage to the son of another prominent family in order to establish or maintain an alliance. Marriages usually took place when the girl was between the ages of 12 and 14. Personal attraction was seldom taken into account; an important decision like marriage was considered too important to leave to the whim of young lovers. Because they married so young, women had frequently given birth to several children by the age of 20 and — if they survived childbirth — were often grandmothers at 30.

Women in Towns

Urban women played an important role in the medieval economic revival. Married women usually worked alongside their husband in his trade. In an age when goods were manufactured by craftspeople in their homes and workshops, wives and daughters were expected to help. As a result, they were also able to participate in guild activities, a privilege that was usually denied to other women. If the husband died, the widow often carried on the trade. If she remarried, however, she was forced to learn the trade of her new husband.

Women's most important contribution may have been in spinning wool, producing silk, weaving, and brewing. From these industries and others come titles such as spinster (a female spinner), webster (a female weaver), brewster (a female brewer), and baxter (a female baker). In some cities, women involved in these crafts formed their own, all-female guilds.

It was not unusual for young children, both boys and girls, to be sent out to work at an early age. In some cases, this would lead to an apprenticeship, although girls were usually apprenticed under the master's wife.

Women in the Countryside

In addition to preparing meals and looking after children, peasant women made cloth and clothing for use by their family and, sometimes, for sale. Outside the home, they helped with nearly everything except ploughing. Alongside their husband and, often, their children, they planted, weeded, and harvested crops. They also milked the cows or goats, looked after the poultry, and did much of the sheep shearing.

The most hard-working women were often the widows of serfs. In addition to farming their own land, they were required to fulfill the obligations owed to the lord. This intensified the hardships faced by widows.

Review...Recall...Reflect

1. Why were many men and women attracted to monastic life during the High Middle Ages?

2. Describe the kind of entertainment commonly found at noble courts during the High Middle Ages.

3. Explain how the life of peasants and serfs differed.

POPULATION GROWTH AND EXPANSION

The expanding population of the High Middle Ages sparked demand for new farming and settlement areas. Forested land was cleared and tilled, and difficult-to-cultivate land in valleys and uplands was ploughed and settled. In some areas, peasant families simply moved to new land with their lord's consent. In others, such as parts of present-day Germany, agricultural expansion was a planned enterprise. Huge areas, which became new principalities as powerful as those of the German heartland, were opened up to colonial settlement in much the same way as the Canadian Prairies were opened in the late nineteenth century.

The small Slav population that had inhabited these areas was killed, enslaved, or driven out when territory was granted to members of the German nobility and clergy. Peasant farmers were attracted to these areas by offers of larger holdings and freer tenure. The German monarchy fostered this settlement, not only because it protected the kingdom against attack by the Slavs but also because they hoped that the newly created principalities would offset the doubtful loyalty of the established duchies and counties, which frequently challenged royal authority.

The eastern frontier of Germany provided one of the most striking examples of twelfth-century colonial expansion, but it was not the only one. In Italy, Norman invaders established the Norman kingdom of Sicily and, later, Anglo-Norman lords crossed into Ireland, where they carved fiefs out of Irish tribal lands. In addition, the Christian kingdoms in the foothills of the Pyrenees took the first steps toward reconquering the Iberian Peninsula from the Muslims. Even the Crusades themselves, which began in 1095, can be viewed as a result of a hunger for land, which could not be satisfied closer to home.

History Continues to Unfold

The High Middle Ages are sometimes called the Age of Faith because the Christian Church played such a central role in European society. This role is reflected in the art and architecture that was dedicated to the greater glory of the Christian God.

By 1300, the countries of Northern Europe had established themselves as the political and cultural powers of the continent. The social order was relatively stable, and towns and cities were growing. On the eve of the fourteenth century, it seemed as if the people of Europe could look forward to continued stability and prosperity. In fact, they did not know that a series of disasters was about to shake the foundations of European society. These disasters would bring the High Middle Ages to an abrupt end. They would also lay the groundwork for the developments that would herald the modern age.

Current Research and Interpretations

The term "feudal" is often used to define the medieval social and political system in which lords and vassals exchanged property in return for military and other services. Contemporary historians dispute this definition. They point out that even where fiefs existed, land was often held in many different ways. What is more, landowners could offer loyalty and service to a lord as an act of homage without turning their land into a fief. They could also receive fiefs without pledging to fulfill obligations to a lord.

Chapter Review

Chapter Summary

In this chapter, we have seen:

- how Europe was shaped by Islamic cultural contributions after the Crusades
- that medieval guilds and universities provided a degree of stability in society
- how medieval Europe contributed to the development of modern Western ideas of citizenship and the rights of individuals
- that women played a variety of vital roles in medieval society

Reviewing the Significance of Key People, Concepts, and Events (Knowledge/Understanding)

1. Understanding the history of the High Middle Ages requires an understanding of the following concepts and events and their significance in the development of medieval society. In your notes, identify and explain the historical significance of three items from each category.

Concepts	Events
Holy Land	Peace of God
Magna Carta	Truce of God
feudalism	Crusades
three estates	Peasants' Crusade
primogeniture	War of Investitures

2. Show how education contributed to stability in medieval society by completing a four-column chart. Title the first column "Educational Institution" and include "Guilds" and "Universities" in this column. Title the second column "Who was educated," the third "Kind of education received," and the fourth "Effect of education on society."

3. List and explain three factors, besides education, that promoted stability during the High Middle Ages. Once you have completed your answer, transfer some of the main ideas to the graphic organizer "Forces That Reinforce Stability and Continuity" in your *World History Handbook*.

Doing History: Thinking About the Past (Thinking/Inquiry)

1. Architecture often reflects the nature of the society that produced it. Stadiums with retractable domes and communications towers that reach to the sky speak volumes about Canada at the beginning of the twenty-first century. What does the architecture of the High Middle Ages reveal about the nature of that society? Respond in a short essay of 500 to 750 words.

2. Considering the objective of the Crusaders, how successful were the Crusades? Considering the effect of the Crusades on the development of European culture and society, how important were the Crusades in the history of Europe? Respond to these questions in a single paragraph.

Applying Your Learning (Application)

1. At both the beginning and end of the second millennium, peace movements sought to ensure peace. On the Venn diagram provided by your teachers, show how these movements were similar and different.

2. Create a series of Great-Women-of-the-Middle-Ages trading cards. On the front of each card, include a picture or image of the woman. On the back, include biographical details, such as birthplace, birthdate, and contributions to medieval society. You may need to consult other sources besides this book.

   Using the information included on the trading cards, identify some important roles played by women in medieval society and record these on the graphic organizer "Women's Roles in Society" in your *World History Handbook*.

Communicating Your Learning (Communication)

1. Create a diagram to illustrate the social hierarchy of the High Middle Ages. On the diagram, include rulers; the nobility; knights; the clergy; merchants; professionals such as doctors; peasants; and serfs. Add illustrations that reflect the position of each group in society. Once you have completed the diagram, transfer some of the ideas to the organizer "Forms of Social Organization" in your *World History Handbook*.

2. Create a map of the medieval world to illustrate the major kingdoms, at least four major events, and trade routes between Europe and the wider world. Add visuals to capture the essence of the events, the nature of the goods exchanged, and a distinctive feature of each kingdom.

CHAPTER SEVENTEEN

The Late Middle Ages

By the end of this chapter, you will be able to:

- explain the forces that started to break down the hierarchical social structure of the Middle Ages

- demonstrate an understanding of how people such as Joan of Arc and Johannes Gutenberg contributed to the process of change

- identify people, such as John Ball, and groups, such as the Lollards and Hussites, who challenged authority

- evaluate the influence of the Church on the political structures of medieval Europe

This manuscript painting from the *Very Rich Book of Hours* shows the calendar for February. Peasants go about their business as farmhands warm themselves by the fire. By the end of the Late Middle Ages, the power of overlords to control peasants' lives had weakened.

As Europe entered the fourteenth century, the outlook was bright. The social order was relatively stable, towns and cities were prospering, cultural pursuits and learning were popular, the population was growing, and harvests were often plentiful. Then a series of disasters struck. Climate change triggered bad weather that ruined harvests, and famine drove many people from their land in search of food. A plague of unprecedented severity swept across the continent. On top of these disasters, wars and rebellions threatened the social order. And the Roman Catholic Church, once a symbol of stability and authority, was split by controversy and confusion.

Because of these events, there is a tendency to describe the Late Middle Ages as a period of disaster, hardship, and decline. It is important to remember, however, that the upheaval and change caused by these events was an important factor in the emergence of dynamic languages and cultures, new economies, new modes of spiritual expression, and new forms of government.

KEY WORDS

Black Death

Peasants' Revolt

Hundred Years' War

Avignonese papacy

Great Schism

Council of Constance

transubstantiation

indulgences

Inquisition

parliament

KEY PEOPLE

Giovanni Boccaccio

Roger Bacon

Joan of Arc

Johannes Gutenberg

Christine de Pisan

Dante Alighieri

Tomás de Torquemada

VOICES FROM THE PAST

If thou follow thy star, thou canst not fail of a glorious haven.
Dante Alighieri,
The Divine Comedy,
1310–1314

TIME LINE: THE LATE MIDDLE AGES

	1310	Dominican Inquisitor Bernard Gui sends heretics to be burned at the stake at the beginning of the Holy Inquisition
Heavy rains devastate crops, leading to widespread famine	**1315**	
	1324	Gunpowder is used in European warfare for the first time
Hundred Years' War begins	**1337**	
	1347	Black Death starts to sweep through Europe
Great Schism begins, temporarily dividing the Christian world	**1378**	
	1381	Peasants rebel in England
Henry V gains control of most of France after Battle of Agincourt	**1415**	
	1429	Joan of Arc leads French forces to victory over English
Joan of Arc is burned at the stake by the English	**1431**	
	1453	Johannes Gutenberg starts a communication revolution by inventing the printing press
Pope Sixtus IV authorizes the Spanish Inquisition	**1478**	
	1492	Jews are expelled from Spain as part of the Spanish Inquisition

PLAGUE AND HARDSHIP

In the twelfth and thirteenth centuries, Europe had enjoyed 200 years of relative prosperity and population growth, spurred, in part, by a warming climate that had resulted in the production of bumper crops. By 1300, however, colder weather had returned. The colder temperatures shortened the growing season and reduced farm production, leading to food shortages. Although famines occurred frequently throughout the medieval period, the worst by far occurred between 1315 and 1317 when heavy rains caused widespread flooding and devastated crops. People were starving. This left them weak and vulnerable to disease.

The Black Death

In 1346, a terrible plague spread through Asia. It is believed that the infection was transmitted by fleas and transported by rats. When a flea carrying the deadly plague bacillus (a kind of bacterium) fed on the blood of a rat, the infection was transferred to the rat's blood, causing the rodent's death. This forced the flea to jump to a new host, which may have been another rat — or a human being.

The symptoms of the plague were painful. The first signs were swollen lymph nodes, which are glands in the groin, armpit, and neck. These swellings are called buboes — and this form of the illness is called the bubonic plague. As the swelling continued to expand, sometimes to the size of an egg or apple, it turned black or purple, giving the plague its dreadful nickname — the **Black Death**. Victims would cough and spit blood because their blood had been thoroughly infected, and their body would exude a foul odour. Eventually, the swellings would burst, and death would soon follow.

If the terrible buboes were lanced and drained completely when they first became visible, victims had a chance of recovery. For those who did not recover, death came quickly, usually within three to five days of infection.

This depiction of the terrible suffering in Florence was based on the eyewitness account of Giovanni Boccaccio.

TIME FRAMES
LATE MIDDLE AGES ca. 1300–1500

Although the two centuries between 1300 and 1500 are often defined as the Late Middle Ages, this term does not accurately describe all of Europe. Many elements of Northern European society remained characteristically medieval during this period; in Italy, however, new economic, social, and cultural influences were already carrying society toward an exciting new era of change and discovery.

The plague also took other forms. If the bacillus transmitted by a flea bite entered the bloodstream directly, it often killed within hours. The death rate from this form of the plague was nearly 100 percent. In winter, a pneumonic form of the plague was spread by coughing and sneezing. Related to pneumonia, the pneumonic plague infected victims' lungs, causing them to drown in their own fluids.

After spreading through Asia, the Black Death was carried to Europe by the caravans that plied the trade routes between China and the Black Sea area. Trading ships transported the infection from the Black Sea to the rest of Europe.

The plague moved along the commercial routes of Europe with devastating speed. During the winter of 1347–1348, it infected inhabitants of the Mediterranean basin. By the summer of 1348, it had reached England, and it was in Scotland the following winter.

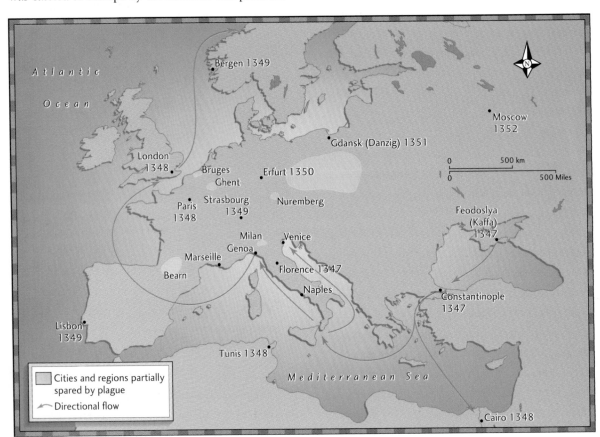

■ Spread of the Black Death, 1347–1352

1. When did people in the Black Sea area start suffering the effects of the Black Death?

2. Once the Black Death appeared in the Black Sea area, how long did it take the plague to reach Southern England?

3. Notice the areas that were only lightly affected. What factors might have helped protect these areas?

Historians estimate that the Black Death killed between one eighth and one half the population of Europe. In some cities, up to two thirds of the population died, while others were only lightly affected. Florence, in northwestern Italy, was hit so hard that two thirds of its population died. Meanwhile, Milan was barely affected, though it was struck by a smaller, second wave of plague in 1361.

Although quarantines were unknown at the time, people who could afford it stayed away from congested cities and towns in summer, when the infection was most common. Stone buildings were inhospitable to rats, and cleanliness helped reduce the presence of rats and fleas. It was the poor, who lived in wooden buildings that lacked sanitary facilities, who suffered most. Still, even royalty and Church officials were not immune. The plague killed, for example, the queen of Aragon, the king of Castile, and a daughter of the king of England, as well as two successive archbishops of Canterbury.

The Black Death profoundly affected the social, religious, and economic environment of Europe. Survivors gained a natural immunity, though there were recurrences of plague in the 1360s, 1370s, 1390s, and in the fifteenth century. The effect of this kind of prolonged and widespread disaster on the human spirit was considerable. Death, symbolized by a skeleton, became a featured character in the art, music, literature, and drama of the time. Elaborate monuments to the dead were created, many of which portrayed rotting corpses, a reminder of the grim realities of the plague.

WEB CONNECTION

http://www.mcgrawhill.ca/links/echoes

Go to the site above to find out more about the Black Death.

An Eyewitness Account of the Black Death

Writer **Giovanni Boccaccio**, a resident of Florence, witnessed firsthand the horror of the Black Death. He recorded his experiences in the *Decameron*, a book of tales that greatly influenced later writers such as Geoffrey Chaucer. In the following passages, Boccaccio describes how people reacted to the plague in Florence:

> In this extremity of our city's sufferings and tribulation the venerable authority of laws, human and divine, was abused and all but totally dissolved, for lack of those who should have administered and enforced them, most of whom, like the rest of the citizens, were either dead or sick or so hard beset... that they were unable to execute any office; whereby every man was free to do what was right in his own eyes.

> Not a few... kept a middle course... living with a degree of freedom sufficient to satisfy their appetites, and not as recluses. They therefore walked abroad, carrying in their hands flowers or fragrant herbs or divers [diverse, various] sorts of spices, which they frequently raised to their noses, deeming it an excellent thing thus to comfort the brain with such perfumes, because the air seemed to be everywhere laden and reeking with the stench emitted by the dead and dying, and the odours of drugs.

> Some again... a multitude of men and women, negligent of all but themselves, deserted their city, their houses, their estates, their kinsfolk, their goods, and went into voluntary exile, or migrated to the country, as if God, in visiting men and women with this pestilence in requital of their iniquities [wickedness], would not pursue them...

Tedious were it to recount how citizen avoided citizen, how among neighbours was scarce found any that showed fellow-feeling for another... in the horror thereof, brother was forsaken by brother, nephew by uncle, brother by sister and, oftentimes, husband by wife... fathers and mothers were found to abandon their own children, untended, unvisited, to their fate, as if they had been strangers...

Many died daily or nightly in the public streets; of many others, who died at home, the departure was hardly observed by their neighbours, until the stench of their putrefying bodies carried the tidings... the whole place was a sepulchre.

It was the common practice... to drag the corpses out of the houses... and to lay them round in front of the doors, where anyone that made the round might have seen, especially in the morning, more of them than he could count... they dug for each graveyard, as soon as it was full, a huge trench in which they laid the corpses as they arrived by hundreds at a time, piling them up as merchandise is stowed in the hold of a ship, tier upon tier, each covered with a little earth, until the trench would hold no more...

How many brave men, how many fair ladies, how many gallant youths... broke fast with their kinsfolk, comrades and friends in the morning, and when evening came, supped with their forefathers in the other world!

Social Effects of the Plague

The social impact of the plague was enormous. The natural order had been upset. Rich and poor, laypeople and clergy, had been indiscriminately swept away by what many interpreted as the wrath of God. In some places, the reaction to death had been a collapse of morals. According to Boccaccio, some Florentines, "finding themselves few and rich," took to "gluttony, taverns, gambling and unbridled lust."

Medieval
MISCELLANY

Young children today still recite a nursery rhyme that was inspired by the Black Death.
Ring around the rosies
Pocket full of posies
Ha-choo! Ha-choo!
We all fall down
Explain the real meaning of this rhyme.

Other people became even more pious. As people became preoccupied with the afterlife and preparing for death, doing penance to earn forgiveness for sins became common. Many people gave gifts and legacies to the Church, hoping that this would secure them a shorter stay in purgatory. Roman Catholics believe that people who have committed minor transgressions must spend time in purgatory, where their spirits are cleansed of sin before they proceed to heaven. A wave of church building also occurred. Despite all this, the Church was considerably weaker, for many clergy and officials had died in the plagues.

Although the plagues were thought by many to be God's judgment, one question remained: Who was spreading it? By early 1348, a "culprit" had been identified: Jews. In Southern France, Jews were massacred as a result. Under torture, a Jewish doctor in Switzerland "confessed" to poisoning local wells. In Basel, Stuttgart, Freiburg, Dresden, Mainz, Cologne, and many other German cities, Jews were burned to death, often before the plague even arrived. Most

A nineteenth-century artist created this depiction of the persecution of the Jews of Strasbourg in 1349.

rulers did little to protect the Jews. Though Pope Clement VI threatened to excommunicate those who persecuted Jews, terrified Christian mobs, urged on by members of extreme cults, were not listening.

This wave of anti-Semitism continued well into the fifteenth century. During this time, Jews were driven out of many countries.

After a period of adjustment, the decline in the population of Europe brought about new social practices. By the fifteenth century, delayed marriages and increased celibacy, rather than war, famine, and disease, had become the main causes of reduced population growth.

Historians have also suggested that the plague-induced labour shortages stimulated the development of labour-saving technology. They also suggest that the failure of prayer to stop the plague promoted distrust of the clergy, which sparked a general reduction in respect for religious institutions and practices. As the power of the Church declined, secular education and vernacular literature assumed greater importance, and people's loyalties were directed

toward their country rather than the Church. This heightened people's sense of nationalism.

Economic Effects of the Plague

It took Europe nearly 150 years to begin to recover from the drastic population decline caused by the Black Death and other fourteenth-century plagues. Agricultural production dropped because there were not enough peasants to work even long-settled tenements. Towns shrank in size, and entire areas of cities were abandoned. The ranks of the clergy were depleted, and the volume of trade was sharply reduced.

As demand for food slumped, so did farm prices, though prices charged for farm labour rose. The price of manufactured goods also rose because many craftspeople had died. According to one English writer, a horse once worth 40 shillings could be bought for half a mark (about one sixth the previous price), and a "fat ox" for four shillings (one third its earlier value). In the autumn, a reaper could not be hired to help with harvesting for less than eight pence (a daily rate that was 50 to 75 percent higher than usual). With labour this expensive, crops were often left to rot. As a result, food prices rose rapidly.

While farm labourers earned more after the plague, others fared even better. Prices charged by craftspeople were sometimes twice as high as they had been before the plague. And the rich who survived often found themselves even richer because there were fewer relatives to claim a share of inheritances.

The plague halted the spirit of economic enterprise that had energized Europe in the twelfth and thirteenth centuries. Merchants and guilds became more restrictive, anxious to protect their share of the market and preserve familiar methods, products, and business practices. To defend their interests, many discouraged innovation, tried to prevent newcomers

This illustration shows a draper's shop. What trade did drapers engage in?

from entering the craft or trade, and blocked the advancement of apprentices who wanted to become masters.

At the same time, economic power was shifting away from cities and towns to the countryside. In England, for example, members of various urban textile guilds, such as weavers, dyers, and fullers (people who cleanse and thicken wool), restricted entry to their craft. To get around these restrictions, which applied only within the the boundaries of the town or city in which the guild was located, people started weaving, dying, and fulling wool in nearby villages, where raw wool has always been cleaned and spun. This encouraged other tradespeople, such as drapers, to set up shop in villages.

This pattern was repeated in other urban centres across Europe. As a result, villages and small towns began to grow and experience a new prosperity. This was signalled by a boom in the construction of marketplaces, stone houses, and new churches and church towers, as well as charitable institutions. At the same time, the population of many established cities and towns was shrinking.

The decline of large urban markets meant that landlords found it less profitable to sell crops that had been produced by serfs. Landowners could make more money by renting their land to peasants, a development that shifted the economic advantage from the landlord to the peasant. Because unoccupied land benefited no one, landlords were eager to find tenants and often competed with other landowners to offer favourable terms to peasant farmers. As a result, peasant farmers assumed a more prominent position in rural life, signalling the beginning of the end of the social hierarchy that had kept them subservient to feudal lords.

Review...Recall...Reflect

1. Describe what happened to people who fell ill with the Black Death.

2. What impact did the Black Death have on wages and prices in Europe?

3. Describe two effects of the Black Death on European society. Were these effects positive or negative? Why?

Peasants' Revolts

Although the catastrophic effects of the plague led to many social and economic changes, these changes did not always come easily. Like craftspeople, landlords strove to maintain their economic and social advantages.

In England, for example, landlords persuaded the rulers to pass laws designed to keep wages at pre-plague levels, to control prices, and to stop the free movement of farm labour by upholding serfs' manorial obligations. As a result of these measures, wage levels were higher than they had been before the plague struck, but they were lower than they might have been.

This situation sparked widespread discontent. When 14-year-old King Richard II imposed a poll tax, which is a tax on every person, the discontent of the peasantry erupted into open rebellion. Led by Wat Tyler and John Ball, the peasants in the countryside around London marched into the city, murdered some Flemish merchants, and destroyed the palace of the king's uncle. They also forced their way into the Tower of London, where they captured — and beheaded — two of the king's advisers.

After Tyler was killed in a confrontation with the king's forces, Richard persuaded the peasants to go home by promising reforms. These reforms were never carried out, and Ball was later captured and hanged. As a result, the **Peasants' Revolt** had little lasting effect, though it is remembered as the first great popular rebellion in English history.

Similar revolts took place in continental Europe. In central France, a series of peasant uprisings started in 1358. The reign of terror they created showed the depth of people's rage against the upper classes, whom the peasants blamed for their problems. In the industrial centres of Florence and Ghent, wool workers rebelled in an attempt to remedy their grievances. All these rebellions were crushed, and many peasants and their leaders were massacred.

This painting depicts John Ball leading the English Peasants' Revolt. A priest who was excommunicated for advocating a classless society, Ball rallied listeners with this famous verse: "When Adam delved [dug] and Eve span [spun], Who was then a gentleman?"

Although these fourteenth-century rebellions were ultimately unsuccessful because they failed to bring about any permanent change, they were a sign that the hierarchical social order was not as stable as those in power might have hoped.

COMMERCE AND TRADE

Although towns and cities did not grow as rapidly as they had during the High Middle Ages, a strong middle class continued to emerge. In some cases, merchant families, such as the banking dynasties of the Medicis of Florence and the Fuggers of Augsburg, a city in Germany, became so wealthy and powerful that they rivalled the traditional aristocracy.

Even though banks had been known in the Roman world and continued in the Byzantine Empire, they had disappeared in the Early Middle Ages when the European economy was dominated by subsistence agriculture. Banks reappeared first in twelfth-century Italy in response to the growth of trade and finance sparked, in part, by the Crusades.

The word "bank" comes from the Old French word *banc*, which refers to a bench or table set up by moneychangers in public markets. In cities such as Genoa, moneychangers undertook to protect their clients' money in addition to changing it. Rather than simply storing clients' money safely, the moneychangers started investing it in other enterprises that might make a profit. Public notaries, who functioned like lawyers by drawing up contracts, ensured the efficiency and legality of these transactions. Banks quickly became popular and grew rapidly, often developing international networks.

During the fourteenth century, the accounting system that is used today was created in Genoa and perfected by the Medicis. In 1494, Luca Pacioli, an Italian mathematician and Franciscan monk, wrote the first explanantion of accounting. His book, which recorded practices that were already widely used, earned Pacioli the nickname Father of Accounting.

This painting shows a money changer and his wife in 1539.

Exchanging coins of many different denominations presented a challenge to the moneychangers. Though various monetary systems were introduced at different times, all were subject to fluctuation as a result of a variety of factors, such as the plagues. The Carolingians devised a widely used system in which 12 pennies equalled one shilling (a solidus or s.) and 20 shillings equalled one pound (a libra or £). This system was used in England until 1971.

CHANGES IN WARFARE

Although the Chinese had used gunpowder in weapons and to create fireworks since the ninth century, it was another 400 years before this compound became known in Europe. In 1254, **Roger Bacon**, a Franciscan monk with a lively interest in experimental science and alchemy, had become the first European to record a recipe for making gunpowder.

The introduction of gunpowder marked a dramatic change in the way wars were conducted. Combat could now be conducted at a distance, and fighting was no longer a personal contest that pitted one soldier against another. Gunpowder could not only propel bullets and cannon balls a great distance, but also be planted under city walls and fortifications to blow them up.

As a result, gunpowder also changed the tactics used in battle. The first recorded use of gunpowder in warfare was at the siege of Metz in 1324, 70 years after Bacon had recorded the recipe. At Metz, the besiegers were armed with iron vases into which they packed the new explosive. Iron or stone balls placed on the top of the vase were then fired at the enemy with great force. Sieges were common in the wars fought in the Middle Ages, and until the introduction of gunpowder, the defenders usually had the advantage. Fewer soldiers were required to defend a fortification than to attack it. If the defenders had enough food and water, they could hold out for a long time.

The use of gunpowder shifted the advantage to the attackers. Rather than trying to scale castle walls with ladders, attacking armies could now blast holes in the fortifications. This meant that monarchs could more easily control rebellious barons, who had been hard to keep in check because of the strength of their fortresses. This increased the power of the monarchies.

Later, advances in the use of gunpowder — larger cannons, and smooth-barrelled, muzzle-loading muskets — would enable bands of European soldiers to overwhelm opposition they encountered overseas. This set the stage for European colonial dominance of the world.

This illustration shows two ways cannons were used during the Late Middle Ages. What special use might each cannon have been put to?

Review...Recall...Reflect

1. Why did peasants' revolts erupt in many parts of Europe during the last half of the fourteenth century?

2. How did Europe's economic system change in the fourteenth century?

3. Describe the impact of gunpowder on European warfare.

THE HUNDRED YEARS' WAR

The Late Middle Ages experienced not one war but a series of wars that were triggered by bitter rivalries between the royalty of England and France. Called the **Hundred Years' War** — even though the fighting actually stretched over a 116-year period — the conflict started in 1337 with a dispute over who was the rightful king of France. Interrupted by an outbreak of the plague, the war consisted mostly of sieges, raids, sea battles, a few land battles, and long periods of tense truce. It also produced epic victories that are still celebrated in England and France.

Plantagenet monarchs had sat on the throne of England since 1154. As descendants of William the Conqueror, the Plantagenets were originally from France — and still controlled territories there. King Edward III of England, for example, was also a French noble. He was Duke of Guyenne, part of Gascony, and Count of Ponthieu. This made him a vassal of the French monarch. Marriages between the two royal families also meant that Edward and the French monarchs were closely related.

When King Charles IV of France died in 1328, Edward believed that he had a legitimate claim to the French throne. His claim was not accepted, however, and Philip VI became king of France.

As Duke of Guyenne, Edward ensured that this duchy in southwestern France maintained close trade ties with England. Most of the wine produced in the region was shipped to England, in exchange for grain, cloth, and other staples. As duke, however, Edward was technically a subject of Philip VI — and Philip, too, wanted to control Gascony.

The competition for control of Gascony worsened Edward and Philip's lingering grudges over the contest for the French throne. These tensions were escalated by piracy in the English Channel and the English desire to control Flanders, a German-ruled duchy on the French border that was an important market for English wool. Edward also resented the fact that Philip had helped the Scots maintain their independence in the face of English claims of sovereignty over Scotland.

The simmering dispute erupted into outright war when Edward challenged Philip's right to rule by declaring himself king of France in 1337. At the time, Edward was not quite 25 years old.

At the outset of the war, which was fought entirely in France, the English forces quickly gained the upper hand. The French kings had continued to meet their military needs by maintaining the feudal tradition of requiring vassals to devote 40 days a year to military service. The English, by contrast, had decided to abandon this tradition and create a contract army in which soldiers were paid for military service. This meant that the English army was more efficient and more motivated than the French troops.

To raise an army, English kings contracted leading nobles to provide a force of a certain size for a specific campaign on prearranged terms. The terms set out the weapons to be used and how the spoils of war were to be divided. The nobles, in turn, subcontracted captains to raise — and pay — the necessary force. Archers, for example, were paid six pence a day, as much as a peasant might earn in six months. Soldiers were also allowed to retain a portion of the booty collected. Not only did this contract army offer soldiers a rewarding income, but it also brought greater professionalism to military service and introduced a command structure based on experience. It also produced bands of mercenaries who preyed on the countryside between wars or during lulls in the fighting.

The war between England and France sputtered along for years, long enough to allow Edward III's eldest son, also named Edward, to join his father in battle. Nicknamed the Black Prince, this popular warrior prince earned his spurs at the Battle of Crécy in 1346, when he was just 16 years old.

In 1347, English forces captured the English Channel port of Calais, just before the Black Death prompted a pause in hostilities. When the war resumed, the Black Prince led the English army to a decisive victory at the Battle of Poitiers in 1356. There, the English captured King John II, who had succeeded Philip to the throne, and many of France's most important knights. A treaty signed in 1360 acknowledged Edward as ruler of Aquitaine, which included Gascony, and required France to pay a large ransom to free the captive king.

Fighting resumed in 1369 when the nobles of Gascony became upset at heavy taxes imposed by the English and sought help from Charles V, who had taken over the French throne. While there were few pitched battles in this phase of the war, the French managed to cut English supply lines, forcing the English to withdraw to their coastal fortresses in 1395.

By this time, both countries were preoccupied with internal power struggles, and the fighting died down. When King Henry V of England assumed the throne in 1413, he decided to take advantage of the discord in France to renew the English claim to the French throne. In 1415, Henry led his army to victory at the famous Battle of Agincourt, an accomplishment

Edward, the Black Prince, leads English forces to victory at the Battle of Poitiers. On his helmet, Edward wears the three ostrich plumes that he adopted as his insignia. As Edward III's eldest son, the popular Black Prince should have inherited the English throne, but he died a year before his father.

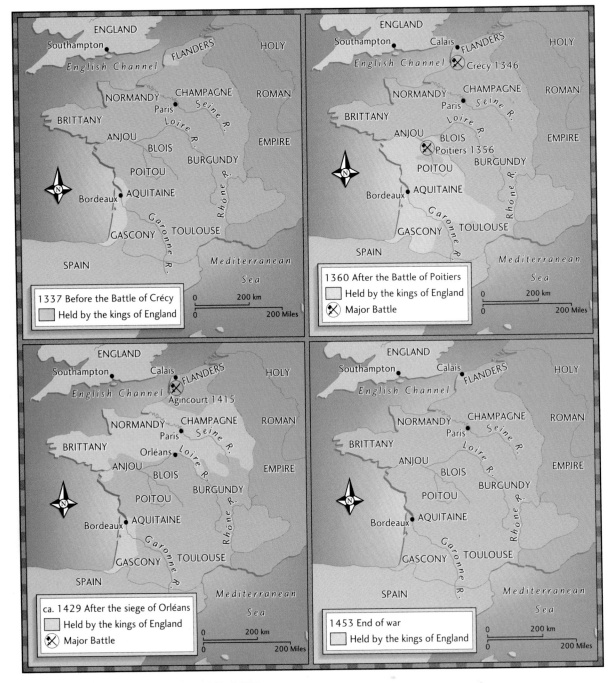

■ **The Hundred Years' War, 1337–1453**

1. Estimate by how much the English had increased their French holdings by 1360.

2. Why would lifting the English siege of Orléans in 1429 have been such an important strategic victory for France?

that is celebrated in William Shakespeare's play *Henry V.* By 1420, English troops had advanced to the gates of Paris, and the French surrendered.

The French king, Charles VI, was humiliated by the treaty he had no choice but to sign. The treaty recognized Henry's right to rule the French lands he had conquered. It also made Charles's daughter Henry's wife and disinherited Charles's eldest son, also named Charles, to make Henry the heir to the French throne. When both Henry and Charles died two years later, Henry's nine-month-old son, Henry VI, became heir to both thrones. At that time, the disinherited dauphin, the French name for the heir to the throne, tried to reclaim the throne of France but failed, leaving the English in almost complete control of the country.

This state of affairs might have continued had it not been for an illiterate French peasant girl named **Joan of Arc.** Claiming to have heard voices that told her to drive the English out of France, the 17-year-old led an army of several thousand French soldiers to victory at Orléans in 1429. This victory gave the dauphin the momentum he needed to reclaim the throne and become Charles VII of France.

Within 20 years, the British had been driven out of France — and the Hundred Years' War was over.

WEB CONNECTION

http://www.mcgrawhill.ca/links/echoes

Go to the site above to find out more about the Hundred Years' War.

THE NEW MEDIA OF THE LATE MIDDLE AGES

When **Johannes Gutenberg** developed a method of using movable type to print books in 1453, his technological innovation revolutionized the printing process. Until then, books had been painstakingly created by hand in monasteries or as special commissions. As a result, they were very expensive and hard to obtain. Before Gutenberg's invention, about 30 000 books existed in all of Europe. By 1500, less than 50 years later, there were about 12 million. Suddenly, literacy and learning were within reach of many more people.

One of the people who embraced Gutenberg's invention was William Caxton. Caxton printed the first book in English and the first English translation of the Bible. By the time Caxton died, he had published about 100 items of various kinds, earning himself the right to be called the first English-language publisher.

Medieval Bestsellers

The first European known to have made a living as a writer was **Christine de Pisan.** Born in Venice in 1364, de Pisan was the daughter of a court astrologer who later worked for King Charles V of France. At the French court, Christine received a solid education. Married at 15, she had three children by the time her husband died when she was 25. To support her children, de Pisan turned to writing.

Because de Pisan lived her entire life in the shadow of the Hundred Years' War, she felt moved to write a poem praising Joan of Arc. Written in 1429, this poem was the first to celebrate the astonishing turn of events that ended the English domination of France.

De Pisan's best-known work, *The Book of the City of Ladies,* was written in 1405. This history of women recalls great women of the past and

Biography
The Hero of Orléans

Born Jehanne Darc in a village in the Lorraine region of northwestern France in 1412, Joan of Arc was an unlikely hero. Yet, this simple, devout peasant girl lit the spark that fired French patriotic sentiment and turned the tide of the Hundred Years' War in favour of France.

As a young teenager, Joan claimed to hear the voices of her favourite saints, as well as that of the archangel Michael, the patron defender of France. These voices convinced her that she was destined to fulfill a prophecy that predicted that, in France's darkest hour, a young woman from Lorraine would save the country.

In February 1429, the 17-year-old travelled to southern France. There, she convinced the dauphin Charles, who desperately wanted to reclaim the French throne, that the angels had given her the divine mission of leading French troops to victory and securing his coronation. Although some members of Charles's court whispered that the peasant girl might be a heretic, a board of theologians declared her sincere. Joan dressed in knight's armour and led a French army to Orléans, a city that had been under siege by the English for six months. Under Joan's command, the French forces drove away the English and recorded other successes. Joan then accompanied Charles to Reims, where he was crowned King Charles VII of France.

In 1430, Joan was captured by Burgundians, who were allies of the English. When Charles did not try to ransom her, she was sold to the English, who charged her with heresy and witchcraft and brought her to trial before a Church court. The Church judges condemned her visions as worthless and her male dress as perverted. Joan defended herself, arguing that her loyalty was to God.

This sketch of Joan of Arc was drawn in the margin of the official history of the siege of Orléans and is the only known contemporary likeness of this French national hero.

After a "confession" was extracted by torture, Joan was sentenced to life in prison. When she resumed wearing men's clothing and appeared to be winning the sympathy of her guards and other people, she was sentenced to be burned at the stake. On 30 May 1431, the sentence was carried out.

In 1450, nearly 20 years after Joan's execution, Charles ordered an investigation into her trial. In 1456, three years after the end of the Hundred Years' War, the pope revoked the Church court's verdict and annulled Joan's sentence. In 1920, Joan of Arc became St. Joan when she was canonized by the Roman Catholic Church, and the French Parliament declared an annual national festival in her honour.

Activities

1. Suggest reasons for Charles's failure to try to rescue Joan from her English captors. Find out whether you were right.

2. Imagine that you are arguing for — or against — canonizing Joan of Arc. What arguments would you use?

Christine de Pisan writes in her study. De Pisan was widely respected for her literary output, which included poetry and prose, as well as treatises on the art of war, good government, and kingship.

examines the role of women in medieval society. As the first woman to speak out in the vernacular about issues affecting women, de Pisan can be called the first feminist historian.

The Late Middle Ages is often called the golden age of vernacular languages because, like de Pisan, many authors chose to write in the vernacular rather than in Latin, the language of scholars. Geoffrey Chaucer, the best-known English writer of the fourteenth century, was one of them. *The Canterbury Tales,* his amusing and often bawdy social commentary, describes a group of very different people who tell stories to entertain one another on a religious pilgrimage.

Sir Gawain and the Green Knight, an epic Arthurian legend by an unknown author, and William Langland's *Piers Plowman* also became well known. *The Book of Margery Kempe* is one of the first autobiographies in the English language. Kempe, a devout but illiterate woman who left her husband and 14 children to make

a pilgrimage to Jerusalem in the late fourteenth century, probably dictated her story to a cleric. Another woman writer was the mystic Julian of Norwich. Born in about 1343, Julian lived as a hermit and wrote *Revelations of Divine Love,* an account of her visions.

Courtly love continued to dominate French literature, which used humour, symbols, and satire in poetry and romance writing. Jean Froissart, who lived from about 1333 to1410, was a leading historian of the Late Middle Ages. Froissart was known for *Chronicles,* a history of the major European countries, and for his lighter writing, such as *Meliador,* a romantic poem about an ideal knight. In the fifteenth century, however, poets like François Villon, who wrote "Ballad of Hanged Men" and the "Debate Between Villon and His Heart," began to write about more realistic subjects.

In Italy, writers such as **Dante Alighieri** and Boccaccio were making their mark. Born in Florence in 1265, Dante was exiled for his role in a bitter political controversy. In 1314, he finished writing *The Divine Comedy,* which tells the story of a poet's journey from despair to salvation as he makes his

To Dante's disappointment, the order exiling him from his native city was not rescinded during his lifetime. After his death, however, Florence commissioned an artist to paint this portrait honouring the writer. Dante is depicted standing outside Florence holding a copy of *The Divine Comedy.*

way through hell and purgatory to paradise. Considered a masterpiece of medieval literature, this book was written in Italian rather than Latin and influenced many later writers.

Boccaccio, another Florentine, was one of the many writers who were influenced by Dante. Boccaccio's eyewitness account of the Black Death, recounted in the *Decameron*, begins the story of ten young people who flee the plague-ridden city for the country, where they amuse themselves by telling tales. Both the *Decameron* and Boccaccio's romantic poetry provided inspiration for later writers, such as Chaucer and Shakespeare. Boccaccio's book *My Lady of the Flame* is considered a very early example of a psychological novel.

The Past AT PLAY

The modern game of tennis owes its name and scoring system to a popular medieval game called real tennis, court tennis, or royal tennis. This was an indoor game in which competitors used pear-shaped rackets to hit hard cloth balls off the court walls. Royalty and nobility enjoyed betting on the outcome of matches, often with disastrous results. "Many people lose and have lost some of their chattels [possessions] and their inheritance," warned the fourteenth-century author of *The Book of Chivalry*.

The Origins of Dracula

One of the most memorable characters in English literature originated in the Late Middle Ages. Vlad III Dracula was a fifteenth-century prince of Walachia, a region in present-day Romania. Famous for his brutal treatment of his enemies, Vlad earned himself the nickname Vlad the Impaler because he liked to impale his foes.

In his 1897 novel Dracula, the Irish author Bram Stoker immortalized Vlad as a blood-sucking monster, who, while still human, had brutally murdered thousands of his subjects.

THE CHURCH IN THE LATE MIDDLE AGES

During the Early and High Middle Ages, Church and state were in a nearly continuous struggle for control of people's hearts and minds. At the beginning of the thirteenth century, it looked as if the Church had gained the upper hand. Those who had challenged Church authority, such as King Henry II of England, had been humbled and the pope was establishing control over both the spiritual and worldly realms. By the beginning of the fourteenth century, however, secular leaders had begun to reassert their control over worldly matters, and the complex struggle between Church and state resumed — with a new intensity.

The Avignonese Papacy

In 1294, Boniface VIII became pope and reopened the longstanding conflict with secular leaders by declaring that kings required his approval to levy taxes on the clergy. These taxes were a rich source of revenue for monarchs, and King Philip IV of France reacted swiftly. His troops arrested and imprisoned Boniface. Although the pope was set free soon afterwards, Philip's action shattered a tradition of respect for, and obedience of, the pope. Boniface died shortly afterwards.

Boniface's death meant that the college of cardinals must elect one of their number to become the new pope. By exerting his power and influence,

Pushing the Boundaries — Science and Technology

The Printing Press: Invention of the Millennium

Johannes Gutenberg was neither the first nor the only person to conceive of a machine that would allow pages of words to be printed using a press, ink, and movable type. Gutenberg's genius lies in the fact that he was able to draw on — and perfect — a variety of technologies, some of which had existed for centuries.

Two of these technologies — paper and movable type — had been invented in China and imported to Europe with Asian trade goods. The invention of movable type is credited to Bi Sheng, who is said to have come up with the idea in 1045. This invention had little noticeable impact on China, however, because representing in movable type the thousands of ideograms that make up Chinese languages was nearly as labour-intensive as hand copying. The effect on Europe, where words were formed by combining a limited number of letters, was much more dramatic.

Gutenberg combined the Chinese inventions with other technologies such as oil-based ink, block-printing techniques, and the wine press. His signature innovation, however, was movable metal type. Each letter of the alphabet was carved into the end of a steel punch that was hammered into copper to make a mould. Hot metal was then poured into the mould to create letters. The letters were attached to a lead base and assembled into words and sentences that were put together in a type tray to print a page. Once the page was printed, the letters could be reused, and letters that wore out or broke could be easily replaced. Gutenberg varied the size of the lead base according to the size of the letter, setting a standard of regularity for printed pages.

Historians believe that the first work Gutenberg printed was a poem, "World Judgement." This was followed by a Latin grammar book and a series of religious letters. His big project, however, was a Bible. By about 1456, Gutenberg had probably printed about 180 copies of what is now called the *Gutenberg Bible*. Unfortunately, this project bankrupted him.

When others took over his print shop, Gutenberg refinanced his business and started again. Others followed suit and, by 1500, printing presses had sprung up throughout Europe. The book business flourished, as did related industries such as papermaking and type foundries. More people learned to read, and books influenced even the many who could not read because travelling readers began reading aloud in public markets as a way of making a living.

The printed word would play a leading role in spreading new ideas across Europe. As a result, some say that Gutenberg's invention paved the way for the ideas about science, religion, politics, and philosophy that have formed contemporary Western society. They call the printing press the invention of the millennium.

Johannes Gutenberg, in the dark cloak, examines a page printed on his flatbed press.

The Granger Collection, New York.

Activities

1. Explain how Gutenberg's inventing the printing press paved the way for major shifts in thinking about science, religion, politics, and philosophy.

2. What twentieth-century invention might be said to have had as dramatic an impact on society as the printing press?

Catherine of Siena was a religious mystic who believed that the papacy belonged in Rome. This painting shows her in Avignon, pleading with Pope Gregory XI to return to Rome. What does the halo around her head signify?

Philip was able to persuade the college to choose a pope who would support French interests.

Philip then invited the new pope, Clement V, to move the papal court to Avignon, a town on the Rhône River within easy reach of the French king. There, a new papal residence was built. This residence resembled a fortress more than the residence of the spiritual leader of Christendom.

The relocation of the papacy to Avignon was viewed with deep suspicion in other countries. Though French ambitions were feared above all in England, where feelings against French rulers ran high, Italy, Germany, and Aragon also protested the move. Italians, in particular, bemoaned what they called contemptuously the "Babylonian captivity" and lobbied for the pope's return to Rome.

Finally, in 1378, Pope Gregory XI decided to end the **Avignonese papacy** and move the papal court back to Rome after an absence of more than 70 years. The prolonged residence outside Rome had

eroded confidence in the papacy, a situation that was not about to improve. Other forces were also contributing to a decline in respect and reverence for the Church and Church officials.

The Great Schism

No sooner had Gregory XI returned to Rome than he died. When the college of cardinals elected an Italian as the new pope, their choice was quickly challenged. A group of dissident French cardinals claimed to have cast their ballots under duress, saying that they had been terrified by crowds that had shouted in the streets and broken into the election chamber. These cardinals elected a second pope, who immediately returned to Avignon, where he set up a papal administration in competition with the first pope.

The rulers of the Christian countries immediately took sides, often based on their feelings toward France. France and its allies backed the pope at Avignon, while the enemies of France and those who were neutral supported the pope at Rome. So began the **Great Schism**, in which two popes claimed Christian obedience as the Vicar of Christ. This debate, which left the Church with two rival heads, was not resolved until November 1417.

The schism (division) in the Church created great problems for the clergy, the bishops, and the universities that advised them. Which pope should they look to for guidance? The schism also presented problems for the people of Europe. Because it had divided people according to national and regional loyalties, the dispute could not be settled until the leading rulers settled their conflicts and sorted out their common interests.

For most of the 40 years of the schism, much effort went into trying to negotiate the withdrawal of

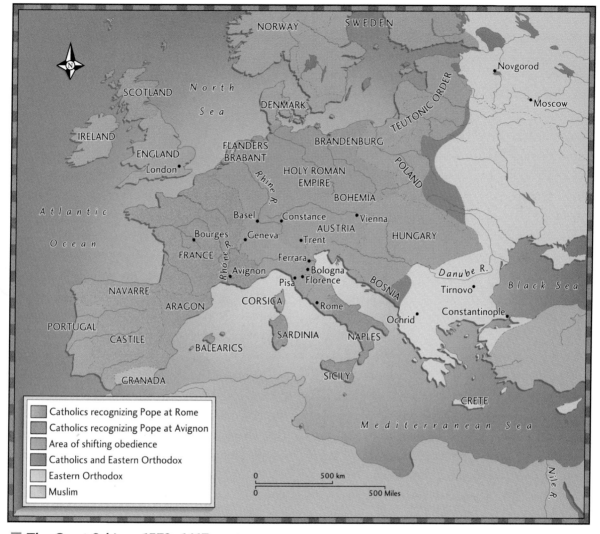

■ **The Great Schism, 1378–1417**

1. What continuing conflict ensured England's support of the pope at Rome?

2. Why might the allegiances of the Holy Roman Empire have shifted between the two sides?

one of the two popes, or both. Finally, cardinals on both sides agreed to call a general council to consider the problem. When this council met at Pisa in 1409, it isolated the two rival popes and elected its own candidate. This only made things worse. When neither of the two original rivals would agree to step down, the Church had three competing popes.

The Council of Constance

Faced with three rival popes, 400 Church leaders agreed to assemble at a council in Constance, north of the Alps, in 1414. After negotiating for three years, the delegates to the **Council of Constance** deposed all three rival popes in 1417. Then they elected a pope, Martin V, who was acceptable to everyone.

As well as restoring Church unity, the council had been charged with the task of introducing reforms. Although modifications to Church administration were approved, no substantial reforms were implemented. This failure to address problems within the Church would echo into the next century when reformers, led by Martin Luther, would break the Church apart.

The Council of Constance was also given a third task: to eliminate heresy. Though the heresy that concerned Church leaders was not as widespread as the movements that had alarmed the Church in earlier centuries, it was still linked to calls for reform that authorities would not accept. Typical of the Late Middle Ages, the movements that were of greatest concern to the Church had a distinct national or regional flavour.

A movement started by John Wycliffe was one example. Until 1378, Wycliffe was a teacher at Oxford University in England. An independent and original thinker, Wycliffe had responded to the Great Schism with a torrent of outspoken works that challenged the pope's authority and the idea of transubstantiation. Transubstantiation, a central belief of the Catholic Church, maintains that the bread and wine served at communion does not simply represent Christ's body and blood: it is Christ's body and blood. Wycliffe's teaching post placed him in a position to influence students, and he attracted fervent disciples, who later became known as Lollards, or "mumblers." Although Wycliffe and his disciples were repressed in England, they were not perceived as a problem for the Church at large.

Some of Wycliffe's students were from Prague in Bohemia. When they returned home, these students spread word of Wycliffe's ideas, fuelling longstanding criticisms of the Church hierarchy. During the early 1400s, the fervent preaching of the charismatic Jan Hus intensified the Bohemian protests. Hus managed to generate a movement that neither the Czech Church nor the monarchy could contain. As a result, Hus and the Hussites became the target of the Council of Constance. It took armed intervention and a bitter social conflict to bring the Hussites under Church control.

Indulgences

The idea of **indulgences** had originated with Pope Urban II, who had recruited volunteers for the First Crusade by promising participants that their sins would be forgiven. The Crusaders were told that when they died, they would spend less time in purgatory before proceeding to heaven.

In the early days of Christianity, people who committed grave sins were required to repent by performing public penance. A sinner might, for example, have been required to stand by the church door all through the 40-day period of Lent. By the Late Middle Ages, public penance had been largely replaced by private prayers and other good works. The value of certain good works was equated with a specific number of days of public penance. By carrying out specific good works, people could earn a partial — or even a full — indulgence. The recipient of a full indulgence would go directly to heaven.

Indulgences could also be earned by, for example, giving money to the poor or building a church. Construction of a new and grander St. Peter's Basilica in Rome was financed by indulgences. Friars, who were often monks from the begging orders, were licensed as "pardoners." After taking a commission, the pardoners passed the money to headquarters. As the Church came to rely on money raised this way, many reformers criticized what they called the sale of indulgences. When their calls for reform went unheeded, it set the stage for the permanent split in the Catholic Church that would occur in the sixteenth century.

This drawing depicts the sale of indulgences. The clergy on the right are official pardoners, a status confirmed by the cross decorated with seals and ribbons. The man at the table issues a certificate of indulgence to the faithful, who place their money in the barrel or on the table.

Inquisitions

The term "inquisition," which comes from the phrase "inquire into," was first applied by William the Conqueror to the method used by officials to record data in the *Domesday Book*. Later, the term was adopted by the Church and used to describe papal **Inquisitions** for suppressing heretics.

In 1252, Pope Innocent IV had decreed that torture and starvation could be used to extract confessions from suspected heretics. Penalties for heresy ranged from prayer and fasting to excommunication, exile, and life imprisonment. Throughout the thirteenth century, suspects who maintained their innocence or heretics who relapsed after repenting were turned over to civil authorities for execution, often by burning at the stake. This is what happened to Joan of Arc when she resumed wearing men's clothing.

One of the most notorious Inquisitors was a Dominican monk named Bernard Gui. Appointed Inquisitor of Toulouse, in France, in 1309, Gui tried more than 900 accused heretics over the next 17 years. Gui also wrote the infamous *Inquisitor's Manual*, a book that would become the guide for conduct in the Spanish Inquisition.

In 1478, Pope Sixtus IV authorized the Spanish Inquisition in Spain. The first Great Inquisitor was **Tomás de Torquemada**, whose zeal resulted in the execution of about 2000 people. Under Torquemada, the Inquisition became a law unto itself. Though they tried, neither the pope nor the Spanish monarch was able to rein in this religious zealot. Unlike earlier Inquisitions, which had been directed chiefly at Christians, the Spanish Inquisition unofficially targeted Muslims and Jews. In 1492, for example, Jews were given a choice: convert to Christianity or leave the country. If they stayed without renouncing their faith, they risked being convicted of heresy. Even Jews and Muslims who claimed to have embraced Christianity often found themselves on trial for converting falsely.

Until the time of the Inquisition, many Spanish kingdoms had enjoyed a standard of religious tolerance that was unknown in other parts of Europe. Christians, Muslims, and Jews had co-existed peacefully. Torquemada's Inquisition ended this period of tolerance.

The Spanish monarchy may have viewed the Inquisition as a means to promote Spanish nationalism with the concept of an ideal Christian state. The Inquisition was very different at different times in different countries, and even at different times in one country. It was an instrument of authority and power that could produce terrible, and perhaps unforeseeable, consequences.

WEB CONNECTION

http://www.mcgrawhill.ca/links/echoes

Go to the site above to find out more about the Inquisitions.

SOCIETY AND GOVERNMENT

Throughout Europe in the Late Middle Ages, the nobility continued to dominate political life and was, as always, preoccupied with war. Still, political change was taking place. In England, for example, institutions that would form the foundation of democratic institutions in countries such as Canada were beginning to take root.

Local Officials

In England, sheriffs provided an important link between the local and national communities. In the twelfth century, sheriffs had functioned as all-purpose county officials who collected taxes, administered justice, and supervised military resources. By the fourteenth century, many of these duties had been taken over by other officials drawn from the local landowners and supported by clerks.

Justices of the peace were typical of these officials, and the fact that this system has survived to this day is evidence of its effectiveness. The first justices of the peace were appointed in the mid-fourteenth century to relieve the central government of responsibility for bringing petty criminals to justice. Although justices of the peace often promoted the interests of their own propertied class, they nevertheless served as an influential lobby for royal interests in local communities. Sheriffs and other local officials functioned as a channel of communication between the local community and the seat of royal government at Westminster in London.

Parliament

Elected representative bodies, such as the Canadian Parliament, form the core of democratic governments

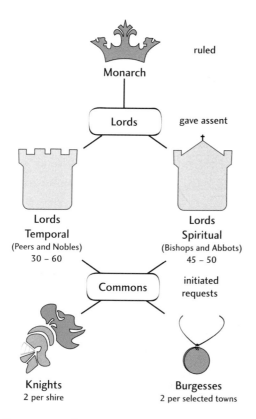

Monarch — ruled

Lords — gave assent

Lords Temporal
(Peers and Nobles)
30 – 60

Lords Spiritual
(Bishops and Abbots)
45 – 50

Commons — initiated requests

Knights
2 per shire

Burgesses
2 per selected towns

Parliamentary Government in Medieval England

1. What elements of medieval parliamentary government exist in Canada today?

2. What are the differences between medieval parliamentary government and the Canadian parliamentary system today?

in the Western world. The idea of parliamentary government, was not a bold departure from the past; rather, it was an adaptation of institutions and practices that originated in England during the Middle Ages.

Throughout his reign, Edward I routinely summoned representatives of the communities of England to **parliaments**, usually held at Westminster. Form the French word *parler,* which means to speak or talk, a parliament is an assembly that makes laws. By summoning parliaments, Edward was protecting his own interests and ensuring that dissent did not

have an opportunity to simmer. He did not wish to repeat the events of 1215 when disgruntled nobles had forced King John to sign the Magna Carta.

The English parliaments were not unique. The rulers of all countries needed popular support to balance the forces that opposed them. The états-généraux (Estates General) of France, the diets of the Holy Roman Empire, and the cortes (courts) held in various parts of Spain met less frequently, but all began to be called in the same general period. All these assemblies depended on basic practicalities to operate. There had to be a way of summoning members, and members had to have a way of travelling to the assembly, as well as assurances that they would be safe. To serve a useful purpose, members had to be confident that they would be heard and given some responsibility in making the decisions that they would report to their communities.

Still, certain distinctive features contributed to the endurance of the English parliament. It met in two unequal groups: the Lords, who were less numerous but had great power; and the Commons, who had less power though their number was greater. Although the two bodies met at the same time and often exchanged views, Lords and Commons held separate meetings. The Lords themselves comprised two groups who met together: the lords temporal and lords spiritual. The first group was composed of leading nobles of the land, while the second was made up of bishops and important abbots.

At the time, Lords and Commons were not known as "Houses." Lords were distinguished from Commons by the fact that each lord received an individual summons to a parliament. The summons reflected the Lords' regular association with the king, and this, in turn, reflected their wealth and power. Before 1500, between 30 and 60 temporal lords — and between 45 and 50 spiritual lords — attended parliaments.

The Commons, on the other hand, were summoned to a parliament by an order issued to each sheriff to elect two knights from his shire, as well as two representatives from each city and borough. Though the Commons included twice as many urban representatives as knights, the urban representatives were subordinate to the 74 elected knights.

This arrangement meant that the landholding aristocracy was represented in both the Lords and the Commons. The greatest landholders, the nobles or barons, sat in the Lords. The lesser landholders were elected to the Commons as knights of the shire, where they mingled with the non-aristocratic burgesses, who represented the cities and boroughs. In the Late Middle Ages, the Lords were an exclusive group, but they mingled, socially and at parliaments, with the lesser aristocracy and the middle class. This helped England avoid the isolation of the classes that was common in the rest of Europe.

Writing and passing laws was one of the jobs of parliaments. At first, most of the laws originated with the king or the Lords, but a growing proportion of English legislation arose from petitions initiated in the Commons. Commons petitions required the assent of the Lords, who then advised the monarch of the parliament's decision. The monarch could accept or reject the Lords' advice.

The Commons helped keep monarchs somewhat informed about the concerns of their subjects, even if it was only politically influential subjects. In exchange, the Commons representatives communicated the monarch's needs to their constituents.

Although the English parliaments met more often than other European assemblies, they were far from democratic in the contemporary sense of the word. They met only when summoned by the king to deal with business that he or his ministers brought up. Still, the English parliaments did meet for several weeks a year, especially in times of trouble, and played a larger role in government than the assemblies of most other countries. During the Hundred Years' War, for example, the king needed money to pay soldiers and buy arms and ships. As a result, a parliament agreed to authorize a tax on wealth.

In France, a much larger country than England, it was harder to summon the états-généraux, and meetings were infrequent. Though meetings of provincial états-généraux were more effective, these bodies were summoned only when the king needed a broader basis of support. Meetings of the Spanish cortes were also few and far between. In the Holy Roman Empire, which was wracked by civil war throughout the Late Middle Ages, the diet was an assembly of princes and nobles rather than a representative body. It was called only when the emperor wanted to use it to promote national unity, which had proved to be an elusive goal.

The New Monarchy

Although representative assemblies had begun to play a role in government, the Late Middle Ages remained an era of monarchs. Some historians use the term "new monarchy" to convey the late medieval idea that the interests of the people and the interests of the monarchs were closely linked — and were different from the interests of the nobles, who often disrupted royal rule and created civil conflict as they jockeyed for power. The civil conflicts initiated by the aristocrats benefited neither monarchs nor the common people, who were often the victims when nobles took up arms against one another.

During the fifteenth century, England, France, and Germany were plagued by periods of civil strife as power struggles played out among the nobility. In England, for example, a bitter dispute over the succession to the throne plunged the country into an on-again, off-again civil war. Starting in 1455, this 30-year conflict pitted the House of Lancaster, a branch of the Plantagenet line of kings, against the House of York, which also claimed descent from the Plantagenets. Called the Wars of the Roses because of the badges — a white rose for York and a red rose for Lancaster — worn by supporters of the two sides, the conflict was not settled until the Lancastrian Henry Tudor, who later became Henry VII, defeated Richard III and the Yorkists at Bosworth Field in 1485.

As the fifteenth century drew to a close, Henry VII strengthened the English throne by employing the best fiscal and administrative measures of his predecessors. He ensured that the nobles did not become strong enough to challenge his rule by setting up the king's council, a powerful group of advisers drawn from the nobility, the lesser nobility, and the professional class. Because the aristocrats on the council shared power with members of the lesser nobility and the professional class, it became harder for the lords to challenge the will of the monarch — and brought much-needed peace to the kingdom. The French also benefited from the absence of war. In Spain, the kingdoms of Castile and Aragon were united in 1474 when Isabella of Castile married Ferdinand of Aragon. The riches that poured into Spain from its overseas empire strengthened this political unity. The unity and wealth of the late fifteenth-century Spanish monarchy helped consolidate its power.

Review...Recall...Reflect

1. How did the production and subject matter of books change during the fourteenth century?

2. Describe the effects of the Avignonese papacy, the Great Schism, and the sale of indulgences on the Roman Catholic Church.

3. What aspects of contemporary Canadian government originated in the Late Middle Ages?

History Continues to Unfold

Despite the ravages of plague, famine, and war, European society emerged from the Late Middle Ages with renewed vitality and energy. Although the Church continued to dominate society, aristocrats continued to dominate the social system, and monarchies became even stronger in the hands of a few competing families — the winds of change were beginning to stir. The political, religious, social, and cultural institutions that characterized the Middle Ages as a whole were beginning to respond to new demands, including a new spirit of nationalism that was starting to be reflected in the vernacular languages that were helping to create new identities and loyalties. These new identities and loyalties would become the foundation for the emergence of present-day European nations.

Current Research and Interpretations

Historians and epidemiologists (people who study epidemics) continue to puzzle over the Black Death. Was it really a bubonic plague? In recent years, some researchers have argued that this pandemic — a world- or country-wide outbreak of disease — could, in fact, have been caused by anthrax, a deadly disease that infects both animals and humans with symptoms similar to the Black Death. Other researchers have suggested that the Black Death may have been caused by forms of the plague bacillus that do not depend on rats or fleas for transmission to humans.

Chapter Review

Chapter Summary

In this chapter, we have seen:

- how innovations such as the development of banking affected Europe's economic structure
- that checks on the power of medieval monarchs contributed to the development of contemporary Western ideas of citizenship and the rights of individuals
- how the Black Death, the introduction of gunpowder, and the invention of the printing press sparked change in medieval Europe
- how changes in the papacy contributed to changes in medieval society
- that the groundwork was being laid for the important political, social, and economic changes that were to occur in subsequent centuries

Reviewing the Significance of Key People, Concepts, and Events (Knowledge/Understanding)

1. Understanding the history of the Late Middle Ages requires an understanding of the following people, concepts, and events and their significance in the development of both medieval society and modern Western concepts of citizenship. In your notes, identify and explain the historical significance of three items from each column.

   People
   Roger Bacon
   Joan of Arc
   Johannes Gutenberg
   Christine de Pisan

   Concepts
   indulgences
   parliament

   Events
   Black Death
   peasants' revolts
   Hundred Years' War
   Avignonese papacy
   Great Schism
   Inquisition

2. The Late Middle Ages was a period of change brought about by the efforts of various people and the introduction of important technological innovations. In your notes, create a three-column chart. Title the first column "Person or Innovation," the second "Description," and the third "Lasting Effect." Enter "Joan of Arc," "Gunpowder," "Johannes Gutenberg," and "Banking" in the first column. Then fill in the rest of the chart to create a summary of some of the significant agents of change.

3. Some changes came about because of scandal, plague, and war. In your notes, create a three-column chart. Title the first column "Calamity," the second "Description," and the third "Change That Resulted." In the first column, enter "Black Death," "Great Schism," "Hundred Years' War," and "Inquisitions." Then fill in the rest of the chart to create a summary of the ways calamities acted as agents of change.

Doing History: Thinking About the Past (Thinking/Inquiry)

1. In Canadian society today, there is a clear separation between Church and state. In the Late Middle Ages, however, the Church and secular governments were closely linked. In a clearly argued, well-supported paragraph, explain whether the close ties between the Catholic Church and European governments was a positive or negative factor in medieval Europe.

2. Historian Barbara Tuchman has described the 1300s as the "calamitous fourteenth century." Despite plague, famine, and war — and the changes in society brought about by these disasters — many aspects of life in Europe remained unchanged. Identify and describe the three most important factors that contributed to continuity in this century of crisis.

Applying Your Learning (Application)

1. Imagine that an English or European monarch agreed to meet with a peasant and a merchant to discuss their concerns. What would they have talked about? Write and record on video- or audio tape a five- to seven-minute discussion reflecting the concerns of the peasantry and the middle class and the power and attitude of the monarch. The monarch selected must be a historical character, but the peasant and merchants can be fictional.

2. Imagine that the Church has asked you to sell indulgences to help raise money to build a cathedral in your community. Design an official certificate of indulgence and write the 400- to 500-word sales pitch that you would use to sell indulgences to the faithful.

Communicating Your Learning (Communication)

1. Create a poster that highlights the life and works of a person who you believe made a significant contribution to the development of religion, politics, military events, or the arts in the Late Middle Ages. Display your poster on the classroom's "Wall of Fame."

2. In pictures, poetry, or a short story, convey three ways in which society changed between 1340 and 1440. You may wish to create a challenge asking viewers or readers to identify the changes you chose to highlight.

Unit Review

Grading the Civilizations

1. Chapter One outlined the essential elements of a civilization and asked you to rank the elements in order of importance. Now that you have studied a civilization in depth, apply your ranking and see how this civilization measures up. Below are three broad categories under which the elements could be clustered. For each of the categories, provide a letter grade (from A+ to F) and a comment of three to five sentences to support the grade. You can complete a fuller assessment of the civilization using your *World History Handbook*.

	Letter Grade	Comments
The Place of People • level of equality • just laws • distribution of wealth • overall quality of life		
Organization of Society • democratic • effective government • meets needs of society • provides security and stability for society		
Lasting Legacy • ideas • works of art • architecture • innovations/inventions • literature		

The Role of Individuals in History

1. Historians often grapple with whether history is shaped by individuals, or if individuals are products of their age and thus shaped by history. Would the history of medieval Europe have been different if Joan of Arc or Charlemagne had not lived? The following is a list of people mentioned in this unit. Select any two. For each, identify his or her role in society, major accomplishments, sphere of greatest impact (e.g., art, ideas, religion, politics), and why you believe the person shaped or was shaped by history. You may want to do additional research on the two individuals you select.

Justinian the Great

King Arthur

Clovis

Charlemagne

William the Conqueror

Joan of Arc

Johannes Gutenberg

Understanding Chronology

1. The study of history, whether the recent or distant past, relies on a sound understanding of the order in which events occurred. Without a clear understanding of how history unfolded, it is difficult to see the relationship between earlier events and later developments. The following questions help to illustrate the importance of chronology:

a) How did the earlier Viking invasions affect the success of William the Conqueror's invasion of Britain?

b) What is the relationship between the Crusades and the rise of a middle class in Europe?

c) Why do all revolutions after 1453 owe a debt of gratitude to Johannes Gutenberg?

d) Could the Black Death have occurred before the Crusades? Why?

Cause and Effect in History

1. History often involves the study of cause and effect. We often find that one cause has several effects, or that several causes lead to one effect. Complete the Cause-and-Effect diagram provided by your teacher. Once you have completed the diagram, use it as a guide in writing a paragraph on the issue addressed.

UNIT SEVEN

Toward the Modern Age

chapter 18
The Renaissance

chapter 19
**Epilogue: Seeds
of the Global Village**

Portrait painting became popular during the Renaissance. This portrait, by Jan van Eyck, shows the wedding of Giovanni Arnolfini, a rich Italian merchant, and Giovanna Cenami.

The fourteenth and fifteenth centuries brought calamities and dramatic changes to Europe — and the world. Plague, famine, wars, and religious persecution led to the death of millions of Europeans. Although the fourteenth century was often marked by despair, the fifteenth century saw Europe move toward the modern age. A rebirth of classicism, the development of the printing press, advances in maritime technology, and the desire to expand trade with Asia contributed to a new world view and the development of a capitalist economy.

The first chapter of this unit explores the emergence of humanist thought and the Renaissance that began in Italy. The final chapter of the unit — and of the book — broadens this examination of the birth of the modern age by considering the effects of the European voyages of exploration on many regions of the world.

UNIT EXPECTATIONS

In this unit, you will:

O analyze the interactions between Europe and other world societies during the fourteenth and fifteenth centuries

O analyze the factors that contributed to change in Europe and the world in the fifteenth and sixteenth centuries

O evaluate the contribution of individuals and groups to the political, cultural, and intellectual traditions of Europe

O analyze diverse economic stuctures and the factors that affected their development

O compare key interpretations of world history

0   3000km

Europe

The Renaissance

CHAPTER EXPECTATIONS

By the end of this chapter, you will be able to:

- explain how European contact with other cultures in the Late Middle Ages contributed to the new ideas of the Renaissance

- identify how technological innovations such as the invention of the printing press contributed to change

- analyze the effects of various new ideas on the development of a capitalist economy

- evaluate the contribution of selected individuals to the development of political, social, artistic, and intellectual traditions in Europe during the Renaissance

Domenico Ghirlandaio painted this picture, titled *An Old Man and His Grandson*, in the realistic style that was typical of Renaissance portraits. The painting captures the old man's warts, wrinkles, and his diseased nose — as well as the affection the child clearly feels for his grandfather.

Europe was radically transformed in the 200 years between 1350 and 1550. During this time, three important movements combined to pull the continent away from its medieval past toward an exciting future. The Renaissance redefined learning and the way Europeans viewed themselves and the world. The Reformation divided Western European Christians, called into question the authority of Church leaders, and led to the development of new ideas about the relationship between Church and state. The emergence of a capitalist economy provided the impetus for adventuresome Europeans to explore and colonize other parts of the world.

By 1600, Europeans were exporting their manufactured goods, their religion, and their culture to all corners of the world. In return, they were receiving an array of raw materials and new foods and had found sources of cheap labour.

Defining the Renaissance in terms of specific years is difficult, as it overlaps both the Late Middle Ages and the Reformation, the period that followed. Still, the Renaissance is usually regarded as the time from about 1350 to 1550. Many historians find it more useful, however, to define the Renaissance by the attitudes and ideas that sparked new intellectual and artistic achievements, as well as social and economic changes.

The word "renaissance" means "rebirth" or "revival," and is most often used in relation to culture and learning. During the Early and High Middle Ages, classical ideas and art forms had been rejected as pagan, while the authority of the Church was emphasized. By the end of the 1300s, however, a renewed interest in classical art, ideas, and the works of ancient writers was setting the stage for a revival of classical culture in Italy. When fused with Christian beliefs, this rebirth of classical ideals triggered a renewed focus on the study of humans and human achievements and produced new and exciting ideas and works of art. The changes that occurred during the Renaissance would ultimately transform not only Europe, but also the entire world.

KEY WORDS

Renaissance

modern age

Peace of Lodi

Sistine Chapel

Revolt of the Ciompi

humanism

The Book of the Courtier

David

popolo minuto

Malleus Maleficarum

KEY PEOPLE

Jacob Burckhardt

Lorenzo de Medici

Francesco Petrarch

Niccolò Machiavelli

Leonardo da Vinci

Michelangelo

Henry VIII

Desiderius Erasmus

VOICES FROM THE PAST

There are three classes of intellects: one which comprehends by itself; another which appreciates what others comprehend; and a third which neither comprehends by itself nor by the showing of others; the first is the most excellent, the second is good, the third is useless.
**Niccolò Machiavelli,
The Prince,
1532**

TIME LINE: THE RENAISSANCE

	1378	Revolt of the Ciompi fails to win concessions for the poor of Florence
Cosimo de Medici becomes head of the Florentine government, starting a family dynasty	1434	
	1453	Invention of the printing press ushers in a communication revolution
Peace of Lodi leads to 40 years of stability in Italy	1454	
	1485	King Henry VII establishes the Tudor dynasty in England
Malleus Maleficarum, a witch-finding guide, is published	1486	
	1504	Michelangelo's *David* is unveiled
King Henry VIII ascends the English throne, bringing Renaissance ideals to his court	1509	
	1512	Michelangelo finishes painting the ceiling of the Sistine Chapel
Spain controls much of Italy, and the Italian Renaissance draws to a close	1525	

FROM MIDDLE AGES TO THE RENAISSANCE

Jacob Burckhardt, a nineteenth-century Swiss historian, was the first to apply the label "**Renaissance**" to fifteenth-century Italy. His work, *The Civilization of the Renaissance in Italy,* "created" the Renaissance as it is often viewed today.

Burckhardt's work had a profound impact on the study of history. Burckhardt began his study of the Renaissance to escape the nineteenth century, which he hated. He believed that liberal ideas were dangerous and that democracy would lead to chaos. As he studied the Renaissance, Burckhardt came to believe that the individualism of this period had laid the foundation for the development of the atheism, democracy, and scientific ideas that he despised in his own society. In addition, he believed that the intellectual and artistic vitality of the Renaissance had arisen at the expense of the Church, leading to what he perceived as the decline of Christian morality.

Burckhardt defined how the Renaissance would be studied, and contemporary historians still respond to his ideas. Historians may challenge Burckhardt's statements, but they seldom study the Renaissance free of the enormous shadow cast by *The Civilization of the Renaissance in Italy.*

Throughout much of the twentieth century, the place of the Renaissance in European history went unchallenged. By the 1970s, however, three developments converged to place the significance — and even the existence — of the Renaissance in doubt.

First, the rise of social history as an area of study revealed that the Renaissance occurred only among the intellectual, artistic, social, and economic elite of Europe. Few of the changes cited as hallmarks of the period affected the lives of ordinary people.

The second development was the emergence of women's history. In an essay titled "Did Women Have a Renaissance?" for example, historian Joan Kelly argued that the Renaissance was a time of declining freedom for women. If this period brought mostly negative effects for half the population of Europe, Kelly said, it was not an era to be celebrated.

The final development challenged the idea of the Renaissance as a period of radical change in the intellectual and artistic life of Europe. Some historians argue that the era represented nothing more than a culmination of trends that had been unfolding throughout the medieval period. They say that the so-called rediscovery of the works of ancients, such as Aristotle and Plato, was exaggerated, pointing out that these works were already well known to many medieval writers and thinkers.

Still, the idea of the Renaissance as a transitional period between the medieval and modern worlds has persisted. Whether this view of history remains relevant continues to spark lively debate today.

TIME FRAMES
RENAISSANCE ca. 1350–1550

People who lived in Northern Italy in this period did not call their time the Renaissance. Though many were aware that radical changes were occurring in intellectual and artistic circles, as well as in society at large, they did not realize that they were living through a period that would later be regarded as the waning of the Middle Ages and the beginning of early modern Europe.

From Medieval to Modern Times

The fourteenth to sixteenth centuries are often seen as an era when Europe began changing from the medieval to the **modern age**. But what is the modern age? Previous chapters have shown that medieval Europe was a very conservative, largely rural society. Medieval Europeans were highly religious and superstitious, and had little contact with other parts of the world. To a great extent, the social hierarchy was determined by birth, and the economy was based on arrangements between peasants or serfs and the lords of large estates.

Early signs that Europe was moving into the modern age included the rise of trade, the development of cities and towns, and the impulse to explore other parts of the world. The power of the nobility was giving way to a growing and increasingly influential middle class. And, perhaps most important, individualism — the belief that people should be able to act freely — had begun to transform European societies.

These changes were evident in nearly all aspects of life, from government and religion to art and education. Although Christianity remained central in the lives of many, it fused with classical ideas, leading to an explosion of artistic and intellectual achievement. Advances in science and technology promoted the spread of knowledge and ideas. At the same time, important changes in economic systems redefined social distinctions, led to a rise in towns, and stimulated the building of global empires.

THE EMERGENCE OF THE RENAISSANCE

Historian Barbara Tuchman has described the 1300s as "the calamitous fourteenth century." Already weakened by recurring crop failures, the people of Europe were devastated by the onslaught of the Black Death in 1347. Further heightening people's misery was the Hundred Years' War, which lasted from 1337 to 1453. It is no wonder that people began to lose faith in established institutions. It was from this age of pessimism and misery, however, that the Renaissance emerged.

There is no doubt that the Renaissance originated in Italy — and in Northern Italy in particular. Why was Italy home to this great cultural revival? Other areas of Europe, such as France and the Holy Roman Empire, had certainly outstripped Italy's wealth and power during the Middle Ages. To fully understand why Italy emerged as the cultural and intellectual heart of Europe, it is necessary to understand the society from which the Renaissance sprang.

During the Middle Ages, the kingdoms of Northern Europe — and their Gothic cultural traditions — had dominated the continent. Italy's culture was not rooted in Gothic traditions; rather, it was closely linked to the achievements of ancient Rome. It is not surprising, then, that Italy would lead a classical revival.

Another factor that contributed to the success of the Renaissance was the peace and stability enjoyed in Italy during the second half of the fifteenth century. At the time, Italy was not a unified country. It was a combination of city-states, which dominated in the north, papal states, which occupied central and northeastern areas, and the Kingdom of Naples, which controlled the southern half of the peninsula.

The stability of the late fourteenth century was a result of the **Peace of Lodi**, signed in 1454. In conjunction with this treaty, which ended a war between Milan and Venice, nearly all the states of the Italian Peninsula joined the Italian League. The terms of the pact that created the league called on the Italian states to maintain existing borders and defend one another in the event of attack. The subsequent peace, which lasted until 1494, enabled Italian culture to flourish. Resources were poured into the arts and civic projects rather than into costly wars.

Changing Economic Structures

Central to the intellectual, artistic, and social changes that characterized the Renaissance was the development of a new economic foundation. The revival of trade and commerce that had taken place in the Late Middle Ages had given people new ways of earning wealth — and the members of the newly wealthy merchant or middle class did not fit into the feudal society that was rooted in land-based wealth. Similarly, the growth of towns and the expansion of markets, as well as the organization of capital, or money, radically altered the economy and society as it had been known. By the early 1500s, the feudal economy of the Middle Ages had been largely replaced by a capitalist economy that had redefined wealth.

The features of the economy that developed at this time remain the pillars of today's capitalist economic system. Of primary importance was using money to make money. In the pre-capitalist era, usury — profiting from lending money to earn interest — was not only frowned upon in society, but also violated Church law. Land was considered the only form of secure wealth, while capital was seen as liquid and volatile.

The emergence of powerful banking families, such as the Medicis of Florence and the Fuggers of Augsburg, changed this view of wealth. Capitalism, which relies on the organization of capital, labour, and raw materials to produce surplus wealth, provided the impetus for powerful merchants to sponsor voyages of exploration and colonization. This brought about a radical change in the nature of long-distance trade. Rather than trading for luxury goods,

merchants began to look for raw, unprocessed materials that could be refined by European manufacturers.

The developing capitalist economy greatly affected the structure of European society. As economic power became increasingly concentrated in the hands of wealthy urban merchants, the importance of cities grew. Some, such as Venice, were important ports through which goods flowed to and from Europe; others, such as Milan, became important manufacturing centres.

The newly rich middle class looked for ways to display their wealth. No longer was conquering land the chief measure of success; rather, the ruling elite

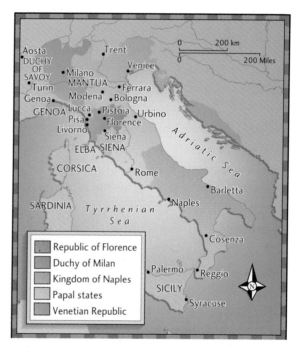

■ Italy, 1454

1. Which Italian states do you think were controlled by hereditary rulers? Is it possible to tell for certain by looking at this map? Why?

2. Why would the Kingdom of Naples have been somewhat isolated from the new ideas that were taking root in the northern states?

of the flourishing cities sought to establish their city as the greatest in Europe. Wealthy merchants became patrons of the arts, commissioning paintings, sculptures, and new buildings to adorn their city. They no longer built palatial homes on sprawling country manors; instead, their homes became an integral part of the cityscape. Merchants tried to entice great artists, scholars, and artisans to work in their city to help boost its claim to artistic and cultural leadership. The vitality of the cities of Northern Italy contributed to their leading role in promoting cultural change.

Urbanization and the Renaissance

By the late 1300s, a significant percentage of the population of Northern Italy lived in urban centres. In England, by contrast, only a small number of people lived in cities. Furthermore, the cities of northern Italy were relatively large, many of them exceeding 100 000 inhabitants.

This is the Palazzo Ducale, the official residence of the doge — or duke — of Venice. Although the doge was appointed for life, the title was not hereditary. The palace was built between 1309 and 1424. What features show the influence of Northern European Gothic architecture?

This urban concentration affected Italian culture in many ways. Unlike the agricultural economies of Northern Europe, the Italian economy was built on urban industries and commercial trade. The secularization of education that occurred during the Renaissance stemmed from the needs of an urban society, because people engaged in urban occupations required more training than farm labourers. To meet this need, many Italian cities established publicly supported schools. Finally, the political organization of the city-states, many of which were an outgrowth of medieval communes, allowed citizens to participate in government.

The Middle Class

The traditional European nobility comprised landowners whose income came from renting out their land. After the Black Death, however, a new nobility began to emerge in Italian cities. These people, called the patriciate, made the middle class way of life — engaging in trade and commerce — the ideal.

Wealth, carefully arranged marriages, and active participation in civic affairs were the keys to power and prestige for members of this new Italian aristocracy. These wealthy merchants and tradespeople became not only the rulers of the Italian cities, with the exception of Rome, but also patrons of the arts and learning. Free from the traditions of the so-called old nobility, the patriciate encouraged new trends in art, literature, and philosophy.

The Italian City-States

Venice: Situated at the north end of the Adriatic Sea, Venice was an important port. Goods arrived there from the Middle East and Asia, and the markets of fourteenth-century Venice were filled with exotic foods, spices, and goods from as far away as China. In addition to its reputation as a trading centre, Venice and its suburb of San Murano also became world famous for producing high-quality glass.

Milan: Unlike Venice, Milan was landlocked. Nevertheless, its aggressive military strength made it a leading city of the Italian Renaissance. Early in the thirteenth century, rival political factions had plunged the city into turmoil. Stability was restored when the Visconti family seized power and replaced the republican government with a hereditary dynasty that ruled from 1278 to 1447.

When the last of the Viscontis died without an heir, a new power struggle erupted. The Sforza family emerged triumphant from this conflict, and the Peace of Lodi recognized Francesco Sforza as ruler of Milan.

While maintaining the city's strong military tradition, the Sforzas also became important patrons of the arts, establishing Milan as one of the leading centres of Renaissance culture. Trade also played an important role in the city's economy. It became the leading producer of high-quality suits of armour, an interesting precursor to its twentieth-century reputation as one of the fashion capitals of the world.

Rome: Though geographically separated from the northern city-states that dominated Italy during the Renaissance, Rome was, nevertheless, one of the leading cities of the era. Just as the ruling families of the northern cities embraced the arts to enhance their prestige, the Renaissance popes, too, became important patrons of the arts. By inviting great artists and thinkers to Rome and freely spending large sums of the money that flowed to the papacy from across Europe, the popes were able to commission some of the most beautiful works of art of the Renaissance.

As members of the leading families of Venice, Florence, and Milan, several popes helped transfer Renaissance influences to Rome. Pope Julius II, for example, was the son of Lorenzo de Medici of Florence. After hearing about the great Renaissance artist Michelangelo Buonarroti, Julius summoned him to Rome to paint the **Sistine Chapel**, the pope's personal place of worship in the Vatican Palace.

Although there is no question that these Renaissance popes helped establish Rome's reputation as a leading arts centre, the price was high. By spending enormous amounts of money on beautifying Rome, the popes angered many Northern Europeans, who began to grumble about sending money to Rome. To some degree, the lavish spending of the popes contributed to the split in the Church that would occur in the sixteenth century.

This photograph shows the Ponte Vecchio, or "Old Bridge," as it looks today. Built in 1345, just before the Black Death ravaged the city, this venerable bridge over the Arno River was the only one spared by the retreating German army during World War II.

Florence: In many ways, Florence is synonymous with the Renaissance. Its stature as the leading cultural and intellectual centre of the late fifteenth century is reflected in the names of the people who called this city home. Francesco Petrarch, Filippo Brunelleschi, Lorenzo de Medici, Sandro Botticelli, Michelangelo Buonarroti, and Niccolò Machiavelli were but a few of the Florentines whose genius contributed to the city's reputation as the heart of the Renaissance.

Politics in Renaissance Florence

During the Renaissance, Florence was the fourth largest city of Italy. Its economy was firmly rooted in trade and banking. By placing a tax on income, the city's government was able to build impressive structures such as the Palazzo Vecchio, which housed the government, and the Ponte Vecchio, a bridge that still spans the Arno River. Most impressive of all was the duomo, or cathedral, with its soaring dome and stunning marble exterior.

When the Black Death struck Florence, the city lost up to two thirds of its 90 000 inhabitants. Compounding the city's woes were famines that struck in 1352–1353, 1369–1370, and 1373–1375. These recurring disasters culminated in a rebellion started by the *ciompi* in 1378. The ciompi were workers who were named for the wooden clogs they wore as shoes.

The **Revolt of the Ciompi** was an uprising against the established guilds, which controlled the

The Creation of Adam was just one of the Biblical stories Michelangelo depicted on the ceiling of the Sistine Chapel. Nearly 500 years later, a painstaking ten-year restoration was undertaken to remove the centuries of dirt, smoke, and varnish that had dulled the famous frescoes, which are considered one of the greatest achievements of Western art.

city's government. The ciompi wanted to establish guilds for themselves and other workers who were not already organized. They also called for reforms to the justice system and tax laws. In July 1378, the ciompi captured the Palazzo Vecchio. A month later, members of the established guilds successfully stormed the building — and hanged the ciompi from its windows. In the end, this revolt failed to win lasting reform; in fact, the major guilds later tightened their control of the city, which fell under the dominance of a few ruling families.

The most powerful of these families was the Medicis. In 1434, Cosimo de Medici was appointed to lead the Florentine government. This event marked the beginning of a dynasty that would dominate Florentine politics for the next three centuries. Although the Medicis were members of the Florentine commercial aristocracy, they were also supported by the commoners because Salvestro de Medici had sided with the ciompi during the 1378 revolt.

The incredible wealth of the Medicis, gained through banking and trade, also contributed to their power and influence. In addition to his dominant role in city politics, Cosimo was a patron of the arts. The stability he brought to Florentine government, coupled with the financial support he provided to artists and writers, was critical in establishing the city as the centre of the Renaissance.

Florence reached its high point under the guidance of Cosimo's grandson, **Lorenzo de Medici**. Called Lorenzo the Magnificent, this Medici expanded the influence and control of Florence through much of Tuscany. Like his grandfather, Lorenzo was a great patron of the arts and sponsored artists such as Ghirlandaio, Botticelli, and the young Michelangelo. In addition to writing vernacular poetry himself, Lorenzo also sponsored poets such as

Pulci and Politian, as well as the philosopher Marsilio Ficino. When he died in 1492, however, the family fortunes had begun to decline as a result of his preoccupation with politics. Even more damaging, he left Florence in the hands of his incompetent son, Piero.

WEB CONNECTION

http://www.mcgrawhill.ca/links/echoes

Go to the site above to find out more about the Medici family.

Shortly after Piero came to power, a dispute arose over the throne of Naples. King Charles VIII of France sided with one of the contenders, and Piero, ignoring the traditional friendship between France and Florence, sided with the other. To offer military support to his candidate, Charles began marching an army south through the Italian Peninsula to Naples. When Charles arrived at Florence, Piero gave up immediately. He begged the French king's forgiveness and gave him Florentine territories, including Pisa. These actions earned Piero the hatred of all Florentines, and he was driven from office by an angry crowd. This incident temporarily ended Medici rule of Florence and marked the beginning of a period of foreign domination in Italy.

The period of peace and stability that had been initiated by the Peace of Lodi and the Italian League was drawing to a close. Though Florence went on to form an alliance with Spain, drive out the French, and restore the republic, these actions simply replaced one dominant power with another. By 1525, Spain was in control of much of Italy, and the Italian Renaissance was nearly over.

HUMANISM

Underlying everything that defined the Renaissance was **humanism**. Humanists were chiefly concerned with the *humaniora,* a Latin term that means "human studies" or "the humanities." As a result, humanists embraced the liberal arts, which included grammar, rhetoric (persuasive speaking or writing), poetry, history, and moral philosophy.

In many ways, the early humanists simply carried on a tradition begun by the teachers of the Middle Ages. Humanists differed from their medieval predecessors, however, in their close adherence to classical models and their focus on earthly actions and the concerns of humans.

Humanist Education

Seldom in history have educational theories and methods faced the kind of scrutiny they did during the Renaissance. Ideas that had been introduced by early humanists were spread by a new breed of humanist teachers. The static medieval curriculum, with its focus on a dialectic approach (logic), was replaced with a liberal-arts curriculum designed to produce well-rounded individuals.

Two of the greatest humanist educators of the late fourteenth and early fifteenth centuries were Vittorino da Feltre and Guarino da Verona. Vittorino opened a school called La Giocosa — "the House of Joy" — in Mantua, where he welcomed sons of the nobility as well as poor boys chosen for their ability. Vittorino believed that studying the works of classical writers built character, and that students must develop both a sound mind and a sound body. As a result, games, swimming, riding, and fencing were included in his school's curriculum.

Guarino da Verona believed that students should enjoy learning, and that mastering Greek and Latin would enable them to read the classics in their original form. His goal was to produce scholars who would continue learning throughout their lives, thereby preparing themselves to play an active role in society and help to further knowledge.

The work of Vittorino, Guarino, and other Renaissance teachers did much to emphasize the importance of the individual, revive interest in classical writers, and focus people's energies on earthly pursuits.

Scripts & Symbols λ μ ν ο π θ υ ρ σ τ υ ϖ ω ξ ψ ζ α β χ ε δ φ γ

Both the sloped cursive handwriting taught in today's schools and the italics often used in printed materials developed from the minuscule (a small cursive script) created by Niccolò Niccoli, one of the accomplished scholars who gathered at the court of Cosimo de Medici. Niccoli, who copied out and organized many ancient manuscripts, also introduced some of the features taken for granted in the books of today. He was the first to include a table of contents and to divide chapters into sections.

Niccoli's italic script

RENAISSANCE IDEAS

The Renaissance was a period dominated by towering geniuses who, through the force of their ideas, brought about significant change in European society. The works of several of these people continue to be studied today and, in some cases, gained wider recognition in the centuries after the Renaissance than when they were first penned.

Francesco Petrarch

Francesco Petrarch, who lived from 1304 to 1374, is often called the first humanist. A man of both medieval Europe and the Renaissance, he is an important figure in this transitional period of European history. Both Petrarch's education and his relationship with the Church reflect his dual nature. As a young man, he spent seven years preparing for a career in law before his interest shifted toward studying classical literature.

In 1326, Petrarch moved to Avignon, where he benefited from the patronage of several high-ranking Church officials. On 26 April 1327, Petrarch first saw the woman who, to this day, is known only as Laura. Struck by Laura's beauty and grace, he fell deeply in love with her and made her the focus of his poetry.

Because Laura was married, Petrarch was able to adore her only from afar. Still, he immortalized her in the 400 sonnets he wrote in her honour. Alas, Laura fell victim to the Black Death in 1348, and Petrarch was left with only the hope of a heavenly reunion.

Petrarch's emphasis on earthly physical love and living an active life represented a significant break with medieval ideas. He believed that the earthly love of women should be encouraged because it would lead to a love of God as the creator of women. He also questioned the value of the contemplative, monastic life, suggesting that members of the clergy would be more useful working in society to save souls.

As the first writer to reject some of the ideas at the heart of medieval philosophy, Petrarch led the way for later Renaissance writers and provided an important link between medieval and Renaissance attitudes.

Niccolò Machiavelli

The most controversial literary work of the Renaissance was **Niccolò Machiavelli**'s *The Prince*. Many people were shocked by the approach of this short work, a guide for governing that emphasized that the end justifies the means. Although *The Prince*, which Machiavelli wrote in 1513, had little in common with the literature of the Middle Ages, it also represented a departure from the works of the Florentine writer's contemporaries. Rather than focusing on the essential goodness of humanity, Machiavelli stressed the need for a successful ruler to act practically. *The Prince* states, for example, that it is better for governments to be miserly than to amass large debts.

Although Machiavelli's views often contrasted sharply with the idealistic views of earlier humanists, there is no doubt that he was a product of the Renaissance. In presenting his ideas, Machiavelli drew heavily on the works of ancient writers, and

Niccolò Machiavelli wrote *The Prince* in response to the political turmoil that gripped Florence after Piero de Medici handed the city over to the French.

power must learn how not to be good and must also learn to use this knowledge, or not use it depending upon the circumstances.

- It is much safer to be feared than loved. In general, men are ungrateful, dishonest, cowardly, and covetous. As long as you help them, they will do your bidding. They will offer you their blood, their goods, their lives, and their children when it appears that you will not need to take them up on the offer. But when you try to collect, they often go back on their word. If a prince has relied solely on the good faith of others, he will be ruined.

- It is not at all necessary for a prince to have all the good qualities which I have named, but it is necessary to seem to have them... Thus it is well to seem merciful, faithful, sincere, religious, and also to be so. But a prince must always be ready to embrace the opposite qualities if the occasion demands it.

worked throughout his life for the good of the city where he was born. He was greatly troubled by the turmoil that resulted from Piero de Medici's actions in the late fifteenth century, and firmly believed that a strong ruler was necessary if Florence was to overcome its problems.

In *The Prince*, Machiavelli wrote that an ideal ruler must unite the people under a single, strong head of state. Neither an aloof idealist nor a power-hungry autocrat, a ruler should be prepared to resort to ruthlessness and deception when it was necessary to preserve the state. Here are some of the ideas set out in *The Prince*:

- In politics, a man should be guided by what is, rather than what it ought to be... Therefore, a prince who wishes to remain in

Despite the apparent cynicism of his advice, Machiavelli's goals were similar to those of earlier civic humanists: the glory, unity, and perfection of the state. By the 1520s, the Renaissance in Italy was waning, and like many writers of the time, Machiavelli was looking for a way to recapture the grandeur and importance Italy had enjoyed in the fifteenth century.

Baldesar Castiglione

As a contemporary of Machiavelli's, Baldesar Castiglione also grappled with restoring Florence's past grandeur. Although he wrote at the same time about many of the same issues as Machiavelli, Castiglione's ideas were very different. Whereas Machiavelli's ideal prince was a pragmatic and sometimes ruthless ruler, the courtier described by Castiglione in *The Book of the*

Courtier is more typical of the humanist ideal: knowledgeable about warfare, yet refined, cultured, and well educated. *The Book of the Courtier* was written as a guide to conduct for members of the aristocracy. Here is some of Castiglione's advice:

- I say, then, that since the princes of today are so corrupted by evil habits and by ignorance and false conceit, and since it is so difficult to acquaint them with truth and entice them to virtue... the Courtier should win for himself the good will of his prince... And if the Courtier is such as he has been described, he will accomplish with little effort and thus always be able to disclose tactfully to his prince the truth of all that matters. In addition to this, the Courtier will be able little by little to instill goodness in the prince's mind and teach him continence [self-restraint], fortitude, justice, and temperance [moderation]...

- I judge that the chief and true profession of the Courtier ought to be that of arms.

- There are also many other exercises which, while not dependent directly on arms, still have close relationship with them and greatly promote manly vigour.

- Our Courtier will be considered excellent and in all things will have grace, especially in speaking, if he shuns affectation.

- Therefore, what chiefly matters and is needful for the Courtier in order that he may speak and write well is, I think, knowledge, because one who knows nothing and who does not have anything in his mind that merits being understood is powerless to say or write anything.

- The Court Lady... is to possess the same virtues as the Courtier... also, she should avoid affectation and cultivate *sprezzatura* [nonchalance or power in repose]. She is to avoid manly exercises and manners and preserve a feminine sweetness and delicacy... Above all, she should acquire a pleasant affability in entertaining men, being neither too bashful nor too bold in company

RENAISSANCE ART AND ARCHITECTURE

The rise of new ideas is often reflected in the art and architecture of a culture. During the Renaissance, the ideas of the civic humanists found expression in the works of the great artists of the age. One hallmark of the Renaissance was the resurgence of fountains and immaculate gardens to adorn the grounds of the homes of the wealthy. Formal gardens such as those of the Pitti Palace in Florence were later copied by King Louis XIV of France when he built his magnificent palace at Versailles.

In the Middle Ages, people were often purposely depicted smaller than religious figures to show the insignificance of humanity. Renaissance artists rejected the conventions of the Middle Ages. Instead, they chose to glorify humans and place them at the centre of the universe.

Painted portraits, seen as vanity during the Middle Ages, became very popular. Perspective was also rediscovered, enabling artists to make their paintings much more realistic. By adding windows to their paintings, artists were able to add depth to their work and move away from the flat, two-dimensional style of the Middle Ages. Finally, the influence of classical antiquity can be seen in the renewed interest in depicting nudes. Renaissance artists began to focus on the ideal human form and the perfectibility of humans rather than their imperfections.

Renaissance Architecture

The greatest achievement of fifteenth-century Florentine architecture was the completion of the duomo, Santa Maria del Fiore. By 1400, this magnificent cathedral was finished except for the dome, which remained incomplete because no architect could figure out how to build an unsupported roof over its 42-m diameter. Finally, Filippo Brunelleschi solved the problem in typically Renaissance fashion: he looked to the ancients. By studying the Pantheon in Rome, Brunelleschi learned how the Romans had

Trained as a sculptor and goldsmith, Filippo Brunelleschi was also fascinated by arithmetic and ancient monuments. These interests made him the ideal person to design an unsupported roof for the dome of Florence's magnificent new cathedral, Santa Maria del Fiore, shown here as it looks today.

spanned long distances and was able to submit a workable plan in 1417.

Once his plan was approved, Brunelleschi began the challenging task of building the roof under the watchful eye of the Florentine crowds. In the end, Brunelleschi's dome made the duomo the dominant feature of the Florentine skyline. Still, the duomo was a transitional building. Its massive size marked it as medieval, but its dome set a bold new standard and direction for architecture.

The civic pride of the Renaissance was also reflected in city planning. The haphazard, unplanned streets of medieval Europe were no longer considered adequate. Instead, planners dreamed of laying out cities in an efficient grid pattern. Few of these idealistic plans were implemented, however, because of the high cost.

The stability of the Renaissance period in Italy enabled leading merchants, bankers, and others to build impressive palazzos, which were quite different from the fortress-like structures of earlier centuries. Palazzos such as the Pitti Palace in Florence and the Doge's Palace in Venice reflected the wealth and power of the new urban aristocracy, as well as the source of their wealth. The ground floor of these structures often served as a storefront for the family business. The three-storey design of many palaces was typical of Renaissance design, as was the use of Greek-style columns and sculpture. Although these palazzos were impressive, they were not overwhelmingly opulent in the way that earlier Gothic architecture had been.

Construction of these large new homes for the patriciate proved to be a boon for artists. The patriciate became leading patrons of the arts, commissioning prominent sculptors and painters to produce works to decorate their homes.

Painting and Sculpture

During the Renaissance, artists had much the same status as artisans, such as leather workers. Because artists worked with their hands, they were considered part of the lower middle class, well beneath the social position of the aristocracy who employed them. Artists received their training as apprentices in workshops that produced paintings, sculptures, and other works of art on commission. At first, these commissions came mainly from churches. As the wealthy middle class began to emerge, more and more commissions came from merchants and bankers. Throughout the Renaissance, the art produced was primarily religious, though the secular influence is apparent in the move towards naturalism.

One of the most renowned artists of the mid-fifteenth century was Sandro Botticelli. As a favourite artist of the Medicis, Botticelli created many paintings for the family. Both *Spring (Primavera)*, painted in 1478, and *Birth of Venus*, completed after 1482, were Medici commissions. *Birth of Venus* was one of the first female nudes of the Renaissance, and depicts the goddess of love emerging from the sea on a shell. The painting combines medieval mysticism, pagan symbols, and Renaissance naturalism to produce an enchanting picture.

Sculpture was also heavily influenced by the renewed interest in classical works and the trend toward naturalism. Two of the great sculptors of the fifteenth century were Lorenzo Ghiberti and Donato Bardi, also known as Donatello.

In *Birth of Venus,* Sandro Botticelli depicted the goddess of love and fertility standing on a scallop shell as she is guided to shore by a gentle breeze created by Zephyr, the god of wind. A mortal woman rushes to cover the nude goddess with a cloak.

Donatello was the best-known sculptor of the first half of the fifteenth century. He worked with both Ghiberti and Brunelleschi, studying the Roman statues at the Pantheon, while Brunelleschi studied its dome. The younger man's careful study of human anatomy enabled him to accurately portray the human body in a variety of poses. His most famous work is his bronze sculpture, *David*, the biblical giant killer. Completed in about 1430, *David* was the first nude sculpture of the Renaissance and the first life-sized sculpture of modern Europe. This statue blended Donatello's appreciation of antiquity with his knowledge of human anatomy to create a work that redefined sculpture in the Renaissance.

Ghiberti's chief claim to fame is the doors he sculpted for the baptistry — a chapel where baptisms are conducted — in Florence. The panels, sculpted over a period of 27 years from 1425 to 1452, depicted scenes from the Old Testament with a startling realism and clarity that set a new standard for bronze work.

Some women artists, such as Sofonisba Anguissola, did work during the Renaissance, but they were exceptions at a time when middle- and upper-class women were encouraged to follow more "ladylike" pursuits. Still, Anguissola persisted and eventually became a portrait painter in the court of King Philip II of Spain.

WEB CONNECTION
http://www.mcgrawhill.ca/links/echoes
Go to the site above to find out about Sofonisba Anguissola and other women artists.

Modelled in wax, cast in bronze, and faced with gold, the east door of the famous Ghiberti doors was nicknamed the Gates of Paradise. In the middle panel of one of the doors, Ghiberti included the self-portrait shown here.

Leonardo da Vinci

If the Renaissance ideal was a person of well-rounded abilities, no one represented this ideal better than **Leonardo da Vinci**. Born in 1452, just as Italy was entering four decades of peace and stability, Leonardo was a gifted painter, sculptor, and engineer with an interest in anatomy, geology, mathematics, and botany. Leonardo was also gifted with horses, a genial courtier, and a superb organizer of celebrations.

Although Leonardo is best remembered for his paintings, few of these survive, and nearly all those that do exist are unfinished, damaged, altered, or decaying. This owes in large part to two facets of

Leonardo's character: his willingness to experiment and his perfectionism. Many of his technical experiments proved disastrous for the preservation of his art, while his perfectionism led him to set aside tasks for years. He never returned to projects that he felt he could not complete to his satisfaction. Unfortunately, his reputation was somewhat damaged by his experiment with a new approach to frescoes. Instead of using plaster, which dries quickly, Leonardo tried a clay base that enabled him to paint fine detail. The experiment failed, however, when the paint cracked, discoloured, and peeled off the clay.

The most famous of Leonardo's paintings, and arguably the most famous painting in the Western world, is the *Mona Lisa*. Francesco del Giocondo, a wealthy Florentine merchant, commissioned Leonardo to create a portrait of his wife, Madonna Lisa Gherhaedini. After working on the painting for four years, Leonardo decided not to part with it and, instead, took it to France when he moved there. When the painter died in 1519, the portrait became part of the French royal collection and remains on exhibit in the Louvre in Paris.

When Leonardo died at the age of 67, he was buried in a Gothic tomb in Amboise, France. Throughout his life, Leonardo had created great art that would influence the work of future masters such as Michelangelo and Raphael. In the process, he had begun to earn artists the respect they deserved.

Michelangelo Buonarroti

The artistic expression of Michelangelo di Lodovico Buonarroti Simoni, better known as **Michelangelo**, exemplified Renaissance humanism. Works such as Michelangelo's larger-than-life-sized sculpture *David* and the painting of the Sistine Chapel are among the greatest achievements in the history of Western art.

The most famous element of Leonardo's *Mona Lisa* is the model's enigmatic smile. One source said that Leonardo hired singers and jesters to keep the smile on the face of his patron's wife while he painted.

Born in 1475 in Caprese, part of the Republic of Florence, Michelangelo was a child of the Renaissance. He built on ideas that had been introduced by Botticelli, Donatello, and Leonardo da Vinci to create masterpieces in his own style. His art, which included painting, sculpture, and poetry, dominated his life. When he died at 89, he was still creating masterpieces.

Michelangelo's greatness lay in his ability to fuse classical style with Christian themes. His *David*, for example, is considered by some to be one of the

Pushing the Boundaries: Developments in Science and Technology

Leonardo da Vinci:
"Tell me if anything at all was done"

Though Leonardo da Vinci's *Mona Lisa* is one of the most celebrated paintings of all time, this infinitely curious Renaissance artist also had many other interests. In many ways, Leonardo da Vinci was truly a "Renaissance man" — someone with many talents. At various times, this gifted painter and sculptor worked as a civil engineer, an architect, a military planner, and a weapons designer. He made discoveries in meteorology and geology, studied hydraulics and botany, and explored the potential of automation.

Like other artists of the time, Leonardo dissected cadavers — dead bodies — to expand his knowledge of anatomy and improve his portrayal of the human form. This study led him to develop an accurate theory about how blood circulates. Yet, as brilliant as Leonardo's genius was, legend says that this was his deathbed plea: "Tell me if anything at all was done."

Leonardo's genius is most evident on paper. His notebooks — those that have been found — were filled with designs for flying machines, submarines, parachutes, and weapons, as well as sketches and notes showing how the human body works. Historians estimate, however, that two thirds of his notebooks may have been lost forever.

Since pieces of Leonardo's manuscripts were first published in the late 1800s, historians and scientists have puzzled over how much his often-brilliant ideas influenced the course of science and technology.

Leonardo was an incurable procrastinator. He planned to publish at least three books, but never did. He also never built most of the ingenious machines shown in his drawings. As a result, some historians have argued that his influence was minimal. Others point out, however, that in Leonardo's time, knowledge and information were communicated personally — from master to pupil, and among peers and colleagues, as well as friends and family.

Historians know that immediately after Leonardo's death, his notebooks were studied by many people. Many of his notes were copied, and many of the notebooks that are now missing were probably stolen.

Though it took detective work, by the end of the twentieth century, researchers had come up with evidence proving that Leonardo's ideas did show up in projects of his era. Though Leonardo may have doubted the lasting value of his research and discoveries, historians now agree that the answer to his deathbed question should have been: "Yes, something was done."

Activities

1. What does this passage suggest about the job of historians?

2. Find out more about one of Leonardo's innovations or inventions and present your findings to a group or the class.

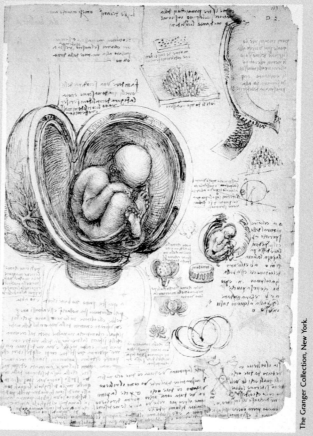

To create this drawing of an embryo in the womb, Leonardo gained permission to dissect a pregnant woman who had died. Consequently, he was able to draw the correct position of the embryo and explain the purpose of the placenta.

The Granger Collection, New York.

greatest sculptures in the history of art. In 1501, Michelangelo won a commission from the city of Florence to sculpt a statue of the Biblical giant killer, David. Three years later, the sculpture was complete.

Although David had been a favourite theme of Renaissance sculptors, Michelangelo's statue was a significant departure from earlier representations.

Politics played an important role in the choice of David as Michelangelo's subject. Just a few years before Florence commissioned the statue, shown here, the actions of Piero di Medici had temporarily handed the city to the French. What symbolic importance would a statue of the Biblical giant killer have for Florence?

Donatello, for example, had portrayed an exultant David with his foot resting in triumph on Goliath's head. Michelangelo chose to portray a meditative David *before* the famous contest, as he wrestled with the decision to act. As a result, David's pose combines stillness with the promise of movement. His intense facial expression reflects his inward search for the strength to face Goliath.

When *David* was unveiled at the entrance to Florence's city hall in September 1504, it brought immediate fame to both Michelangelo and the city. For the artist, this fame was a mixed blessing. Michelangelo's reputation brought him to the attention of Pope Julius II, who wanted the best artist of the time to paint the twelve apostles and some ornamental designs on the ceiling of the Vatican's Sistine Chapel. Though Michelangelo tried to turn down the commission, he was persuaded to accept it.

In taking the project, Michelangelo transformed a relatively simple commission into 520 m² of figures, scenes, and architectural elements. The painting took four years to complete, and Michelangelo spent most of this time atop specially constructed scaffolding with his head thrown back and paint dripping in his eyes. Although the scenes are Biblical, the work is typical of the Renaissance. The paintings focus on the physical and spiritual beauty of human beings. Many of the pictures, such as the famous *Creation of Adam,* are nudes that would have been unheard of two centuries earlier.

The completion of the Sistine Chapel ceiling in 1512 firmly established Michelangelo as the leading sculptor and painter of the time — and his life was but half over. The Renaissance ideas first expressed by humanists such as Petrarch received their clearest expression in the art of this Renaissance master whose art became a lasting testament to the vibrant culture of Renaissance Italy.

WEB
CONNECTION
http://www.mcgrawhill.ca/links/echoes
Go to the site above to find out more about Renaissance art and architecture.

Review...Recall...Reflect

1. Why is Petrarch considered the first humanist of the Italian Renaissance?

2. If you were to visit Florence today, how would you distinguish Renaissance buildings from medieval structures?

3. Why was Michelangelo's *David* considered the greatest sculpture of the Renaissance?

THE RENAISSANCE AND THE INDIVIDUAL

Beneath the classical styles and religious themes of Renaissance art was a clear expression of the individualism and secular spirit that marked the period. The quest for a definition of the human ideal was a constant theme in Renaissance writing, painting, and sculpture caused by the disasters.

After the despair of the fourteenth century, the Renaissance reflected an optimism about humanity that had not been known since classical times. Many people genuinely believed that reason and education would help them improve their own lives and the cities where they made their homes.

The Ideal Renaissance Man

The political stability of the High Middle Ages, the rise of the Italian city-states, and the emergence of the new urban aristocracy all contributed to the rise of a new concept of the ideal man. This new ideal was the opposite of the medieval ideal. The universal man of the Renaissance was to be cultured, educated, and well versed in the classics; a gentleman, comfortable both on the battlefield and in the ballroom; a poet and artist; and a man of eloquence, wit, satire, and music. The leading thinkers of the Renaissance rejected the idea of the superiority of the hereditary aristocracy, stressing instead the importance of intellect.

The Ideal Renaissance Woman

Gone, too, was the medieval concept of the ideal woman who was placed on a pedestal at the same time as she was dismissed as an inferior — even evil — being. Although women of the Renaissance were discouraged from taking part in physically demanding sports, they were, on the whole, better educated than their medieval predecessors. Still, women were discouraged from using their knowledge publicly. When Isotta Nogarola, for example, tried to engage in an intellectual debate by writing a series of public letters, she was sternly rebuked for her "immoral" behaviour.

Many women of the Renaissance were cultured, and participated in activities such as dance, theatre, and music. It also appears that Renaissance women had more say about their marriage partner than their medieval predecessors. They were often advised not to fall in love unless it was likely to lead to marriage. Once married, they were expected to attend to the needs of their husbands. Some of the advice passed from mother to daughter regarding marriage included:

- Be good to [your husband's] family and friends.
- Do not do anything important without seeking his advice.
- Be attractive, fresh, clean, modest in appearance, and chaste in behaviour.
- Do not go out too often; the man's domain is outside, whereas the woman's is in the home.

The average age of marriage during the Renaissance was 27 for men and 18 for women. In his book, *The Father of the Family*, Torquato Tasso offered this advice:

> I say that a husband should try to find a young wife rather than an old one. Not only are young women more fit for bearing children, but they are also, according to Hesiod, better at receiving and adopting the habits that a husband wants to impart to them… If a man takes a wife under the conditions that I have just described, it will be much easier for him to exercise the superiority that nature has granted men, and if he cannot make his natural superiority felt, he will sometimes find his wife so recalcitrant and disobedient that, in place of the companion whom he expected to help lighten the burden that our humanity brings with it, he will confront a perpetual enemy who is as contrary to him as unbridled desire to reason.

The age difference between husbands and wives had important implications for the role of women in society. Because husbands were often older, many women had become widows by the time they reached the age of 40 or 50 — and had inherited large sums of money or thriving businesses. These inheritances enhanced the importance of these women and gave them a voice in establishing the new values of the Renaissance.

Raising Children

The Renaissance optimism and belief in the potential goodness of humanity was reflected in child-rearing practices. During the Renaissance, wealthy parents played a much more active role in their children's lives than they had during medieval times, when child rearing was often left to servants. Before the Renaissance, most upper-class babies were breastfed by a wet nurse. During the Renaissance, this practice was discouraged, and mothers were urged to feed their own children. Parents were also encouraged to handle infants lovingly and to nurture their development without fear of spoiling them.

Child rearing became the subject of books, which encouraged parents to show children how to choose good behaviour rather than to punish them for bad behaviour. Michele Savonarola, a celebrated Renaissance doctor, instructed parents to "encourage good speech and begin [the toddler's] moral upbringing. Do this by being reverent mothers and fathers, and also insisting upon this in all your relatives, according to their closeness; above all, get on your knees to call piously for help from Jesus and Mary. Say the Hail Mary and the Our Father every day, and teach him to make the sign of the cross…"

Savonarola went on to suggest that children should start school at the age of five. There, they should develop good habits and learn to read. He warned, however, that schoolchildren should not be kept cooped up all day. They should have opportunities to go outside to play and exercise, and should go home for an hour at midday. In selecting a teacher, Savonarola suggested that parents seek someone who used rewards to motivate and hit students only rarely. "Reverential awe for the teacher should never come solely from fear of getting beaten," he wrote.

Adolescents

During the Renaissance, adolescence was defined as the period between the end of childhood and the age of 28. Childhood was said to end at the age of discretion, when young people's actions became the product of conscious choices. The "age of discretion" was thought of as the moral and spiritual transformation that developed over a period that varied from person to person. Still, it was often marked by the arrival of puberty, and would have occurred in most children by age 14.

Drawing on the work of ancients such as Plutarch and Quintilian, secular writers viewed adolescence as a critical point in life. They believed that it was the time at which individuals would make the personal choices that would lead them toward vice or virtue. The humanist writer Matteo Palmieri offered this advice to parents of adolescents:

> ...physical punishment is contrary to nature and not good. Furthermore, it is likely to turn natural filial love into hatred. Rebuke should be enough, and even this according to age; cite good examples of other youths he knows, vilify the bad ones, have him converse with the good ones... Whippings give only brief suffering; quickly forgotten, they wrongly give the impression that the bad behaviour is now fully paid for and, therefore, the sin is easily repeated. Choosing good comes not from fear of a painful beating, but from the desire to flee from sin.

In contrast to Palmieri, Cardinal Silvio Antoniano viewed adolescence as the period when sin reaches its peak. He described adolescents as "self-indulgent, greedy, and ever ready to grab for more, even though this constant grasping is often volatile and contradictory, changing from one moment to the next, quickly tiring of the old and ready for anything new... They are easily deceived, malleable as wax, sociable only with their own kind, quick to make friends if it leads to pleasure seeking, merrymaking, and gaming."

Despite this negative view of youth, Antoniano's advice to fathers on raising sons was surprisingly moderate. He reminded fathers that the best time to instill virtue in their sons was at a young age, and urged parents to ensure that their children's playmates were of good moral character. He also suggested that children be rewarded for good behaviour.

Antoniano warned mothers of daughters to be vigilant. A daughter should not be sent out in the company of old maids, nor allowed to hang out windows or off balconies to show herself off or flirt with passersby. Most important, Antoniano said, mothers should keep their daughters busy with chores so that they have no time for idle thoughts and sinfulness. "The female sex by nature is lewd and frivolous and at this age of little consequence. But there is always hope that good early upbringing, along with fear of God and a saintly example from her mother, will bring a good result anyway," Antoniano wrote.

The Past AT PLAY

Knucklebones, a popular game with Renaissance children, had been played since ancient times and still exists today, in the form of jacks. Knucklebones was played with the dried ankle bones of sheep. These bones have four distinct sides — one flat, one concave, one convex, and one sinuous. Each side was assigned a numerical value. Players tossed the bones in the air and let them fall. The winner was the player whose toss added up to the highest score.

This 1560 painting by Pieter Bruegel is titled *Young Folk at Play*. It shows more than 200 children engaged in more than 80 play activities, of which more than 20 are games. Examine the painting. Find the two young women playing knucklebones. Pick out other familiar activities.

Even secular writers such as Niccolò Vito di Gozze, of the Dubrovnik Republic (now a city in Croatia), judged young women harshly. Gozze argued that the four necessary virtues in young women were modesty, piety, chastity, and beauty. "Women generally are too loquacious and would be better off staying mute than babbling on as they do," he added.

Renaissance feminists such as Moderata Fonte of Venice challenged these negative views of women. Though Fonte acknowledged that young women did, at times, seem shallow and fickle, she argued that this resulted from being raised without proper discipline. In her writing, Fonte asserted that women were not only equal, but also superior, to men.

Although Renaissance thinkers, writers, and parents may have disagreed over the best way of raising children, they nevertheless viewed children as unique individuals whose needs were different from those of adults. This view was a departure from medieval attitudes toward children. It was, however, a view that applied only to the children of prosperous families. Few people worried about what happened to the children of the poor.

Lives of the Popolo Minuto

In nearly all societies, there is a large gap between the powerful elite and the masses. Renaissance Florence was no exception. The *popolo minuto*, or "little people," made up nearly 50 percent of the city's population. They included domestic servants, porters, messengers, unorganized labourers, criminals, vagabonds, beggars, the elderly, widows, the disabled, and others unable to find employment.

Economically, the popolo minuto were highly vulnerable. Inflation ravaged their meagre wages, and forced loans and taxes often placed them in dire straits. When the poor were unable to pay their debts, their property, which often included their means of employment, was confiscated. This made them even more desperate. For example, Giusto di Luca Petrini, a wool carder, owned a loom for weaving woollen cloth, a bed, a chest with two locks, a cupboard, and a mattress. When he could not pay a 19-florin debt, these possessions were all seized. Similarly, Niccolò di Salvi was forced to sell everything he owned, including his cobbler's shop, to pay a tax levied by the government.

The wealthy often regarded the popolo minuto with a mixture of fear and compassion. A sense of Christian duty and the threat of a mass uprising, such as the Revolt of the Ciompi in 1378, forced the upper classes to pay some attention to the plight of the poor. Occasionally, men too old to work were given a small pension by the city government. In

This painting by Lorenzo Lotto shows St. Anthony distributing alms to the poor.

Florence and elsewhere, alms were often distributed to the poor in an attempt to please God. For many of the popolo minuto, however, life was an endless struggle to eke out a living, with little or no hope of getting ahead. Workers' attempts to improve their conditions by organizing guilds were harshly — and often violently — suppressed.

TECHNOLOGY AND THE MODERN AGE

Technological advances were a central factor in the success of the emerging capitalist economy and the spread of Renaissance ideas to Northern Europe. Significant changes in the technology of ocean-going ships, for example, enabled Europeans to travel long distances more safely. The introduction of large, square sails and the lateen, a triangular, mobile stern sail that could be set at an angle to the wind, increased the speed at which ships travelled. The development of the Catalan rudder, which was mounted on the sternpost in place of the two side rudder oars, as well as compasses, nautical charts, and pilots' books, also improved navigation.

These technological advances made sailing on the open seas much easier. It was no longer necessary to keep land in sight, nor were clear skies essential for navigation. By the sixteenth century, wealthy merchants were willing to sponsor voyages of exploration and colonization to find supplies of cheap raw materials, cheap labour, and markets for their manufactured goods.

The social, cultural, and economic changes that marked the Italian Renaissance eventually started to spread to the rest of Europe, contributing to the emergence of the modern age. Two fifteenth-century technological innovations — the introduction of paper and the development of the printing press — were essential

The History of the Imagination: Myths and Legends

Hunting Witches

Snow White. Little Red Riding Hood. Rumpelstiltsken. European fairy tales are full of wicked witches. But where — and when — did this mythical image originate?

In the late fifteenth century, at about the same time as the Spanish Inquisition was starting, a different kind of Inquisition was getting under way in Northern Europe. There, new outbreaks of plague, bad weather that ruined crops, and bloody wars had disrupted society and created hardship. As a result, people began to question the authority of the Church and the nobility and even blame them for causing these problems. To deflect this blame, a scapegoat was needed. Who better than women?

Two German Inquisitors, Heinrich Kramer and Johann Sprenger, persuaded Pope Innocent VIII to allow them to pursue witches in the same way as heretics. In 1486, the two published *Malleus Maleficarum* (*Hammer Against Witches*). This book became a handbook for identifying, torturing, and killing witches. *Malleus Maleficarum* was not the only book its kind. In France, for expample, 345 books about witchcraft were published between 1550 and 1650.

The Inquisitors claimed that nearly every calamity — blighted crops, cows that failed to give milk, the death of a child — was the work of witches.

Although men were not immune to charges of witchery, 80 percent of those executed were women. Historians now estimate that hundreds of thousands of women were executed. Most were burned at the stake.

Why were women the chief targets of this hysteria? The reasons are complex. One is that Kramer, who wrote most of *Malleus Maleficarum*, was a misogynist, or woman hater. His hatred burns from the pages of the book, which says things like:

- [Women] have slippery tongues, and are unable to conceal from their fellow-women those things which by evil arts they know.

- For [witches] raise hailstorms and hurtful sterility in men and animals; offer to devils, or otherwise kill, the children whom they do not devour... They can also, before the eyes of their parents, and when no one is in sight, throw into the water children walking by the waterside; they make horses go mad under their riders; they can transport themselves from place to place through the air, either in body or in imagination…

The witch hunt lasted for about 200 years. By the time the worst was over, the image of the wicked witch was fixed in people's imaginations and had become a powerful symbol in the fairy tales told to generations of European children.

Activities

1. The witch hunts made women scapegoats for the ills that plagued society. Do societies need scapegoats? Why? Name a person or group who might be considered a scapegoat today. Why has this happened?

2. Explain how this feature has added to your understanding of historiography, the story of history.

Many of the women accused of witchcraft were old, and many, though not all, were poor. Examine this seventeenth-century painting called *Witches at Their Incantations*. What images might spark fear in viewers?

This detail from the *Fall of Icarus* painted by Pieter Bruegel shows a sixteenth-century carrack getting under way. Notice the large, square foresail billowing in the wind and the lateen-rigged mizzen.

to spreading Renaissance ideas. The communication revolution sparked by these developments allowed books to be produced relatively cheaply and easily, an important factor in the circulation of humanist ideas. People could now read the works of ancient and contemporary writers, learn Greek and Latin, and participate in the learning that characterized the Renaissance.

The printing press ensured that the Italian Renaissance would not be a passing phase like the eighth-century Carolingian Renaissance, but would extend its influence throughout Europe.

RENAISSANCE IDEAS IN NORTHERN EUROPE

Humanistic ideas and other influences of the Italian Renaissance began to move into Northern Europe toward the end of the fifteenth century. In many areas, these humanistic ideals were being imported from Italy at the same time as a religious revolution called the Reformation was occurring. The Reformation was a movement that resulted in the founding of Protestantism, which added a third branch to the Christian church.

As the Italian Renaissance began to wane under the pressure of external invasions, well-known Italian humanists were hired by royal courts in France and England. Because the countries north of the Alps had sprung from different roots, however, they adapted the Renaissance ideals to fit their character, history, and culture. In these northern countries, the new ideas represented not so much a renaissance, or rebirth, of classical ideals as a northern version of humanism.

The English Renaissance

When King Henry VII ascended the English throne in 1485 after winning the Wars of the Roses, he inherited a largely medieval kingdom with an unruly nobility. During his reign, he was able to establish a strong central government, setting the stage for the English Renaissance.

It was Henry's son, **Henry VIII**, however, who became an active patron of the arts and established England as a leading intellectual and cultural centre. Few kings in the history of England are as well known or as misunderstood as Henry VIII. Most people think of this king as an obese man who "went through" six wives. His tremendous mental and physical abilities and his contribution to bringing the Renaissance to England are often overlooked.

As the second son of Henry VII, the tall, handsome, and athletic young prince was not the designated heir to the throne; that role fell to his older brother, Arthur. Instead, Henry was given a broad education, which included academic studies, theology, and athletics, in preparation for a career as a high Church official. He spoke English, French, and Latin, and was an accomplished musician and composer, who is often credited with writing the song "Greensleeves."

When his older brother died, Henry became heir to the throne and began his rule in 1509. Unlike his father, who had focused on securing the Tudor dynasty and ensuring stability at home, Henry VIII's reign would be distinguished by expensive foreign wars, ruthless suppression of opposition, and a lavish court life that embraced the ideals of the Renaissance.

Throughout Henry VIII's reign, war with France dominated England's continental ambitions. The foundations of England's naval supremacy were also laid at this time. The naval war with France, despite some setbacks, enabled England to establish mastery of the English Channel. This mastery would later be extended to the high seas.

By the time Hans Holbein painted this portrait of Henry VIII in 1538, the once-athletic king was plagued by ill health and had grown enormously fat. His popularity with the people had also declined, and he had become bitter, depressed, and short-tempered.

The Art of the Northern Humanists

Until England, France, and the German principalities that were nominally part of the Holy Roman Empire began to embrace Renaissance ideals during the sixteenth century, the art of Northern Europe had been entrenched in the Gothic style. As humanism took hold in Northern Europe, however, art began to break with Gothic tradition. Conventions were disregarded, and realism took over.

Jan van Eyck, in his portraits and scenes, exemplifies this realistic style. He was painting for a new audience in the flourishing commercial centres, such as Brugge (Bruges) and Ghent in present-day Belgium. There, wealthy merchants commissioned paintings and portraits. One of van Eyck's most famous paintings is the wedding portrait of Giovanni Arnolfini and his bride.

Hans Holbein the Younger, an artist from Basel in present-day Switzerland, exemplified Northern humanism in his complete break from the Gothic tradition. After encountering leading humanists such as Erasmus, who encouraged him to abandon religious painting, Holbein travelled to the court of Henry VIII to paint and to design clothes and costumes.

The approach of Albrecht Dürer, a German artist, combined the Eyckian school's meticulous detail with Renaissance ideas of proportion and mathematical precision. The Renaissance spirit of inquiry is obvious in Dürer's detailed scientific observations of people and landscapes, which he encountered on his journeys. Some of the first pure landscapes evolved from his sketches, in which the landscape is no longer a mere backdrop. To Dürer, nature was art, and he drew people and places as they were. He also struggled to free art from the restrictions of religion and to make it mirror humanity. Dürer's works cover a wide range of subjects, from traditional themes to the introspective humanistic psyche.

Review...Recall...Reflect

1. Why were technological developments critical to the birth of the modern age?

2. Why do some historians believe that the idea of the Renaissance is elitist and that there was no "renaissance" for women and the poor?

3. How was the Northern Renaissance similar to and different from the Italian Renaissance?

Literature of the Northern Renaissance

As humanism flourished in Northern Europe, the literature was often directed at winning Church reform. Thomas More of England, Desiderius Erasmus of Rotterdam, and Martin Luther of Germany were all leaders of the northern humanist movement.

More was a kind, refined, charismatic, and devout statesman, as well as a man of conscience, who gave his life for his beliefs. When he was 20, a spiritual crisis led him to seriously consider withdrawing to a monastery. Although he did not do this, he voluntarily adopted the regimented discipline of the monks. He attempted to address humanity's inadequacies as well as his own, and attacked the excesses and inconsistencies of both the Church and state.

More made his views known through the printed word. His ability as a writer is demonstrated in *Utopia,* published in 1516. In this book, More engages in a conversation with an imaginary traveller who had visited the New World. While there, the traveller discovered a city-state governed by reason where everyone was well educated and lived in peace and harmony, without corruption. In the book, More satirized European society while setting out his idea of the ideal humanistic state.

More continued writing at the same time as he pursued a career in the king's service, rising to the powerful position of Lord Chancellor in King Henry VIII's court. This was his downfall. When More refused to approve Henry's marriage to Anne Boleyn, the angry king had the chancellor tried, convicted of treason, and beheaded. Centuries later, More was canonized by the Roman Catholic Church.

More met and became friends with **Desiderius Erasmus**, a monk and cosmopolitan humanist and intellectual nomad. Erasmus might be called the first journalist for taking advantage of the printing press to communicate his ideas and present his knowledge and opinions in a way that encouraged readers to participate in his thought processes. *In Praise of Folly,* a book he wrote while staying with More in England, reflects on the absurdity of human nature and the importance of folly in balancing reason. Humorous yet profound, the book sometimes pokes fun at Erasmus' friends. At other times, it sharply criticizes the Church. Believing that the trappings, routines, and conventions of Christianity had overwhelmed people's beliefs, Erasmus said that a return to sincere faith was needed.

Erasmus reacted to the Renaissance by developing a keen interest in the classics, though this interest gave way to theological pursuits.

Erasmus examined the earliest Greek versions of the *Gospels* and *Epistles* of the New Testament and produced a new Latin translation correcting many of the errors in the Vulgate, the standard Latin version.

Erasmus' ideas strongly influenced Martin Luther, who was a German priest and scholar. When Luther translated the New Testament into German, for example, he worked from Erasmus' text. As a result, Luther hoped to make Erasmus an ally in the

Often nicknamed the Prince of Humanists, Desiderius Erasmus was consulted by scholars, artists, and politicians across Europe. Although he was a monk, Erasmus felt confined by monastic discipline and embarked on a life of travel that took him to the major intellectual centres of the continent.

campaign to win Church reform. Erasmus chose not to become caught up in the religious tumult of the times. As a result, this quiet idealist who had been the intellectual "star" of Europe came to be despised in the years that followed by both the Church and reformers. His quiet moderation was contrary to the revolutionary beliefs that would be unleashed by Luther to sweep across Europe.

History Continues to Unfold

Through the Late Middle Ages and the early sixteenth century, Europe underwent a significant transformation. The advent of a capitalist system, the rebirth of classicism, and the birth of humanism led to dramatic changes in the social, economic, artistic, and cultural life of Europe. These changes would be felt from the marketplace to the Church, and from the homes of many Europeans to the schools in which children were educated.

To a large degree, Renaissance ideas affected only Europe's elite — those who commissioned works of art, received an education, or earned their wealth from overseas trade. Over time, however, the ideals of the Renaissance would percolate through society, affecting nearly all Europeans. Beliefs about the perfectibility of people and the place of individuals in society would have their clearest expression in the democratic revolutions of the eighteenth century. The effects of these revolutions are still being felt today. Although the popolo minuto may not have realized that they were living in a period of radical change, their descendants undoubtedly felt the effects of the new ideas of the Renaissance.

Current Research and Interpretations

When historians first began using the term "Renaissance," they applied it only to the Renaissance in Italy. In the twentieth century, the term was broadened to include other revivals of classical culture in Europe, such as the ninth-century Carolingian Renaissance and the Twelfth-Century Renaissance, which were discussed in earlier chapters. Some historians opposed applying the term to these medieval periods because they believed that it undermined the idea of the Italian Renaissance as a distinctive time.

Chapter Review

Chapter Summary

In this chapter, we have seen:

- that historians' conflicting interpretations have led to contrasting views about the existence of the Renaissance
- that innovations in art, technology, and intellectual thought led to dramatic changes in European society during the Renaissance
- how capitalism began to shift the basis of wealth and authority in European society
- that humanism led to changes in educational practices that continue to influence schools today

Reviewing the Significance of Key People, Concepts, and Events (Knowledge/Understanding)

1. Understanding the history of the Renaissance requires an understanding of following people, concepts, and events and their significance in the development of both medieval society and modern Western concepts of citizenship. In your notes, identify and explain the historical significance of three items from each column.

People	*Concepts*	*Events*
Lorenzo de Medici	modern age	Peace of Lodi
Francesco Petrarch	renaissance	Revolt of the Ciompi
Niccolò Machiavelli	humanism	painting of the Sistine Chapel
Leonardo da Vinci	*Malleus Maleficarum*	
Michelangelo	*David*	

2. Identify and explain how technological innovations affected European economic structures by creating a three-column chart in your notes. Title the first column "Innovation," the second "Description," and the third "Effect on Economic Structure of Europe." In the first column, place these innovations: "Catalan rudder and large, square sails," "Printing press," and "Capitalism." Then complete the chart. Transfer the main ideas for two of these innovations to the graphic organizer "Economic Impact of Innovations" in your *World History Handbook*.

3. Identify the significance of several important artists of the Renaissance by completing a three-column chart in your notes. Title the first column "Artist," the second "Work," and the third "Significance." Enter these names in the first column: "Botticelli," "Michelangelo," "Ghiberti," and "Leonardo da Vinci." Then complete the chart.

Doing History: Thinking About the Past (Thinking/Inquiry)

1. Write a paragraph explaining why the Renaissance was essentially a Northern Italian phenomenon. Be sure to identify and explain three reasons the city-states of Northern Italy emerged as the leading cultural centres of the fifteenth century. Transfer the main idea of your paragraph to the graphic organizer "Why Some Societies Rose to Dominance" in your *World History Handbook*.

2. Write a 400- to 500-word essay in response to this statement: *Humanism was the most important factor in the changes that occurred during the fourteenth and fifteenth centuries.* The statement may serve as the thesis of your essay. If you wish to dispute the statement, you will need to create a clear thesis.

Applying Your Learning (Application)

1. Prepare a calendar titled "Agents of Change: Great People of the Renaissance." Include six people, samples of their work, and a brief explanation of their contribution to the birth of the modern age. The six people must reflect three different aspects of the age, such as the arts, politics, literature, poetry, architecture, and economics.

2. Write an imaginary dialogue between yourself and a Renaissance teenager. Discuss the treatment of boys and girls, social mobility, hopes for the future, education, and views about the direction the world is heading. The dialogue can be written or recorded on audio tape.

Communicating Your Learning (Communication)

1. Assume that you have been hired to advise the Prime Minister of Canada. Your task is to help the Prime Minister govern effectively while maintaining the support of the people. Draw on the works of Machiavelli or Castiglione to create a list of ten tips for political survival.

2. Create a map of Italy in about 1500. Indicate the major centres of the Renaissance. For each centre, include images that capture or define the essence of the city during the Renaissance.

CHAPTER NINETEEN

Epilogue
Seeds of the Global Village

By the end of this chapter, you will be able to:

- *assess the many forms of economic organization that existed before the sixteenth century*

- *identify the forces that contributed to worldwide change during the fifteenth century*

- *explain the reaction of various societies to external influences*

- *demonstrate an understanding of the factors that influenced relations among groups*

This sixteenth-century Portuguese harbour was typical of European ports that thrived as a result of the long-distance sea-going trade that developed after 1500.

Today's world is often called a global village. Stores are filled with products from around the world, many of the foods we eat are imported from other countries, and the people of Canada reflect the country's diverse cultural heritage. The foundations of this global interdependence were laid during the age of European exploration, which began more than five centuries ago.

In late-fifteenth-century Europe, the developing capitalist economy had created a desire for new sources of raw material and markets for manufactured goods. This sent Europeans on voyages of exploration to places they viewed as the ends of the earth. These voyages would have a profound effect on both Europeans and the peoples they encountered. Unfortunately, the effects seldom benefited the peoples encountered as much as the Europeans. Many of the peoples who came into contact with Europeans were exploited, and some were destroyed by disease and warfare. By the eighteenth century, few areas of the world were untouched by European exploration.

KEY WORDS

globalization

world economy

natural slaves

chattel slavery

grand exchange

acculturation

KEY PEOPLE

Christopher Columbus

Bartolomé de Las Casas

VOICES FROM THE PAST

What a great language I have, [Spanish is] a fine language we inherited from the fierce Conquistadors... They carried everything off and left us everything... They left us the words.
Pablo Neruda, Confieso Que He Vivido: Memorias [Memoirs], 1974

TIME LINE: SEEDS OF THE GLOBAL VILLAGE

| | 1367 | China suspends foreign exploration and limits contact with the outside world |

Turkish conquest of Constantinople disrupts East-West overland trade — **1453**

1487 — Portuguese establish settlements at Madeira and on Arguin Island, and begin to explore the mouth of the Congo River

Christopher Columbus encounters the Americas while searching for a route to Asia — **1492**

1513 — Vasco Núñez de Balboa crosses the Isthmus of Panama and reaches the Pacific Ocean

First shipload of African slaves arrives in the Caribbean — **1518**

1522 — Juan Sebastián de Elcano completes the circumnavigation of the globe started by Ferdinand Magellan

Led by Francisco Pizarro, Spaniards begin conquest of the Inca — **1530**

THE MODERN AGE ARRIVES

For years, Western historians thought of the years between 1480 and 1780 as the birth of the modern age. This 300-year period was considered a watershed, for both Europeans and the rest of the world. By 1480, the Middle Ages were drawing to a close and Europe was rebounding from the effects of the Black Death and the Hundred Years' War. The optimistic new ideas that had originated in the Renaissance had created a new faith in human potential. This was the spirit that sparked Europeans to carry out the voyages of exploration and colonization that would lead to profound changes in both Europe and elsewhere.

During this time, it was widely accepted that Europe's passage into the so-called modern age represented a step forward for the entire world. Europeans thought that what was good for Europe must be good for the rest of the world, and few questioned the idea that the spread of European culture represented progress. They simply assumed that the expansion of European culture would be welcomed because it brought the so-called benefits of European civilization to more people.

One historian, for example, wrote that "the Europeanization of a country was to be synonymous with its modernization" and suggested that those who accepted European civilization could only benefit from modernization. The same historian said that societies that were either isolated from Europe or resisted following Europe's lead were left behind as the world continued to "progress."

This view of history ignores two important facts: the first is that vibrant civilizations flourished before contact with the Europeans; the second, that contact with Europeans destroyed many cultures.

Few Western historians today accept the idea that the European conquests occurred because European civilization was superior to that of the conquered peoples. Rather, they believe that the conquests occurred because a unique combination of circumstances, including technological advances, the ravages of disease, the dislocation of regional wars, and the abuses of the slave trade, placed the European colonizers in a position to dominate some of the civilizations they encountered.

Historians now recognize that European colonization was often accomplished at the expense of peoples who had built their own complex societies. The achievements of these societies were largely ignored as Europeans, supremely confident in the superiority of their own culture, visited untold misery on the peoples they conquered and destroyed their civilizations. Hundreds of years later, peoples around the world are still feeling the negative effects of the European conquests.

FROM ISOLATION TO GLOBAL VILLAGE

By tracing the rise from village to empire of various cultures, the preceding chapters have demonstrated how interaction among cultures helped create unique and diverse societies. What distinguishes the time since 1500 from earlier periods, however, is the degree of **globalization** that has occurred. Though definitions of globalization vary, it is often considered to be a process that draws the people of the world together in economic, political, social, or cultural relationships. Whether globalization is a positive or negative force is an issue that is — and will continue to be — hotly debated.

Although the cultures and civilizations that existed before 1500 were by no means homogeneous, the regions of the world remained relatively isolated from one another. Since 1500, however, the world has changed a great deal. During the three centuries from 1480 to 1780, European voyages of exploration and colonization brought the peoples of the world into contact with one another. The impact of this increased contact was felt by everyone.

EARLY TRADING NETWORKS

Extensive trading networks and contact between civilizations was not a phenomenon peculiar to the 1500s. Far-reaching commercial networks had existed for thousands of years. Whenever an area had surplus produce, the people sought markets where they could trade this surplus for goods or services. Until the sixteenth century, however, goods were transported over land by beasts of burden or, for relatively short distances, over water by small ships that could accommodate only a limited amount of cargo. As a result, luxury items, which could earn merchants enormous profits, tended to dominate long-distance trade. Goods for everyday use were usually traded only among the towns and villages of a small area.

The five centuries before the era of European exploration represented the heyday of the caravan and of the pastoral nomads who lived along the overland trading routes. The pastoral nomads, who included Turks, Mongols, Arabs, and Berbers, raised livestock by continually moving their herds in search of pasture and water. These groups played an important role in the transcontinental caravan trade, for they demanded tribute in exchange for allowing the caravans to pass safely through their territory. The emergence of sea routes for conducting long-distance trade relegated the pastoral nomads to a marginal role in world affairs.

The case of the pastoral nomads demonstrates that even pre-sixteenth-century societies were interconnected to some extent. No society — from the highly centralized Chinese civilization to the loosely independent city-states of Greece or the Maya of the Central American lowlands — existed in complete isolation. All cultures were products of some interaction among societies.

On the eve of the age of European exploration, at least three world economies existed. A **world economy**, like a world war, does not include all countries of the world. It is called a world economy because it involves a number of states and is larger than any single, defined political unit. In the fifteenth century, the Asian and Russian world economies coexisted with the European world economy. In the centuries after 1500, long-distance trade developed and brought cultures from around the world into contact with one another.

EUROPEAN KNOWLEDGE OF THE WORLD

The empires of Asia, Africa, and Europe had traded with one another since ancient times. Despite this, European knowledge of Asia and Africa was fragmentary until the sixteenth century. It was shaped more by classical mythology than reality. Herodotus, a Greek historian who lived from 480 to 425 BCE, recorded improbable accounts of Africans in his *History*, which chronicled the Greco-Persian Wars; Roman trade goods have been excavated in Eastern India; and the Venetian adventurer Marco Polo, who claimed to have lived in Asia from 1271 to 1295, heard tales of the existence of the Japanese islands.

The earliest known European settlement in North America was by the Vikings at L'Anse aux Meadows, Newfoundland, in about 1000. For centuries after this, however, Europeans ignored the Americas.

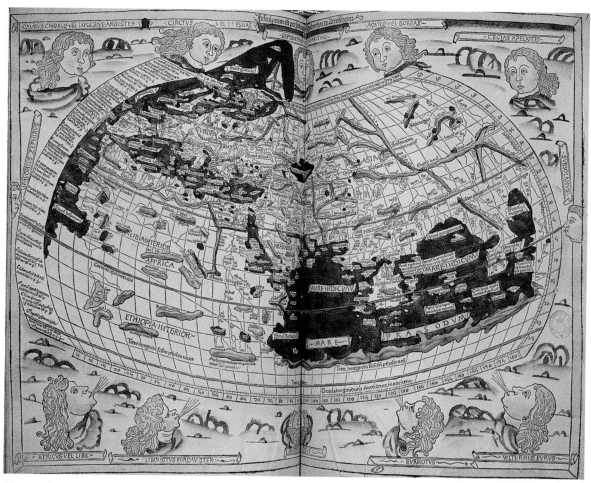

This map, from Ptolemy's *Geography,* shows a world consisting of three continents — Asia, Africa, and Europe — and two oceans — the Indian Ocean and the Western Ocean. Find the three continents. How accurate was Ptolemy's depiction of world geography?

The new European interest in exploration was led by the Spaniards and Portuguese. During the fifteenth century, the *Geography* of Ptolemy, an ancient astronomer, geographer, and mathematician, was translated from Greek and printed on the new printing presses. This meant that many more Europeans were able to take part in the debate over the accuracy of Ptolemaic geography, as well as the shape of the globe. Nowhere were these issues more hotly debated than in Madrid, the capital of Spain, and Lisbon, the capital of Portugal.

As a result, it was in Spain and Portugal that explorers were most likely to find investors willing to finance risky overseas exploration. The kings and queens of Spain and Portugal sponsored explorers such as **Christopher Columbus**, Vasco da Gama, Ferdinand Magellan, and Juan Sebastián de Elcano. Because of the many voyages of exploration that took place during the late fifteenth and sixteenth centuries, Europeans gradually came to accept that the world was round and that the continents of North and South America lay between Europe and Asia.

FOUNDATIONS OF EUROPEAN EXPLORATION

The famous voyage of Christopher Columbus in 1492 was but one of many journeys of exploration undertaken by Europeans between 1487 and 1780. During this 300-year period, Europeans altered the history of many societies around the world. At the same time, Europe was itself experiencing profound change.

What factors both motivated and enabled Europeans to sail around the world? The four most important were

- a resurgence in learning led by the Florentine humanists
- advances in seafaring technology
- the closing of overland trade routes to the Orient by the Ottoman Turks
- the development of capitalism

Medieval Europe's preoccupation with spiritual growth and religious learning had left little room for exploring the world. The Crusades, however, greatly expanded the horizons of medieval Europeans and played an important role in reopening the trade routes that had once connected the Roman Empire and Asia. Of equal importance in setting the stage for European exploration were the Renaissance humanists, who ushered in a new age of learning. The humanists' focus on ancient texts, their faith in the potential of humanity, and their interest in science sparked an interest in devising methods of exploring the world using the stars as a guide. Rather than dismissing far-off lands as the home of pagans, Europeans were beginning to realize the economic potential of Africa and Asia.

By the Late Middle Ages, trade with India and Asia was supplying Europe with spices for flavouring and preserving foods, silks for fine clothing, and herbs essential for medicine. The exotic nature of the goods imported from Africa and the Orient led many to imagine the existence of a terrestrial paradise. This splendid land was thought to be enclosed within a high wall of crystal or diamonds, and was believed to be the source of what Europeans considered the great rivers of the world: the Nile, the Ganges, the Tigris, and the Euphrates. Europeans thought that the banks of these rivers were lined with the plants and trees that produced spices and aromatic resins such as balsam, cinnamon, myrrh, cardamom, and benzoin. Although the terrestrial paradise was a myth, it reflected people's view of the East and the increasing importance of trade between Europe and Asia.

The Turkish conquest of Constantinople in 1453 created a serious problem for European merchants who imported goods from Asia. Although the Ottomans did not shut down East-West trade, they did try to regulate it by imposing high duties on goods. As a result, goods imported from Asia became scarce and very expensive. This situation caused European merchants to look elsewhere for sources.

The spread of secular learning, new pressures on land routes to Asia, and changes in seafaring technology

The varied wares displayed in this busy fourteenth-century spice-seller's shop reflect the European demand for luxury goods from Asia. How would the scarcity of spices have affected prices?

all contributed to the spirit of European exploration. The driving force behind European expansion between 1480 and 1780, however, was economics — the quest for new markets and sources of raw material to fuel the emerging capitalist economy.

GLOBALIZATION

The age of European exploration and expansion began in 1414 when the Portuguese captured the Muslim port of Ceuta on the African side of the Strait of Gibraltar. Although the main objective of the Portuguese was to secure their access to the Mediterranean, their presence on the North African coast opened the door to European exploration of the southern Atlantic. The need for raw materials to fuel Europe's emerging capitalist economy and the blockade of the traditional caravan routes prompted Europeans to search for a sea route to the riches of Asia.

The Atlantic Ocean would prove to be the key to this search. During the two centuries after the Portuguese seizure of Ceuta, Europeans launched many Atlantic voyages in search of Asia. By 1487, the Portuguese had established settlements at Madeira (a group of islands west of Morocco) and on Arguin Island (off the coast of present-day

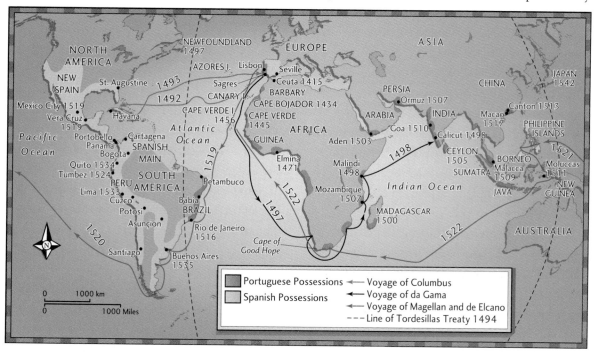

■ Spanish and Portuguese Exploration and Conquest: 1400–1550

In 1493, the pope divided the "undiscovered" world between Spain and Portugal. To cement this agreement, the two countries signed the Treaty of Tordesillas in 1494.

1. If you were the Portuguese monarch, would you have been pleased or displeased with the Treaty of Tordesillas? Why?

2. If you were the Spanish monarch, would you have been pleased or displeased with the treaty? Why?

3. Whose interests were completely ignored when the treaty was signed? Why?

Mauritania), explored the mouth of the Congo River, and rounded the Cape of Good Hope (at the southern tip of Africa). In 1497, Vasco da Gama's voyage around the African cape to East Africa and the Malabar Coast of India opened a route to India.

The Portuguese were not alone in seeking new sources of wealth. In 1492, Columbus — sailing west under the sponsorship of the Spanish monarchs in search of an alternative route to Asia — had come upon the islands of the Caribbean. The Spaniards followed up Columbus's voyage by exploring the mainland of South and Central America. In 1513, Vasco Núñez de Balboa crossed the Isthmus of Panama and reached the Pacific Ocean; in 1519, Hernán Cortés began the conquest of Mexico; and in 1530, Francisco Pizarro set out to conquer Peru.

The Spaniards also continued their quest to find a western route to Asia. This route was discovered by Ferdinand Magellan, who located a passage — later named the Straits of Magellan — around the southern tip of South America. Although Magellan died during the voyage, Juan Sebastián de Elcano took over the expedition and completed the first circumnavigation of the globe in 1522.

The Portuguese voyages around the Cape of Good Hope and the Spanish voyages around the southern tip of South America proved that the oceans of the Southern Hemisphere were connected, and opened up sea routes to Asia. Throughout the sixteenth century, the Spaniards and Portuguese zealously guarded these passages to Asia, using force to maintain their monopoly on the spice trade.

Anxious to share in the lucrative trade with Asia, other countries, including England, France, and the Netherlands, sought their own routes. This search led men such as Giovanni Caboto (John Cabot) in 1497, Jacques Cartier in 1534 and 1535, Martin Frobisher in 1574, and Henry Hudson in 1610 to explore the coast of North America. Although these explorers never found an alternative passage to Asia, their voyages did reveal the extent of the North American land mass and opened up eastern North America to exploration and colonization.

The richness of the resources of Asia, Africa, and the Americas meant that clashes between European powers would no longer be restricted to the European continent. After the sixteenth century, European conflicts would affect peoples around the world. This is the essence of the modern age, in which continents have been drawn into a global system of interdependence. The effects of events that take place in one area are often felt a world away.

EARLY CONTACT

Many of the cultures the Europeans came into contact with — and with whom Europe established trading relationships — have been the focus of earlier chapters. Advanced societies existed in many parts of the world, and the eventual dominance of Europeans was neither inevitable nor the product of cultural or racial superiority. In many cases, Europeans were superior only in their ability to travel great distances.

The eventual dominance of Europeans in the Americas, for example, was largely the result of diseases that decimated the Aboriginal population. "European diseases did more than European technology to vanquish the American Indian in the early years of colonization," Karen Kuperman wrote in *Settling with the Indians*. Estimates of the scale of this disaster suggest that 75 to 90 percent of the Aboriginal population — eight to ten million people — may have died as a result of contact with the Europeans. Most of these deaths were from diseases contracted by people who had no natural immunity against them.

European weapons and military strategies were seldom superior to those of the peoples they came into contact with. In fact, European technology and systems were often completely unsuited to waging war in non-European environments. Consequently, the main aim of most European expeditions was to establish trading relationships with the societies they encountered. In order to establish these relationships, however, terms acceptable to both parties had to be negotiated.

To view these negotiations as weighted in favour of the Europeans would be inaccurate. The fur trade between Europeans and the Aboriginal peoples of present-day Canada and the northern United States, for example, served the interests of both parties.

Europeans preferred furs that had been worn for some time, as wearing loosened and helped remove the coarse outer fur. Fur was plentiful enough in these northern regions that Aboriginal people attached little value to it. In exchange for furs of little value, Aboriginal people received glass beads and metal utensils, which they did value. In the same way, the Europeans attached little value to the glass beads and metal utensils that they traded for furs, which they considered very valuable. As a result, the fur trade — in its initial stages, at least — involved a mutually beneficial trading relationship.

European reaction to the peoples they encountered was largely shaped by the role these people might play in the European world economy. This often sparked a tragic paradox in European relationships with people of other cultures. Europeans often spoke of the people they encountered as barbaric savages. At the same time, many Europeans committed atrocities that can only be described as savage and inhumane.

Bartolomé de Las Casas, a Spanish historian who took part in the conquest of Cuba in 1513 and was disgusted by the cruelties he witnessed,

recorded some of the atrocities committed by his fellow soldiers: "The Spaniards with their Horses, their Speares and Lances, began to commit murders, and strange cruelties: they entered into Townes, Borowes, and Villages, sparing neither children nor old men, neither women with childe..."

Though he participated willingly in the Spanish conquest of Cuba, Bartolomé de Las Casas later regretted his action. He became the first European to speak out against the enslavement of the Aboriginal peoples conquered by the Spaniards.

In an attempt to justify enslaving the Aboriginal peoples they encountered, some Spanish intellectuals classified them as "**natural slaves**." This classification was based on ideas found in the works of the Greek philosopher Aristotle, who divided slaves into two groups: civil slaves and natural slaves. Aristotle wrote that civil slaves were those captured in war and who chose slavery over death. He said that natural slaves were subhuman beings whose purpose was to be enslaved.

The Spanish intellectuals argued that becoming slaves to the Spaniards was the natural fate of the Aboriginal peoples, who were, in fact, better off because slavery exposed them to the influence of European civilization. In time, this argument was rejected, and the Aboriginal peoples came to be viewed as fully human, though the idea that they were part of a younger civilization lingered. By this time, however, their numbers had been slashed by disease and Spanish atrocities.

In areas such as China, Japan, and India, the ravages of European diseases were not a factor. Consequently, Europeans were less able to dominate. Unlike Europe in the seventeenth century, China was a highly centralized nation in which people adhered strictly to the directives of the government in Beijing. This frustrated the Dutch, who repeatedly tried to establish a trading base in that country. To ensure that the Dutch would not become essential to trade, the Chinese refused to allow them to do anything more than transport goods in an already established trade circle. Once the Manchu dynasty was firmly established and the threat of Japanese piracy had decreased, the Chinese limited contact with foreigners to commercial relations only and allowed trading relationships to be established only at selected ports. As a result, no European power ever established a trading monopoly in China.

THE ROLE OF SLAVERY

For centuries, the continent of Africa had remained remote and mysterious to Europeans. Eventually, Europeans classified Africans as savages and inferior beings, perhaps to justify the slave trade, which became a crucial element in the European world economy. This view reveals the depth of European ignorance of this continent, where ancient civilizations had thrived. Cities such as the legendary

The Granger Collection, New York.

A sixteenth-century artist depicted some of the fantastic creatures that he imagined Marco Polo had seen during his travels. Pictures like this shaped European ideas about far-off lands.

Timbuktu (Tombouctou), where merchants made their greatest profits from selling books because so many people were scholars, and Benin, which was a thriving commercial and cultural centre, attest to the richness and vitality of the civilizations of Africa.

Europeans who visited West Africa in the late fifteenth century found not a savage wilderness but prosperous city-states linked by a vibrant system of trade. Inhabiting these cities were merchants, artisans, clerks, and labourers who lived comfortable lives. Although the technical knowledge of the Africans may not have been as great as that of the Europeans, Africans excelled in many other areas such as mining, metalworking, and tropical farming. They were also astute businesspeople, and had established sophisticated social and political systems.

The early Portuguese voyages to West Africa were prompted by the search for gold and spices. At first, the relationship between Portugal and the kingdoms of West Africa involved investigating each other's resources and making a decision to start trading. In exchange for textiles, wheat, brass utensils, and glass beads, the Portuguese received gold, pepper, ivory, gum, beeswax, leather, and timber — as well as slaves.

Initially, the slave trade was not an important element of this trading relationship. In time, however, the new plantations that were springing up in the Americas began to generate a demand for cheap labour. When this happened, the slave trade came to dominate African-Portuguese relations.

As early as 1501, Africans had been brought to the Caribbean island of Hispaniola. The slave trade did not begin in earnest until 1518, however, when the first cargo of African captives arrived in the Caribbean. The Dutch joined the slave trade after winning independence from Spain, and in 1626, the French built the fort of Saint Louis in Senegal, marking their entry into the trade in humans. When the English captured a Portuguese castle on the west coast of Africa, they too became slave traders.

Some historians have defended European participation in the slave trade by saying that Europeans did little more than take advantage of an existing trade that was embedded in African culture. Although it is true that trade in people was not new in either Africa or Europe, it had never been conducted on the scale of the trade that developed during the 1500s and continued in later centuries. In the 100 years between 1701 and 1801, for example, more than six million people were forcibly removed from Africa to supply the demand for slaves in Europe and the Americas.

What is more, the idea of **chattel slavery**, in which a slave and his or her children became nothing but property, had been unknown in Africa, though it had been common in Europe. Before contact with the Portuguese, a West African could become a slave in one of three ways:

- through pawnship, which means in settlement of a debt
- through crime, as a means of punishment
- through warfare, in which captives were enslaved

People who became slaves through pawnship did so only for a set period. Even those who were enslaved as criminals or captives could become functioning members of society.

This was not the case once Europeans entered the slave trade. Europeans introduced chattel slavery, provided a huge market for slaves, and encouraged a century of strife between African kingdoms. This warfare produced the prisoners who were sold into slavery.

The slave trade led to the massive depopulation of West Africa and the conscious underdevelopment

African slaves are shown working on a sugar plantation in Barbados. The slaves cut the sugar cane, and then processed it to produce molasses, which was distilled into rum. Notice the overseer in the foreground.

of the region. Exchanging only cheap manufactured goods for slaves, Europeans did not contribute to the region's infrastructure, a situation that contributed to West Africa's current status as part of the developing world.

THE GRAND EXCHANGE

When Columbus set sail in 1493 on his return visit to the Americas, he had no way of knowing how much this voyage would change the world. Aboard his 17 ships were seeds, fruit trees, and livestock. This cargo would start a revolution that would change forever the diet of the world — and form the basis of a trading process that is sometimes called the **grand exchange**.

The process is illustrated by sunflowers, which are native to the Great Plains of North America.

Exported to Europe, sunflowers thrived in cold northern areas and provided Russians with a welcome new cooking oil. In return, wheat, barley, and oats from Europe and the Middle East arrived in North America, eventually making the Great Plains the "breadbasket of the world."

Coffee and chocolate were other important crops in the grand exchange. Coffee had been cultivated in Africa and, later, Arabia before it was imported to the New World, where it became one of the most important crops of the Caribbean and Brazil. Cacao chocolate, which originated in tropical America, was exported to Europe where it was used to make cocoa and chocolate. Peanuts, vanilla, sweet and hot peppers, lima beans, pineapple, and tobacco are some of the many other crops that arrived in Europe and Asia from the New World. In addition to the grains mentioned earlier, cattle, horses, poultry, and pigs were exported from Europe to the New World, where they have become staples in contemporary diets.

Maize, a variety of corn native to the Americas, entered the peasant food chain in northern Spain, Portugal, and Italy in the form of animal food. It was also ground into flour. Columbus noted that in Cuba, corn was boiled, roasted, or ground into flour. The Spaniards took corn to the Philippines in the sixteenth century, and Chinese merchants there imported it to China. The Portuguese took it to Africa, where it was widely cultivated and used on slave ships. Tomatoes, which were first encountered by Spaniards in the valley of Mexico, also became a staple of the peasant diet in northern Spain, Portugal, and Italy.

Potatoes were another New World crop that changed European diets. Potatoes were used to provision ships returning to Europe and by 1573, the Seville poorhouse was buying them for the inmates. Knowledge of the potato spread to Spain's Italian possessions, and then to France, Germany, and Britain. At first, some people resisted growing potatoes, though enlightened monarchs of the eighteenth century encouraged their use as a food source. Potatoes were nutritious, could be grown on land not suitable for other crops, and helped ease the demand for wheat, which was more expensive to cultivate.

The "re-transmission" of foods from one area of the world to another occurred quickly. Within a century of Columbus's arrival in the New World, pineapples, papaya, and sweet potatoes had been transported across the Pacific to Asia. Manioc (cassava plant roots), rice, yams, cowpeas (edible plant seeds), and previously unknown citrus fruits were being imported to Africa before 1700. As well, by the sixteenth century, the turkey, a bird native to North and Central America, was well domesticated in Western Europe.

Sugar cane was planted in the New World as early as 1506. Although Arabs had cultivated sugar in the Mediterranean area since at least 750, most Europeans relied on honey to sweeten their food. This began to change when sugar was transported to the New World, where growing conditions were ideal. By 1550, at least five sugar plantations had been established in Brazil, and by 1623, this number had jumped to more than 350. By 1580, the sugar plantations of northeastern Brazil were a major source of revenue. When the Dutch attacked the Portuguese colony of Pernambuco, in present-day Brazil, during the seventeenth century, their goal was to take over this rich source of revenue. Coffee, tea, sugar, and spices were soon generating huge revenues and providing new sources of taxation for governments. The diet of the average European was now healthier and more varied than it had been a few centuries earlier.

THE PROCESS OF ACCULTURATION

European expansion and the globalization that resulted brought about significant change to most cultures. The process of **acculturation** altered all areas in which distinct cultures met. "Acculturation" is a term used to describe the process of change that occurs when societies with different cultural traditions come into contact and are altered because of this contact. Because elements of both cultures are preserved, acculturation is distinct from assimilation, which refers to the overwhelming of one culture by another.

Acculturation sometimes leads to the development of a new culture. This is what happened in

North America. As a result of European contact with the Aboriginal peoples, a new culture developed. This culture blended European and Aboriginal traditions.

The early European colonists brought with them the Christian religion, a new concept of land ownership, and European government and law, traditions, and foods. They also introduced a number of plants and animals to North America. Horses, sheep, cattle, and pigs were imported, as was the dandelion, which was brought over as a food source, and the starling, which was brought over to make Canada seem more like England.

For these early colonists, survival meant adapting to a new environment. This was most often

In the late 1500s, John White, an artist, accompanied expeditions to North America. His illustrations, such as the one shown here, provide an important record of Aboriginal life before it was changed forever by contact with the Europeans. Examine the picture. What information about Aboriginal society does it provide?

accomplished by learning from the native inhabitants. Maize became a regular part of the settlers' diet, smoking was a favourite pastime, and canoes and snowshoes were essential for travel. In this way, European customs blended with Aboriginal traditions. This process continues today, as Canadian culture becomes increasingly diverse.

The acculturation process was not as beneficial for the Aboriginal peoples. Although they initially benefited from trade with the Europeans, they were in time drawn into a market economy that led to a growing dependence on European traders. Many of the nomadic peoples altered their traditional patterns of hunting in order to maintain their trading relationships with Europeans. This led to clashes between Aboriginal groups and sometimes left them ill-prepared for winter, as they had been preoccupied with trading furs rather than with gathering winter food supplies.

As European diseases ravaged the Aboriginal population, their religious leaders began losing prestige because they could not prevent the tragedy that gripped their people. Traditional Aboriginal religions were supplanted by Christianity, which undermined Aboriginal social structures. The introduction of alcohol also contributed to the erosion of their society. Though the settlers successfully blended elements of European and Aboriginal cultures to create a strong, new culture, Aboriginal peoples suffered from their experience with acculturation.

Some cultures resisted contact with other societies, wishing to remain pure. Until the fourteenth century, China, for example, maintained extensive contacts with the outside world. During the Tang dynasty (618–906), the Chinese contact with India allowed Buddhism to make major inroads. During the Song dynasty, trade in the South Seas expanded greatly, and under the Mongols, trade with the West was reopened along the old Silk Roads. This brought

Muslim, Jewish, and Christian merchants to China.

China's increasing contact with the outside world came to an abrupt halt when the Ming drove out the Mongols and seized power in 1367. Seeking to return China to its traditional roots, the Ming stopped foreign exploration and contact with the outside world to promote stability at home. Severe restrictions were imposed on foreign trade.

The European demand for spices and tea, which had become a favourite drink in the West, brought European merchants back in search of trade. When the Manchu dynasty came to power in 1644, East-West trade resumed, but under very strict imperial control.

Still, the commercial activity that developed under the Manchu dynasty, and earlier, was to have important effects within China. By the sixteenth century, trade with the Portuguese and Spaniards along the southern coast had led businesses to start producing sugar, textiles, porcelain, and metal wares specifically for export to the West. In exchange, the Chinese received tobacco, sweet potatoes, and peanuts, all from the Americas.

Despite China's reluctance to engage in extensive foreign trade, its culture was drawn into a very complex international economy. In *Europe and the People Without History*, Eric Wolf noted: "To pay for tea, otter skins from the Northwest Coast of North America, sea cucumbers and sandalwood from the Pacific, silver from America, and Indian raw cotton and opium all began to flow toward China in a gigantic escalation of mercantile activity."

The worldwide exchange of goods and the increasing dependence of nations on international trade represented the early stages of the development of today's global village. Economies were becoming integrated, and the cultures of various regions were influencing one another. By the nineteenth century, food, clothing, music, art, and many other facets of life in many areas of the world had taken on an international flavour.

Echoes from the Past

This study of world history to the sixteenth century has now come full circle, and the echoes of the past resound all about us. Though each chapter has focused on a specific civilization, all have acknowledged the importance of outside influences on the culture studied.

Contact among peoples and the process of acculturation were not new in the fifteenth century. What was new was the extent of contact and the rapid changes that occurred because of the meeting of very distinct worlds. The modern age is, perhaps, best defined as the era in which the world ceased to be home to distinct cultures, which existed in relative isolation, and became an interconnected, global village.

No country better exemplifies the modern age than Canada. Home to people from a multitude of cultures, Canada is a product of the events that have reshaped the world since the fifteenth century. One need only stroll through cities such as Vancouver, Calgary, Toronto, Montreal, and Halifax to experience the cosmopolitan flavour of this country. Here, East and West, New World and Old, have integrated to create a rich, vibrant, and culturally diverse country. To truly understand and appreciate the histories and cultures that have come together to create this rich diversity, it is necessary to study the civilizations of the world. This is the way to become educated, not only about the history of the world, but also about the heritage of Canada.

Chapter Review

Chapter Summary

In this chapter, we have seen:

- that interaction among societies during the fifteenth and sixteenth centuries produced a variety of results
- how technological innovations and voyages of exploration contributed to the process of change
- how the processes of globalization and acculturation brought about change in many societies
- that understanding bias is critical to assessing the period of European exploration and expansion

Reviewing the Significance of Key People, Concepts, and Events (Knowledge/Understanding)

1. Understanding the history of the age of exploration requires an understanding of the following concepts and events and their significance in the development of early modern European society and the wider world. In your notes, identify and explain the historical significance of three items from each column.

Concepts	*Events*
world economy	voyages of Columbus
natural slaves	Spanish conquest of parts of Central America and the Caribbean
chattel slavery	grand exchange
acculturation	

2. In your notes, create a three-column chart that assesses the effect of globalization on various parts of the world. Title the first column "Area," the second "Effect of Globalization," and the third "Assessment of Effect (Positive or Negative)." In the first column, enter "Africa," "China," "India," "The Americas," and "Europe." Then complete the chart. Transfer three key ideas from the chart to the graphic organizer "Response to External Influences" in your *World History Handbook*.

Doing History: Thinking About the Past (Thinking/Inquiry)

1. What single factor do you believe was most important in deciding whether Europeans would dominate in their trading relationships with other peoples of the world? Write a paragraph describing and defending your choice.

2. Europeans believed that they were helping colonized peoples by exposing them to the benefits of Western civilization and the Christian faith. Write two paragraphs explaining why this belief was mistaken. In each paragraph, focus either on one area of the world or on one negative consequence of European contact.

Applying Your Learning (Application)

1. Create a Famous (or Infamous) Explorers trading card for each of the people on the following list. On the front of each card, include a picture or image of the person. On the back, include biographical details such as birthdate, birthplace, areas explored, and details of the person's interactions with indigenous peoples. To complete this activity, you may need to conduct additional research.

   Christopher Columbus
   Francisco Pizarro
   Hernán Cortés
   Bartolomé de Las Casas
   Giovanni Caboto (John Cabot)
   Ferdinand Magellan
   Vasco Núñez de Balboa

2. Select ten foods from your cupboards or refrigerator and determine where they were grown or processed. Next, find out where each food originated (e.g., potatoes are originally from South America). Once you have gathered this information, create a map of the grand exchange. Show the foods you selected, where they originated, and where they were grown or processed. Locate your community on the map and, for each food, use arrows to show how it made its way to your community. Write a paragraph summing up how the grand exchange has affected your life and attach the paragraph to the map.

Communicating Your Learning (Communication)

1. From the perspective of an early sixteenth-century European explorer, write a diary entry describing your first encounter with someone from the Americas, Asia, or Africa. Be sure that the cultural identity of the person selected is clear. Write a second diary entry describing the encounter from the non-European's perspective. Ensure that the two entries capture how the two views of this encounter might have differed.

2. Create a collage of images that capture the essence of the emerging capitalist world economy. Choose images that depict who or what was involved, the effects of capitalism on various groups, the importance of technology, and the global nature of capitalism. Transfer the central theme or idea of your collage to the graphic organizer "Economic Organization" in your *World History Handbook*.

Unit Review

Grading the Civilizations

1. In Chapter One, the essential elements of a civilization were outlined, and you were asked to rank each element in order of importance. Now that you have studied the Renaissance and early modern Europe, apply your ranking to this civilization. Below are three broad categories under which the elements can be clustered. For each category, provide a letter grade (from A+ to F) and an anecdotal comment of three to five sentences to support the grade. A fuller assessment of the civilization can be completed in your *World History Handbook*.

	Letter Grade	Comments
The Place of People • level of equality • just laws • distribution of wealth • overall quality of life		
Organization of Society • democratic • effective government • meets needs of society • provides security and stability for society		
Lasting Legacy • ideas • works of art • architecture • innovations/inventions • literature		

The Role of Individuals in History

1. Historians often grapple with whether history is shaped by individuals, or if individuals are products of their age and thus shaped by history. Would the history of Europe have been different if Leonardo da Vinci had not lived? Did Christopher Columbus change the direction of European history or the history of the Americas? The following is a list of people mentioned in this unit. Select any two. For each, identify his or her role in society, major accomplishments, sphere of greatest impact (e.g., art, ideas, religion, politics), and why you believe the person shaped or was shaped by history. You may want to do additional research on the two individuals you select.

Lorenzo de Medici   Leonardo da Vinci   Francesco Petrarch   Johannes Gutenberg

Michelangelo Buonarroti   Christopher Columbus   Niccolò Machiavelli

Understanding Chronology

1. The study of history relies on a sound understanding of the order in which events occurred. Without this understanding, it is difficult to make links between earlier events and later developments. The following questions help to illustrate the importance of understanding the chronology of history:

   a) Why does studying the Renaissance provide important background for students of modern European history?

   b) Why were humanist ideas essential to Michelangelo's creation of *David*?

   c) Though a Viking settlement existed in northern Newfoundland five hundred years before Columbus's voyage, little significance is attached to this early contact. Why?

Cause and Effect in History

1. History often involves the study of cause and effect. One cause may have several effects, or several causes may have one effect. Complete the cause-and-effect diagram provided by your teacher. Once you have completed the diagram, use it as a guide to write a paragraph on the issue addressed.

I. Methods of Historical Inquiry

Archaeological Interpretation and the Historian

Archaeology provides historical researchers with data that can help them reconstruct the past. Hollywood films such as *Raiders of the Lost Ark* leave the general public with the mistaken impression that most archaeological research takes place in the field. In fact, post-excavation analysis occupies most of the archaeologist's time, and is arguably the most important part of the work. Without careful analysis and documentation of finds, the material recovered during a dig would be nothing more than a random collection of artifacts and data of little value to historians.

Generally, archaeologists spend a few months at a dig site recovering objects, mapping and photographing sites, and gathering data from their excavations. The raw data is then taken back to laboratories, offices, and workrooms, where it is transformed into meaningful information. The post-excavation analysis usually takes at least twice as long as the excavation itself. The stages in the analysis of raw data are as follows:

1. As objects are recovered, they are sorted to determine which need conservation. Wood and leather objects often require immediate attention, and this may take place right at the site. Other objects, such as metalwork, are treated later.

2. Objects are carefully washed, recorded, and sorted into groups such as pottery sherds, worked flint, and bones from middens (garbage mounds). The artifacts are then sent to specialists to be studied. The specialists will identify the materials and determine their use, date, and other vital information.

3. In addition to the objects recovered, documentation of an excavation helps to reconstruct a comprehensive picture of the site. The documentation includes photographs, grid drawings of the site that also record stains in the soil (indicating post holes), and notes made by the archaeologists during the excavation.

4. Written and photographic documentation of an excavation is vitally important. During the excavation of any site, the soil is carefully removed in layers and records are made of what was found at each level. To get an accurate understanding of the past, it is critical that each level of occupation is clearly recorded and illustrated.

5. Each level of an excavation is referred to as a *context*. Separate records are made for each context. The relationship between contexts is recorded in a diagram like the one shown here. In a diagram such as this, it is possible to see the relationship of any one context to the rest of the site. The diagram also provides a visual representation of the history of the site. For example, the careful excavation and analysis of the Ball Site in Orillia, Ontario, revealed the length of habitation at the site — where buildings were built on top of earlier buildings — and the nature and purpose of some buildings.

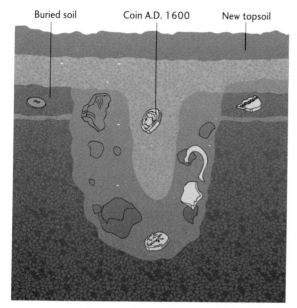

Buried soil   Coin A.D. 1600   New topsoil

Before excavating, the site is prepared by establishing a grid system over the entire area. This allows the archaeologists to accurately record where artifacts or stains in the soil were found. The first task is to remove the topsoil while watching for artifacts or changes in the colour of the soil. The technique used is called shovel shining, which involves carefully scraping the soil away using the edge of the shovel. Once artifacts begin to appear, a more meticulous method called troweling is used. Troweling is done by carefully scraping the edge of a trowel along the earth so as to remove the soil slowly.

6. Once the specialists have completed their reports, and the archaeologists have completed their analysis of a site and its contexts, a detailed technical report is published and made available to other archaeologists. This ensures that a permanent record of the excavation will be kept.

7. The final stage in the documentation of an archaeological site is the publication of a book or article for public reading. This general summary of the site replaces the technical terminology with language suitable for the public. This source is often the one that historians draw on

as they attempt to reconstruct the past. An archaeological excavation provides a detailed snapshot of a particular site over a given period of time. By reviewing evidence from a variety of sites for the same period, historians can reconstruct a general picture of a society at a particular time and place.

The Relationship Between Archaeology and History

In the Prologue and Chapter Three, the exploits of Heinrich Schliemann are discussed. At the time of his excavation, he received much criticism and opposition from archaeologists who feared that, as an amateur, Schliemann could cause irreparable damage to a site of enormous importance. The excavations at Troy revealed many layers of habitation of an ancient city that Schliemann did not properly record. Moreover, Schliemann photographed his wife Sophia wearing the priceless gold jewelry he had found in tombs.

Activities

Review the steps in analyzing an archaeological site and reflect on the importance of analysis and documentation in developing an accurate understanding of the past. Write a one-page letter to Schliemann commenting on his archaeological and historical methods.

II. Methods of Historical Inquiry

Writing Historical Biographies

The writing of historical biographies, while closely related to other forms of historical writing, poses unique challenges. Historical biographies attempt to reconstruct the lives of particular individuals within a historical context. This requires both an understanding of the time in which the individual lived and insights into the individual's life. Whereas other forms of historical writing consider general trends, biographies must scrutinize the lives of individuals in minute detail. Furthermore, it is crucial that writers of historical biographies examine the lives of their subjects through the eyes of the subject's era, not ours. One must become immersed in the times in which the subject lived to write a fair and successful biography. In addition, the biographer must never lose sight of the fact that the subject was a living human being whose emotions and idiosyncrasies may have, at times, led to actions that defy logical explanation.

A biography is not merely an account of the events of someone's life. The most engaging biography presents a clear point of view about the individual, supported and illustrated with historical evidence. Follow these practical suggestions when you try your hand at the art of historical biography:

- Immerse yourself in the time and place in which the individual lived. To understand the subject of your biography, you must understand the era and society in which she or he lived.

- Pay careful attention to contemporary views of the subject — how did those who knew and interacted with him or her view the individual's character and accomplishments?

- Carefully consider whether the individual was a product of the times (shaped by the forces of the society in which she or he lived) or a revolutionary figure who changed the course of history.

- Be sure to view the individual in the context of her or his own era. It is unfair to judge people of the past according to our values. Be careful not to make unsupported assumptions about the past.

- Pay close attention to your research sources. Who wrote the account of an event? Is there an obvious bias in favour of or against the individual? What was the purpose of the document you are using? Was it propaganda created to enhance or tarnish the image of the individual? If you are using a particular historian's account, how might his or her views have been influenced? Was there a hidden agenda underlying the text? Be aware that the era in which historians write has an impact on how they recreate the past.

- Use pictorial as well as written records. How has the individual been portrayed in painting or sculpture? Why was the work of art created? Was it commissioned by the subject? By someone else? Where would the work have been seen? In public? In a private place? What purposes did it serve?

- When you are ready to write your biography, formulate a thesis that clearly states the importance of the individual in history. Did the subject meet the personal challenges she or he set?

- Do more than present a chronology of your subject's life. Remember that a historical biography is an analysis of the individual's place in history.

- Provide relevant and necessary background, but avoid lengthy and unnecessary detail. Ensure that the information is needed to clarify or lay foundations to support your point of view.

- Make sure that the historical evidence you gather is used effectively to support the point of view set out in your thesis. Given the complex nature of the individual, be sure to explain any paradoxes or contradictions. If your research uncovers a character that was a tormented genius prone to violent fits, or a political leader whose decisions seemed inconsistent, make this part of your thesis. Present the individual as an enigma.

- Above all, do not lose sight of the subject of your biography as a human being. The individual's humanity may be the fact that best explains any irrational or contradictory behaviour.

This painting is from the Memoirs of Emperor Jahangir. Memoirs are a type of historical biography — an auto biography. How might this have affected the artist's approach to his subject.

III. Methods of Historical Inquiry

Analyzing Art: A Window on the Past

Prior to the invention of the camera in the mid-nineteenth century, art provided an important record of the past. Unlike written records, visual art served as a constant reminder of our ancestors, of great feats and great calamities, viewed in both public and private spaces. Much can be learned about a society through the art it produced. Art often mirrors the values and aspirations of a people and can provide a glimpse into their daily lives. Throughout *Echoes from the Past: World History to the 16th Century*, numerous works of art are displayed, and from them you can learn a great deal about the civilizations you are studying. Take the time to look carefully at the images in this text. You may be surprised at what you find. Here are some suggestions to help you get the most out these works of art.

1. **Identify the work of art:**
   Just as interpreting political cartoons requires an understanding of the issue it represents, so the analysis of a work of art depends on knowing its context. When and where was the artwork completed? Who was the artist? How might this individual's personal life have affected the work?

2. **Reflect on the audience and purpose of the work of art:**
   As with writing, audience and purpose often determine the nature of an artwork. For example, a portrait commissioned by a ruling monarch will attempt to portray her or him as positively as possible. A painting of an enemy in war will probably be less flattering. When viewing a work of art, consider its *patronage*

(who had it made) and its purpose (a portrait, as propaganda, for religious purposes, as a commemoration).

3. **Reflect on the importance of religion in the society that produced the art:**
   Art produced by very religious societies will most often employ religious imagery and symbols. Less religious societies are more likely to produce a larger body of secular (non-religious) art.

4. **Note the content of the work of art:**
   What has the artist chosen, or been told to depict? How have the central elements of the work been portrayed? Has religion or politics influenced the work of art? Look at all the details, in the foreground and the background, what do they tell you?

5. **Consider why the artist chose to use certain images:**
   Once you have carefully reflected on the purpose and content of the painting, consider the conventions (traditional styles or images) the artist used. Has the artist tried to show reality? Used symbols or traditional images to represent ideas? For example, the image of a skull may suggest death. A dove might be used to symbolize peace.

6. **Consider the artist's use of *chiaroscuro* (light and dark) to convey ideas:**

   The use of light and dark (as well as the use of colours) can convey important messages in a painting. Bright light and colours may suggest rebirth or happy subjects or ideas, while dark, heavy colours may suggest fear or evil. In many artworks you will see, light shining on a subject may represent a deity, or divine presence. How figures are portrayed in a painting (light or dark, etc.) can reveal a painter's bias.

7. **Consider the sizes of objects or people shown in a work of art:**

   In much of ancient art especially, the relative sizes of people or beings portrayed is highly significant. A god will typically be shown as larger than life. A ruler may have him- or herself depicted as much larger than an enemy.

8. **What is the value of the piece of art?**

   Works of art are valued by whole societies, even when a single individual commissioned the art. When viewing an artwork, consider the way in which that particular piece might be valued. Some works carry a material value; that is, they are valued primarily for the material with which they are made (i.e., gold, jewels). Other works of art have an intrinsic value in a given society. Paintings such as the *Mona Lisa* are valued because they are seen to have a timeless beauty. In some cases, the greatest value attached to an artwork is religious. A wooden sculpture of a god may be neither a masterpiece nor made of precious material, but be highly valued by those who worship and believe in the god. Similarly, some works of art carry a highly nationalistic or patriotic value, for example, a statue of Mao Zedong, the Parthenon, or the Statue of Liberty. Finally, some works of art may have a psychological value, unleashing a wide range of emotions from fright and outrage to amusement and pleasure. Of course, an artwork could be valued for one or several of these reasons.

Activities

Below are two works of art from very different societies. Write a paragraph comparing and contrasting them using the points above. Examine the pictures and captions carefully. Several of the steps outlined above should be covered in your paragraph.

Hunting in the Afterlife. Tomb fresco, Thebes, Egypt, ca. 1400 BCE.

Shiva, cast in bronze, from southern India, ca. 1000.

IV. Methods of Historical Inquiry

Techniques for Historical Research

Tackling a research essay in grade eleven can be a daunting task. How many sources do I need? How can I possibly read several long books? How come some sources seem to be different from others? These and many other questions flood the minds of students as they grapple with this task. Try the following useful strategies for carrying out historical research.

1. **Focus your research:**

   Before beginning your research, make sure you have narrowed down your topic to a manageable size. "World War II" is too broad a topic, whereas researching "The Role of Canada in the Development of Nuclear Weapons" is a more focused, manageable topic.

2. **Work from general to specific:**

   Never begin your research with a large, in-depth treatment of your topic. This will overwhelm you. Begin with general sources such as your textbook, encyclopedias, or general histories. Once you have a general grasp of your topic, you can begin your search for more specific information and make efficient use of in-depth sources.

3. **Make use of notes and bibliographies in other sources:**

   All the work done by other researchers is a goldmine for historical researchers. Most history books include a bibliography of sources, and notes (endnotes, footnotes or internal citations). Scan these to see what relevant sources are available on your topic. If you find a reference to the topic you are researching that is documented, check the citation (note); it may give you a great lead to a useful source.

4. **Begin with an extensive working bibliography:**

   When compiling a list of sources for your research, begin with an extensive working bibliography of 10 to 15 sources. A working bibliography is a list of sources that may be useful in researching your topic. It also assures you that there is ample information available on the topic. Once you have compiled a working bibliography and your sources, briefly scan them to see if each source is relevant, understandable, and useful.

5. **Use oral history where possible:**

   Do not forget that people are an invaluable source of information. If you know of anyone who lived through the period you are researching, be sure to arrange an interview to get this person's perspective on the topic.

6. **Use visual sources such as historical photographs and political cartoons:**

   Much can be learned about the past through historical photographs and political cartoons. Sources with visuals are much more interesting to work with and can help you visualize the information you are reading. Carefully examine cartoons and photographs to see what they reveal about the time period you are studying.

7. **Use film, music, literature, and art:**
There are documentary films and videos on many topics. Music, literature, and visual arts can also provide insights into the issues and attitudes of a generation. Do not limit your sources to the traditional print materials.

8. **Make effective use of the table of contents and index:**
Once you have narrowed your sources down to those most useful, you are ready to begin making research notes. The table of contents and index in a book are vital tools. Skim the table of contents to find relevant chapters, and look for specific topics in the index. It can save you a lot of research time.

9. **Use key words and phrases when doing electronic searches:**
Much like knowing how to use the table of contents and index of a book, the ability to use key words and phrases when searching electronic sources is an indispensable tool. Your School Librarian will be able to teach you some search techniques.

10. **Consider who wrote each source you use and what biases they may have had:**
As you are doing your research, be sure to reflect on the source of information. Does the author have a bias? Have you used a variety of sources to ensure that you have examined different viewpoints? When you find conflicting interpretations, consider the evidence used to support the point of view and the consistency with other sources. Remember, using one source is only a book review. A properly researched essay must draw on a variety of sources by a variety of authors.

V. Methods of Historical Inquiry

Working with Primary Documents

Primary sources take many forms, including the primary data gathered by archaeologists, diaries, journals, ships logs, letters, visual art, manuscripts, and government documents. You have already looked at visual arts and archaeology as primary sources; it is now time to consider the printed word.

Given their critical role in the study of history, knowing how to use written primary documents is essential. Incorrect or inadequate use of primary documents can have serious consequences. Imagine the view of the world in the 1930s we would have if the only primary sources we studied were those left by Nazi Germany. The same danger lies in any period of history. To study the life and times of Joan of Arc only through words left by her enemies, or Suleyman the Magnificent only through his official documents would surely create biased views of their lives. If historians are to construct as objective a view of the past as possible, they must explore as many versions of the events as possible. They must examine each source in light of the period in which it was created. One of the greatest challenges facing historians is the temptation to interpret the past through the eyes of the present. When we attempt to interpret the past based on present values, we invariably run the risk of writing biased history. For example, in this textbook you have read about several civilizations in which slavery was a normal practice, and in some cases, an indispensable factor in a civilization's survival. Is it fair for us to say that all these civilizations were evil or morally wrong, simply because our society finds slavery unacceptable today?

To avoid such pitfalls and meet the challenge of using primary documents, follow these guidelines:

1. Make sure you understand unfamiliar words. Look up any new words or phrases, or ask your teacher to help you define them.

2. How does the document fit in with what you believe you already know about the period? If the document seems to contradict what you believe, how will you test it and your assumptions about the period?

3. Who wrote the document, and why? How did the author's perspective and intentions shape the document?

4. Who was the intended audience? How might the document reflect or contradict the views of the audience?

5. Are other accounts of the same event available? If so, do they confirm the views held in the document being studied or challenge them? If there are differences between the documents, can they be explained by reviewing points 1 to 4 above?

Accounts from Different Perspectives: The Fall of Tenochtitlán

One of the most startling defeats in the history of the Americas was the rapid conquest of the Aztec capital of Tenochtitlán by the Spaniards under the leadership of Hernán Cortés. How do we explain the defeat of the powerful and larger Aztec force at the hands of a relatively small group of Spaniards? What can we learn about this conquest from the accounts of Spanish and Aztec observers? Below are two separate accounts of the fall of Tenochtitlán. Bernal Díaz, who had accompanied Cortés on his march on Tenochtitlán, wrote the first. Díaz describes an early assault on the Aztecs in which the Spaniards were driven back. The second source is the Florentine Codex, written in Nahuatl, the language of the Aztecs, and based on accounts by Aztec survivors. This document provides some insights into what happened between the attack described by Díaz and the final assault. How might these documents change or confirm your ideas about what actually happened during the Spanish Conquest?

Bernal Díaz, *The Conquest of New Spain* (1568)

[June 1520] The battle was fierce and the fighting was intense. It was a memorable sight to see us all streaming with blood and covered with wounds; and some of us were slain... And when we reached the top, some of us fighting and some lighting the fire, the papas who belonged to that cue were a sight to see! As we retired, however, four or five thousand Indians, every one a leading warrior, tumbled us down the steps six or ten at a time. Then there were some enemy bands posted on the battlements and in the embrasures of the cue, many who shot so many darts and arrows at us that we could face

neither one group of squadrons nor the other. So we resolved, with much toil and risk to our lives, to return to our quarters.

The Florentine Codex (ca. 1550)

[July 1520–May 1521] After the Spaniards had left the city of Mexico, and before they had made any preparations to attack us again, there came amongst us a great sickness, a general plague. It began in the month of Tepeilhuitl. It raged amongst us, killing vast numbers of people. It covered many all over with sores: on the face, on the chest, everywhere. It was devastating... Nobody could move himself, nor turn his head, nor flex any part of his body. The sores were so terrible that the victims could not lie face down, nor on their backs, nor move from one side to the other. And when they tried to move even a little, they cried out in agony...

Many died of the disease, and many others died merely of hunger. They starved to death because there was no one left alive to care for them... Many had their faces ravaged; they were pockmarked, they were pitted for life. Others lost their sight, they became blind.

The worst phase of this pestilence lasted sixty days, sixty days of horror... then it diminished, but it never stopped entirely... And when this happened, the Spaniards returned.

Activities

1. Apply steps one through five to both these documents.

2. What do your results tell you about the writing of history?

VI. Methods of Historical Inquiry

Writing a History Essay

Once you have gathered all your research materials, including primary and secondary sources, you are almost ready to begin writing your essay. The final two steps are formulating a thesis and preparing an essay outline.

Formulating a Thesis

A thesis is a statement of intent that clearly defines the argument presented in the essay. A good thesis does not merely identify the topic or state the obvious; it sets out an argument in two or three sentences. To be effective, a thesis must not only be clearly stated in the introduction, it also should be the focus of the entire essay. The purpose of the evidence presented throughout the essay is to support the thesis.

Examples

Weak Thesis: The pyramids of Egypt took many people to build. (This statement would be obvious to most people; there is no issue.)

Strong Thesis: Building the pyramids of Egypt would have been impossible without the slave labour made available through military and political conquests. (This thesis takes a clear stand on an issue that could be debated. You must now provide evidence to support this point of view.)

Preparing an Essay Outline

A strong history essay opens with an effective introduction that establishes the topic, the nature of the issue to be discussed, and the central thesis of the essay. The introduction is followed by a series of paragraphs that directly relate to the thesis and provide historical evidence and analysis that support it. An effective conclusion restates the thesis and connects the main arguments to the central argument, and brings the essay to a close. Remember, any idea or information borrowed from other sources must be given credit in your essay. This documenting of sources can be done in a variety of ways. Ask your teacher which method she or he wants you to use.

Writing Effective Introductions

A good introduction does much more than grab the reader's attention. It also states the intent of the essay by clearly defining the topic, the thesis, and the issues. An effective way to write a good introduction is to follow the "coffee filter" approach.

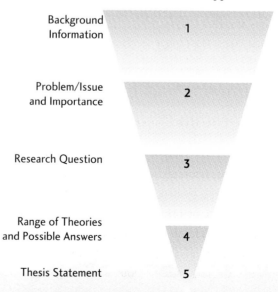

Background Information — 1

Problem/Issue and Importance — 2

Research Question — 3

Range of Theories and Possible Answers — 4

Thesis Statement — 5

The "coffee filter" model for an essay introduction.

Keeping the Thesis at the Forefront of Your Essay

To ensure that all your hard work pays off in an excellent essay, you will need to make effective use of your research to support your thesis. For each paragraph, carefully consider what historical evidence you will use and how you will relate this information to your thesis. Use this model as a guide to make sure that your essay has sound analysis.

Thesis: _____

_____

_____

Historical Evidence: _____

_____

_____

How I will relate the Historical Evidence

to my thesis: _____

_____

_____

Writing Effective Conclusions

An effective conclusion reviews the main points of the essay and draws them together in its final paragraph. A properly structured conclusion begins with a restatement of the thesis. This is followed by a brief discussion of major supporting points. The final statement should link all the above points and provide a final thrust to your thesis. A conclusion that works is a conclusion that stands on its own. If readers read only the conclusion, they should get a very clear sense of what the argument is and how it is presented and reinforced in the body of the essay.

In formulating your own conclusion, structure it by filling in the spaces under the following headings.

Restate Thesis: _____

_____

_____

List Major Supporting Points: _____

_____

_____

_____

Concluding Statement: _____

_____

_____

_____

_____

You may want to ask the following three questions after you have formulated your conclusion:

1. Can you identify the author's thesis?

2. What appear to be the major sections of the essay?

3. Is this approach an effective way to organize the main ideas in support of the thesis?

VII. Methods of Historical Inquiry

History's Place in Your Future Career

Consider the difference between thinking about careers in history and history's role in preparing you for a career. When we think about careers in history, we think about the many jobs that apply historical knowledge and skills. This can range from jobs in teaching at various levels, to working in museums and historic sites. But thinking about the role of history in preparing you for a career opens up a whole new range of possibilities.

Careers in History

If you have a passion for history, consider a career that enables you to apply your historical skills and knowledge directly. Examine the history web to see what captures your interest. Once you have identified a few careers you would like to know more about, do some research, talk to your teacher about contacting people in the field, and surf the Internet.

History's Role in Preparing You for A Career

History's importance in preparing you for a variety of careers extends well beyond those directly related to history. Think of the problems we would face if everyone who studied history in high school decided to get a history degree and work in a history-related field. The fact that most students sitting in the classroom at this time will not proceed to university to earn a history degree in no way diminishes the value of studying history. Below are the expectations for this course relating to the Methods of Historical Inquiry strand and the Employability Skills Profile prepared by the Conference Board of Canada. Notice how many of the skills and attributes that major cor-

porations identify as important in the workplace are reflected in the Methods of Historical Inquiry strand. While learning about the past, you also learn many vital skills, such as how to think creatively and critically, how to work collaboratively, and how to manage time effectively. Regardless of the career path you choose, the skills you develop while studying history will contribute to your future success.

Methods of Historical Inquiry
Overall Expectations

- demonstrate an ability to locate, select, and organize information from a variety of sources

- demonstrate an understanding of the steps in the process of historical interpretation and analysis

- communicate opinions based on effective research clearly and concisely

- demonstrate an ability to think creatively, manage time efficiently, and work effectively in independent and collaborative study

Specific Expectations
Research

- formulate significant questions for research and inquiry, drawing on examples from world history to the sixteenth century

- conduct organized research, using a variety of information sources

- organize research findings, using a variety of methods and forms

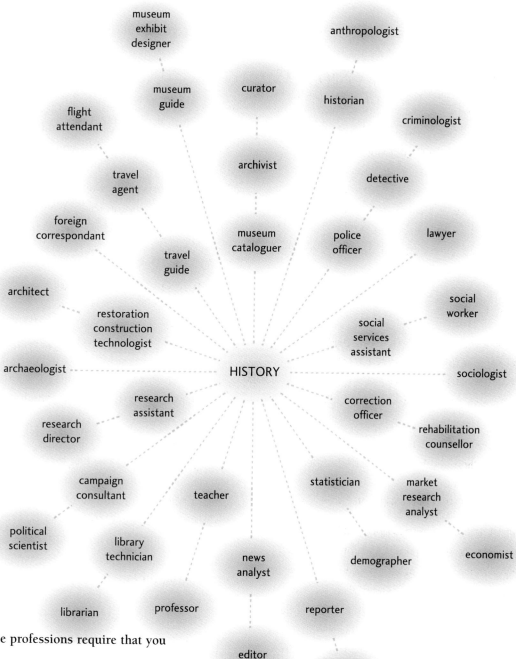

museum exhibit designer
anthropologist
museum guide
curator
historian
flight attendant
criminologist
archivist
travel agent
detective
foreign correspondant
museum cataloguer
lawyer
travel guide
police officer
architect
restoration construction technologist
social worker
archaeologist
HISTORY
social services assistant
sociologist
research assistant
research director
correction officer
rehabilitation counsellor
campaign consultant
statistician
market research analyst
teacher
political scientist
library technician
demographer
economist
news analyst
librarian
professor
reporter
editor
journalist

All these professions require that you

- work co-operatively with people
- have effective communication skills
- understand cause and effect relationships
- are able to formulate and ask good questions
- have research skills
- have the knowledge to establish a context for your thinking

Interpretation and Analysis

- demonstrate an ability to distinguish bias, prejudice, stereotyping, or a lack of substantiation in statements, arguments, and opinions

- compare key interpretations of world history

- identify and describe relationships and connections in the data studied

- draw conclusions based on effective evaluation of sources, analysis of information, and awareness of diverse historical interpretations

- demonstrate an ability to develop a cogent thesis substantiated by effective research

Communication

- communicate effectively, using a variety of styles and forms

- use an accepted form of academic documentation effectively and correctly

- express opinions and conclusions clearly, articulately, and in a manner that respects the opinions of others

Creativity, Collaboration, and Independence

- demonstrate an ability to think creatively in reaching conclusions about both assigned questions and issues and those conceived independently

- use a variety of time-management strategies effectively

- demonstrate an ability to work independently and collaboratively and to seek and respect the opinions of others

- identify career possibilities related to the study of history

A Convergence of Skills and Knowledge

Some of the most exciting opportunities to apply history skills and knowledge are provided by the convergence of history with other skill sets. For example over the past decade, many of the most popular Hollywood films have been based on historical events: *Schindler's List*, *Titanic*, *Gladiator*, and even *Star Wars*.

Despite its futuristic setting, much of the *Star Wars* series borrows heavily from the past. The pod race in *The Phantom Menace* was an adaptation of a Roman chariot race, while the costume design drew heavily from ancient China. Computer games such as *Civilization*, and theatrical productions such as *Les Miserables*, are more enjoyable with an understanding of the past they reflect. The blending of historical knowledge and skills with other skill sets creates highly sought-after individuals. Michael Crichton's 1999 novel *Timeline* features a billionaire computer genius with a passion for history who finances the archaeological excavation of a medieval town in France. Using the historical expertise of a select team (and an understanding of quantum physics), the billionaire's company manages to transport people to France in the year 1357. Fiction? Of course, but this scenario certainly highlights the exciting potential for those with imagination and an understanding of the present, future, and *past*.

Activities

1. Choose five Employability Skills and match them up with five Methods of Historical Inquiry expectations.

2. Can you think of any other careers to add to the History Web?

Employability Skills 2000+

These are the skills you need to enter, stay in, and progress in the world of work— whether you work on your own or as part of a team. These skills can be acquired and used beyond the workplace in a range of daily activities.

Fundamental Skills

The skills needed as a base for further development. You will be better prepared to progress in the world of work when you can:

Communicate

- Read and understand information presented in a variety of forms (e.g., words, graphs, charts, diagrams)
- Write and speak so others pay attention and understand
- Listen and ask questions to understand and appreciate the points of view of others
- Share information using a range of information and communications technologies (e.g., voice, e-mail, and computers)
- Use relevant scientific, technological and mathematical knowledge and skills to explain or clarify ideas

Manage Information

- Locate, gather and organize information using appropriate technology and information systems
- Access, analyze and apply knowledge and skills from various disciplines (e.g., the arts, languages, science, technology, mathematics, social sciences and the humanities)

Use Numbers

- Decide what needs to be measured or calculated
- Observe and record data using appropriate methods, tools and technology
- Make estimates and verify calculations

Think & Solve Problems

- Assess situations and identify problems
- Seek different points of view and evaluate them based on facts
- Recognize the human, interpersonal, technical, scientific and mathematical dimensions of a problem
- Identify the root cause of a problem
- Be creative and innovative in exploring possible solutions
- Readily use science, technology and mathematics as ways to think, gain and share knowledge, solve problems and make decisions
- Evaluate solutions to make recommendations or decisions
- Implement solutions
- Check to see if a solution works, and act on opportunities for improvement

Personal Management Skills

The personal skills, attitudes and behaviours that drive one's potential for growth. You will be able to offer yourself greater possibilities for achievement when you can:

Demonstrate Positive Attitudes and Behaviours

- Feel good about yourself and be confident
- Deal with people, problems and situations with honesty, integrity and personal ethics
- Recognize your own and other people's good efforts
- Take care of your personal health
- Show interest, initiative and effort

Be Responsible

- Set goals and priorities, balancing work and personal life
- Plan and manage time, money and other resources to achieve goals
- Assess, weigh and manage risk
- Be accountable for your actions and the actions of your group
- Be socially responsible and contribute to your community

Be Adaptable

- Work independently or as part of a team
- Carry out multiple tasks or projects
- Be innovative and resourceful: identify and suggest alternative ways to achieve goals and get the job done
- Be open and respond constructively to change
- Learn from your mistakes and accept feedback
- Cope with uncertainty

Learn Continuously

- Be willing to continuously learn and grow
- Assess personal strengths and areas for development
- Set your own learning goals
- Identify and access learning sources and opportunities
- Plan for and achieve your learning goals

Work Safely

- Be aware of personal and group health and safety practices and procedures, and act in accordance with these

Teamwork Skills

The skills and abilities needed to contribute productively. You will be better prepared to add value to the outcomes of a task, project or team when you can:

Work with Others

- Understand and work within the dynamics of a group
- Ensure that a team's purpose and objectives are clear
- Be flexible: respect, be open to and supportive of the thoughts, opinions and contributions of others in a group
- Recognize and respect people's diversity, individual differences and perspectives
- Accept and provide feedback in a constructive and considerate manner
- Contribute to a team by sharing information and expertise
- Lead or support when appropriate, motivating a group for high performance
- Understand the role of conflict in a group to reach solutions
- Manage and resolve conflict when appropriate

Participate in Projects & Tasks

- Plan, design or carry out a project or task from start to finish with well defined objectives and outcomes
- Develop a plan, seek feedback, test, revise and implement
- Work to agreed quality standards and specifications
- Select and use appropriate tools and technology for a task or project
- Adapt to changing requirements and information
- Continuously monitor the success of a project or task and identify ways to improve

Glossary

Acculturation The blending of two or more cultures that results in the creation of a new culture.

Adze A heavy hand tool with a steel cutting blade attached at right angles to a wooden handle. Used especially for squaring timber.

Alluvial plain Extensive accumulations of clay, silt, sand, or gravel deposited by running water forming a level or gently sloping surface.

Alms Food, money, clothing, or other items given as charitable gifts to help the poor.

Amalgamation An independent whole that results from the uniting and combining of various factors or elements.

Ancestor veneration Honouring the spirits of dead ancestors with the intent of avoiding evil and being granted good fortune.

Animism The belief that everything, such as plants, stones, or natural phenomena like thunderstorms, has a spirit that is able to affect situations by exerting a positive or negative influence.

Anthropology The study of the anatomical and mental make-up of humanity, by examining historic and present geographical distribution, cultural history, acculturation, cultural relationships, and racial classification.

Anthropomorphic Attributing, in description or representation, human characteristics and/or appearance to non-human things.

Apostate One who has abandoned his or her religious faith or given up moral allegiance.

Artisans Craftspeople involved in a variety of trades, such as potters, cobblers, tailors, and clockmakers.

Assimilation The cultural absorption of one group into another.

Autocracy A form of government in which one person holds absolute and unlimited power and authority.

Autonomy The political control and moral freedom possessed by a political unit, community, or group as it relates to the larger political structure of which it is a part.

Ayllus (*ay-yous*) Ayllus were Inca descent groups — people descended from a single ancestor or male/female pair. Ayllus were composed of varying numbers of families. Ayllus held land in common and allocated plots to individual families within the ayllu each year. Members of an ayllu marry other members of the same ayllu.

Beneficium Property bestowed on a person by a lord in return for unspecified work; in a religious context it can also mean the granting of a church office.

Benevolent Being kind and generous and taking pleasure in doing good works, which may result in the happiness and prosperity of others.

Bishopric The administrative area under the jurisdiction of the bishop; the office of a bishop, or the bishop's seat or residence.

Borough In medieval times, a group of fortified houses forming a town, having duties and privileges, courts, representatives in councillor parliament, and holding an inheritable charter from the king.

Bridgehead An area seized in hostile territory and used as a foothold in further advancements.

Bronze Age The period of human culture between the Stone and Iron Ages, distinguished by the use of bronze tools and weapons and intensive trade; beginning in the Middle East about 4500 BCE and lasting in Britain from about 2000 to 500 BCE.

Bureaucracy A structured, centralized, and inflexible system of government or rule characterized by a hierarchy of authority with a powerful group of officials basing their actions on fixed rules.

Burgess A representative of the small minority who held full legal rights in a British town or city. The duties included holding public office, entertaining visiting officials, and granting loans to the king. The governing body of the town gave the status of burgess as prescribed in a town's charter. A comparable modern office would be membership in a chamber of commerce.

Canon law A written group of religious laws for the government of a church or for the members of a particular faith.

Capitalism An economic system based on the private ownership of the means of production, distribution, and exchange. Also characterized by the use of money to earn money through usury or trade.

Caste A division within a society based on wealth, inherited rank or privilege, profession or occupation.

Chattel slavery A type of slavery that assumes the slaves are items of personal and moveable property.

Slaves and their descendants are held as slaves in perpetuity and are not held in lieu of debt for a specified period of time.

Chivalry The system of knighthood based on the character of the ideal knight who exhibits honour, protective kindness to the weak, generosity to friends as well as enemies, and flawless gallantry.

City-state An independent, self-governing city such as ancient Athens or Renaissance Florence.

Classical Age While many civilizations have periods referred to as "Classical," the term "Classical Age" has generally been used by most Western historians to mean the civilizations of ancient Greece and Rome.

Confederacy A group or league formed by people or political units for mutual support or for achieving common goals.

Conquistadors Usually refers to the Spanish conquerors of the Americas in the sixteenth century.

Cosmopolitan Being sophisticated and knowledgeable about the world; having a wide vision and not restricted by regional beliefs, attitudes, prejudice, or interests.

Cultural diffusion The spread of the characteristics and traits of a culture to other cultures and inhabitants in other areas.

Deify The process of giving someone the status of a god with divine power.

Demigod A divine or semi-divine being, sometimes the offspring of a mortal and a god, who carries less power than a god; e.g., Herakles.

Desiccation The process of drying.

Despotism A system of government in which the ruler has absolute power and authority.

Dhow A two-masted sailing vessel commonly used in the Arab and Asian worlds.

Diaspora A dispersion of people of a common national origin or of common beliefs into other countries; often used with reference to the dispersion of the Jews.

Diocese An administrative division of the Roman Catholic church, usually the district where the bishop had authority.

Duchy The dukedom or lands ruled by a duke or duchess, nobles of the highest hereditary rank.

Dynasty A succession of rulers coming from the same family or the same line of descent.

Ecosystem A unit that combines the living and non-living elements of an ecological system.

Egalitarian Used to describe a group or society wherein everyone is equal and equally entitled to the rights and privileges of the group or society.

Enfranchisement The freeing, and giving of political rights to a town or a city under feudal law; the freeing of lands previously held as a fiefdom; giving the vote to someone or a group.

Entrepreneur A person who organizes, owns or manages an economic venture and who usually assumes all the risks, financial or otherwise.

Ethnohistory A means of studying the past through aspects of culture such as folklore, religion, oral traditions, and customs.

Ethnology The science that deals with the racial or national divisions of humanity through comparison and analysis of origins, distribution, relations, characteristics, cultures, and societies.

Etymology The origin of a sound or a word based on its earliest recorded use and by identifying cognates (similar words) in other languages.

Eunuch A castrated man, often employed in a harem or holding some other occupation in a palace.

Eurocentric A world view that measures aspects of all civilizations in relation to European standards; implying a belief in the intrinsic superiority of European culture.

Faïence Pottery or porcelain decorated with coloured opaque glazes.

Feudalism A social system that encompassed the legal and social organization of medieval Europe. This included the granting of fiefs and a series of contractual obligations between the lord and his vassals.

Fief (also **feoff**) A grant of land held in return for a specified service (usually military).

Fiefdom A feudal estate or territory held by a vassal.

Fluvial deposits The deposits produced by the flowing action of a river.

Fratricide The act of murdering a brother or sister or someone who is very close.

Fresco The painting of fresh moist plaster with water-based paints, often done on large surfaces (walls) resulting in brightly coloured murals.

Friar A member of a religious order in which monastic life and religious activity are combined, and the possession of property is forbidden.

Genealogy A historical account, in the order of succession, of the descent of a person or family.

Gentry The people of the upper class wielding large economic and social influence. Wealth and power generally derived from political appointments, since they are not part of the nobility. Although of the upper class, the position of the gentry is more volatile than that of members of the aristocracy.

Genus A class or group marked by one or several common characteristics.

Hieroglyph (also **hieroglyphics**) A picture or symbol that represents an idea, sound, or object.

Hominid Any primate belonging to the family *Hominidae* (includes modern humans).

Humanoid Resembling a human in appearance.

Iconoclasm The attacking of established and traditional beliefs, often including the destruction of religious icons or sacred objects.

Iconography The symbols used in a work of art or art movement.

Ideology A body of ideas and concepts.

Impress To commandeer or coerce people or their property into government service.

Indigenous Having originated, developed, or been produced in a particular land, region, or environment.

Infidel A person who has no religious belief or who rejects a specific religion, especially Christianity or Islam.

Insular Being remote or isolated.

Investiture The act of granting an office or a title. This act is often accompanied by a ceremony and by the transfer of the symbols of this particular office or position.

Jurisprudence The science or philosophy of law.

Kingdom A territory or state ruled by a monarch (king or queen).

Koran See **Qur'an.**

Linguistics The scientific study of language.

Lord A male member of the nobility or someone of whom a fee or estate is held in feudal tenure, often the master of the manor or a person who holds power and authority over others.

Machu Pichu (*ma-chew pea-chew*) An Inca settlement on the eastern slopes of the Andes near Cuzco. Machu Pichu was one of the royal estates of the emperor Pacha Kutiq.

Manumission Formal release from slavery or from feudal obligations.

Martyrdom The suffering or death of a person, caused by their refusal to renounce beliefs or adherence to a particular religious faith.

Matriarch The female head of a family, tribe, community, or dynasty who rules by dictatorship and without male influence.

Mausoleum A building that serves as a tomb, usually for a number of people.

Megalomania A mental state in which a person believes they have the ability to perform great feats, and characterized by delusions of grandeur, power, and wealth.

Mendicants People who beg and live by begging.

Mercenary A soldier hired into foreign service in an army to which he holds no allegiance.

Metaphysical Dealing with ideas or elements that lie outside the realm of everyday life.

Millennium A period spanning 1000 years.

Mindalaes (*mean-dah-lah-ace*) These were traders sponsored by the Ecuadorian chiefs, and later the Incas. The term is related to the verb "to walk" and indicates that members of this class of trader were also porters, carrying their goods from place to place. Sponsored by the elite, they specialized in transporting high-valued, lightweight items. Strings of beads made from the Spondylus shell served as a form of currency, a standardized measure of value.

Mitmaq (*meet-mawck*) Colonists who were moved from one part of the empire to another by the Inca government. Loyal subjects were moved into newly conquered areas to help pacify them, teach the inhabitants Quechua (the Incan language), and serve as garrison troops. Sometimes people were moved to exploit specific resources.

Monolithic Consisting of a large, complete unit that is uniform and has no diversity or variation.

Monotheism The belief or doctrine that states that there is only one god.

Moors The Muslim people of North Africa who trace their heritage to the Arabs and Berbers.

Mosque A Muslim place of worship.

Muslims Followers of the religion of Islam.

Myth A story involving gods and/or superhuman beings, which was seen by early humanity as a true account of how a natural phenomenon or social custom came into being.

Neolithic The new or latest period of the Stone Age, which was characterized by developments such as the grinding stone, making pottery, domesticating animals, cultivating grain, weaving linen, and the beginnings of a settled village life.

Ochre Earth containing natural pigments that are used in creating yellow, orange, or red colours for paints.

Oracle An agent of divine or supernatural communication; also the place where this communication occurs.

Pagan A person who follows a polytheistic religion. The term was generally applied to worshippers of religions other than Christianity, Judaism, or Islam.

Paleoanthropology The branch of anthropology relating to primitive humanity.

Paleolithic The second period of the Stone Age when primitive humanity emerged and manufactured unpolished stone tools. The time period was from about 2.5 to 3 million years ago up to about 12 000 BCE.

Paleontologist A person who studies prehistoric life forms through the study of plant and animal fossils.

Pandemic Affecting an exceptionally large percentage of the population over a wide geographic area; often an extensive epidemic.

Pantheon The collective gods of a religion; a temple built to all the gods.

Papal see The jurisdiction, such as the seat or centre, of the power and authority of a pope.

Pastoral nomadism A nomadic lifestyle based on the search for pastureland for herds of livestock.

Patriarchy A system based on the male head of a family, community, tribe, or dynasty.

Patrimony An inheritance from one's father or ancestors.

Peasant A broad term that encompasses both free peasants and servile peasants. Free peasants could own their own land and legally owed no obligation to a lord other than the king. Servile peasants, also known as serfs or villeins, did not own their own land but held a tenement from a lord. These people were tied to the soil in that they owed feudal obligations to a lord and were not free to leave the manor. Serfs could obtain the status of freemen if the lord chose to grant manumission.

Pharaonic Relating to, or of, a Pharaoh of ancient Egypt.

Philanthropy Goodwill towards humanity demonstrated by performing charitable or benevolent actions, or donating money.

Pi The symbol π, representing the ratio of the circumference of a circle to its diameter.

Pilgrimage A journey to a shrine or other sacred site undertaken for religious or spiritual reasons.

Polity Refers to a political organization, a form of government, or the constitution of a political unit.

Polyandry A form of marriage wherein a woman has more than one husband at the same time.

Polytheist A person who believes in or worships more than one god.

Pottage Oatmeal or vegetables cooked to the consistency of a stew or thick soup.

Primates An order of mammals that includes humans, apes, monkeys, and lemurs.

Primeval Relating to or being from the earliest stages of the world or human history.

Primogeniture The exclusive right of the first child of the same parents to inherit the property or estate of their ancestors.

Priory A community of religious people led by a prior living under the jurisdiction of an abbey.

Proto-human Any of the prehistoric primates that are related to or resembled early modern humans.

Qombi (*kom-bee*) The finest quality Inca cloth, usually woven by specialists. The finest qombi was multicoloured tapestry.

Qoya (*koy-ya*) The term used to designate the Inca queen. The Qoya was, at least during the late part of the Inca dynasty, the full sister of the Sapa Inca.

Quechua (*quech-wa*) Quechua is what we now call the language of the Inca. To the Inca themselves, the quechua was an ecological zone in the highlands, located approximately 3300 m above sea level, where it was possible to grow maize (a form of corn). It was also used to refer to the people who lived in that ecological zone.

Qur'an The sacred book of Islam composed of the revelations of the Prophet Muhammad.

Realpolitik Politics based on practical and material factors, political realities, or the realities of national interest and power.

Regionalism The development of a political or social system based on smaller political units or regions that may divide the country.

Relief Sculpture in which figures are distinguished by being raised from or sunk into the surrounding flat surface.

Rhetoric The art of expressive speech and effective communication.

Sapa Inca (*sap-pa een-ka*) The word "Inca" is used in several different ways. The term sometimes refers to the emperor himself. In this sense, the Inca used the term "Sapa Inca" to mean the only or unique Inca, as one title for the Inca emperor.

Secular Relating to worldly as opposed to things or ideas concerned with or related to religion.

Semitic A branch of the Afro-Asiatic family of languages that includes Arabic, Hebrew, Aramaic, Amharic, as well as ancient languages such as Akkadian and Phoenician.

Sericulture The production of raw silk by the cultivation of silkworms.

Servility Being obedient to or dominated by a person or thing, usually as a slave.

Shamanist A person who practises or believes in the powers of a shaman, a priest doctor who uses magic to cure the sick, to divine the future, to control the good and evil spirits of the world.

Simony The selling or buying of a church office.

Social contract An agreement that results in the creation of an organized society with a ruler and a community, and defines the rights and duties of its people.

Species A biological class of related living organisms having common attributes and the ability to breed.

Stele (plural **stelae**) An upright stone slab decorated with pictures or inscriptions.

Strata A succession of deposits one on top of another so that the uppermost deposits, or layers, are later in date than the lower ones.

Suzerain A feudal lord or a political state or sovereignty exercising some degree of control over a dependent state, often in the control of its foreign affairs.

Synod The meeting of an ecclesiastical council, a church governing or advisory body, usually of a diocese to discuss church matters.

Tambo (*tahm-bow*) A stopping place along the royal roads of the Inca where provisions and other facilities were found. Some of the largest tambos also served as the administrative centres for entire provinces.

Tawantinsuyu (*ta-wan-tin-sue-you*) The Inca name for their empire. The word emphasizes the wholeness of the Inca empire: tawa means "four," suyu is a territorial division, and tin indicates that the four divisions are all taken together as one whole.

Tectonic plates It is believed that Earth's crust is made up of a number of plates known as tectonic plates. Since Earth's core is fluid, these plates occasionally shift, creating mountain ranges, volcanic activity, earthquakes, and tidal waves.

Temporal Relating to secular as opposed to spiritual or religious affairs; of or relating to a particular time.

Tenement Property held in tenure by one person or another. Also, buildings in a city divided into units or rooms, usually for poor people.

Theocracy A government or a state under religious rule, directed by or administered by a god or religious officials such as priests or clergy.

Theologian A specialist in, or a person engaged in, the study of religion.

Third Estate In medieval Europe, society was broadly divided into three estates: the First Estate was the Estates Temporal (the aristocracy); the Second Estate was the Estates Spiritual (religious leaders); the Third Estate was the Estates Common (the common people, including the gentry). Later, journalists were called the Fourth Estate.

Tithe A tenth of the yearly agricultural yield, personal income, or profits contributed as a tax or voluntarily for religious purposes and for the support of the Church and clergy.

Transubstantiation The doctrine or belief that the substance of bread and wine changes into the substance of the body and the blood of Christ when consecrated by the Eucharist.

Tribute Homage or payment made by a vassal to his lord, or a sum of money or valuables paid by one ruler or nation to another as acknowledgement of submission, and often as payment for peace and protection.

Triremes Greek warships from the fifth century BCE that were fast, manoeuvrable, and powered by three tiers of rowers.

Usury The practice of loaning money and charging interest for its use.

Vassal A person who holds a fief (or feoff) from a superior lord. Vassals do not include peasants, as they held a tenement.

Vernacular The commonly spoken language or dialect of a particular people of a region or country, which contrasts with the literary or cultured form of the language.

Virgins of the Sun Girls who were selected by Inca officials to serve the state religion. They were chosen as the most beautiful and unblemished girls of the empire when they were about 12 years old. They were placed in special houses where they were taught the skills appropriate to high-status women, especially fine weaving and preparation of ceremonial foods. Later, the Sapa Inca took some as concubines, while others were given to favoured nobles and warriors as wives. Others dedicated their lives in chastity to the service of the cult of the sun.

Wak'a (*wa-ka*) Among the Inca, wak'as were powerful spiritual forces. Many things were seen as wak'as, including: large rocks, springs, lakes, mountains, twins, babies born feet first, unusual ears of maize or oddly shaped chili peppers, the sun, the moon, some stars, the ocean, and the earth.

Xenophobic To be afraid of or to hate strangers or foreigners, their politics, and their culture; fearing or hating anything strange or foreign.

Yeoman A member of the most respected class of common people, the small freeholders who ranked below the gentry and cultivated and farmed their own land.

Credits

Photos

page 2 Comstock Images/Bill Wittman; page 5 Tony Stone Images/Terry Vine; page 6 Garfield Newman; page 7 CP Picture Archive/Leila Gorchev; page 9 Maria Stenzel/National Geographic Society Image Collection; page 10 O. Louis Mazzatenta/National Geographic Society Image Collection; page 13 left Private Collection/Bridgeman Art Library, right Christopher A. Klein/National Geographic Society Image Collection; page 15 Réunion des Musées Nationaux/Art Resource, NY; page xii top, xiii top left, 20 top and centre right, 22 top, 24 top, 52 top, 54 top Robert Harding Picture Library; page 22 bottom right Ancient Art & Architecture Collection; page xvi bottom right, 25 Jay Matternes/National Geographic Society Image Collection; page 28 Mary Jellisse/Ancient Art & Architecture Collection; page 29 Natural History Museum, London UK/Bridgeman Art Library; page 30 Erich Lessing/Art Resource, NY; page 32 Art Resource, NY; page 34 Naturhistorisches Museum, Vienna, Austria/Ali Meyer/Bridgeman Art Library; page 36 Erich Lessing/Art Resource, NY; page 41 Courtesy of the Oriental Institute of the University of Chicago; page 42 Erich Lessing/Art Resource, NY; page 45 British Museum, London, UK/Bridgeman Art Library; page 46 Erich Lessing/Art Resource, NY; page 48 Ur, Iraq/Bridgeman Art Library; page xii bottom, 20 bottom, 52 bottom left, bottom right Scala/Art Resource, NY; page 58 SEF/Art Resource, NY; page xiv bottom left, 63 Giraudon/Art Resource, NY; page 64 Erich Lessing/Art Resource, NY; page 65 top Giraudon/Art Resource, NY, bottom Erich Lessing/Art Resource, NY; page 66 Erich Lessing/Art Resource, NY; page 67 Scala/Art Resource, NY; page 69, 655 centre Werner Forman/Art Resource, NY; page xiii middle, 70 Erich Lessing/Art Resource, NY; page 71 *Mummy of a Man with funerary portrait*, c. CE 200. Human remains/linen/wood with encaustic painting, length: 167 cm (65 3/4 in.). Gift of Egyptian Research Account, Courtesy Museum of Fine Arts, Boston; page 72 Werner Forman/Art Resource, NY; page xiv top centre, 75 Giraudon/Art Resource, NY; page 80 Vanni/Art Resource, NY; page xiv bottom centre, 81 Art Resource, NY; page 85 © Gianni Dagli Orti/CORBIS/MAGMA; page 86 Art Resource, NY; page xiii bottom right, 87 The Jewish Museum, NY/Art Resource, NY (detail); page 94 Nimatallah/Art Resource, NY; page 96 Garfield Newman; page 102 Michos Tzovaras/Art Resource, NY; page 103 Erich Lessing/Art Resource, NY; page 104 Erich Lessing/Art Resource, NY; page 105 Garfield Newman; page xiii top centre, 107 Image Select/Art Resource, NY; page 108 Nimatallah/Art Resource, NY; page 110 Scala/Art Resource, NY; page 112 Garfield Newman; page 114 Nimatallah/Art Resource, NY; page 115 Scala/Art Resource, NY; page 122 Erich Lessing/Art Resource, NY; page 124 left Nimatallah/Art Resource, NY, right Erich

page 278 Robert Aberman/Barbara Heller/Art Resource, NY. Great Zimbabwe, Zimbabwe (Rhodesia); page 283 Giraudon/Art Resource, NY; page 292 bottom right, 655 bottom right Réunion des Musées Nationaux/Art Resource, NY, page 292, 294, 296, 326, 328, 364, 366 top right, 302, Giraudon/Art Resource, NY; page 294 bottom right, 297, 298, 301 Borromeo/Art Resource, NY; page 304 SEF/Art Resource, NY; page 305 left Borromeo/Art Resource, NY, right SEF/Art Resource, NY; page 309, 653 Giraudon/Art Resource, NY; page 310 Tony Stone Images/Chris Noble; page 311 Werner Forman/Art Resource, NY; page 314 © Earl & Nazima Kowall/CORBIS/MAGMA; page 316 Image Bank/Andrea Pistolesi; page 320 Borromeo/Art Resource, NY; 292, 294, 296, 326, 328, 364, 266 bottom left, 326, 364 bottom left Ontario Science Centre; page 331 left Erich Lessing/Art Resource, NY, right Photograph courtesy of Royal Ontario Museum © ROM; page 333 Vanni/Art Resource, NY; page 335 Photograph courtesy of Royal Ontario Museum © ROM; page 337 Art Resource, NY; page 338, 339 Erich Lessing/Art Resource, NY; page 340 Tony Stone Images/Keren Su; page 343 Giraudon/Art Resource, NY; page 345 © The British Museum; page 346 Private Collection/Bridgeman Art Library; page 348 left, right Ontario Science Centre; page 349 Photograph courtesy of Royal Ontario Museum © ROM; page 350 Ontario Science Centre; 351 Courtesy of The Bata Shoe Museum; page 352 Ontario Science Centre; page 353 Victoria & Alberta Museum, London/Art Resource, NY; page 357 Tony Stone Images/Michael McQueen; page 360 © CORBIS/MAGMA; page 364 The Newark Museum/Art Resource, NY; page 369 Scala/Art Resource, NY; page 370 Giraudon/Art Resource, NY; page 371 Werner Forman/Art Resource, NY; page 373 First Light/Dallas and John Heaton; page 376 Art Resource, NY; page 377 Scala/Art Resource, NY; page 379 © Burstein Collection/CORBIS/MAGMA; page 381 Ancient Art & Architecture Collection; page 384 Werner Forman/Art Resource, NY; page 385 Victoria & Albert Museum, London/Art Resource, NY; page 387 left, right Werner Forman/Art Resource, NY; page 394 SEF/Art Resource, NY; page 396 Werner Forman/Art Resource, NY; page 403, 406 Kay Badcock; page 408, 394 bottom left, 396 bottom left, 424 bottom left, 456 bottom left, 398 bottom left, 426 bottom left, 458 bottom left Giraudon/Art Resource, NY; page 411 Erich Lessing/Art Resource, NY; page 413 SEF/Art Resource, NY; page 414 Palenque, Chiapas State, Mexico/Sean Sprague/Mexicolore/Bridgeman Art Library; page 415 SEF/Art Resource, NY; page 416 Werner Forman/Art Resource, NY; page 417 British Museum, London, UK/Bridgeman Art Library; page 424 Erich Lessing/Art Resource, NY; page 430 Werner Forman/Art Resource, NY; page 433 Scala/Art Resource, NY; page 435 Museo Nacional de Antropologia, Mexico City, Mexico/Ian Mursell/Mexicolore/Bridgeman Art Library; page 437, 438 Werner Forman/Art Resource, NY; page 440 Michel Zabe/Art Resource, NY; page 442 Werner Forman/Art Resource, NY; page 444 John Bigelow Taylor/Art Resource, NY; page 445 Werner Forman/Art Resource, NY; page 447 Mexico City, Mexico/Clive Coward/Bridgeman Art Library; page 448 Michel Zabe/Art Resource, NY; page 450 Private Collection/The Stapleton Collection/Bridgeman Art Library; page 452 left, right Museo de America, Madrid, Spain/Bridgeman Art Library; page 456, 394 top right, 396 top right, 398 top right, 424 top right, 426 top right, 458 top right, 456 top right American Museum of Natural History, New York, USA/Bridgeman Art Library; page 460 John Topic; page 462 Nick Saunder/Barbara Heller Photo Library, London/Art Resource, NY; page 463 Machu Picchu, Peru/Ali Meyer/Bridgeman Art Library; page 465 Tony Stone Images/William J. Hebert; page 469 Werner Forman/Art Resource, NY; page 470, 471 John Topic; page 474 Winay Wayna, near Machu Picchu, Peru/Katie Attenborough/Bridgeman Art Library; page 475 Werner Forman/Art Resource, NY; page 476 Nick Saunders /Barbara Heller Photo Library, London/Art Resource, NY; page 477 British Museum, London, UK/Bridgeman Art Library; page 478 Werner Forman/Art Resource, NY; page 481 John Topic; page 482 Scala/Art Resource, NY; page 483, 484 Werner Forman/Art Resource, NY; page 492 Erich Lessing/Art Resource, NY; page 496 Vanni/Art Resource, NY; page 499 Scala/Art Resource, NY; page 503 Vanni/Art Resource, NY; page 504 © Fulvio Roiter/CORBIS/MAGMA; page 513 © Nik Wheeler/CORBIS/MAGMA; page 517 © David Reed/CORBIS/MAGMA; page 519 © Bettmann/CORBIS/MAGMA; page 520 Werner Forman/Art Resource, NY; page 526 Anthony Scibilia/Art Resource, NY; page 530 © Bettmann/CORBIS/MAGMA; page 534, 490 bottom left, 492 bottom left, 494 bottom left, 526 bottom left, 528 bottom left, 560 bottom left 562 bottom left Giraudon/Art Resource, NY; page 533 Alecto Historical Editions, London, UK/Bridgeman Art Library; page 535 Anthony Scibilia/Art Resource, NY; page 537 Bibliotheque Nationale, Paris, France/Bridgeman Art Library; page 540 Scala/Art Resource, NY; page 541 © Gianni Dagli Orti/CORBIS/MAGMA; page 542 ©

Leonard de Selva/CORBIS/MAGMA; page 543 left Anthony Scibilia/Art Resource, NY, right Scala/Art Resource, NY; page 546 Scala/Art Resource, NY; page 549 Christie's Images, London, UK/Art Resource, NY; page 551 Giraudon/Art Resource, NY; page 552 John Bethell/Bridgeman Art Library; page 555 © Christel Gerstenberg/CORBIS/MAGMA; page 560 bottom right Réunion des Musées Nationaux/Art Resource, NY; page 563 © Bettmann/CORBIS/MAGMA; page 567 Archiv Für Kunst Und Geschichte, Berlin/AKG London; page 568 Scala/Art Resource, NY; page 569 British Library, London, UK/Bridgeman Art Library; page 570 © Archivo Iconografico, S. A./CORBIS/MAGMA; page 571 Erich Lessing/Art Resource, NY; page 572 © Bettmann/CORBIS/MAGMA; page 576, 490 top right, 492 top right, 494 top right, 526 top right, 528 top right, 560 top right, 562 top right, Réunion des Musées Nationaux/Art Resource, NY; page 578 right Scala/Art Resource, NY, left Giraudon/Art Resource, NY; page 582 Erich Lessing/Art Resource, NY; page 585 Art Resource, NY; page 594 bottom right © CORBIS/MAGMA; page 596 Erich Lessing/Art Resource, NY; page 602 Scala/Art Resource, NY; page 603 Garfield Newman; page 604 Scala/Art Resource, NY; page 608 Erich Lessing/Art Resource, NY; page 610 Garfield Newman; page 611, 612, 613, 594 bottom left, 596 bottom left, 598 bottom left, 630 bottom left, 632 bottom left Erich Lessing/Art Resource, NY; page 616 Nimatallah/Art Resource, NY; page 620 Erich Lessing/Art Resource, NY; page 621 AKG London Camera photo; page 623 © National Gallery Collection, By kind permission of the Trustees of the National Gallery, London/CORBIS/MAGMA; page 624, 625

Scala/Art Resource, NY; **page 627** Réunion des Musées Nationaux/Art Resource, NY; **page 630** Giraudon/Art Resource, NY; **page 594 top right, 596 top right, 598 top right, 630 top right, 632 top right, 635** Giraudon/Art Resource, NY; **page 636** Scala/Art Resource, NY; **page 639** © Bettmann/CORBIS/MAGMA; **page 642** New York Public Library/Art Resource, NY; **page 644** Giraudon/Art Resource, NY;

Text and Illustrations

Page xiv, 44, 57, 77, 83, 334, 459 From *World Adventures in Time and Place* by James A. Banks, McGraw-Hill, 1999; **page 8** From *The Hamilton Spectator*, April 24, 1990, p. AA5; **page 11** From *Penguin Dictionary of Archaeology*, Penguin Press, 1982; **page 26** From *Human Evolution* by Roger Lewin, © 1984, 1989 Blackwell Science Ltd. Reprinted by permission; **page xiv, 73, 74** From *A History of Western Art*, Second Edition, by Laurie Schneider Adams, McGraw-Hill, 1997; **page 123** From "The Trireme Sets Sail" by George Retseck from *Scientific American*, April 1989. Reprinted by permission of George Retseck; **page 131** © Oxford University Press 1988. Reprinted from *The Oxford History of the Classical World* edited by John Boardman, Jasper Griffin and Oswyn Murray (1988), by permission of Oxford University Press; **page 134, 141, 497, 501, 510, 511, 514, 516, 538, 583, 601, 637** From *The West in the World: A Mid-Length Narrative History* by Dennis Sherman, McGraw-Hill, © 2001; **page 148** *From Art Across Time, Vol. 1,* by Laurie Schneider Adams, McGraw-Hill, 1999; **page 174** *World History: Traditions and New Directions* by Peter N. Stearns, Donald R. Schwartz, Barry K. Beyer, © 1989 by

Addison-Wesley Publishing Company Inc.; **page 185** F.O.Copley, *Catullus: The Complete Poetry* (Ann Arbor: University of Michigan, 1957) **page 175, 187** Reprinted from Frank Sear: *Roman Architecture*, Copyright © Frank Sear 1982. Used by permission of the publisher, Cornell University Press; **page 204** From *Pompeii: The Day a City was Buried*, Stoddart Publishing, 1999; **page 217** From *World History* by Jerome R. Reich, © 1987 HBJ Canada Inc., original edition published by Coronado Publishing, 1984; **page 264, 284** From B. Davidson, *African Kingdoms*, Time Life Books, 1971; **page 271, 281** From *Africa in the Iron Age* by Ronald Oliver, Cambridge University Press, 1975; **page 351** Jacques Gernet, *Daily Life in China on the Eve of the Mogol Invasion, 1250–1276* (London: George Allen and Unwin Ltd, 1962) **page 385** A. L. Fadler, Trans., *Ten Foot Hut and Tales of the Heike* (Sydney: Angus and Robertson, 1928), p. 154; **page 399, 427, 431** Drawings by Emil Hustiu; **page 401** George Stuart/National Geographic Society Image Collection; **page 404** Drawing by H. Stanley Loten and Michael P. Closs. Courtesy of the Royal Ontario Museum © ROM; **page 405** Deer, monkey, longtailed creature — Drawings by Georgina Hosek. Courtesy of the Royal Ontario Museum © ROM. Jaguar with bundle — Redrawn by Emil Hustiu from Thompson, *The Rise and Fall of Maya Civilization*. Courtesy of the Royal Ontario Museum © ROM; **page 445** Bernal Diaz, *The Conquest of New Spain*, J. M. Cohen translation (Harmondsworth: Penguin Books, 1972), pp. 214-216; **page 446** Miguel Leon Portilla, *Los Antiguos Mexicanos* (Mexico City: Fondo De Cultural Economica, 1961), p. 63; **page 467** Drawn by James Loates from *Mayas, Aztecs, and Incas: Mysteries of Ancient Civilizations of Central* and *South America* by Mark J. Dworkin, 1990; page 449 Frances Berdan, *The Aztecs of Central Mexico: An Imperial Society* (Toronto: Holt, Rinehart, Winston, 1982), p. 36; **page 496** From *Emperors Gratian, Valentinian, and Theodosius Augustuses: An Edict to the People of the City of Constantinople* **page 507** From *From Roman to Merovingian Gaul: A Reader* edited and translated by Alexander Callander Murray, Broadview Press, © 2000; **page 553, 574** McKay, John P., Bennet Hill, and John Buckler, *A History of World Societies*, Second Edition. Copyright © 1988 Houghton Mifflin Company. Used with permission; **page 544** Andromeda Oxford Ltd.; **page 546** Methuen and Company: A. G. Ferrers Howell, *The Lives of S. Francis of Assisi* by Brother Thomas of Celano (London, 1908); **page 565** From *The Black Death*, Second Edition, by Philip Ziegler, Penguin Books, 1998; **page 608** Niccolo Machiavelli, *The Prince*, translated by George Bull, Penguin Classics, Third Edition, 1981, London, pp. 90, 93, 95-100. Copyright © George Bull, 1961, 1975, 1981;

page 609 From James Harvey Robinson and Merrick Whitcomb, eds., "Period of the Early Reformation in Germany," in *Translations and Reprints from the Original Sources of European History,* vol. II, no. 6, ed., Department of History of the University of Pennsylvania (Philadelphia: University of Pennsylvania Press, 1989), pp. 4-5; **page 618 top** Diane Bornstein, *The Lady in the Tower: Medieval Courtesy Literature for Women* (Hamden, 1983), translated from Pietro Gori, ed., *Dodici avvertimenti che deve dare la madre alla figliuola quando la manda a marito* (Florence, 1885), **left** Torquato Tasso, "The Father of the Family," in Carnes Lord and Dain Trafton, trans. and eds., *Tasso's Dialogues: A Selection with the Discourse on the Art of Dialogue* (Berkeley, 1982), pp. 83-85; **page 618 right, 619** From *How to Do It Guides to Good Living for Renaissance Italians* by Rudolph M. Bell, University of Chicago Press, 1999 **page 665** *Employability Skills 2000+*, Brochure 2000E/F (Ottawa: The Conference Board of Canada, 2000)

About the Cover Image

The world's first detector of distant earthquakes, this bronze urn has eight dragons holding balls between their jaws. If the urn is tilted by an earth tremor, a pendulum tilts inside it and opens the jaws of the dragon facing the source of the tremor. The ball drops into the mouth of the frog sitting below. The clanging of the pendulum and the fall of the ball indicate the time and the direction of the earthquake. This seismograph was invented in 132 AD by Zhang Heng.

Cover Credit: Ontario Science Centre

Index

Page numbers in italics indicate illustrations

Abacus, 479
Abbasids, 237–238, 239–240, 252
Abelard, Peter, 546–547
Aboriginal peoples of North America, 639, 644
Abraham, 82
Acculturation, 643–645
Acropolis at Athens, *137*
Actium, Battle of, 195
Acupuncture, 352
Adolescents in Renaissance, 619–620
Aegospotami, Battle of, 135
Aeneid, 200
Aeschylus, 122
Aetolian League, 144
Africa. *See* Axumites; East Africa; Great Zimbabwe; Kushites; West Africa
Afterlife, concept in Egypt, 69–72
Agriculture:
    Aztecs, 427–428, 450–451
    Egypt, 76–77
    India, 323
    intensification, 37
    Neolithic Revolution, 35
Ainu people, 368
Akbar, 308
Akhenaton, 65–66
Akkadians, 42
Alaric, 220
Albigensians, 537
Alcibiades, 134–135
Alcuin, 511
Alexander the Great, 129, 139–141, 142–143
Alfred the Great, 516, *517*
Algebra, 248, 254, 255
Ajanta Caves, *305*
Alla-ud-din, 308
Alphabet, 110
Alvares, Jorge, 389
Amharas, 268, 269
Amon-Re, 58
Amphitheatres, 205
Amphorae, 215
Analects, The (Confucius), 334
Ancestor reverence, 182, 332, 353, 469
Andalusia, 515

Anglo-Saxons:
    conversion to Christianity, 517
    kingdoms and land divisions, 516
Anguissola, Sofonisba, 612
Annales (Ennius), 185
Anthony the Hermit (St. Anthony), 504, 505
Antoniano, Cardinal Silvio, 619–620
Antoninus Pius, 216
Appian Way, 176
Aqueducts, 203, 205
Aquinas, Thomas, 527, 541
Arabian Nights, 250–251
Arabic language, 286
Arabic numerals, 248–249, 254, 539
Archaean League, 144
Archaeology and history, 6–11, 13, 189
    archaeological dig, 6–7
    Hamilton and *Scourge* project, 8–9
    interview with an archaeologist, 478–479
    underwater archaeology, 7–9
Archimedes, 152
Architecture:
    Aztecs, 445–446
    Gothic, 542–544
    Inca, 461, 470, 480–481
    Maya, 412–414
    Middle East, 249, 252–253
    Renaissance in Europe, 610
Arc of the Covenant, 86
Arians, 498
Aristeides, 131
Aristophanes, 136–137
Aristotle, 146, 152, 639
Armies. *See* Warfare
Arthur, King, 516, 518–519, 523
Artifacts, 9–10
Aryabhatta, 318
Ashikaga shogunate, 383–386
Ashoka, 302–303
Askia Muhammad, 285, 286
Assemblies, Roman Republic, 169–171
Assyrians, 43
Aswan Dam, 263
Atawallpa, 457, 467, 485
Athens:
    Athenian Empire, *131,* 133
    daily life, 150–151
    democracy, 113, 114–115, 116, 131–132

    plague, 133
    population, 132
    rivalry with Sparta, 117, 132–133
    slavery, 115, 117, 144–145
Attila, 220, 502
Augustine, 505
Augustus, 189, 195, 196–200
Aurangjeb, 310
Avignonese Papacy, 579, 582
Axum, 267–268
Axumites:
    geography, 267
    language and writing, 270
    people, 269
    religion, 269
    trade, 267–268
Ayllus, 473
Ayurveda, 304
Aztecs:
    agriculture, 427–428, 450–451
    architecture, 445–446
    art, 437
    clothing, 437, 442–444
    family life, 439, 442
    geography, 427–428
    law, 436
    literature and music, 444–445
    markets, 451–452
    medicine, 447
    religion, 434–435
    sculpture, 446
    social structure, 436–439
    Time Line, 426
    trade, 437–438, 449
    writing, 447
Aztlán, 430

Babylonians, 39, 42–43
Bacon, Roger, 570
Baghdad, 239–240
Bai Juyi, 347
Balboa, Vasco Núñez de, 638
Ball, John, 569
Banks, 570
Bantus, 273
Barbarians:
    Celtic peoples, 501
    Germanic peoples, 501–502, 515–516
    invasions of Roman Empire, 219, 220
    migrations, *500,* 501, 516

Slavic peoples, 502
Bar Mitzvah, 87–88
Barter system, 32, 60
Bath complexes in Roman Empire, 203, 204
Bathild, 522
Bat Mitzvah, 88
Bayeux Tapestry, 533, 534
Becket, Thomas, 534–535
Bede, 517
Before the Common Era (BCE), 15
Béguine movement, 547
Benedict of Nursia (St. Benedict), 504, 505
Beowulf, 523
Berelekh, 33
Bernard of Clairveaux, 537
Bhagavad-Gita, 320
Bhakti doctrines, 317
Bias in history, 12–13
Black Death, 355, 563–568, 600, 604
    economic effects, 567–568
    eyewitness account, 565–566
    method of transmission, 563, 564, 580
    social effects, 566–567
    spread (text and map), 564
    symptoms, 563
Black Prince, 576
Boccaccio, Giovanni, 565–566
Boniface, 508
Book burning in China, 337, 340
Book of Kells, 505
Book of the Courtier (Castiglione), 608–609
Botticelli, Sandro, 611
Brahmagupta, 318
Brahmanas, 300
Brahmins, 312, 317, 323
Brava, 273
Brigit of Kildare, 520
British Isles, in Early Middle Ages, 515–520
Bronze, 99, 482
Bruegel, Pieter, 619, 624
Brunelleschi, Filippo, 610
Bubonic plague. See Black Death
Buddha (Gotama Buddha), 313, 316–317
Buddhism, 302, 313, 316–317, 380–381
    in China, 345
    in Japan, 371, 372, 373
    Zen Buddhism, 381, 383
Buildings. See Architecture
Bull-jumping by Minoans, 103–104
Burckhardt, Jacob, 599
Burial customs, Etruscans, 166
Burning of the books, 340

Bushido Code, 384–385
Byzantine Empire, 495–500
    and Christian Church, 496–498
    Justinian the Great, 497–499
    language changed from Latin to Greek, 499
Byzantium, 217

Cadbury Castle, 518–519
Cairo, 240
Calendar:
    Aztecs, 448–449
    Inca, 479
    Julian Calendar, 180
    Maya, 406, 416
Caligula, 200
Caliphs, 236–238
Calligraphy, Islamic, 233, 234, 240, 245
Camelot, 518–519
Canada, 645
Canterbury Tales (Chaucer), 577
Capet (Hugh), and Capetians, 529
Capitalism, 601, 637
Capitoline, 167
Capitolium (Capitol), 175
Caracalla, 214, 215, 216
Caravanserai, 253
Caravan trade, 246, 634
Carolingian minuscule, 511
Carolingians, 508–511, 514
Carthaginians, 172–173
Castiglione, Baldesar, 608–609
Castles, 384, 530, 551, 552
Catalan rudder, 621
Cathedrals, 526
Caton-Thompson, Gertrude, 278–279
Catullus, 185
Cause-and-effect relationships, 14
Cave paintings, 20, 22, 32, 34
Caxton, William, 577
Celtic peoples, 501
Cenote of Sacrifice, 406–407
Censors, 171
Central Africa. See Great Zimbabwe; Mutapa Empire
Centralized government, 36–37
Chandragupta II, 305
Chandragupta Maurya, 322
Chang'an, 346
Chanson de Roland, 512–513
Charlemagne, 492, 509–511
    Empire in about 800 (map), 510
Charles Martel, 508
Chattel slavery, 641
Chaucer, Geoffrey, 577
Chichen Itzá, 396, 400
Children:

Heian Period of Japan, 376–377
High Middle Ages, 554, 555, 556
    Renaissance, 618
Chimu, 465
China:
    art, 335, 337, 343, 345, 346
    class divisions, 332
    Classical Age, 332–336
    First Empire, 337–344
    Formative Period, 330–332
    geography, 329–330
    Last Empire, 355, 358–359
    literature, 347, 354–355
    Second Empire, 345–347
    stability, 330, 361
    technology, 333, 356–357
    Third Empire, 347–355
    warfare, 333
    world view, 359–360
    writing, 334
Chinampas, 427, 450
Chingghis Khan, 308, 353, 354
Chivalry, 547
Cholas, 307
"Chosen Women" (Inca), 468, 470–473, 483
Chrétien de Troyes, 542
Christianity, 193, 208–209, 221
    Axumites, 268, 269
    in Byzantine Empire, 496–498
    Edict of Toleration, 218
    High Middle Ages, 527, 545, 554, 557
    icons, 499–501
    in Japan, 389
    Late Middle Ages, 581
    persecution, 200–201, 209, 212, 218
    Reformation, 624
    schism between East and West, 496, 532, 582, 583
    spread, 209, 212, 503–504, 507
Christine de Pisan, 577
Cicero, 185
Cid (El Cid), 515
Circus Maximus in Rome, 206
Cities, 35, 41, 514, 601–602
    High Middle Ages, 539–540, 541
    women in, 555–556
Citizenship in Roman Empire, 214
Citizenship in Roman Republic, 176–177
City planning in Renaissance, 610
City-states:
    Greek, 110
    Italian, 602–605
    Mayan, 400–401
Civilizations:

characteristics, 36–39
evaluating, 49
Class structure, 35, 37
Classical Moment, 136-138
Claudius, 200, 214
Cleisthenes, 115
Cleopatra, 195
Clothing:
    Aztecs, 442–444
    Egypt, 78–79
    Japan of Heian Period, 375
Clovis I, 506
Coinage, 157, 189. *See also* Money
Colonization:
    by Europe, 633
    colonies in Roman Republic, 175–176
Colosseum in Rome, 188, 205
Columba and Columbanus, 520
Columbus, Christopher, 635, 636, 638
Common Era (CE), 15
Commons in English parliament, 587
Communes, 541
Concordat of Worms, 532
Concrete, 187–188
Confucianism, 330
Confucius, 327, 333–335, 359
Constantine the Great, 209, 216, 218, 495, 496, 503
Constantinople, 218–219, 241, 495, 496, 636
Consuls, 169
Corinth, 174, 175, 186
Corn, 459–60, 643
Cortés, Hernán, 432, 440, 451, 452–453, 638
Council of Constance, 583
Courtly love, 580
Covenant, 87
Crassus, 179
Crete, 99
Croesus, 119
Cro-Magnons, 32–33
Cross-cultural influences and Minoans, 101
Crusades, 238–239, 529, 536–538, 556, 584
    effects, 537–538, 636
    routes (map), *538*
Culhuacán, 430–431
Cult of beauty in Heian period, 376–377
Cuneiform, 44
Cuzco, 462
Cyrus the Great, 43, 120

Damascus, 24, 232, 237, 252
Damnatio memoriae, 215

Danelaw, 516, 517, 521
Dante Alighieri, 561, 578
Daoist (Taoist) philosophy, 335–336
Dark Ages of China, 344
Dark Ages of Greece, 109
David (sculpture by Michelangelo), 613, 616
Death masks, 182
Decameron (Boccaccio), 565–566, 580
Decimal system, 318
Delhi Sultanate, 307
Delian League, 131
Delphi, 111, 155
Democracy, 144, 189
    in Athens, 113, 114–115, 116, 131–132
Demotic writing, 73
Dervishes, 235
Desert regions in Middle East, 243
Dhows, 271
Diaspora (dispersion) of Jews, 84, 89, 212
Diaz del Castillo, Bernal, 445, 446
Dictator (Roman Republic), 169
Diocletian, 216–218, 221
Diseases, European, effect on American peoples, 638
Divination, 470
Djoser, 57
Dome of the Rock, 249, 252
Domesday Book, 533–534
Domestication of animals, 35
Domitian, 201, 210
Domna, Julia, 213, 214
Donatello, 611–612
Donatists, 505
Dracula, 579
Dürer, Albrecht, 625–626

Earthquakes, 102
East Africa:
    city states, 272
    geography, 270–271
    Kilwa, 273–274
    offshore islands, 271
    people, 274
    trade, 272
Eastern (Greek) Orthodox Church, 496
Eastern Roman Empire. *See* Byzantine Empire
Economy, changing structures in the Renaissance, 601–602
Edict of Toleration (Edict of Milan), 218
Education:
    in ancient Egypt, 80
    in ancient India, 317–318

Aztecs, 439
China, 342–343
humanist, 606
public schools in Italian cities, 601
in Roman Republic, 183
Edward I, 586
Egypt, 52–82, 124
    agriculture, 76–77
    army, 59, 64–65
    art, 75–76
    clothing, 78–79
    economic system, 61–63
    education, 80
    family, 77
    foods and festivals, 79
    funerals, 72–73
    geography, 55–56
    jewelry and cosmetics, 79–80
    law, 61
    legacy, 82
    medicine, 81–82
    Middle Kingdom, 58–59
    New Kingdom, 63–67
    Old Kingdom, 56–58
    political structures, 59–61
    religion, 58, 65, 66, 67–73
    role of women and men, 77–78
    science and technology, 80
    skilled trades, 62–63
    social structure, 76–80
    temples, 74
    trade, 59, 62
    writing, 73, 80, 81
Egyptian civilization, 263
Eid al-Adha, 245, 248
Elcano, Juan Sebastián de, 638
Emperors of China, 342
Emperors of Rome, 189
Empress Wu, 346
Ennius, 184–185
Epics:
    Beowulf, 523
    Gilgamesh and Enkidu, 46–47
    Homer, 105, 106, 109
    Mahabharata, 320
    Virgil, 200
Erasmus, Desiderius, 626
Ethiopia, ancient. *See* Axumites
Ethiopian Highlands, 267, 269
Etruscans, 110, 166–168
    burial customs, 166
    influence on Roman life, 168
European colonization, 633
Examination system (China), 343
Exploration by Europeans, 635, 636–638
Ezana, 265, 268, 269

Fables, 550–551
Faiyum, 56
Family life:
 Egypt, 77
 Roman Empire, 193, 213
 Roman Republic, 181, 183–184
Fasces, 168
Fatimids, 238
Fa Xian, 305
Feltre, Vittorino da, 606
Festivals, Greece, 155
Feudalism, 530–531, 557
Fiefs, 531
Filial piety, 334
Firecrackers, 356
First Triumvirate, 179
Florence, 604–605, 620
Fonte, Moderata, 620
Foot binding, 350–351
Forbidden City, 344
Formularies, 507
Francis of Assisi, 546
Froissart, Jean, 580
Fujiwara, 374, 377
Fur trade, 639

Galla Placidia, 221
Gama, Vasco da, 638
Games:
 Africa, 268
 Aztecs, 442, 443
 China, 358
 Egypt, 60
 Greece, 147
 Inca, 471
 India, 318
 Japan, 387
 Late Middle Ages, 580
 Maya, 421
 Mesopotamia, 43
 Middle East, 241
 Renaissance in Europe, *619*, 620
Gauls, 172
Ge'ez language, 269
Geisha, 386
Gemmyo, Empress, 373
Germanic peoples, 501–502, 515–516
Ghana, ancient, 277, 280
 government, 281
 people, 280
 trade, 280–281
Ghiberti, Lorenzo, 611
Ghirlandaio, Domenico, *596*
Gibbon, Edward, 493
Gilgamesh and Enkidu, 46–47
Gladiators, 205–206
Globalization, 633–634, 637–638

Go-Daigo, 383
Goffart, Walter, 493
Gokstad ship, *520*
Golden Age of China, 346–347
Gotama Buddha, 313, 316–317
Gothic architecture, 542–544
Goths, 219, 502
Government:
 China, 342–344, 358–359
 Inca, 472
 Roman Republic, 169, *170* (chart), 171
Gozze, Niccolò Vito di, 620
Gracchus brothers, 176
Grand exchange, 642–643
Great Leap Forward, 30–31
Great Pyramid at Giza, 73
Great Schism, 496, 532, 582, *583*
Great Wall of China, 340
Great Zimbabwe:
 archaeological exploration, 284–285
 geography, 274–275
 ruins, *260, 284*
Greece:
 Archaic Period, 110
 art and architecture, 123–125,
  137–138, 147–149, 158
 classical movement, 136–138
 coinage, 157
 colonization, 110, 111–113
 festivals, 155
 games and sports, 147, 150
 geography, 110
 Hellenistic Age, 141, 144–145
 language, 104–105, 158
 literature, 105, 106, 109, 110, 125,
  136–137, 158
 map, *100*
 medicine, 149
 myths and legends, 154
 philosophy, 145–146, 158
 political life, 155, 158
 religion, 153–154, 155
 science and technology, 125, 152
 sexuality, 149, 152
 slavery, 115, 117
 temples, 124–125, 155
 trade, 110, 156–157
 women, 129, 152–153
 writing, 152
Gregory VII, Pope, 532, 545
Gui, Bernard, 585
Guilds, 540, *541,* 604–605
Gunpowder, 356–357
Gupta Empire, 304–306, *307*
Gutenberg, Johannes, 575, 580–581
Gymnasium in ancient Greece,
 150

Hadrian, 201–202
Hagia Sophia church, *503*
Hajj (pilgrimage to Mecca), 233, 245
 Mansa Musa's famous Hajj, 283–284
Halicarnassus, tomb at, 148–149
Hamilton and *Scourge* project, 8–9
Hammurabi, 42–43
Handwriting, 511
Han Dynasty in China, 341–344
Han Fei Zi, 337
Hanging Gardens of Babylon, 84, *85*
Hangzhou, 348, 350, 353
Haniwa, 369, 370
Han law code, 343–344
Hannibal, 172–173
Hara-kiri, 384
Harold, King of England, 533
Harsha, King, 305–306
Hastings, Battle of, 533–534
Hatshepsut, 63–64
Heian-kyo (known today as Kyoto), 374
Héloïse, 546–547
Helots, 117, 132
Henry II of England, 534–535
Henry V of England, 576
Henry VII of England, 588, 624
Henry VIII of England, 624–625
Herculaneum, *10,* 206
Heresy, 496–497, 498, 582
Herodotus, 70, 97, 121, 153, 159, 634
Hieroglyphs, 73, 81, 416–417, 447
High Middle Ages:
 architecture, 542–544
 birth, marriage, death, 554, 555
 literature, 542
 painting, 544–545
 population growth, 556
 religious spirit, 545–547, 554, 557
 sculpture, 544
 social organization, 547–554
 women, 546–547, 554–556
Hindi, 310
Hinduism, *292,* 299
 bhakti doctrines, 317
 class system, 312
 Hindus and Muslims, 317
 household ceremonies, 311
 life rituals, 312–313, 323
 Puranas, 311
 Rig-Veda, 311–312
 wedding ceremony, 314–315
Hippocrates, 149
Historiography, 4, 14–15
Hiuen Tsiang, 306, 307
Holbein, Hans, the Younger, 625
Holy Roman Empire, 509
Homer, 105, 106, 109, 150

Hominids, 25
Homo erectus, 25
Homo sapiens, 25–26
Homo sapiens sapiens, 26, 30, 31
Honestiores (upper class in Roman
  Empire), 214
Hoplites, 113, *114*
Horace, 200
Huitzilopochtli, 431
Humanists, 606, 636
Human sacrifice, 406–407, 431,
  432–434, 463
Humiliores (common folk in Roman
  Empire), 214
Hunas, 305
Hundred Years' War, 572–575, 600
  events, 572–573
  Joan of Arc, 575, 576–577
  maps, *574*
Huns, 220, 501
Hunting, Paleolithic Age, 32, 33
Hus (Jan), and Hussites, 583–584
Hyksos, 59

Iberia, 514–515
Ibn Battuta, 272, 273, 281
Iconoclastic Controversy, 499–501
Ikebana, 387
Iliad, 105, 109, 110, 150
Il-Khan, 240
Illuminated manuscripts, 505–506, *560*
Imams, 235
Imhotep, 57–58
Inca:
  architecture, 461, 470, 479, 482
  art, *456, 476,* 478–479
  calendar, 479
  census categories (age grades), 472
  cloth and clothing, 484
  devastated by old-world diseases, 466
  dynastic succession, 461–462
  food and drink, 459, 461, 468
  geography, 459–460
  government, 472
  households, 473–474
  land tenure, 474
  metallurgy, 483–484
  military history, 468–469
  mythology, 461–462
  no written language, 465
  occupational specialization, 475
  origins, 460–461
  religion and ritual, 464, 470–471
  road system, 482–483
  social history, 471–477
  split inheritance, 474
  taxation, 476

  trade, 460, 474–475
India:
  art and literature, 320
  daily life in ancient India, 321–322
  legacy, 322–323
  science and technology, 318
  trade, 318–320
  writing, 310
Indian Ocean trade network, 271, 273
Indo-European languages, 310
Indulgences, 584–585
Indus Valley civilization, 295, 297–299
  discoveries, 297–298
  rise and fall, 298–299
  town planning, 297, 298
  writing, 298
Innocent III, Pope, 545
In Praise of Folly (Erasmus), 626
Inquisitions, 585
Instructions in Wisdom, 77
Ireland, in Early Middle Ages, 520
Irene, Empress, 523
Irrigation systems, Inca, 461
Isis, 208
Islam, 232–240, 268
  Abbasids, 237–238, 239–240
  conquests, 236
  crusades, 238–239
  Five Demands, 233
  law, 235–236, 244
  Mongols, 239–240
  Muhammad, 232–233
  philosophy, 236
  spread, *231*
  Sunni and Shi'i division, 234–235
  today, 256
  Umayyads, 236–237
Islamic civilization, 248–249, 255
Islamic Middle East, Time Line, 230
Israel, 82-89
Italian city-states, 602–605
Italian League, 600–601
Italy:
  in 1454 (map), *601*
  beginnings of Renaissance in, 600–601
Itzcoatl, 432

Japan:
  aristocratic society, 368, 369–370,
    374
  art, *364, 376, 381,* 387
  Chinese influence, 371–374
  cult of beauty, 376–377
  daily life in Heian period, 374–375
  education, 381
  European contacts, 388–389
  geography, 367

  law codes, 372–373, 380
  literature, 375
  religion, 370–371
  trade, 388
  writing, 375
Jenne, 283
Jesuits, 358
Jesus, 208–209
Jews, 585. *See also* Israel; Judaism
  blamed for plague, 566–567
  diaspora, 84, 87, 212
  in Roman Empire, 202, 212, 214
Jimmu, 365
Joan of Arc, 575, 576–577
John, King of England, 535
Jomon in Japan, 368–369
Josephus, 84
Judaism (Jewish faith), 86–87, 208
Judas Pasta, 287
Julian Calendar, 180
Julian of Norwich, 580
Julius Caesar, 177, 179–180, 196
Julius II, Pope, 603, 616
Justinian Code, 498
Justinian the Great, 497–499

Kamakura shogunate in Japan, 377–383
  Buddhism during, 380–81
  Minamoto Yoritomo, 378–379, 380
Kami (deities of Shinto), 370
Kamikaze, 382
Kana, 375
Kanishka, 303, 304
Karma, 311
Kelly, Joan, 599
Kempe, Margery, 577, 580
Khadija, 243, 246–247
Khan, Chingghis, 239
Khubilai Khan, 353, 354, 382
Kilwa, 273
Kimon, 131, 132
Kipu, 478–479
Knights, *490,* 547–550
Knossos, palaces at, 101, 102, 103
Kojoki, 365
Koken, Empress, 373–374
Kowtowing, 358, 360
Kuperman, Karen, 638
Kushans, 303–304
Kushites, 263, 264–267
  arts and architecture, *266,* 266
  geography, 263–264
  religion, 266
  science and technology, 267
  trade, 264–265
  writing, 266
Kusi Yupanki, 464

Lake Titicaca, 459, 460
Lamu Island, 274
Languages:
    Axumites, 269
    Early Middle Ages, 523
L'Anse aux Meadows, 634
Las Casas, Bartolomé de, 639
Lascaux Caves, 34
Late Middle Ages. *See also* Black Death
    plague, 563–568
Latin language, 184, 185
    reform by Charlemagne, 509, 511
Latin literature, 184–185
Law:
    Athenian code, 114
    Aztecs, 436
    Babylonia, 42–43
    Egypt, 61
    English parliament, 587
    Han law code, 343–344
    Islam, 235–236, 244
    other codes in Japan, 380
    Roman Empire, 214
    Roman Republic, 177–178
    Taiho Code, 372–373
Law schools, 248
Leakey family, 27–28
Legalists, 336-337
Legends, 5, 46–47
    Alexander the Great, 142–143
    Chanson de Roland, 512–513
    Greece, 154
    Trojan War, 106
Leonardo da Vinci, 612–613, 614–615
Lepidus, 195
Levees, 40
Liberal historians, 15
Linear A, 101, 102, 103, 106
Linear B, 102–103, 106, 109
Lions Gate at Mycenae, *96*
Li Si, 337
Literature:
    Greece, 125
    High Middle Ages, 542
    Mesopotamia, 46–47
    Middle East, 249, 250–251
    Renaissance in Europe, 626–627
    Roman Empire, 200
    Roman Republic, 184–185, 189
Livy, 189
Local officials, Late Middle Ages, 586
Lords, 586–587
Lothair, 514
Louis the Pious, 511, 521
Louis XIV of France, 15, 609
Lo Zi, 335–336
Lucretius, 185

Lull, Ramón, 550
Luther, Martin, 582, 626–627
Lycurgus, 117–118

Ma'at, 60
Macedonia, 144
Machiavelli, Niccolò, 597, 607–608
Machu Pichu, 474, *482*
Madrasas, 248
Magellan, Ferdinand, 638
Magna Carta, 535–536, 586
Mahabharata, 320
Mali kingdom, 282–283
Malleus Maleficarum, 622–623
Mama Waqu, 462
Mamluks, 240
Mandate of Heaven, 342
Manors, 552, *553*
Manqu, 461
Mansa Musa, 283–284
Manumission, 215
Manuscript illumination, *245, 253, 255*
Marathon, Battle of, 121
Marc Antony, 180, 195
Marco Polo, 350, 354, 634
Marcus Aurelius, 216
Marie de France, 542, 550–551
Marius, Gaius, 178
Marriage:
    Aztecs, 439, 442
    Vedic wedding, 314–315
Marxist view, 15
Mastabas, 73
Mauryan Empire, 301–303
Maya:
    architecture, art, sculpture, *404,*
        412–415, 417, 420
    calendar, 406
    city-states, 400–401
    cross-cultural influence, 411–412
    development and collapse of civiliza-
        tion, 402–404
    discoveries and inventions, 416
    excavation, 400, *401*
    food and drink, 410–411, 420
    geography, 399–400
    government and law, 400–401
    human sacrifice, 406–407
    literature, 412
    mathematics, 418–419
    medicine, 415–416
    morals and values, 407–408
    music and games, festivals, 409–410
    mythology, 404, 405
    religion, 402, 404, 406–407
    social customs and structure, 408–409
    sources for history, 400

    Spanish Conquest, 404, 421
    temples, *406,* 407
    trade, 420–421
    water supply, 399–400
    writing, 402, 416–417
Mecca, 232, 233
Mechtild of Magdeburg, 547
Medici, Cosimo de, 605
Medici, Lorenzo de, 605
Medicine:
    Aztecs, 447
    China, 344, 352
    Egypt, 81–82
    Maya, 415–416
Medina, 233, 234
Mediterranean Sea, 56
Megaliths, *36*
Megasthenes, 302
Menes, 57
Meroë, 266
Merovingians, 506–508
Mesopotamia, 39–49
    Akkadians, 42
    Assyrians, 43
    Babylonians, 39, 42–43
    central government, 41
    the land, 39–41
    lasting legacy, 48–49
    laws, 42–43
    literature, 46–47
    the people, 41
    Persian Empire, 43
    religion, 45, 48
    science and technology, 44
    society, 41–42
    writing, 43–44, 81
Mexico. *See* Aztecs
Michelangelo, 603, 604, 613, 616
Middle class and Renaissance in
    Europe, 601–602
Middle East:
    architecture, 249, 252–253
    cross-cultural influences, 248–249,
        254
    customs and festivals, 245, 248
    education, 248
    geography and trade, 231–232
    literature, 249, 250–251
    painting, 252, 255
    social structure, 242–243
    women, 243–245, 246–247
Middle Kingdom of Egypt, 58–59
Migration of early humans (map), *25*
Milan, 601, 603
Minamoto Yoritomo, 378–379, 380
Mindalaes, 475
Ming dynasty in China, 355, 358–359

Ming Huang, 347
Minoans:
 cross-cultural influences, 101
 influence on Mycenae, 106, 109
 palaces, 101–102
 trade, 99
 writing, 101, 102–103
Minotaur, 103
Minuscule, 606
Mithraism, 208
Mitmaq, 477
Modern age, 600
Mogadishu, 273
Mohenjo-daro, 297
Mona Lisa (painting by Leonardo), 613
Monarchy, in Late Middle Ages Europe,
 588
Monasticism, 504
 in High Middle Ages, 545–547
 Irish monasteries, 520
 women, 546–547
Money. *See also* Coinage
 China, *348*
 Roman Empire, 216
Moneychangers, 570
Mongols, 239–240, 353–355
 invasions of Japan, 368, 382
Monophysites, 498
Monotheism, 83, 87
Monsoon trade winds, 271
Montezuma II, 436, 440–441, 446, 452
Moors, 515
Morality, 181
More, Thomas, 626
Mosaics, *140,* 199, 249, 252
Moses, 82–83
Mosque, 249
Mountain regions in Middle East, 242
Moxibustion, 352
Mozarabs, 515
Muhamad bin Tughluq, 308
Muhammad, 232–233, 243
Mummification, 56, 69–72, 462, 469
Murasaki Shikibu, 375
Muslims, 232. *See also* Islam
 bureaucratic-patrimonial states,
  240–241
 rule in India, 307–308
Mutapa Empire, 276
Mutota, 276
Mycenaeans, 102, 103, 104–106,
 109–110
Myths, 5, 46–47. *See also* Legends
 Aztecs, 433
 Egypt, 67–68
 Inca, 461–462
 Greece, 154, 158

Mayan, 404, 405
 Theseus and the Minotaur, 103–104

Names in High Middle Ages, 531
Nara, 373
Neanderthals, 26, 29–30
 appearance, 26
 extinction, 30
Nebuchadrezzar II (or
  Nebuchadnezzar), 84–85
Neo-Confucianism, 347
Neolithic Revolution, 35–36
Nero, 200–201, 209
Neruda, Pablo, 631
New Kingdom of Egypt, 63–67
New Stone Age. *See* Neolithic Revolution
Niccoli, Niccolò, 606
Nicene Creed, 220
Nika Riot (C.E. 532), 499
Nile Delta, 56
Nile River, 55–56, 76, 263, 264
Nogarola, Isotta, 617
Noh theatre, 386–387
Norman Conquest of England, 532–533
Normandy and Normans, 521
Notre Dame de Paris Cathedral, *526*
Nubia, civilization. *See* Kushites

Occupations, specialized, 37, 62–63
Octavian. *See* Augustus
Odyssey, 105, 106, 109, 110, 150
Old English (Anglo-Saxon) language, 516
Old Kingdom of Egypt, 56–58
Old Stone Age. *See* Paleolithic Age
Olduvai Gorge, 28
Olympic Games, 111, 155
Oman, Charles, 493
Onin War, 388
Oracle bones, 331
Ostracism, 115
Ostrogoths, 502
Ottomans, 241, 252
Overlords, 531
Ovid, 200

Pacha Kutiq, 462–463, 471
Pacioli, Luca, 570
Paganism, 497–498
Palaces, Minoans, 101–102, 106
Palazzos, 610
Paleolithic Age:
 artistic sense, 31, 33–34
 hunting, 32, 33
 religion, 34
 roles in society, 31, 33
 tools and weapons, 31, 32, 33–34
Paleopathology, 9–10

Palmieri, Matteo, 619
Pantheon, 188, 202–203
Paper, 621, 624
Parliaments in Late Middle Ages, 586–588
Parthenon, 137
Pastoral nomads, 634
Patriarch of Constantinople, 496
Patriarchy, 244–245
Patricians and plebeians, 168, 171–172,
 176
Patriciate, 602, 610
Patrick, Saint, 520
Pax Romana, 193, 213
Peace of God, 529
Peace of Lodi, 600, 603
Peasants:
 serfs, 522, 552-553
 social pressure in High Middle
  Ages, 530
 subservience to lords decreases, 568
Peasants' Crusade, 536
Peasants' Revolts, 568–570
Peisistratus, 114–115
Peking Opera, 355
Peloponnesian League, 133
Peloponnesian War, 133–136
Pepin the Short, 508–509
Pericles, 131–132, 133
Persians:
 Empire, 43
 conquered by Alexander, 140
 Persian War with Greece, 119–123
Petrarch, Francesco, 607
Pharaohs of Egypt, 59–60
Pheidias, 137
Philip of Macedon, 139
Phoenicians, 110
Pilgrimages, 505
Pilgrimage to Mecca. *See* Hajj
Pimiko, 369
Pisan, Christine de, 575
Pizarro, Francisco, 457, 467, 485, 638
Plague. *See* Black Death
Plantagenet kings of England, 534
Plataea, 123
Plato, 129, 145, 146, 149
Plautus, 185
Plebeian tribunes, 171–172
Pliny the Elder, 200
Political structures, Egypt, 59–61
Poll tax, 569
Poma de Ayala, Guaman, 472, 480
Pompeii, 206–207
Pompey the Great, 179, 180, 185
Pontifex Maximus, 180, 195, 196, 197
Popes, 496, 603. *See also* popes' names
 (e.g. *Julius*)

Popolo minuto in Renaissance, 620–621
Population growth, High Middle Ages, 556
Porcelain, 349
Porète, Marguerite, 547
Post-modernism, 16
Potatoes, 459, 643
Pottery, 10, 115, 266, 368, 415, 417, 420, *438*, 476
Praetors, 171
Primary sources, 4–5. *See also* Archaeology
Primogeniture, 530, 554
Prince, The (Machiavelli), 597, 607, 608
Principate, 197–198
Printing with movable type, 577, 580–581, 621, 624
Ptolemy, 144, 635
Pulakeshin II, 306–307
Punic Wars, 172–173
Puranas, 311
Pyramids in ancient Egypt, 14, 57, 73
Pythagoras, 152

Qin Dynasty in China, 337
Qing dynasty, 355
Qoya, 472
Quechua (the Inca language), 465, 467
Quetzalcoatl, 433, 435, 441
Quiché Creation Myth, 405
Qur'an, 233, 234, 243, 244, 286, 522

Radegund, 522–523
Radiocarbon dating, 11
Ramadan, 233, 245
Ramses II, 67
Reformation, 624, 626–627
Relics, 522
Religion, 180–181.
    Axumites, 268–269
    Egypt, 58, 65, 66, 67–73
    Greece, 153–154, 155
    High Middle Ages, 545–547
    Judaism (Jewish faith), 86–87
    Kushites, 266
    Mesopotamia, 45, 48
    monotheism, 83, 87
    Neanderthals, 29
    Neolithic Revolution, 36
    Paleolithic Age, 34
    Roman Empire, 208–209, 212
    Roman Republic, 189, 196
    Shinto, 370–371
    in Song China, 352–353
    state religion in early civilizations, 38
Renaissance in Europe:
    architecture, 610

children and adolescents, 618–620
economy, changing, 601–602
historical view of, 599
humanism, 606
ideal man, 617
Italian city-states, 602–605
literature, 626–627
Middle Ages to Renaissance, 599–600
middle class and, 601–602
optimism, 617, 618, 627
origins in Italy, 600–601
painting, *594, 596,* 609, 611–613, *619,* 625–626
people and ideas, 607–609
poor people, 620–621
science and technology, 614–615
sculpture, 611–613, 616
technological advances, 621, 624
urbanization, 602
women, 612, 617–618, 620, 622–623
Revolt of the Ciompi, 604–605, 621
Richard II of England, 569
Rich-poor gap in Renaissance, 620–621
Rig-Veda, 311–312
Ritsuryo system. *See* Taiho Code
River basins in Middle East, 242
Rivers, in China, 329–330
Rollo, 521
Roman Catholic Church. *See* Christianity; Great Schism
Roman Empire:
    art and architecture, 198–199
    circus, 206
    citizenship, 214
    coinage, 216
    daily life for men and women, 213–214
    Empire divided, 193, 217
    games and sports, 202
    gladiators, 205–206
    housing, 206–208
    law, 214
    literature, 200
    Pax Romana, 193, 213
    Principate, 197–198
    provinces, 198
    public baths, 203, *204*
    religions, 208–209, 212
    from Republic to Empire, 195–197
    sculpture, *192, 197, 198, 210, 219*
    slavery, 215
    theatres and amphitheatres, 205
    trade and commerce, 215
    water supply, 203, 205
    Western Empire ends, *217,* 219–221
Romanesque architecture, 542, *543*
Roman numerals, 218
Roman Republic, 168–189

armies, 178–179
art and architecture, 186–188
assemblies, 169, 170
citizenship, 176–177
civil war, 195
collapse, 189
expansion of territory, 174–176
family life, 181, 183
First Triumvirate, 179
government structure, 169, *170,* 171
growth and maturity, 172
Latin language, 184, 185
laws, 177–178
literature, 184–185, 189
patricians and plebeians, 168, 171–172, 176
public buildings, typical, *175*
religion, 180–181, 189, 196
Senate, 169
women, 183–184
Rome, 144, 167. *See also* Roman Empire; Roman Republic
    Etruscans, 166–168
    geography and climate, 165
    sacked by Visigoths, 502
    trade, 165
Romulus and Remus, *162, 167,* 200
Rosetta stone, *81*
Rule of St. Benedict, 504, 546

Sadducees, 209
Safavids, 241
Saicho (Monk Saicho), 381
Sailing ships, *271,* 349, 621, *624*
Saints, 504–505
Saladin, 238, *239,* 537
Salamis, 122–123
Salic Law, 507
Samurai, 377, 379, 381, 383, 384–386
Sanctuaries, 101, 124–125
Sanskrit, 310
Santa Maria del Fiore Cathedral, 610
Sapa Inca, 472, 476
Sappho, 125, 152
Saqia, 267
Sargon, 42
Savonarola, Michele, 618
Saxons, 516
Schliemann, Heinrich, 105, 107–108
Schools. *See* Education
Science and technology:
    China, 333, 344, 349, 356–357
    early development, 38
    Egypt, 80
    Greece, 125
    Islamic civilization, 255
    Kushites, 266–267

Mesopotamia, 44
Renaissance in Europe, 614–615
Roman use of concrete, 187–188
Scipio Africanus, 173
Scribes in Egypt, 60–61
Seals, 298, 360
Secondary sources, 4
Second Triumvirate, 195
Seleucus, 144
Senate of Rome, 169, 196
Seppuka, 384
Septimius Severus, 216
Serfs, 522, 552–553
Sextus Pompey, 195
Sforza family, 603
Shang dynasty in China, 330–332
Shi Huangdi, 337–340
    tomb, 338-339
Shi'i Islam, 234–235, 241
Shinto, 370–371
Shogun, 380
Shona Empire, 274
Shotoku, Prince, 372
Sicily, 172
Sieges, 571
Silk Road, 341, 342
Single-stone churches, 269
Sistine Chapel, 603, 604, 613, 616
Slavery, 640–642
    Aztecs, 438–439
    chattel slavery, 641
    in China, 332
    Early Middle Ages, 522
    Greece, 115, 117
    "natural slaves", 639
    Roman Empire, 215, 221
Slavic peoples, 502
Smallpox, 466
Social changes in Late Middle Ages, 568
Social history, 13
Social upheaval in High Middle Ages,
    530–531
Society:
    defined, 29
    Great Leap Forward, 30–31
Society and government in Late Middle
    Ages, 586–588
Socrates, 145–146, 155
Soga clan, 372
Solon, 114
Song dynasty in China, 347–353
    art, 349
    daily life, 350
    food, 351–352
    medicine, 352
    religion, 352–353
    technology, 348

trade, 348–349
women, 350–351
Songhay Empire:
    decline and fall, 286–287
    education and government, 286
    growth, 284–285
Soninke, 278
Sophocles, 136
Spaniards, 404, 421
Spanish Conquest:
    of the Inca, 457, 466–467, 468, 484
    of the Maya, 404, 421
    of Mexico, 429, 440–441, 445–446,
        452
Spanish Inquisition, 585
Sparta, 115, 117–119
    government, 118–119
    rivalry with Athens, 132–133
Spartacus, 179, 215
SPQR, 168
Statues, 182
Stelae, 402, 414
Steppes in Middle East, 242
Step Pyramid of Djoser, 58, 73
Stilicho, 220
Stratification of society, 32
Stratigraphy, 11
Stupas, 304
Subsistence agriculture, 539
Sufi mystics, 236
Sugar cane, 643
Suiko, Empress, 372
Sui Wendi, 345
Sultan of Morocco, 286–287
Sundiata Keita, 282
Sun Goddess, 370
Sun-line of Japan, 370
Sunni Ali, 285
Sunni Islam, 234–235, 241
Sun Si Miao, 356
Swahili Civilization. See East Africa
Swords, 386

Tacitus, 210–211
Taiho Code, 372–373
Taika, 372
Taizong, 346
Taizu, 355
Taj Mahal, 310
Tale of Genji, 375
Tambos, 469
Tang dynasty in China, 346–347
Tarquin the Proud, 167
Tasso, Torquato, 618
Tawantinsuyu, 472
Tea ceremony, 387
Technology. See Science and technology

Tecuilatl, 429
Temples:
    Aztecs, 445
    Greece, 124–125, 155
    Jerusalem, 86, 212
    Maya, 406, 407
    Roman Empire, 198, 199
Ten Commandments, 83
Tenochtitlán, 427, 431
Teotihuacán, 403, 429
Tepanecs, 431–432
Terence, 185
Terrace systems, Inca, 473, 474
Tezcatlipoca (Aztec deity), 434
Thales, 145
Theoderic the Great, 221
Theodora, 498–499
Theodosius the Great, 219–220
Thera, 102
Thermopylae, 121–122
Theseus, 103
Three estates, 531
Thucydides, 133, 135–136, 159
Thupa Inca, 463, 469, 472
Tiberius, 200
Tigris and Euphrates rivers, 39, 56
Timbuktu, 282, 283, 286, 641
Time Line:
    African Kingdoms, 262
    ancient Egypt and Israel, 54
    Aztecs, 426
    China, 328
    classical Greece, 130
    Early Middle Ages, 494
    Greece in the Heroic age, 98
    High Middle Ages, 528
    Inca, 458
    India, 296
    Islamic Middle East, 230
    Japan, 366
    Late Middle Ages, 562
    march to civilization, 24
    Maya, 398
    Renaissance, 598
    Roman Empire, 194
    Roman Republic, 164
    seeds of the global village, 632
Tithes, 550
Tlacaelel, 434
Tlaloc, 435
Tokugawa shogunate, 389
Toltecs, 429, 430
Tomoe, 385
Tools, 10
    Neolithic Revolution, 35
    Paleolithic Age, 31, 32, 33–34
Topic, John, 480–481